BEGINNING OF DUBLIN *Quem quaeritis*, FROM BODLEIAN RAWLINSON LITURGICAL MS. D. 4
(14TH CENTURY)

THE
MEDIAEVAL STAGE

BY

E. K. CHAMBERS

VOLUME I

OXFORD UNIVERSITY PRESS

Oxford University Press, Walton Street, Oxford OX2 6DP

OXFORD LONDON GLASGOW
NEW YORK TORONTO MELBOURNE WELLINGTON
IBADAN NAIROBI DAR ES SALAAM LUSAKA CAPE TOWN
KUALA LUMPUR SINGAPORE JAKARTA HONG KONG TOKYO
DELHI BOMBAY CALCUTTA MADRAS KARACHI

ISBN 0 19 811512 1

First published 1903
Eighth impression 1978

Printed in Great Britain by
Lowe & Brydone Printers Limited, Thetford, Norfolk

TO N. C.

PREFACE

SOME years ago I was thinking of a little book, which now may or may not ever get itself finished, about Shakespeare and the conditions, literary and dramatic, under which Shakespeare wrote. My proper task would have begun with the middle of the sixteenth century. But it seemed natural to put first some short account of the origins of play-acting in England and of its development during the Middle Ages. Unfortunately it soon became apparent that the basis for such a narrative was wanting. The history of the mediaeval theatre had never, from an English point of view, been written. The initial chapter of Collier's *Annals of the Stage* is even less adequate than is usual with this slovenly and dishonest antiquary. It is with some satisfaction that, in spite of the barrier set up by an incorrect reference, I have resolved one dramatic representation elaborately described by Collier into a *soteltie* or sweetmeat. More scholarly writers, such as Dr. A. W. Ward, while dealing excellently with the mediaeval drama as literature, have shown themselves but little curious about the social and economic facts upon which the mediaeval drama rested. Yet from a study of such facts, I am sure, any literary history, which does not confine itself solely to the analysis of genius, must make a start.

An attempt of my own to fill the gap has grown into these two volumes, which have, I fear, been unduly swelled by the inclusion of new interests as, from time to time, they took hold upon me ; an interest, for example, in the light-hearted and coloured life of those *poverelli* of letters, the minstrel folk ; a very deep interest in the track across the ages of certain customs and symbols of rural gaiety which bear with them the inheritance of a remote and ancestral heathenism. I can only hope that this disproportionate treatment of parts has not wholly destroyed the unity of purpose at which, after all, I aimed. If I may venture to define for myself the formula of my work, I would say that it endeavours to state and explain the pre-existing conditions which, by the latter half of the sixteenth century, made the great Shakespearean stage possible. The story is one of a sudden dissolution and a slow upbuilding. I have arranged the material in four Books. The First Book shows how the organization of the Graeco-Roman theatre broke down before the onslaught of Christianity and the indifference of barbarism, and how the actors became wandering minstrels, merging with the gleemen of their Teutonic conquerors, entertaining all classes of mediaeval society with *spectacula* in which the dramatic element was of the slightest, and in the end, after long endurance, coming to a practical compromise with the hostility of the Church. In the Second Book I pass to *spectacula* of another type, which also had to struggle against ecclesiastical disfavour, and which also made their ultimate peace with all but the most austere forms of the dominant religion. These are the *ludi* of the village feasts, bearing witness, not only to their origin in heathen ritual, but also, by their constant tendency to break out into primitive forms of drama, to the deep-rooted mimetic instinct of the folk. The Third Book is a study of the process by which the Church itself, through the introduction of dramatic elements into its liturgy, came to make its own appeal to this same mimetic instinct; and of that by which, from such beginnings, grew up the great popular religious drama of the miracle-plays, with its offshoots in the moralities and the dramatic pageants. The Fourth and final Book deals summarily with the transformation of the mediaeval stage, on the literary side under the influence of humanism, on the social and economic side by the emergence from amongst the ruins of minstrelsy of a new class of professional players, in whose hands the theatre was destined to recover a stable organization upon lines which had been departed from since the days of Tertullian.

I am very conscious of the manifold imperfections of these volumes. They are the work, not of a professed student, but of one who only plays at scholarship in the rare intervals of a busy administrative life. They owe much to the long-suffering officials of the British Museum and the London Library, and more recently to the aid and encouragement of the Delegates of the Clarendon Press and their accomplished staff. The literary side of the mediaeval drama, about which much remains to be said, I have almost wholly neglected. I shall not, I hope, be accused of attaching too much importance in the first volume to the vague and uncertain results of folk-lore research. One cannot be always giving expression to the minuter shades of probability. But in any investigation the validity of the inferences must be relative to the nature of the subject-matter; and, whether I qualify it in words or not, I do not, of course, make a statement about the intention, say, of primitive sacrifice, with the same confidence which attaches to one about matters of historic record. The burden of my notes and appendices sometimes appears to me intolerable. My excuse is that I wanted to collect, once for all, as many facts with as precise references as possible. These may, perhaps, have a value independent of any conclusions which I have founded upon them. And even now I do not suppose that I have been either exhaustive or accurate. The remorseless ideal of the historian's duties laid down in the *Introduction aux Études Historiques* of MM. Langlois and Seignobos floats before me like an accusing spirit. I know how very far I am from having reached that austere standard of scientific completeness. To begin with, I had not the necessary training. Oxford, my most kindly nurse, maintained in my day no *École des Chartes*, and I had to discover the rules of method as I went along. But the greater difficulty has been the want of leisure and the spacious life. Shades of Duke Humphrey's library, how often, as I jostled for my turn at the crowded catalogue-shelves of the British Museum, have I not envied those whose lot it is to tread your ample corridors and to bend over your yellowing folios! Amongst such happy scholars, the canons of Clio may claim implicit obedience. A silent company, they 'class' their documents and 'try' their sources from morn to eve, disturbed in the pleasant ways of research only by the green flicker of leaves in the Exeter garden, or by the statutory inconvenience of a terminal lecture.—

'Tanagra! think not I forget!'

E. K. C.

LONDON, *May*, 1903.

CONTENTS

VOLUME I

BOOK I. MINSTRELSY

BOOK II. FOLK DRAMA

VOLUME II

BOOK III. RELIGIOUS DRAMA

BOOK IV. THE INTERLUDE

APPENDICES

CONTENTS

LIST OF AUTHORITIES

[*General Bibliographical Note.* I mention here only a few works of wide range, which may be taken as authorities throughout these two volumes. Others, more limited in their scope, are named in the preliminary notes to the sections of the book on whose subject-matter they bear.—An admirable general history of the modern drama is W. Creizenach's still incomplete *Geschichte des neueren Dramas* (Band i, *Mittelalter und Frührenaissance*, 1893; Bände ii, iii, *Renaissance und Reformation,* 1901–3). R. Prölss, *Geschichte des neueren Dramas* (1881–3), is slighter. The earlier work of J. L. Klein, *Geschichte des Dramas* (13 vols. 1865–76), is diffuse, inconvenient, and now partly obsolete. A valuable study is expected from J. M. Manly in vol. iii of his *Specimens of the Pre-Shakespearean Drama*, of which two volumes, containing selected texts, appeared in 1897. C. Hastings, *Le Théâtre français et anglais* (1900, Eng. trans. 1901), is a compilation of little merit.—Prof. Creizenach may be supplemented for Germany by R. Froning, *Das Drama des Mittelalters* (1891). For France there are the exhaustive and excellent volumes of L. Petit de Julleville's *Histoire du Théâtre en France au Moyen Âge* (*Les Mystères*, 1880; *Les Comédiens en France au Moyen Âge*, 1885; *La Comédie et les Mœurs en France au Moyen Âge*, 1886; *Répertoire du Théâtre comique au Moyen Âge*, 1886). G. Bapst, *Essai sur l'Histoire du Théâtre* (1893), adds some useful material on the history of the stage. For Italy A. d' Ancona, *Origini del Teatro italiano* (2nd ed., 1891), is also excellent.—The best English book is A. W. Ward's *History of English Dramatic Literature to the death of Queen Anne* (2nd ed., 1899). J. P. Collier, *History of English Dramatic Poetry* (new ed., 1879), is full of matter, but, for various reasons, not wholly trustworthy. J. J. Jusserand, *Le Théâtre en Angleterre* (2nd ed., 1881), J. A. Symonds, *Shakespeare's Predecessors in the English Drama* (1884), and G. M. Gayley, *Representative English Comedies* (1903), are of value. Texts will be found in Manly's and Gayley's books, and in A. W. Pollard, *English Miracle Plays, Moralities and Interludes* (3rd ed., 1898); W. C. Hazlitt, *Dodsley's Old Plays* (15 vols. 1874–6); A. Brandl, *Quellen des weltlichen Dramas in England* (1898). F. H. Stoddard, *References for Students of Miracle Plays and Mysteries* (1887), and K. L. Bates and L. B. Godfrey, *English Drama; a Working Basis* (1896), are rough attempts at bibliographies.—In addition the drama of course finds treatment in the general histories of literature. The best are: for Germany, R. Kögel, *Geschichte der deutschen Literatur bis zum Ausgange des Mittelalters* (1894-7, a fragment); K. Gödeke, *Grundriss zur Geschichte der deutschen Dichtung aus den Quellen* (2nd ed., 1884-1900); W. Scherer, *Geschichte der deutschen Litteratur* (8th ed., 1899): for France, L. Petit de Julleville (editor), *Histoire de la Langue et de la Littérature françaises* (1896-1900); G. Paris, *La Littérature française au Moyen Âge* (2nd ed., 1890): for Italy, A. Gaspary, *Geschichte der italienischen Litteratur* (1884-9, Eng. transl. 1901): for England, T. Warton, *History of English Poetry* (ed. W. C. Hazlitt, 1871); B. Ten Brink, *History of English Literature* (Eng. trans. 1893-6); J. J. Jusserand, *Literary History of the English People* (vol. i. 1895); W. J. Courthope, *History of English Poetry* (vols. i, ii. 1895-7); G. Saintsbury, *Short History of English Literature* (1898), and, especially for bibliography, G. Körting, *Grundriss der Geschichte der englischen Litteratur* (3rd ed., 1899). The *Periods of European Literature*, edited by Prof. Saintsbury, especially G. Gregory Smith, *The Transition Period* (1900), and the two great *Grundrisse*, H. Paul, *Grundriss der germanischen Philologie* (2nd ed., 1896-1903), and G. Gröber, *Grundriss der romanischen Philologie* (1888-1903), should also be consulted.—The beginnings of the mediaeval drama are closely bound up with liturgy, and the nature of the liturgical books referred to is explained by W. Maskell, *A Dissertation upon the Ancient Service-Books of the Church of England* (in *Monumenta Ritualia Ecclesiae Anglicanae*, 2nd ed., 1882, vol. iii); H. B. Swete, *Church Services and Service-Books before the Reformation* (1896); Procter-Frere, *New History of the Book of Common Prayer* (1901). The beginnings of Catholic ritual are studied by L. Duchesne, *Origines du Culte chrétien* (3rd ed., 1902, Eng. trans. 1903), and its mediaeval forms described by D. Rock, *The Church of our Fathers* (1849-53), and J. D. Chambers, *Divine Worship in England in the Thirteenth and Fourteenth Centuries* (1877).

The following list of books is mainly intended to elucidate the references in the footnotes, and has no claim to bibliographical completeness or accuracy. I have included the titles of a few German and French dissertations of which I have not been able to make use.]

Aberdeen Records. Extracts from the Council Register of the Burgh of Aberdeen. Edited by J. Stuart. 2 vols. 1844-8. [*Spalding Club*, xii, xix.]

Acta SS. Acta Sanctorum quotquot toto orbe coluntur, quas collegit

I. Bollandus. Operam continuavit G. Henschenius [et alii], 1734–1894. [In progress.]

AHN. English Mysteries and Miracle Plays. By Dr. Ahn. Trier, 1867. [Not consulted.]

ALCUIN. See DÜMMLER.

ALLARD. Julien l'Apostat. Par P. Allard. 3 vols. 1900–3.

ALLEN. The Evolution of the Idea of God : an Enquiry into the Origins of Religion. By Grant Allen, 1897.

ALT. Theater und Kirche in ihrem gegenseitigen Verhältniss. Von H. Alt, 1846.

Anal. Hymn. Analecta Hymnica Medii Aevi. Ediderunt C. Blume et G. M. Dreves. 37 parts, 1886–1901. [In progress.]

ANCONA. Origini del Teatro italiano. Per A. d'Ancona, 2nd ed. 2 vols. 1891.

ANCONA, *Sacr. Rappr.* Sacre Rappresentazioni dei secoli xiv, xv e xvi, raccolte e illustrate per cura di A. d'Ancona, 1872.

Anglia. Anglia : Zeitschrift für englische Philologie. 24 vols. 1878–1903. [In progress.]

Ann. Arch. Annales Archéologiques, dirigées par Didron aîné. 28 vols. 1844–81.

Antiquarian Repertory. The Antiquarian Repertory : A Miscellaneous assemblage of Topography, History, Biography, Customs and Manners. Compiled by F. Grose and T. Astle. 2nd ed. 4 vols. 1807.

ARBOIS DE JUBAINVILLE, *Civ. Celt.* La Civilisation des Celtes et celle de l'Épopée homérique. Par H. d'Arbois de Jubainville, 1899. [Vol. vi of *Cours de littérature celtique.*]

ARBOIS DE JUBAINVILLE, *Cycl. Myth.* Le Cycle mythologique irlandais et la Mythologie celtique. Par H. d'Arbois de Jubainville, 1884. [Vol. ii of same.]

Archaeologia. Archaeologia : or Miscellaneous Tracts relating to Antiquity. Published by the Society of Antiquaries of London. 57 vols. 1770–1901. [In progress.]

ARNOLD. The Customs of London, otherwise Arnold's Chronicle. Edited by F. Douce, 1811.

ASHTON. A Righte Merrie Christmasse ! ! ! By J. Ashton, n. d.

BAHLMANN, *Ern.* Die Erneuerer des antiken Dramas und ihre ersten dramatischen Versuche : 1314–1478. Von P. Bahlmann, 1896.

BAHLMANN, *L. D.* Die lateinischen Dramen von Wimpheling's Stylpho bis zur Mitte des sechzehnten Jahrhunderts : 1480–1550. Von P. Bahlmann, 1893.

BALE. Scriptorum illustrium maioris Britanniae, quam nunc Angliam et Scotiam vocant, Catalogus. Autore Ioanne Baleo Sudouolgio Anglo. 2 vols. Basileae, Oporinus, 1557–9. [Enlarged from the edition in one vol. of 1548.]

BALE, *Index.* Index Britanniae Scriptorum quos ex variis bibliothecis non parvo labore collegit Ioannes Baleus. Edited by R. L. Poole and

M. Bateson, 1902. [*Anecdota Oxoniensia, Mediaeval and Modern Series*, ix, from a MS. compiled 1549–1557.]

BAPST. Essai sur l'Histoire du Théâtre. Par G. Bapst, 1893.

BARBAZAN-MÉON. Fabliaux et Contes des Poètes françois des xi, xii, xiii, xiv et xv siècles. Publiés par E. Barbazan. Nouvelle édition, par M. Méon. 4 vols. 1808.

BARRETT. Riding Skimmington and Riding the Stang. By C. R. B. Barrett, 1895. [*Journal of British Archaeological Association*, N. S. vol. i.]

BARTHÉLEMY. Rational ou Manuel des divins Offices de Guillaume Durand, Évêque de Mende au treizième siècle. Traduit par M. C. Barthélemy. 5 vols. 1854.

BARTSCH. Altfranzösische Romanzen und Pastourellen. Par K. Bartsch, 1870.

BATES. The English Religious Drama. By K. L. Bates, 1893.

BATES-GODFREY. English Drama: a Working Basis. By K. L. Bates and L. B. Godfrey, 1896.

BEDE, *D. T. R.* Venerabilis Bedae Opera quae Supersunt Omnia. Edidit J. A. Giles. 12 vols. 1843–4. [The *De Temporum Ratione* forms part of vol. vi.]

BEDE, *E. H. See* PLUMMER.

BÉDIER. Les Fabliaux. Études de Littérature populaire et d'Histoire littéraire du Moyen Âge. Par J. Bédier, 2nd ed. 1895.

BELETHUS. Rationale Divinorum Officiorum Auctore Joanne Beletho Theologo Parisiensi, 1855. [In *P. L.* ccii.]

BELL. Ancient Poems, Ballads, and Songs of the Peasantry of England. Edited by R. Bell, 1857.

BÉRENGER-FÉRAUD. Superstitions et Survivances étudiées au point de vue de leur Origine et de leurs Transformations. Par L. J. B. Bérenger-Féraud. 4 vols. 1896.

BERNHARD. Recherches sur l'Histoire de la Corporation des Ménétriers ou Joueurs d'Instruments de la Ville de Paris. Par B. Bernhard. [*Bibl. de l'École des Chartes*, iii. 377, iv. 525, v. 254, 339.]

BERTRAND. Nos Origines : iv. La Religion des Gaulois ; Les Druides et le Druidisme. Par A. Bertrand, 1897.

Bibl. des Chartes. Bibliothèque de l'Ecole des Chartes. Revue d'Érudition consacrée spécialement à l'étude du Moyen Âge. [I quote the numbers of the annual volumes, without regard to the *Séries*.]

BINGHAM. The Works of Joseph Bingham. Edited by R. Bingham. New ed. 10 vols.

BLOMEFIELD. An Essay towards a Topographical History of the County of Norfolk. By F. Blomefield. 2nd ed. 11 vols. 1805–10.

BÖHCK. Die Anfänge des englischen Dramas. Von Dr. Böhck, 1890. [Not consulted.]

BOLTON. The Counting-Out Rhymes of Children. By H. C. Bolton, 1888.

BORETIUS. Capitularia Regum Francorum. Ediderunt A. Boretius et V. Krause. 2 vols. 1883-7. [*M. G. H. Leges*, Sectio ii.]

BOURQUELOT. Office de la Fête des Fous. Publié par F. Bourquelot, 1858. [*Bulletin de la Société archéologique de Sens*, vol. vi. Not consulted at first hand.]

BOWER. The Elevation and Procession of the Ceri at Gubbio. By H. M. Bower, 1897. [*F. L. S.*]

BRAND. Observations on Popular Antiquities, chiefly illustrating the Origin of our Vulgar Customs, Ceremonies, and Superstitions. By J. Brand. Enlarged by Sir H. Ellis. 3 vols. 1841-2.

BRAND-HAZLITT. Observations on Popular Antiquities. By J. Brand. Edited with additions by W. C. Hazlitt. 3 vols. 1870.

BRANDL. Quellen des weltlichen Dramas in England vor Shakespeare. Ein Ergänzungsband zu Dodsley's Old English Plays. Herausgegeben von A. Brandl, 1898. [*Quellen und Forschungen*, lxxx.]

BREWER. Letters and Papers, Foreign and Domestic, of the Reign of Henry VIII. Arranged and catalogued by J. S. Brewer [and afterwards J. Gairdner and R. H. Brodie]. 18 vols. 1862-1902. [*Calendars of State Papers.*]

BROOKE. The History of Early English Literature : being the History of English Poetry to the Accession of King Alfred. By S. A. Brooke. 2 vols. 1892.

BROOKE, *Eng. Lit.* English Literature from the Beginning to the Norman Conquest. By S. A. Brooke, 1898.

BROTANEK. Die englischen Maskenspiele. Von R. Brotanek, 1902. [*Wiener Beiträge zur englischen Philologie*, xv.]

BROWN. Calendar of State Papers and Manuscripts relating to English Affairs, in the Archives and Collections of Venice and in other Libraries of North Italy. Edited by H. F. Brown and R. Brown. 10 vols. 1864-1900.

BRYLINGER. Comoediae et Tragoediae aliquot ex Novo et Vetere Testamento desumptae. Basileae, Brylinger, 1540.

BURCHARDUS. Burchardi Wormaciencis Ecclesiae Episcopi Decretorum Libri xx, 1853. [In *P. L.* cxl.]

BURNE-JACKSON. Shropshire Folk-lore: A Sheaf of Gleanings. Edited by C. S. Burne, from the collections of G. F. Jackson, 1883.

BURNET. A History of the Reformation of the Church of England. By G. Burnet. Edited by N. Pocock. 7 vols. 1865.

BURTON. Rushbearing. By A. Burton, 1891.

BURY-GIBBON. *See* GIBBON.

CAMPBELL. Materials for a History of the Reign of Henry VII, from documents in the Public Record Office. By W. Campbell. 2 vols. 1873-7. [*R. S.* lx.]

CANEL. Recherches historiques sur les Fous des Rois de France. Par A. Canel, 1873.

Captain Cox. See LANEHAM.

Carmina Burana. *See* SCHMELLER.

CASPARI. Eine Augustin fälschlich beilegte Homilia de Sacrilegiis. Herausgegeben von C. P. Caspari, 1886. [*Gesellschaft der Wissenschaften zu Christiania.*]

CASSIODORUS. Cassiodori Senatoris Variae. Recensuit Theodorus Mommsen, 1894. [*M. G. H. Auctores Antiquissimi*, vol. xii.]

Catholicon Anglicum. Catholicon Anglicum : an English-Latin Wordbook (1483). Edited by S. J. Herrtage, 1881. [*C. S.* N. S. xxx.]

CAVENDISH. The Life of Cardinal Wolsey. By J. Cavendish. Edited by S. W. Singer. 2 vols. 1825.

CHAMBERS. Divine Worship in the Thirteenth and Fourteenth Centuries, contrasted with the Nineteenth. By J. D. Chambers, 1877.

CHAMPOLLION-FIGEAC. *See* HILARIUS.

CHAPPELL. Old English Popular Music. By W. Chappell. A new edition by H. E. Wooldridge. 2 vols. 1893.

C. H. B. Corpus Scriptorum Historiae Byzantinae. Editio emendatior, consilio B. G. Niebuhrii instituta, 1828-97.

CHÉREST. Nouvelles Recherches sur la Fête des Innocents et la Fête des Fous. Par A. Chérest, 1853. [*Bulletin de la Société des Sciences de l'Yonne*, vol. vii.]

CHILD. The English and Scottish Popular Ballads. Edited by F. J. Child. 10 vols. 1882-98.

Christmas Prince. *See* HIGGS.

C. I. C. Corpus Iuris Civilis. Editio altera, 1877-95. [Vol. i contains the *Institutiones*, ed. P. Krueger, and the *Digesta*, ed. Th. Mommsen; vol. ii the *Codex Iustiniani*, ed. P. Krueger; vol. iii the *Novellae Iustiniani*, ed. Schoell and Kroll.]

C. I. Can. Corpus Iuris Canonici. Editio Lipsiensis secunda : post A. L. Richter curas . . . instruxit A. Friedberg. 2 vols. 1879-81. [Contains the *Decretum* of Gratian (†1139), the *Decretales* of Gregory IX (1234), the *Liber Sextus* of Boniface VIII (1298), the *Decretales* of Clement V and John XXII (1317), and the *Extravagantes* (down to 1484).]

CIVIS. Minutes, collected from the ancient Records and Accounts in the Chamber of Canterbury. [By C. R. Bunce or W. Welfitt. These documents, bound in B. M. under press-mark 10,358, h. i., appear to be reprints or proof-sheets of articles, signed *Civis*, in the *Kentish Chronicle* for 1801-2.]

CLARKE. The Miracle Play in England, an account of the Early Religious Drama. By S. W. Clarke, n. d.

CLÉDAT. Le Théâtre en France au Moyen Âge. Par L. Clédat, 1896. [*Classiques Populaires.*]

CLÉMENT. Histoire générale de la Musique religieuse. Par F. Clément, 1860.

CLÉMENT-HÉMERY. Histoire des Fêtes civiles et religieuses du Département du Nord. Par Mme Clément (née Hémery), 1832.

CLOETTA. Beiträge zur Litteraturgeschichte des Mittelalters und der

Renaissance. Von W. Cloetta. i. Komödie und Tragödie im Mittelalter, 1890. ii. Die Anfänge der Renaissancetragödie, 1892.

Cod. Th. Codex Theodosianus. Edidit G. Haenel, 1844. [*Corpus Iuris Romani Ante-Iustiniani*, vol. ii.]

COLLIER. The History of English Dramatic Poetry to the Time of Shakespeare : and Annals of the Stage to the Restoration. By J. P. Collier. New ed. 1879.

COLLIER, *Five Plays.* Five Miracle Plays, or Scriptural Dramas. Edited by J. P. Collier, 1836.

COLLIER, *P. J.* Punch and Judy, with illustrations by G. Cruikshank. Accompanied by the Dialogue of the Puppet-Show, an account of its Origin, and of Puppet-Plays in England. [By J. P. Collier.] 5th ed. 1870.

CONYBEARE. The History of Christmas. By F. C. Conybeare, 1899 [*Journal of American Theology*, vol. iii.]

CONYBEARE, *Key of Truth.* The Key of Truth : a Manual of the Paulician Church. Edited and translated by F. C. Conybeare, 1898.

CORTET. Essai sur les Fêtes religieuses, et les Traditions populaires qui s'y rattachent. Par E. Cortet, 1867.

COTGRAVE. A French-English Dictionary, with another in English and French. By R. Cotgrave, 1650.

County Folk-Lore. Examples of printed Folk-Lore. Vol. i (Glouces-
tershire, Suffolk, Leicestershire, and Rutland), 1892-5. Vol. ii (North Riding of Yorkshire, York, and the Ainsty), 1901. [*F. L. S.*]

COURTHOPE. A History of English Poetry. By W. J. Courthope. Vols. i, ii. 1895-7. [In progress.]

COUSSEMAKER. Drames liturgiques du Moyen Âge. Par E. de Coussemaker, 1860.

COUSSEMAKER, *Harm.* Histoire de l'Harmonie au Moyen Âge. Par E. de Coussemaker, 1852.

COX. Introduction to Folk-Lore. By M. R. Cox. 2nd ed. 1897.

C. P. B. Corpus Poeticum Boreale : the Poetry of the Old Northern Tongue from the Earliest Times to the Thirteenth Century. Edited by G. Vigfusson and F. Y. Powell. 2 vols. 1883.

CREIZENACH. Geschichte des neueren Dramas. Von W. Creizenach. Vols i–iii, 1893-1903. [In progress.]

CROWEST. The Story of British Music, from the Earliest Times to the Tudor Period. By F. J. Crowest, 1896.

C. S. Camden Society, now incorporated with the Royal Historical Society.

C. S. E. L. Corpus Scriptorum Ecclesiasticorum Latinorum. Editum consilio Academiae Litterarum Caesareae Vindobonensis. 41 vols. 1866-1900. [In progress.]

CUMONT. Textes et Monuments figurés relatifs aux Mystères de Mithra. Par F. Cumont. 2 vols. 1896-9.

CUNLIFFE. The Influence of Seneca on Elizabethan Tragedy. An Essay by J. W. Cunliffe, 1893. [Manchester dissertation.]

CUNNINGHAM. Extracts from the Accounts of Revels at Court in the Reigns of Queen Elizabeth and King James I. By P. Cunningham, 1842. [*Shakespeare Society.*]

CUSHMAN. The Devil and the Vice in the English Dramatic Literature before Shakespeare. By L. W. Cushman, 1900. [*Studien zur englischen Philologie*, vi.]

CUTTS. Parish Priests and their People in the Middle Ages in England. By E. L. Cutts, 1898.

DANKÓ. Die Feier des Osterfestes. Von J. Dankó, 1872. [Not consulted.]

DANKÓ, *Hymn.* Vetus Hymnarium Ecclesiasticum Hungariae. Edidit J. Dankó, 1893.

DAVID. Études historiques sur la Poésie et la Musique dans la Cambrie. Par E. David, 1884.

DAVIDSON. Studies in the English Mystery Plays. By C. Davidson, 1892. [Yale dissertation, in *Transactions of Connecticut Academy*, ix. 1.]

DAVIES. Extracts from the Municipal Records of the City of York during the Reigns of Edward IV, Edward V, and Richard III. By R. Davies, 1843.

DAWSON. Christmas: Its Origin and Associations. By W. F. Dawson, 1902.

D. C. A. A Dictionary of Christian Antiquities. Edited by Sir W. Smith and S. Cheetham. 2 vols. 1875-80.

DEIMLING. The Chester Plays. Re-edited from the MSS. by the late H. Deimling, 1893. [*E. E. T. S.*, Part i, with Plays 1-13, only published.]

DE LA FONS-MELICOCQ. Cérémonies dramatiques et anciens Usages dans les Églises du Nord de la France. Par A. de la Fons-Melicocq, 1850.

DENIFLE. Chartularium Universitatis Parisiensis. Collegit H. Denifle. 4 vols. 1889-97.

DESJARDINS. Histoire de la Cathédrale de Beauvais. Par G. Desjardins, 1865.

DESLYONS. Traitez singuliers et nouveaux contre le Paganisme du Roy Boit. Par J. Deslyons, 1670.

DEVRIENT. Geschichte der deutschen Schauspielkunst. Von E. Devrient. 2 vols. 1848.

DIDRON. See *Annales Archéologiques.*

DIETERICH. Pulcinella; pompejanische Wandbilder und römische Satyrspiele. Von A. Dieterich, 1897.

DIEZ. Die Poesie der Troubadours. Von F. C. Diez, 1826.

DIEZ-BARTSCH. Leben und Werke der Troubadours. Von F. C. Diez. Zweite Auflage, von K. Bartsch, 1882.

Digby Plays. See FURNIVALL; SHARP.

DILL. Roman Society in the last Century of the Western Empire. By S. Dill. 2nd ed. 1899.

DITCHFIELD. Old English Customs extant at the present Time. By P. H. Ditchfield, 1896.

DIXON. A History of the Church of England from the Abolition of the Roman Jurisdiction. By R. W. Dixon. 6 vols. 1878–1902.

D. N. B. Dictionary of National Biography. Edited by L. Stephen and S. Lee. 66 vols. 1885–1901.

DORAN. A History of Court Fools. By J. Doran, 1858.

DOUCE. Illustrations of Shakspeare, and of Ancient Manners : with Dissertations on the Clowns and Fools of Shakspeare, and on the English Morris Dance. By F. Douce, 1839.

DOUHET. Dictionnaire des Mystères. Par Jules, Comte de Douhet, 1854. [J. P. Migne, *Encyclopédie Théologique*, Series II, vol. xliii.]

DRAKE. Shakespeare and his Times. By N. Drake. Paris, 1838.

DREUX DE RADIER. Histoire des Fous en titre d'Office. Par J. F. Dreux de Radier, 1768. [In *Récréations Historiques.*]

DREVES. Zur Geschichte der Fête des Fous. Von G. M. Dreves, 1894. [*Stimmen aus Maria-Laach*, vol. xlvii.]

See also *Analecta Hymnica.*

DUCANGE. Glossarium mediae et infimae Latinitatis conditum a Du Cangio, auctum a monachis Ordinis S. Benedicti, cum supplementis Carpenterii suisque digessit G. A. L. Henschel. Editio nova, aucta a L. Favre. 10 vols. 1883–7.

DUCHESNE. Origines du Culte chrétien : Étude sur la Liturgie avant Charlemagne. Par l'Abbé L. Duchesne. 2nd ed. 1898. [A 3rd ed. was published in 1902, and a translation, by M. L. McLure, under the title of Christian Worship : its Origin and Evolution, in 1903.]

DUGDALE. Origines Iuridiciales : or, Historical Memorials of the English Laws ... Inns of Court and Chancery. By W. Dugdale. 2nd ed. 1671.

DUGDALE, *Monasticon.* Monasticon Anglicanum : or, the History of the Ancient Abbies and other Monasteries, Hospitals, Cathedral and Collegiate Churches in England and Wales. By Sir W. Dugdale. A new edition by J. Caley, Sir H. Ellis, and the Rev. B. Bandinel. 6 vols. 1846.

DU MÉRIL. Origines latines du Théâtre moderne, publiées et annotées par M. Édélestand Du Méril, 1849. [Has also a Latin title-page, Theatri Liturgici quae Latina superstant Monumenta, etc. A facsimile reprint was issued in 1896.]

DU MÉRIL, *La Com.* Histoire de la Comédie. Par É. du Méril. Période primitive, 1864. [All published.]

DÜMMLER. Epistolae Merowingici et Karolini Aevi. Recensuit E. L. Dümmler. 3 vols. 1892–9. [*M. G. H. Epistolae*, iii–v. The 2nd vol. contains Alcuin's letters.]

DURANDUS. Rationale Divinorum Officiorum editum per . . . . Gulielmum Duranti. Haec editio a multis erroribus diligenter correcta. [Edidit N. Doard.] Antwerpiae, 1614. See BARTHÉLEMY.

Durham Accounts. Extracts from the Account Rolls of the Abbey of Durham. Edited by Canon Fowler. 3 vols. 1898–1901. [*Surtees Soc.* xcix, c, ciii.]

DÜRR. Commentatio Historica de Episcopo Puerorum, vulgo von Schul Bischoff. Von F. A. Dürr, 1755. [In J. Schmidt, *Thesaurus Iuris Ecclesiastici* (1774), iii. 58.]

DU TILLIOT. Mémoires pour servir à l'Histoire de la Fête des Foux. Par M. Du Tilliot, Gentilhomme Ordinaire de S. A. R. Monseigneur le Duc de Berry, 1751.

DYER. British Popular Customs, Present and Past. By T. F. Thiselton Dyer, 1876.

EBERT. Die englischen Mysterien. Von A. Ebert, 1859. [*Jahrbuch für romanische und englische Literatur*, vol. i.]

ECKHARDT. Die lustige Person im älteren englischen Drama (bis 1642). Von E. Eckhardt, 1903. [*Palaestra*, xvii; not consulted.]

E. H. Review. The English Historical Review. 18 vols. 1886–1903. [In progress.]

ELTON. Origins of English History. By C. I. Elton. 2nd ed. 1890.

EVANS. English Masques. With an introduction by H. A. Evans, 1897. [*Warwick Library.*]

FABIAN. The New Chronicles of England and France. By R. Fabyan. Edited by H. Ellis, 1811.

FAIRHOLT. Lord Mayor's Pageants. Edited by F. W. Fairholt. 2 vols. 1843–4. [*Percy Soc.* xxxviii, xlviii.]

FEASEY. Ancient English Holy Week Ceremonial. By H. J. Feasey, 1897.

FISCHER. Zur Kunstentwickelung der englischen Tragödie von ihren ersten Anfängen bis zu Shakespeare. Von R. Fischer, 1893.

FITCH. Norwich Pageants. The Grocers' Play. From a manuscript in possession of R. Fitch, 1856. [Extract from *Norfolk Archaeology*, vol. v.]

F. L. Folk-Lore: a Quarterly Review of Myth, Tradition, Institution, and Custom. 14 vols. 1890–1903. [Organ of *F. L. S.*, in progress.]

F. L. Congress. The International Folk-Lore Congress, 1891. Papers and Transactions. Edited by J. Jacobs and A. Nutt, 1892.

F. L. Journal. The Folk-Lore Journal, 7 vols. 1883–9. [Organ of *F. L. S.*]

F. L. Record. The Folk-Lore Record. 5 vols. 1878–82. [Organ of *F.L.S.*]

FLEAY. *C. H.* A Chronicle History of the London Stage, 1559–1642. By F. G. Fleay, 1890.

FLÖGEL. Geschichte der Hofnarren. Von C. F. Flögel, 1789.

F. L. S.=Folk-Lore Society.

FOWLER. The Roman Festivals of the Period of the Republic : an Introduction to the Study of the Religion of the Romans. By W. W. Fowler, 1899. [*Handbooks of Archaeology and Antiquities.*]

FOURNIER. Le Théâtre français avant la Renaissance. Par E. Fournier, 1872.

FOXE. The Acts and Monuments of John Foxe. With a Life of the Martyrologist by G. Townsend. [Edited by S. R. Cattley.] 8 vols. 1843–9.

FRAZER. The Golden Bough: a Study in Comparative Religion. By J. G. Frazer. 2nd ed. 3 vols. 1900.

FRAZER, *Pausanias.* Pausanias's Description of Greece. Translated with a commentary by J. G. Frazer. 6 vols. 1898.

FRERE. The Winchester Troper. Edited by W. H. Frere, 1894. [*Henry Bradshaw Society.*]

FRERE, *Use of Sarum.* The Use of Sarum. Edited by W. H. Frere. 2 vols. 1898–1901.

See also PROCTER-FRERE.

FREYMOND. Jongleurs und Menestrels. Von E. Freymond, 1883. [Halle dissertation.]

FRIEDLÄNDER. Darstellungen aus der Sittengeschichte Roms in der Zeit von August bis zum Ausgang der Antonine. Von L. Friedländer. 6th ed. 3 vols. 1888–90. [*Das Theater* is in vol. ii.]

FRONING. Das Drama des Mittelalters. Herausgegeben von R. Froning. 3 Parts, 1891. [*Deutsche National-Litteratur,* xiv.]

FROUDE. History of England from the Fall of Wolsey to the Defeat of the Spanish Armada. By J. A. Froude. 2nd ed. 1889–95.

FURNIVALL. The Digby Plays, with an Incomplete Morality of Wisdom, who is Christ. Edited by F. J. Furnivall, 1882. [*N. S. S.* Series vii, 1: re-issue for *E. E. T. S.* 1896.]

See also LANEHAM, MANNYNG, STAFFORD, STUBBES.

Furnivall Miscellany. An English Miscellany Presented to Dr. Furnivall in Honour of his Seventy-fifth Birthday, 1901.

GAIDOZ. Études de Mythologie gauloise. Par H. Gaidoz. I. Le Dieu gaulois du Soleil et le Symbolisme de la Roue, 1886. [Extrait de la *Revue Archéologique,* 1884–85.]

GASPARY. The History of Early Italian Literature to the Death of Dante. Translated from the German of A. Gaspary, by H. Oelsner, 1901.

GASTÉ. Les Drames liturgiques de la Cathédrale de Rouen. Par A. Gasté, 1893. [Extrait de la *Revue Catholique de Normandie.*]

GAUTIER. Les Épopées françaises. Par L. Gautier, vol. ii. 2nd edition, 1892. [Lib. ii. chh. xvii-xxi form the section on *Les Propagateurs des Chansons de Geste.* References to this work may be distinguished from those to *Les Tropaires* by the presence of a volume-number.]

GAUTIER, *Bibl.* Bibliographie des Chansons de Geste. Par L. Gautier, 1897. [A section on *Les Propagateurs des Chansons de Geste.*]

GAUTIER, *Orig.* Origines du Théâtre moderne. Par L. Gautier, 1872. [In *Le Monde.*]

GAUTIER, *Tropaires.* Histoire de la Poésie liturgique au Moyen Âge. Par L. Gautier. Vol. i. *Les Tropaires,* 1886. [All published.]

GAYLEY. Representative English Comedies: from the Beginnings to Shakespeare. Edited by C. M. Gayley, 1903.

GAZEAU. Les Bouffons. Par A. Gazeau, 1882.

GENÉE. Die englischen Mirakelspiele und Moralitäten als Vorläufer des englischen Dramas. Von R. Genée, 1878. [Serie xiii, Heft 305 of

Sammlung gemeinverständlicher wissenschaftlicher Vorträge, herausgegeben von R. Virchow und Fr. v. Holtzendorff.]

GIBBON. The History of the Decline and Fall of the Roman Empire. By E. Gibbon. Edited by J. B. Bury. 7 vols. 1897–1900.

GILPIN. The Beehive of the Romish Church. By G. Gilpin, 1579. [Translated from Isaac Rabbotenu, of Louvain, 1569.]

Gloucester F. L. See *County Folk-Lore.*

GOEDEKE. Grundriss zur Geschichte der deutschen Dichtung, aus den Quellen. Von K. Goedeke. 2nd ed. 7 vols. 1884–1900. [In progress.]

Golden Legend. The Golden Legend: or, Lives of the Saints, as Englished by W. Caxton. Edited by F. S. Ellis, 1900, &c. [*Temple Classics.*]

GÖLTHER. Handbuch der germanischen Mythologie. Von W. Gölther, 1895.

GOMME. Ethnology in Folk-lore. By G. L. Gomme, 1892.

GOMME, *Brit. Ass.* On the Method of determining the Value of Folklore as Ethnological Data. By G. L. Gomme, 1896. [In *Report* of *British Association for the Advancement of Science.*]

GOMME, *Nature.* Christmas Mummers. By G. L. Gomme, 1897. [*Nature*, vol. lvii.]

GOMME, *Vill. Comm.* The Village Community: with special Reference to the Origin and Form of its Survivals in Britain. By G. L. Gomme, 1890. [*Contemporary Science Series.*]

GOMME, MRS. The Traditional Games of England, Scotland, and Ireland, with Tunes. Collected and annotated by A. B. Gomme. 2 vols. 1894–8. [Part i of *Dictionary of British Folk-Lore*, Edited by G. L. Gomme.]

GOOGE. See KIRCHMAYER.

GRACIE. The Presentation in the Temple: A Pageant, as originally represented by the Corporation of Weavers in Coventry, 1836. [Edited by J. B. Gracie for the *Abbotsford Club*.]

GRASS. Das Adamsspiel: anglonormannisches Gedicht des xii. Jahrhunderts. Mit einem Anhang 'Die fünfzehn Zeichen des jüngsten Gerichts.' Herausgegeben von K. Grass, 1891. [*Romanische Bibliothek*, vi.]

GRATIAN. See *C. I. Can.*

GREENIDGE. Infamia: Its Place in Roman Public and Private Law. By A. H. J. Greenidge, 1894.

GREG, *Masques.* A list of Masques, Pageants, &c. Supplementary to a list of English Plays. By W. W. Greg, 1902. [*Bibliographical Society.*]

GREG, *Plays.* A List of English Plays written before 1643, and published before 1700. By W. W. Greg, 1900. [*Bibliographical Society.*]

GREGORY. Gregorii Posthuma: on Certain Learned Tracts written by John Gregory. Published by his Dearest Friend J. G. 1683. [Part II of his *Works*: A separate title-page for *Episcopus Puerorum in Die Innocentium: or, A Discovery of an Ancient Custom in the Church of Sarum, of making an Anniversary Bishop among the Choristers.*]

Gregory's Chronicle. The Historical Collections of a Citizen of London in the Fifteenth Century. Edited by J. Gairdner, III, William Gregory's Chronicle of London. [*C. S.* N. S. xvii.]

GREIN-WÜLCKER. Bibliothek der angelsächsischen Poesie. Herausgegeben von C. W. M. Grein. Neu bearbeitet, vermehrt und herausgegeben von R. P. Wülcker. 3 vols. 1883–98.

GRENIER. Introduction à l'Histoire générale de la Province de Picardie. Par Dom Grenier, 1856. [*Mémoires de la Société des Antiquaires de Picardie. Documents inédits,* iii.]

GRIMM. Teutonic Mythology. By J. Grimm. Translated from the 4th ed. with notes and appendix by J. S. Stallybrass. 4 vols. 1880–8.

GRÖBER. Zur Volkskunde aus Concilbeschlüssen und Capitularien. Von G. Gröber. 1894.

GRÖBER, *Grundriss.* Grundriss der romanischen Philologie. Herausgegeben von G. Gröber. 1888–1902. [In progress. Vol. ii has article by G. Gröber on *Französische Litteratur.*]

GROOS. *Play of Animals.* The Play of Animals : a Study of Animal Life and Instinct. By K. Groos. Translated by E. L. Baldwin, 1898.

GROOS. *Play of Man.* The Play of Man. By K. Gross. Translated by E. L. Baldwin, 1901.

GROSSE. Les Débuts de l'Art. Par E. Grosse. Traduit par E. Dirr. Introduction par L. Marillier. 1902. [*Bibliothèque Scientifique Internationale.*]

GROVE. Dancing. By L. Grove, and other writers. With Musical examples. 1895. [*Badminton Library.*]

GUMMERE, *B. P.* The Beginnings of Poetry. By F. B. Gummere, 1901.

GUMMERE, *G. O.* Germanic Origins : a Study in Primitive Culture. By F. B. Gummere, 1892.

GUTCH. A Lytell Geste of Robin Hood, with other Ballads relative to Robin Hood. Edited by J. M. Gutch. 2 vols. 1847.

GUY. Essai sur la Vie et les Œuvres littéraires du Trouvère Adan de le Hale. Par H. Guy, 1898.

HADDAN-STUBBS. Councils and Ecclesiastical Documents relating to Great Britain and Ireland. Edited, after Spelman and Wilkins, by A. W. Haddan and W. Stubbs. 3 vols. 1869–78.

HADDON. The Study of Man. By A. C. Haddon, 1898. [*Progressive Science Series.*]

HAIGH. The Tragic Drama of the Greeks. By A. E. Haigh, 1896.

HALL. The Union of the Families of Lancaster and York. By E. Hall. Edited by H. Ellis. 1809.

HALLIWELL-PHILLIPPS. Outlines of the Life of Shakespeare. By J. O. Halliwell-Phillipps. 9th ed. 2 vols. 1890.

HALLIWELL-PHILLIPS. *Revels.* A Collection of Ancient Documents respecting the Office of Master of the Revels, and other Papers relating to the Early English Theatre. [By J. O. Halliwell-Phillipps.] 1870.

HAMPSON. Medii Aevi Kalendarium: or Dates. Charters and Customs of the Middle Ages, &c. By R. T. Hampson. 2 vols. 1841.

Handlyng Synne. See MANNYNG.

HARLAND. Lancashire Folk-Lore. By J. Harland and T. T. Wilkinson, 1867.

HARRIS. Life in an Old English Town: a History of Coventry from the Earliest Times. Compiled from Official Records by M. D. Harris, 1898. [*Social England Series.*]

HARTLAND. The Legend of Perseus: a Study of Tradition in Story, Custom and Belief. By E. S. Hartland. 3 vols. 1894-6.

HARTLAND. *Fairy Tales.* The Science of Fairy Tales: an Inquiry into Fairy Mythology. By E. S. Hartland, 1891. [*Contemporary Science Series.*]

HARTZHEIM. *See* SCHANNAT.

HASE. Miracle Plays and Sacred Dramas. By C. A. Hase. Translated by A. W. Jackson, 1880.

HASTINGS. Le Théâtre français et anglais: ses Origines grecques et latines. Par C. Hastings, 1900.

HASTINGS. The Theatre: its Development in France and England. By C. Hastings. Translated by F. A. Welby, 1901.

HAUCK. Kirchengeschichte Deutschlands. Von A. Hauck. 2nd ed. 3 vols. 1896-1900.

HAVARD. Les Fêtes de nos Pères. Par O. Havard, 1898.

HAZLITT. Remains of the Early Popular Poetry of England. Collected and edited, with introductions and notes, by W. Carew Hazlitt. 4 vols. 1864-6. [*Library of Old Authors.*]

HAZLITT, *E. D. S.* The English Drama and Stage under the Tudor and Stuart Princes, 1543-1664, illustrated by a series of Documents, Treatises, and Poems. Edited by W. C. Hazlitt, 1869. [*Roxburghe Library.*]

HAZLITT, *Liv.* The Livery Companies of London. By W. C. Hazlitt, 1892.

HAZLITT, *Manual.* A Manual for the Collector and Amateur of Old English Plays. By W. C. Hazlitt, 1892.

HAZLITT-DODSLEY. A Select Collection of Old Plays. By R. Dodsley. Chronologically arranged, revised and enlarged by W. C. Hazlitt. 4th ed. 15 vols. 1874-6.

HAZLITT-WARTON. History of English Poetry, from the Twelfth to the close of the Sixteenth Century. By T. Warton. Edited by W. C. Hazlitt. 4 vols. 1871.

H. B. S. = Henry Bradshaw Society.

HEALES. Easter Sepulchres: their Object, Nature, and History. By A. Heales, 1868. [*Archaeologia*, vol. xlii.]

HEINZEL. Beschreibung des geistlichen Schauspiels im deutschen Mittelalter. Von R. Heinzel, 1898. [*Beiträge zur Ästhetik*, iv.]

HENDERSON. Notes on the Folk-Lore of the Northern Counties of England and the Borders. By W. Henderson. 2nd ed. 1879. [*F. L. S.*]

HERBERT. Antiquities of the Inns of Court and Chancery. By W. Herbert, 1804.

HERBERT, *Liv.* History of the Twelve Great Livery Companies of London. By W. Herbert. 2 vols. 1836-7.

Hereford Missal. Missale ad usum percelebris Ecclesiae Herfordensis. Edidit W. G. Henderson, 1874.

HERFORD. The Literary Relations of England and Germany in the Sixteenth Century. By C. H. Herford, 1886.

HERRTRICH. Studien zu den York Plays. Von O. Herrtrich, 1886. [Breslau dissertation ; not consulted.]

HIGGS. The Christmas Prince. By Griffin Higgs, 1607. [In *Miscellanea Antiqua Anglicana*, 1816.]

HILARIUS. Hilarii Versus et Ludi. Edidit J. J. Champollion-Figeac, 1838.

HIRN. The Origins of Art : a Psychological and Sociological Enquiry. By Yrjö Hirn, 1900.

Hist. d'Autun. Histoire de l'Église d'Autun. Autun, 1774.

Hist. Litt. Histoire littéraire de la France. Par des Religieux bénédictins de la Congrégation de S. Maur. Continuée par des Membres de l'Institut. 32 vols. 1733-1898. [In progress.]

Hist. MSS. Reports of the Historical Manuscripts Commission, 1883-1902. [In progress.]

HOBHOUSE. Churchwardens' Accounts of Croscombe, Pilton, Yatton, Tintinhull, Morebath, and St. Michael's, Bath, 1349-1560. Edited by E. Hobhouse, 1890. [*Somerset Record Society*, vol. iv.]

HODGKIN. Italy and her Invaders. By T. Hodgkin. 8 vols. 1892-9.

HOHLFELD. Die altenglischen Kollektivmisterien, unter besonderer Berücksichtigung des Verhältnisses der York- und Towneley-Spiele. Von A. Hohlfeld, 1889. [*Anglia*, vol. xi.]

HOLINSHED. Holinshed's Chronicles of England, Scotland, and Ireland. 6 vols. 1807-8.

HOLTHAUSEN. Noah's Ark : or, the Shipwright's Ancient Play or Dirge. Edited by F. Holthausen, 1897. [Extract from *Göteborg's Högskola's Årsskrift.*]

HONE. Ancient Mysteries described, especially the English Miracle Plays, founded on Apocryphal New Testament Story, extant among the unpublished Manuscripts in the British Museum. By W. Hone, 1823.

HONE, *E. D. B.* The Every Day Book and Table Book. By W. Hone. 3 vols. 1838.

Household Ordinances. A Collection of Ordinances and Regulations for the Government of the Royal Household, made in divers Reigns from King Edward III to King William and Mary, 1790. [*Society of Antiquaries of London.*]

HROTSVITHA. Hrotsvithae Opera. Recensuit et emendavit P. de Winterfeld, 1902. [In *Scriptores Rerum Germanicarum in usum Scholarum ex Monumentis Germaniae Historicis separatim editi.*]

HUBATSCH. Die lateinischen Vagantenlieder des Mittelalters. Von O. Hubatsch, 1870.

Indiculus. See SAUPE.

JAHN. Die deutschen Opfergebräuche bei Ackerbau und Viehzucht. Ein Beitrag von U. Jahn, 1884. [*Germanistische Abhandlungen*, herausgegeben von Karl Weinhold, iii.]

JEANROY. Les Origines de la Poésie lyrique en France au Moyen Âge : Études de Littérature française et comparée, suivies de Textes inédits. Par A. Jeanroy, 1889.

JEVONS. An Introduction to the History of Religion. By F. B. Jevons, 1896.

JEVONS, *Plutarch.* Plutarch's Romane Questions. Translated A.D. 1603 by Philemon Holland. Now again edited by F. B. Jevons. With Dissertations on Italian Cults, 1892.

See also SCHRÄDER.

JONES, *Fasti.* Fasti Ecclesiae Sarisburiensis, or A Calendar of the Bishops, Deans, Archdeacons, and Members of the Cathedral Body at Salisbury, from the Earliest Times to the Present. By W. H. Jones, 1881. [Pages 295-301 contain an account of the Boy Bishop at Salisbury.]

JORDAN. The Creation of the World. By W. Jordan. Edited with a translation by Whitley Stokes, 1863. [*Transactions of Philological Society.*]

JUBINAL. Jongleurs et Trouvères : Choix de Pièces des xiiie et xive Siècles. Par M. L. A. Jubinal, 1835.

JUBINAL, *Myst.* Mystères inédits du xve Siècle. Par M. L. A. Jubinal. 2 vols. 1837.

JUBINAL, *N. R.* Nouveau Recueil de Contes, Dits, Fabliaux, et autres Pièces inédites des xiiie, xive, et xve Siècles. Par M. L. A. JUBINAL. 2 vols. 1839-42.

JULIAN. Iuliani Imperatoris quae supersunt. Recensuit F. C. Hertlein. 2 vols. 1875-6.

JULLEVILLE. *See* PETIT DE JULLEVILLE.

JUSSERAND. Le Théâtre en Angleterre depuis la Conquête jusqu'aux Prédécesseurs immédiats de Shakespeare. Par J. J. Jusserand. 2nd ed. 1881.

JUSSERAND, *E. L.* A Literary History of the English People from the Origins to the Renaissance. By J. J. Jusserand. Vol. i, 1895. [In progress.]

JUSSERAND, *E. W. L.* English Wayfaring Life in the Middle Ages. By J. J. Jusserand. Translated by L. T. Smith. 4th ed. 1892. [The English translation has valuable illustrations.]

KEARY. The Vikings in Western Christendom : A.D. 789 to A.D. 888. By C. F. Keary, 1891.

KELLER. Fastnachtspiele aus dem 15. Jahrhundert. Von A. von Keller, 1853-8.

KELLY. Notices Illustrative of the Drama, and other Popular Amusements, chiefly in the Sixteenth and Seventeenth Centuries, incidentally illustrating Shakespeare and his Contemporaries; extracted from the Chamberlain's Accounts and other Manuscripts of the Borough of Leicester. With an introduction and notes by W. Kelly, 1865.

KEMBLE. The Saxons in England : a History of the English Commonwealth till the Period of the Norman Conquest. By J. M. Kemble. 2 vols. 1849.

KEMPE. Manuscripts and other rare Documents from the Reign of Henry VIII to that of James I, preserved in the Muniment Room at Loseley House. Edited by A. J. Kempe, 1835.

KIRCHMAYER. The Popish Kingdom, or reigne of Antichrist, written in Latine verse by Thomas Naogeorgus (or Kirchmayer), and englyshed by Barnabe Googe, 1570. [See STUBBES.]

KLEIN. Geschichte des Dramas. Von J. L. Klein. 13 vols. 1865-76. Register-Band von T. Ebner, 1886. [Vol. ii contains 'Das Drama der Römer,' vol. iii 'Die lateinischen Schauspiele,' vols. xii, xiii 'Das englische Drama.']

KNAPPERT. Le Christianisme et le Paganisme dans l'Histoire ecclésiastique de Bède le Vénérable. Par L. Knappert, 1897. [In *Revue de l'Histoire des Religions*, vol. xxxv.]

KÖGEL. Geschichte der deutschen Litteratur bis zum Ausgange des Mittelalters. Von R. Kögel. 2 vols. 1894-7. [All published.]

KÖPPEN. Beiträge zur Geschichte der deutschen Weihnachtsspiele. Von W. Köppen, 1893.

KÖRTING. Geschichte des Theaters in seinen Beziehungen zur Kunstentwickelung der dramatischen Dichtkunst. Erster Band : Geschichte des griechischen und römischen Theaters. Von G. Körting, 1897.

KÖRTING, *Grundriss*. Grundriss der Geschichte der englischen Litteratur von ihren Anfängen bis zur Gegenwart. Von G. Körting. 3rd ed. 1899.

KRAMER. Sprache und Heimath der Coventry-Plays. Von M. Kramer. [Not consulted.]

KRUMBACHER. Geschichte der byzantinischen Litteratur von Justinian bis zum Ende des oströmischen Reiches (527-1423). Von K. Krumbacher. 2nd ed. 1897. [Vol. ix. Pt. I of *Handbuch der klassischen Altertumswissenschaft*, herausgegeben von Dr. I. von Müller.]

LABBÉ. Sacrosancta Concilia. Studio Philippi Labbei et Gabrielis Cossartii. 17 vols. 1671-2.

LACROIX. Dissertation sur les Fous des Rois de France. Par P. Lacroix. [*pseud.* P. L. Jacob.]

LANEHAM. Captain Cox, his Ballads and Books: or Robert Laneham's Letter. Re-edited by F. J. Furnivall, 1871. [*Ballad Society*, vii. Reprinted with slight alterations for *N. S. S.*, series vi. 14 in 1890.]

Lang. et Litt. Histoire de la Langue et de la Littérature française, des Origines à 1900. Publiée sous la direction de L. Petit de Julleville, 1896-1900. [Tom. i, in two parts, covers the Moyen Âge : the articles are by various specialists.]

LANG, *M. of R.* The Making of Religion. By A. Lang. 2nd ed. 1900.

LANG, *M. R. R.* Myth, Ritual, and Religion. By A. Lang. 2 vols. 1887. 2nd ed. 1899.

LANGE. Die lateinischen Osterfeiern : Untersuchungen über den Ursprung und die Entwickelung der liturgisch-dramatischen Auferstehungsfeier. Von C. Lange, 1887.

LAVOIX. La Musique au Siècle de Saint-Louis. Par H. Lavoix. [Contributed to G. Raynaud, *Recueil de Motets français*, vol. ii.]

LEACH. The Schoolboys' Feast. By A. F. Leach, 1896. [*Fortnightly Review*, vol. lix.]

LEACH, *Beverley MSS.* Report on the Manuscripts of the Corporation of Beverley. By A. F. Leach, 1900. [*Hist. MSS.*]

LEBER. Collection des meilleures Dissertations, Notices, et Traités particuliers, relatifs à l'Histoire de France. Par C. Leber, J. B. Salgues et J. Cohen. 20 vols. 1826-38.

Leicester F. L. See *Country Folk-Lore.*

LELAND. Iohannis Lelandi de Rebus Britannicis Collectanea. Cum T. Hearnii praefationibus, notis, &c. Accedunt de Rebus Anglicis Opuscula varia. 2nd ed. 6 vols. 1774.

LE ROY. Études sur les Mystères. Par O. Le Roy, 1837.

L. H. T. Accounts. Accounts of the Lord High Treasurer of Scotland. Edited by Thomas Dickson (vol. i, 1473-1498) and Sir J. B. Paul (vols. ii, 1500-1504 ; iii, 1506-1507), 1877-1901.

Lincoln Statutes. Statutes of Lincoln Cathedral. Arranged by H. Bradshaw ; with Illustrative Documents, edited by C. Wordsworth. 2 vols. 1892-7.

LIPENIUS. Martini Lipenii Strenarum Historia, 1699 [in J. G. Graevius. *Thesaurus Antiquitatum Romanarum*, xii. 409.]

LOLIÉE. La Fête des Fous. Par F. Loliée, 1898. [In *Revue des Revues*, vol. xxv.]

London Chronicle. A Chronicle of London, from 1089 to 1483. [Edited by N. H. Nicolas or Edward Tyrrell], 1827.

Ludus Coventriae. Ludus Coventriae. A Collection of Mysteries, formerly represented at Coventry on the Feast of Corpus Christi. Edited by J. O. Halliwell, 1841 [*Shakespeare Society*].

LUICK. Zur Geschichte des englischen Dramas im xvi. Jahrhundert. Von K. Luick, 1898. [In *Forschungen zur neueren Litteraturgeschichte : Festgabe für Richard Heinzel.*]

MAASSEN. Concilia Aevi Merovingici. Recensuit F. Maassen, 1893. [*M. G. H. Leges*, Sectio iii.]

MACHYN. The Diary of Henry Machyn, Citizen and Merchant-Taylor of London, 1550-63. Edited by J. G. Nichols, 1848. [*C. S.* o. s. xlii.]

MACLAGAN. The Games and Diversions of Argyleshire. By R. C. Maclagan, 1901. [*F. L. S.*]

MAGNIN. Les Origines du Théâtre moderne, ou Histoire du Génie dramatique depuis le 1ᵉʳ jusqu'au xviᵉ Siècle. Par C. Magnin, 1838. [Vol. i only published, containing introductory ' Études sur les Origines du Théâtre antique.' Notes of Magnin's lectures in the *Journal général de l'Instruction publique* (1834-6) and reviews in the *Journal des Savants* (1846-7) partly cover the ground of the missing volumes.]

MAGNIN, *Marionnettes*. Histoire des Marionnettes en Europe. Par C. Magnin. 2nd ed. 1862.

MALLESON-TUKER. Handbook to Christian and Ecclesiastical Rome. By H. M[alleson] and M. A. R. T[uker]. 3 vols. 1897-1900.

MANLY. Specimens of the Pre-Shaksperean Drama. With an introduction, notes, and a glossary. By J. M. Manly. 3 vols. 1897. [*Athenæum Press Series*; 2 vols. only yet published.]

MANNHARDT. Wald- und Feld-Kulte. Von W. Mannhardt. 2 vols. 1875-7.

MANNING. Oxfordshire Seasonal Festivals. By P. Manning, 1897. [*Folk-Lore*, vol. viii.]

MANNYNG. Roberd [Mannyng] of Brunnè's Handlyng Synne. Edited by F. J. Furnivall, 1862. [*Roxburghe Club*; a new edition promised for *E. E. T. S.*]

MANSI. Sacrorum Conciliorum Nova et Amplissima Collectio. Editio novissima a patre J. D. Mansi. 30 vols. Florence, 1769-92.

MAP. *See* WRIGHT.

MARKLAND. Chester Mysteries. De deluvio Noe, De occisione innocentium. Edited by J. H. Markland, 1818. [*Roxburghe Club.*]

MARQUARDT-MOMMSEN. Handbuch der römischen Alterthümer. Von J. Marquardt und T. Mommsen. 3rd ed. 7 vols. 1881-8.

MARRIOTT. A Collection of English Miracle-Plays or Mysteries. Edited by W. Marriott. Basle, 1838.

MARTENE. De Antiquis Ecclesiae Ritibus Libri Tres collecti atque exornati ab Edmundo Martene. Editio novissima, 1783. [This edition has a 4th vol., De Monachorum Ritibus.]

MARTIN OF BRAGA. Martin von Bracara's Schrift: De Correctione Rusticorum, herausgegeben von C. P. Caspari, 1883. [*Videnskabs-Selskab* of Christiania.]

MARTINENGO-CESARESCO. Essays in the Study of Folk-Songs. By the Countess E. Martinengo-Cesaresco, 1886.

MARTONNE. La Piété du Moyen Âge. Par A. de Martonne, 1855.

MASKELL. The Ancient Liturgy of the Church of England according to the Uses of Sarum, York, Hereford, Bangor, and the Roman Liturgy. By W. Maskell. 3rd ed. 1882.

MASKELL, *Mon. Rit.* Monumenta Ritualia Ecclesiae Anglicanae. Occasional Offices according to the ancient Use of Salisbury, &c. By W. Maskell. 2nd ed. 3 vols. 1882.

MAUGRAS. Les Comédiens hors la Loi. Par G. Maugras, 1887.

MAYER. Ein deutsches Schwerttanzspiel aus Ungarn. Von F. A. Mayer, 1889. [*Zeitschrift für Völkerpsychologie.*]

Mélusine. Mélusine : Recueil de Mythologie, Littérature populaire, Traditions et Usages, 1878, 1883, &c.

MERBOT. Aesthetische Studien zur angelsächsischen Poesie. Von R. Merbot, 1883.

Merc. Fr. Le Mercure de France. 974 vols. 1724–91.

MEYER. Fragmenta Burana. Herausgegeben von W. Meyer aus Speyer, 1901. [Sonderabdruck aus der Festschrift zur Feier des 150-jährigen Bestehens der *Königlichen Gesellschaft der Wissenschaften zu Göttingen.*]

MEYER, *Germ. Myth.* Germanische Mythologie. Par E. H. Meyer, 1891.

M. G. H. Monumenta Germaniae Historiae. Auspiciis Societatis Aperiendis Fontibus Rerum Germanicarum Medii Aevi. Edidit G. H. Pertz, T. Mommsen, et alii, 1826–1902. [In progress, under various series, as *Auctores Antiquissimi, Epistolae, Leges, Scriptores,* &c. Indices, 1890.]

MICHELS. Studien über die ältesten deutschen Fastnachtspiele. Von V. Michels, 1896. [*Quellen und Forschungen,* lxxvii.]

MICKLETHWAITE. The Ornaments of the Rubric. By J. T. Micklethwaite, 1897. [*Alcuin Club Tracts,* 1.]

MILCHSACK. Die Oster- und Passionsspiele : literar-historische Untersuchungen über den Ursprung und die Entwickelung derselben bis zum siebenzehnten Jahrhundert, vornehmlich in Deutschland. Von G. Milchsack. i, Die lateinischen Osterfeiern, 1880. [All published.]

Miracles de Nostre Dame. Miracles de Nostre Dame par Personnages. Publiés d'après le manuscrit de la Bibliothèque Nationale par G. Paris et U. Robert. 8 vols. 1876–93. [*Société des Anciens Textes Français.*]

MOGK. Mythologie. Von E. Mogk. 2nd ed. 1897–8. [In Paul, *Grundriss,* 2nd ed. vol. iii.]

MOMMSEN, *C. I. L.* Inscriptiones Latinae Antiquissimae. Editio Altera. Pars Prior. Cura Theodori Mommsen [et aliorum], 1893. [*Corpus Inscriptionum Latinarum,* vol. i. part 1.]

See MARQUARDT-MOMMSEN.

MONACI. Appunti per la Storia del Teatro italiano. Per E. Monaci, 1872–5. [*Rivista di Filologia Romanza,* i, ii.]

Monasticon. See DUGDALE.

MONE. Schauspiele des Mittelalters. Herausgegeben und erklärt von F. J. Mone. 2 vols. 1846.

MONE. Altteutsche Schauspiele. Herausgegeben von F. J. Mone, 1835.

MONMERQUÉ-MICHEL. Théâtre français au Moyen Âge. Publié d'après les Manuscrits de la Bibliothèque du Roi par L. J. N. Monmerqué et F. Michel, 1839.

MONTAIGLON-RAYNAUD. Recueil général et complet des Fabliaux des treizième et quatorzième Siècles. Par A. de Montaiglon et G. Raynaud. 6 vols. 1872–90.

MONTAIGLON-ROTHSCHILD. Recueil de Poésies françaises des quinzième et seizième Siècles. Par A. de Montaiglon et J. de Rothschild. 13 vols. 1855–78.

MOREAU. Fous et Bouffons. Étude physiologique, psychologique et historique par P. Moreau, 1885.

MORLEY. Memoirs of Bartholomew Fair. By H. Morley, 1859.

MORLEY, *E. W.* English Writers : an Attempt towards a History of English Literature. By H. Morley. 11 vols. 1887–95.

MORRIS. Chester in the Plantagenet and Tudor Reigns. By Rupert Morris, 1893.

MORTENSEN, Medeltidsdramat i Frankrike. By Dr. Mortensen, 1899. [Not consulted.]

MÜLLENHOFF. Ueber den Schwerttanz. Von K. Müllenhoff, 1871. [In *Festgaben für Gustav Homeyer, zum 28. Juli* 1871 (Berlin). Müllenhoff's essay is contained in pages 111 to 147 ; he published additions to it in *Zeitschrift für deutsches Alterthum*, xviii. 9 ; xx. 10.]

MÜLLER, E. Le Jour de l'An et les Étrennes, chez tous les Peuples dans tous les Temps. Par E. Müller, n. d.

MÜLLER, P. E. Commentatio Historica de Genio, Moribus et Luxu Aevi Theodosiani. By P. E. Müller. 2 parts, 1797–8.

N. E. D. A New English Dictionary on Historical Principles, founded mainly on the Materials collected by the Philological Society. Edited by J. A. H. Murray, H. Bradley, and W. A. Craigie. Vols. 1–6, 1888–1903. [In progress.]

NEWELL. Games and Songs of American Children. By W.W.Newell,1884.

NICHOLS, *Elizabeth.* Progresses and Public Processions of Queen Elizabeth. With historical notes, &c., by J. Nichols. 2nd ed. 3 vols. 1823.

NICHOLS, *James I.* Progresses, Processions, and Festivities of James I, his Court, &c. By J. Nichols. 4 vols. 1828.

NICHOLS, *Pageants.* London Pageants. By J. G. Nichols, 1837.

NICHOLSON. Golspie : Contributions to its Folklore. Edited by E. W. B. Nicholson, 1897.

NICK. Hof- und Volksnarren. Von A. F. Nick, 1861.

Noctes Shaksperianae. Noctes Shaksperianae : Papers edited by C. H. Hawkins, 1887. [*Winchester College Shakespere Society.*]

NÖLDECHEN. Tertullian und das Theater. Von E. Nöldechen, 1894. [*Zeitschrift für Kirchengeschichte*, xv. 161.]

Norf. Arch. Norfolk Archaeology : or, Miscellaneous Tracts relating to the Antiquities of the County of Norfolk, 1847–1903. [In progress : transactions of *Norfolk and Norwich Archaeological Society.*]

NORRIS. The Ancient Cornish Drama. Edited and translated by E. Norris. 2 vols. 1859.

NORTHALL. English Folk-Rhymes : a Collection of Traditional Verses relating to Places and Persons, Customs, Superstitions, &c. By G. F. Northall, 1892.

Northern F. L. See HENDERSON.

N. Q. Notes and Queries : a Medium of Intercommunication for Literary Men and General Readers. 107 vols. 1850–1903. [Ninth decennial series in progress.]

N. S. S. = New Shakspere Society.

OLRIK. Middelalderens vandrende Spillemænd. By A. Olrik, 1887. [In *Opuscula Philologica*, Copenhagen; not consulted.]

OPORINUS. Dramata Sacra, Comoediae et Tragoediae aliquot e Veteri Testamento desumptae. 2 vols. Basileae, Oporinus, 1547.

ORDISH. English Folk-Drama. By T. F. Ordish, 1891–3. [*Folk-Lore*, vols. ii, iv.]

OROSIUS. Pauli Orosii Historiarum adversus Paganos libri vii. Recensuit C. Zangemeister, 1882. [*C. S. E. L.* vol. v.]

OWEN-BLAKEWAY. A History of Shrewsbury. [By H. Owen and J. B. Blakeway.] 2 vols. 1825.

PADELFORD. Old English Musical Terms. By F. M. Padelford, 1899.

PARIS. La Littérature française au Moyen Âge. Par G. Paris. 2nd edition, 1890. [A volume of the *Manuel d'ancien Français*.]

PARIS, *Orig.* Les Origines de la Poésie lyrique en France au Moyen Âge. Par G. Paris, 1892. [Extrait du *Journal des Savants*.]

Paston Letters. The Paston Letters; 1422–1509 A.D. Edited by J. Gairdner. 2nd ed. 4 vols. 1900.

PAUL, *Grundriss.* Grundriss der germanischen Philologie. Herausgegeben von H. Paul. 2nd ed. 1896–1902. [In progress.]

PEARSON. The Chances of Death and other Studies in Evolution. By K. Pearson. 2 vols. 1897.

PERCY. Reliques of Ancient English Poetry. By Thomas Percy. Edited by H. B. Wheatley. 3 vols. 1876. [Vol. i contains an *Essay on the Ancient Minstrels in England*.]

PERCY, *N. H. B.* The Regulations and Establishment of the Household of Henry Algernon Percy, the fifth Earl of Northumberland, &c. Edited by T. Percy, 1827.

PERTZ. See *M. G. H.*

PETIT DE JULLEVILLE. Les Mystères. Par L. Petit de Julleville. 2 vols. 1880. [Forms, with three following, the *Histoire du Théâtre en France*.]

PETIT DE JULLEVILLE, *La Com.* La Comédie et les Mœurs en France au Moyen Âge. Par L. Petit de Julleville, 1886.

PETIT DE JULLEVILLE, *Les Com.* Les Comédiens en France au Moyen Âge. Par L. Petit de Julleville, 1889.

PETIT DE JULLEVILLE, *Rép. Com.* Répertoire du Théâtre Comique en France au Moyen Âge. Par L. Petit de Julleville, 1886.

See also *Lang. et Litt.*

PFANNENSCHMIDT. Germanische Erntefeste im heidnischen und christlichen Cultus mit besonderer Beziehung auf Niedersachsen. Von H. Pfannenschmidt, 1878.

P. G. Patrologiae Cursus Completus, seu Bibliotheca Universalis, Integra, Uniformis, Commoda, Oeconomica, Omnium SS. Patrum, Doctorum Scriptorumve Ecclesiasticorum, &c.; Series Graeca. Accurante J. P. Migne. 161 vols. 1857–66.

PHILPOT. The Sacred Tree: or the Tree in Religion and Myth. By Mrs. J. H. Philpot, 1897.

PICOT. La Sottie en France. Par E. Picot, 1878. [In *Romania*, vol. vii.]

PILOT DE THOREY. Usages, Fêtes, et Coutumes, existant ou ayant existé en Dauphiné. Par J. J. A. Pilot de Thorey. 2 vols. 1884.

P. L. Patrologiae Cursus Completus, &c. Series Latina. Accurante J. P. Migne. 221 vols. 1844-64.

PLUMMER. *See* BEDE, *E. H.*

POLLARD. English Miracle Plays, Moralities, and Interludes: Specimens of the Pre-Elizabethan Drama. Edited by A. W. Pollard. 3rd ed. 1898.

See also *Towneley Plays.*

PRELLER. Römische Mythologie. Von L. Preller. 3rd ed. by H. Jordan. 2 vols. 1881-3.

PROCTER-FRERE. A New History of the Book of Common Prayer. By F. Procter. Revised and rewritten by W. H. Frere, 1901.

PRÖLSS. Geschichte des neueren Dramas. Von R. Prölss. 3 vols. 1881-3.

Promptorium Parvulorum. Promptorium Parvulorum seu Clericorum: Lexicon Anglo-Latinum Princeps, Auctore Fratre Galfrido Grammatico Dicto, circa 1440. Recensuit A. Way. 3 vols. 1843-65. [*C. S.* O. S. xxv, liv, lxxxix.]

PRYNNE. Histrio-Mastix. The Players Scourge or Actors Tragedie. By W. Prynne, 1633.

PUECH. St. Jean Chrysostome et les Mœurs de son Temps. Par A. Puech, 1891.

RAMSAY, *F. E.* The Foundations of England, or Twelve Centuries of British History; B.C. 55-A.D. 1154. By Sir J. H. Ramsay. 2 vols. 1898.

RAMSAY, *L. Y.* Lancaster and York: 1399-1485. By Sir J. H. Ramsay. 2 vols. 1892.

RASHDALL. The Universities of the Middle Ages. By H. Rashdall. 2 vols. 1895.

RAYNAUD. Recueil de Motets français des douzième et treizième Siècles, avec notes, &c., par G. Raynaud. Suivi d'une Étude sur la Musique au Siècle de S. Louis par H. Lavoix fils. 2 vols. 1881-3.

Regularis Concordia. De Consuetudine Monachorum. Herausgegeben von W. S. Logemann, 1891-3. [*Anglia*, vols. xiii, xv.]

REIDT. Das geistliche Schauspiel des Mittelalters in Deutschland. Von H. Reidt, 1868.

REINERS. Die Tropen-, Prosen- und Präfations-Gesänge des feierlichen Hochamtes im Mittelalter. Von A. Reiners, 1884. [Not consulted.]

Reliquiae Antiquae. See WRIGHT-HALLIWELL.

Rev.° Celt. Revue Celtique, dirigée par H. Gaidoz [afterwards H. D'Arbois de Jubainville]. 24 vols. 1890-1903. [In progress.]

Rev. Hist. Rel. Annales du Musée Guimet. Revue de l'Histoire des Religions. 46 vols. 1880–1902. [In progress.]

Rev. T. P. Revue des Traditions populaires, 1886, &c. [Organ of *Société des Traditions populaires.*]

RHYS, *C. F.* Celtic Folklore: Welsh and Manx. By J. Rhys. 2 vols. 1901.

RHYS, *C. H.* Lectures on the Origin and Growth of Religion as illustrated by Celtic Heathendom. By J. Rhys, 1888. [The *Hibbert Lectures* for 1886.]

RIBTON-TURNER. A History of Vagrants and Vagrancy. By C. J. Ribton-Turner, 1887.

RIGOLLOT. Monnaies inconnues des Evêques des Innocens, des Fous, et de quelques autres Associations singulières du même Temps. Par M. J. R[igollot] d'Amiens. Avec une introduction par C. L[eber]. 2 vols. (Texte et Planches), 1837.

RILEY. Memorials of London and London Life : a series of Extracts from the Archives of the City of London, 1276–1419. Translated and edited by H. T. Riley, 1868.

RIMBAULT. Two Sermons Preached by the Boy Bishop. Edited by J. G. Nichols. With an introduction giving an account of the Festival of the Boy Bishop in England. By E. F. Rimbault, 1875. [*Camden Miscellany*, vol. vii. *C. S.*]

RITSON. Ancient English Metrical Romanceës. Selected and published by J. Ritson. 2 vols. 1802. [Vol. I contains a *Dissertation on Romance and Minstrelsy.*]

RITSON, *Bibl. Poet.* Bibliographia Poetica : a Catalogue of English Poets, from the twelfth to the sixteenth centuries, with an account of their Works. By J. Ritson, 1802.

RITSON, *Robin Hood.* Robin Hood : a Collection of all the Ancient Poems, Songs, and Ballads now extant, relative to that Outlaw. Edited by J. Ritson, 1795.

RITSON, *Songs.* Ancient Songs and Ballads, from Henry II to the Revolution. By J. Ritson. 3rd ed., revised by W. C. Hazlitt, 1877.

Ritual Commission. Second Report of the Commissioners Appointed to Inquire into the Rubrics, Orders, and Directions for Regulating the Course and Conduct of Public Worship, &c., 1868. [A Parliamentary paper. *Appendix E* (pp. 399–685) is a reprint of Injunctions and Visitation Articles from 1561 to 1730.]

ROCK. The Church of our Fathers, in St. Osmund's Rite for Salisbury, &c. By D. Rock. 3 vols. 1849–53.

Romania. Romania : Recueil trimestriel consacré à l'Étude des Langues et des Littératures romanes. 32 vols. 1872–1903. [In progress.]

ROSCHER, *Lexicon.* Ausführliches Lexicon der griechischen und römischen Mythologie. Herausgegeben von W. H. Roscher, 1884–97. [In progress.]

ROVENHAGEN. Alt-englische Dramen. I. Die geistlichen Schauspiele. Von Prof. Dr. Rovenhagen, 1879.

R. S.=Rerum Britannicarum Medii Aevi Scriptores, or, Chronicles and Memorials of Great Britain and Ireland during the Middle Ages. Published under the direction of the Master of the Rolls, 1858-99. [*Rolls Series.*]

RYMER. Foedera, Conventiones, Literae, et cuiuscumque generis Acta Publica. Accurante Thoma Rymer. 20 vols. 1704-35.

SAINTSBURY. A Short History of English Literature. By G. Saintsbury, 1898.

SAINTSBURY, *Ren.* The Earlier Renaissance. By G. Saintsbury, 1901. [*Periods of European Literature,* v.]

SALVIAN. Salviani Presbyteri Massiliensis Opera Omnia. Recensuit Franciscus Pauly, 1883. [*C. S. E. L.* viii. The references in the text are to the *De Gubernatione Dei.*]

SANDYS. Christmastide : its History, Festivities, and Carols. By W. Sandys, n. d.

SANDYS, *Carols.* Christmas Carols, Ancient and Modern, &c. With an introduction and notes by W. Sandys, 1833.

Sarum Breviary. Breviarium ad usum insignis Ecclesiae Sarum. Labore F. Procter et C. Wordsworth. 3 vols. 1882-6.

Sarum Manual. See *York Manual.*

Sarum Missal. Missale ad usum insignis et praeclarae Ecclesiae Sarum. Labore et studio F. H. Dickinson, 1861-83.

Sarum Processional. Processionale ad usum Sarum. Edited by W. G. Henderson, 1882. [From Rouen edition of 1508.] *See* WORDSWORTH, *Proc.*

SATHAS. Ἱστορικὸν δοκίμιον περὶ τοῦ θεάτρου καὶ τῆς μουσικῆς τῶν βυζαντινῶν. By K. N. Sathas, Venice, 1878.

SAUPE. Der Indiculus Superstitionum et Paganiarum : ein Verzeichnis heidnischer und abergläubischer Gebräuche und Meinungen aus der Zeit Karls des Grossen. Von H. A. Saupe, 1891. [Leipziger Programm.]

SCHACK. Geschichte der dramatischen Litteratur und Kunst in Spanien. Von A. F. von Schack. 3 vols. 1845-6.

SCHAFF. History of the Christian Church. By P. Schaff. 2nd ed. 12 vols. 1883-93.

SCHÄFFER. Geschichte des spanischen Nationaldramas. Von A. Schäffer, 1890.

SCHANNAT. Concilia Germaniae, quae J. F. Schannat primum collegit, deinde J. Hartzheim auxit. 11 vols. 1759-90.

SCHELLING. The English Chronicle Play : a Study in the Popular Historical Literature environing Shakespeare. By F. E. Schelling, 1902.

SCHERER. Geschichte der deutschen Litteratur. Von W. Scherer. 8th ed. 1899. [Eng. transl. from 3rd ed. by Mrs. F. C. Conybeare, 1886.]

SCHMELLER. Carmina Burana : lateinische und deutsche Lieder und Gedichte einer Handschrift des xiii. Jahrhunderts aus Benedictbeuern. Herausgegeben von J. A. Schmeller, 3rd edition, 1894.

SCHMIDT. Die Digby-Spiele. Von K. Schmidt, 1884. [Berlin dissertation : continued in *Anglia*, vol. viii.]

SCHMITZ. Die Bussbücher und die Bussdisciplin der Kirche. Von H. J. Schmitz, 1883.

SCHÖNBACH. Über die Marienklagen. Ein Beitrag zur Geschichte der geistlichen Dichtung in Deutschland. Von A. E. Schönbach, 1874.

SCHRÄDER. Reallexicon der indo-germanischen Altertumskunde. Von O. Schräder, 1901.

SCHRÄDER-JEVONS. Prehistoric Antiquities of the Aryan People. Translated from the 'Sprachvergleichung und Urgeschichte' of O. Schräder by F. B. Jevons, 1890.

SCHÜCKING. Studien über die stofflichen Beziehungen der englischen Komödie zur italienischen bis Lilly. Von L. L. Schücking, 1901. [*Studien zur englischen Philologie*, ix.]

SCHULTZ. Das höfische Leben zur Zeit der Minnesinger. Von A. Schultz. 2 vols. 2nd edition, 1889.

SEIFERT. Wit-und-Science Moralitäten. Von J. Seifert, 1892. [Not consulted.]

SEPET. Les Prophètes du Christ. Étude sur les Origines du Théâtre au Moyen Âge. Par Marius Sepet, 1878. [First published in *Bibl. des Chartes*, vols. xxviii, xxix, xxxviii, from which I quote.]

SEPET, *D. C.* Le Drame chrétien au Moyen Âge. Par Marius Sepet, 1878.

SEPET, *Or.* Origines catholiques du Théâtre moderne. Par Marius Sepet, 1901.

SHARP. A Dissertation on the Pageants or Dramatic Mysteries, anciently performed at Coventry. By T. Sharp, 1825.

SHARP. *Digby Plays.* Ancient Mysteries from the Digby Manuscripts in the Bodleian. Edited by T. Sharp, 1835. [*Abbotsford Club.*]

Sh.-Jahrbuch. Jahrbuch der Deutschen Shakespeare-Gesellschaft. 38 vols. 1865–1902.

SIMPSON. The Buddhist Praying-wheel : a Collection of Material bearing upon the Symbolism of the Wheel and Circular Movements in Custom and Religious Ritual. By W. Simpson, 1896.

SITTL. Die Gebärden der Griechen und Römer. Von C. Sittl, 1890.

SMITH, GREGORY. The Transition Period. By G. Gregory Smith, 1900. [*Periods of European Literature.*]

SMITH, ROBERTSON. Lectures on the Religion of the Semites : First Series, The Fundamental Institutions. By W. Robertson Smith. 2nd ed. 1894.

SMITH, TOULMIN. English Gilds : Original Ordinances of more than a Hundred Gilds. Edited with notes by J. T. Smith, 1870. [*E. E. T. S.* xl.]

SÖRGEL. Die englischen Maskenspiele. Von G. Sörgel, 1882. [Halle dissertation.]

S. P. Dom. Calendar of State Papers, Domestic Series, of the Reigns of Edward VI, Mary, Elizabeth, and James I. 12 vols. 1856–72.

SPECHT. Geschichte des Unterrichtswesens in Deutschland. Von F. A. Specht, 1885.

SPENCE. Shetland Folk-Lore. By J. Spence, 1899.

STAFFORD. A Compendious or Brief Examination of Certain Ordinary Complaints. By W. Stafford, 1581. Edited by F. J. Furnivall, 1876. [*N. S. S.* Series vi. 3.]

STEPHENS-HUNT. A History of the English Church. Edited by W. R. W. Stephens and W. Hunt. 4 vols. 1899-1902. [In progress.]

STODDARD. References for Students of Miracle Plays and Mysteries. By F. H. Stoddard, 1887. [*University of California Library Bulletin*, No. viii.]

STOWE, *Annals*. Annales, or a general Chronicle of England. By J. Stowe. Continued to the end of 1631 by E. Howes, 1631.

STOWE, *Survey*. A Survey of London. By J. Stowe. Edited by W. J. Thoms, 1876.

STRUTT. The Sports and Pastimes of the People of England : including the Rural and Domestic Recreations, May Games, Mummeries, Shows, Processions, Pageants, and Pompous Spectacles, from the earliest Period to the present Time. By J. Strutt. New ed. by W. Hone, 1833.

STUBBES. The Anatomie of Abuses. By Phillip Stubbes, 1583. Edited by F. J. Furnivall, 1877-82. [*N. S. S.* Series vi. 4, 6, 12. Part I contains Barnaby Googe's translation (1570) of Kirchmayer's *Regnum Papismi* (1553), Bk. iv.]

Suffolk F. L. See *County Folk-Lore*.

SWETE. Church Services and Service-Books before the Reformation. By H. B. Swete, 1896.

SWOBODA. John Heywood als Dramatiker. Ein Beitrag zur Entwicklungsgeschichte des englischen Dramas. Von W. Swoboda, 1888. [*Wiener Beiträge zur deutschen und englischen Philologie*, iii : not consulted.]

SYMONDS. Shakspere's Predecessors in the English Drama. By J. A. Symonds, 1884.

TABOUROT. Orchésographie; par Thoinot Arbeau [*pseud.* for Jehan Tabourot], 1588. Réimpression précédée d'une notice sur les Danses du xvie Siècle, par Laure Fonta, 1888.

TEN BRINK. History of English Literature. By B. Ten Brink. Translated from the German. 3 vols. 1893-6. [All published ; a 2nd German edition, by A. Brandl, in progress.]

TERTULLIAN. Quinti Septimi Florentis Tertulliani Opera. Ex recensione Augusti Reifferscheid et Georgii Wissowa. Pars i. 1890 [vol. xx of *Corpus Scriptorum Ecclesiasticorum Latinorum*. The *De Spectaculis* and *De Idololatria* are in this vol., and are translated, with the *Apologeticus*, in vol. xi of the *Ante-Nicene Christian Library*, 1869. The complete works of Tertullian are also in *P. L.* vols. i and ii.]

TEUFFEL. Teuffel's History of Roman Literature. Revised and enlarged by L. Schwabe. Authorized translation from the 5th German edition by G. C. W. Warr. 2 vols. 1891.

THIERS. Iohannis Baptistae Thiers, de Festorum Dierum Imminutione Liber, 1668.

THIERS. Traité des Jeux et des Divertissemens qui peuvent être permis. Par J.-B. Thiers, 1686.

TICKNOR. History of Spanish Literature. By G. Ticknor. 6th American ed. 3 vols. 1888.

TIERSOT. Histoire de la Chanson populaire en France. Par J. Tiersot, 1889.

TILLE, *D. W.* Die Geschichte der deutschen Weihnacht. Von A. Tille, 1893.

TILLE, *Y and C.* Yule and Christmas: Their Place in the Germanic Year. By G. Tille, 1899.

TORRACA. Il Teatro italiano dei Secoli xiii, xiv, e xv. Per F. Torraca, 1885.

Towneley Plays. The Towneley Mysteries. Edited by J. Raine, with preface by J. Hunter and glossary by J. Gordon, 1836. [*Surtees Soc.* iii.]

Towneley Plays. Re-edited from the unique MS. by G. England, with side-notes and introduction by A. W. Pollard, 1897. [*E. E. T. S.* E. S. lxxi.]

Trad. La Tradition: Revue générale des Contes, Légendes, Chants, Usages, Traditions et Arts populaires.

UNGEMACHT. Die Quellen der fünf ersten Chester Plays. Von H. Ungemacht, 1890.

USENER. Religionsgeschichtliche Untersuchungen. Von H. Usener. 3 vols. 1889-99.

Use of Sarum. See FRERE.

VACANDARD. L'Idolâtrie dans la Gaule. Par E. Vacandard, 1899. [In *Revue des Questions historiques,* vol. lxv.]

Variorum. The Plays and Poems of William Shakespeare. With a Life of the Poet and an Enlarged History of the Stage. By the late E. Malone. Edited by J. Boswell. 21 vols. 1821.

VAUX. Church Folklore. By the Rev. J. E. Vaux, 1894. [A 2nd ed. was published in 1902.]

Venetian Papers. See BROWN.

Viel Testament. Le Mistère du Viel Testament. Publié avec introduction, notes et glossaire par le Baron J. de Rothschild. 6 vols. 1878-91. [*Société des Anciens Textes Français.*]

VIOLLET-LE-DUC. Ancien Théâtre françois: depuis les Mystères jusqu'à Corneille. Par E. L. N. Viollet-le-Duc. 10 vols. 1854-7.

VOGT. Leben und Dichten der deutschen Spielleute im Mittelalter. Von F. Vogt, 1876.

WACKERNAGEL. Geschichte der deutschen Litteratur. Ein Handbuch von W. Wackernagel. 2nd ed. by E. Martin, 1879.

WACKERNELL. Altdeutsche Passionsspiele aus Tirol. Von J. E. Wackernell, 1897.

WALLASCHEK. Primitive Music: an Inquiry into the Origin and

Development of Music, Songs, Instruments, Dances, and Pantomimes of Savage Races. By R. Wallaschek, 1893.

WALTER. Das Eselsfest. Von A. Walter, 1885. [In *Caecilien-Kalender*, 75.]

WARD. A History of English Dramatic Literature to the Death of Queen Anne. By A. W. Ward. 2nd ed. 3 vols. 1899.

WARTON. *See* HAZLITT-WARTON.

WASSERSCHLEBEN. Die Bussordnungen der abendländischen Kirche. Von F. W. H. Wasserschleben, 1851.

WEBER. Geistliches Schauspiel und kirchliche Kunst in ihrem Verhältnis erläutert an einer Ikonographie der Kirche und Synagoge. Von P. Weber, 1894.

WECHSSLER. Die romanischen Marienklagen. Ein Beitrag zur Geschichte des Dramas im Mittelalter. Von E. Wechssler, 1893.

WESTERMARCK. A History of Human Marriage. By E. Westermarck. 2nd ed. 1894.

WETZER-WELTE. Kirchenlexicon. Von H. J. Wetzer und B. Welte. 2nd ed. by J. Hergenröther and F. Kaulen. 12 vols. 1882-1900. [In progress.]

WIECK. Der Teufel auf der mittelalterlichen Mysterienbühne. Von H. Wieck, 1887. [Marburg dissertation : not consulted.]

WILKEN. Geschichte der geistlichen Spiele in Deutschland. Von E. Wilken, 1872.

WILKINS. Concilia Magnae Britanniae et Hiberniae, 446-1717. Accedunt Constitutiones et alia ad Historiam Ecclesiae Anglicanae Spectantia. 4 vols. 1737.

WILMOTTE. Les Passions allemandes du Rhin dans leur Rapport avec l'ancien Théâtre français. Par M. Wilmotte, 1898. [*Ouvrages couronnés et autres Mémoires publiés par l'Académie Royale de Belgique*, lv.]

Winchester Troper. *See* FRERE.

WIRTH. Die Oster- und Passionsspiele bis zum xvi. Jahrhundert. Von L. Wirth, 1889.

WISSOWA. Religion und Kultus der Römer. Von G. Wissowa, 1902. [Vol. v, Part 4 of I. von Müller's *Handbuch der classischen Altertums-wissenschaft.*]

WOOD, *Athenae.* Athenae Oxonienses, an Exact History of all Writers and Bishops who have had their Education in the University of Oxford. By Anthony à Wood. 2nd ed. by P. Bliss. 4 vols. 1813-20.

WOOD, *Hist. Univ.* History and Antiquities of the University of Oxford. By Anthony à Wood. Now first published in English with continuation by J. Gutch. 2 vols. 1792-6.

WOOD-MARTIN. Traces of the Elder Faiths of Ireland. By W. G. Wood-Martin. 2 vols. 1902.

WORDSWORTH. Notes on Mediaeval Services in England, with an index of Lincoln Ceremonies. By C. Wordsworth, 1898.

WORDSWORTH, *Proc.* Ceremonies and Processions of the Cathedral Church of Salisbury. Edited by C. Wordsworth, 1901. [From *Salisbury Chapter MS.* 148 of †1445, a book for use by the *principalis persona* in the choir, and supplementary to the printed Processional.]

WRIGHT. Early Mysteries and other Latin Poems of the Twelfth and Thirteenth Centuries. By T. Wright, 1838.

WRIGHT, *Chester Plays.* The Chester Plays. Edited by Thomas Wright. 2 vols. 1843. [*Shakespeare Society.*]

WRIGHT, *Map.* The Latin Poems commonly attributed to Walter Mapes. Collected and edited by T. Wright, 1841. [*C. S.* o. s. xvii.]

WRIGHT-HALLIWELL. Reliquiae Antiquae: Scraps from Ancient Manuscripts, illustrating chiefly Early English Literature and the English Language. By T. Wright and J. O. Halliwell. 2 vols. 1841.

WRIGHT-WÜLCKER. Anglo-Saxon and Old English Vocabularies. By T. Wright. Edited and collated by R. P. Wülcker. 2 vols. 1884.

WÜLCKER. Grundriss zur Geschichte der angelsächsischen Litteratur: mit einer Übersicht der angelsächsischen Sprachwissenschaft. Von R. Wülcker, 1885.

WYLIE. A History of England under Henry IV. By J. H. Wylie. 4 vols. 1884–98.

York Breviary. Breviarium ad usum insignis Ecclesiae Eboracensis. Edidit S. W. Lawley. 2 vols. 1880–2. [*Surtees Soc.* lxxi, lxxv.]

York Manual. Manuale et Processionale ad usum insignis Ecclesiae Eboracensis. Edidit W. G. Henderson, 1875. [*Surtees Soc.* lxiii. Contains also *Sarum Manual.*]

York Missal. Missale ad usum insignis Ecclesiae Eboracensis. Edidit W. G. Henderson. 2 vols. 1874. [*Surtees Soc.* lix, lx.]

York Plays. The Plays performed by the Crafts or Mysteries of York on the Day of Corpus Christi. Edited by L. T. Smith, 1885.

Z. f. d. A. Zeitschrift für deutsches Alterthum [*afterwards added* und deutsche Literatur], 1841–1903. [In progress.]

Z. f. rom. Phil. Zeitschrift für romanische Philologie, 1877–1903. [In progress.]

ZSCHECH. Die Anfänge des englischen Dramas. Von Dr. Zschech, 1886. [Not consulted.]

BOOK I

MINSTRELSY

C'est une étrange entreprise que celle de faire rire les honnêtes gens.—J.-B. POQUELIN DE MOLIÈRE.

Molière est un infâme histrion.—J.-B. BOSSUET.

CHAPTER I

THE FALL OF THE THEATRES

[*Bibliographical Note.* — A convenient sketch of the history of the Roman stage will be found in G. Körting, *Geschichte des griechischen und römischen Theaters* (1897). The details given in L. Friedländer, *Sittengeschichte Roms in der Zeit von August bis zum Ausgang der Antonine* (vol. ii, 7th ed. 1901), and the same writer's article on *Die Spiele* in vol. vi of Marquardt and Mommsen's *Handbuch der römischen Alterthümer* (2nd ed. 1885), may be supplemented from E. Nöldechen's article *Tertullian und das Theater* in *Zeitschrift für Kirchengeschichte*, xv (1894), 161, for the *fabulae Atellanae* from A. Dieterich, *Pulcinella* (1897), chs. 4-8, and for the *pantomimi* from C. Sittl, *Die Gebärden der Griechen und Römer* (1890), ch. 13. The account in C. Magnin, *Les Origines du Théâtre moderne* (vol. i, all published, 1838), is by no means obsolete. Teuffel and Schwabe, *History of Latin Literature*, vol. i, §§ 3-18 (trans. G. C. W. Warr, 1891), contains a mass of imperfectly arranged material. The later history of the Greek stage is dealt with by P. E. Müller, *Commentatio historica de genio, moribus et luxu aevi Theodosiani* (1798), vol. ii, and A. E. Haigh, *Tragic Drama of the Greeks* (1896), ch. 6. The ecclesiastical prohibitions are collected by W. Prynne, *Histriomastix* (1633), and J. de Douhet, *Dictionnaire des Mystères* (1854), and their general attitude summarized by H. Alt, *Theater und Kirche in ihrem gegenseitigen Verhältniss* (1846). S. Dill, *Roman Society in the Last Century of the Roman Empire* (2nd ed. 1899), should be consulted for an admirable study of the conditions under which the pre-mediaeval stage came to an end.]

CHRISTIANITY, emerging from Syria with a prejudice against disguisings [1], found the Roman world full of *scenici*. The mimetic instinct, which no race of mankind is wholly without, appears to have been unusually strong amongst the peoples of the Mediterranean stock. A literary drama came into being in Athens during the sixth century, and established itself in city after city. Theatres were built, and tragedies and comedies acted on the Attic model, wherever a Greek foot trod, from Hipola in Spain to Tigranocerta in Armenia. The great capitals of the later Greece, Alexandria,

---

[1] *Deuteronomy*, xxii. 5, a commonplace of anti-stage controversy from Tertullian (*de Spectaculis*, c. 23) to *Histrio-Mastix*. Tertullian (*loc. cit.*) asserts, 'non amat falsum auctor veritatis; adulterium est apud illum omne quod fingitur.'

Antioch, Pergamum, rivalled Athens itself in their devotion
to the stage. Another development of drama, independent
of Athens, in Sicily and Magna Graecia, may be distinguished
as farcical rather than comic. After receiving literary treatment at the hands of Epicharmus and Sophron in the fifth
century, it continued its existence under the name of mime
(μῖμος), upon a more popular level. Like many forms of
popular drama, it seems to have combined the elements of
farce and morality. Its exponents are described as buffoons
(γελωτοποιοί, παιγνιογράφοι) and dealers in indecencies (ἀναι-
σχυντογράφοι), and again as concerning themselves with questions of character and manners (ἠθολόγοι, ἀρεταλόγοι). They
even produced what sound singularly like problem plays
(ὑποθέσεις). Both qualities may have sprung from a common
root in the observation and audacious portrayal of contemporary life. The mime was still flourishing in and about
Tarentum in the third century[1].

Probably the Romans were not of the Mediterranean stock,
and their native *ludi* were athletic rather than mimetic. But
the drama gradually filtered in from the neighbouring peoples.
Its earliest stirrings in the rude farce of the *satura* are
attributed by Livy to Etruscan influence[2]. From Campania
came another type of farce, the *Oscum ludicrum* or *fabula
Atellana*, with its standing masks of Maccus and Bucco,
Pappus and Dossennus, in whom it is hard not to find a
kinship to the traditional personages of the Neapolitan *com-
media dell' arte*. About 240 B.C. the Greek Livius Andro-
nicus introduced tragedy and comedy. The play now
became a regular element in the *spectacula* of the Roman
festivals, only subordinate in interest to the chariot-race and
the gladiatorial show. Permanent theatres were built in the
closing years of the Republic by Pompey and others, and
the number of days annually devoted to *ludi scenici* was constantly on the increase. From 48 under Augustus they
grew to 101 under Constantius. Throughout the period of

---

[1] J. Denis, *La Comédie grecque*
(1886), i. 50, 106; ii. 535. The so-
called mimes of Herodas (third
cent. B.C.) are literary pieces, based
probably on the popular mime but
not intended for representation
(Croiset, *Hist. de la Litt. grecque*,
v. 174).

[2] Livy, vii. 2; Valerius Maximus,
ii. 4. 4 (364 B.C.).

the Empire, indeed, the theatre was of no small political importance. On the one hand it was the rallying point of all disturbers of the peace and the last stronghold of a public opinion debarred from the senate and the forum; on the other it was a potent means for winning the affection of the populace and diverting its attention from dynastic questions. The *scenici* might be thorns in the side of the government, but they were quite indispensable to it. If their perversities drove them from Italy, the clamour of the mob soon brought them back again. Trajan revealed one of the *arcana imperii* when he declared that the *annona* and the *spectacula* controlled Rome[1]. And what was true of Rome was true of Byzantium, and in a lesser degree of the smaller provincial cities. So long as the Empire itself held together, the provision firstly of corn and secondly of novel *ludi* remained one of the chief preoccupations of many a highly placed official.

The vast popular audiences of the period under consideration cared but little for the literary drama. In the theatre of Pompey, thronged with slaves and foreigners of every tongue, the finer histrionic effects must necessarily have been lost[2]. Something more spectacular and sensuous, something appealing to a cruder sense of humour, almost inevitably took their place. There is evidence indeed that, while the theatres stood, tragedy and comedy never wholly disappeared from their boards[3]. But it was probably only the ancient masterpieces that got a hearing. Even in Greece performances of new plays on classical models cannot be traced beyond about the time of Hadrian. And in Rome the tragic poets had long before then learnt to content themselves with recitations and to rely for victims on the good nature, frequently inadequate, of their friends[4]. The stilted dramas of Seneca were the

---

[1] Juvenal, x. 81; Dion Chrysostom, *Or.* xxxii. 370, 18 M.; Fronto, *Princip. hist.* v. 13. A fourth-century inscription (*Bull. d. Commis. arch.comun.di Roma*, 1891, 342) contains a list of small Roman *tabernarii* entitled to *locum spectaculis et panem.*

[2] The holding capacity of the theatre of Pompey is variously given at from 17,580 to 40,000, that of the theatre of Balbus at from 11,510 to 30,085, that of the theatre of Marcellus as 20,000.

[3] Friedländer, ii. 100; Haigh, 457; Krumbacher, 646; Welcker, *Die griechischen Tragödien* (1841), iii. 1472.

[4] Juvenal, i. 1; Pliny, *Epist.* vi.

delight of the Renaissance, but it is improbable that, until the Renaissance, they were ever dignified with representation. Roughly speaking, for comedy and tragedy the Empire substituted farce and pantomime.

Farce, as has been noticed, was the earliest traffic of the Roman stage. The Atellane, relegated during the brief vogue of comedy and tragedy to the position of an interlude or an afterpiece, now once more asserted its independence. But already during the Republic the Atellane, with its somewhat conventional and limited methods, was beginning to give way to a more flexible and vital type of farce. This was none other than the old mime of Magna Graecia, which now entered on a fresh phase of existence and overran both West and East. That it underwent considerable modifications, and probably absorbed much both of Atellane and of Attic comedy, may be taken for granted. Certainly it extended its scope to mythological themes. But its leading characteristics remained unchanged. The ethical element, one may fear, sank somewhat into the background, although it was by no means absent from the work of the better mimewriters, such as Laberius and Publilius Syrus[1]. But that the note of shamelessness was preserved there is no doubt whatever[2]. The favourite theme, which is common indeed to farce of all ages, was that of conjugal infidelity[3]. Unchaste scenes were represented with an astonishing realism[4].

15; vii. 17; Tacitus, *de Oratoribus*, 9, 11.

[1] The *Sententiae* of Publilius Syrus were collected from his mimes in the first century A.D., and enlarged from other sources during the Middle Ages (Teuffel-Schwabe, § 212). Cf. the edition by W. Meyer, 1880. The other fragments of the mimographs are included in O. Ribbeck, *Comicorum Romanorum Fragmenta* (3rd ed. 1898). Philistion of Bithynia, about the time of Tiberius, gave the mime a literary form once more in his κωμῳδίαι βιολογικαί (J. Denis, *La Com. grecque*, ii. 544; Croiset, *Hist. de la Litt. grecque*, v. 449).

[2] *Incerti* (fourth century) *ad Terentium* (ed. Giles, i. xix) 'mimos ab diuturna imitatione vilium rerum et levium personarum.' Diomedes (fifth century), *Ars Grammatica*, iii. 488 'mimus est sermonis cuiuslibet imitatio et motus sine reverentia, vel factorum et dictorum turpium cum lascivia imitatio.'

[3] Ovid, *Tristia*, ii. 497:
'quid, si scripsissem mimos obscoena iocantes,
qui semper vetiti crimen amoris habent.'

[4] *Hist. Augusta*, *Vita Heliogabali*, 25 'in mimicis adulteriis ea quae solent simulato fieri effici ad verum iussit'; cf. the *pyrrichae*

Contrary to the earlier custom of the classical stage, women took part in the performances, and at the *Floralia*, loosest of Roman festivals, the spectators seem to have claimed it as their right that the *mimae* should play naked[1]. The *mimus*—for the same term designates both piece and actor— was just the kind of entertainer whom a democratic audience loves. Clad in a parti-coloured *centunculus*, with no mask to conceal the play of facial gesture, and *planipes*, with no borrowed dignity of sock or buskin, he rattled through his side-splitting scenes of low life, and eked out his text with an inexhaustible variety of rude dancing, buffoonery and horse-play[2]. Originally the mimes seem to have performed in monologues, and the action of their pieces continued to be generally dominated by a single personage, the *archimimus*, who was provided with certain *stupidi* and *parasiti* to act as foils and butts for his wit. A satirical intention was frequently present in both mimes and Atellanes, and their outspoken allusions are more than once recorded to have wrung the withers of persons of importance and to have brought serious retribution on the actors themselves. Caligula, for instance, with characteristic brutality, had a ribald playwright burnt alive in the amphitheatre[3].

The farce was the diversion of the proletariat and the *bourgeoisie* of Rome. Petronius, with all the insolence of the literary man, makes Trimalchio buy a *troupe* of comedians, and insist on their playing an Atellane[4]. The golden and

---

described by Suetonius, *Nero*, 12. The Roman taste for bloodshed was sometimes gratified by mimes given in the amphitheatre, and designed to introduce the actual execution of a criminal. Martial, *de Spectaculis*, 7, mentions the worrying and crucifixion of a brigand in the mime *Laureolus*, by order of Domitian :

'nuda Caledonio sic pectora praebuit urso

non falsa pendens in cruce Laureolus.'

[1] Martial, i. 1 ; Ausonius, *Ecl.* xviii. 25 ; Lactantius (†300), *de Inst. div.* i. 20. 10. Probably the influence of a piece of folk-ritual is

to be traced here.

[2] The 'mimus' type is exactly reproduced by more than one popular performer on the modern 'variety' or 'burlesque' stage.

[3] Macrobius, *Sat.* ii. 7 ; Cicero, *ad Atticum*, xiv. 3 ; Suetonius, *Augustus*, 45, 68 ; *Tiberius*, 45 ; *Caligula*, 27 ; *Nero*, 39 ; *Galba*, 13 ; *Vespasian*, 19 ; *Domitian*, 10 ; *Hist. Augusta, Vita Marc. Aurel.* 8. 29 ; *Vita Commodi*, 3 ; *Vita Maximini*, 9.

[4] Petronius, *Satyricon*, liii ; cf. *Taming of the Shrew*, i. 1. 258 ''Tis a very excellent piece of work, madam lady ; would 'twere done ! '

cultured classes preferred the pantomimic dance. This arose out of the ruins of the literary drama. On the Roman stage grew up a custom, unknown in Greece, by which the lyric portions of the text (*cantica*) were entrusted to a singer who stood with the flute-player at the side of the stage, while the actor confined himself to dancing in silence with appropriate dumb show. The dialogue (*diverbia*) continued to be spoken by the actors. The next step was to drop the *diverbia* altogether; and thus came the *pantomimus* who undertook to indicate the whole development of a plot in a series of dramatic dances, during the course of which he often represented several distinct *rôles*. Instead of the single flute-player and singer a full choir now supplied the musical accompaniment, and great poets—Lucan and Statius among the number—did not disdain to provide texts for the *fabulae salticae*. Many of the *pantomimi* attained to an extreme refinement in their degenerate and sensuous art. They were, as Lucian said, χειρόσοφοι, erudite of gesture [1]. Their subjects were, for the most part, mythological and erotic, not to say lascivious, in character [2]. Pylades the Cilician, who, with his great rival Bathyllus the Alexandrian, brought the dance to its first perfection under Augustus, favoured satyric themes; but this mode does not appear to have endured. Practically the dancers were the tragedians, and the mimes were the comedians, of the Empire. The old Etruscan name for an actor, *histrio*, came to be almost synonymous with *pantomimus* [3]. Rome, which could lash itself into a fury over the contests between the Whites and Reds or the Blues and Greens in the circus, was not slow to take sides upon the respective merits of its scenic entertainers. The

---

[1] Lucian, *de Saltatione*, 69.

[2] Juvenal, *Sat.* vi. 63; Zosimus (450-501 A.D.), i. 6 (*Corp. Script. Hist. Byz.* xx. 12) ἥ τε γὰρ παντό-μιμος ὄρχησις ἐν ἐκείνοις εἰσήχθη τοῖς χρόνοις . . . πολλῶν αἴτια γεγονότα μέχρι τοῦδε κακῶν.

[3] This is not wholly so, at any rate in Tacitus, who seems to include the players both of mimes and of Atellanes amongst *histriones* (*Ann.* i. 73; iv. 14). For the

origin of the name, cf. Livy, vii. 2 'ister Tusco verbo ludius vocaba-tur.' Besides *ludius*, *actor* is good Latin. But it is generally used in some such phrase as *actor prima-rum personarum*, protagonist, and by itself often means *dominus gregis*, manager of the *grex* or company. *Mimus* signifies both performer and performance, *panto-mimus* the performer only. He is said *saltare fabulas*.

histrionalis favor led again and again to brawls which set the rulers of the city wondering whether after all the *pantomimi* were worth while. Augustus had found it to his advantage that the spirit of partisanship should attach itself to a Pylades or a Bathyllus rather than to more illustrious antagonists[1]. But the personal instincts of Tiberius were not so genial as those of Augustus. Early in his principate he attempted to restrain the undignified court paid by senators and knights to popular dancers, and when this measure failed, he expelled the *histriones* from Italy[2]. The example was followed by more than one of his successors, but Rome clamoured fiercely for its toys, and the period of exile was never a long one[3].

Both *mimi* and *pantomimi* had their vogue in private, at the banquets and weddings of the great, as well as in public. The class of *scenici* further included a heterogeneous variety of lesser performers. There were the rhapsodes who sung the tragic *cantica*, torn from their context, upon the stage. There were musicians and dancers of every order and from every land[4]. There were jugglers (*praestigiatores, acetabuli*), ropewalkers (*funambuli*), stilt-walkers (*grallatores*), tumblers (*cernui, petauristae, petaminarii*), buffoons (*sanniones, scurrae*), beast-tamers and strong men. The pick of them did their 'turns' in the theatre or the amphitheatre; the more humble were content with modest audiences at street corners or in the vestibule of the circus. From Rome the entertainers of the imperial race naturally found their way into the theatres of the provinces. Tragedy and comedy no doubt held their own longer in Greece, but the stage of Constantinople under Justinian does not seem to have differed notably from the stage of Rome under Nero. Marseilles alone distinguished itself by the honourable austerity which forbade the *mimi* its gates[5].

[1] Dion Cassius, liv. 17.

[2] Tacitus, *Annales*, i. 77; iv. 14; Dion Cassius, lvii. 21; Suetonius, *Tiberius*, 37.

[3] Tacitus, *Annales*, xiii. 25; xiv. 21; Dion Cassius, lix. 2; lxi. 8; lxviii. 10; Suetonius, *Nero*, 16, 26; *Titus*, 7; *Domitian*, 7; Pliny, *Paneg.* 46; *Hist. Augusta, Vita Hadriani*, 19; *Vita Alex. Severi*, 34.

[4] The *pyrricha*, a Greek concerted dance, probably of folk origin (cf. ch. ix), was often given a mythological *argumentum*. It was danced in the amphitheatre.

[5] Valerius Maximus, ii. 6. 7 'eadem civitas severitatis custos

It must not be supposed that the profession of the *scenici* ever became an honourable one in the eyes of the Roman law. They were for the most part slaves or at best freedmen. They were deliberately branded with *infamia* or incapacity for civil rights. This *infamia* was of two kinds, depending respectively upon the action of the censors as guardians of public dignity and that of the praetors as presidents in the law courts. The censors habitually excluded actors from the *ius suffragii* and the *ius honorum*, the rights of voting and of holding senatorial or equestrian rank ; the praetors refused to allow them, if men, to appear as attorneys, if women, to appoint attorneys, in civil suits [1]. The legislation of Julius Caesar and of Augustus added some statutory disabilities. The *lex Iulia municipalis* forbade actors to hold municipal *honores* [2] : the *lex Iulia de adulteriis* set the example of denying them the right to bring criminal actions [3] ; the *lex Iulia et Papia Poppaea* limited their privileges when freed, and in particular forbade senators or the sons of senators to take to wife women who had been, or whose parents had been, on the stage [4]. On the other hand Augustus confined the *ius virgarum*, which the praetors had formerly had over *scenici*, to the actual place and time of performances [5] ; and so far as the censorian *infamia* was concerned, the whole tendency of the late Republic and early Empire was to relax its application to actors. It came to be possible for senators and knights to appear on the stage without losing caste. It was a grievous insult when Julius Caesar

---

acerrima est : nullum aditum in scenam mimis dando, quorum argumenta maiore in parte stuprorum continent actus ; ne talia spectandi consuetudo etiam imitandi licentiam sumat.'

[1] A. H. J. Greenidge, *Infamia* (*passim*) ; Bouché-Leclercq, *Manuel des Institutions romaines*, 352, 449 ; *Edictum praetoris* in *C. I. C. Digest*, iii. 2. 1 ' infamia notatur qui . . . artis ludicrae pronuntiandive causa in scaenam prodierit.' The jurists limited the application of the rule to professional actors. *Thymelici*, or orchestral musicians, were exempt. Diocletian made a

further exemption for persons appearing in their minority (*C. I. C. Cod. Iust.* ii. 11. 21). The censors, on the other hand, spared the *Atellani*, whose performances had a traditional connexion with religious rites.

[2] *C. I. L.* i. 122.

[3] *C. I. C. Digest*, xlviii. 5. 25. A husband may kill an actor with whom his wife is guilty.

[4] *Ibid.* xxiii. 2. 42, 44 ; xxxviii. 1. 37 ; Ulpian, *Fragm.* xiii.

[5] Tacitus, *Annales*, i. 77. An attempt to restore the old usage under Tiberius was unsuccessful.

compelled the mimograph Laberius to appear in one of his own pieces. But after all Caesar restored Laberius to his rank of *eques*, a dignity which at a still earlier date Sulla had bestowed on Roscius [1]. Later the restriction broke down altogether, although not without an occasional reforming effort to restore it [2]. Nero himself was not ashamed to take the boards as a singer of *cantica* [3]. And even an *infamis*, if he were the boon companion of a prince, might be appointed to a post directly depending on the imperial dignity. Thus Caracalla sent a *pantomimus* to hold a military command on the frontier, and Heliogabalus made another *praefectus urbi* in Rome itself [4]. Under Constantine a reaction set in, and a new decree formally excluded *scenici* from all *dignitates* [5]. The severe class legislation received only reluctant and piecemeal modification, and the praetorian *infamia* outlived the Empire itself, and left its mark upon Carolingian jurisprudence [6].

The relaxation of the old Roman austerity implied in the popularity of the *mimi* and *histriones* did not pass uncensured by even the pagan moralists of the Empire. The stage has a share in the denunciations of Tacitus and Juvenal, both of whom lament that princes and patricians should condescend to practise arts once relegated to the *infames*. Martial's hypocrite rails at the times and the theatres. Three centuries later the soldierly Ammianus Marcellinus finds in the gyrations of the dancing-girls, three thousand of whom were allowed to remain in Rome when it was starving, a blot upon the fame of the state ; and Macrobius contrasts the sober evenings of Praetextatus and his friends with revels dependent for their mirth on the song and wanton motions of

---

[1] Caesar was tolerably magnanimous, for Laberius had already taken his revenge in a scurrilous prologue. It had its touch of pathos, too :

'eques Romanus lare egressus meo
　　domum revertar mimus.'

[2] Cicero, *ad Fam.* x. 32 ; Dion Cassius, xlviii. 33 ; liii. 31 ; liv. 2 ; lvi. 47 ; lvii. 14 ; lix. 10 ; lxi. 9 ; lxv. 6 ; Tacitus, *Ann.* xiv. 20 ; *Hist.* ii. 62 ; Suetonius, *Augustus*, 45 ;

Domitian, 8.

[3] Suetonius, *Nero*, 21 ; Tacitus, *Ann.* xiv. 14 ; Juvenal, viii. 198 ; Pseudo-Lucian, *Nero*, 9.

[4] Dion Cassius, lxxvii. 21 ; *Hist. Augusta, Vita Heliogabali*, 12. Yet in the time of Severus a soldier going on the stage was liable to death (*C. I. C. Digest*, xlviii. 19. 14).

[5] *C. I. C. Cod. Iust.* xii. 1. 2.

[6] Cf. p. 38.

the *psaltria* or the jests of *sabulo* and *planipes*[1]. Policy compelled the emperors to encourage *spectacula*, but even they were not always blind to the ethical questions involved. Tiberius based his expulsion of the *histriones*, at least in part, on moral grounds. Marcus Aurelius, with a philosophic regret that the high lessons of comedy had sunk to mere mimic dexterity, sat publicly in his box and averted his eyes to a state-paper or a book[2]. Julian, weaned by his tutor Mardonius from a boyish love of the stage, issued strict injunctions to the priests of the Sun to avoid a theatre which he despaired of reforming[3]. Christian teachers, unconcerned with the interests of a dynasty, and claiming to represent a higher morality than that either of Marcus Aurelius or of Julian, naturally took even stronger ground. Moreover, they had their special reasons for hostility to the stage. That the actors should mock at the pagan religion, with whose *ludi* their own performances were intimately connected, made a good dialectical point. But the connexion itself was unpardonable, and still more so the part taken by the mimes during the war of creeds, in parodying and holding up to ridicule the most sacred symbols and mysteries of the church. This feeling is reflected in the legends of St. Genesius, St. Pelagia and other holy folk, who are represented as turning from the scenic profession to embrace Christianity, the conversion in some cases taking place on the very boards of the theatre itself[4].

---

[1] Tacitus, *Ann.* xiv. 20; Juvenal, vi. 60; viii. 183; Martial, ix. 28. 9; Ammianus Marcellinus, xiv. 6. 18; xxviii. 4. 32; Macrobius, ii. 1. 5, 9.

[2] M. Aurelius, *Comm.* xi. 6; *Hist. Augusta, Vita M. Aurel.* 15. This refers directly to the *circus*.

[3] Gibbon, ii. 447; Schaff, v. 49; Dill, 34, 100; P. Allard, *Julien l'Apostat*, i. 272; Alice Gardner, *Julian the Apostate*, 201; G. H. Rendall, *The Emperor Julian* (1879), 106. The most interesting passage is a fragmentary 'pastoral letter' to a priest (ed. Hertlein, *Fragm. Ep.* p. 304 B; cf. *Ep.* 49, p. 430 B); Julian requires the priests to abstain even from reading the Old Comedy (*Fragm. Ep.* p. 300 D).

He also thinks that the moral layman should avoid the theatre (*Misopogon*, p. 343 c).

[4] On the critical problem offered by such *vitae* cf. Prof. Bury in Gibbon, i. l. B. von der Lage, *Studien zur Genesius - legende* (1898), attempts to show that the legends of St. Genesius (*Acta SS. Aug.* v. 122), St. Gelasius (*Acta SS. Feb.* iii. 680), St. Ardalio (*Acta SS. Apr.* ii. 213), St. Porphyrius (*Acta SS. Sept.* v. 37), and another St. Porphyrius (*Acta SS. Nov.* ii. 230) are all variants of a Greek story originally told of an anonymous *mimus*. The *Passio* of St. Genesius represents him as a *magister mimithemelae artis*, converted while he

So far as the direct attack upon the stage is concerned, the key-note of patristic eloquence is struck in the characteristic and uncompromising treatise *De Spectaculis* of Tertullian. Here theatre, circus, and amphitheatre are joined in a three-fold condemnation. Tertullian holds that the Christian has explicitly forsworn *spectacula*, when he renounced the devil and all his works and vanities at baptism. What are these but idolatry, and where is idolatry, if not in the *spectacula*, which not only minister to lust, but take place at the festivals and in the holy places of Venus and Bacchus? The story is told of the demon who entered a woman in the theatre and excused himself at exorcism, because he had found her in his own demesne. A fervid exhortation follows. To worldly pleasures Christians have no claim. If they need *spectacula* they can find them in the exercises of their Church. Here are nobler poetry, sweeter voices, maxims more sage, melodies more dulcet, than any comedy can boast, and withal, here is truth instead of fiction. Moreover, for Christians is reserved the last great *spectaculum* of all. 'Then,' says Tertullian, 'will be the time to listen to the tragedians, whose lamentations will be more poignant for their proper pain. Then will the comedians turn and twist, rendered nimbler than ever by the sting of the fire that is not quenched [1].' With Tertullian asceticism is always a passion, but the vivid African rhetoric is no unfair sample of a *catena* of outspoken comment which extends across the third century from Tatian to Lactantius [2].

was mimicking a baptism before Diocletian and martyred. It professes to give part of the dialogue of the mime. The legends of St. Philemon (*Menologium Basilii*, ii. 59; cf. *Acta SS. Mar.* i. 751) and St. Pelagia or Margarita (*Acta SS. Oct.* iv. 248) appear to be distinct. Palladius, *Vita Chrysostomi*, 8, records how the stage of Antioch in the fifth century rang with the scandals caused by the patriarch Severus and other Monophysite heretics.

[1] Tertullian, *De Spect.*, especially cc. 4, 26, 30. Schaff, iv. 833, dates the treatise †200. An earlier Greek writing by Tertullian on the same subject is lost; cf. also his *Apologeticus*, 15 (*P. L.* i. 357). The information as to the contemporary stage scattered through Tertullian's works is collected by E. Nöldechen, *Tertullian und das Theater* (*Z. f. Kirchengeschichte* (1894), xv. 161). An anonymous *De Spectaculis*, formerly ascribed to St. Cyprian, follows on Tertullian's lines (*P. L.* iv. 779, transl. in *Ante-Nicene Christian Libr.* xiii. 221).

[2] Tatian, *ad Graecos*, 22 (*P. G.* vi. 856); Minucius Felix, *Octavius*, 27 (*P. L.* iii. 352); Cyprian, *Epist.* i. 8 (*P. L.* iv. 207); Lactantius, *de Inst. div.* vi. 20 (*P. L.* vi. 710), 'quid de mimis loquar, corruptelarum praeferentibus disciplinam, qui do-

The judgement of the Fathers finds more cautious expression
in the disciplinary regulations of the Church. An early formal
condemnation of actors is included in the so-called *Canons* of
Hippolytus [1], and the relations of converts to the stage were
discussed during the fourth century by the councils of Elvira
(306) and of Arles (314) and by the third and fourth councils
of Carthage (397–398) [2]. It was hardly possible for practical
legislators to take the extreme step of forbidding Christian
laymen to enter the theatre at all. No doubt that would be the
counsel of perfection, but in dealing with a deep-seated popular
instinct something of a compromise was necessary [3]. An
absolute prohibition was only established for the clergy: so
far as the laity were concerned, it was limited to Sundays and
ecclesiastical festivals, and on those days it was enforced by
a threat of excommunication [4]. No Christian, however, might
be a *scenicus* or a *scenica*, or might marry one ; and if a member
of the unhallowed profession sought to be baptized, the
preliminary of abandoning his calling was essential [5].

cent adulteria, dum fingunt, et
simulatis erudiunt ad vera?'; cf.
Du Méril, *Or. Lat.* 6 ; Schaff, iii.
339. A remarkable collection of
all conceivable authorities against
the stage is given by Prynne, 566,
685, &c.

[1] *Canones Hippolyti*, 67 (Duchesne, 509) 'Quicumque fit θεα-
τρικός vel gladiator et qui currit vel
docet voluptates vel [*illegible*] vel
[*illegible*] vel κυνηγός vel ἱπποδρό-
μος [?], vel qui cum bestiis pugnat
vel idolorum sacerdos, hi omnes
non admittuntur ad sermones
sacros nisi prius ab illis immundis
operibus purgentur.' This is from
an Arabic translation of a lost
Greek original. M. Duchesne says
' ce recueil de prescriptions liturgiques et disciplinaires est sûrement
antérieur au ivᵉ siècle, et rien ne
s'oppose à ce qu'il remonte à la
date indiquée par le nom d'Hippo-
lyte' [†198–236].

[2] *Conc. Illib.* cc. 62, 67 (Mansi,
ii. 16) ; *Conc. Arelat.* c. 5 (Mansi,
ii. 471) ; 3 *Conc. Carth.* cc. 11, 35
(Mansi, iii. 882, 885) ; 4 *Conc.
Carth.* cc. 86, 88 (Mansi, iii. 958).

[3] The strongest pronouncement
is that of Augustine and others in
3 *Conc. Carth.* c. 11 'ut filii episcoporum vel clericorum spectacula
saecularia non exhibeant, sed non
spectent, quandoquidem ab specta-
culo et omnes laici prohibeantur.
Semper enim Christianis omnibus
hoc interdictum est, ut ubi blasphe-
mi sunt, non accedant.'

[4] 4 *Conc. Carth.* c. 88 'Qui die
solenni, praetermisso solenni ecclesiae conventu, ad spectacula vadit,
excommunicetur.'

[5] *D. C. A.* s.vv. *Actor*, *Theatre* ;
Bingham, vi. 212, 373, 439 ; Alt,
310 ; Prynne, 556. Some, however, of the pronouncements of the
fathers came to have equal force
with the decrees of councils in
canon law. The *Code* of Gratian
(†1139), besides 3 *Conc. Carth.*
c. 35 'scenicis atque ystrionibus,
ceterisque huiusmodi personis, vel
apostaticis conversis, vel reversis
ad Deum, gratia vel reconcilia-
tio non negetur' (*C. I. Can.* iii.
2. 96) and 7 *Conc. Carth.* (419) c. 2
(Mansi, iv. 437) 'omnes etiam infamiae maculis aspersi, id est histrio-

It is curious to notice that a certain sympathy with the stage seems to have been characteristic of one of the great heresiarchs. This was none other than Arius, who is said to have had designs of setting up a Christian theatre in rivalry to those of paganism, and his strange work, the *Thaleia*, may perhaps have been intended to further the scheme. At any rate an orthodox controversialist takes occasion to brand his Arian opponents and their works as 'thymelic' or 'stagy'[1]. But it would probably be dangerous to lay undue stress upon what, after all, is as likely as not to be merely a dialectical metaphor.

After the edict of Milan (313), and still more after the end of the pagan reaction with the death of Julian (363), Christian influences began to make themselves felt in the civil legislation of the Empire. But if the councils themselves were chary of utterly forbidding the theatre, a stronger line was not likely to be taken in rescripts from Constantinople or Ravenna. The emperors were, indeed, in a difficult position. They stood between bishops pleading for decency and humanity and populaces now traditionally entitled to their *panem et spectacula*. The theatrical legislation preserved in the *Code* of Theodosius is not without traces of this embarrassment[2]. It

nes ... ab accusatione prohibentur' (*C. I. Can.* ii. 4. 1. 1), includes two patristic citations. One is Cyprian, *Ep.* lxi. (*P. L.* iv. 362), which is 'de ystrione et mago illo, qui apud vos constitutus adhuc in suae artis dedecore perseverat,' and forbids 'sacra communio cum ceteris Christianis dari' (*C. I. Can.* iii. 2. 95); the other Augustine, *Tract. C. ad c.* 16 *Iohannis* (*P. L.* xxxv. 1891) 'donare res suas histrionibus vitium est immane, non virtus' (*C. I. Can.* i. 86. 7). Gratian adds Isidorus Hispalensis, *de Eccl. Off.* ii. 2 (*P. L.* lxxxiii. 778) 'his igitur lege Patrum cavetur, ut a vulgari vita seclusi a mundi voluptatibus sese abstineant ; non spectaculis, non pompis intersint' (*C. I. Can.* i. 23. 3).

[1] Sathas, 7 ; Krumbacher, 644. Anastasius Sinaita (bp. of Antioch, 564) in his tract, *Adversus*

Monophysitas ac Monothelitas (Mai, *Coll. Nov. Script. Vet.* vii. 202), speaks of the συγγράμματα of the Arians as θυμελικὰς βίβλους, and calls the Arian Eunomius πρωτοστάτης τῆς Ἀρείου θυμελικῆς ὀρχήστρας. I doubt if these phrases should be taken too literally ; possibly they are not more than a criticism of the buffoonery and levity which the fragments of the Θάλεια display. Krumbacher mentions an orthodox Ἀντιθάλεια of which no more seems to be known.

[2] Alt, 310 ; Bingham, vi. 273 ; Schaff, v. 106, 125 ; Haigh, 460 ; Dill, 56 ; P. Allard, *Julien l'Apostat.* i. 230. The *Codex Theodosianus*, drawn up and accepted for both empires +435, contains imperial edicts from the time of Constantine onwards.

is rather an interesting study. The views of the Church were
met upon two points. One series of rescripts forbade performances on Sundays or during the more sacred periods of the
Christian calendar[1]: another relaxed in favour of Christians
the strict caste laws which sternly forbade actresses or their
daughters to quit the unhappy profession in which they were
born[2]. Moreover, certain sumptuary regulations were passed,
which must have proved a severe restriction on the popularity
as well as the liberty of actors. They were forbidden to wear
gold or rich fabrics, or to ape the dress of nuns. They must
avoid the company of Christian women and boys. They must
not come into the public places or walk the streets attended
by slaves with folding chairs[3]. Some of the rescripts contain
phrases pointed with the bitterest contempt and detestation of
their victims[4]. Theodosius will not have the portraits of
scenici polluting the neighbourhood of his own *imagines*[5]. It
is made very clear that the old court favourites are now to
be merely tolerated. But they *are* to be tolerated. The idea
of suppressing them is never entertained. On the contrary
the provision of *spectacula* and of performers for them
remains one of the preoccupations of the government[6]. The
praetor is expected to be lavish on this item of his budget[7],

---

[1] *Spectacula* are forbidden on
Sunday, unless it is the emperor's
birthday, by *C. Th.* xv. 5. 2 (386),
which also forbids judges to rise
for them, except on special occasions, and *C. Th.* ii. 8. 23 (399).
The exception is removed by *C. Th.*
ii. 8. 25 (409) and *C. Iust.* iii. 12. 9
(469). The Christian feasts and
fasts, Christmas, Epiphany, the
first week in Lent, Passion and
Easter weeks are added by *C. Th.*
ii. 8. 23 (400) and *C. Th.* xv. 5. 5
(425). According to some MSS.
this was done by *C. Th.* ii. 8. 19
(389), but the events of 399 recorded
below seem to show that 400 is the
right date.

[2] *C. Th.* xv. 7. 1, 2 (371); xv. 7.
4 (380); xv. 7. 9 (381). Historians
have seen in some of these rescripts
which are dated from Milan the
influence of St. Ambrose. *C. Th.*
xv. 7. 13 (414) seems to withdraw

the concessions, in the interest of
the public *voluptates*, but this may
have been only a temporary or local
measure.

[3] *C. Th.* xv. 7. 11 (393); xv. 7. 12
(394); xv. 13. 1 (396).

[4] *C. Th.* iv. 6. 3 (336) 'scenicae
. . . quarum venenis inficiuntur
animi perditorum'; xv. 7. 8 (381),
of the relapsing *scenica*, 'perma-
neat donec anus ridicula, senectute
deformis, nec tunc quidem absolu-
tione potiatur, cum aliud quam
casta esse non possit.'

[5] *C. Th.* xv. 7. 12 (394).

[6] *C. Th.* xv. 6. 2 (399) is explicit,
'ludicras artes concedimus agitari,
ne ex nimia harum restrictione
tristitia generetur.'

[7] *C. Th.* vi. 4. 2 (327); vi. 4. 4
(339); vi. 4. 29 (396); vi. 4. 32 (397).
It appears from the decree of 396
that the 'theatralis dispensio' of the
praetors had been diverted to the

and special municipal officers, the *tribuni voluptatum*, are appointed to superintend the arrangements[1]. Private individuals and rival cities must not deport actors, or withdraw them from the public service[2]. The bonds of caste, except for the few freed by their faith, are drawn as tight as ever[3], and when pagan worship ceases the shrines are preserved from demolition for the sake of the theatres built therein[4].

The love of even professing Christians for *spectacula* proved hard to combat. There are no documents which throw more light on the society of the Eastern Empire at the close of the fourth century than the works of St. Chrysostom; and to St. Chrysostom, both as a priest at Antioch before 397 and as patriarch of Constantinople after that year, the stage is as present a danger as it was to Tertullian two centuries earlier[5]. A sermon preached on Easter-day, 399, is good evidence of this. St. Chrysostom had been attacking the stage for a whole year, and his exhortations had just come to nought. Early in Holy Week there was a great storm, and the people joined the rogatory processions. But it was a week of *ludi*. On Good Friday the circus, and on Holy Saturday the theatre, were thronged and the churches were empty. The Easter sermon was an impassioned harangue, in which the preacher dwelt once more on the inevitable corruption bound up with things theatrical, and ended with a threat to enforce the sentence of excommunication, prescribed only a few months before by the council of Carthage, upon whoever should again venture to defy the Church's law in like fashion on Sunday or holy day[6]. Perhaps one may trace the controversy which

building of an aqueduct; they are now to give 'scenicas voluptates' again. Symmachus, *Ep.* vi. 42, describes his difficulties in getting *scenici* for his son's praetorship, which cost him £80,000. They were lost at sea; cf. Dill, 151.

[1] See Appendix A.

[2] *C. Th.* xv. 7. 5 (380); xv. 7. 10 (385); *C. Iust.* xi. 41. 5 (409).

[3] *C. Th.* xv. 7. 8 (381); xiv. 7. 3 (412).

[4] *C. Th.* xvi. 10. 3 (346). But *C. Th.* xvi. 10. 17 (399) forbids 'voluptates' to be connected with

sacrifice or superstition.

[5] A. Puech, *St. Jean Chrysostome et les Mœurs de son Temps* (1891), 266, has an interesting chapter on the *spectacula*. He refers to *Hom. in Matt.* 6, 7, 37, 48; *Hom. in Ioann.* 18; *Hom. in Ep.* 1 *ad Thess.* 5; *Hom. de Dav. et Saul,* 3; *Hom. in Prisc. et Aquil.* 1, &c. Most of these works belong to the Antioch period; cf. also Allard, i. 229. In *de Sacerdotio* 1, Chrysostom, like Augustine, records his own delight in the stage as a young man.

[6] *P. G.* lvi. 263.

St. Chrysostom's deliverance must have awakened, on the one hand in the rescript of the autumn of 399 pointedly laying down that the *ludicrae artes* must be maintained, on the other in the prohibition of the following year against performances in Holy week, and similar solemn tides.

More than a century after the exile and death of St. Chrysostom the theatre was still receiving state recognition at Constantinople. A regulation of Justinian as to the *ludi* to be given by newly elected consuls specified a performance on the stage ominously designated as the 'Harlots'[1]. By this date the *status* of the theatrical profession had at last undergone further and noticeable modification. The ancient Roman prohibition against the marriage of men of noble birth with *scenicae* or other *infames* or the daughters of such, had been re-enacted under Constantine. A partial repeal in 454 had not extended to the *scenicae*[2]. During the first half of the sixth century, however, a series of decrees removed their disability on condition of their quitting the stage, and further made it an offence to compel slaves or freed women to perform against their will[3]. In these humane relaxations of the rigid laws of theatrical caste has often been traced the hand of the empress Theodora, who, according to the contemporary gossip of Procopius, was herself, before her conversion, one of the most shameless of mimes. But it must be noted that the most important of the decrees in question preceded the accession of Justinian, although it may possibly have been intended to facilitate his own marriage[4]. The history of the stage in

---

[1] *C. I. C. Nov. Iust.* cv. 1 (536) 'faciet processum qui ad theatrum ducit, quem pornas vocant, ubi in scena ridiculorum est locus tragoedis et thymelicis choris'; cf. Choricius, *Apology for Mimes*, ed. Ch. Graux, in *R. d. Philologie*, i. 209; Krumbacher, 646.

[2] *C. Th.* iv. 6. 3 (336); *C. Iust.* v. 5. 7 (454).

[3] *C. Iust.* v. 4. 23 (520-3) allows the marriage on condition of an imperial rescript and a *dotale instrumentum*. *C. Iust.* i. 4. 33 (534) waives the rescript. It also imposes penalties on *fideiussores* or

sureties of actresses who hinder them from conversion and quitting the stage. For similar legislation cf. *Nov.* li; lxxxix. 15; cxvii. 4. By *Nov.* cxvii. 8. 6 a man is permitted to turn his wife out of doors and afterwards repudiate her, if she goes to theatre, circus, or amphitheatre without his knowledge or against his will.

[4] Gibbon, iv. 212, 516 (with Prof. Bury's additions); C. E. Mallet in *E. H. Review*, ii. 1; A. Debidour, *L'Impératrice Théodora*, 59. Neither Prof. Bury nor the editor of the *C. I. C.* accepts M. Debi-

the East cannot be traced much further with any certainty. The canons of the Quinisextine council, which met in the Trullan chamber to codify ecclesiastical discipline in 692, appear to contemplate the possibility of performances still being given [1]. A modern Greek scholar, M. Sathas, has made an ingenious attempt to establish the existence of a Byzantine theatrical tradition right through the Middle Ages ; but Dr. Krumbacher, the most learned historian of Byzantine literature, is against him, and holds that, so far as our know-ledge goes, the theatre must be considered to have perished during the stress of the Saracen invasions which, in the seventh and eighth centuries, devastated the East [2].

The ending of the theatre in the West was in very similar fashion. Chrysostom's great Latin contemporaries, Augustine and Jerome, are at one with him and with each other in their condemnation of the evils of the public stage as they knew it [3]. Their divergent attitude on a minor point may perhaps be explained by a difference of temperament. The fifth century saw a marked revival of literary interests from which even dignitaries of the Church did not hold themselves wholly aloof. Ausonius urged his grandson to the study of Menander. Sidonius, a bishop and no undevout one, read both Menander and Terence with his son [4]. With this movement Augustine had some sympathy. In a well-known passage of the *Confessions* he records the powerful influence exercised by tragedy,

---

dour's dating of *C. Iust.* v. 4. 23 under Justinian in 534.

[1] Mansi, xi. 943. Canon 3 ex-cludes one who has married a σκηνική from orders. C. 24 forbids priests and monks θυμελικῶν παι-γνίων ἀνέχεσθαι, and confirms a de-cree of the council of Laodicea (cf. p. 24, n. 4) obliging them, if present at a wedding, to leave the room before τὰ παίγνια are intro-duced. C. 51 condemns, both for clergy and laity, τοὺς λεγομένους μίμους καὶ τὰ τούτων θέατρα and τὰς ἐπὶ σκηνῶν ὀρχήσεις. For clergy the penalty is degradation, for laity ex-communication. C. 61 provides a six-years' excommunication for bear-leaders and such. C. 62 deals with

pagan religious festivals of a semi-theatrical character ; cf. ch. xiv. C. 66 forbids the circus or any δη-μώδης θέα in Easter week.

[2] Sathas, *passim* ; Krumbacher, 644.

[3] Jerome, *in Ezechiel* (410–15) 'a spectaculis removeamus oculos arenae circi theatri' (*P. L.* xxv. 189) ; Augustine, *de Fide et Sym-bolo* (393) 'in theatris labes morum, discere turpia, audire inhonesta, videre perniciosa' (*P. L.* xl. 639 ; cf. the sermon quoted in Appendix N, N⁰. x.

[4] Ausonius, *Idyl.* iv. 46 ; Sido-nius, *Ep.* iv. 12 'legebamus, pariter laudabamus, iocabamurque.'

and particularly erotic tragedy, over his tempestuous youth[1]. And in the *City of God* he draws a careful distinction between the higher and the lower forms of drama, and if he does not approve, at least does not condemn, the use of tragedies and comedies in a humane education[2]. Jerome, on the other hand, although himself like Augustine a good scholar, takes a more ascetic line, and a letter of his protesting against the reading of comedies by priests ultimately came to be quoted as an authority in Roman canon law[3].

The references to the stage in the works of two somewhat younger ecclesiastical writers are of exceptional interest. Orosius was a pupil of both Jerome and Augustine; and Orosius, endeavouring a few years after the sack of Rome by the Goths to prove that that startling disaster was not due to Christianity, lays great and indeed exaggerated importance on the share of the theatre in promoting the decay of the Empire[4]. About the middle of the fifth century the same note is struck by Salvian in his remarkable treatise *De Gubernatione Dei*[5]. The sixth book of his work is almost entirely devoted to the *spectacula*. Like Tertullian, Salvian insists on the definite renunciation of *spectacula* by Christians in their baptismal vow[6]. Like Orosius, he traces to the weakening of

---

[1] Augustine, *Conf.* iii. 2, 3 (*P. L.* xxxii. 683). The whim took him once 'theatrici carminis certamen inire.'

[2] Aug. *de Civ. Dei*, ii. 8 (*P. L.* xli. 53) 'et haec sunt scenicorum tolerabiliora ludorum, comoediae scilicet et tragoediae ; hoc est, fabulae poetarum agendae in spectaculis, multa rerum turpitudine sed nulla saltem sicut alia multa verborum obscoenitate compositae ; quas etiam inter studia quae honesta ac liberalia vocantur pueri legere et discere coguntur a senibus.'

[3] Jerome, *Ep.* 21 (*alii* 146) *ad Damasum*, written 383 (*P. L.* xxii. 386) 'at nunc etiam sacerdotes Dei, omissis evangeliis et prophetis, videmus comoedias legere, amatoria bucolicorum versuum verba canere, tenere Vergilium, et id quod in pueris necessitatis est, crimen in se

facere voluptatis' (*C. I. Can.* i. 37. 2).

[4] Orosius, *Hist. adv. Paganos* (417), iv. 21. 5 'theatra incusanda, non tempora.' On the character of the treatise of Orosius cf. Dill, 312; Gibbon, iii. 490. Mr. Dill shows in the third book of his admirable work that bad government and bad finance had much more to do with the breakdown of the Empire than the bad morals of the stage.

[5] Dill, 58, 137 ; Hodgkin, i. 930. Salvian was a priest of Marseilles, and wrote between 439 and 451.

[6] Salvian, vi. 31 'quae est enim in baptismo salutari Christianorum prima confessio ? quae scilicet nisi ut renuntiare se diabolo ac pompis eius et spectaculis atque operibus protestentur ?' The natural interpretation of this is that the word 'spectaculis' actually occurred in

moral fibre by these accursed amusements the failure of the West
to resist the barbarians. *Moritur et ridet* is his epigram on the
Roman world. The citizens of Tréves, three times destroyed,
still called upon their rulers for races and a theatre. With the
Vandals at the very gates of Cirta and of Carthage, *ecclesia
Carthaginiensis insaniebat in circis, luxuriebat in theatris* [1].
Incidentally Salvian gives some valuable information as to
the survival of the stage in his day. Already in 400 Augustine
had been able to say that the theatres were falling on every
side [2]. Salvian, fifty years later, confirms the testimony, but
he adds the reason. It was not because Christians had learnt
to be faithful to their vows and to the teachings of the Church ;
but because the barbarians, who despised *spectacula*, and therein
set a good example to degenerate Romans [3], had sacked half
the cities, while in the rest the impoverished citizens could no
longer pay the bills. He adds that at Rome a circus was still
open and a theatre at Ravenna, and that these were thronged
with delighted travellers from all parts of the Empire [4]. There
must, however, have been a theatre at Rome as well, for
Sidonius found it there when he visited the city, twelve years
after it had been sacked for the second time, in 467. He was
appointed prefect of the city, and in one of his letters expresses
a fear lest, if the corn-supply fail, the thunders of the theatre
may burst upon his head [5]. In a poem written a few years
earlier he describes the *spectacula theatri* of mimes, pantomimes, and acrobats as still flourishing at Narbonne [6].

The next and the latest records of the stage in the West

the *formula abrenuntiationis*. Was
this so ? It was not when Tertullian wrote (†200). He gives the
formula as 'renunciare diabolo et
pompae et angelis eius,' and goes
on to argue that visiting 'spectacula'
amounts to 'idolatria,' or worship of
the ' diabolus ' (*de Spectaculis*, c. 4).
Nor is the word used in any of the
numerous versions of the *formula*
given by Schaff, iii. 248 ; Duchesne,
293 ; Martene, i. 44 ; Martin von
Bracara, *de Caeremoniis* (ed. Caspari), c. 15.
  [1] Salvian, vi. 69, 87.
  [2] Augustine, *de Cons. Evang.* i.
33 (*P. L.* xxxiv. 1068) 'per omnes

pene civitates cadunt theatra . . .
cadunt et fora vel moenia, in quibus
demonia colebantur. Unde enim
cadunt, nisi inopia rerum, quarum
lascivo et sacrilego usu constructa
sunt.'
  [3] This point was made also by
Chrysostom in the Easter-day sermon, already cited on p. 15.
  [4] Salvian, vi. 39, 42, 49.
  [5] Sidonius, *Ep.* i. 10. 2 ' vereor
autem ne famem Populi Romani
theatralis caveae fragor insonet et
infortunio meo publica deputetur
esuries '; cf. *Ep.* i. 5. 10.
  [6] Sidonius, *Carm.* xxiii. 263
(†460) ; cf. *Ep.* ix. 13. 5.

date from the earlier part of the sixth century, when the
Ostrogoths held sway in Italy. They are to be found in
the *Variae* of Cassiodorus, who held important official posts
under the new lords of Rome, and they go to confirm the inference which the complaint of Salvian already suggests that
a greater menace to the continuance of the theatre lay in the
taste of the barbarians than even in the ethics of Christianity.

The Ostrogoths had long dwelt within the frontiers of the
Empire, and Theodoric, ruling as 'King of the Goths and
Romans in Italy,' over a mixed multitude of Italians and
Italianate Germans, found it necessary to continue the
spectacula, which in his heart he despised. There are many
indications of this in the state-papers preserved in the *Variae*,
which may doubtless be taken to express the policy and temper
of the masters of Cassiodorus in the rhetorical trappings of
the secretary himself. The *scenici* are rarely mentioned without a sneer, but their performances and those of the *aurigae*,
or circus-drivers, who have now come to be included under
the all-embracing designation of *histriones*, are carefully
regulated[1]. The gladiators have, indeed, at last disappeared,
two centuries after Constantine had had the grace to suppress them in the East[2]. There is a letter from Theodoric
to an architect, requiring him to repair the theatre of Pompey,
and digressing into an historical sketch, imperfectly erudite,
of the history of the drama, its invention by the Greeks, and
its degradation by the Romans[3]. A number of documents
deal with the choice of a *pantomimus* to represent the *prasini*
or 'Greens,' and show that the rivalry of the theatre-factions

---

[1] Cassiodorus, *Variae*, iii. 51
'quantum histrionibus rara con-
stantia honestumque votum, tanto
pretiosior est, cum in eis probabilis
monstratur affectus'; this is illustrated by the conduct of one
'Thomas Auriga'; *Var.* ii. 8 'Sa-
binus auriga . . . quamvis histrio
honesta nos supplicatione per-
movit'; *Var.* vi. 4 'tanta enim est
vis gloriosae veritatis, ut etiam in
rebus scenicis aequitas desideretur.'

[2] Schaff, v. 122; Dill, 55. The
rescript of Constantine is *C. Th.*

xv. 12. 1 'cruenta spectacula in
otio civili et domestica quiete non
placent; quapropter omnino gladiatores esse prohibemus (325).'

[3] Cassiodorus, *Var.* iv. 51. Of
the mime is said 'mimus etiam,
qui nunc modo derisui habetur,
tanta Philistionis cautela repertus
est ut eius actus poneretur in litteris'
(cf. p. 4, n. 1); of the pantomime,
'orchestrarum loquacissimae manus, linguosi digiti, silentium cla-
mosum, expositio tacita.'

remained as fierce as it had been in the days of Bathyllus and Pylades. Helladius is given the preference over Thorodon, and a special proclamation exhorts the people to keep the peace[1]. Still more interesting is the *formula*, preserved by Cassiodorus, which was used in the appointment of the *tribunus voluptatum*, an official whom we have already come across in the rescripts of the emperors of the fourth century. This is so characteristic, in its contemptuous references to the nature of the functions which it confers, of the whole German attitude in the matter of *spectacula*, that it seems worth while to print it in an appendix[2]. The passages hitherto quoted from the *Variae* all seem to belong to the period between 507 and 511, when Cassiodorus was *quaestor* and secretary to Theodoric at Rome. A single letter written about 533 in the reign of Athalaric shows that the populace was still looking to its Gothic rulers for *spectacula*, and still being gratified[3]. Beyond this the Roman theatre has not been traced. The Goths passed in 553, and Italy was reabsorbed in the Empire. In 568 came the Lombards, raw Germans who had been but little under southern influence, and were far less ready than their predecessors to adopt Roman manners. Rome and Ravenna alone remained as outposts of the older civilization, the latter under an exarch appointed from Constantinople, the former under its bishop. At Ravenna the theatre may conceivably have endured; at Rome, the Rome of Gregory the Great, it assuredly did not. An alleged mention of a theatre at Barcelona in Spain during the seventh century resolves itself into either a survival of pagan ritual or a bull-fight[4].

---

[1] Cassiodorus, *Var.* i. 20, 31-3.

[2] Cf. Appendix A.

[3] Cassiodorus, *Var.* ix. 21 'opes nostras scaenicis pro populi oblectatione largimur.'

[4] Du Méril, *Or. Lat.* 13, quotes from Mariana, *Hist. of Spain*, vi. 3, the statement that Sisebut, king of the Visigoths, deposed Eusebius, bishop of Barcelona, in 618, 'quod in theatro quaedam agi concessisset quae ex vana deorum superstitione traducta aures Christianae abhorrere videantur.' Sisebuthus, *Ep.* vi (*P. L.* lxxx. 370), conveys his decision to the bishop. He says, 'obiectum hoc, quod de ludis theatriis taurorum, scilicet, ministerio sis adeptus nulli videtur incertum; quis non videat quod etiam videre poeniteat.' But I cannot find in Sisebut or in Mariana, who writes Spanish, the words quoted by Du Méril. For 'taurorum' one MS. has 'phanorum.' I suspect the former is right. A bull-fight sounds so Spanish, and such festivals of heathen origin as the *Kalends* (ct. ch. xi) were not held in theatres. A. Gassier, *Le Théâtre espagnol*

Isidore of Seville has his learned chapters on the stage, but they are written in the imperfect tense, as of what is past and gone [1]. The bishops and the barbarians had triumphed.

(1898), 14, thinks such a festival is intended; if so, 'theatriis' probably means not literally, 'in a theatre,' but merely 'theatrical'; cf. the 'ludi theatrales' of the Feast of Fools (ch. xiii). In any case there is no question of 'scenici.'

[1] Isidorus Hispalensis, *Etymologiarum* (600–636), xviii. 42 (*P. L.* lxxxii. 658).

CHAPTER II

MIMUS AND SCÔP

[*Bibliographical Note* (for chs. ii–iv).—By far the best account of minstrelsy is the section on *Les Propagateurs des Chansons de Gestes* in vol. ii of L. Gautier, *Les Épopées françaises* (2nd ed. 1892), bk. ii, chs. xvii–xxi. It may be supplemented by the chapter devoted to the subject in J. Bédier, *Les Fabliaux* (2nd ed. 1895), and by the dissertation of E. Freymond, *Jongleurs und Menestrals* (Halle, 1883). I have not seen A. Olrik, *Middelalderens vandrende Spillemænd* (*Opuscula Philologica*, Copenhagen, 1887). Some German facts are added by F. Vogt, *Leben und Dichten der deutschen Spielleute im Mittelalter* (1876), and A. Schultz, *Das höfische Leben zur Zeit der Minnesinger* (2nd ed. 1889), i. 565, who gives further references. The English books are not good, and probably the most reliable account of English minstrelsy is that in the following pages; but materials may be found in J. Strutt, *Sports and Pastimes of the People of England* (1801, ed. W. Hone, 1830); T. Percy, *Reliques of Ancient English Poetry* (ed. H. B. Wheatley, 1876, ed. Schroer, 1889); J. Ritson, *Ancient English Metrical Romances* (1802), *Ancient Songs and Ballads* (1829); W. Chappell, *Old English Popular Music* (ed. H. E. Wooldridge, 1893); F. J. Crowest, *The Story of British Music, from the Earliest Times to the Tudor Period* (1896); J. J. Jusserand, *English Wayfaring Life in the Middle Ages* (trans. L. T. Smith, 4th ed. 1892). The early English data are discussed by R. Merbot, *Aesthetische Studien zur angelsächsischen Poesie* (1883), and F. M. Padelford, *Old English Musical Terms* (1899). F. B. Gummere, *The Beginnings of Poetry* (1901), should be consulted on the relations of minstrelsy to communal poetry; and other special points are dealt with by O. Hubatsch, *Die lateinischen Vagantenlieder des Mittelalters* (1870); G. Maugras, *Les Comédiens hors la Loi* (1887), and H. Lavoix, *La Musique au Siècle de Saint-Louis* (in G. Raynaud, *Recueil de Motets français*, 1883, vol. ii). To the above list of authorities should of course be added the histories of literature and of the drama enumerated in the *General Bibliographical Note*.]

THE fall of the theatres by no means implied the complete extinction of the *scenici*. They had outlived tragedy and comedy: they were destined to outlive the stage itself. Private performances, especially of *pantomimi* and other dancers, had enjoyed great popularity under the Empire, and had become an invariable adjunct of all banquets and other festivities. At such revels, as at the decadence of the theatre and of public morals generally, the graver pagans had looked askance[1]: the Church naturally included them in its universal condemnation of *spectacula*. Chrysostom in the East[2], Jerome in the West[3], are hostile to them, and a canon of the fourth-century council of Laodicea, requiring the clergy who might be present at weddings and similar rejoicings to rise and leave the room before the actors were introduced, was adopted by council after council and took its place as part of the ecclesiastical law[4]. The permanence of the regulation proves the strength of the habit, which indeed the Church might ban, but was not able to subdue, and which seems to have commended itself, far more than the theatre, to Teutonic manners. Such irregular performances proved a refuge for the dispossessed *scenici*. Driven from their theatres, they had still a vogue, not only at banquets, but at popular merry-makings or wherever in street or country they could gather together the remnant of their old audiences. Adversity and change of masters modified many of their characteristics. The *pantomimi*, in particular, fell upon evil times. Their subtle art had had its origin in an exquisite if corrupt taste, and adapted itself with difficulty to the ruder conditions of the new civilizations[5]. The *mimi* had always appealed to a common and gross humanity. But even they must now rub shoulders and contend for *denarii* with jugglers and with rope-dancers, with out-at-elbows gladiators and beast-tamers. More than ever they learnt to turn their hand to anything that might amuse; learnt to tumble, for instance; learnt to tell the long stories which the Teutons loved. Nevertheless, in essentials they remained the same; still jesters and buffoons,

---

[1] Macrobius, *Saturnalia*, ii. 1. 5, 9.
[2] Chrysostom, *Hom. in Ep. ad Col. cap.* 1, Hom. i. cc. 5, 6 (*P. G.* lxii. 306).
[3] Jerome, *Ep.* 117 (*P. L.* xxii. 957) 'difficile inter epulas servatur pudicitia'; cf. Dill, 110.
[4] *Conc. of Laodicea* (†343-81) can. 54 (Mansi, ii. 574) ὅτι οὐ δεῖ ἱερατικοὺς ἢ κληρικοὺς τινας θεωρίας θεωρεῖν ἐν γάμοις ἢ δείπνοις, ἀλλὰ πρὸ τοῦ εἰσέρχεσθαι τοὺς θυμελικοὺς ἐγείρεσθαι αὐτοὺς καὶ ἀναχωρεῖν. Cf. *Conc. of Braga* (†572) c. 60 (Mansi, v. 912),

Conc. of Aix-la-Chapelle (816) c. 83 (Mansi, vii. 1361); and finally, *C. I. Can.* iii. 5. 37 'non oportet ministros altaris vel quoslibet clericos spectaculis aliquibus, quae aut in nuptiis aut scenis exhibentur, interesse, sed ante, quam thymelici ingrediantur, surgere eos de convivio et abire.' It is noteworthy that 'scenis' here translates δείπνοις.
[5] Muratori *Antiq. Ital. Med. Aev.* ii. 847, traces the *pantomimi* in the Italian *mattaccini*.

still irrepressible, still obscene. In little companies of two or three, they padded the hoof along the roads, travelling from gathering to gathering, making their own welcome in castle or tavern, or, if need were, sleeping in some grange or beneath a wayside hedge in the white moonlight. They were, in fact, absorbed into that vast body of nomad entertainers on whom so much of the gaiety of the Middle Ages depended. They became *ioculatores, jougleurs,* minstrels[1].

The features of the minstrels as we trace them obscurely from the sixth to the eleventh century, and then more clearly from the eleventh to the sixteenth, are very largely the features of the Roman *mimi* as they go under, whelmed in the flood which bore away Latin civilization. But to regard them as nothing else than *mimi* would be a serious mistake. On another side they have a very different and a far more reputable ancestry. Like other factors in mediaeval society, they represent a merging of Latin and the Teutonic elements. They inherit the tradition of the *mimus*: they inherit also the tradition of the German *scôp*[2]. The earliest Teutonic poetry, so far as can be gathered, knew no *scôp*. As will be shown in a later chapter, it was communal in character, closely bound up with the festal dance, or with the rhythmic movements of labour. It was genuine folk-song, the utterance of no select caste of singers, but of whoever in the ring of worshippers or workers had the impulse and the gift to link the common movements to articulate words. At the festivals such a spokesman would be he who, for whatever reason, took the lead in the ceremonial rites, the *vates*, germ at once of priest and bard. The subject-matter of communal song was naturally determined by the interests ruling on the occasions when it was made. That of daily life would turn largely on the activities of labour itself: that of the high days on the emotions of religion, feasting, and love which were evoked by the primitive revels of a pastoral or agricultural folk.

Presently the movements of the populations of Europe brought the Germanic tribes, after separating from their Scandinavian kinsmen, into contact with Kelts, with Huns,

---

[1] Cf. Appendix B.   *Romania* (1876), 260 ; G. Paris,
[2] Ten Brink, i. 11 ; P. Meyer in   36 ; Gautier, ii. 6 ; Kögel, i. 2. 191.

with the Roman Empire, and, in the inevitable recoil, with each other. Then for the first time war assumed a prerogative place in their life. To war, the old habits and the old poetry adapted themselves. Tiwaz, once primarily the god of beneficent heaven, became the god of battles. The chant of prayer before the onset, the chant of triumph and thanksgiving after the victory, made themselves heard [1]. From these were disengaged, as a distinct species of poetry, songs in praise of the deeds and deaths of great captains and popular heroes. Tacitus tells us that poetry served the Germans of his day for both chronology and history [2]. Jordanis, four centuries later, has a similar account to give of the Ostrogoths [3]. Arminius, the vanquisher of a Roman army, became the subject of heroic songs [4]: Athalaric has no higher word of praise for Gensimund than *cantabilis* [5]. The glories of Alboin the Lombard [6], of Charlemagne himself[7], found celebration in verse, and Charlemagne was at the pains to collect and record the still earlier *cantilenae* which were the chronicle of his race. Such historical *cantilenae*, mingled with more primitive ones of mythological import, form the basis of the great legendary epics [8]. But the process of epic-making is one of self-conscious and deliberate art, and implies a considerable advance from primitive modes of literary composition. No doubt the earliest heroic *cantilenae* were still communal in character. They were *rondes* footed and sung at festivals by bands of young men and maidens. Nor was such folk-song quick to disappear. Still in the

[1] Tacitus, *Ann.* i. 65; iv. 47; *Hist.* ii. 22; iv. 18; v. 15; *Germ.* 3; Ammianus Marcellinus, xvi. 12. 43; xxxi. 7. 11; Vegetius, *de re militari*, iii. 18; cf. Kögel, i. 1. 12, 58, 111; Müllenhoff, *Germania*, ch. 3. The *barditus* or *barritus* of the Germans, whatever the name exactly means, seems to have been articulate, and not a mere noise.

[2] Tacitus, *Germ.* 2 'quod unum apud illos memoriae et annalium genus est.'

[3] Jordanis, *de orig. Getarum* (in *M. G. H.*), c. 4 'in priscis eorum carminibus pene storico ritu in commune recolitur.'

[4] Tacitus, *Ann.* ii. 88 'canitur adhuc barbaras apud gentes.'

[5] Cassiodorus, *Var.* viii. 9.

[6] Kögel, i. 1. 122, quoting Paulus Diaconus, i. 27.

[7] Kögel, i. 1. 122; i. 2. 220; Gautier, i. 72; G. Paris, *Hist. Poét. de Charlemagne*, 50; cf. *Poeta Saxo* (†890) in *M. G. H. Scriptores*, i. 268 'est quoque iam notum; vulgaria carmina magnis laudibus eius avos et proavos celebrant. Pippinos, Karolos, Hludiwicos et Theodricos, et Carlomannos Hlothariosque canunt.'

[8] Gautier, i. 37; Gröber, ii. 1. 447. The shades of opinion on the exact relation of the *cantilenae* to the *chansons de gestes* are numerous.

eleventh century the deeds of St. William of Orange resounded amongst the *chori iuvenum*[1]; and spinning-room and village green were destined to hear similar strains for many centuries more[2]. But long before this the *cantilenae* had entered upon another and more productive course of development: they were in the mouths, not only of the folk, but also of a body of professional singers, the fashioners of the epic that was to be[3]. Like heroic song itself, the professional singers owed

[1] *Vita S. Willelmi* (*Acta SS. Maii*, vi. 801) ' qui chori iuvenum, qui conventus populorum, praecipue militum ac nobilium virorum, quae vigiliae sanctorum dulce non resonant, et modulatis vocibus decantant qualis et quantus fuerit'; cf. Gautier, i. 66. The merest fragments of such folk-song heroic *cantilenae* are left. A German one, the Ludwigslied, on the battle of Saucourt (881) is in Müllenhoff und Scherer, *Denkmäler deutscher Poesie und Prosa* (1892), N°. xi ; cf. Kögel, i. 2. 86; Gautier, i. 62. And a few lines of a (probably) French one on an event in the reign of Clotaire (†620) are translated into Latin in Helgarius (†853–76), *Vita S. Faronis* (*Historiens de France*, iii. 505; Mabillon, *Acta SS. Benedictinorum*, ii. 610). Helgarius calls the song a 'carmen rusticum' and says 'ex qua victoria carmen publicum iuxta rusticitatem per omnium pene volitabat ora ita canentium, feminaeque choros inde plaudendo componebant.' The *Vita S. Faronis* in *Acta SS.* lx. 612, which is possibly an abridgement of Helgarius, says ' carmine rustico . . . suavi cantilena de-cantabatur'; cf. Gautier, i. 47; Gröber, ii. 1. 446.

[2] Ten Brink, i. 148, quotes from *Hist. Ely*, ii. 27 (†1166), a fragment of a song on Canute, 'quae usque hodie in choris publice cantantur,' and mentions another instance from Wm. of Malmesbury. Cf. *de Gestis Herewardi Saxonis* (Michel, *Chron. Anglo-Norm.* ii. 6) ' mulieres et puellae de eo in choris canebant,' and for Scotland the song on Ban-nockburn(1314)which, says Fabyan,

Chronicle (ed. Ellis), 420, 'was after many days sungyn in dances, in carolles of ye maydens and myn-strellys of Scotlande'; cf. also Gummere, *B. P.* 265.

[3] It is important to recognize that the *cantilenae* of the folk and those of the professional singers existed side by side. Both are, I think, implied in the account of the St. William songs quoted above: the folk sung them in choruses and on wake-days, the professional singers in the assemblies of warriors. At any rate, in the next (twelfth) cent. Ordericus Vitalis, vi. 3 (ed. *Soc. de l'Hist. de France*, iii. 5), says of the same Willelmus, 'Vulgo canitur a ioculatoribus de illo cantilena.' M. Gautier (ii. 6) will not admit the filiation of the *ioculatores* to the *scôpas*, and therefore he is led to suppose (i. 78) that the *cantilenae* and *vulgaria carmina* were all folk-song up to the end of the tenth cent. and that then the *ioculatores* got hold of them and lengthened them into *chansons de gestes*. But, as we shall see (p. 34), the Franks certainly had their professional singers as early as Clovis, and these cannot well have sung anything but heroic lays. Therefore the *cantilenae* and *vulgaria carmina* of the Mero-vingian and Carolingian periods may have been either folk-song, or *scôp*-song, or, more probably, both (Gröber, ii. 1. 449). *Cantilena* really means no more than 'chant' of any kind ; it includes ecclesiastical chant. So Alcuin uses it in (e. g. *Ep.* civ in Dümmler, ii. 169) ; and what Gautier, ii. 65, prints as a folk-song *cantilena* of S. Eulalia is treated by Gröber, ii. 1. 442, as a sequence.

their origin to war, and to the prominence of the individual, the hero, which war entailed. Around the person of a great leader gathered his individual following or *comitatus*, bound to him by ties of mutual loyalty, by interchange of service and reward[1]. Amongst the *comitatus* room was found for one who was no spearman, but who, none the less honoured for that, became the poet of the group and took over from the less gifted *chorus* the duty of celebrating the praises of the chieftain. These he sung to the accompaniment, no longer of flying feet, but of the harp, struck when the meal was over in tent or hall. Such a harper is the characteristically Germanic type of professional entertainer. He has his affinities with the Demodokos of a Homeric king. Rich in dignities and guerdons, sitting at the foot of the leader, consorting on equal terms with the warriors, he differs wholly from the *scenicus infamis*, who was the plaything and the scorn of Rome. Precisely when the shifting of social conditions brought him into being it is hard to say. Tacitus does not mention him, which is no proof, but a presumption, that amongst the tribes on the frontier he had not yet made his appearance in the first century of the Empire. By the fifth century he was thoroughly established, and the earliest records point to his existence at least as early as the fourth. These are not to be found in Latin sources, but in those early English poems which, although probably written in their extant forms after the invasion of these islands, seem to date back in substance to the age when the Angles still dwelt in a continental home around the base of the Jutish peninsula. The English remained to a comparatively late stage of their history remote from Roman influence, and it is in their literature that both the original development of the Teutonic *scôp* and his subsequent contamination by the Roman *mimus* can most easily be studied.

The earliest of all English poems is almost certainly *Widsith*, the 'far-traveller.' This has been edited and interpolated in Christian England, but the kernel of it is heathen and continental[2]. It is an autobiographic sketch of the life of Widsith, who was himself an actual or ideal *scôp*, or rather *gleómon*, for the precise term *scôp* is not used in the

---

[1] Gummere, *G. O.* 260. [2] Grein, i. 1.

poem. Widsith was of the Myrgings, a small folk who dwelt hard by the Angles. In his youth he went with Ealhhild, the 'weaver of peace,' on a mission to Eormanric the Ostrogoth. Eormanric is the Hermanric of legend, and his death in 375 A.D. gives an approximate date to the events narrated. Then Widsith became a wanderer upon the face of the earth, one who could 'sing and say a story' in the 'mead-hall.' He describes the nations and rulers he has known. Eormanric gave him a collar of beaten gold, and Guthhere the Burgundian a ring. He has been with Caesar, lord of jocund cities, and has seen Franks and Lombards, Finns and Huns, Picts and Scots, Hebrews, Indians, Egyptians, Medes and Persians. At the last he has returned to the land of the Myrgings, and with his fellow Scilling has sung loud to the harp the praises of his lord Eadgils and of Ealhhild the daughter of Eadwine. Eadgils has given him land, the inheritance of his fathers. The poem concludes with an eulogy of the life of gleemen. They wander through realm upon realm, voice their needs, and have but to give thanks. In every land they find a lord to whom songs are dear, and whose bounty is open to the exalters of his name. Of less undeniable antiquity than *Widsith* are the lines known as the *Complaint of Deor*. These touch the seamy side of the singer's life. Deor has been the *scôp* of the Heodenings many winters through. But one more skilled, Heorrenda by name—the Horant of the Gudrun saga—has outdone him in song, and has been granted the land-right that once was Deor's. He finds his consolation in the woes of the heroes of old. 'They have endured: may not I endure[1]?' The outline drawn in *Widsith* and in *Deor* is completed by various passages in the epic of *Beowulf,* which may be taken as representing the social conditions of the sixth or early seventh century. In Heorot, the hall of Hrothgar, there was sound of harp, the gleewood. Sweetly sang the *scôp* after the mead-bench. The lay was sung, the gleeman's *gyd* told. Hrothgar's thanes, even Hrothgar himself, took their turns to unfold the wondrous tale. On the other hand, when a folk is in sorrow, no harp is heard, the glee-beam is silent in the halls[2]. In these three poems, then, is fully

[1] Grein, i. 278.   [2] *Beowulf,* 89, 499, 869, 1064, 1162, 2106, 2259, 2449.

limned the singer of Teutonic heathenism. He is a man
of repute, the equal of thanes. He holds land, even the
land of his fathers. He receives gifts of gold from princes
for the praise he does them. As yet no distinction appears
between *scôp* and *gleómon*. Widsith is at one time the resident
singer of a court ; at another, as the mood takes him, a wanderer
to the ends of the earth. And though the *scôp* leads the song,
the warriors and the king himself do not disdain to take part
in it. This is noteworthy, because it gives the real measure
of the difference between the Teutonic and the Roman entertainer. For a Nero to perform amongst the *scenici* was to
descend : for a Hrothgar to touch the harp was a customary
and an honourable act.

The singing did not cease when the English came to these
islands. The long struggle with the Britons which succeeded
the invasions assuredly gave rise to many new lays, both in
Northumbria and Wessex. 'England,' says Mr. Stopford
Brooke, ' was conquered to the music of verse, and settled
to the sound of the harp.' But though Alfred and Dunstan
knew such songs, they are nearly all lost, or only dimly
discerned as the basis of chronicles. At the end of the sixth
century, just as the conquest was completed, came Christianity.
The natural development of English poetry was to some
extent deflected. A religious literature grew up at the hands
of priests. Eadhelm, who, anticipating a notion of St. Francis
of Assisi, used to stand on a bridge as if he were a gleeman,
and waylay the folk as they hurried back from mass, himself
wrote pious songs. One of these, a *carmen triviale*, was still
sung in the twelfth century[1]. This was in Wessex. In
Northumbria, always the most literary district of early
England, the lay brother Cædmon founded a school of divine
poetry. But even amongst the disciples of Cædmon, some,
such as the author of the very martial *Judith*, seem to have
designed their work for the mead-hall as well as the monastery[2]. And the regular *scôp* by no means vanished. The
Wanderer, a semi-heathen elegiac poem of the early eighth

[1] William of Malmesbury, *de
gestis Pontif. Angl.* (R. S.), 336
' quasi artem cantitandi professum,

. . . sensim inter ludicra verbis
scripturarum insertis.'
[2] Grein, ii. 294.

century, seems to be the lament of a *scôp* driven from his haunts, not by Christianity, but by the tumults of the day[1]. The great poet of the next generation, Cynewulf, himself took treasure of appled gold in the mead-hall. A riddle on 'the wandering singer' is ascribed to him[2], and various poems of his school on the fates or the crafts of man bear witness to the continued existence of the class[3]. With the eighth century, except for the songs of war quoted or paraphrased in the *Anglo-Saxon Chronicle*, the extant Early English poetry reaches a somewhat inexplicable end. But history comes to the rescue, and enables us still to trace the *scôp*. It is in the guise of a harp-player that Alfred is reported to have fooled the Danes, and Anlaf in his turn to have fooled the Saxons[4]: and mythical as these stories may be, they would not have even been plausible, had not the presence of such folk by the camp-fire been a natural and common event.

Certainly the *scôp* survived heathenism, and many Christian bishops and pious laymen, such as Alfred[5], were not ashamed of their sympathy with secular song. Nevertheless, the entertainers of the English folk did not find favour in the eyes of the Church as a whole. The stricter ecclesiastics especially attacked the practice of harbouring them in religious houses. Decrees condemning this were made by the council on English affairs which sat at Rome in 679[6], and by the council of Clovesho in 747[7]. Bede, writing at about the latter date on the

---

[1] Grein, i. 284. A similar poem is *The Sea-farer* (Grein, i. 290).

[2] Cynewulf, *Elene*, 1259 (Grein, ii. 135); *Riddle* lxxxix (Grein, iii. 1. 183). But A. S. Cook, *The Christ* (1900), lv, lxxxiii, thinks that Cynewulf was a thane, and denies him the *Riddle*.

[3] Cynewulf, *Christ* (ed. Gollancz), 668; *Gifts of Men* (Grein, iii. 1. 140); *Fates of Men* (Grein, iii. 1. 148).

[4] William of Malmesbury, *Gesta Reg. Angl.* (R. S.), i. 126, 143.

[5] Asserius, *de rebus gestis Alfredi* (Petrie-Sharp, *Mon. Hist. Brit.* i. 473). Alfred was slow to learn as a boy, but loved 'Saxonica poemata,' and remembered them. His first

book was a 'Saxonicum poematicae artis librum,' and 'Saxonicos libros recitare et maxime carmina Saxonica memoriter discere non desinebat.'

[6] Haddan-Stubbs, iii. 133 'Statuimus atque decernimus ut episcopi vel quicunque ecclesiastici ordinis religiosam vitam professi sunt . . . nec citharoedas habeant, vel quaecunque symphoniaca, nec quoscunque iocos vel ludos ante se permittant, quia omnia haec disciplina sanctae ecclesiae sacerdotes fideles suos habere non sinit.'

[7] *Ibid.* iii. 369 (can. 20) ' ut monasteria . . . non sint ludicrarum artium receptacula, hoc est, poetarum, citharistarum, musico-

condition of church affairs in Northumbria complains of those
who make mirth in the dwellings of bishops [1]; and the complaint is curiously illustrated by a letter of Gutbercht, abbot
of Newcastle, to an episcopal friend on the continent, in which
he asks him for a *citharista* competent to play upon the *cithara*
or *rotta* which he already possesses [2]. At the end of the eighth
century, Alcuin wrote a letter to Higbald, bishop of Lindisfarne,
warning him against the snares of *citharistae* and *histriones* [3]:
and some two hundred years later, when Edgar and Dunstan [4]
were setting themselves to reform the religious communities
of the land, the favour shown to such ribald folk was one of
the abuses which called for correction [5]. This hostile attitude
of the rulers of the Church is not quite explained by anything
in the poetry of the *scôpas*, so far as it is left to us. This had
very readily exchanged its pagan for a Christian colouring: it
cannot be fairly accused of immorality or even coarseness, and

rum, scurrorum.' Can. 12 shows
a fear of the influence of the *scôp*
on ritual: 'ut presbyteri saecularium
poetarum modo in ecclesia non
garriant, ne tragico sono sacrorum
verborum compositionem et dis-
tinctionem corrumpant vel con-
fundant.' Cf. the twelfth-century
account of church singers who used
'histrionicis quibusdam gestis,'
quoted by Jusserand, *E.L.* 455, from
the *Speculum Caritatis* of Abbot
Ælred of Rievaulx.

[1] Bede to Egbert in 734 (Haddan-
Stubbs, iii. 315) 'de quibusdam
episcopis fama vulgatum est ...
quod ipsi ... secum habeant ...
illos qui risui, iocis, fabulis ...
subigantur.'

[2] Gutberchtus to Lullus in 764
(Dümmler, *Epist. Mer. et Car.* in
M. G. H. i. 406).

[3] Alcuin, *Ep.* 124 (797) 'melius
est pauperes edere de mensa tua
quam istriones vel luxuriosos quoslibet ... verba Dei legantur in
sacerdotali convivio. ibi decet lec-
torem audiri, non citharistam; sermones patrum, non carmina gentium. quid Hinieldus cum Christo?
angusta est domus; utrosque tenere non poterit ... voces legentium

audire in domibus tuis, non riden-
tium turbam in plateis.' The allusion to a lost epic cycle of Hinieldus (Ingeld) is highly interesting;
on it cf. Haupt in *Z. f. d. A.* xv. 314.

[4] The *Vitae* of Dunstan (Stubbs,
Memorials of Dunstan, R. S. 11, 20,
80, 257) record that he himself
learnt the 'ars citharizandi.' One
day he hung 'citharam suam quam
lingua paterna hearpam vocamus'
on the wall, and it discoursed an
anthem by itself. Anthems, doubtless, were his mature recreation, but
as a young clerk he was accused
'non saluti animae profutura sed
avitae gentilitatis vanissima didi-
cisse carmina, et historiarum frivo-
volas colere incantationum nae-
nias.'

[5] *Anglo-Saxon Canons of Edgar*
(906), can. 58 (Wilkins, i. 228), *sic
Latine*, 'docemus artem, ut nullus
sacerdos sit cerevisarius, nec aliquo
modo scurram agat secum ipso, vel
aliis'; *Oratio Edgari Regis* (969)
pro monachatu propaganda (Wilkins, i. 246) 'ut iam domus clericorum putentur ... conciliabulum
histrionum ... mimi cantant et sal-
tant.'

the Christian sentiment of the time is not likely to have been much offended by the prevailing theme of battle and deeds of blood. The probable explanation is a double one. There is the ascetic tendency to regard even harmless forms of secular amusement as barely compatible with the religious life. And there is the fact, which the language of the prohibitions themselves makes plain, that a degeneration of the old Teutonic gleemen had set in. To singing and harping were now added novel and far less desirable arts. Certainly the prohibitions make no exception for *poetae* and *musici*; but the full strength of their condemnation seems to be directed against *scurrae* and their *ioca*, and against the *mimi* and *histriones* who danced as well as sang. These are new figures in English life, and they point to the fact that the merging of the Teutonic with the Latin entertainer had begun. To some extent, the Church itself was responsible for this. The conversion of England opened the remote islands to Latin civilization in general: and it is not to be wondered at, that the *mimi*, no less than the priests, flocked into the new fields of enterprise. If this was the case already in the eighth century, we can hardly doubt that it was still more so during the next two hundred years of which the literary records are so scanty. Such a view is supported by the numerous miniatures of dancers and tumblers, jugglers and bear-leaders, in both Latin and Early English manuscripts of this period [1], and by the glosses which translate such terms as *mimus, iocista, scurra, pantomimus* by *gligmon*, reserving *scôp* for the dignified *poeta* [2].

---

[1] Strutt, 172 and *passim*.

[2] Wright-Wülker, 150, 311, 539. A synonym for *scôp* is *leodwyrhta*. On 188 *lyricus* is glossed *scôp*. But the distinctive use of *scôp* is not in all cases maintained, e.g. *tragicus vel comicus unwurð scôp* (188), *comicus scôp* (283), *comicus id est qui comedia scribit, cantator vel artifex canticorum seculorum, idem satyricus, i. scôp, ioculator, poeta* (206). Other western peoples in contact with Latin civilization came to make the same classification of poet and buffoon. Wackernagel, i. 51, says that the German *liuderi* or poet is opposed to the *skirnun* or *tûmarâ, scurra* or *mimus*. The buffoon is looked askance at by the dignified Scandinavian men of letters (Saxo Grammaticus, *Hist. Danica*, transl. Elton, vi. 186); and Keltic bardism stands equally aloof from the *clerwr* (cf. p. 76). Of course Kelts and Teutons might conceivably have developed their buffoons for themselves, independently of Roman influence, but so far as the Germans go, Tacitus, *Germ.* 24, knows no *spectaculum* but the *sweorda-gelá.c* or sword-dance (ch. ix).

This distinction I regard as quite a late one, consequent upon the degeneracy introduced by *mimi* from south Europe into the lower ranks of the gleemen. Some writers, indeed, think that it existed from the beginning, and that the *scôp* was always the resident court poet, whereas the *gleómon* was the wandering singer, often a borrower rather than a maker of songs, who appealed to the smaller folk[1]. But the theory is inconsistent with the data of *Widsith*. The poet there described is sometimes a wanderer, sometimes stationary. He is evidently at the height of his profession, and has sung before every crowned head in Europe, but he calls himself a *gleómon*. Nor does the etymology of the words *scôp* and *gleómon* suggest any vital difference of signification[2].

The literary records of the continental Teutons are far scantier than those of the English. But amongst them also Latin and barbaric traditions seem to have merged in the *ioculator*. Ancestral deeds were sung to the harp, and therefore, it may be supposed, by a *scôp*, and not a *chorus*, before the Ostrogoths in Italy, at the beginning of the sixth century[3]. In the year 507 Clovis the Frank sent to Theodoric for a *citharoedus* trained in the musical science of the South, and Boethius was commissioned to make the selection[4]. On the other hand, little as the barbarians loved the theatre, the *mimi* and *scurrae* of the conquered lands seem to have tickled their fancy as they sat over their wine. At the banquet with which Attila entertained the imperial ambassadors in 448, the guests

[1] Brooke, i. 12; Merbot, 11. The *gleómon*, according to Merbot, became mixed with the *plegman* or *mimus*. In the glosses *pleȝa=ludus* in the widest sense, including athletics; and *pleȝ-stowe = amphitheatrum* (Wright-Wülker, 342). A synonym of *pleȝa* is the etymological equivalent of *ludus*, *lâc* (cf. ch. viii). *Spil* is not A. S., *spilian*, a loan-word (Kögel, i. 1. 11).

[2] *Scôp*, the O. H. G. *scopf* or *scof* is the 'shaper,' 'maker,' from *skapan*, 'to make'; it is only a West-German word, and is distinct from *scopf*, a 'scoff,' 'mock,' and also from O.N. *skald*. This is not West-German, but both 'sing' and 'say'

are from the same root *seg* (Kögel, i. 1. 140). *Gleómon* is from *gleo*, *gleow*, *gliw*, *glig* = 'glee,' 'mirth.' The harp, in *Beowulf* and elsewhere, is the 'glee-beam,' 'glee-wood.'

[3] Jordanis, *de hist. Get.* (in *M. G. H.*), c. 5 'ante quos etiam cantu maiorum facta modulationibus citharisque cantabant.'

[4] Cassiodorus, *Variae*, ii. 40, 41. Kögel, i. 1. 130, thinks that the professional singer, as distinct from the *chorus*, first became known to the Franks on this occasion. But one may rather infer from Theodoric's letter to Boethius that the *citharoedus* was to replace barbaric by civilized music.

were first moved to martial ardour and to tears by the recital of ancient deeds of prowess, and then stirred to laughter by the antics of a Scythian and a Moorish buffoon[1]. Attila was a Hun and no German; but the Vandals who invaded Africa in 429 are recorded to have taken to the *spectacula* so extravagantly popular there[2], and Sidonius tells how *mimici sales*, chastened in view of barbaric conceptions of decency, found a place in the festivities of another Theodoric, king from 462 to 466 of the Visigoths in Gaul[3]. Three centuries later, under Charlemagne, the blending of both types of entertainer under the common designation of *ioculator* seems to be complete. And, as in contemporary England, the animosity of the Church to the *scenici* is transferred wholesale to the *ioculatores*, without much formal attempt to discriminate between the different grades of the profession. Alcuin may perhaps be taken as representing the position of the more rigid disciplinarians on this point. His letter to the English bishop, Higbald, does not stand alone. In several others he warns his pupils against the dangers lurking in *ludi* and *spectacula*[4], and he shows himself particularly exercised by

---

[1] Priscus, *Hist. Goth.* (ed. Bonn) 205 ἐπιγενομένης δὲ ἑσπέρας δᾷδες ἀνήφθησαν, δύο δὲ ἀντικρὺ τοῦ Ἀττήλα παρελθόντες βάρβαροι ᾄσματα πεποιημένα ἔλεγον, νίκας αὐτοῦ καὶ τὰς κατὰ πόλεμον ᾄδοντες ἀρετάς· ἐς οὓς οἱ τῆς εὐωχίας ἀπέβλεπον, καὶ οἱ μὲν ἥδοντο τοῖς ποιήμασιν, οἱ δὲ τῶν πολέμων ἀναμιμνησκόμενοι διηγείροντο τοῖς φρονήμασιν, ἄλλοι δὲ ἐχώρουν ἐς δάκρυα, ὧν ὑπὸ τοῦ χρόνου ἠσθένει τὸ σῶμα καὶ ἡσυχάζειν ὁ θυμὸς ἠναγκάζετο. μετὰ δὲ τὰ ᾄσματα Σκύθης τις παρελθὼν φρενοβλαβής, . . . ἐς γέλωτα πάντας παρεσκεύασε παρελθεῖν. μεθ' ὃν . . . Ζέρκων ὁ Μαυρούσιος . . . πάντας . . . ἐς ἄσβεστον ὁρμῆσαι γέλωτα παρεσκεύασε, πλὴν Ἀττήλα. Cf. Gibbon, iii. 440; Hodgkin, ii. 86; Kögel, i. 1. 114.

[2] Procopius, *de bell. Vandol.* ii. 6; Victor Vitensis, *de persec. Vandal.* i. 15. 47.

[3] Sidonius, *Ep.* i. 2. 9 'sane intromittuntur, quanquam raro, inter coenandum mimici sales, ita ut nullus conviva mordacis linguae felle

feriatur.' There are no musicians, 'rege solum illis fidibus delenito, quibus non minus mulcet virtus animum quam cantus auditum.' In *Carm.* xii Sidonius mentions Gothic songs, ' without specifying whether they are professional or choric.

[4] Alcuin, *Ep.* cclxxxi (793–804), to a disciple in Italy, 'melius est Deo placere quam histrionibus, pauperum habere curam quam mimorum'; *Ep.* ccl (†801), to the monks of Fulda, 'non sint [adulescentuli] luxuriosi, non ebrietati servientes, non contemptuosi, non inanes sequentes ludos'; *Ep.* ccxliv (†801), to Fredegis, master of the palace school, 'non veniant coronatae columbae ad fenestras tuas, quae volant per cameras palatii, nec equi indomiti inrumpant ostia camerae; nec tibi sit ursorum saltantium cura, sed clericorum psallentium.' The 'coronatae columbae' were Charlemagne's wanton daughters. Dümmler (*Ep. Mer. et Car.* ii. 541)

the favour which they found with Angilbert, the literary and far from strict-lived abbot of St. Richer[1]. The influence of Alcuin with Charlemagne was considerable, and so far as ecclesiastical rule went, he had his way. A capitulary (†787) excluded the Italian clergy from uncanonical sports[2]. In 789 bishops, abbots, and abbesses were forbidden to keep *ioculatores*[3], and in 802 a decree applying to all in orders required abstinence from idle and secular amusements[4]. These prohibitions were confirmed in the last year of Charlemagne's reign (813) by the council of Tours[5]. But as entertainers of the lay folk, the minstrels rather gained than lost status at the hands of Charlemagne. Personally he took a distinct interest in their performances. He treasured up the heroic *cantilenae* of his race[6], and attempted in vain to

prints a *responsio* of Leidradus, Abp. of Lyons, to Charles. This is interesting, because it contrasts the 'mobilitas histrionum' which tempts the eye, with the 'carmina poetarum et comediarum mimorumque urbanitates et strophae,' which tempt the ear. This looks as if *histriones*, in the sense of *pantomimi*, were still known, but the piece also mentions 'teatrorum moles' and 'circenses,' and is, I suspect, quite antiquarian.

[1] *Ep.* clxxv (799), to Adalhart, Bp. of Old Corbey, 'Vereor, ne Homerus [Angilbert] irascatur contra cartam prohibentem spectacula et diabolica figmenta. quae omnes sanctae scripturae prohibent, in tantum ut legebam sanctum dicere Augustinum, "nescit homo, qui histriones et mimos et saltatores introducit in domum suam, quam magna eos immundorum sequitur turba spirituum." sed absit ut in domo christiana diabolus habeat potestatem' (the quotation from Augustine cannot be identified): *Ep.* ccxxxvii (801), also to Adalhart, 'quod de emendatis moribus Homeri mei scripsisti, satis placuit oculis meis ... unum fuit de histrionibus, quorum vanitatibus sciebam non parvum animae sui periculum imminere, quod mihi non placuit, ... mirumque mihi visum est, quomodo

tam sapiens animus non intellexisset reprehensibilia dignitati suae facere et non laudabilia.' Angilbert also seems to have had relations unbecoming an abbot with one of the 'coronatae columbae.'

[2] *Capit. of Mantua* (Boretius, i. 195), can. 6 'neque ulla iocorum genera ante se fieri permittant quae contra canonum auctoritatem eveniunt.'

[3] *Capit. Generale* (Boretius, i. 64; *P. L.* xcvii. 188), c. 31 'ut episcopi et abbates et abbatissae cupplas canum non habeant, nec falcones, nec accipitres, nec ioculatores.' If this is the *carta* of Alcuin's *Ep.* clxxv, and I know of no other which it can be, Dümmler's date for the letter of 799 seems too late. Mabillon's 791 is nearer the mark.

[4] *Capit. Gen.* (Boretius, i. 96), can. 23 'cleri ... non inanis lusibus vel conviviis secularibus vel canticis vel luxuriosis usum habeant.'

[5] *Conc. of Tours* (Mansi, xiv. 84), c. 7 'histrionum quoque turpium et obscoenorum insolentiis iocorum et ipsi [sacerdotes] animo effugere caeterisque sacerdotibus effugienda praedicare debent.'

[6] Einhard, *Vita Caroli Magni*, c. 29 'barbara et antiquissima carmina, quibus veterum regum actus et bella canebantur, scripsit memoriaeque mandavit.'

inspire the *saevitia* of his sons with his own enthusiasm for these[1]. The chroniclers more than once relate how his policy was shaped or modified by the chance words of a *ioculator* or *scurra*[2]. The later tradition of the *jougleurs* looked back to him as the great patron of their order, who had given them all the fair land of Provence in fee[3]: and it is clear that the songs written at his court form the basis not only of the *chansons de gestes*, but also, as we found to be the case with the English war-songs, of many passages in the chronicles themselves[4]. After Charlemagne's death the minstrels fell for a time on evil days. Louis the Pious by no means shared his father's love for them. He attempted to suppress the *cantilenae* on which he had been brought up, and when the *mimi* jested at court would turn away his head and refuse to smile[5]. To his reign may perhaps be ascribed a decree contained in the somewhat dubious collection of Benedictus Levita, forbidding idle dances, songs and tales in public places and at crossways on Sundays[6], and another which continued

---

[1] Alcuin, *Ep.* cxlix (798), to Charlemagne, ' ut puerorum saevitia vestrorum cuiuslibet carminis dulcedine mitigaretur, voluistis'; Alcuin, who doubtless had to *ménager* Charlemagne a little, is apparently to write the poem himself.

[2] Kögel, i. 2. 222. The *Chronicon Novaliciense*, iii. 10, describes how after crossing Mt. Cenis in 773, Charlemagne was guided by a Lombard *ioculator* who sung a ' cantiunculam a se compositam de eadem re rotando in conspectu suorum.' As a reward the *ioculator* had all the land over which his *tuba* sounded on a hill could be heard. The *Monachus S. Galli* (Jaffé, *Bibl. rer. Germ.* iv), i. 13, tells how (†783) a *scurra* brought about a reconciliation between Charlemagne and his brother-in-law Uodalrich. The same writer (i. 33) mentions an ' incomparabilis clericus' of the 'gloriosissimus Karolus,' who ' scientia ... cantilenae ecclesiasticae vel iocularis novaque carminum compositione sive modulatione ... cunctos praecelleret.'

[3] Philippe Mouskes, *de Poetis*

Provincialibus (quoted Ducange, s. v. *leccator*):

' Quar quant li buens Rois Karlemaigne
Ot toute mise à son demaine
Provence, qui mult iert plentive
De vins, de bois, d'aigue, de rive,
As lecours, as menestreus,
Qui sont auques luxurieus,
Le donna toute et departi.'

[4] Kögel, i. 2. 220.

[5] Theganus, *de gestis Ludovici Pii* (*M. G. H. Scriptores*, ii. 594), c. 19 ' Poetica carmina gentilia, quae in iuventute didicerat, respuit, nec legere nec audire nec docere voluit,' and ' nunquam in risu exaltavit vocem suam, nec quando in festivitatibus ad laetitiam populi procedebant thymelici, scurrae, et mimi cum choraulis et citharistis ad mensam coram eo, tunc ad mensuram ridebat populus coram eo, ille nunquam vel dentes candidos suos in risu ostendit.' The 'carmina gentilia,' so much disliked by Louis, were probably Frankish and not classic poems.

[6] Benedictus Levita, vi. 205

for the benefit of the minstrels the legal incapacity of the Roman *scenici*, and excluded *histriones* and *scurrae* from all privilege of pleading in courts of justice [1].

The ill-will of a Louis the Pious could hardly affect the hold which the minstrels had established on society. For good or for bad, they were part of the mediaeval order of things. But their popularity had to maintain itself against an undying ecclesiastical prejudice. They had succeeded irrevocably to the heritage of hate handed down from the *scenici infames*. To be present at their performances was a sin in a clerk, and merely tolerated in a layman. Largesse to them was declared tantamount to robbery of the poor [2]. It may be fairly said that until the eleventh century at least the history of minstrelsy is written in the attacks of ecclesiastical legislators, and in the exultant notices of monkish chroniclers when this or that monarch was austere enough to follow the example of Louis the Pious, and let the men of sin go empty away [3]. Throughout the Middle Ages proper the same standpoint was officially maintained [4]. The canon law, as codified by Gratian, treats

(*M. G. H. Leges*, ii. 2. 83), ' ne in illo sancto die vanis fabulis aut locutionibus sive cantationibus vel saltationibus stando in biviis et plateis ut solet inserviant.' On this collection see Schaff, v. 272.

[1] This capitulary is of doubtful date, but belongs to the reign either of Louis the Pious, or Lothair (Boretius, i. 334; Pertz, i. 324; Ben. Levita, ii. 49) ' ut in palatiis nostris ad accusandum et iudicandum et testimonium faciendum non se exhibeant viles personae et infames, histriones scilicet, nugatores, manzeres, scurrae, concubinarii, . . . aut servi aut criminosi'; cf. R. Sohm, *Die fränk. Reichs- und Gerichtsverfassung*, 354.

[2] For ninth-century prohibitions see *Statutes* of Haito, Bp. of Basle (807–23), c. 11 (Boretius, i. 364); *Conc. of Maintz* (847), c. 13 (Boretius, ii. 179); *Conc. of Maintz* (852), c. 6 (Boretius, ii. 187); *Capit.* of Walter of Orleans (858), c. 17 (Mansi, xv. 507), *Capit.* of Hincmar

of Rheims (*P. L.* cxxv. 776); and cf. Prynne, 556. Stress is often laid on the claims of the poor; e. g. Agobardus († 836), *de Dispens. Eccles. Rer.* 30 (*P. L.* civ. 249) ' satiat praeterea et inebriat histriones, mimos, turpissimosque et vanissimos ioculares, cum pauperes ecclesiae fame discruciati intereant.'

[3] Otto Frisingensis, *Chronicon*, vi. 32, records of the Emperor Henry III in 1045 that ' quumque ex more regio nuptias Inglinheim celebraret, omne balatronum et histrionum collegium, quod, ut assolet, eo confluxerat, vacuum abire permisit, pauperibusque ea quae membris diaboli subtraxerat, large distribuit.' After the death of the Emperor Henry I of Germany his widow Matilda ' neminem voluit audire carmina saecularia cantantem' (*Vita Machtildis Antiquior* in *M. G. H. Scriptores*, iv. 294).

[4] Honorius Augustodunensis, *Elucidarium* († 1092), ii. 18 (*P. L.*

as applicable to minstrels the pronouncements of fathers and councils against the *scenici,* and adds to them others more recent, in which clergy who attend *spectacula,* or in any way by word or deed play the *ioculator,* are uncompromisingly condemned [1]. This temper of the Church did not fail to find its expression in post-Conquest England. The ·council of Oxford in 1222 adopted for this country the restatement of the traditional rule by the Lateran council of 1215 [2]; and the stricter disciplinary authorities at least attempted to enforce the decision. Bishop Grosseteste of Lincoln, for instance, pressed it upon his clergy in or about 1238 [3]. The reforming provisions of Oxford in 1259 laid down that, although minstrels might receive charitable doles in monasteries, their *spectacula* must not be given [4]; and a similar prohibition, couched in very

clxxii. 1148) 'Habent spem ioculatores? nullam; tota namque intentione sunt ministri Satanae'; on the vogue of this book cf. *Furnivall Miscellany,* 88.

[1] The following passages of the *Decretum Gratiani,* besides those already quoted, bear on the subject: (*a*) i. 23. 3, *ex Isid. de Eccl. Officiis,* ii. 2 'His igitur lege Patrum cavetur, ut a vulgari vita seclusi a mundi voluptatibus sese abstineant; non spectaculis, non pompis intersint': (*b*) i. 44. 7, *ex Conc. Nannetensi* 'Nullus presbyterorum ... quando ad collectam presbyteri convenerit . . . plausus et risus inconditos, et fabulas inanes ibi referre aut cantare praesumat, aut turpia ioca vel urso vel tornatricibus ante se fieri patiatur'; I cannot identify the Council of Nantes referred to: the canon is not amongst those supposed to belong to the Council of 660, and given by Mansi, xviii. 166: (*c*) i. 46. 6, *ex Conc. Carthag.* iv. c. 60 [398. Mansi, iii. 956] 'Clericum scurrilem et verbis turpibus ioculatorem ab officio retrahendum censemus': (*d*) ii. 4. 1. 1, *ex Conc. Carthag.* vii (419) 'Omnes etiam infamiae maculis aspersi, id est histriones . . . ab accusatione prohibentur.' The *Decretum Gratiani* was drawn up † 1139. The *Decretales* of Gregory IX (1234) incorporate can. 16 of

the *Lateran Council* (Mansi, xxii. 1003), held in 1215 (*Decr. Greg. IX,* iii. 1. 15) '[Clerici] mimis, ioculatoribus, et histrionibus non intendant'; and the *Liber Sextus* of Boniface VIII (1298) adds the following decree of that Pope (*Sext. Decr.* iii. 1. 1) 'Clerici qui, clericalis ordinis dignitati non modicum detrahentes, se ioculatores seu goliardos faciunt aut bufones, si per annum artem illam ignominiosam exercuerint, ipso iure, si autem tempore breviori, et tertio moniti non resipuerint, careant omni privilegio clericali.'

[2] Wilkins, i. 585. For can. 16 of the Lateran council see last note. The prohibition is again confirmed by can. 17 of the Synod of Exeter in 1287 (Wilkins, ii. 129).

[3] *Constitutiones* of Bp. Grosseteste in his *Epistolae* (R. S.), 159 'ne mimis, ioculatoribus, aut histrionibus intendant.' In 1230, Grosseteste's predecessor, Hugh of Wells, had bid his archdeacons inquire, 'an aliqui intendant histrionibus' (Wilkins, i. 627).

[4] *Annales de Burton* (*Ann. Monast.* R. S. i. 485) 'histrionibus potest dari cibus, quia pauperes sunt, non quia histriones; et eorum ludi non videantur, vel audiantur, vel permittantur fieri coram abbate vel monachis.'

uncomplimentary terms, finds a place in the new statutes drawn up in 1319 for the cathedral church of Sarum by Roger de Mortival[1]. A few years later the statutes of St. Albans follow suit[2], while in 1312 a charge of breaking the canons in this respect brought against the minor clergy of Ripon minster had formed the subject of an inquiry by Archbishop Greenfield[3]. Such notices might be multiplied[4]; and the tenor of them is echoed in the treatises of the more strait-laced amongst monkish writers. John of Salisbury[5], William Fitz Stephen[6], Robert Mannyng of Brunne[7], are at one in their disapproval of *ioculatores*. As the fourteenth century draws to its close, and the Wyclifite spirit gets abroad, the freer critics of church

[1] *Const.* of Roger de Mortival, § 46 (Dayman and Jones, *Sarum Statutes*, 76) 'licet robustos corpore, laborem ad quem homo nascitur subire contemnentes, et in delicato otio sibi victum quaerere sub inepta laetitia saeculi eligentes, qui "menestralli" et quandoque "ludorum homines" vulgari eloquio nuncupantur, non quia tales sunt, sed quia opus Dei nostramque naturam conspicimus in eisdem, nostris domibus refectionis gratia aliquotiens toleremus,' yet no money or goods convertible into money may be given them; 'nec ad fabulas quas referunt, et quae in detractationibus, turpiloquio, scurrilitate consistunt, ullus voluntarium praebeat auditum, nec ad eas audiendas aures habeat prurientes, sed per obauditionem ab huiusmodi relatibus, quin potius latratibus, in quantum fieri poterit, excludantur, tamen nemo libenter invito referat auditori.' They may, if they are not women, have their dole of bread, and keep peace from evil words. 'Nec debet de huiusmodi personarum, quae infames sunt, laude, immo verius fraude, seu obloquio, aut alias vanae laudis praeconio, ecclesiasticus vir curare, cum nihil eo miserius sit praelato, qui luporum laudibus gloriatur.' The statute is headed 'De maledicis, adulatoribus, histrionibus, et detractoribus respuendis.'

[2] Thomas Walsingham, *Gesta Abbatum S. Albani* (ed. Riley, R. S. ii. 469) 'illicita spectacula prorsus evitent' (1326-35).

[3] J. T. Fowler, *Memorials of Ripon Minster*, ii. 68 (Surtees Soc.); the charge was that 'vicarii, capellani, et caeteri ministri . . . spectaculis publicis, ludibriis et coreis, immo teatricalibus ludis inter laicos frequentius se immiscent.'

[4] The *Statutes*, i. 5. 4, of St. Paul's, as late as †1450, direct the beadles 'quod menestrallos coram altaribus Virginis et Crucis indevote strepitantes arceant et eiiciant' (W. S. Simpson, *Register of St. Paul's*, 72).

[5] John of Salisbury, *Polycraticus* (†1159), i. 8 (*P.L.* cxcix. 406) 'satius enim fuerat otiari quam turpiter occupari. Hinc mimi, salii vel saliares, balatrones, aemiliani, gladiatores, palaestritae, gignadii, praestigiatores, malefici quoque multi, et tota ioculatorum scena procedit.'

[6] Cf. *Representations*, s.v. London.

[7] R. Mannyng de Brunne (†1303), *Handlyng Synne* (ed. Furnivall), 148. 'Here doyng ys ful perylous' he translates William of Wadington's 'Qe unt trop perilus mester'; and tells a tale of divine judgement on 'a mynstralle, a gulardous,' who disturbed a priest at mass.

and state, such as William Langland [1] or the imagined author of Chaucer's *Parson's Tale* [2], take up the same argument. And they in their turn hand it on to the interminable pamphleteering of the Calvinistic Puritans [3].

[1] *Piers the Plowman, C. text,* viii. 97:

'Clerkus and knyȝtes · wel-cometh kynges mynstrales,
And for loue of here lordes · lithen hem at festes;
Muche more, me thenketh · riche men auhte
Haue beggars by-fore hem · whiche beth godes myn-strales.'

[2] *Cant. Tales* (ed. Skeat), § 69 'Soothly, what thing that he yeveth for veyne glorie, as to minstrals and to folk, for to beren his renoun in the world, he hath sinne ther-of, and noon almesse.'

[3] e. g. Stubbes, *Anatomy,* i. 169.

CHAPTER III

THE MINSTREL LIFE

THE perpetual *infamia* of the minstrels is variously reflected in the literature of their production. Sometimes they take their condemnation lightly enough, dismissing it with a jest or a touch of bravado. In *Aucassin et Nicolete*, that marvellous romance of the *viel caitif*, when the hero is warned that if he takes a mistress he must go to hell, he replies that, to hell will he go, for thither go all the goodly things of the world. 'Thither go the gold and the silver, and the vair and the grey, and thither too go harpers and minstrels and the kings of the world. With these will I go, so that I have Nicolete, my most sweet friend, with me'[1]. At other times they show a wistful sense of the pathos of their secular lot. They tell little stories in which heaven proves more merciful than the vice-gerents of heaven upon earth, and Virgin or saint bestows upon a minstrel the sign of grace which the priest denies[2]. But often, again, they turn upon their persecutors

[1] *Aucassin et Nicolete* († 1150–1200), ed. Bourdillon (1897), 22. The term 'caitif' has puzzled the editors. Surely the minstrel has in mind the abusive epithets with which the clergy bespattered his profession. See Appendix B.

[2] See especially *Le Tombeor de Notre Dame* (*Romania*, ii. 315). Novati (*Rom.* xxv. 591) refers to a passage quoted by Augustine, *de Civ. Dei*, vi. 10, from the lost work of Seneca, *de Superstitionibus*, 'doctus archimimus, senex iam decrepitus, cotidie in Capitolio mimum agebat, quasi dii libenter spectarent quem illi homines desierant.' Somewhat similar are *Don Cierge qui descendi au Jougleour* (Gautier de Coincy), *Miracles de Nostre Dame* († 1223, ed. Poquet, 1859), and *Le Harpeor de Roncestre* (Michel, *Roms.*, *Contes*, *Dits*, *Fabl.* ii. 108). *Saint Pierre et le Jongleur* (Montaiglon Raynaud, v. 117) is a witty tale, in which a minstrel, left in charge of hell, loses so many souls to St. Peter at dice, that no minstrel has been allowed there since. B. Joannes Bonus (*Acta SS. Oct.* ix. 693) was a minstrel in his youth, but the patron saints of the minstrels were always St. Genesius the mime (cf. p. 10), and St. Julian Hospitator (*Acta SS. Jan.* iii. 589), who built a hospital and once entertained an angel unawares.

and rend them with the merciless satire of the *fabliaux*, wherein it is the clerk, the theologian, who is eternally called upon to play the indecent or ridiculous part [1].

Under spiritual disabilities the minstrels may have been, but so far as substantial popularity amongst all classes went, they had no cause from the eleventh to the fourteenth century to envy the monks. As a social and literary force they figure largely both on the continent and in England. The distinctively Anglo-Saxon types of *scôp* and *gleômon* of course disappear at the Conquest. They do not cease to exist; but they go under ground, singing their defiant lays of Hereward [2]; and they pursue a more or less subterranean career until the fourteenth century brings the English tongue to its own again. But minstrelsy was no less popular with the invaders than with the invaded. Whether the *skald* had yet developed amongst the Scandinavian pirates who landed with Rollo on the coasts of France may perhaps be left undetermined [3]: for a century and a half had sufficed to turn the Northmen into Norman French, and with the other elements of the borrowed civilization had certainly come the *ioculator*. In the very van of William's army at Senlac strutted the minstrel Taillefer, and went to his death exercising the double arts of his hybrid profession, juggling with his sword, and chanting an heroic lay of Roncesvalles [4]. Twenty years later, Domesday Book records how Berdic the *ioculator regis* held three vills and five carucates of land in Gloucestershire, and how in Hamp-

---

[1] Paris, 113; Bédie‑ 333.

[2] Brooke, *Eng. Lit.* 305; Ten Brink, i. 149.

[3] Sophus Bugge, in *Bidrag til den aeldste Skaldedigtnings Historie* (1894; cf. L. Duvau in *Rev. Celt.* xvii. 113), holds that Skaldic poetry began in the Viking raids of the eighth and ninth centuries, under the influence of the Irish *filid*. The tenth-century skald as described in the *Raven-Song* of Hornklofi at the court of Harold Fair-hair is very like the *scôp* (*C. P. B.* i. 254), and here too tumblers and buffoons have found their way. Cf. Kögel, i. 1. 111; E. Mogk, in Paul, *Grundriss*[2], iii. 248.

[4] Guy of Amiens, *de Bello Hastingensi* (†1068), 391, 399:
'Histrio, cor audax nimium quem nobilitabat. . .
. . . Incisor-ferri mimus cognomine dictus.'
Wace, *Roman de Rou* (†1170) (ed. Andresen, iii. 8035):
'Taillefer, ki mult bien chantout,
Sor un cheval ki tost alout,
Devant le duc alout chantant
De Karlemaigne et de Rolant
Et d'Oliver et des vassals
Qui morurent en Rencevals.'
Cf. Freeman, *Norman Conquest*, iii. 477.

shire Adelinda, a *ioculatrix*, held a virgate, which Earl Roger had given her [1]. During the reigns of the Angevin and Plantagenet kings the minstrels were ubiquitous. They wandered at their will from castle to castle, and in time from borough to borough, sure of their ready welcome alike in the village tavern, the guildhall, and the baron's keep [2]. They sang and jested in the market-places, stopping cunningly at a critical moment in the performance, to gather their harvest of small coin from the bystanders [3]. In the great castles, while lords and ladies supped or sat around the fire, it was theirs to while away many a long bookless evening with courtly *geste* or witty sally. At wedding or betrothal, baptism or knight-dubbing, treaty or tournament, their presence was indispensable. The greater festivities saw them literally in their hundreds [4], and rich was their reward in money and in jewels, in costly garments [5], and in broad acres. They were licensed vagabonds, with free right of entry into the presence-chambers of the land [6]. You might know them from afar by their coats of many colours, gaudier than any knight might respectably wear [7], by the instruments upon their backs and those of their

---

[1] Domesday Book, *Gloc.* f. 162 ; *Hants*, f. 38 (b). Before the Conquest, not to speak of Widsith and Deor, Edmund Ironside had given the hills of Chartham and Walworth 'cuidam ioculatori suo nomine Hitardo' (Somner-Battely, *Antiq. of Canterbury*, app. 39). Hitardus, wishing to visit Rome, gave it to Christ Church, Canterbury.

[2] Bernhard, iii. 378, gives a thirteenth-century regulation for the Petit Pont entry of Paris : 'Et ausi tot li jougleur sunt quite por i ver de chançon.'

[3] Gautier, ii. 124.

[4] There were 426 at the wedding of Margaret of England with John of Brabant in 1290 (Chappell, i. 15, from *Wardrobe Bk.* 18 Edw. I).

[5] Rigordus, *de gestis Philippi Augusti* (1186) 'vidimus quondam quosdam principes qui vestes diu excogitatas et variis florum picturationibus artificiossisimis elaboratas,

pro quibus forsan viginti vel triginta marcas argenti consumpserant, vix revolutis septem diebus, histrionibus, ministris scilicet diaboli, ad primam vocem dedisse.'

[6] The *Annales* (†1330) of Johannes de Trokelowe (R. S.), 98, tell *s. a.* 1317, how when Edward II was keeping Pentecost in Westminster 'quaedam mulier, ornatu histrionali redimita, equum bonum, histrionaliter phaleratum, ascensa, dictam aulam intravit, mensas more histrionum circuivit.' She rode to the king, placed an insulting letter in his hands, and retired. The 'ianitores et hostiarii,' when blamed, declared 'non esse moris regii, alicui menestrallo, palatium intrare volenti, in tanta solemnitate aditum denegare' ; cf. Walsingham, *Hist. Angl.* (R. S.). i. 149.

[7] Strutt, 189, has a fourteenth-century story of a youth rebuked for coming to a feast in a coat bardy, cut German fashion like a minstrel's;

servants, and by the shaven faces, close-clipped hair and flat shoes proper to their profession [1]. This kenspeckle appearance, together with the privilege of easy access, made the minstrel's dress a favourite disguise in ages when disguise was often imperative. The device attributed by the chroniclers to Alfred and to Anlaf becomes in the romances one of the commonest of *clichés* [2]. The readiness with which the minstrels won the popular ear made them a power in the land. William de Longchamp, the little-loved chancellor of Richard I, found it worth his while to bring a number of them over from France, that they might sing his praises abroad in the public places [3]. Nor were they less in request for satire than for eulogy. The English speaking minstrels, in particular, were responsible for many songs in derision of unpopular causes and personalities [4]; and we need not doubt that 'the lay that Sir Dinadan made by King Mark, which was the worst lay that ever harper sang with harp or with any other instruments,' must have had its precise counterparts in actual life [5]. The Sarum statutes of 1319 lay especial stress on the flattery and the evil speaking with which the minstrels rewarded their

cf. the complaint against knights in *A Poem on the times of Edward II* (Percy Soc. lxxxii), 23:

'Now thei beth disgysed,
    So diverselych i-diȝt,
That no man may knowe
    A mynstrel from a knyȝt
        Wel ny.'

The miniatures show minstrels in short coats to the knees and sometimes short capes with hoods. The *Act of Apparel* (1463, 3 *Edw. IV*, c. 5) excepts minstrels and 'players in their interludes.' The Franciscan story (p. 57) shows that some of the humbler minstrels went shabby enough.

[1] Klein, iii. 635; Du Méril, *Or. Lat.* 30; Gautier, ii. 104; Geoffrey of Monmouth, *Historia Britonum*, ix. 1 'rasit capillos suos et barbam, cultumque ioculatoris cum cithara cepit.' Cf. the canon quoted on p. 61 requiring Goliardic clerks to be shorn or shaven, to obliterate the tonsure. The flat shoe had been a mark of the *mimi planipedes* at Rome.

[2] Gautier, ii. 105. Thus Nicolete (*Aucassin et Nicolete*, ed. Bourdillon, 120) 'prist une herbe, si en oinst son cief et son visage, si qu'ele fu tote noire et tainte. Et ele fist faire cote et mantel et cemisse et braies, si s'atorna a guise de jogleor'; cf. *King Horn* (ed. Hall, 1901), 1471–2:

'Hi sede, hi weren harpurs,
    And sume were gigours.'

[3] Roger de Hoveden, *Chronicon* (R. S), iii. 143 'De regno Francorum cantores et ioculatores muneribus allexerat, ut de illo canerent in plateis; et iam dicebatur quod non erat talis in orbe.'

[4] Ten Brink, i. 314.

[5] Malory, *Morte d'Arthur*, x. 27, 31. Even King Mark let the minstrel go quit, because he was a minstrel.

entertainers[1]. Sometimes, indeed, they over-reached themselves, for Henry I is related to have put out the eyes of Lucas de Barre, a Norman *jougleur*, or perhaps rather *trouvère*, who made and sang songs against him[2]. But Lucas de Barre's rank probably aggravated his offence, and as a rule the minstrels went scot-free. A wiser churchman here and there was not slow to perceive how the unexampled hold of minstrelsy on the popular ear might be turned to the service of religion. Eadhelm, standing in gleeman's attire on an English bridge to mingle words of serious wisdom with his *carmina trivialia*, is one instance[3]. And in the same spirit St. Francis, himself half a troubadour in youth, would call his Minorites *ioculatores Domini*, and send them singing over the world to beg for their fee the repentance and spiritual joy of their hearers[4]. A popular hymn-writer of the present day is alleged to have thought it 'hard that the devil should have all the good tunes'; but already in the Middle Ages religious words were being set to secular music, and graced with the secular imagery of youth and spring[5].

But if the minstrels were on the one hand a force among the people, on the other they had the ear of kings. The

[1] Cf. p. 40.

[2] Ordericus Vitalis, *Hist. Eccles.* xii. 19 'pro derisoriis cantionibus... quin etiam indecentes de me cantilenas facetus choraula composuit, ad iniuriam mei palam cantavit, malevolosque mihi hostes ad cachinnos ita saepe provocavit.' Lucas de Barre seems to have been of noble birth, but 'palam cantavit cantilenas.'

[3] Cf. p. 30.

[4] *Speculum Perfectionis* (ed. Sabatier), 197. When Francis had finished his Canticle of the Sun, he thought for a moment of summoning 'frater Pacificus qui in saeculo vocabatur rex versuum et fuit valde curialis doctor cantorum,' and giving him a band of friars who might sing it to the people at the end of their sermons : 'finitis autem laudibus volebat quod praedicator diceret populo : "Nos sumus ioculatores Domini, et pro his volumus remu-

nerari a vobis, videlicet ut stetis in vera paenitentia." Et ait : "Quid enim sunt servi Dei nisi quidam ioculatores eius qui corda hominum erigere debent et movere ad laetitiam spiritualem."' Cf. Sabatier, *Life of St. Francis*, 9, 51, 307. Perhaps Francis may have heard of Joachim of Flora, his contemporary, who wrote in his *Commentary on the Apocalypse*, f. 183. a. 2 'qui vere monachus est nihil reputat esse suum nisi citharam.'

[5] The MS. of the famous thirteenth-century canon *Sumer is icumen in* has religious words written beneath the profane ones ; cf. Wooldridge, *Oxford Hist. of Music*, i. 326. Several religious adaptations of common motives of profane lyric are amongst the English thirteenth-century poems preserved in Harl. MS. 2253 (*Specimens of Lyrical Poetry* : Percy Soc., 1842, no. 19, and ed. Böddeker, Berlin, 1878).

English court, to judge by the payments recorded in the exchequer books, must have been full of them [1]. The fullest and most curious document on the subject dates from the reign of Edward I. It is a roll of payments made on the occasion of a Whitsuntide feast held in London in the year 1306, and a very large number of the minstrels recorded are mentioned by name [2]. At the head of the list come five minstrels with the high-sounding title of *le roy* [3], and these get five marks apiece. A number of others follow, who received sums varying from one mark upwards. Most of these have French names, and many are said to be in the company of this or that noble or reverend guest at the feast. Finally, two hundred marks were distributed in smaller sums amongst the inferior minstrels, *les autres menestraus de la commune*, and some of these seem to have been of English birth. Below the *roys* rank two minstrels, Adam le Boscu and another, who are dignified with the title of *maistre*, which probably signifies that they were clerks [4]. The other names are mainly descriptive, 'Janin le Lutour,' 'Gillotin le Sautreour,' 'Baudec le Taboureur,' and the like ; a few are jesting stage names, such as the inferior performers of our music halls bear to-day [5]. Such are ' Guillaume sanz Maniere,' ' Reginaldus le Menteur,' 'le Petit Gauteron,' 'Parvus Willielmus,' and those of the attractive comedians Perle in the Eghe, and Matill ' Makejoye. The last, by the way, is the only woman performer named. The resources of Edward I could no doubt stand the strain of rewarding with royal magnificence the entertainers of his guests. There is plenty of evidence, however, that even on secular grounds the diatribes of the moralists against the minstrels were often enough justified. To the lavish and unthrifty of purse they became

---

[1] Jusserand, *E. W. L.* 195, 199, 215 ; Strutt, 194-5, 210, 227 ; Hazlitt-Warton, ii. 119; Chappell, i. 15 ; Collier, i. 22 ; *Wardrobe Accounts of Edward I* (Soc. Antiq.), 163, 166, 168.

[2] Cf. Appendix C.

[3] Cf. Appendix D.

[4] This cannot be the famous Adan de le Hale (cf. ch. viii), known as 'le Bossu,' if Guy, 178, is right in saying that his nephew, Jean Mados,

wrote a lament for his death in 1288. He quotes *Hist. Litt.* xx. 666, as to this.

[5] Gautier, ii. 103 ; Bédier, 405, quote many similar names ; e.g. Quatre Œufs, Malebouche, Rongefoie, Tourne-en-fuie, Courtebarbe, Porte-Hotte, Mal Quarrel, Songe-Feste a la grant viele, Mal-appareillié, Pelé, Brise-Pot, Simple d'Amour, Chevrete, Passereau.

blood-suckers. Matilda, the wife of Henry I, is said to have squandered most of her revenues upon them[1]; while the unfortunate Robert of Normandy, if no less a chronicler than Ordericus Vitalis may be believed, was stripped by these rapacious gentry to the very skin[2]. Yet for all the days of honour and all the rich gifts the minstrel life must have had its darker side. Easily won, easily parted with; and the lands and laced mantles did not last long, when the elbow itched for the dice-box. This was the incurable ruin of the minstrel folk[3]. And even that life of the road, so alluring to the fever in the blood, must have been a hard one in the rigours of an English climate. To tramp long miles in wind and rain, to stand wet to the skin and hungry and footsore, making the slow *bourgeois* laugh while the heart was bitter within; such must have been the daily fate of many amongst the humbler minstrels at least[4]. And at the end to die like a dog in a ditch, under the ban of the Church and with the prospect of eternal damnation before the soul.

Kings and nobles were not accustomed to depend for their entertainment merely upon the stray visits of wandering minstrels. Others more or less domiciled formed a permanent part of the household. These indeed are the minstrels in the stricter sense of that term—*ministri, ministeriales*. In Domesday Book, as we have seen, one Berdic bears the title of the *ioculator regis*. Shortly afterwards Henry I had his *mimus regis*, by name Raherus, who made large sums by his *suavitas iocularis*, and founded the great priory of St. Bartholomew at Smithfield[5]. Laying aside his parti-coloured

[1] William of Malmesbury, *Gesta Reg. Angl.* (R. S.), ii. 494.

[2] Ordericus Vitalis, v. 12, &c. On one occasion 'ad ecclesiam, quia nudus erat, non pervenit.'

[3] Bédier, 359.

[4] Gautier, chs. xx, xxi, gives an admirable account of the *jougleur's* daily life, and its seamy side is brought out by Bédier, 399–418. A typical *jougleur* figure is that of the poet Rutebeuf, a man of genius, but often near death's door from starvation. See the editions of his works by Jubinal and Kressner, and the biography by Clédat in the series of *Grands Écrivains français*.

[5] Morley, *Bartholomew Fair*, 1–25, from *Liber Fundacionis* in *Cott. Vesp. B. ix*; Leland, *Collectanea*, I, 61, 99; Dugdale, *Monasticon*, ii. 166; Stow, *Survey*, 140; C. Knight, *London*, ii. 34; Percy, 406. No minstrels, however, appear in the formal list of Henry I's Norman Household (†1135), which seems to have been the nucleus of the English Royal

coat, he even became himself the first prior of the new community. The old spirit remained with him, however ; and it is recorded that the fame of the house was largely magnified by means of some feigned miracles which Raherus put forth. Richard I was a noted lover of song, and the names of more than one minstrel of his are preserved. There was Ambroise, who was present at Richard's coronation in 1189 and at the siege of Acre in 1191, and who wrote a history, still extant, of the third crusade [1]. And there was that Blondiaux or Blondel de Nesle, the story of whose discovery of his captive master, apocryphal though it may be, is in all the history books [2]. Henry III had. his *magister Henricus versificator* in 1251 [3], and his *magister Ricardus citharista* in 1252 [4]. A harper was also amongst the *ministri* of Prince Edward in the Holy War [5], and when the prince became Edward I, he still retained one in his service. He is mentioned as Walter de Stourton, the king's harper, in 1290 [6], and as the *citharista regis* in 1300 [7]. Edward II had several minstrels, to one of whom, William de Morlee, known as *Roy. de North*, he made a grant of land [8]. By this time the royal minstrels seem to have become a regular establishment of no inconsiderable numbers. Under Edward III they received 7½*d.* a day [9]. A little later in the reign, between 1344 and 1347, there were nineteen who received 12*d.* a day in war, when they doubtless formed a military band, and 20*s.* a year in peace. These included five trumpeters, one citoler, five pipers, one tabouretter, two clarions, one nakerer, and one fiddler, together with three

Household as it existed up to 1782 (Hall, *Red Book of Exchequer*, R.S., iii. cclxxxvii, 807).

[1] Gautier, ii. 47, 54 ; G. Paris, § 88 ; Ambroise, *L'Estoire de la Guerre Sainte*, ed. G. Paris (*Documents inédits sur l'Hist. de France*, 1897).

[2] Percy, 358.

[3] Madox, *Hist. of Exchequer*, 268.

[4] Percy, 365.

[5] Walter Hemmingford, *Chronicon*, c. 35 (*Vet. Hist. Angl. Script.* ii. 591).

[6] Chappell, i. 15, from *Wardrobe Book*, 18 Edw. I.

[7] *Wardrobe Accounts of Edw. I* (Soc. Antiq.), 323.

[8] Anstis, *Register of Order of the Garter*, ii. 303, from *Pat. de terr. forisfact.* 16 Edw. III. Cf. *Gesta Edw. de Carnarvon* in *Chron. of Edw. I and II* (R. S.), ii. 91 'adhaesit cantoribus, tragoedis, aurigis, navigiis et aliis huiuscemodi artificiis mechanicis.'

[9] Strutt, 194 ; *Issue Roll of Thomas de Brantingham* (ed. Devon), 54-57, 296-8.

additional minstrels, known as waits[1]. The leader of the minstrels bore the title of *rex*, for in 1387 we find a licence given by Richard II to his *rex ministrallorum*, John Caumz, permitting him to pass the seas[2]. Henry V had fifteen minstrels when he invaded France in 1415, and at a later date eighteen, who received 12*d.* a day apiece[3]. At the end of his reign his minstrels received 100*s.* a year, and this annuity was continued under Henry VI, who in 1455 had twelve of them, besides a wait. In the next year this king issued a commission for the impressing of boys to fill vacancies in the body[4]. Edward IV had thirteen minstrels and a wait[5]. By 1469 these had been cut down to eight. At their head was a chief, who was now called, not as in Richard II's time *rex*, but *marescallus*[6]. The eight king's minstrels and their *marescallus* can be traced through the reign of Henry VII, and so on into the sixteenth century[7].

Nor was the royal household singular in the maintenance of a permanent body of minstrels. The *citharista* of Margaret, queen of Edward I, is mentioned in 1300, and her *istrio* in 1302[8]. Philippa, queen of Edward III, had her minstrels in 1337[9], and those of Queen Elizabeth were a regular establishment in the reign of Henry VII[10]. The Scottish court, too, had its recognized troupe, known by the early years of the sixteenth century as the 'minstrels of the chekkar[11].' As with kings and queens so with lesser men. The list of minstrels at court in 1306 includes the harpers and other musicians of several lords, both English and foreign[12]. In 1308 the earl of Lancaster had a body of *menestralli* and an *armiger menestrallorum*[13]. During

---

[1] *Household Ordinances*, 4, 11.
[2] Rymer, vii. 555.
[3] Ibid. ix. 255, 260, 336.
[4] Ibid. x. 287; xi. 375.
[5] *Household Ordinances*, 48.
[6] Rymer, xi. 642; cf. Appendix D.
[7] Ibid. xiii. 705; Collier, i. 45; Campbell, i. 407, 516, 570; ii. 100, 224.
[8] *Wardrobe Accounts of Edw. I* (Soc. Antiq.), 7, 95; *Calendar of Anc. Deeds*, ii. A, 2050, 2068, 2076.
[9] Strutt, 189.
[10] Collier, i. 46; Campbell, i. 407,

542, 572; ii. 68, 84, 176.
[11] The entry 'ad solvendum histrionibus' occurs in 1364 (*Compoti Camerarii Scot.* i. 422). The Exchequer Rolls from 1433–50 contain payments to the 'mimi,' 'histriones,' 'ioculatores regis'; and in 1507–8 for the 'histriones in scaccario' or 'minstrels of the chekkar' (*Accounts of Treasurer of Scotland*, i. xx, cxcix; ii. lxxi).
[12] Cf. Appendix C.
[13] Collier, i. 21, from *Lansd. MS.* 1.

the fourteenth and fifteenth centuries entries of payments
to the minstrels of a vast number of *domini*, small and
great, are common in the account books[1]. Henry, earl
of Derby, took minstrels with him in his expeditions abroad
of 1390 and 1392[2]; while the *Houschold Book* of the earl of
Northumberland († 1512) shows that he was accustomed to
entertain 'a Taberett, a Luyte, and a Rebecc,' as well as six
'trompettes[3].' Minstrels are also found, from the beginning
of the fifteenth century, in the service of the municipal corporations. London, Coventry, Bristol, Shrewsbury, Norwich,
Chester, York, Beverley, Leicester, Lynn, Canterbury had
them, to name no others. They received fixed fees or dues,
wore the town livery and badge of a silver scutcheon, played
at all local celebrations and festivities, and were commonly
known as *waits*[4]. This term we have already found in use
at court, and the ' Black Book,' which contains the household
regulations of Edward IV, informs us that the primary duty
of a wait was to ' pipe the watch,' summer and winter, at
certain fixed hours of the night[5].

It must not be supposed that established minstrels, whether
royal, noble, or municipal, were always in constant attendance
on their lords. Certain fixed services were required of them,

Two of this lord's *menestriers* were
entertained by Robert of Artois,
who also had his own (Guy, 154).

[1] Gautier, ii. 51 ; cf. the extracts
from various *computi* in Appendix
E. There are many entries also in
the accounts of King's Lynn (*Hist.
MSS.* xi. 3. 213) ; Beverley (Leach,
Beverley MSS. 171), &c.

[2] L. T. Smith, *Derby Accounts*
(C. S.), xcvi.

[3] Percy, *N. H. B.* 42, 344.

[4] Stowe, *Survey*, 39 (London) ;
Smith, *English Guilds*, 423, 447
(Bristol, Norwich) ; Davies, 14
(York) ; Kelly, 131 (Leicester) ;
Morris, 348 (Chester) ; Civis, No.
xxi (Canterbury) ; Sharpe, 207
(Coventry) ; *Hist. MSS.* xi. 3. 163
(Lynn) ; Leach, *Beverley MSS.*
105, &c. (Beverley); for Shrewsbury
cf. Appendix E. On *Waits' Badges*,
cf. Ll. Jewitt, in *Reliquary*, xii. 145.

Gautier, ii. 57, describes the communal *cantorini* of Perugia, from
the fourteenth to the sixteenth century. The usual Latin term for
the Beverley waits is *speculatores* ;
but they are also called *ministralli*,
histriones and *mimi*. Apparently
waits are intended by the *satrapi*
of the Winchester Accounts (App.
E. (iv)). Elsewhere *histriones* is
the most usual term. The signa-
tories to the 1321 statutes of the
Paris guild include several *guètes*
(Bernhard, iii. 402).

[5] *Household Ordinances*, 48 ' A
Wayte, that nyghtly, from Mighel-
masse till Shere-Thursday, pipeth
the watche within this courte fower
tymes, and in the somer nyghtes
three tymes.' He is also to attend
the new Knights of the Bath when
they keep watch in the chapel the
night before they are dubbed.

which were not very serious, except in the case of waits[1];
for the rest of their time they were free. This same 'Black
Book' of Edward IV is very explicit on the point. The
minstrels are to receive a yearly fee and a livery[2]. They
must attend at court for the five great feasts of the year. At
other times, two or three out of their number, or more if the
king desire it, are to be in waiting. The last regulation on
the subject is curious. The king forbids his minstrels
to be too presumptuous or familiar in asking rewards of
any lord of the land; and in support of this he quotes a
similar prohibition by the Emperor Henry II[3]. Doubtless,
in the intervals of their services, the household minstrels

---

[1] The Lynn waits had to go
through the town from All Saints
to Candlemas. Those of Coventry
had similar duties, and in 1467 were
forbidden 'to pass this Cite but to
Abbotts and Priors within x myles
of this Cite.'

[2] The six minstrels of the Earl
of Derby in 1391 had a livery of
'blod ray cloth and tanne facings'
(Wylie, iv. 160).

[3] *Household Ordinances*, 48:
'Mynstrelles, xiii, whereof one is
verger, that directeth them all in
festivall dayes to theyre stations, to
bloweings and pipynges, to suche
offices as must be warned to pre-
pare for the king and his houshold
at metes and soupers, to be the
more readie in all servyces; and all
these sittinge in the hall togyder;
whereof sume use trumpettes, sume
shalmuse and small pipes, and
sume as strengemen, comyng to
this courte at five festes of the yere,
and then to take theyre wages of
houshold after iiij[d] ob. a day, if they
be present in courte, and then they
to avoyde the next day after the
festes be done. Besides eche of
them anothyr reward yerely, taking
of the king in the resceyte of the
chekker, and clothing wynter and
somer, or xx[s] a piece, and lyverey
in courte, at evyn amonges them
all, iiij gallons ale; and for wynter
season, iij candels wax, vj candells
peris', iiij talwood, and sufficiaunt

logging by the herberger, for them
and theyre horses, nygh to the
courte. Also havyng into courte
ij servauntes honest, to beare theyre
trumpettes, pipes, and other instru-
mentes, and a torche for wynter
nyghts, whyles they blowe to souper,
and other revelles, delyvered at the
chaundrey; and allway ij of these
persons to continue in courte in
wages, beyng present to warne at the
kinge's rydinges, when he goeth to
horse-backe, as ofte as it shall require,
and by theyre blowinges the houshold meny may follow in the countries. And if any of these two
minstrelles be sicke in courte, he
taketh ij loves, one messe of grete
mete, one gallon ale. They have
no part of any rewardes gevyn to
the houshold. And if it please the
kinge to have ij strenge Minstrelles
to contynue in like wise. The kinge
wull not for his worshipp that his
Minstrelles be too presumptuous,
nor too familier to aske any rewardes
of the lordes of his londe, remem-
bring De Henrico secundo im-
peratore [1002 – 24] qui omnes
Ioculatores suos et Armaturos mo-
nuerit, ut nullus eorum in eius
nomine vel dummodo steterint in
servicio suo nihil ab aliquo in regno
suo deberent petere donandum;
sed quod ipsi domini donatores pro
Regis amore citius pauperibus ero-
garent.'

travelled, like their unattached brethren of the road, but with the added advantage of a letter of recommendation from their lord, which ensured them the hospitality of his friends[1]. Such letters were indeed often given, both to the minstrels of a man's own household and as testimonials to other minstrels who may have especially pleased the giver. Those interesting collections of mediaeval epistolary formulae, the *summae dictaminis*, contain many models for them, and judging by the lavish eulogy which they employ, the minstrels themselves must have had a hand in drawing them up[2]. Many minstrels probably confined themselves to short tours in the vicinity of their head quarters; others, like Widsith, the Anglo-Saxon *scôp*, were far travellers. John Caumz received a licence from Richard II to cross the seas, and in 1483 we find Richard III entertaining minstrels of the dukes of Austria and Bavaria[3]. Possibly the object of John Caumz was to visit one of the *scolae ministrallorum* in France, where experiences might be exchanged and new songs learnt. Beauvais, Lyon, Cambrai were famous for these schools, which were held year by year in Lent, when performances were stopped ; and the wardrobe accounts of Edward III record grants of licences and expenses to Barbor and Morlan, two bagpipers, to visit the *scolas ministrallis in partibus trans mare*[4].

---

[1] Percy, *N. H. B.* (†1512), 339. The king's shawms, if they came yearly, got 10s., the king's jugler and the king's or queen's bearward, 6s. 8d.; a duke's or earl's trumpeters, if they came six together, also got 6s. 8d., an earl's minstrels only 3s. 4d. If the troupe came only once in two or three years, and belonged to a 'speciall Lorde, Friende, or Kynsman' of the earl, the rate was higher.

[2] Gautier, ii. 107, from *Bibl. de l'Arsenal MS.* 854; e.g. '*Deprecatio pro dono instrioni impendendo.* Salutem et amoris perpetui firmitatem. R. latorem praesentium, egregium instrionem qui nuper meis interfuit nuptiis, ubi suum officium exercuit eleganter, ad vos cum magna confidentia destinamus, rogantes precibus, quibus possumus, quatinus aliquid subsidium gracie specialis eidem impendere debeatis.' Collier, i. 42, gives a letter of Richard III for his bearward.

[3] Collier, i. 41.

[4] Strutt, 194 ; Gautier, ii. 173–8; H. Lavoix, ii. 198. They are called *Scolae ministrorum, Scolae mimorum.* They can be traced to the fourteenth century. Genève and Bourg-en-Bresse also had them. The Paris statutes of 1407 (cf. Appendix F) require a licence from the *roi des ménestrels* for such an assembly. A Beauvais *computus* (1402) has 'Dati sunt de gratia panes ducenti capitulares mimis in hac civitate de diversis partibus pro cantilenis novis addiscendis confluentibus.'

From the fourteenth century it is possible to trace the growth of the household minstrels as a privileged class at the expense of their less fortunate rivals. The freedom of access enjoyed by the entertainers of earlier days was obviously open to abuse. We have seen that in 1317 it led to the offering of an insult to Edward II by an emissary clad as a minstrel at his own table. It was only two years before that a royal proclamation had considerably restrained the liberty of the minstrels. In view of the number of idle persons who 'under colour of mynstrelsie' claimed food, drink, and gifts in private houses, it was ordered 'that to the houses of prelates earls and barons none resort to meate and drynke, unless he be a mynstrel, and of these mynstrels that there come none except it be three or four minstrels of honour at the most in one day, unlesse he be desired of the lorde of the house.' The houses of meaner men are to be altogether exempt, except at their desire[1]. I think it is probable that by 'minstrels of honour' we must here understand 'household minstrels[2]'; and that the severity of the ordinance must have come upon those irresponsible vagrants who had not the shelter of a great man's name. With the Statutes of Labourers in the middle of the fourteenth century begins a history of legislation against 'vacabonds and valiant beggars,' which put further and serious difficulties in the way of the free movement of the migratory classes through the country[3]. Minstrels, indeed, are not specifically declared to be 'vacabonds' until this legislation was codified by William Cecil in 1572[4]; but there is evidence that they were none

---

[1] Hearne, *Appendix ad Lelandi Collectanea*, vi. 36; Percy, 367. The proclamation is dated Aug. 6, 9 Edw. II (i. e. 1315).

[2] No technical term seems, however, intended in *Launfal* (ed. Ritson), 668:
'They hadde menstrales of moch honours,
  Fydelers, sytolyrs, and trompours.'

[3] C. J. Ribton-Turner, *Vagrants and Vagrancy*, chs. 3, 4, 5. The proclamation of 1284 against 'Westours, Bards, and Rhymers and other idlers and vagabonds, who live on the gifts called Cymmortha,' and the Act of 1402 (4 *Hen. IV*, c. 27) in the same sense, seem only to refer to the Welsh bards (cf. p. 77).

[4] Ribton-Turner, 107 (14 *Eliz.* c. 5). Whipping is provided for 'all Fencers Bearewardes Comon Players in Enterludes & Minstrels, not belonging to any Baron of this Realme or towards any other honourable personage of greater Degree; all Juglers Pedlars Tynkers and Petye Chapmen; whiche

the less liable to be treated as such, unless they had some protection in the shape of livery or licence. At Chester from the early thirteenth century, and at Tutbury in Stafford-shire from 1380, there existed courts of minstrelsy which claimed to issue licences to all performers within their pur-view. It is not probable that this jurisdiction was very effective. But a step taken by Edward IV in 1469 had for its avowed object to strengthen the hands of what may be called official minstrelsy. Representation had been made to the king that certain rude husbandmen and artificers had usurped the title and livery of his minstrels, and had thus been enabled to gather an illegitimate harvest of fees. He therefore created or revived a regular guild or fraternity of minstrels, putting his own household performers with their *marescallus* at the head of it, and giving its officers a disciplinary authority over the profession throughout the country, with the exception of Chester. It is not improbable, although it is not distinctly stated, that admission into the guild was practically confined to 'minstrels of honour.' Cer-tainly one of the later local guilds which grew up in the sixteenth century, that of Beverley, limited its membership to such as could claim to be 'mynstrell to some man of honour or worship or waite of some towne corporate or other ancient town, or else of such honestye and conyng as shalbe thought laudable and pleasant to the hearers [1].' In any case the whole drift of social development was to make things difficult for the inde-pendent minstrels and to restrict the area of their wanderings.

The widespread popularity of the minstrels amongst the mediaeval laity, whether courtiers, burghers, or peasants, needs no further labouring. It is more curious to find that in spite of the formal anathemas of the Church upon their art, they were not, as a matter of fact, rigorously held at arm's length by the clergy. We find them taking a prominent part in the

said Fencers Bearewardes comon Players in Enterludes Myn-strels Juglers Pedlars Tynkers & Petye Chapmen, shall wander abroade and have not Lycense of two Justices of the Peace at the leaste, whereof one to be of the Quorum, wher and in what Shier they shall happen to wander.' The terms of 39 *Eliz.* c. 4 (1597-8) are very similar, but 1 *Jac. I*, c. 7 (1603-4), took away the exemption for noblemen's servants.

[1] Appendix F.

holyday festivities of religious guilds[1]; we find them solacing
the slow progress of the pilgrimages with their ready wit and
copious narrative or song[2]; we find them received with favour
by bishops, even upon their visitations[3], and not excluded
from a welcome in the hall of many a monastery. As early
as 1180, one Galfridus, a *citharoedus*, held a 'corrody,' or right
to a daily commons of food and drink in the abbey of Hyde
at Winchester[4]. And payments for performances are frequent
in the accounts of the Augustinian priories at Canterbury[5],
Bicester, and Maxtoke, and the great Benedictine houses of
Durham, Norwich, Thetford, and St. Swithin's, Winchester[6],
and doubtless in those of many another cloistered retreat. The

[1] Gautier, ii. 156; Ducange, s.v. *Ministelli*.

[2] Gautier, ii. 158. Strutt, 195, quotes from *Cott. MS. Nero*, c. viii a payment of Edw. III 'ministrallo facienti ministralsiam suam coram imagine Beatae Mariae in Veltam, rege praesente.'. Chaucer's pilgrims had no professional minstrels, but the miller did as well:

'He was a janglere and a goliardeys, ...
...A baggepype wel koude he blowe and sowne,
And therwithal he broghte us out of towne.'

It was in the absence of regular minstrels that the pilgrims fell to telling one another stories.

[3] Gautier, ii. 160. Richard Swinfield, bishop of Hereford, more than once rewarded minstrels on his episcopal rounds (J. Webb, *Household Expenses of Richard de Swinfield*, C. S. i. 152, 155). The bishops of Durham in 1355, Norwich in 1362, and Winchester in 1374, 1422, and 1481 had 'minstrels of honour,' like any secular noble (see Appendix E, &c.). Even the austere Robert Grosseteste had his private harper, if we may credit Mannyng, 150:

'He louede moche to here the harpe;
For mannys wyt hyt makyth sharpe.
Next hys chaumbre, besyde hys stody,

Hys harpers chaumbre was fast therby.'

Mannyng represents Grosseteste as excusing his predilection by a reference to King David.

[4] Madox, *Hist. of Exchequer*, 251.

[5] *Norfolk Archaeology*, xi. 339 (Norwich); Hazlitt-Warton, ii. 97; Kennet, *Parochial Antiq.* ii. 259 (Bicester); *Decem Scriptores*, 2011 (Canterbury); for the rest cf. Appendix E.

[6] Hazlitt-Warton, ii. 97; iii. 118, quotes from the *Register* of St. Swithin's amongst the *Wolvesey MSS.*; in 1338 'cantabat ioculator quidam nomine Herebertus canticum Colbrondi, necdum gestum Emmae reginae a iudicio ignis liberatae, in aula prioris': in 1374 'In festo Alwynis episcopi ... in aula conventus sex ministralli, cum quatuor citharisatoribus, faciebant ministralcias suas. Et post cenam, in magna camera arcuata domini Prioris, cantabant idem gestum ... Veniebant autem dicti ioculatores a castello domini regis et ex familia episcopi.' The 'canticum Colbrondi' was doubtless a romance of Guy of Warwick, of which Winchester is the locality. Fragments of early fourteenth-century English versions exist (Ten Brink, i. 246; Jusserand, *E. L.* i. 224; Zupitza, *Guy of Warwick*, E. E. T. S.; G. L. Morrill, *Speculum Gy de Warewyke*, E. E. T. S. lxxxi).

Minorite chroniclers relate, how at the time of the coming of
the friars in 1224 two of them were mistaken for minstrels by
the porter of a Benedictine grange near Abingdon, received
by the prior and brethren with unbecoming glee, and when
the error was discovered, turned out with contumely[1]. At
such semi-religious foundations also, as the college of St. Mary
at Winchester, or Waynflete's great house of St. Mary
Magdalen in Oxford, minstrels of all degrees found, at least
by the fifteenth century, ready and liberal entertainment[2].

How, then, is one to reconcile this discrepancy between the
actual practice of the monasteries and the strict, the uncompromising prohibition of minstrelsy in rule and canon? An
incomplete answer readily presents itself. The monks being
merely human, fell short of the ideal prescribed for them.
We do not now learn for the first time, that the ambitions
of the pious founder, the ecclesiastical law-giver, the patristic
preacher, were one thing; the effective daily life of churchmen
in many respects quite another. Here, as in matters of even
more moment, did mediaeval monasticism 'dream from deed
dissever'—

> 'The reule of Seint Maure or of Seint Beneit,
> By-cause that it was old and som-del streit
> This ilke monk leet olde thinges pace,
> And held after the newe world the space.'

True enough, but not the whole truth. It doubtless explains
the behaviour of the Benedictines of Abingdon; but we can
hardly suppose that when Robert de Grosseteste, the sworn
enemy of ecclesiastical abuses, kept his harper's chamber next
his own, he was surreptitiously allowing himself an illegitimate
gratification which he denied to his clergy. The fact is that the
condemnations of the Church, transferred, as we have seen,
wholesale from the *mimi* and *histriones* of the decaying

---

[1] Bartholomaeus (Albizzi) de Pisis
(1385–99), *Liber Conformitatum*
(ed. 1590, i. 94^b); Antoninus Episc.
Florentiae (1389–1459), *Chronicon*
(ed. 1586, iii. 752) 'alterius linguae
ioculatores eos existimans'; cf. A.
Wood, *Hist. et Antiq. Univ. Oxon.*
(1674), i. 69; *City of Oxford*
(O. H. S.), ii. 349.

[2] See Appendix E. At Paris the
Statutes of Cornouaille College
(1380) required abstinence from
'ludis mimorum, ioculatorum, histrionum, goliardorum, et consimi-
lium.' Bulaeus, v. 782, gives another
Paris regulation allowing 'mimi, ad
summum duo' on Twelfth Night
(Rashdall, ii. 674).

Empire, were honestly not applicable without qualification, even from the ecclesiastical point of view, to their successors, the *mimi* and *histriones* of the Middle Ages. The traditions of the Roman stage, its manners, its topics, its ethical code, became indeed a large part of the direct inheritance of minstrelsy. But, as we have seen, they were far from being the whole of that inheritance. The Teutonic as well as the Latin element in the civilization of western Europe must be taken into account. The minstrel derives from the disreputable *planipes*; he derives also from the *scôp*, and has not altogether renounced the very different social and ethical position which the *scôp* enjoyed. After all, nine-tenths of the secular music and literature, something even of the religious literature, of the Middle Ages had its origin in minstrelsy. Practically, if not theoretically, the Church had to look facts in the face, and to draw a distinction between the different elements and tendencies that bore a single name. The formularies, of course, continued to confound all minstrels under the common con-demnation of *ioculatores*. The Church has never been good at altering its formularies to suit altered conditions. But it has generally been good at practical compromises. And in the case of minstrelsy, a practical compromise, rough enough, was easily arrived at.

The effective conscience of the thirteenth-century Church had clearly come to recognize degrees in the ethical status of the minstrels. No more authoritative exponent of the official morals of his day can be desired than St. Thomas Aquinas, and St. Thomas Aquinas is very far from pronouncing an unqualified condemnation of all secular entertainment. The profession of an *histrio*, he declares, is by no means in itself unlawful. It was ordained for the reasonable solace of humanity, and the *histrio* who exercises it at a fitting time and in a fitting manner is not on that account to be regarded as a sinner [1]. Another contemporary document is still more

---

[1] Thomas Aquinas, *Summa Theologiae* (†1274), ii. 2, quaest. 168, art. 3 'Sicut dictum est, ludus est necessarius ad conversationem vitae humanae. ad omnia autem, quae sunt utilia conversationi hu-manae, deputari possunt aliqua officia licita. et ideo etiam officium histrionum, quod ordinatur ad sola-tium hominibus exhibendum, non est secundum se illicitum, nec sunt in statu peccati: dummodo moderate

explicit. This is the *Penitential* written at the close of the thirteenth century by Thomas de Cabham, sub-dean of Salisbury and subsequently archbishop of Canterbury[1]. In the course of his analysis of human frailty, Thomas de Cabham makes a careful classification from the ethical point of view, of minstrels. There are those who wear horrible masks, or entertain by indecent dance and gesture. There are those again who follow the courts of the great, and amuse by satire and by raillery. Both these classes are altogether damnable. Those that remain are distinguished by their use of musical instruments. Some sing wanton songs at banquets. These too are damnable, no less than the satirists and posture-mongers. Others, however, sing of the deeds of princes, and the lives of the saints. To these it is that the name *ioculatores* more strictly belongs, and they, on no less an authority than that of Pope Alexander himself[2], may be tolerated.

Of the three main groups of minstrels distinguished by Thomas de Cabham, two correspond roughly to the two broad types which, from the point of view of racial tradition, we have already differentiated. His musicians correspond to the Teutonic gleemen and their successors ; his posture-mongers and buffoons to the Roman *mimi* and their successors.

---

ludo utantur, id est, non utendo aliquibus illicitis verbis vel factis ad ludum, et non adhibendo ludum negotiis et temporibus indebitis ... unde illi, qui moderate iis subveniunt, non peccant, sed iusta faciunt, mercedem ministerii eorum iis attribuendo. si qui autem superflue sua in tales consumunt, vel etiam sustentant illos histriones qui illicitis ludis utuntur, peccant, quasi eos in peccatis foventes. unde Augustinus dicit, *super Ioan.* quod *donare res suas histrionibus vitium est immane,*' &c., &c.

[1] Cf. Appendix G.

[2] Another version of this story is given by Petrus Cantor (ob. 1197), *Verbum Abbreviatum,* c. 84 (*P. L.* ccv. 254) ' Ioculatori cuidam papa Alexander (Alex. III) nec concessit vivere de officio suo, nec ei penitus interdixit.' In c. 49 of the same work Petrus Cantor inveighs learnedly *Contra dantes histrionibus.* Doubtless the Alexander in question is Alexander III (1159-81), though the (Alex. III) above may be due to the seventeenth-century editor, Galopinus. A hasty glance at the voluminous and practically unindexed decrees and letters of Alexander III in *P. L.* cc. and Jaffé, *Regesta Pontificum Romanorum* (ed. 2, 1885-8), ii. 145-418, has not revealed the source of the story ; and I doubt whether the Pope's decision, if it was ever given, is to be found in black and white. The two reports of it by Thomas de Cabham and Petrus Cantor are barely consistent. In any case, it never got into the Gregorian Decretals.

Who then are Thomas de Cabham's third and intermediate
group, the satirists whose lampoons beset the courts of the
great ? Well, raillery and invective, as we have seen, were
common features of minstrelsy ; but Gautier may very likely
be right when he surmises that Thomas de Cabham has particularly in mind the *scolares vagantes*, who brought so much
scandal upon the Church during the twelfth and thirteenth
centuries [1]. Some of these were actually out at elbows and
disfrocked clerks ; others were scholars drifting from university to university, and making their living meantime by their
wits ; most of them were probably at least in minor orders.
But practically they lived the life of the minstrels, tramping
the road with them, sharing the same temptations of wine,
women, and dice, and bringing into the profession a trained
facility of composition, and at least a flavour of classical learning [2]. They were indeed the main intermediaries between the
learned and the vernacular letters of their day ; the spilth of
their wit and wisdom is to be found in the burlesque Latin verse
of such collections as the *Carmina Burana*, riotous lines, by no
means devoid of poetry, with their half-humorous half-pathetic
burden,

<blockquote>
' In taberna quando sumus
Non curamus quid sit humus [3].'
</blockquote>

And especially they were satirists, satirists mainly of the
hypocrisy, cupidity and evil living of those in the high places
of the Church, for whom they conceived a grotesque expression
in Bishop Golias, a type of materialistic prelate, in whose
name they wrote and whose *pueri* or *discipuli* they declared
themselves to be [4]. *Goliardi*, *goliardenses*, their reputation in

---

[1] Gautier, ii. 42 ; Bédier, 389 ;
Ten Brink, i. 186 ; Ducange, s. vv.
Golia, &c.; O. Hubatsch, *Lat. Va-
gantenlieder des Mittelalters* (1870).

[2] *Le Département des Livres*
(Méon, *N. R.* i. 404) :

'A Bouvines delez Dinant
Li perdi-je Ovide le grant . . .
Mon Lucan et mon Juvenal
Oubliai-je a Bonival,
Eustace le grant et Virgile
Perdi aus dez a Abeville.'

[3] The chief collections of goliardic
verse are Schmeller, *Carmina
Burana* (ed. 3, 1894), and T. Wright,
*Latin Poems attributed to Walter
Mapes* (C. S. 1841) : for others cf.
Hubatsch, 16. Latin was not un-
known amongst lay minstrels : cf.
Deus Bordeors Ribauz (Montai-
glon-Raynaud, i. 3) :

'Mais ge sai aussi bien conter,
Et en roumanz et en latin.'

[4] Hubatsch, 15. The origin,
precise meaning, and mutual relations of the terms *Golias, goliardi*

the eyes of the ecclesiastical authorities was of the worst, and their ill practices are coupled with those of the minstrels in many a condemnatory decree [1].

It is not with the *goliardi* then, that Thomas de Cabham's relaxation of the strict ecclesiastical rigours is concerned. Neither is it, naturally enough, with the lower minstrels of the *mimus* tradition. Towards these Thomas de Cabham, like his predecessors, is inexorable. And even of the higher minstrels the musicians and singers, his toleration has its limits. He discriminates. In a sense, a social and professional sense, all these higher minstrels fall into the same class. But from the ethical point of view there is a very marked distinction amongst them. Some there are who haunt taverns and merry-

---

are uncertain. Probably the goliardic literature arose in France, rather than in England with Walter Mapes, the attribution to whom of many of the poems is perhaps due to a confusion of G[olias] with G[ualterus] in the MSS. Giraldus Cambrensis (ob. 1217), *Speculum Ecclesiae*, says 'Parasitus quidam Golias nomine nostris diebus gulositate pariter et leccacitate famosissimus . . . in papam et curiam Romanam carmina famosa . . . evomuit': but the following note points to a much earlier origin for Golias and his *pueri*, and this is upheld by W. Scherer, *Gesch. d. deutsch. Dichtung im* 11. *und* 12. *Jahrh.* 16.

[1] Early decrees forbidding the clergy to be *ioculatores* are given on p. 39. More precise is the order of Gautier of Sens († 913) in his *Constitutiones*, c. 13 (Mansi, xviii. 324) 'Statuimus quod clerici ribaldi, maxime qui dicuntur de familia Goliae, per episcopos, archidiaconos, officiales, et decanos Christianitatis, tonderi praecipiantur vel etiam radi, ita quod eis non remaneat tonsura clericalis: ita tamen quod sine periculo et scandalo ita fiant.' If Mansi's date is right, this precedes by three centuries the almost identical *Conc. of Rouen*, c. 8 (Mansi, xxiii. 215), and *Conc. of Castle Gonther* (Tours), c. 21 (Mansi, xxiii. 237), both in 1231. Gautier, *Les Tropaires*, i. 186, dwells on the influence of the *goliardi* on the late and ribald development of the tropes, and quotes *Conc. of Treves* (1227), c. 9 (Mansi, xxiii. 33) 'praecipimus ut omnes sacerdotes non permittant trutannos et alios vagos scholares aut goliardos cantare versus super *Sanctus* et *Agnus Dei*.' On their probable share in the Feast of Fools cf. ch. xiv. For later legislation cf. Hubatsch, 14, 95, and the passage from the *Liber Sextus* of Boniface VIII on p. 39. It lasts to the *Conc. Frisingense* (1440) 'statuimus ne clerici mimis, ioculatoribus, histrionibus, buffonibus, galliardis, largiantur' (Labbe, xiii. 1286). By this time 'goliard' seems little more than a synonym for 'minstrel.' The 'mynstralle, a gulardous,' of Mannyng, 148, does not appear to be a clerk, while Chaucer's 'goliardeys' is the Miller (*C. T.* prol. 560). On the other hand, Langland's 'Goliardeys, a glotoun of wordes' (*Piers Plowman*, prol. 139), speaks Latin. Another name for the *goliardi* occurs in an *Epistola Guidonis S. Laurentii in Lucina Cardinalis*, xx (1266, Hartzheim, iii. 807) against 'vagi scolares, qui Eberdini vocantur,' and who 'divinum invertunt officium, unde laici scandalizantur.'

makings with loose songs of love and dalliance. These it is
not to be expected that the holy mother Church should in any
way countenance. Her toleration must be reserved for those
more reputable performers who find material for their verse
either in the life and conversation of the saints and martyrs
themselves, or at least in the noble and inspiring deeds of
national heroes and champions. Legends of the saints and
gests of princes : if the minstrels will confine themselves to
the celebration of these, then, secure in the pronouncement of
a pope, they may claim a hearing even from the devout. It
would be rash to assert that even the comparatively liberal
theory of Thomas de Cabham certainly justified in all cases
the practice of the monasteries. But it is at least noteworthy
that in several instances where the subjects of the minstrelsy
presented for the delectation of a cowled audience remain
upon record, they do fall precisely within the twofold definition which he lays down. At Winchester in 1338 the minstrel
Herbert sang the song of Colbrond (or Guy of Warwick), and
the gest of the miraculous deliverance of Queen Emma ;
while at Bicester in 1432 it was the legend of the Seven
Sleepers of Ephesus that made the Epiphany entertainment
of the assembled canons.

If now we set aside the very special class of ribald *galiardi*,
and if we set aside also the distinction drawn by Thomas de
Cabham on purely ethical grounds between the minstrels of
the love-songs and the minstrels of saintly or heroic gest, the
net result is the twofold classification of higher and lower
minstrels already familiar to us. Roughly—it must always be
borne in mind how roughly—it corresponds on the one hand
to the difference between the Teutonic and the Roman tradition, on the other to the distinction between the established
' minstrel of honour ' and his unattached rival of the road.
And there is abundant evidence that such a distinction was
generally present, and occasionally became acute, in the consciousness of the minstrels themselves. The aristocrats of
minstrelsy, a Baudouin or a Jean de Condé, or a Watriquet de
Couvin, have very exalted ideas as to the dignity of their
profession. They will not let you, if they can help it, put the
grans menestreus on the same level with every-day *jang-*

leur of poor attainments and still poorer repute [1]. In the *Dit des Taboureurs* again it is a whole class, the *joueurs de vielle*, who arise to vindicate their dignity and to pour scorn upon the humble and uninstructed drummers [2]. But the most instructive and curious evidence comes from Provence. It was in 1273, when the amazing growth of Provençal poetry was approaching its sudden decay, that the last of the great troubadours, Guiraut de Riquier, addressed a verse *Supplicatio* to Alphonso X of Castile on the state of minstrelsy. He points out the confusion caused by the indiscriminate grouping of poets, singers, and entertainers of all degrees under the title of *joglars*, and begs the king, as high patron of letters, to take order for it. A reply from Alphonso, also in verse, and also, one may suspect, due to the fertile pen of Guiraut Riquier, is extant. Herein he establishes or confirms a fourfold hierarchy. At the head come two classes, the *doctors de trobar* and the *trobaires*, who are composers, the former of didactic, the latter of ordinary songs and melodies. Beneath these are the *joglars* proper, instrumentalists and reciters of delightful stories, and beneath these again the *bufos*, the entertainers of common folk, who have really no claim to be considered as *joglars* at all [3]. One of the distinctions here made is new to us. The difference between *doctor de trobar* and *trobaire* is perhaps negligible. But that between the *trobaire*

[1] Baudouin de Condé in his *Contes des Hiraus* contrasts the 'grans menestreus,' the

'Maistres de sa menestrandie,
Qui bien viele ou ki bien die
De bouce'

with the 'felons et honteux,' who win pence,

'l'un por faire l'ivre,
L'autre le cat, le tiers le sot,'

while in *Les États du Monde* his son Jean sets up a high standard of behaviour for the true minstrels:

'Soies de cuer nes et polis,
Courtois, envoisiés, et jolis,
Pour les boinnes gens solacier'

(Scheler, *Dits et Contes de Baudouin de Condé et de son fils Jean de Condé*, i. 154; ii. 377). Cf. Watriquet de Couvin, *Dis du fol menestrel* (ed. Scheler, 367):

'Menestriex se doit maintenir
Plus simplement c'une pucele, ...
Menestrel qui veut son droit faire
Ne doit le jangleur contrefaire,
Mais en sa bouche avoir tous dis
Douces paroles et biaus dis,
Estre nés, vivre purement.'

These three writers belong to the end of the thirteenth and the beginning of the fourteenth century.

[2] A. Jubinal, *Jongleurs et Trouvères*, 165. Cf. Gautier, ii. 78; Bédier, 418.

[3] F. Diaz, *Poesie der Troubadours* (ed. Bartsch), 63; K. Bartsch, *Grundriss der provenzalischen Literatur*, 25; F. Hueffer, *The Troubadours*, 63. Diaz, *op. cit.* 297, prints the documents.

or composer and the *joglar* or executant of poetry, is an important one. It is not, however, so far as the Teutonic element in minstrelsy goes, primitive. The *scôpas* and the French or Anglo-Norman *ioculatores* up to the twelfth century composed their verses as a class, and sang them as well[1]. In Provence, however, the Teutonic element in minstrelsy must have been of the slightest, and perhaps the Roman tradition, illustrated by the story of Laberius, of a marked barrier between composing and executing, had vaguely lingered. At any rate it is in Provence, in the eleventh century, that the distinction between *trobaire* and *joglar* makes its appearance. It never became a very complete one. The *trobaire* was generally, not always, of gentle or burgess birth; sometimes actually a king or noble. In the latter case he contented himself with writing his songs, and let the *joglars* spread them abroad. But the bulk of the *trobaires* lived by their art. They wandered from castle to castle, alone with a *vielle*, or with *joglars* in their train, and although they mingled with their hosts on fairly equal terms, they did not disdain to take their rewards of horse or mantle or jewel, just like any common performer. Moreover, they confined themselves to lyric poetry, leaving the writing of epic, so far as epic was abroad in Provence, to the *joglars*[2]. From Provence, the *trobaire* spread to other countries, reappearing in the north of France and England as the *trouvère*. We seem to trace an early *trouvère* in Lucas de Barre in the time of Henry I. But it is Eleanor of Poitiers, daughter of the *trobaire* count William of Poitiers, and mother of the *trouvère* Richard Cœur de Lion, who appears as the chief intermediary between north and south. The intrusion of the *trouvère* was the first step in the degradation of minstrelsy. Amongst the Anglo-Saxons, even apart from the *cantilenae* of the folk, the professional singer had no monopoly of song. Hrothgar and Alfred harped with their *scôpas*. But if there had been a similar tendency amongst the

[1] There is nothing to show that Scilling, the companion of Widsith (*Widsith*, 104), was of an inferior grade.
[2] Hueffer, 52; G. Paris, 182: A. Stimming in Grober's *Grundriss*, ii. 2. 15; Gautier, ii. 45, 58. The commonest of phrases in troubadour biography is 'cantet et trobet.' The term *trobador* is properly the accusative case of *trobaire*.

continental Teutons who merged in the French and Norman-French, it had been checked by the complete absorption of all literary energies, outside the minstrel class, in neo-Latin. It was not until the twelfth century, and as has been said, under Provençal influence, that secular-minded clerks, and exceptionally educated nobles, merchants, or officials, began to devote themselves to the vernacular, and by so doing to develop the *trouvère* type. The *trouvère* had the advantage of the minstrel in learning and independence, if not in leisure ; and though the latter long held his own by the side of his rival, he was fated in the end to give way, and to content himself with the humbler task of spreading abroad what the *trouvère* wrote [1]. By the second quarter of the fourteenth century, the conquest of literature by the *bourgeoisie* was complete. The interest had shifted from the minstrel on the hall floor to the burgher or clerk in the *puy* ; the prize of a successful poem was no longer a royal mantle, but a laureate crown or the golden violet of the *jeux floraux* ; and its destiny less to be recited at the banquet, than read in the bower. In England the completion of the process perhaps came a little later, and was coincident with the triumph of English, the tongue of the *bourgeois*, over French, the tongue of the noble. The full flower of minstrelsy had been the out-at-elbows vagabond, Rutebeuf. The full flower of the *trouvère* is the comptroller of the customs and subsidies of the port of London, Geoffrey Chaucer.

The first distinction, then, made by Guiraut Riquier, that between *trobaire* and *joglar*, implies a development from within minstrelsy itself that was destined one day to overwhelm it. But the second, that between the *joglar* and the *bufo*, is precisely the one already familiar to us, between the minstrels of the

---

[1] Petrarch, *Epist. Rerum Senil.* v. 3 ' sunt homines non magni ingenii, magnae vero memoriae, magnaeque diligentiae, sed maioris audaciae, qui regum ac potentum aulas frequentant, de proprio nudi, vestiti autem carminibus alienis, dumque quid ab hoc, aut ab illo exquisitius materno praesertim charactere dictum sit, ingenti expressione pronunciant, gratiam sibi nobilium, et pecunias quaerunt, et vestes et munera.' Fulke of Marseilles, afterwards bishop of Toulouse, wrote songs in his youth. He became an austere Cistercian ; but the songs had got abroad, and whenever he heard one of them sung by a *joglar*, he would eat only bread and water (*Sermo* of Robert de Sorbonne in Hauréau, *Man. Fr.* xxiv. 2. 286).

scôp and the minstrels of the *mimus* tradition. And, as has been said, it is partly, if not entirely, identical with that which grew up in course of time between the protected minstrels of the court and of great men's houses, and their vagrant brethren of the road. This general antithesis between the higher and lower mintrelsy may now, perhaps, be regarded as established. It was the neglect of it, surely, that led to that curious and barren logomachy between Percy and Ritson, in which neither of the disputants can be said to have had hold of more than a bare half of the truth[1]. And it runs through the whole history of minstrelsy. It became acute, no doubt, with the growth in importance of the minstrels of honour in the thirteenth and fourteenth centuries. But it had probably been just as acute, if not more so, at the very beginning of things, when the clash of Teutonic and Roman civilization first brought the bard face to face with the serious rivalry of the mime. Bard and mime merged without ever becoming quite identical; and even at the moment when this process was most nearly complete, say in the eleventh century, the *jouglerie seigneuriale*, to use Magnin's happy terms, was never quite the same thing as the *jouglerie foraine et populaire*[2], least of all in a country like England where differences of tongue went to perpetuate and emphasize the breach.

Nevertheless, the antithesis may easily be pushed too far. After all, the minstrels were entertainers, and therefore their business was to entertain. Did the lord yawn over a gest or a saintly legend? the discreet minstrel would be well advised to

---

[1] In the first edition of his *Reliques* (1765), Percy gave the mediaeval minstrel as high a status as the Norse *scald* or Anglo-Saxon *scôp*. This led to an acrid criticism by Ritson who, in his essay *On the ancient English Minstrels* in *Ancient Songs and Ballads* (1829), easily showed the low repute in which many minstrels were held. See also his elaborate *Dissertation on Romance and Minstrelsy* in his *Ancient English Metrical Romances* (1802). The truth really lay between the two, for neither appreciated the wide variety covered by a common name. On the controversy, cf. Minto in *Enc. Brit.* s. v. *Minstrels*, Courthope, i. 426–31, and H. B. Wheatley's Introduction to his edition of Percy's *Reliques*, xiii–xv. Percy in his later editions profited largely by Ritson's criticism; a careful collation of these is given in Schroer's edition (1889).

[2] Magnin, *Journal des Savants* (1846), 545.

drop high art, and to substitute some less exacting, even if less refined fashion of passing the time. The instincts of boor and baron were not then, of course, so far apart as they are nowadays. And as a matter of fact we find many of the most eminent minstrels boasting of the width and variety of their accomplishments. Thus of Baudouin II, count of Guisnes (1169–1206), it is recorded that he might have matched the most celebrated professionals, not only in *chansons de gestes* and *romans d'aventure* but also in the *fabliaux* which formed the delight of the vulgar *bourgeoisie*[1]. Less aristocratic performers descended even lower than Baudouin de Guisnes. If we study the répertoires of such *jougleurs* as the diabolic one in Gautier de Coincy's miracle[2], or Daurel in the romance of *Daurel et Beton*[3], or the disputants who vaunt their respective proficiencies in *Des Deus Bordeors Ribauz*[4], we shall find that they cover not only every conceivable form of minstrel literature proper, but also tricks with knives and strings, sleight of hand, dancing and tumbling. Even in Provence, the *Enseignamens* for *joglars* warn their readers to learn the arts of imitating birds, throwing knives, leaping through hoops, showing off performing asses and dogs, and dangling marionettes[5]. So that

---

[1] Lambertus Ardensis, *Chronicon*, c. 81 (ed. Godefroy Menilglaise, 175) 'quid plura? tot et tantorum ditatus est copia librorum ut Augustinum in theologia, Areopagitam Dionysium in philosophia, Milesium fabularium in naeniis gentium, in cantilenis gestoriis, sive in eventuris nobilium, sive etiam in fabellis ignobilium, ioculatores quosque nominatissimos aequiparare putaretur.'

[2] Freymond, *Jongleurs et Menestrels*, 34:
'Il est de tout bons menesterieux:
Il set peschier, il set chacier,
Il set trop bien genz solacier;
Il set chançons, sonnez et fables,
Il set d'eschez, il set des tables,
Il set d'arbalestre et d'airon.'

[3] *Daurel et Beton* (ed. Meyer, *Soc. des anc. textes fr.* 1886), 1206:
'El va enant, a lor des jocz mostratz,
Dels us e dels altres, qu'el ne sap pro asatz.

Pueis pres l[a] arpa, a .ij. laisses notatz,
Et ab la viola a los gen deportat[z],
Sauta e tomba; tuh s'en son alegratz.'

[4] Montaiglon-Raynaud, i. 1:
'Ge sai contes, ge sai flabeax;
Ge sai conter beax dix noveax,
Rotruenges viez et noveles,
Et sirventois et pastorels.
Ge sai le flabel du Denier,

.   .   .   .   .

Si sai de Parceval l'estoire,

.   .   .   .   .

Ge sai joer des baasteax,
Et si sai joer des costeax,
Et de la corde et de la fonde,
Et de toz les beax giex du monde,

.   .   .   .   .

De totes les chansons de geste.'

[5] Three of these *Enseignamens*, by Guiraut de Cabreira († 1170), Guiraut de Calanso († 1200), and Bertran de Paris († 1250), are

one discerns the difference between the lower and the higher minstrels to have been not so much that the one did not sink so low, as that the other, for lack of capacity and education, did not rise so high.

The palmy days of minstrelsy were the eleventh, twelfth and thirteenth centuries. The germ of decay, however, which appeared when the separation grew up between *trouvère* and *jougleur*, and when men began to read books instead of listening to recitations, was further developed by the invention of printing. For then, while the *trouvère* could adapt himself readily enough to the new order of things, the *jougleur's* occupation was gone. Like Benedick he might still be talking, but nobody marked him. Eyes cast down over a page of Chaucer or of Caxton had no further glitter or tear for him to win [1]. The fifteenth, and still more the sixteenth century, witness the complete break-up of minstrelsy in its mediaeval form. The mimes of course endured. They survived the overthrow of mediaevalism, as they had survived the overthrow of the Empire [2]. The Tudor kings and nobles had still their jugglers, their bearwards, their domestic buffoons, jesters or fools [3]. Bearbaiting in Elizabethan London rivalled the drama in its vogue. Acrobats and miscellaneous entertainers never ceased to crowd to every fair, and there is applause even to-day in

---

printed by K. Bartsch, *Denkmäler der provenzalischen Litteratur*, 85–101. Cf. Bartsch, *Grundriss der prov. Lit.* 25 ; Hueffer, *The Troubadours*, 66 ; *Hist. Litt.* xvii. 581.

[1] Bernhard, iii. 397, gives some French references, one dated 1395, for 'menestriers de bouches,' a term signifying minstrels who sang as well as played instruments.

[2] There are numerous payments to jugglers, tumblers and dancers in the Household Accounts of Henry VII (Bentley, *Excerpta Historica*, 85–113 ; Collier, i. 50). A letter to Wolsey of July 6, 1527, from R. Croke, the tutor of Henry VIII's natural son, the Duke of Richmond, complains of difficulties put in his way by R. Cotton, the Clerk-comptroller of the duke's household, and

adds : ' At hic tamen in praeceptore arcendo diligens, libenter patitur scurras et mimos (qui digna lupanari in sacro cubiculo coram principe cantillent)admitti' (Nichols,*Memoir of Henry Fitzroy* in *Camden Miscellany*, iii. xxxviii).

[3] For the *ioculator regis*, cf. Appendix E, and Leach,*Beverley MSS.* 179. He is called 'jugler' in *N.H.B.* 67. Is he distinct from the royal *gestator* (*gestour*, *jester*) ? Both appear in the Shrewsbury accounts (s. ann. 1521, 1549). In 1554 both *le jugler* and *le gester* were entertained. The *gestator* seems to have merged in the *stultus* or court fool (ch. xvi). The accounts in App. E often mention the royal bearward, who remained an important official under Elizabeth.

circus and music-hall for the old jests and the old somersaults
that have already done duty for upwards of twenty centuries.
But the *jougleur* as the thirteenth century knew him was by
the sixteenth century no more. Professional musicians there
were in plenty ; 'Sneak's noise' haunted the taverns of East-
cheap [1], and instrumentalists and vocalists in royal palaces
and noble mansions still kept the name and style of minstrels.
But they were not minstrels in the old sense, for with the production of literature, except perhaps for a song here and there,
they had no longer anything to do. That had passed into
other hands, and even the lineaments of the *trouvère* are
barely recognizable in the new types of poets and men of letters
whom the Renaissance produced. The old fashioned minstrel
in his style and habit as he lived, was to be presented before
Elizabeth at Kenilworth as an interesting anachronism [2]. Some
of the discarded entertainers, as we shall see, were absorbed into
the growing profession of stage-players ; others sunk to be ballad
singers. For to the illiterate the story-teller still continued to
appeal. The ballad indeed, at least on one side of it, was the
detritus, as the *lai* had been the germ, of romance [3], and at
the very moment when Spenser was reviving romance as
a conscious archaism, it was still possible for a blind fiddler
with a ballad to offend the irritable susceptibilities of a Puritan,
or to touch the sensitive heart-strings of a Sidney [4]. But as
a social and literary force, the glory of minstrelsy had
departed [5].

---

[1] 2 *Hen. IV*, ii. 4. 12.

[2] Cf. Appendix H (i).

[3] Courthope, i. 445 ; A. Lang,
s. v. *Ballad* in *Enc. Brit.* and in *A
Collection of Ballads*, xi ; *Quarterly
Review* (July, 1898) ; Henderson,
335 ; G. Smith, 180. But I think
that Gummere, *B. P. passim*, succeeds in showing that the element of
folk-poetry in balladry is stronger
than some of the above writers recognize.

[4] Sidney, *Apologie for Poetrie*
(ed. Arber), 46 'Certainly I must
confess my own barbarousness. I
never heard the old song of *Percy
and Douglas*, that I found not my
heart moved more than with a

trumpet. And yet is it sung but by
some blind Crowder, with no rougher
voice than rude style.' For the
Puritan view, see Stubbes, i. 169.

[5] Ritson, ccxxiv, quotes the follow-
ing lines, ascribed to Dr. Bull
(†1597), from a *Harl. MS.*, as the
epitaph of minstrelsy :
'When Jesus went to Jairus'
    house
    (Whose daughter was about to
    dye),
He turned the minstrels out of
    doors,
    Among the rascal company :
Beggars they are, with one
    consent,
And rogues, by Act of Parliament.'

CHAPTER IV

THE MINSTREL REPERTORY

THE floor of a mediaeval court, thronged with minstrels of every degree, provided at least as various an entertainment as the Roman stage itself [1]. The performances of the mimes, to the accompaniment of their despised tabor or wry-necked fife, undoubtedly made up in versatility for what they lacked in decorum. There were the *tombeors, tombesteres* or *tumbleres*, acrobats and contortionists, who twisted themselves into incredible attitudes, leapt through hoops, turned somersaults, walked on their heads, balanced themselves in perilous positions. Female tumblers, *tornatrices*, took part in these feats, and several districts had their own characteristic modes of tumbling, such as *le tour français, le tour romain, le tour de Champenois*[2].' Amongst the *tombeors* must be reckoned the rarer *funambuli*

[1] *Du Vilain au Buffet* (Mont-aiglon-Raynaud, iii. 202) :
'Li quens manda les menestrels,
Et si a fet crier entr'els
Qui la meillor truffe sauroit
Dire ne fere, qu'il auroit
Sa robe d'escarlate nueve.
L'uns menestrels a l'autre rueve
Fere son mestier, tel qu'il sot,
L'uns fet l'ivre, l'autre le sot ;
Li uns chante, li autres note,
Et li autres dit la riote,
Et li autres la jenglerie ;
Cil qui sevent de jouglerie
Vielent par devant le conte ;
Aucuns i a qui fabliaus conte,
Où il ot mainte gaberie,
Et li autres dit l'*Erberie*,
Là où il ot mainte risée.'
Cf. p. 67 ; also the similar list in Wace, *Brut*, 10823, and *Piers Plowman*, Passus xvi. 205 :
'Ich can nat tabre ne trompe · ne telle faire gestes,
Farten, ne fithelen · at festes, ne harpen,
Iapen ne iogelen · ne gentelliche pipe,
Nother sailen ne sautrien · ne singe with the giterne.'

[2] Gautier, ii. 63 ; Strutt, 207. L. T. Smith, *Derby Accounts* (Camden Soc.), 109, records a payment by Henry of Bolingbroke when in Prussia in 1390-1 'cuidam tumblere facienti ministralciam suam.' See miniatures of tumblers (Strutt, 211, 212), stilt-dancing (ibid. 226), hoop-vaulting (ibid. 229), balancing (ibid. 232-4), a contortionist (ibid. 235).

or rope-walkers, such as he whom the Corvei annals record to have met with a sorry accident in the twelfth century[1], or he who created such a *furore* in the thirteenth by his aerial descent from the cathedral at Basle[2]. Nor are they very distinct from the crowd of dancers, male and female, who are variously designated as *saltatores* and *saltatrices*, 'sautours,' 'sailyours,' 'hoppesteres.' Indeed, in many mediaeval miniatures, the daughter of Herodias, dancing before Herod, is represented rather as tumbling or standing on her head than in any more subtle pose[3]. A second group includes the jugglers in the narrower sense, the *jouers des costeax* who tossed and caught knives and balls[4], and the practitioners of sleight of hand, who generally claimed to proceed by *nigremance* or sorcery[5]. The two seem to have shared the names of *prestigiatores* or *tregetours*[6]. Other mimes, the *bastaxi*, or *jouers des basteax*, brought round, like the Punch and Judy men of our own day, little wooden performing puppets or marionettes[7]. Others, to whom Thomas de Cabham more particularly refers, came in masked as animals, and played the dog, the ass or the bird with appropriate noises and behaviour[8].

---

[1] *Annales Corbeienses*, s.a. 1135 (Leibnitz, *Rer. Brunsv. Script.* ii. 307) 'funambulus inter lusus suos in terram deiectus.'

[2] Gautier, ii. 64, quotes *Annales Basilienses*, s.a. 1276 'Basileam quidam corpore debilis venit, qui funem protensum de campanili maioris ecclesiae ad domum cantoris manibus et pedibus descendebat'; for later English examples cf. ch. xxiv.

[3] Strutt, 172, 176, 209; Jusserand, i. 214, and *E. W. L.* 23.

[4] Strutt, 173, 197; Jusserand, *E. W. L.* 212; Wright, 33-7.

[5] Gautier, ii. 67, quotes *Joufrois*, 1146:
'Ainz veïssiez toz avant traire
Les jogleors et maint jou faire.
Li uns dançoit . . .
Li autre ovrent de nigremance.'

[6] Strutt, 194, quotes from Cott. MS. *Nero*, c. viii, a payment 'Janins le Cheveretter (bagpiper) called le Tregettour,' for playing

before Edw. II. Collier, i. 30, quotes Lydgate, *Daunce de Macabre* (Harl. 116):
'Maister John Rykell, sometyme
      tregitoure
Of noble Henry kynge of Eng-
      londe,
And of Fraunce the myghty
      conqueroure,
For all the sleightes and turn-
      yngs of thyne honde,
Thou must come nere this
      daunce to understonde.
      .   .   .   .   .
Lygarde de mayne now helpeth
      me right nought.'

[7] Ducange, s.v. *bastaxi*; Gautier, ii. 11; C. Magnin, *Hist. des Marionnettes en Europe* (ed. 2, 1862); cf. ch. xxiv. *Bastaxus* seems to be the origin of the modern *bateleur*, used in a wide sense of travelling entertainers.

[8] Du Méril, *Com.* 74; Strutt, 253; Jusserand, *E. W. L.* vi. 218. Amongst the letters commendatory

Others, again, led round real animals ; generally bears or apes, occasionally also horses, cocks, hares, dogs, camels and even lions [1]. Sometimes these beasts did tricks ; too often they were baited [2], and from time to time a man, lineal descendant of the imperial gladiators, would step forward to fight with them [3]. To the gladiatorial shows may perhaps also be traced the fight with wooden swords which often formed a part of the fun.[4] And, finally, whatever the staple of the performance, there was the *parade* or preliminary patter to call the audience together, and throughout the ' carping,' a continuous flow of rough witticism and repartee, such as one is accustomed to hear Joey, the clown, in the pauses of a circus, pass off on Mr. Harris, the ring-master [5]. Here came in the especial talents of the *scurra, bordeor* or *japere*, to whom the moralists took such marked exception. ' *L'uns fet l'ivre, l'autre le sot,*' says the *fabliau* ; and indeed we do not need the testimony of Thomas de Cabham or of John of Salisbury to conclude that such buffoonery was likely to be of a ribald type [6].

Even in the high places of minstrelsy there was some measure of variety. A glance at the pay-sheet of Edward I's

of minstrels quoted by Gautier, ii. 109, is one ' De illo qui scit volucrum exprimere cantilenas et voces asininas.' Baudouin de Condé mentions a minstrel who 'fait le cat ' (cf. p. 63, n. 1).

[1] See figures of bears (Strutt, 176, 214, 239, 240), apes (ibid. 240, 241 ; Jusserand, *E. W. L.* 218), horses (Strutt, 243, 244), dog (ibid. 246, 249), hare (ibid. 248), cock (ibid. 249). For the *ursarius* and for lion, marmoset, &c., cf. pp. 53, 68, and Appendix E.

[2] Strutt, 256. A horse-baiting is figured in Strutt, 243.

[3] Strutt, 244, figures a combat between man and horse. Gautier, ii. 66, cites *Acta SS. Jan.* iii. 257 for the intervention of St. Poppo when a naked man smeared with honey was to fight bears before the emperor Henry IV († 1048).

[4] Strutt, 260, 262.

[5] *Adam Davie* († 1312) :
' Merry it is in halle to here the harpe,

The minstrelles synge, the jogelours carpe.'

[6] John of Salisbury, *Polycraticus,* i. 8 ' Quorum adeo error invaluit, ut a praeclaris domibus non arceantur, etiam illi qui obscenis partibus corporis oculis omnium eam ingerunt turpitudinem, quam erubescat videre vel cynicus. Quodque magis mirere, nec tunc eiiciuntur, quando tumultuantes inferius crebro sonitu aerem foedant, et turpiter inclusum turpius produnt'; Adam of Bremen (*M. G. H.*), iii. 38 ' Pantomimi, qui obscoenis corporis motibus oblectare vulgus solent.' Raine, *Hist. Papers from Northern Registers* (R. S.), 398, prints a letter of Archbishop Zouche of York on the indecent behaviour of some clerks of the bishop of Durham in York Minster on Feb. 6, 1349, ' subtus imaginem crucifixi ventositates per posteriora dorsi cum foedo strepitu more ribaldorum emittere fecerunt pluries ac turpiter et sonore.'

Whitsuntide feast will show that the minstrels who aspired to be musicians were habitually distinguished by the name of the musical instrument on which they played. They are *vidulatores, citharistae, trumpatores, vilours, gigours, crouderes, harpours, citolers, lutours, trumpours, taboreurs* and the like. The harp (*cithara*), played by twitching the strings, had been the old instrument of the Teutons, but in the Middle Ages it came second in popularity to the *vielle* (*vidula*), which was also a string instrument, but, like the modern fiddle, was played with a bow. The drum (*tympanum, tabour*) was, as we have seen, somewhat despised, and relegated to the mimes. The trumpeters appear less often singly than in twos and threes, and it is possible that their performances may have been mainly ceremonial and of a purely instrumental order. But the use of music otherwise than to accompany the voice does not seem to have gone, before the end of the thirteenth century, much beyond the signals, flourishes and fanfares required for wars, triumphs and processions. Concerted instrumental music was a later development [1]. The ordinary function of the harp or *vielle* in minstrelsy was to assist the voice of the minstrel in one of the many forms of poetry which the middle ages knew. These were both lyric and narrative. The distinction is roughly parallel to that made by Thomas de Cabham when he subdivides his highest grades of minstrels into those who sing wanton songs at taverns, and those more properly called *ioculatores* who solace the hearts of men with reciting the deeds of the heroes and the lives of the saints. The themes of mediaeval lyric, as of all lyric, are largely wantonness and wine; but it must be borne in mind that Thomas de Cabham's classification is primarily an ethical one, and does not necessarily imply any marked difference of professional status between the two classes. The haunters of taverns and the solacers of the virtuous were after all the same minstrels, or at least minstrels of the same order. That the *chansons*, in their innumerable varieties, caught up from folk-song, or devised by Provençal ingenuity, were largely in the mouths of the minstrels, may be taken for granted. It was here,

[1] Gautier, ii. 69; Lavoix, *La Musique au Siècle de Saint-Louis*, i. 315; cf. Appendix C.

however, that the competition of *trobaire* and *trouvère* began earliest, and proved most triumphant, and the supreme minstrel *genre* was undoubtedly the narrative. This was, in a sense, their creation, and in it they held their own, until the laity learned to read and the *trouvères* became able to eke out the shortness of their memories by writing down or printing their stories. With narrative, no doubt, the minstrels of highest repute mainly occupied themselves. Harp or *vielle* in hand they beguiled many a long hour for knight and *châtelaine* with the interminable *chansons de gestes* in honour of Charlemagne and his heroic band [1], or, when the vogue of these waned, as in time it did, with the less primitive *romans d'aventure*, of which those that clustered round the Keltic Arthur were the widest famed. Even so their repertory was not exhausted. They had *lais*, *dits* and *contes* of every kind; the devout *contes* that Thomas de Cabham loved, historical *contes*, romantic *contes* of less alarming proportions than the genuine *romans*. And for the *bourgeoisie* they had those improper, witty *fabliaux*, so racy of the French soil, in which the *esprit gaulois*, as we know it, found its first and not its least characteristic expression. In most of these types the music of the instrument bore its part. The shorter *lais* were often accompanied musically throughout [2]. The longer poems were delivered in a chant or recitative, the monotony of which was broken at intervals by a phrase or two of intercalated melody, while during the rest of the performance a few perfunctory notes served to sustain the voice [3]. And at times, especially in the later days of minstrelsy, the harp or *vielle* was laid aside altogether, and the singer became a mere story-teller. The antithesis, no infrequent one, between minstrel, and *fabulator*, *narrator*, *fableor*, *conteor*,

---

[1] W. Mapes, *de Nugis Curialium* (Camden Soc.), dist. v. prol., 'Caesar Lucani, Aeneas Maronis, multis vivunt in laudibus, plurimum suis meritis et non minimum vigilantia poetarum; nobis divinam Karolorum et Pepinorum nobilitatem vulgaribus rithmis sola mimorum concelebrat nugacitas.'

[2] Lavoix, ii. 295.

[3] Ibid. ii. 344. The Paris MS. (*B. N.* f. fr. 2168) of *Aucassin et Nicolete* preserves the musical notation of the verse sections. Only three musical phrases, with very slight variations, are used. Two of these were probably repeated, alternately or at the singer's fancy, throughout the tirade; the third provided a cadence for the closing line (Bourdillon, *Aucassin et Nicolette* (1897), 157).

gestour, disour, segger, though all these are themselves elsewhere classed as minstrels, sufficiently suggests this [1]. It was
principally, one may surmise, the *dits* and *fabliaux* that lent
themselves to unmusical narration ; and when prose crept in,
as in time it did, even before reading became universal, it can
hardly have been sung. An interesting example is afforded
by *Aucassin et Nicolete*, which is what is known as a *cante-
fable*. That is to say, it is written in alternate sections of
verse and prose. The former have, in the Paris manuscript,
a musical accompaniment, and are introduced with the words
' *Or se cante* ' ; the latter have no music, and the introduction
' *Or content et dient et fablent.*'

A further differentiation amongst minstrels was of linguistic
origin. This was especially apparent in England. The mime
is essentially cosmopolitan. In whatever land he finds himself the few sentences of patter needful to introduce his *tour*
or his *nigremance* are readily picked up. It is not so with
any entertainer whose performances claim to rank, however
humbly, as literature. And the Conquest in England brought
into existence a class of minstrels who, though they were by
no means mimes, were yet obliged to compete with mimes,
making their appeal solely to the *bourgeoisie* and the peasants,
because their speech was not that of the Anglo-Norman lords
and ladies who formed the more profitable audiences of the
castles. The native English gleemen were eclipsed at courts
by the Taillefers and Raheres of the invading host. But they
still held the road side by side with their rivals, shorn of their
dignities, and winning a precarious livelihood from the shrunken

---

[1] Chaucer, *House of Fame*, 1197:
' Of alle maner of minstrales,
  And gestiours, that tellen tales,
  Bothe of weping and of game.'
Cf. *Sir Thopas*, 134; and Gower,
Confessio Amantis, vii. 2424 :
' And every menstral hadde pleid,
  And every disour hadde seid.'
The evidence of Erasmus is late, of
course, for the hey-day of min-
strelsy, but in his time there were
certainly English minstrels who
merely recited, without musical
accompaniment; cf. *Ecclesiastes*

(*Opera*, v. col. 958) 'Apud Anglos
est simile genus hominum, quales
apud Italos sunt circulatores, de
quibus modo dictum est; qui irrum-
punt in convivia magnatum, aut in
cauponas vinarias ; et argumentum
aliquod, quod edidicerunt, recitant ;
puta mortem omnibus dominari,
aut laudem matrimonii. Sed quoniam ea lingua monosyllabis fere
constat, quemadmodum Germanica ;
atque illi studio vitant cantum,
nobis latrare videntur verius quam
loqui.'

purses of those of their own blood and tongue[1]. It was they
who sang the unavailing heroisms of Hereward, and, if we
may judge by the scanty fragments and records that have
come down to us, they remained for long the natural focus and
mouthpiece of popular discontent and anti-court sentiment.
In the reign of Edward III a gleeman of this type, Laurence
Minot, comes to the front, voicing the spirit of an England
united in its nationalism by the war against France ; the rest
are, for the most part, nameless[2]. Naturally the English
gleemen did not remain for ever a proscribed and isolated
folk. One may suspect that at the outset many of them
became bilingual. At any rate they learnt to mingle with
their Anglo-Norman *confrères* : they borrowed the themes of
continental minstrelsy; translating *roman, fabliau* and *chanson*
into the metres and dialects of the vernacular ; and had their
share in that gradual fusion of the racial elements of the land,
whose completion was the preparation for Chaucer.

Besides the Saxons, there were the Kelts. In the provinces
of France that bordered on Armorica, in the English counties
that marched with Wales, the Keltic harper is no unusual or
negligible figure. Whether such minstrels ranked very high
in the bardic hierarchy of their own peoples may be doubted ;
but amid alien folk they achieved popularity[3]. Both Giraldus

[1] Ten Brink, i. 193, 225, 235,
314, 322 ; Jusserand, i. 219. The
Old gleeman tradition was probably less interfered with in the
lowlands of Scotland than in England proper ; cf. Henderson, *Scottish Vernacular Literature*, 16.

[2] Ten Brink, i. 322 ; Jusserand,
i. 360 ; Courthope, i. 197. Minot's
poems have been edited by J. Hall
(Oxford, 1887). See also Wright,
Political Songs (C.S.) and *Political
Poems and Songs* (R.S.). Many of
these, however, are Latin.

[3] On Welsh bardism see H.
d'Arbois de Jubainville, *Intr. à
l'Étude de la Litt. celtique*, 63 ;
Stephens, *Literature of the Kymry*,
84, 93, 97, 102 ; Ernest David,
*Études historiques sur la Poésie et
la Musique dans la Cambrie*, 13,
62-103, 147-64. In Wales, an

isolated corner of Europe, little
touched by Latin influences, the
bards long retained the social and
national position which it is probable they once had held in all the
Aryan peoples. Their status is
defined in the laws of Howel Dha
(†920) and in those of Gruffyd ab
Cynan (1100). The latter code
distinguishes three orders of bards
proper, the *Pryddyd* or Chair bards,
the *Teuluwr* or Palace bards, and
the *Arwyddfardd* or heralds, also
called *Storiawr*, the *cantores hi-
storici* of Giraldus Cambrensis. The
Pryddyd and *Teuluwr* differ precisely as poets and executants,
trouvères and *jougleurs*. Below
all these come the *Clerwr*, against
whom official bardism from the
sixth to the thirteenth century
showed an inveterate animosity.

Cambrensis and Thomas the author of *Tristan* speak of a certain *famosus fabulator* of this class, Bledhericus or Breri by name[1]. Through Breri and his like the Keltic traditions filtered into Romance literature, and an important body of scholars are prepared to find in *lais* sung to a Welsh or Breton harp the *origines* of Arthurian romance[2]. In England the Welsh, like the English-speaking minstrels, had a political, as well as a literary significance. They were the means by which the spirit of Welsh disaffection under English rule was kept alive, and at times fanned into a blaze. The fable of the massacre of the bards by Edward I is now discredited, but an ordinance of his against Keltic 'bards and rhymers' is upon record, and was subsequently repeated under Henry IV[3].

An important question now presents itself. How far, in this heterogeneous welter of mediaeval minstrelsy, is it possible to distinguish any elements which can properly be called dramatic? The minstrels were entertainers in many *genres*. Were they also actors? An answer may be sought first of all in their literary remains. The first condition of drama is dialogue, and dialogue is found both in lyric and in narrative minstrelsy. Naturally, it is scantiest in lyric. But there is a group of *chansons* common to northern France and to southern France or Provence, which at least tended to develop in this direction. There are the *chansons à danser*, which are frequently a semi-dialogue between a soloist and a chorus, the one singing the verses, the other breaking into

---

These are an unattached wandering folk, players on flutes, tambourines, and other instruments meaner than the *telyn* or harp, and the *crwth* or viol which alone the bards proper deigned to use. Many of them had also picked up the mime-tricks of the foreigners. It was probably with these *Clerwr* that the English and French neighbours of the Kelts came mainly into contact. Padelford, 5, puts this contact as early as the Anglo-Saxon period.

[1] Giraldus Cambrensis, *Descriptio Cambriae*, i. 17 'famosus ille fabulator Bledhericus, qui tempora nostra paulo praevenit.' Thomas,

Tristan († 1170, ed. Michel, ii. 847):
'Mès sulum ço que j'ai oy
N'el dient pas sulum Breri,
Ky solt les gestes e les cuntes
De tuz les reis, de tuz les cuntes
Ki orent esté en Bretaingne.'

[2] G. Paris, in *Hist. Litt.* xxx. 1–22; *Litt. Fr.* §§ 53–5; Nutt, *Legend of the Holy Grail*, 228; Rhys, *Arthurian Legend*, 370–90. These views have been vigorously criticized by Prof. Zimmer in *Göttingische gelehrte Anzeigen* (1891), 488, 785, and elsewhere.

[3] David, *op. cit.* 13, 235; cf. p. 54.

a burden or refrain. There are the *chansons à personnages* or *chansons de mal mariée*, complaints of unhappy wives, which often take the form of a dialogue between the woman and her husband, her friend or, it may be, the poet, occasionally that of a discussion on courtly love in general. There are the *aubes*, of which the type is the morning dialogue between woman and lover adapted by Shakespeare with such splendid effect in the third act of *Romeo and Juliet*. And finally there are the *pastourelles*, which are generally dialogues between a knight and a shepherdess, in which the knight makes love and, successful or repulsed, rides away. All these *chansons*, like the *chansons d'histoire* or *de toile*, which did not develop into dialogues, are, in the form in which we have them, of minstrel origin. But behind them are probably folk-songs of similar character, and M. Gaston Paris is perhaps right in tracing them to the *fêtes du mai*, those agricultural festivals of immemorial antiquity in which women traditionally took so large a part. A further word will have to be said of their ultimate contribution to drama in a future chapter[1].

Other lyrical dialogues of very different type found their way into the literature of northern France from that of Provence. These were the elaborate disputes about abstract questions, generally of love, so dear to the artistic and scholastic mind of the *trobaire*. There was the *tenso* (Fr. *tençon*) in which two speakers freely discussed a given subject, each taking the point of view which seems good to him. And there was the *joc-partitz* or *partimen* (Fr. *jeu-parti* or *parture*), in which the challenger proposed a theme, indicated two opposed attitudes towards it, and gave his opponent his choice to maintain one or other[2]. Originally, no doubt the *tensons* and the *jocs-partitz* were, as they professed to be, improvised verbal tournaments: afterwards they became little more than academic exercises[3]. To the drama they have nothing to say.

---

[1] Paris, §§ 118, 122, and *Orig.* (*passim*); Jeanroy, 1, 84, 102, 387; *Lang. et Litt.* i. 345 ; cf. ch. viii. Texts of *chansons à personnages* and *pastourelles* in Bartsch, *Altfranzösische Romanzen und Pastourellen*; of *aubes* in Bartsch, *Chrestomathie de l'ancien français*.

[2] Paris, § 126; *Orig.* (*passim*); Jeanroy, 45, and in *Lang. et Litt.* i. 384 ; Bartsch, *Grundriss der prov. Lit.* 34; Hueffer, *The Troubadours*, 112; Stimming in Gröber's *Grundriss*, ii. 2. 24.

[3] In 1386 we hear of ' des compaingnons, pour de jeux de parture

The dialogue elements in lyric minstrelsy thus exhausted, we turn to the wider field of narrative. But over the greater space of this field we look in vain. If there is anything of dialogue in the *chansons de gestes* and the *romans* it is merely reported dialogue such as every form of narrative poetry contains, and is not to the purpose. It is not until we come to the humbler branches of narrative, the unimportant *contes* and *dits*, that we find ourselves in the presence of dialogue proper. *Dits* and *fabliaux dialogués* are not rare [1]. There is the already quoted *Deus Bordeors Ribauz* in which two *jougleurs* meet and vaunt in turn their rival proficiencies in the various branches of their common art [2]. There is Rutebeuf's *Charlot et le Barbier*, a similar 'flyting' between two gentlemen of the road [3]. There is *Courtois d'Arras*, a version of the Prodigal Son story [4]. There is *Le Roi d'Angleterre et le Jongleur d'Ely*, a specimen of witty minstrel repartee, of which more will be said immediately. These dialogues naturally tend to become of the nature of disputes, and they merge into that special kind of *dit*, the *débat* or *disputoison* proper. The *débat* is a kind of poetical controversy put into the mouths of two types or two personified abstractions, each of which pleads the cause of its own superiority, while in the end the decision is not infrequently referred to an umpire in the fashion familiar in the eclogues of Theocritus [5]. The *débats* thus bear a strong

---

juer et esbattre' at Douai (Julleville, *Rép. Com.* 323), which looks as if, by the end of the fourteenth century, the *partures* were being professionally performed.

[1] Paris, § 109; Bédier, 31. A *fabliau* is properly a 'conte à rire en vers'; the term *dit* is applied more generally to a number of short poems which deal, 'souvent avec agrément, des sujets empruntés à la vie quotidienne.' Some *dits* are satirical, others eulogistic of a class or profession, others descriptive. But the distinction is not very well defined, and the *fabliaux* are often called *dits* in the MSS.

[2] Montaiglon-Raynaud, i. 1 ; ii. 257. The *dit* is also called *La Jengle au Ribaut et la Contrejengle*.

[3] Rutebeuf (ed. Kressner), 99.

[4] Barbazan-Méon, i. 356. Bédier, 33, considers *Courtois d'Arras* as the oldest French comedy, a *jeu dramatique* with intercalated narrative by a *meneur de jeu*. But the fact that it ends with the words *Te Deum* leads one to look upon it as an adaptation of a religious play ; cf. ch. xix.

[5] On the *débats* in general, see *Hist. Litt.* xxiii. 216 sqq.; Paris, *Litt. fr.* §§ 110, 155 ; Arthur Piaget, *Littérature didactique* in *Lang. et Litt.* ii. 208 ; Jeanroy, 48 ; R. Hirzel, *Der Dialog*, ii. 382 ; *Literaturblatt* (1887), 76. A full list is given by Petit, *Rép. Com.* 405-9. The *débats* merge into such allegorical poems as Henri d'Andeli's

resemblance to the lyric *tençons* and *jeux-partis* already mentioned. Like the *chansons*, they probably owe something to the folk festivals with their 'flytings' and seasonal songs. In any case they are common ground to minstrelsy and to the clerkly literature of the Middle Ages. Many of the most famous of them, such as the *Débat de l'Hiver et de l'Été*, the *Débat du Vin et de l'Eau*, the *Débat du Corps et de l'Âme*, exist in neo-Latin forms, the intermediaries being naturally enough those *vagantes* or wandering scholars, to whom so much of the interaction of learned and of popular literature must be due [1]. And in their turn many of the *débats* were translated sooner or later into English. English literature, indeed, had had from Anglo-Saxon days a natural affinity for the dialogue form [2],

Bataille des Vins (Barbazon-Méon, i. 152) or *Le Mariage des Sept Arts et des Sept Vertus* (Jubinal, *Œuvres de Rutebeuf*, ii. 415) ; cf. Paris, *Litt. fr.* 158.

[1] Ten Brink, i. 215 ; Hubatsch, 24 ; Gummere, *B. P.* 200, 306. The *Débat de l'Yver et de l'Esté* has the nearest folk-lore origin ; cf. ch. ix. Paris, *Origines*, 28, mentions several Greek and Latin versions beginning with Aesop (Halm, 414). The most important is the ninth-century *Conflictus Veris et Hiemis* (Riese, *Anth. Lat.* i. 2. 145), variously ascribed to Bede (Wernsdorff, *Poetae Latini Minores*, ii. 239), Alcuin (*Alc. Opera*, ed. Froben, ii. 612) and others. French versions are printed in Montaiglon-Rothschild, *Anc. Poés. fr.* vi. 190, x. 41, and Jubinal, *N. R.* ii. 40. There are imitations in all tongues : cf. M. Émile Picot's note in Mont.-Rothsch. *op. cit.* x. 49 ; *Hist. Litt.* xxiii. 231 ; Douhet, 1441.—*La Disputoison du Vin et de l'Iaue* is printed in Jubinal, *N. R.* i. 293 ; Wright, *Lat. Poems of Walter Mapes*, 299 ; *Carmina Burana*, 232. It is based on the *Goliae Dialogus inter Aquam et Vinum* (Wright, *loc. cit.* 87) ; cf. *Hist. Litt.* xxiii. 228 ; *Romania*, xvi. 366.—On the complicated history of the *Débat du Corps et de l'Âme*, see T. Batiouchkof in *Romania*, xx. 1. 513 ; G.

Kleinert, *Ueber den Streit von Leib und Seele* ; *Hist. Litt.* xxii. 162 ; P. de Julleville, *Répertoire Comique*, 5, 300, 347 ; Wright, *Latin Poems*, xxiii. 95, 321. Latin, French and other versions are given by Wright, and by Viollet-Leduc, *Anc. Thé. fr.* iii. 325.—*Phillis et Flora*, or *De Phyllis qui aime un chevalier et de Flora qui aime un prêtre*, is also referred by Paris, *Orig.* 28, to a folksong beginning ; cf. *H. L.* xxii. 138, 165 ; *Romania*, xxii. 536. Latin versions are in *Carmina Burana*, 155 ; Wright, *Latin Poems of W. Mapes*, 258.—A possible influence of the Theocritean and Virgilian eclogues upon these *débats*, through their neo-Latin forms, must be borne in mind.

[2] Wülker, 384 ; Brooke, i. 139, ii. 93, 221, 268 ; Jusserand, i. 75, 443. The passages of dialogue dwelt on by these writers mostly belong to the work of Cynewulf and his school. It has been suggested that some of them, e.g. the A.-S. *Descent into Hell* (Grein, iii. 175 ; cf. *Anglia*, xix. 137), or the dialogue between Mary and Joseph in Cynewulf's *Christ*, 163 (ed. Gollancz, p. 16), may have been intended for liturgical use by half-choirs ; but of this there is really no proof. Wülker, *loc. cit.*, shows clearly that the notion of a dramatic representation was unfamiliar to the Anglo-Saxons.

and presents side by side with the translated *débats* others—
strifs or *estrifs* is the English term—of native origin [1]. The
thirteenth-century *Harrowing of Hell* is an *estrif* on a subject
familiar in the miracle plays : and for an early miracle play it
has sometimes been mistaken [2]. Two or three other *estrifs*
of English origin are remarkable, because the interlocutors
are not exactly abstractions, but species of birds and
animals [3].

Dialogue then, in one shape or another, was part of the
minstrel's regular stock-in-trade. But dialogue by itself is not
drama. The notion of drama does not, perhaps, necessarily
imply scenery on a regular stage, but it does imply impersonation and a distribution of rôles between at least two performers.
Is there anything to be traced in minstrelsy that satisfies these
conditions? So far as impersonation is concerned, there are
several scattered notices which seem to show that it was not
altogether unknown. In the twelfth century for instance,
Ælred, abbot of Rievaulx, commenting on certain unpleasing
innovations in the church services of the day, complains that
the singers use gestures just like those of *histriones*, fit rather
for a *theatrum* than for a house of prayer [4]. The word *theatrum*

---

[1] Ten Brink, i. 312. Several
English versions of the *Debate be-
tween Body and Soul* are given by
Wright, *loc. cit.* 334. An English
*Debate and Stryfe betwene Somer
and Wynter* is in W. C. Hazlitt,
Early Popular Poetry, iii. 29.

[2] Cf. ch. xx.

[3] Ten Brink, i. 214, 309. *The
Owl and the Nightingale* (c. 1216–
72), was printed by J. Stevenson
(Roxburghe Club) ; *the Thrush and
the Nightingale* and *the Fox and
the Wolf*, by W. C. Hazlitt, *Early
Popular Poetry*, i. 50, 58. There
are also a *Debate of the Carpenter's
Tools* (Hazlitt, i. 79) and an English
version of a Latin *Disputacio inter
Mariam et Crucem* (R. Morris,
Legends of the Holy Rood, 131) ;
cf. Ten Brink, i. 259, 312. An A.-S.
version of the *Debate between Body
and Soul* is in the *Exeter Book*
(Grein, ii. 92).

[4] Ælred (†1166), *Speculum Cha-*

ritatis, ii. 23 (*P. L.* cxcv. 571) ' Videas aliquando hominem aperto ore
quasi intercluso halitu expirare,
non cantare, ac ridiculosa quadam
vocis interceptione quasi minitari
silentium ; nunc agones morientium,
vel extasim patientium imitari. Interim histrionicis quibusdam gestibus
totum corpus agitatur, torquentur
labia, rotant, ludunt humeri ; et ad
singulas quasque notas digitorum
flexus respondet. Et haec ridiculosa dissolutio vocatur religio ! . . .
Vulgus . . . miratur . . . sed lasci-
vas cantantium gesticulationes, me-
retricias vocum alternationes et
infractiones, non sine cachinno risu-
que intuetur, ut eos non ad orato-
rium sed ad theatrum, non ad oran-
dum, sed ad spectandum aestimes
convenisse.' Cf. *op. cit.* ii. 17 ' Cum
enim in tragediis vanisve carminibus
quisquam iniuriatus fingitur, vel
oppressus . . . si quis haec, vel cum
canuntur audiens, vel cernens si

G

is, however, a little suspicious, for an actual theatre in the twelfth century is hardly thinkable, and with a learned ecclesiastic one can never be sure that he is not drawing his illustrations rather from his knowledge of classical literature than from the real life around him. It is more conclusive, perhaps, when *fabliaux* or *contes* speak of minstrels as 'doing' *l'ivre*, or *le cat*, or *le sot*[1]; or when it appears from contemporary accounts that at a performance in Savoy the manners of England and Brittany were mimicked[2]. In Provence *contrafazedor* seems to have been a regular name for a minstrel[3]; and the facts that the minstrels wore masks 'with intent to deceive'[4], and were forbidden to wear ecclesiastical dresses[5], also point to something in the way of rudimentary impersonation.

As for the distribution of rôles, all that can be said, so far as the *débats* and *dits dialogués* go, is, that while some of them

recitentur . . . moveatur'; and Johannes de Janua, s.v. *persona* (cited Creizenach, i. 381) 'Item persona dicitur histrio, repraesentator comoediarum, qui diversis modis personat diversas repraesentando personas.' All these passages, like the ninth-century *responsio* of archbishop Leidradus referred to on p. 36, may be suspected of learning rather than actuality. As for the epitaph of the mime Vitalis (Riese, *Anth. Lat.* i. 2. 143; Baehrens, *P. L. M.* iii. 245), sometimes quoted in this connexion, it appears to be classical and not mediaeval at all; cf. Teuffel-Schwabe, §§ 8. 11; 32. 6. Probably this is also the case with the lines *De Mimo iam Sene* in Wright, *Anecdota Literaria*, 100, where again 'theatra' are mentioned.

[1] Cf. p. 71. The mention of a 'Disare that played the sheppart' at the English court in 1502 (Nicolas, *Privy Purse Expenses of Elizabeth of York*) is too late to be of importance here.

[2] Creizenach, i. 383, citing at second-hand from fourteenth-century accounts of a Savoy treasurer 'rappresentando i costumi delle compagnie inglesi e bretoni.'

[3] Creizenach, i. 380.

[4] Thomas de Cabham mentions the *horribiles larvae* of some minstrels. A. Lecoy de la Marche, *La Chaire française* (ed. 2, 1886), 444, quotes a sermon of Étienne de Bourbon in *MS. B. N. Lat.* 15970, f. 352 'ad similitudinem illorum ioculatorum qui ferunt facies depictas quae dicuntur artificia gallicè, cum quibus ludunt et homines deludunt.' Cf. Liudprand, iii. 15 (Pertz, iii. 310) 'histrionum mimorumve more incedere, qui, ut ad risum facile turbas illiciant, variis sese depingunt coloribus.' The *monstra larvarum*, however, of various ecclesiastical prohibitions I take to refer specifically to the Feast of Fools (cf. ch. xiii).

[5] Schack, *Gesch. der dram. Litt. und Kunst in Spanien*, i. 30, quotes a Carolingian capitulary, from Heineccius, *Capit.* lib. v. c. 388 'si quis ex scenicis vestem sacerdotalem aut monasticam vel mulieris religiosae vel qualicunque ecclesiastico statu similem indutus fuerit, corporali poena subsistat et exilio tradatur.' This prohibition is as old as the *Codex Theodosianus*; cf. p. 14.

may conceivably have been represented by more than one performer, none of them need necessarily have been so, and some of them certainly were not. There is generally a narrative introduction and often a sprinkling of narrative interspersed amongst the dialogue. These parts may have been pronounced by an *auctor* or by one of the interlocutors acting as *auctor*, and some such device must have been occasionally necessitated in the religious drama. But there is really no difficulty in supposing the whole of these pieces to have been recited by a single minstrel with appropriate changes of gesture and intonation, and in *The Harrowing of Hell*, which begins ' A strif will I tellen of,' this was clearly the case. The evidences of impersonation given above are of course quite consistent with such an arrangement ; or, for the matter of that, with sheer monologue. The minstrel who recited Rutebeuf's *Dit de l'Erberie* may readily be supposed to have got himself up in the character of a quack [1].

But the possibilities of secular mediaeval drama are not quite exhausted by the *débats* and *dits dialogués*. For after all, the written literature which the minstrels have left us belongs almost entirely to those higher *strata* of their complex fraternity which derived from the thoroughly undramatic Teutonic *scôp*. But if mediaeval farce there were, it would not be here that we should look for it. It would belong to the inheritance, not of the *scôp*, but of the *mimus*. The Roman *mimus* was essentially a player of farces ; that and little else. It is of course open to any one to suppose that the *mimus* went down in the seventh century playing farces, and that his like appeared in the fifteenth century playing farces, and that not a farce was played between. But is it not more probable on the whole that, while occupying himself largely with other matters, he preserved at least the rudiments of the art of acting, and that when the appointed time came, the despised and forgotten farce, under the stimulus of new conditions, blossomed forth once more as a vital and effective form of literature? In the absence of data we are reduced to conjecture. But the mere absence of data itself does not render

---

[1] *Œuvres* de Rutebeuf (ed. Kress-   Julleville, *Les Com.* 24 ; *Rép. Com.*
ner), 115 ; cf. *Romania*, xvi. 496 ;   407.

the conjecture untenable. For if such rudimentary, or, if you please, degenerate farces as I have in mind, ever existed in the Middle Ages, the chances were all against their literary survival. They were assuredly very brief, very crude, often improvised, and rarely, if ever, written down. They belonged to an order of minstrels far below that which made literature[1]. And one little bit of evidence which has not yet been brought forward seems to point to the existence of something in the way of a secular as well as a religious mediaeval drama. In the well-known Wyclifite sermon against miracle plays, an imaginary opponent of the preacher's argument is made to say that after all it is ' lesse yvels that thei have thyre recreaceon by pleyinge of myraclis than bi pleyinge of other japis'; and again that ' to pley in rebaudye ' is worse than ' to pley in myriclis[2].' Now, there is of course no necessary dramatic connotation either in the word 'pley' or in the word ' japis,' which, like ' bourde' or 'gab' is frequently used of any kind of rowdy merriment, or of the lower types of minstrelsy in general[3]. But on the other hand the whole tone of the passage seems to draw a very close parallel between the 'japis' and the undeniably dramatic ' myriclis,' and to imply something in the former a little beyond the mere recitation, even with the help of impersonation, of a solitary mime.

Such rude farces or 'japis' as we are considering, if they

[1] Creizenach, i. 386, further points out that a stage was not indispensable to the Latin *mimus*, who habitually played before the curtain and probably with very little setting; that the favourite situations of fifteenth-century French farce closely resemble those of the mimes; and that the use of marionettes is a proof of some knowledge of dramatic methods amongst the minstrels.

[2] On this treatise, cf. ch. xx.

[3] A ' japer' is often an idle talker, like a 'jangler' which is clearly sometimes confused with a 'jongleur'; cf. Chaucer, *Parson's Tale*, 89 ' He is a japere and a gabber and no verray repentant that eftsoone dooth thing for which hym oghte repente.' Langland uses the term in a more technical sense. *Activa Vita* in *Piers Plowman*, xvi. 207, is no minstrel, because ' Ich can not . . . japen ne jogelen.' No doubt a ' jape' would include a *fabliau*. It is equivalent etymologically to 'gab,' and Bédier, 33, points out that the *jougleurs* use *gabet*, as well as *bourde, trufe*, and *risée* for a *fabliau.*—The use of ' pleye' as 'jest' may be illustrated by Chaucer, *Pardoner's Tale* (*C. T.* 12712) ' My wit is greet, though that I bourde and pleye.'— The ' japis ' of the *Tretise* are probably the ' knakkes ' of the passage on ' japeris ' in *Parson's Tale*, 651 ' right so conforten the vileyns wordes and knakkes of japeris hem that travaillen in the service of the devel.'

formed part of the travelling equipment of the humbler mimes, could only get into literature by an accident; in the event, that is to say, of some minstrel of a higher class taking it into his head to experiment in the form or to adapt it to the purposes of his own art. And this is precisely what appears to have happened. A very natural use of the farce would be in the *parade* or preliminary patter, merely about himself and his proficiency, which at all times has served the itinerant entertainer as a means whereby to attract his audiences. And just as the very similar *boniment* or patter of the mountebank charlatan at a fair became the model for Rutebeuf's *Dit de l'Erberie*, so the *parade* may be traced as the underlying motive of other *dits* or *fabliaux*. The *Deus Bordeors Ribauz* is itself little other than a glorified *parade*, and another, very slightly disguised, may be found in the discomfiture of the king by the characteristic repartees of the wandering minstrel in *Le Roi d'Angleterre et le Jougleur d'Ely*[1]. The *parade*, also, seems to be the origin of a certain familiar type of dramatic prologue in which the author or the presenters of a play appear in their own persons. The earliest example of this is perhaps that enigmatic *Terentius et Delusor* piece which some have thought to point to a representation of Terence somewhere in the dark ages between the seventh and the eleventh century[2]. And there is a later one in the *Jeu du Pèlerin* which was written about 1288 to precede Adan de la Hale's *Jeu de Robin et Marion*.

The renascence of farce in the fifteenth century will call for consideration in a later chapter. It is possible that, as is here suggested, that renascence was but the coming to light again of an earth-bourne of dramatic tradition that had

---

[1] Montaiglon-Raynaud, ii. 243. Cf. *Hist. Litt.* xxiii. 103; Jusserand, *Lit. Hist.* i. 442. A shorter prose form of the story is found in *La Riote du Monde* (ed. Fr. Michel, 1834), a popular *facétie* of which both French and Anglo-Norman versions exist; cf. Paris, *Litt. fr.* 153. And a Latin form, *De Mimo et Rege Francorum* is in Wright, *Latin Stories*, No. 137. The point consists in the quibbling replies with which the *jougleur* meets the king's questions. Thus, in *La Riote du Monde* : 'Dont ies tu?—Je suis de no vile.—U est te vile?—Entor le moustier.—U est li moustiers?— En l'atre.—U est li atres?—Sor terre.—U siet cele terre? — Sor l'iaue.—Comment apiel-on l'iaue? —On ne l'apiele nient; ele vient bien sans apieler.'

[2] Cf. Appendix V.

worked its way beneath the ground ever since the theatres of the Empire fell. In any case, rare documents of earlier date survive to show that it was at least no absolutely sudden and unprecedented thing. The *jeux* of Adan de la Hale, indeed, are somewhat irrelevant here. They were not farces, and will fall to be dealt with in the discussion of the popular *fêtes* from which they derive their origin[1]. But the French farce of *Le Garçon et l'Aveugle*, ascribed to the second half of the thirteenth century, is over a hundred years older than any of its extant successors[2]. And even more interesting to us, because it is of English *provenance* and in the English tongue, is a fragment found in an early fourteenth-century manuscript of a dramatic version of the popular mediaeval tale of Dame Siriz[3]. This bears the heading *Hic incipit interludium de Clerico et Puella*. But the significance of this fateful word *interludium* must be left for study at a later period, when the history of the secular drama is resumed from the point at which it must now be dropped.

[1] Cf. ch. viii.

[2] Ed. P. Meyer, in *Jahrbuch für romanische und englische Litera-tur*, vi. 163. The piece was pro-bably written in Flanders, between 1266 and 1290. Cf. Creizenach, i. 398.

[3] See Appendix U. References for the earlier non-dramatic versions in Latin, French, and English of the story are given by Jusserand, *Lit. Hist.* i. 447. A Cornish dra-matic fragment of the fourteenth century is printed in the *Athenæum* for Dec. 1, 1877, and *Revue celtique*, iv. 259; cf. Creizenach, i. 401.

BOOK II

FOLK DRAMA

Stultorum infinitus est numerus.
ECCLESIASTES.

CHAPTER V

THE RELIGION OF THE FOLK

[*Bibliographical Note.*—The conversion of heathen England is described in the *Ecclesiastical History* of Bede (C. Plummer, *Baedae Opera Historica*, 1896). Stress is laid on the imperfect character of the process by L. Knappert, *Le Christianisme et le Paganisme dans l'Histoire ecclésiastique de Bède le Vénérable* (in *Revue de l'Histoire des Religions*, 1897, vol. xxxv). A similar study for Gaul is E. Vacandard, *L'Idolatrie dans la Gaule* (in *Revue des Questions historiques*, 1899, vol. lxv). Witness is borne to the continued presence of pre-Christian elements in the folk-civilization of western Europe both by the general results of folk-lore research and by the ecclesiastical documents of the early Middle Ages. Of these the most important in this respect are—(1) the *Decrees* of Councils, collected generally in P. Labbe and G. Cossart, *Sacrosancta Concilia* (1671-2), and J. D. Mansi, *Sacrorum Conciliorum nova et amplissima Collectio* (1759-98), and for England in particular in D. Wilkins, *Concilia Magnae Britanniae et Hiberniae* (1737) and A. W. Haddan and W. Stubbs, *Councils and Ecclesiastical Documents relating to Great Britain and Ireland* (1869-78). An interesting series of extracts is given by G. Gröber, *Zur Volkskunde aus Concilbeschlüssen und Capitularien* (1894) :—(2) the *Penitentials*, or catalogues of sins and their penalties drawn up for the guidance of confessors. The most important English example is the *Penitential of Theodore* (668-90), on which the *Penitentials of Bede* and *of Egbert* are based. Authentic texts are given by Haddan and Stubbs, vol. iii, and, with others of continental origin, in F. W. H. Wasserschleben, *Die Bussordnungen der abendländischen Kirche* (1851), and H. J. Schmitz, *Die Bussbücher und die Bussdisciplin der Kirche* (1883). The most interesting for its heathen survivals is the eleventh-century *Collectio Decretorum* of Burchardus of Worms (Migne, *P. L.* cxl, extracts in J. Grimm, *Teutonic Mythology*, iv. 1740) :—(3) *Homilies* or *Sermons*, such as the *Sermo* ascribed to the seventh-century St. Eligius (*P. L.* lxxxvii. 524, transl. Grimm, iv. 1737), and the eighth-century Frankish pseudo-Augustinian *Homilia de Sacrilegiis* (ed. C. P. Caspari, 1886):—(4) the *Vitae* of the apostles of the West, St. Boniface, St. Columban, St. Gall, and others. A critical edition of these is looked for from M. Knappert. The *Epistolae* of Boniface are in *P. L.* lxxxix. 593 :—(5) *Miscellaneous Documents*, including the sixth-century *De correctione Rusticorum* of Bishop Martin of Braga in Spain (ed. C. P. Caspari, 1883) and the so-called *Indiculus Superstitionum et Paganiarum* (ed. H. A. Saupe, 1891), a list of heathen customs probably drawn up in eighth-century Saxony.—The view of primitive religion taken in this book is largely, although not altogether in detail, that of J. G. Frazer, *The Golden Bough* (1890, 2nd ed. 1900), which itself owes much to E. B. Tylor, *Primitive Culture* (1871) ; W. Robertson Smith, *Religion of the Semites* (2nd ed. 1894) ; W. Mannhardt, *Der Baumkultus der Germanen* (1875) ; *Antike Wald- und Feldkulte* (1875-7). A more systematic work on similar lines is F. B. Jevons, *An Introduction to the History of Religion* (1896): and amongst many others may be mentioned A. Lang, *Myth, Ritual, and Religion* (1887, 2nd ed. 1899), the conclusions of which are somewhat modified in the same writer's *The Making of Religion* (1898); Grant Allen, *The Evolution of the Idea of God* (1897); E. S. Hartland, *The Legend of Perseus* (1894–6); J. Rhys, *The Origin and Growth of Religion as illustrated by Celtic Heathendom* (1888). The last of these deals especially with Keltic *data*, which may be further studied in H. D'Arbois de Jubainville, *Le Cycle mythologique irlandais et la Mythologie celtique* (1884), together with the chapter on *La Religion* in the same writer's *La Civilisation des Celtes et celle de l'Épopée homérique* (1899) and A. Bertrand, *La Religion des Gaulois* (1897). Teutonic religion has been more completely investigated. Recent works of authority are E. H. Meyer, *Germanische Mythologie* (1891); W. Golther, *Handbuch der germanischen Mythologie* (1895); and the article by E. Mogk on *Mythologie* in H. Paul's *Grundriss der germanischen Philologie*, vol. iii (2nd ed. 1897). The collection of material in J. Grimm's *Teutonic Mythology* (transl. J. S. Stallybrass, 1880–8) is still of the greatest value. The general facts of early German civilization are given by F. B. Gummere, *Germanic Origins* (1892), and for the Aryan-speaking peoples in general by O. Schräder, *Prehistoric Antiquities of the Aryan Peoples* (transl. F. B. Jevons, 1890), and *Reallexicon der indo-germanischen Altertumskunde* (1901). In dealing with the primitive calendar I have mainly, but not wholly, followed the valuable researches of A. Tille, *Deutsche Weihnacht* (1893) and *Yule and Christmas* (1899), a scholar the loss of whom to this country is one of the lamentable results of the recent war.]

MINSTRELSY was an institution of the folk, no less than of the court and the *bourgeoisie*. At many a village festival, one may be sure, the taberers and buffoons played their conspicuous part, ravishing the souls of Dorcas and Mopsa with merry and doleful ballads, and tumbling through their amazing programme of monkey tricks before the ring of wide-mouthed rustics on the green. Yet the soul and centre of such revels always lay, not in these alien professional *spectacula*, but in other entertainments, home-grown and racy of the soil, wherein the peasants shared, not as onlookers only, but as performers, even as their fathers and mothers, from immemorial antiquity, had done before them. A full consideration of the village *ludi* is important to the scheme of the present book for more than one reason. They shared with the *ludi* of the minstrels the hostility of the Church. They bear witness, at point after point, to the deep-lying dramatic instincts of the folk. And their substantial contribution to mediaeval and Renaissance drama and dramatic *spectacle* is greater than has been fully recognized.

Historically, the *ludi* of the folk come into prominence with the attacks made upon them by the reforming ecclesiastics of the thirteenth century and in particular by Robert Grosseteste, bishop of Lincoln [1]. Between 1236 and 1244 Grosseteste issued a series of disciplinary pronouncements, in which he condemned many customs prevalent in his diocese. Amongst these are included miracle plays, 'scotales' or drinking-bouts, 'ram-raisings' and other contests of athletic prowess, together with ceremonies known respectively as the *festum stultorum* and the *Inductio Maii sive Autumni* [2]. Very similar are the prohibitions contained in the *Constitutions* (1240) of Walter de Chanteloup, bishop of Worcester [3]. These particularly specify the *ludus de Rege et Regina*, a term which may be taken as generally applicable to the typical English folk-festival, of which the *Inductio Maii sive Autumni*, the 'May-game' and 'mell-supper,' mentioned by Grosseteste, are varieties [4]. Both this *ludus*, in its various forms, and the

---

[1] Stephens-Hunt, ii. 301; F. S. Stevenson, *Robert Grosseteste*, 126. The disciplinary attack seems to have begun with Grosseteste's predecessor, Hugh de Wells, in 1230 (Wilkins, i. 627), but he, like Roger Weseham, bishop of Coventry and Lichfield, in 1252 (*Annales Monastici*, R. S. i. 296), merely condemns *ludi*, a term which may mean folk-festivals or minstrelsy, or both. A similar ambiguity attaches to the obligation of the anchoresses of Tarrant Keyneston not to look on at a *ludus* (*pleouwe*) in the church-yard (*Ancren Riwle*, C. S. 318).

[2] In 1236 Grosseteste wrote to his archdeacons forbidding 'arietum super ligna et rotas elevationes, caeterosque ludos consimiles, in quo decertatur pro bravio; cum huius-modi ludorum tam actores quam spectatores, sicut evidenter demon-strat Isidorus, immolant daemoni-bus, ... et cum etiam huiusmodi ludi frequenter dant occasiones irae, odii, pugnae, et homicidii.' His *Constitutiones* of 1238 say 'Praecipimus etiam ut in singulis ecclesiis denun-cietur solenniter ne quisquam levet arietes super rotas, vel alios ludos statuat, in quibus decertatur pro bravio: nec huiusmodi ludis quis-quam intersit, &c.' About 1244 he

wrote again to the archdeacons: 'Faciunt etiam, ut audivimus, clerici ludos quos vocant miracula: et alios ludos quos vocant Inductionem Maii sive Autumni; et laici scotales ... miracula etiam et ludos supra nominatos et scotales, quod est in vestra potestate facili, omnino exter-minetis' (Luard, *Letters of Robert Grosseteste* (R. S.) *Epp.* xxii, lii, cvii, pp. 74, 162, 317). For his condem-nations of the Feast of Fools cf. ch. xiv.

[3] *Const. Walt. de Cantilupo* (Wilkins, i. 673) 'prohibemus cleri-cis ... nec sustineat ludos fieri de Rege et Regina, nec arietas levari, nec palaestras publicas fieri, nec gildales inhonestas.' The clergy must also abstain and dissuade the laity from 'compotationibus quae vocantur scottales' (Wilkins, i. 672). On 'ram-raisings,' &c., cf. ch. vii; on 'gildales' and 'scotales' ch. viii.

[4] Surely the reference is to the mock kings and queens of the village festivals, and not, as Guy, 521; Jusserand, *Litt. Hist.* i. 444, suggest, to the question-and-answer game of *Le Roi qui ne ment* described in Jean de Condé's *Sentier Batu* (Montaiglon-Raynaud, iii. 248), although this is called playing 'as

less strictly popular *festum stultorum*, will find ample illustration in the sequel. Walter de Chanteloup also lays stress
upon an aggravation of the *ludi inhonesti* by the performance of them in churchyards and other holy places, and on
Sundays or the vigils and days of saints [1].

The decrees of the two bishops already cited do not stand
alone. About 1250 the University of Oxford found it necessary
to forbid the routs of masked and garlanded students in the
churches and open places of the city [2]. These appear to have
been held in connexion with the feasts of the ' nations ' into
which a mediaeval university was divided. Articles of visitation
drawn up in connexion with the provisions of Oxford in 1253
made inquiry as to several of the obnoxious *ludi* and as to
the measures adopted to check them throughout the country [3].
Prohibitions are upon record by the synod of Exeter in 1287 [4],
and during the next century by the synod of York in 1367 [5],
and by William of Wykeham, bishop of Winchester, in
1384 [6]; while the denunciations of the rulers of the church

rois et as reines' in Adan de la
Hale's *Robin et Marion* (ed. Monmerqué-Michel, 121) and elsewhere
(cf. Guy, 222), and possibly grew
out of the festival custom. Yet
another game of *King and Queen*,
of the practical joke order, is described as played at Golspie by
Nicholson, 119.

[1] Wilkins, i. 666.

[2] Anstey, *Munimenta Academica*
(R. S.), i. 18 'ne quis choreas cum
larvis seu strepitu aliquo in ecclesiis
vel plateis ducat, vel sertatus, vel
coronatus corona ex foliis arborum,
vel florum vel aliunde composita
alicubi incedat ... prohibemus.'

[3] *Inquisitiones ... de vita et con-
versatione clericorum et laicorum*
in *Annales de Burton* (*Ann.Monast.*
R. S. i. 307) 'an aliqui laici mercata,
vel ludos, seu placita peculiaria fieri
faciant in locis sacris, et an haec
fuerint prohibita ex parte episcopi
... An aliqui laici elevaverint
arietes, vel fieri faciant schothales,
vel decertaverint de praeeundo cum
vexillis in visitatione matricis ecclesiae.'

[4] Wilkins, ii. 129 'c. 13 ... Ne
quisquam luctas, choreas, vel alios
ludos inhonestos in coemeteriis
exercere praesumat; praecipue in
vigiliis et festis sanctorum, cum
huiusmodi ludos theatrales et ludibriorum spectacula introductos
per quos ecclesiarum coinquinatur
honestas, sacri ordines detestan-
tur.'

[5] Wilkins, iii. 68 'c. 2 ... nec
in ipsis [locis sacris] fiant lucta-
tiones, sagittationes, vel ludi.' A
special caution is given against ludi
'in sanctorum vigiliis' and 'in exe-
quiis defunctorum.'

[6] T. F. Kirby, *Wykeham's Register* (Hampshire Record Soc.), ii.
410, forbids ' ad pilas ludere, iacta-
ciones lapidum facere ... coreas
facere dissolutas, et interdum canere
cantilenas, ludibriorum spectacula
facere, saltaciones et alios ludos
inhonestos frequentare, ac multas
alias insolencias perpetrare, ex quibus cimeterii huiusmodi execracio
seu pollucio frequencius verisimiliter
formidetur.'

find an unofficial echo in that handbook of ecclesiastical morality, Robert Mannyng of Brunne's *Handlyng Synne*[1]. There is, however, reason to suppose that the attitude thus taken up hardly represents that of the average ecclesiastical authority, still less that of the average parish priest, towards the *ludi* in question. The condemnatory decrees should probably be looked upon as the individual pronouncements of men of austere or reforming temper against customs which the laxer discipline of their fellows failed to touch ; perhaps it should rather be said, which the wiser discipline of their fellows found it better to regulate than to ban. At any rate there is evidence to show that the village *ludi*, as distinct from the *spectacula* of the minstrels, were accepted, and even to some extent directed, by the Church. They became part of the parochial organization, and were conducted through the parochial machinery. Doubtless this was the course of practical wisdom. But the moralist would find it difficult to deny that Robert Grosseteste and Walter de Chanteloup had, after all, some reason on their side. On the one hand they could point to the ethical lapses of which the *ludi* were undoubtedly the cause—the drunkenness, the quarrels, the wantonings, by which they were disgraced[2]. And on the other they could—if they

---

[1] *Handlyng Synne* (ed. Furnivall), p. 148, l. 4684 :
' Daunçes, karols, somour games,
   Of many swych come many
      shames.'
This poem is a free adaptation (†1303) of the thirteenth-century Anglo-Norman *Manuel de Péché*, which is probably by William de Wadington, but has been ascribed to Bishop Grosseteste himself. The corresponding lines in this are
' Muses et tieles musardries,
   Trippes, dances, et teles folies.'
Cf. also *Handlyng Synne*, p. 278, l. 8989 :
' Karolles, wrastlynges, or somour
      games,
   Who so euer haunteþ any swyche
      shames,
   Yy cherche, oþer yn cherche-
      ȝerde,
   Of sacrylage he may be a ferde ;

Or entyrludës, or syngynge,
Or tabure bete, or oþer pypynge,
Alle swychë þyng forbodyn es,
Whyle þe prest stondeþ at
   messe ' ;
where the *Manuel de Péché* has
' Karoles ne lutes nul deit fere,
   En seint eglise qe me veut
      crere ;
Car en çymiter neis karoler
Est outrage grant, ou luter :
Souent lur est mes auenu
Qe la fet tel maner de iu ;
Qe grant peche est, desturber
Le prestre quant deit celebrer.'
[2] The Puritan Fetherston, in his *Dialogue agaynst light, lewde, and lascivious Dancing* (1583), sign. D. 7, says that he has ' hearde of tenne maidens which went to set May, and nine of them came home with childe.' Stubbes, i. 149, has a very similar observation. Cf. the adventures of

were historically minded—recall the origin of the objectionable
rites in some of those obscure survivals of heathenism in the
rustic blood, which half a dozen centuries of Christianity had
failed to purge[1]. For if the comparative study of religions
proves anything it is, that the traditional beliefs and customs
of the mediaeval or modern peasant are in nine cases out of
ten but the *detritus* of heathen mythology and heathen worship,
enduring with but little external change in the shadow of an
hostile creed. This is notably true of the village festivals
and their *ludi*. Their full significance only appears when they
are regarded as fragments of forgotten cults, the naïve cults
addressed by a primitive folk to the beneficent deities of field
and wood and river, or the shadowy populace of its own
dreams. Not that when even the mediaeval peasant set up
his Maypole at the approach of summer or drove his cattle
through the bonfire on Midsummer eve, the real character of
his act was at all explicit in his consciousness. To him, as to
his descendant of to-day, the festival was at once a practice
sanctioned by tradition and the rare amusement of a strenuous
life : it was not, save perhaps in some unplumbed recesses of
his being, anything more definitely sacred. At most it was
held to be 'for luck,' and in some vague general way, to the
interest of a fruitful year in field and fold. The scientific
anthropologist, however, from his very different point of view,
cannot regard the conversion to Christianity as a complete
solution of continuity in the spiritual and social life of western
Europe. This conversion, indeed, was clearly a much slower
and·more incomplete process than the ecclesiastical chroniclers
quite plainly state. It was so even on the shores of the
Mediterranean. But there the triumph of Christianity began
from below. Long before the edict of Milan, the new religion,
in spite of persecutions, had got its firm hold upon the masses
of the great cities of the Empire. And when, less than a

Dr. Fitzpiers and Suke Damson on
Midsummer Eve in Thomas Hardy's
novel, *The Woodlanders*, ch. xx.

[1] Grosseteste, in 1236, quotes
'Isidorus' as to the pagan origin
of '*ludi, in quo decertatur de bravio.*'
The reference is to Isidore of Seville
(560–636), *Etymologiarum*, xviii. 27,
De ludis circensibus (P. L. lxxxii.
653). This, of course, refers directly
to the religious associations of
Roman rather than Celto-Teutonic
ludi.

century later, Theodosius made the public profession of any
other faith a crime, he was but formally acknowledging
a *chose jugée*.   But even in these lands of the first ardour the
old beliefs and, above all, the old rituals died hard.   Lingering
unacknowledged in the country, the pagan, districts, they
passed silently into the dim realm of folk-lore.   How could
this but be more so when Christianity came with the missionaries of Rome or of Iona to the peoples of the West ?   For
with them conversion was hardly a spontaneous, an individual
thing.   As a rule, the baptism of the king was the starting-
point and motive for that of his followers : and the bulk of
the people adopted wonderingly an alien cult in an alien
tongue imposed upon them by the will of their rulers.
Such a Christianity could at best be only nominal.   Ancient
beliefs are not so easily surrendered : nor are habits and
instincts, deep-rooted in the lives of a folk, thus lightly laid
down for ever, at the word of a king.   The churches of the
West had, therefore, to dispose somehow of a vast body of
practical heathenism surviving in all essentials beneath a new
faith which was but skin-deep.   The conflict which followed
is faintly adumbrated in the pages of Bede : something more
may be guessed of its fortunes by a comparison of the
customs and superstitions recorded in early documents of
church discipline with those which, after all, the peasantry
long retained, or even now retain.

Two letters of Gregory the Great, written at the time of the
mission of St. Augustine, are a key to the methods adopted
by the apostles of the West.   In June 601, writing to Ethelbert
of Kent by the hands of abbot Mellitus, Gregory bade the
new convert show zeal in suppressing the worship of idols, and
throwing down their fanes[1].   Having written thus, the pope
changed his mind.   Before Mellitus could reach England, he
received a letter instructing him to expound to Augustine
a new policy.   ' Do not, after all,' wrote Gregory, ' pull down
the fanes.   Destroy the idols ; purify the buildings with holy
water ; set relics there ; and let them become temples of the
true God.   So the people will have no need to change their

---

[1] Haddan-Stubbs, iii. 30 ' idolorum cultus insequere, fanorum aedificia
everate.'

places of concourse, and where of old they were wont to sacrifice cattle to demons, thither let them continue to resort on the day of the saint to whom the church is dedicated, and slay their beasts no longer as a sacrifice, but for a social meal in honour of Him whom they now worship [1].' There can be little doubt that the conversion of England proceeded in the main on the lines thus laid down by Gregory. Tradition has it that the church of Saint Pancras outside the walls of Canterbury stands on the site of a fane at which Ethelbert himself once worshipped [2]; and that in London St. Paul's replaced a temple and grove of Diana, by whom the equivalent Teutonic wood-goddess, Freyja, is doubtless intended [3]. Gregory's directions were, perhaps, not always carried out quite so literally as this. When, for instance, the priest Coifi, on horseback and sword in hand, led the onslaught against the gods of Northumbria, he bade his followers set fire to the fane and to all the hedges that girt it round [4]. On the other hand, Reduald, king of East Anglia, must have kept his fane standing, and indeed he carried the policy of amalgamation

[1] Bede, *Hist. Eccl.* i. 30; Haddan-Stubbs, iii. 37 ' Dicite [Augustino], quid diu mecum de causa Anglorum cogitans tractavi : videlicet quia fana idolorum destrui in eadem gente minime debeant ; sed ipsa quae in illis sunt idola destruantur, aqua benedicta fiat, in eisdem fanis aspergatur, altaria construantur, reliquiae ponantur : quia si fana eadem bene constructa sunt, necesse est ut a cultu daemonum in obsequium veri Dei debeant commutari, ut dum gens ipsa eadem fana sua non videt destrui, de corde errorem deponat, et Deum verum cognoscens ac adorans, ad loca, quae consuevit, familiarius concurrat. Et quia boves solent in sacrificio daemonum multos occidere, debet eis etiam hac de re aliqua solemnitas immutari : ut die dedicationis, vel natalitii sanctorum martyrum quorum illic reliquiae ponuntur, tabernacula sibi circa easdem ecclesias quae ex fanis commutatae sunt, de ramis arborum faciant, et religiosis conviviis sollemnitatem celebrent ; nec diabolo iam animalia immolent, sed ad laudem Dei in esum suum animalia occidant, et donatori omnium de satietate sua gratias referant : ut dum eis aliqua exterius gaudia reservantur, ad interiora gaudia consentire facilius valeant. Nam duris mentibus simul omnia abscindere impossibile esse non dubium est, quia et is qui summum locum ascendere nititur gradibus vel passibus non autem saltibus elevatur '. . .

[2] Stanley, *Memorials of Canterbury*, 37.

[3] H. B. Wheatley, *London, Past and Present*, iii. 39 ; Donne, *Poems* (Muses' Library), ii. 23.

[4] Bede, ii. 13 ' iussit sociis destruere ac succendere fanum cum omnibus septis suis.' In Essex in a time of plague and famine (664), Sigheri and his people ' coeperunt fana, quae derelicta sunt, restaurare, et adorare simulacra.' Bp. Jaruman induced them to reopen the churches, ' relictis sive destructis fanis arisque ' (Bede, iii. 30).

further than its author intended, for he wavered faint-heartedly between the old religion and the new, and maintained in one building an *altare* for Christian worship and an *arula* for sacrifice to demons[1]. Speaking generally, it would seem to have been the endeavour of the Christian missionaries to effect the change of creed with as little dislocation of popular sentiment as possible. If they could extirpate the essentials, or what they considered as the essentials, of heathenism, they were willing enough to leave the accidentals to be worn away by the slow process of time. They did not, probably, quite realize how long it would take. And what happened in England, happened also, no doubt, on the continent, save perhaps in such districts as Saxony, where Christianity was introduced *vi et armis*, and therefore in a more wholesale, if not in the end a more effectual fashion[2].

The measure of surviving heathenism under Christianity must have varied considerably from district to district. Much would depend on the natural temper of the converts, on the tact of the clergy and on the influence they were able to secure. Roughly speaking, the old worships left their trace upon the new society in two ways. Certain central practices, the deliberate invocation of the discarded gods, the deliberate acknowledgement of their divinity by sacrifice, were bound to be altogether proscribed[3]. And these, if they did not precisely

[1] Bede, ii. 15. So too in eighth-century Germany there were priests who were equally ready to sacrifice to Wuotan and to administer the sacrament of baptism (Gummere, 342). See also Grimm, i. 7, and the letter of Gregory the Great to queen Brunichildis in *M. G. H. Epist.* ii. 1. 7 'pervenit ad nos, quod multi Christianorum et ad ecclesias occurrant, et a culturis daemonum non abscedant.'

[2] Willibald (*Gesch.-Schreiber der deutschen Vorzeit*, 27) relates that in Germany, when Boniface felled the sacred oak of Thor (robur Iovis) he built the wood into a church.

[3] A Saxon *formula abrenuntiationis* of the ninth century (Müllenhoff-Scherer, *Denkmäler deutscher Poesie und Prosa aus dem* 8.–12. *Jahrhundert*, 1892, No. li) specifically renounces 'Thuner ende Uuôden ende Saxnôte ende allum thêm unholdum thê hira genôtas sint.' Anglo-Saxon laws and council decrees contain frequent references to sacrifices and other lingering remnants of heathenism. Cf. *Councils of Pincanhale and Cealcythe* (787), c. 19 (Haddan-Stubbs, iii. 458) 'si quid ex ritu paganorum remansit, avellatur, contemnatur, abiiciatur.' *Council of Gratlea* (928), c. 3 (Wilkins, i. 205) 'diximus. . . de sacrificiis barbaris. . . si quis aliquem occiderit . . . ut vitam suam perdat.' *Council of London* (1075) (Wilkins, i. 363) 'ne offa mortuorum animalium, quasi

vanish, at least went underground, coming to light only as shameful secrets of the confessional[1] or the witch-trial[2], or when the dominant faith received a rude shock in times of especial distress, famine or pestilence[3]. Others again were absorbed into the scheme of Christianity itself. Many of the protective functions, for instance, of the old pantheon were taken over bodily by the Virgin Mary, by St. John, St. Michael, St. Martin, St. Nicholas, and other personages of the new dispensation[4]. And in particular, as we have seen shadowed forth in Pope Gregory's policy, the festal customs of heathenism, purified so far as might be, received a generous amount of toleration. The chief thing required was that the outward and visible signs of the connexion with the hostile religion

pro vitanda animalium peste, alicubi suspendantur; nec sortes, vel aruspicia, seu divinationes, vel aliqua huiusmodi opera diaboli ab aliquo exerceantur.' Also *Leges* of Wihtred of Kent (696), c. 12 (Haddan-Stubbs, iii. 235), and other A.-S. laws quoted by Kemble, i. 523.

[1] *Penitential of Theodore* (Haddan-Stubbs, iii. 189), i. 15, *de Cultura Idolorum*; *Penitential of Egbert* (H.-S. iii. 424), 8, *de Auguriis vel Divinationibus.*

[2] Pearson, ii. 1 (Essay on *Woman as Witch*); cf. A.-S. spells in Kemble, i. 528, and Cockayne, *Leechdoms* (R. S.), iii. 35, 55. Early and mediaeval Christianity did not deny the existence of the heathen gods, but treated them as evil spirits, demons.

[3] An Essex case of 664 has just been quoted. Kemble, i. 358, gives two later ones from the *Chronicle of Lanercost*. In 1268 'cum hoc anno in Laodonia pestis grassaretur in pecudes armenti, quam vocant usitate Lungessouth, quidam bestiales, habitu claustrales non animo, docebant idiotas patriae ignem confrictione de lignis educere et simulachrum Priapi statuere, et per haec bestiis succurrere.' In 1282 'sacerdos parochialis, nomine Johannes, Priapi prophana parans, congregatis ex villa puellulis, cogebat ejs,

choreis factis, Libero patri circuire.' By Priapus-Liber is probably meant Freyr, the only Teutonic god known to have had Priapic characteristics (Adam of Bremen, *Gesta Hammaburgensis Eccles. Pontif.* iv. 26 in *M. G. H. Script.* vii. 267).

[4] Grimm, i. 5, 11, 64, 174; iii. xxxiv–xlv; Keary, 90; Pearson, ii. 16, 32, 42, 243, 285, 350. The Virgin Mary succeeds to the place of the old Teutonic goddess of fertility, Freyja, Nerthus. So elsewhere does St. Walpurg. The toasts or *minni* drunk to Odin and Freyja are transferred to St. John and St. Gertrude. The travels of Odin and Loki become the travels of Christ and St. Peter. Many examples of the adaptation of pre-existing customs to Christianity will be found in the course of this book. A capitulary of Karlmann, drawn up in 742 after the synod of Ratisbon held by Boniface in Germany, speaks of 'hostias immolatitias, quas stulti homines iuxta ecclesias ritu pagano faciunt sub nomine sanctorum martyrum vel confessorum' (Boretius, *Capitularia Reg. Franc.* i. 24 in *M. G. H.*; Mansi, xii. 367). At Kirkcudbright in the twelfth century bulls were killed 'as an alms and oblation to St. Cuthbert (*F. L.* x. 353).

should be abandoned. Nor was this such a difficult matter. Cult, the sum of what man feels it obligatory upon him to do in virtue of his relation to the unseen powers, is notoriously a more enduring thing than belief, the speculative, or mythology, the imaginative statement of those relations. And it was of the customs themselves that the people were tenacious, not of the meaning, so far as there was still a meaning, attached to them, or of the names which their priests had been wont to invoke. Leave them but their familiar revels, and the ritual so indissolubly bound up with their hopes of fertility for their flocks and crops, they would not stick upon the explicit consciousness that they drank or danced in the might of Eostre or of Freyr. And in time, as the Christian interpretation of life became an everyday thing, it passed out of sight that the customs had been ritual at all. At the most a general sense of their 'lucky' influence survived. But to stop doing them ; that was not likely to suggest itself to the rustic mind. And so the church and the open space around the church continued to be, what the temple and the temple precinct had been, the centre, both secular and religious, of the village life. From the Christian point of view, the arrangement had its obvious advantages. It had also this disadvantage, that so far as obnoxious elements still clung to the festivals, so far as the darker practices of heathenism still lingered, it was precisely the most sacred spot that they defiled. Were incantations and spells still muttered secretly for the good will of the deposed divinities ? it was the churchyard that was sure to be selected as the nocturnal scene of the unhallowed ceremony. Were the clergy unable to cleanse the yearly wake of wanton dance and song ? it was the church itself, by Gregory's own decree, that became the focus of the riot.

The partial survival of the village ceremonies under Christianity will appear less surprising when it is borne in mind that the heathenism which Christianity combated was itself only the final term of a long process of evolution. The worshippers of the Keltic or Teutonic deities already practised a traditional ritual, probably without any very clear conception of the *rationale* on which some at least of the acts which they performed were based. These acts had their origin far back in the history of the religious consciousness ; and it must not be supposed, because modern scholarship, with its comparative methods, is able to some extent to reconstruct the mental conditions out of which they arose, that these conditions were still wholly operative in the sixth, any more than in the thirteenth or the twentieth century. Side by side with customs which had still their definite and intelligible significance, religious conservatism had certainly preserved others of a very primitive type, some of which survived as mere fossils, while others had undergone that transformation of intention, that pouring of new wine into old bottles, which is one of the most familiar features in the history of institutions. The heathenism of western Europe must be regarded, therefore, as a group of religious practices originating in very different strata of civilization, and only fused together in the continuity of tradition. Its permanence lay in the law of association through which a piece of ritual originally devised by the folk to secure their practical well-being remained, even after the initial meaning grew obscure, irrevocably bound up with their expectations of that well-being. Its interest to the student is that of a development, rather than that of a system. Only the briefest outline of the direction taken by this development can be here indicated. But it must first be pointed out that, whether from a common derivation, or through a similar intellectual structure reacting upon similar conditions of life, it seems, at least up to the point of emergence of the fully formed village cult, to have proceeded on uniform lines, not only amongst the Teutonic and Keltic tribes who inhabited western and northern Europe and these islands, but also amongst all the Aryan-speaking peoples. In particular, although the Teutonic and the Keltic priests and bards elaborated, probably in comparatively late stages of their history, very different god-names and very different mythologies, yet these are but the superstructure of religion ; and it is possible to infer, both from the results of folk-lore and from the more scanty documentary evidence, a substantial identity throughout the whole Kelto-Teutonic group, of the underlying institutions of ritual and of the fundamental theological conceptions [1]. I am aware that it is no longer permissible to sum up all the facts of European civilization in an Aryan formula. Ethnology has satisfactorily established the existence on the continent of at least two important racial strains besides that of the blonde invader from Latham-land [2]. But I do not think that any of the attempts hitherto made to distinguish Aryan from pre-Aryan elements in folk-lore have met with any measure of success [3]. Nor is it quite clear that any such distinction need have been implied by the difference of blood. Archaeologists speak of a remarkable uniformity of material culture throughout the whole of Europe during the neolithic period; and there appears to be no special reason why this uniformity may not have extended to the comparatively simple notions which man was led to form of the not-man by his early contacts with his environment. In any case the social amalgamation of Aryan and pre-Aryan

[1] In the present state of Gaulish and still more of Irish studies, only a glimmering of possible equations between Teutonic and Keltic gods is apparent.

[2] Recent ethnological research is summed up in G. Vacher de Lapouge, *L'Aryen* (1899); W. Z. Ripley, *The Races of Europe* (1900); A. H. Keane, *Ethnology* (1896); *Man, Past and Present* (1899); J. Deniker, *The Races of Man* (1900); G. Sergi, *The Mediterranean Race* (1901). The three racial types that, in many pure and hybrid forms, mainly compose the population of Europe may be distinguished as (1) *Homo Europaeus*, the tall blonde long-headed (dolichocephalic) race of north Europe, (including Teutons and red-haired 'Kelts'), to which the Aryan speech seems primarily to have belonged; (2) *Homo alpinus*, the medium coloured and sized brachycephalic (round-headed) race of central Europe; (3) *Homo meridionalis* (Lapouge) or *mediterranensis* (Keane), the small dark dolichocephalic race of the Mediterranean basin and the western isles (including dark 'Kelts'). During the formative pe-

riod of European culture (2) was probably of little importance, and (1) and (3) are possibly of closer racial affinity to each other than either of them is to (2).

[3] Gomme, *Ethnology in Folklore*, 21; *Village Community*, 69; *Report of Brit. Ass.* (1896), 626; *F. L. Congress*, 348; *F. L.* x. 129, ascribes the fire customs of Europe to Aryans and the water customs to the pre-Aryans. A. Bertrand, *Religion des Gaulois*, 68, considers human sacrifice characteristically pre-Aryan. There seems to me more hope of arriving at a knowledge of specific Mediterranean cults, before the Aryan intermixture, from a study of the stone amulets and cup-markings of the megaliths (Bertrand, *op. cit.* 42) or from such investigations into 'Mycenaean' antiquity as that of A. J. Evans, *Mycenaean Tree and Pillar Cult* (1901). The speculations of Nietzsche, in *A Genealogy of Morals* and elsewhere, as to the altruistic 'slave' morality of the pre-Aryan and the self-regarding morality of the conquering Aryan 'blond beast' are amusing or pitiful reading, according to one's mood.

was a process already complete by the Middle Ages; and for the purpose of this investigation it seems justifiable, and in the present state of knowledge even necessary, to treat the village customs as roughly speaking homogeneous throughout the whole of the Kelto-Teutonic area.

An analysis of these customs suggests a mental history somewhat as follows. The first relations of man to the not-man are, it need hardly be said, of a practical rather than a sentimental or a philosophic character. They arise out of an endeavour to procure certain goods which depend, in part at least, upon natural processes beyond man's own control. The chief of these goods is, of course, food; that is to say, in a primitive state of civilization, success in hunting, whether of berries, mussels and 'witchetty grubs,' or of more elusive and difficult game; and later, when hunting ceases to be the main-stay of existence, the continued fertility of the flocks and herds, which form the support of a pastoral race, and of the cornfields and orchards which in their turn come to supple-ment these, on the appearance of agriculture. Food once supplied, the little tale of primitive man's limited conception of the desirable is soon completed. Fire and a roof-tree are his already. But he asks for physical health, for success in love and in the begetting of offspring, and for the power to anticipate by divination that future about which he is always so childishly curious. In the pursuit, then, of these simple goods man endeavours to control nature. But his earliest essays in this direction are, as Dr. Frazer has recently pointed out, not properly to be called religion[1]. The magical charms by

[1] Frazer, *G. B.* i. 9 'The fun-damental principles on which it [savage magic] is based would seem to be reducible to two: first, that like produces like, or that an effect resembles its cause; and second, that things which have once been in contact, but have ceased to be so, continue to act upon each other as if the contact still persisted. From the first of these principles, the savage infers that he can pro-duce any desired effect merely by imitating it; from the second he concludes that he can influence at pleasure and at any distance any person of whom, or any thing of which, he possesses a particle. Magic of the latter sort, resting as it does on the belief in a certain secret sympathy which unites indis-solubly things that have once been connected with each other may appropriately be termed sympathe-tic in the strict sense of the term. Magic of the former kind, in which the supposed cause resembles or simulates the supposed effect, may conveniently be described as imi-tative or mimetic.' Cf. Jevons, 31

which he attempts to make the sun burn, and the waters fall, and the wind blow as it pleases him, certainly do not imply that recognition of a quasi-human personality outside himself, which any religious definition may be supposed to require as a minimum.   They are rather to be regarded as applications of primitive science, for they depend upon a vague general notion of the relations of cause and effect.   To assume that you can influence a thing through what is similar to it, or through what has been in contact with it, which, according to Dr. Frazer, are the postulates of magic in its mimetic and its sympathetic form respectively, may be bad science, but at least it is science of a sort, and not religion.

The magical charms play a large part in the village ritual, and will be illustrated in the following chapter.   Presently, however, the scientific spirit is modified by that tendency of animism through which man comes to look upon the external world not as mere more or less resisting matter to be moved hither or thither, but rather as a debateable land peopled with spirits in some sense alive.   These spirits are the active forces dimly discerned by human imagination as at work behind the shifting and often mysterious natural phenomena—forces of the moving winds and waters, of the skies now clear, now overcast, of the animal races of hill and plain, of the growth waxing and waning year by year in field and woodland.   The control of nature now means the control of these powers, and to this object the charms are directed.   In particular, I think,

' The savage makes the generalization that like produces like ; and then he is provided with the means of bringing about anything he wishes, for to produce an effect he has only to imitate it.   To cause a wind to blow, he flaps a blanket, as the sailor still whistles to bring a whistling gale. . . . If the vegetation requires rain, all that is needed is to dip a branch in water, and with it to sprinkle the ground.   Or a spray of water squirted from the mouth will produce a mist sufficiently like the mist required to produce the desired effect ; or black clouds of smoke will be followed by black clouds of rain.'   I do not feel that magic is altogether a happy term for this sort of savage science. In its ordinary sense (the ' black art '), it certainly contains a large element of what Dr. Frazer distinguishes from magic as religion, ' a propitiation or conciliation of powers superior to man which are believed to direct and control the course of nature and of human life.'   True, these powers are not to whom the orthodox religion is directed, but the approach to them is religious in the sense of the above definition.   Such magic is in fact an amalgam of charms, which are Dr. Frazer's ' magic,' and spells, which are his ' religion.'   But so are many more recognized cults.

at this stage of his development, man conceives a spirit of that food which still remains in the very forefront of his aspirations, of his actual food-plant, or of the animal species which he habitually hunts[1]. Of this spirit he initiates a cult, which rests upon the old magical principle of the mastering efficacy of direct contact. He binds the spirit literally to him by wearing it as a garment, or absorbs it into himself in a solemn meal, hoping by either process to acquire an influence or power over it. Naturally, at this stage, the spirit becomes to the eye of his imagination phytomorphic or theriomorphic in aspect. He may conceive it as especially incarnate in a single sacred plant or animal. But the most critical moment in the history of animism is that at which the elemental spirits come to be looked upon as anthropomorphic, made in the likeness of man himself. This is perhaps due to the identification of them with those other quasi-human spirits, of whose existence man has by an independent line of thought also become aware. These are the ghostly spirits of departed kinsmen, still in some shadowy way inhabiting or revisiting the house-place. The change does not merely mean that the visible phytomorphic and theriomorphic embodiments of mental forces sink into subordination ; the plants and animals becoming no more than symbols and appurtenances of the anthropomorphic spirit, or temporary forms with which from time to time he invests himself. A transformation of the whole character of the cult is involved, for man must now approach the spirits, not merely by charms, although conservatism preserves these as an element in ritual, but with modifications of the modes in which he approaches his fellow man. He must beg their favour with submissive speech or buy it with bribes. And here, with prayer and oblation, religion in the stricter sense makes its appearance.

The next step of man is from the crowd of animistic spirits to isolate the god. The notion of a god is much the old notion of an anthropomorphic elemental spirit, widened,

---

[1] Some facts of European animal worship are dealt with in two important recent papers, one by S. Reinach in *Revue celtique*, xxi. 269, the other by N. W. Thomas, in *F. L.* xi. 227. The relation of such worship to the group of savage social institutions classed as totemism is a difficult and far from solved problem, which cannot be touched upon here.

exalted, and further removed from sense. Instead of a local and limited home, the god has his dwelling in the whole expanse of heaven or in some distant region of space. He transcends and as an object of cult supplants the more bounded and more concrete personifications of natural forces out of which he has been evolved. But he does not annul these : they survive in popular credence as his servants and ministers. It is indeed on the analogy of the position of the human chief amongst his *comitatus* that, in all probability, the conception of the god is largely arrived at. Comparative philology seems to show that the belief in gods is common to the Aryan-speaking peoples, and that at the root of all the cognate mythologies there lies a single fundamental divinity. This is the Dyaus of the Indians, the Zeus of the Greeks, the Jupiter of the Romans, the Tiwaz (O.H.G. Zíu, O.N. Týr, A.-S. Tîw) of the Teutons. He is an embodiment of the great clear sunlit heavens, the dispenser of light to the hunts-man, and of warmth and moisture to the crops. Side by side with the conception of the heaven-god comes that of his female counterpart, who is also, though less clearly, indicated in all the mythologies. In her earliest aspect she is the lady of the woods and of the blossoming fruitful earth. This primary dualism is an extremely important factor in the explanation of early religion. The all-father, the heaven, and the mother-goddess, the earth, are distinct personalities from the begin-ning. It does not appear possible to resolve one into a mere doublet or derivative of the other. Certainly the marriage of earth and heaven in the showers that fertilize the crops is one of the oldest and most natural of myths. But it is generally admitted that myth is determined by and does not determine the forms of cult. The heaven-god and the earth-goddess must have already had their separate existence before the priests could hymn their marriage. An explanation of the dualism is probably to be traced in the merging of two cults originally distinct. These will have been sex-cults. Tillage is, of course, little esteemed by primitive man. It was so with the Germans, even up to the point at which they first came into contact with the Romans[1]. Yet all the Aryan languages

[1] Gummere, 39; Caesar, *de B. G.* iv. 1. 7; vi. 22. 2; Tacitus, *Germ.* 26.

show some acquaintance with the use of grains [1]. The analogy
with existing savages suggests that European agriculture in
its early stages was an affair of the women. While the men
hunted or afterwards tended their droves of cattle and horses,
the women grubbed for roots, and presently learnt to scratch
the surface of the ground, to scatter the seed, and painfully to
garner and grind the scanty produce [2]. As the avocations of
the sexes were distinct, so would their magic or their religion
be. Each would develop rites of its own of a type strictly
determined by its practical ambitions, and each would stand
apart from the rites of the other. The interest of the men
would centre in the boar or stag, that of the women in the
fruit-tree or the wheat-sheaf. To the former the stone altar
on the open hill-top would be holy; to the latter the dim
recesses of the impenetrable grove. Presently when the god
concept appeared, the men's divinity would be a personification of the illimitable and mysterious heavens beneath which
they hunted and herded, from which the pools were filled with
water, and at times the pestilence was darted in the sun rays;
the women's of the wooded and deep-bosomed earth out of
which their wealth sprang. This would as naturally take
a female as that a male form. Agriculture, however, was
not for ever left solely to the women. In time pasturage and
tillage came to be carried on as two branches of a single pursuit, and the independent sex-cults which had sprung out of
them coalesced in the common village worship of later days.
Certain features of the primitive differentiation can still be
obscurely distinguished. Here and there one or the other sex

---

[1] Schräder-Jevons, 281, says that
the Indo-Europeans begin their
history 'acquainted with the rudiments of agriculture,' but 'still
possessed with nomadic tendencies.'
He adds that considerable progress
must have been made before the
dispersion of the European branches,
and points out that agriculture
would naturally develop when the
migratory hordes from the steppes
reached the great forests of central
Europe. For this there would be
two reasons, the greater fertility of

the soil and the narrowed space
for pasturage. On the other hand,
V. Hehn, *Culturpflanzen und
Haustiere*, and Mommsen, *Hist. of
Rome*, i. 16, find the traces of agriculture amongst the undivided
Indo-Europeans very slight; the
word γάνα-ζέα, which is common
to the tongues, need mean nothing
more than a wild cereal.

[2] Jevons, 240, 255; Pearson, ii.
42; O. T. Mason, *Woman's Share
in Primitive Culture*, 14.

is barred from particular ceremonies, or a male priest must perform his mystic functions in woman's garb. The heaven-god perhaps remains the especial protector of the cattle, and the earth-goddess of the corn. But generally speaking they have all the interests of the farm in a joint tutelage. The stone altar is set up in the sacred grove ; the mystic tree is planted on the hill-top [1]. Theriomorphic and phytomorphic symbols shadow forth a single godhead [2]. The earth-mother becomes a divinity of light. The heaven-father takes up his abode in the spreading oak.

The historic religions of heathenism have not preserved either the primitive dualistic monotheism, if the phrase may be permitted, or the simplicity of divine functions here sketched. With the advance of civilization the objects of worship must necessarily take upon them new responsibilities. If a tribe has its home by the sea, sooner or later it trusts frail barks to the waters, and to its gods is committed the charge of sea-faring. When handicrafts are invented, these also become their care. When the pressure of tribe upon tribe leads to war, they champion the host in battle. Moral ideas emerge and attach themselves to their service : and ultimately they become identified with the rulers of the dead, and reign in the shadowy world beyond the tomb. Another set of processes combine to produce what is known as polytheism. The constant application of fixed epithets to the godhead tends in the long run to break up its unity. Special aspects of it begin to take on an independent existence. Thus amongst the Teutonic peoples Tiwaz-Thunaraz, the thunderous sky, gives rise to Thunar or Thor, and Tiwaz-Frawiaz, the bounteous sky, to Freyr. And so the ancient heaven-god is replaced by distinct gods of rain and sunshine, who, with the mother-goddess, form that triad of divinities so prominent in several European cults [3]. Again as tribes come into contact with each other,

---

[1] Burne-Jackson, 352, 362; Rhys, C. F. i. 312 ; F. L. v. 339; Dyer, 133 ; Ditchfield, 70 ; cf. ch. vi. One of the hills so visited is the artificial one of Silbury, and perhaps the custom points to the object with which this and the similar 'mound' at Marlborough were piled up.

[2] Frazer, ii. 261, deals very fully with the theriomorphic corn-spirits of folk belief.

[3] On these triads and others in which three male or three female

there is a borrowing of religious conceptions, and the tribal deities are duplicated by others who are really the same in origin, but have different names. The mythological speculations of priests and bards cause further elaboration. The friendly national gods are contrasted with the dark hostile deities of foreign enemies. A belief in the culture-hero or semi-divine man, who wrests the gifts of civilization from the older gods, makes its appearance. Certain cults, such as that of Druidism, become the starting-point for even more philosophic conceptions. The personal predilection of an important worshipper or group of worshippers for this or that deity extends his vogue. The great event in the later history of Teutonic heathenism is the overshadowing of earlier cults by that of Odin or Wodan, who seems to have been originally a ruler of the dead, or perhaps a culture-hero, and not an elemental god at all [1]. The multiplicity of forms under which essentially the same divinity presents itself in history and in popular belief may be illustrated by the mother-goddess of the Teutons. As Freyja she is the female counterpart of Freyr; as Nerthus of Freyr's northern doublet, Njordr. When Wodan largely absorbs the elemental functions, she becomes his wife, as Frîja or Frigg. Through her association with the heaven-gods, she is herself a heaven- as well as an earth-goddess [2], the Eostre of Bede [3], as well as the Erce of the Anglo-Saxon ploughing charm [4]. She is probably the Tanfana

---

figures appear, cf. Bertrand, 341; A. Maury, *Croyances et Légendes du Moyen Âge* (1896), 6; *Matronen-Kultus* in *Zeitschrift d. Vereins f. Volkskultur*, ii. 24. I have not yet seen L. L. Paine, *The Ethnic Trinities and their Relation to the Christian Trinity* (1901).

[1] Mogk, iii. 333; Golther, 298; Grimm, iv. 1709; Kemble, i. 335; Rhys, *C. H.* 282; H. M. Chadwick, *Cult of Othin* (1899).

[2] Mogk, iii. 366; Golther, 428.

[3] Mogk, iii. 374; Golther, 488; Tille, *Y. and C.* 144; Bede, *de temp. ratione*, c. 15 (*Opera*, ed. Giles, vi. 179) 'Eostur-monath qui nunc paschalis mensis interpretatur, quondam a dea illorum, quae Eostre vocabatur, et cui in illo festa celebrabant, nomen habuit; a cuius nomine nunc paschale tempus cognominant, consueto antiquae observationis vocabulo gaudia novae solemnitatis vocantes.' There seems no reason for thinking with Golther and Tille, that Bede made a mistake. Charlemagne took the name *Ôstarmânoth* for April, perhaps only out of compliment to the English, such as Alcuin, at his court.

[4] *A Charm for unfruitful or bewitched land* (O. Cockayne, *Leechdoms of Early England*, R. S. i. 399); cf. Grimm. i. 253; Golther, 455; Kögel, i. 1. 39. The ceremony has taken on a Christian colouring, but retains many primitive features.

of Tacitus and the Nehellenia of the Romano-Germanic votive
stones. If so, she must have become a goddess of mariners,
for Nehellenia seems to be the Isis of the *interpretatio Romana.*
As earth-goddess she comes naturally into relation with the
dead, and like Odin is a leader of the rout of souls. In
German peasant-lore she survives under various names, of
which Perchta is the most important ; in witch-lore, as Diana,
and by a curious mediaeval identification, as Herodias [1]. And
her more primitive functions are largely inherited by the
Virgin, by St. Walpurg and by countless local saints.

Most of the imaginative and mythological superstructure so
briefly sketched in the last paragraph must be considered as
subsequent in order of development to the typical village cult.
Both before and in more fragmentary shape after the death
of the old Keltic and Teutonic gods, that continued to be in
great measure an amalgam of traditional rites of forgotten
magical or pre-religious import. So far as the consciousness of the mediaeval or modern peasant directed it to unseen
powers at all, which was but little, it was rather to some of
these more local and bounded spirits who remained in the
train of the gods, than to the gods themselves. For the purposes of the present discussion, it is sufficient to think of it
quite generally as a cult of the spirits of fertilization, without
attaching a very precise connotation to that term. Unlike
the domestic cult of the ancestral ghosts, conducted for each
household by the house-father at the hearth, it was communal
in character. Whatever the tenure of land may have been,

Strips of turf are removed, and
masses said over them. They are
replaced after oil, honey, barm,
milk of every kind of cattle, twigs
of every tree, and holy water have
been put on the spot. Seed is
bought at a double price from
almsmen and poured into a hole
in the plough with salt and herbs.
Various invocations are used, including one which calls on ' Erce,
Erce, Erce, Eorthan modor,' and
implores the Almighty to grant her
fertility. Then the plough is driven,
and a loaf, made of every kind of
corn with milk and holy water, laid
under the first furrow. Kögel considers *Erce* to be derived from *ero,*
' earth.' Brooke, i. 217, states on
the authority of Montanus that a
version of the prayer preserved in
a convent at Corvei begins ' Eostar,
Eostar, Eordhan modor.' He adds :
' nothing seems to follow from this
clerical error.' But why an error ?
The equation Erce-Eostre is consistent with the fundamental identity
of the light-goddess and the earth-
goddess.

[1] Tacitus, *Ann.* i. 51 ; Mogk,
iii. 373 ; Golther, 458 ; cf. ch. xii.

there seems no doubt that up to a late period 'co-aration,' or co-operative ploughing in open fields, remained the normal method of tillage, while the cattle of the community roamed in charge of a public herd over unenclosed pastures and forest lands[1]. The farm, as a self-sufficing agricultural unit, is a comparatively recent institution, the development of which has done much to render the village festivals obsolete. Originally the critical moments of the agricultural year were the same for the whole village, and the observances which they entailed were shared in by all.

The observances in question, or rather broken fragments of them, have now attached themselves to a number of different outstanding dates in the Christian calendar, and the reconstruction of the original year, with its seasonal feasts, is a matter of some difficulty[2]. The earliest year that can be traced amongst the Aryan-speaking peoples was a bipartite one, made up of only two seasons, winter and summer. For some reason that eludes research, winter preceded summer, just as night, in the primitive reckoning, preceded day. The divisions seem to have been determined by the conditions of a pastoral existence passed in the regularly recurring seasons of central Europe. Winter began when snow blocked the pastures and the cattle had to be brought home to the stall: summer when the grass grew green again and there was once more fodder in the open. Approximately these dates would correspond to mid-November and mid-March[3]. Actually, in the absence of a calendar, they would vary a little from year

[1] Gomme, *Village Community*, 157; B. C. A. Windle, *Life in Early Britain*, 200; F. W. Maitland, *Domesday Book and Beyond*, 142, 337, 346.

[2] I have followed in many points the views on Teutonic chronology of Tille, *Deutsches Weihnacht* (1893) and *Yule and Christmas* (1899), which are accepted in the main by O. Schräder, *Reallexicon der indogermanischen Altertumskunde*, s.vv. Jahr, Jahreszeiten, and partly correct those of Weinhold, *Ueber die deutsche Jahrtheilung* (1862), and Grotefend, *Die Zeitrechnung des*

deutschen Mittelalters (1891).

[3] In Scandinavia the winter naturally began earlier and ended later. Throughout, Scandinavian seasons diverged from those of Germany and the British Isles. In particular the high summer feast and the consequent tripartition of the year do not seem to have established themselves (*C. P. B.* i. 430). Further south the period of stall-feeding was extended when a better supply of fodder made it possible (Tille, *Y. and C.* 56, 62; Burne-Jackson, 380).

to year and would perhaps depend on some significant annual event, such as the first snowstorm in the one case[1], in the other the appearance of the first violet, butterfly or cockchafer, or of one of those migratory birds which still in popular belief bring good fortune and the summer, the swallow, cuckoo or stork[2]. Both dates would give occasion for religious cere-monies, together with the natural accompaniment of feasting and revel. More especially would this be the case at mid-November, when a great slaughtering of cattle was rendered economically necessary by the difficulty of stall-feeding the whole herd throughout the winter. Presently, however, new conditions established themselves. Agriculture grew in importance, and the crops rather than the cattle became the central interest of the village life. Fresh feasts sprang up side by side with the primitive ones, one at the beginning of ploughing about mid-February, another at the end of harvest, about mid-September. At the same time the increased supply of dry fodder tended to drive the annual slaughtering farther on into the winter. More or less contemporaneously with these processes, the old bipartite year was changed into a tripartite one by the growth of yet another new feast during that dangerous period when the due succession of rain and sun for the crops becomes a matter of the greatest moment to the farmer. Early summer, or spring, was thus set apart from late summer, or summer proper[3]. This development

---

[1] Cf. ch. xi, where the winter feasts are discussed in more detail.

[2] Grimm, ii. 675, 693, 762, notes the heralds of summer.

[3] Jahn, 34; Mogk, iii. 387; Golther, 572; Schräder-Jevons, 303. The Germans still knew three seasons only when they came into contact with the Romans; cf. Tacitus, *Germ.* 26 'annum quoque ipsum non in totidem digerunt species: hiems et ver et aestas intellectum ac vocabula habent, autumni perinde nomen ac bona ignorantur.' I do not agree with Tille, *Y. and C.* 6, that the tripartition of the year, in this pre-calendar form, was 'of foreign extraction.' Schräder shows that it is common to the Aryan languages. The Keltic seasons, in particular, seem to be closely parallel to the Teutonic. Of the three great Keltic feasts described by Rhys, *C. H.* 409, 513, 676; *C. F.* i. 308, the Lugnassad was probably the harvest feast, the Samhain the old beginning of winter feast, and the Beltain the high summer feast. The meaning of 'Beltain' (cf. *N. E. D.* s.v. Beltane) seems quite uncertain. A connexion is possible but certainly unproved with the Abelio of the Pyrenean inscriptions, the Belenus-Apollo of those of the eastern Alps, and, more rarely, Provence (Röscher, *Lexicon*, s.v. Belenus; Holder, *Alt-celtischer Sprachschatz*, s.vv. Belenus, Abelio;

also may be traced to the influence of agriculture, whose interest runs in a curve, while that of herding keeps comparatively a straight course. But as too much sun or too much wet not only spoils the crops but brings a murrain on the cattle, the herdsmen fell into line and took their share in the high summer rites. At first, no doubt, this last feast was a sporadic affair, held for propitiation of the unfavourable fertilization spirits when the elders of the village thought it called for. And to the end resort may have been had to exceptional acts of cult in times of especial distress. But gradually the occasional ceremony became an annual one, held as soon as the corn was thick in the green blade and the critical days were at hand.

So far, there has been no need to assume the existence of a calendar. How long the actual climatic conditions continued to determine the dates of the annual feasts can hardly be said. But when a calendar did make its appearance, the five feasts adapted themselves without much difficulty to it. The earliest calendar that can be inferred in central Europe was one, either of Oriental or possibly of Mediterranean *provenance*, which divided the year into six tides of three-score days each[1]. The beginnings of these tides almost certainly fell at about the middle of corresponding months of the Roman calendar[2]. The first would thus be marked by the beginning of winter feast in mid-November; two others by the beginning of summer feast and the harvest feast in mid-March and mid-August respectively. A little accommodation of the seasonal feasts of the farm would be required to adapt them to the remaining three. And here begins a process of dislocation of the original dates of customs, now becoming traditional rather than vital, which

Ausonius, *Professores*, iv. 7), or the Bel of Bohemia mentioned by Allso (ch.xii). The Semitic Baal, although a cult of Belus, found its way into the Roman world (cf. Appendix N, No. xxxii, and Wissowa, 302), is naturally even a less plausible relation. But it is dear to the folk-etymologist; cf. e.g. S. M. Mayhew, *Baalism* in *Trans. of St. Paul's Ecclesiological Society*, i. 83.

[1] Tille, *Y. and C.* 7, 148, suggests an Egyptian or Babylonian origin, but the equation of the Gothic *fiuleis* and the Cypriote ἰλαῖος, ἰουλαῖος, ἰουλήιος, ἰούλιος as names for winter periods makes a Mediterranean connexion seem possible.

[2] Cf. ch. xi.

was afterwards extended by successive stages to a bewildering degree. By this time, with the greater permanence of agriculture, the system of autumn ploughing had perhaps been invented. The spring ploughing festival was therefore of less importance, and bore to be shifted back to mid-January instead of mid-February. Four of the six tides are now provided with initial feasts. These are mid-November, mid-January, mid-March, and mid-September. There are, however, still mid-May and mid-July, and only the high summer feast to divide between them. I am inclined to believe that a division is precisely what took place, and that the hitherto fluctuating date of the summer feast was determined in some localities to mid-May, in others to mid-July [1].

The European three-score-day-tide calendar is rather an ingenious conjecture than an ascertained fact of history. When the Germano-Keltic peoples came under the influence of Roman civilization, they adopted amongst other things the Roman calendar, first in its primitive form and then in the more scientific one given to it under Julius Caesar. The latter divided the year into four quarters and twelve months, and carried with it a knowledge of the solstices, at which the astronomy neither of Kelts nor of Germans seems to have previously arrived [2]. The feasts again underwent a process of dis-

---

[1] Grimm, ii. 615, notes that Easter fires are normal in the north, Midsummer fires in the south of Germany. The Beltane fires both of Scotland and Ireland are usually on May 1, but some of the Irish examples collected by J. Jamieson, *Etym. Dict. of the Scottish Language*, s. v., are at midsummer.

[2] Tille, *Y. and C.* 71 ; Rhys, *C. H.* 419. The primitive year was thermometric, not astronomic, its critical moments, not the solstices, a knowledge of which means science, but the sensible increase and diminution of heat in spring and autumn. The solstices came through Rome. The *Sermo Eligii* (Grimm, iv. 1737) has 'nullus in festivitate S. Ioannis vel quibuslibet sanctorum solemnitatibus solstitia... exerceat,' but Eligius was a seventh-century bishop,

and this *Sermo* may have been interpolated in the eighth century (O. Reich, *Über Audoen's Lebensbeschreibung des heiligen Eligius* (1872), cited in *Rev. celtique*, ix. 433). It is not clear that the un-Romanized Teuton or Kelt made a god of the sun, as distinct from the heaven-god, who of course has solar attributes and emblems. In the same *Sermo* Eligius says 'nullus dominos solem aut lunam vocet, neque per eos iuret.' But the notion of ' domini' may be post-Roman, and the oath is by the permanent, rather than the divine ; cf. A. de Jubainville, *Intr. à l'Étude de la Litt. celt.* 181. It is noticeable that German names for the sun are originally feminine and for the moon masculine.

location in order to harmonize them with the new arrangement.
The ceremonies of the winter feast were pulled back to November 1 or pushed forward to January 1. The high summer feast
was attracted from mid-May and mid-July respectively to
the important Roman dates of the *Floralia* on May 1 and the
summer solstice on June 24. Last of all, to complete the confusion, came, on the top of three-score-day-tide calendar and
Roman calendar alike, the scheme of Christianity with its
host of major and minor ecclesiastical festivals, some of them
fixed, others movable. Inevitably these in their turn began
to absorb the agricultural customs. The present distribution
of the five original feasts, therefore, is somewhat as follows.
The winter feast is spread over all the winter half of the year
from All Souls day to Twelfth night. A later chapter will
illustrate its destiny more in detail. The ploughing feast is
to be sought mainly in Plough Monday, in Candlemas and
in Shrovetide or Carnival [1]; the beginning of summer feast in
Palm Sunday, Easter and St. Mark's day; the early variety
of the high summer feast probably also in Easter, and certainly
in May-day, St. George's day, Ascensiontide with its Rogations, Whitsuntide and Trinity Sunday; the later variety of
the same feast in Midsummer day and Lammastide; and the
harvest feast in Michaelmas. These are days of more or less
general observance. Locally, in strict accordance with the
policy of Gregory the Great as expounded to Mellitus, the
floating customs have often settled upon conveniently neighbouring dates of wakes, rushbearings, kirmesses and other
forms of vigil or dedication festivals [2]; and even, in the utter

---

[1] Mogk, iii. 393; Golther, 584;
Jahn, 84; Caspari, 35; Saupe, 7;
Hauck, ii. 357; Michels, 93. The
ploughing feast is probably the
spurcalia of the *Indiculus* and of
Eadhelm, *de laudibus virginitatis*,
c. 25, and the *dies spurci* of the
Hom. de Sacrilegiis. This term
appears in the later German name
for February, *Sporkele*. It seems
to be founded on Roman analogy
from *spurcus*, 'unclean.' Pearson,
ii. 159, would, however, trace it to an
Aryan root *spherag*, 'swell,' 'burst,'

'shoot.' Bede, *de temp. rat.* c. 15,
calls February *Sol-monath*, which he
explains as 'mensis placentarum.'
September, the month of the harvest-
festival, is *Haleg-monath*, or 'mensis
sacrorum.'

[2] Pfannenschmidt, 244; Brand,
ii. 1; Ditchfield, 130; Burne-Jackson, 439; Burton, *Rushbearing*,
147; Schaff, vi. 544; Duchesne,
385. The dedication of churches
was solemnly carried out from the
fourth century, and the anniversary observed. Gregory the Great

oblivion of their primitive significance, upon the anniversaries of historical events, such as Royal Oak day on May 29 [1], or Gunpowder day. Finally it may be noted, that of the five feasts that of high summer is the one most fully preserved in modern survivals. This is partly because it comes at a convenient time of year for the out-of-door holiday-making which serves as a preservative for the traditional rites; partly also because, while the pastoral element in the feasts of the beginnings of winter and summer soon became comparatively unimportant through the subordination of pasturage to tillage, and the ploughing and harvest feasts tended more and more to become affairs of the individual farm carried out in close connexion with those operations themselves, the summer feast retained its communal character and continued to be celebrated by the whole village for the benefit of everybody's crops and trees, and everybody's flocks and herds [2]. It is therefore mainly, although not wholly, upon the summer feast that the analysis of the agricultural ritual to be given in the next chapter will be based.

ordered 'solemnitates ecclesiarum dedicationum per singulos annos sunt celebrandae.' The A.-S. *Canons* of Edgar (960), c. 28 (Wilkins, i. 227), require them to be kept with sobriety. Originally the anniversary, as well as the actual dedication day, was observed with an all night watch, whence the name *vigilia*, wakes. Belethus, *de rat. offic.* (*P. L.* ccii. 141), c. 137, says that the custom was abolished owing to the immorality to which it led. But the 'eve' of these and other feasts continued to share in the sanctity of the 'day,' a practice in harmony with the European sense of the precedence of night over day (cf. Schräder-Jevons, 311; Bertrand, 267, 354,

413). An Act of Convocation in 1536 (Wilkins, iii. 823) required all wakes to be held on the first Sunday in October, but it does not appear to have been very effectual.

[1] S. O. Addy, in *F. L.* xii. 394, has a full account of 'Garland day' at Castleton, Derbyshire, on May 29; cf. *F. L.* xii. 76 (Wishford, Wilts); Burne-Jackson, 365.

[2] The classification of agricultural feasts in U. Jahn, *Die deutschen Opfergebräuche*, seems throughout to be based less on the facts of primitive communal agriculture, than on those of the more elaborate methods of the later farms with their variety of crops.

CHAPTER VI

VILLAGE FESTIVALS

[*Bibliographical Note.*—A systematic calendar of English festival usages by a competent folk-lorist is much needed. J. Brand, *Observations on Popular Antiquities* (1777), based on H. Bourne, *Antiquitates Vulgares* (1725), and edited, first by Sir Henry Ellis in 1813, 1841-2 and 1849, and then by W. C. Hazlitt in 1870, is full of valuable material, but belongs to the age of pre-scientific antiquarianism. R. T. Hampson, *Medii Aevi Kalendarium* (1841), is no less unsatisfactory. In default of anything better, T. F. T. Dyer, *British Popular Customs* (1891), is a useful compilation from printed sources, and P. H. Ditchfield, *Old English Customs* (1896), a gossipy account of contemporary survivals. These may be supplemented from collections of more limited range, such as H. J. Feasey, *Ancient English Holy Week Ceremonial* (1897), and J. E. Vaux, *Church Folk-Lore* (1894); by treatises on local folk-lore, of which W. Henderson, *Notes on the Folk-Lore of the Northern Counties of England and the Borders* (2nd ed. 1879), C. S. Burne and G. F. Jackson, *Shropshire Folk-Lore* (1883-5), and J. Rhys, *Celtic Folk-Lore, Welsh and Manx* (1901), are the best; and by the various publications of the Folk-Lore Society, especially the series of *County Folk-Lore* (1895-9) and the successive periodicals, *The Folk-Lore Record* (1878-82), *Folk-Lore Journal* (1883-9), and *Folk-Lore* (1890-1903). Popular accounts of French *fêtes* are given by E. Cortet, *Essai sur les Fêtes religieuses* (1867), and O. Havard, *Les Fêtes de nos Pères* (1898). L. J. B. Bérenger-Féraud, *Superstitions et Survivances* (1896), is more pretentious, but not really scholarly. C. Leber, *Dissertations relatives à l'Histoire de France* (1826-38), vol. ix, contains interesting material of an historical character, largely drawn from papers in the eighteenth-century periodical *Le Mercure de France*. Amongst German books, J. Grimm, *Teutonic Mythology* (transl. J. S. Stallybrass, 1880-8), H. Pfannenschmidt, *Germanische Erntefeste* (1878), and U. Jahn, *Die deutschen Opfergebräuche bei Ackerbau und Viehzucht* (1884), are all excellent. Many of the books mentioned in the bibliographical note to the last chapter remain useful for the present and following ones; in particular J. G. Frazer, *The Golden Bough* (2nd ed. 1900), is, of course, invaluable. I have only included in the above list such works of general range as I have actually made most use of. Many others dealing with special points are cited in the notes. A fuller guide to folk-lore literature will be found in M. R. Cox, *Introduction to Folklore* (2nd ed. 1897).]

THE central fact of the agricultural festivals is the presence in the village of the fertilization spirit in the visible and tangible form of flowers and green foliage or of the fruits of the earth. Thus, when the peasants do their 'observaunce to a morn of May,' great boughs of hawthorn are cut before daybreak in the woods, and carried, with other seasonable leafage and blossom, into the village street. Lads plant branches before the doors of their mistresses. The folk deck themselves, their houses, and the church in green. Some of them are clad almost entirely in wreaths and tutties, and become walking bushes, 'Jacks i' the green.' The revel centres in dance and song around a young tree set up in some open space of the village, or a more permanent May-pole adorned for the occasion with fresh garlands. A large garland, often with an anthropomorphic representation of the fertilization spirit in the form of a doll, parades the streets, and is accompanied by a 'king' or 'queen,' or a 'king' and 'queen' together. Such a garland finds its place at all the seasonal feasts; but whereas in spring and summer it is naturally made of the new vegetation, at harvest it as naturally takes the form of a sheaf, often the last sheaf cut, of the corn. Then it is known as the 'harvest-May' or the 'neck,' or if it is anthropomorphic in character, as the 'kern-baby.' Summer and harvest garlands alike are not destroyed when the festival is over, but remain hung up on the May-pole or the church or the barn-door until the season for their annual renewing comes round. And sometimes the grain of the 'harvest-May' is mingled in the spring with the seed-corn [1].

The rationale of such customs is fairly simple. They depend upon a notion of sympathetic magic carried on into the animistic stage of belief. Their object is to secure the beneficent influence of the fertilization spirit by bringing the persons or places to be benefited into direct contact with the physical embodiment of that spirit. In the burgeoning quick set up on the village green is the divine presence. The worshipper clad in leaves and flowers has made himself a garment of the god, and is therefore in a very special sense under his protection. Thus efficacy in folk-belief of physical contact may be illustrated by another set of practices in which recourse is had to the fertilization spirit for the cure of disease. A child suffering from croup, convulsions, rickets,

[1] Frazer, i. 193; ii. 96; Brand, i. 125; Dyer, 223; Ditchfield, 95; Philpot, 144; Grimm, ii. 762; &c., &c. A single example of the custom is minutely studied by S. O. Addy, *Garland Day at Castleton*, in *F. L.* xii. 394.

or other ailment, is passed through a hole in a split tree, or beneath a bramble rooted at both ends, or a strip of turf partly raised from the ground. It is the actual touch of earth or stem that works the healing[1].

May-pole or church may represent a focus of the cult at some specially sacred tree or grove in the heathen village. But the ceremony, though it centres at these, is not confined to them, for its whole purpose is to distribute the benign influence over the entire community, every field, fold, pasture, orchard close and homestead thereof. At ploughing, the driving of the first furrow; at harvest, the home-coming of the last wain, is attended with ritual. Probably all the primitive festivals, and certainly that of high summer, included a lustration, in which the image or tree which stood for the fertilization spirit was borne in solemn procession from dwelling to dwelling and round all the boundaries of the village. Tacitus records the progress of the earth-goddess Nerthus amongst the German tribes about the mouth of the Elbe, and the dipping of the goddess and the drowning of her slaves in a lake at the term of the ceremony[2]. So too at Upsala in Sweden the statue of Freyr went round when winter was at an end[3]; while Sozomenes tells how, when Ulfilas was preaching Christianity to the Visigoths, Athanaric sent the image of his god abroad in a wagon, and burnt the houses of all who refused to bow down and sacrifice[4]. Such lustrations continue to be a prominent feature of the folk survivals. They are preserved in a number of processional customs in all parts of England; in the municipal 'ridings,' 'shows,' or 'watches' on St. George's[5] or Midsummer[6]

---

[1] A. B. Gomme, ii. 507; Hartland, *Perseus*, ii. 187; Grimm, iv. 1738, 1747; Gaidoz, *Un vieux rite médical* (1893).

[2] Tacitus, *Germania*, 40.

[3] Vigfusson and Ungar, *Flateyjarbok*, i. 337; Grimm, i. 107; Gummere, *G. O.* 433; Mogk, iii. 321; Golther, 228.

[4] Sozomenes, *Hist. Eccles.* vi. 37. Cf. also *Indiculus* (ed. Saupe, 32) 'de simulacro, quod per campos portant,' the fifth-century *Vita S.*

Martini, c. 12, by Sulpicius Severus (*Opera*, ed. Halm, in *Corp. Script. Eccl. Hist.* i. 122) 'quia esset haec Gallorum rusticis consuetudo, simulacra daemonum, candido tecta velamine, misera per agros suos circumferre dementia,' and Alsso's account of the fifteenth-century *calendisationes* in Bohemia (ch. xii).

[5] Cf. ch. x.

[6] Cf. *Representations* (Chester, London, York). There were similar watches at Nottingham (Deering,

days; in the 'Godiva' procession at Coventry[1], the 'Bezant' procession at Shaftesbury[2]. Hardly a rural merry-making or wake, indeed, is without its procession; if it is only in the simple form of the *quête* which the children consider themselves entitled to make, with their May-garland, or on some other traditional pretext, at various seasons of the calendar. Obviously in becoming mere *quêtes*, collections of eggs, cakes and so forth, or even of small coins, as well as in falling entirely into the hands of the children, the processions have to some extent lost their original character. But the notion that the visit is to bring good fortune, or the 'May' or the 'summer' to the household, is not wholly forgotten in the rhymes used[3]. An interesting version of the ceremony is the 'furry' or 'faddy' dance formerly used at Helston wake; for in this the oak-decked dancers claimed the right to pass in at one door and out at another through every house in the village[4].

Room has been found for the summer lustrations in the scheme of the Church. In Catholic countries the statue of the local saint is commonly carried round the village, either annually on his feast-day or in times of exceptional trouble[5]. The inter-relations of ecclesiastical and folk-ritual in this respect are singularly illustrated by the celebration of St. Ubaldo's eve (May 15) at Gubbio in Umbria. The folk procession of the *Ceri* is a very complete variety of the summer festival. After vespers the clergy also hold a procession in honour of the saint. At a certain point the two companies meet. An interchange of courtesies takes place. The priest elevates the host; the bearers of the *Ceri* bow them to the ground; and each procession passes on its way[6]. In England the summer lustrations take an ecclesiastical form in the Roga-

---

Hist. of Nott. 123), Worcester (Smith, *English Gilds*, 408), Lydd and Bristol (Green, *Town Life in the Fifteenth Century*, i. 148), and on St. Thomas's day (July 7) at Canterbury (*Arch. Cant.* xii. 34; *Hist. MSS.* ix. 1. 148).

[1] Harris, 7; Hartland, *Fairy Tales*, 71.

[2] Dyer, 205.

[3] Cf. ch. viii.

[4] Dyer, 275; Ditchfield, 111; cf. the phrase 'in and out the windows' of the singing game *Round and Round the Village* (A. B. Gomme, s. v.).

[5] M. Deloche, *Le Tour de la Lunade*, in *Rev. celtique*, ix. 425; Bérenger-Féraud, i. 423; iii. 167.

[6] Bower, 13.

tions or 'bannering' of 'Gang-week,' a ceremony which itself appears to be based on very similar folk-customs of southern Europe[1]. Since the Reformation the Rogations have come to be regarded as little more than a 'beating of the bounds.' But the declared intention of them was originally to call for a blessing upon the fruits of the earth ; and it is not difficult to trace folk-elements in the 'gospel oaks' and 'gospel wells' at which station was made and the gospel read, in the peeled willow wands borne by the boys who accompany the procession, in the whipping or 'bumping' of the said boys at the stations, and in the choice of 'Gang-week' for such agricultural rites as 'youling' and 'well-dressing[2].'

Some anthropomorphic representation of the fertilization spirit is a common, though not an invariable element in the lustration. A doll is set on the garland, or some popular 'giant' or other image is carried round[3]. Nor is it surprising that at the early spring festival which survives in

---

[1] Duchesne, 276 ; Usener, i. 293 ; Tille, *Y. and C.* 51 ; W. W. Fowler, 124 ; Boissier, *La Religion romaine*, i. 323. The Rogations or *litaniae minores* represent in Italy the Ambarvalia on May 29. But they are of Gallican origin, were begun by Mamertus, bishop of Vienne (†470), adapted by the *Council of Orleans* (511), c. 27 (Mansi, viii. 355), and required by the English *Council of Clovesho* (747), c. 16 (Haddan-Stubbs, iii. 368), to be held 'non admixtis vanitatibus, uti mos est plurimis, vel negligentibus, vel imperitis, id est in ludis et equorum cursibus, et epulis maioribus.' Jahn, 147, quotes the German abbess Marcsuith (940), who describes them as 'pro gentilicio Ambarvali,' and adds, 'confido autem de Patroni huius misericordia, quod sic ab eo gyrade terrae semina uberius provenient, et variae aeris inclementiae cessent.' Mediaeval Rogation litanies are in *Sarum Processional*, 103, and York Processional (*York Manual*, 182). The more strictly Roman *litania major* on St. Mark's day (March 25) takes the place of the *Robigalia*, but is not of great importance in English folk-custom.

[2] *Injunctions*, ch. xix, of 1559 (Gee-Hardy, *Docts. illustrative of English Church History*, 426). Thanks are to be given to God 'for the increase and abundance of his fruits upon the face of the earth.' The *Book of Homilies* contains an exhortation to be used on the occasion. The episcopal injunctions and interrogatories in *Ritual Commission*, 404, 409, 416, &c., endeavour to preserve the Rogations, and to eliminate 'superstition' from them ; for the development of the notion of 'beating of bounds,' cf. the eighteenth-century notices in Dyer, *Old English Social Life*, 196.

[3] The image is represented by the doll of the May-garland, which has sometimes, according to Ditchfield, 102, become the Virgin Mary, with a child doll in its arms, and at other times (e. g. Castleton, *F. L.* xii. 469) has disappeared, leaving the name of 'queen' to a particular bunch of flowers ; also by the 'giant' of the midsummer watch. The Salisbury giant, St. Christopher, with his hobby-horse, Hob-nob, is described in *Rev. d. T. P.* iv. 601.

Plough Monday, the plough itself, the central instrument of the opening labour, figures. A variant of this custom may be traced in certain maritime districts, where the functions of the agricultural deities have been extended to include the oversight of seafaring. Here it is not a plough but a boat or ship that makes its rounds, when the fishing season is about to begin. Ship processions are to be found in various parts of Germany[1]; at Minehead, Plymouth, and Devonport in the west of England, and probably also at Hull in the north[2].

The magical notions which, in part at least, explain the garland customs of the agricultural festival, are still more strongly at work in some of its subsidiary rites. These declare themselves, when understood, to be of an essentially practical character, charms designed to influence the weather, and to secure the proper alternation of moisture and warmth which is needed alike for the growth and ripening of the crops and for the welfare of the cattle. They are probably even older than the garland-customs, for they do not imply the animistic conception of a fertilization spirit immanent in leaf and blossom; and they depend not only upon the 'sympathetic' principle of influence by direct contact already illustrated, but also upon that other principle of similarity distinguished by Dr. Frazer as the basis of what he calls 'mimetic' magic. To the primitive mind the obvious way of obtaining a result in nature is to make an imitation of it on a small scale. To achieve rain, water must be splashed about, or some other characteristic of a storm or shower must be reproduced. To achieve sunshine, a fire must be lit, or some other representation of the appearance and motion of the sun must be devised. Both rain-charms and sun-charms are very clearly recognizable in the village ritual.

As rain-charms, conscious or unconscious, must be classified

[1] Grimm, i. 257; Golther, 463; Mogk, iii. 374; Hahn, *Demeter und Baubo*, 38; Usener, *Die Sintfluthsagen*, 115. There are parallels in south European custom, both classical and modern, and Usener even derives the term 'carnival,' not from *carnem levare*, but from the *currus navalis* used by Roman women. A modern survival at Fréjus is described in *F. L.* xii. 307.

[2] Ditchfield, 103; *Transactions of Devonshire Association*, xv. 104; cf. the Noah's ship procession at Hull (*Representations*, s. v.).

the many festival customs in which bathing or sprinkling holds
an important place. The image or bough which represents
the fertilization spirit is solemnly dipped in or drenched with
water. Here is the explanation of the ceremonial bathing
of the goddess Nerthus recorded by Tacitus. It has its
parallels in the dipping of the images of saints in the feast-
day processions of many Catholic villages, and in the buckets
of water sometimes thrown over May-pole or harvest-May.
Nor is the dipping or drenching confined to the fertilization
spirit. In order that the beneficent influences of the rite
may be spread widely abroad, water is thrown on the fields
and on the plough, while the worshippers themselves, or
a representative chosen from among them, are sprinkled or
immersed. To this practice many survivals bear evidence;
the virtues persistently ascribed to dew gathered on May
morning, the ceremonial bathing of women annually or in
times of drought with the expressed purpose of bringing
fruitfulness on man or beast or crop, the 'ducking' customs
which play no inconsiderable part in the traditions of many
a rural merry-making. Naturally enough, the original sense
of the rite has been generally perverted. The 'ducking' has
become either mere horse-play or else a rough-and-ready
form of punishment for offences, real or imaginary, against
the rustic code of conduct. The churl who will not stop
working or will not wear green on the feast-day must be
'ducked,' and under the form of the 'cucking-stool,' the
ceremony has almost worked its way into formal jurisprudence as an appropriate treatment for feminine offenders.
So, too, it has been with the 'ducking' of the divinity. When
the modern French peasant throws the image of his saint
into the water, he believes himself to be doing it, not as
a mimetic rain-charm, but as a punishment to compel a
power obdurate to prayer to grant through fear the required
boon.

The rain-charms took place, doubtless, at such wells,
springs, or brooks as the lustral procession passed in its
progress round the village. It is also possible that there may
have been, sometimes or always, a well within the sacred
grove itself and hard by the sacred tree. The sanctity

derived by such wells and streams from the use of them in
the cult of the fertilization spirit is probably what is really
intended by the water-worship so often ascribed to the
heathen of western Europe, and coupled closely with tree-
worship in the Christian discipline-books. The goddess of
the tree was also the goddess of the well. At the conversion her wells were taken over by the new religion. They
became holy wells, under the protection of the Virgin or one
of the saints. And they continued to be approached with
the same rites as of old, for the purpose of obtaining the
ancient boons for which the fertilization spirit had always
been invoked. It will not be forgotten that, besides the public
cult of the fertilization spirit for the welfare of the crops
and herds, there was also a private cult, which aimed at
such more personal objects of desire as health, success in
love and marriage, and divination of the future. It is this
private cult that is most markedly preserved in modern holy
well customs. These may be briefly summarized as follows [1].
The wells are sought for procuring a husband or children,
for healing diseases, especially eye-ailments or warts, and for
omens, these too most often in relation to wedlock. The
worshipper bathes wholly or in part, or drinks the water.
Silence is often enjoined, or a motion *deasil*, that is, with
the sun's course, round the well. Occasionally cakes are
eaten, or sugar and water drunk, or the well-water is splashed
on a stone. Very commonly rags or bits of wool or hair are
laid under a pebble or hung on a bush near the well, or pins,
more rarely coins or even articles of food, are thrown into it.
The objects so left are not probably to be regarded as offerings ;
the intention is rather to bring the worshipper, through the
medium of his hair or clothes, or some object belonging to
him, into direct contact with the divinity. The close connexion between tree- and well-cult is shown by the use of
the neighbouring bush on which to hang the rags. And the

---

[1] Brand, ii. 223; Grimm, ii. 584; Elton, 284; Gomme, *Ethnology*, 73; Hartland, *Perseus*, ii. 175; Haddon, 362; Vaux, 269; Wood-Martin, ii. 46; Bérenger-Féraud, iii. 291; R. C. Hope, *Holy Wells*; M.-L. Quiller-Couch, *Ancient and Holy Wells of Cornwall* (1894); J. Rhys, *C. F.* i. 332, 354, and in *F. L.* iii. 74, iv. 55; A. W. Moore, in *F. L.* v. 212; H. C. March, in *F. L.* x. 479 (Dorset).

practice of dropping pins into the well is almost exactly paralleled by that of driving nails 'for luck' into a sacred tree or its later representative, a cross or saintly image. The theory may be hazarded that originally the sacred well was never found without the sacred tree beside it. This is by no means the case now; but it must be remembered that a tree is much more perishable than a well. The tree once gone, its part in the ceremony would drop out, or be transferred to the well. But the original rite would include them both. The visitant, for instance, would dip in the well, and then creep under or through the tree, a double ritual which seems to survive in the most curious of all the dramatic games of children, 'Draw a Pail of Water[1].'

The private cult of the fertilization spirit is not, of course, tied to fixed seasons. Its occasion is determined by the needs of the worshipper. But it is noteworthy that the efficacy of some holy wells is greatest on particular days, such as Easter or the first three Sundays in May. And in many places the wells, whether ordinarily held 'holy' or not, take an important place in the ceremonies of the village festival. The 'gospel wells' of the Rogation processions, and the well to which the 'Bezant' procession goes at Shaftesbury are cases in point; while in Derbyshire the 'well-dressings' correspond to the 'wakes,' 'rushbearings,' and 'Mayings' of other districts. Palm Sunday and Easter Sunday, as well as the Rogation days, are in a measure Christian versions of the heathen agricultural feasts, and it is not, therefore, surprising to find an extensive use of holy water in ecclesiastical ritual, and a special rite of *Benedictio Fontium* included amongst the Easter ceremonies[2]. But the Christian custom has been moralized, and its avowed aim is purification rather than prosperity.

The ordinary form of heat-charm was to build, in semblance

---

[1] A. B. Gomme, s. v.; Haddon, 362.

[2] Schaff, iii. 247 ; Duchesne, 281, 385 ; Rock, iii. 2. 101, 180; Maskell, i. cccxi ; Feasey, 235 ; Wordsworth, 24; Pfannenschmidt, *Das Weihwasser im heidnischen und christlichen Cultus* (1869). The *Benedictio Fontium* took place on Easter Saturday, in preparation for the baptism which in the earliest times was a characteristic Easter rite. The formulae are in *York Missal*, i. 121; *Sarum Missal*, 350; Maskell, i. 13.

of the sun, the source of heat, a great fire[1]. Just as in the rain-charm the worshippers must be literally sprinkled with water, so, in order that they may receive the full benefits of the heat-charm, they must come into direct physical contact with the fire, by standing in the smoke, or even leaping through the flames, or by smearing their faces with the charred ashes[2]. The cattle too must be driven through the fire, in order that they may be fertile and free from pestilence throughout the summer; and a whole series of observances had for their especial object the distribution of the preserving influence over the farms. The fires were built on high ground, that they might be visible far and wide. Or they were built in a circle round the fields, or to windward, so that the smoke might blow across the corn. Blazing arrows were shot in the air, or blazing torches carried about. Ashes were sprinkled over the fields, or mingled with the seed corn or the fodder in the stall[3]. Charred brands were buried or stuck upright in the furrows. Further, by a simple symbolism, the shape and motion of the sun were mimicked with circular rotating bodies. A fiery barrel or a fiery wheel was rolled down the hill on the top of which the ceremony took place. The lighted torches were whirled in the air, or replaced by lighted disks of wood, flung on high. All these customs still linger in these islands or in other parts of western Europe, and often the popular imagination finds in their successful performance an omen for the fertility of the year.

On *a priori* grounds one might have expected two agricultural festivals during the summer; one in the earlier part of it, when moisture was all-important, accompanied with rain-charms; the other later on, when the crops were well grown

---

[1] Frazer, iii. 237; Gomme, in *Brit. Ass. Rep.* (1896), 626; Simpson, 195; Grenier, 380; Gaidoz, 16; Bertrand, 98; Gummere, *G. O.* 400; Grimm, ii. 601; Jahn, 25; Brand, i. 127, 166; Dyer, 269, 311, 332; Ditchfield, 141; Cortet, 211.

[2] To this custom may possibly be traced the black-a-vised figures who are persistent in the folk *ludi*, and also the curious tradition which makes May-day especially the chimney-sweeps' holiday.

[3] The reasons given are various, 'to keep off hail' (whence the term *Hagelfeuer* mentioned by Pfannenschmidt, 67), 'vermin,' 'caterpillars,' 'blight,' 'to make the fields fertile.' In Bavaria torches are carried round the fields 'to drive away the wicked sower' (of tares?). In Northumberland raids are made on the ashes of neighbouring villages (Dyer, 332).

and heat was required to ripen them, accompanied with sun-charms. But the evidence is rather in favour of a single original festival determined, in the dislocation caused by a calendar, to different dates in different localities[1]. The Midsummer or St. John's fires are perhaps the most widely spread and best known of surviving heat-charms. But they can be paralleled by others distributed all over the summer cycle of festivals, at Easter[2] and on May-day, and in con-nexion with the ploughing celebrations on Epiphany, Candle-mas, Shrovetide, Quadragesima, and St. Blaize's day. It is indeed at Easter and Candlemas that the *Benedictiones*, which are the ecclesiastical versions of the ceremony, appear in the ritual-books[3]. On the other hand, although, perhaps owing to the later notion of the solstice, the fires are greatly prominent on St. John's day, and are explained with con-siderable ingenuity by the monkish writers[4], yet this day was never a fire-festival and nothing else. Garland customs are common upon it, and there is even evidence, though slight

---

[1] Cf. p. 113.

[2] I know of no English Easter folk-fires, but St. Patrick is said to have lit one on the hill of Slane, opposite Tara, on Easter Eve, 433 (Feasey, 180).

[3] Schaff, v. 403; Duchesne, 240; Rock, iii. 2. 71, 94, 98, 107, 244; Feasey, 184; Wordsworth, 204; Frazer, iii. 245; Jahn, 129; Grimm, ii. 616; Simpson, 198. The formulae of the *benedictio ignis* and *benedictio cereorum* at Candlemas, and the *benedictio ignis*, *benedictio incensi*, and *benedictio cerei* on Easter Eve, are in *Sarum Missal*, 334, 697; *York Missal*, i. 109; ii. 17. One York MS. has 'Paschae ignis de berillo vel de silice exceptus … accenditur.' The correspondence between Pope Zacharias and St. Boniface shows that the lighting of the *ignis* by a crystal instead of from a lamp kept secretly burning distinguished Gallican from Roman ceremonial in the eighth century (Jaffé, 2291). All the lights in the church are previously put out, and this itself has become a ceremony in the *Tenebrae*. Ecclesiastical symbolism explained the extinction and rekindling of lights as typifying the Resurrection. Sometimes the *ignis* provides a light for the folk-fire outside.

[4] Belethus († 1162), *de Div. Offic.* c. 137 (*P. L.* ccii. 141), gives three customs of St. John's Eve. Bones are burnt, because (1) there are dragons in air, earth, and water, and when these ' in aere ad libidi-nem concitantur, quod fere fit, saepe ipsum sperma vel in puteos vel in aquas fluviales eiiciunt, ex quo le-thalis sequitur annus,' but the smoke of the bonfires drives them away; and (2) because St. John's bones were burnt in Sebasta. Torches are carried, because St. John was a shining light. A wheel is rolled, because of the solstice, which is made appropriate to St. John by *St. John* iii. 30. The account of Bele-thus is amplified by Durandus, *Ra-tionale Div. Offic.* (ed. corr. Antwerp, 1614) vii. 14, and taken in turn from Durandus by a fifteenth-century monk of Winchelscombe in a ser-mon preserved in *Harl. MS.* 2345, f. 49 (b).

evidence, for rain-charms[1]. It is perhaps justifiable to infer that the crystallization of the rain- and heat-charms, which doubtless were originally used only when the actual condition of the weather made them necessary, into annual festivals, took place after the exact rationale of them had been lost, and they had both come to be looked upon, rather vaguely, as weather-charms.

Apart from the festival-fires, a superstitious use of sun-charms endured in England to an extraordinarily late date. This was in times of drought and pestilence as a magical remedy against mortality amongst the cattle. A fire was built, and, as on the festivals, the cattle were made to pass through the smoke and flames[2]. On such occasions, and often at the festival-fires themselves, it was held requisite that, just as the water used in the rain-charms would be fresh water from the spring, so the fire must be fresh fire. That is to say, it must not be lit from any pre-existing fire, but must be made anew. And, so conservative is cult, this must be done, not with the modern device of matches, or even with flint and steel, but by the primitive method of causing friction in dry work. Such fire is known as 'need-fire' or 'forced fire,' and is produced in various ways, by rubbing two pieces of wood together, by turning a drill in a solid block, or by rapidly rotating a wheel upon an axle. Often certain precautions are observed, as that nine men must work at the job, or chaste boys; and often all the hearth-fires in the village are first extinguished, to be rekindled by the new flame[3].

The custom of rolling a burning wheel downhill from the

[1] Gaidoz, 24, 109; Bertrand, 122; Dyer, 323; Stubbes, i. 339, from Naogeorgos; Usener, ii. 81; and the mediaeval calendar in Brand, i. 179.

[2] Gomme, in *Brit. Ass. Rep.*(1896), 636 (Moray, Mull); *F. L.* ix. 280 (Caithness, with illustration of wood used); Kemble, i. 360 (Perthshire in 1826, Devonshire).

[3] Grimm, ii. 603; Kemble, i. 359; Elton, 293; Frazer, iii. 301; Gaidoz, 22; Jahn, 26; Simpson, 196; Bertrand, 107; Golther, 570. The English term is *needfire*, Scotch *neidfyre*, German *Noth-feuer*. It is variously derived from *nôt* 'need,' *niuwan* 'rub,' or *hniotan* 'press.' If the last is right, the English form should perhaps be *knead-fire* (Grimm, ii. 607, 609; Golther, 570). Another German term is *Wildfeuer*. The Gaelic *tin-egin* is from *tin* 'fire,' and *egin* 'violence' (Grimm, ii. 609). For ecclesiastical prohibitions cf. *Indiculus* (Saupe, 20) 'de igne fricato de ligno, i. e. *nodfyr*'; *Capit. Karlmanni* (742), c. 5 (Grimm, ii. 604) 'illos sacrilegos ignes quos *niedfyr* vocant.'

festival-fire amongst the vineyards has been noted. The wheel is, of course, by no means an uncommon solar emblem [1]. Sometimes round bannocks or hard-boiled eggs are similarly rolled downhill. The use of both of these may be sacrificial in its nature. But the egg plays such a large part in festival customs, especially at Easter, when it is reddened, or gilt, or coloured yellow with furze or broom flowers, and popularly regarded as a symbol of the Resurrection, that one is tempted to ask whether it does not stand for the sun itself [2]. And are we to find the sun in the 'parish top [3],' or in the ball with which, even in cathedrals, ceremonial games were played [4]?

[1] Gaidoz, 1; Bertrand, 109, 140; Simpson, 109, 240; Rhys, *C. H.* 54. The commonest form of the symbol is the swastika, but others appear to be found in the 'hammer' of Thor, and on the altars and statues of a Gaulish deity equated in the *interpretatio Romana* with Jupiter. There is a wheel decoration on the *barelle* or cars of the Gubbio *ceri* (Bower, 4).

[2] Brand, i. 97; Dyer, 159; Ditchfield, 78. Eggs are used ceremonially at the Scotch Beltane fires (Frazer, iii. 261; Simpson, 285). Strings of birds' eggs are hung on the Lynn May garland (*F. L.* x. 443). In Dauphiné an omelette is made when the sun rises on St. John's day (Cortet, 217). In Germany children are sent to look for the Easter eggs in the nest of a hare, a very divine animal. Among the miscellaneous Benedictions in the *Sarum Manual*, with the *Ben. Seminis* and the *Ben. Pomorum in die Sti Iacobi* are a *Ben. Carnis Casei Butyri Ovorum sive Pastillarum in Pascha* and a *Ben. Agni Paschalis, Ovorum et Herbarum in die Paschae*. These Benedictions are little more than graces. The *Durham Accounts*, i. 71–174, contain entries of fifteenth- and sixteenth-century payments 'fratribus et sororibus de Wytton pro eorum Egsilver erga festum pasche.'

[3] *Tw. N.* i. 3. 42 'He's a coward and a coystrill, that will not drink to my niece till his brains turn o' the toe like a parish-top.' Steevens says 'a large top was formerly kept in every village, to be whipt in frosty weather, that the peasants might be kept warm by exercise and out of mischief while they could not work.' This is evidently a 'fake' of the 'Puck of commentators.' Hone, *E. D. B.* i. 199, says 'According to a story (whether true or false), in one of the churches of Paris, a choir boy used to whip a top marked with *Alleluia*, written in gold letters, from one end of the choir to the other.' The 'burial of Alleluia' is shown later on to be a mediaeval perversion of an agricultural rite. On the whole question of tops, see Haddon, 255; A. B. Gomme, s. v.

[4] Leber, ix. 391; Barthélemy, iv. 447; Du Tilliot, 30; Grenier, 385; Bérenger-Féraud, iii. 427; Belethus, c. 120 'Sunt nonnullae ecclesiae in quibus usitatum est, ut vel etiam episcopi et archiepiscopi in coenobiis cum suis ludant subditis, ita ut etiam se ad lusum pilae demittant. atque haec quidem libertas ideo dicta est decembrica.... quamquam vero magnae ecclesiae, ut est Remensis, hanc ludendi consuetudinem observent, videtur tamen laudabilius esse non ludere'; Durandus, vi. 86 'In quibusdam locis hac die, in aliis in Natali, praelati cum suis clericis ludunt, vel in claustris, vel in domibus episcopalibus; ita ut etiam descendant

If so, perhaps this game of ball may be connected with the curious belief that if you get up early enough on Easter morning you may see the sun dance[1].

In any case sun-charms, quite independent of the fires, may probably be traced in the circular movements which so often appear invested with a religious significance, and which sometimes form part of the festivals[2]. It would be rash to regard such movements as the basis of every circular dance or *ronde* on such an occasion; a ring is too obviously the form which a crowd of spectators round any object, sacred or otherwise, must take. But there are many circumambulatory rites in which stress is laid on the necessity for the motion to be *deasil*, or with the right hand to the centre, in accordance with the course of the sun, and not in the opposite direction, *cartuaitheail* or *withershins*[3]. And these, perhaps, may be legitimately considered as of magical origin.

ad ludum pilae, vel etiam ad choreas et cantus, &c.' Often the ball play was outside the church, but the canons of Evreux on their return from the *procession noire* of May 1, played ' ad quillas super voltas ecclesiae '; and the Easter *pilota* of Auxerre which lasted to 1538, took place in the nave before vespers. Full accounts of this ceremony have been preserved. The dean and canons danced and tossed the ball, singing the *Victimae paschali*. For examples of Easter hand-ball or marbles in English folk-custom, cf. Brand, i. 103; Vaux, 240; *F. L.* xii. 75; Mrs. Gomme, s. v. *Hand-ball*.

[1] Brand, i. 93; Burne-Jackson, 335. A Norfolk version (*F. L.* vii. 90) has ' dances as if in agony.' On the Mendips (*F. L.* v. 339) what is expected is ' a lamb in the sun.' The moon, and perhaps the sun also, is sometimes ' wobbly,' ' jumping ' or ' skipping,' owing to the presence of strata of air differing in humidity or temperature, and so changing the index of refraction (Nicholson, *Golspie*, 186). At Pontesford Hill in Shropshire (Burne-Jackson, 330) the pilgrimage was on Palm Sunday, actually to pluck a sprig from a

haunted yew, traditionally ' to look for the golden arrow,' which must be solar. In the Isle of Man hills, on which are sacred wells, are visited on the Lugnassad, to gather ling-berries. Others say that it is because of Jephthah's daughter, who went up and down on the mountains and bewailed her virginity. And the old folk now stop at home and read *Judges* xi (Rhys, *C. F.* i. 312). On the place of hill-tops in agricultural religion cf. p. 106, and for the use of elevated spots for sun-worship at Rome, ch. xi.

[2] Simpson, *passim* ; cf. *F. L.* vi. 168; xi. 220. *Deasil* is from Gaelic *deas*, ' right,' ' south.' Mediaeval ecclesiastical processions went ' contra solis cursum et morem ecclesiasticum ' only in seasons of woe or sadness (Kock, iii. 2. 182).

[3] Dr. Murray kindly informs me that the etymology of *withershins* (A.-S. *wiþersynes*) is uncertain. It is from *wiþer*, ' against,' and either some lost noun, or one derived from *séon*, ' to see,' or *sinþ*, ' course.' The original sense is simply ' backwards,' and the equivalence with *deasil* not earlier than the seventeenth century. A folk-etymology from *shine* may account for the aspirate.

With the growth of animistic or spiritual religion, the mental tendencies, out of which magical practices or charms arise, gradually cease to be operative in the consciousness of the worshippers. The charms themselves, however, are preserved by the conservative instinct of cult. In part they survive as mere bits of traditional ritual, for which no particular reason is given or demanded; in part also they become material for that other instinct, itself no less inveterate in the human mind, by which the relics of the past are constantly in process of being re-explained and brought into new relations with the present. The sprinkling with holy water, for instance, which was originally of the nature of a rain-charm, comes to be regarded as a rite symbolical of spiritual purification and regeneration. An even more striking example of such transformation of intention is to be found in the practice, hardly yet referred to in this account of the agricultural festivals, of sacrifice. In the ordinary acceptation of the term, sacrifice implies not merely an animistic, but an anthropomorphic conception of the object of cult. The offering or oblation with which man approaches his god is an extension of the gift with which, as suppliant, he approaches his fellow men. But the oblational aspect of sacrifice is not the only one. In his remarkable book upon *The Religion of the Semites*, Professor Robertson Smith has formulated another, which may be distinguished as 'sacramental.' In this the sacrifice is regarded as the renewal of a special tie between the god and his worshippers, analogous to the blood-bond which exists amongst those worshippers themselves. The victim is not an offering made to the god; on the contrary, the god himself is, or is present in, the victim. It is his blood which is shed, and by means of the sacrificial banquet and its subsidiary rites, his personality becomes, as it were, incorporated in those of his clansmen[1]. It is not necessary to determine here the general priority of the two types or

[1] Robertson Smith, *Religion of the Semites*, 196; Jevons, 130; Frazer, ii. 352; Grant Allen, 318; Hartland, ii. 236; Turnbull, *The Blood Covenant*. Perhaps, as a third type of sacrifice, should be distinguished the 'alimentary' sacrifice of food and other things made to the dead. This rests on the belief in the continuance of the mortal life with its needs and desires after death.

conceptions of sacrifice described. But, while it is probable that the Kelts and Teutons of the time of the conversion consciously looked upon sacrifice as an oblation, there is also reason to believe that, at an earlier period, the notion of a sacrament had been the predominant one. For the sacrificial ritual of these peoples, and especially that used in the agricultural cult, so far as it can be traced, is only explicable as an elaborate process of just that physical incorporation of the deity in the worshippers and their belongings, which it was the precise object of the sacramental sacrifice to bring about. It will be clear that sacrifice, so regarded, enters precisely into that category of ideas which has been defined as magical. It is but one more example of that belief in the efficacy of direct contact which lies at the root of sympathetic magic. As in the case of the garland customs, this belief, originally pre-animistic, has endured into an animistic stage of thought. Through the garland and the posies the worshipper sought contact with the fertilization spirit in its phytomorphic form ; through sacrifice he approaches it in its theriomorphic form also. The earliest sacrificial animals, then, were themselves regarded as divine, and were naturally enough the food animals of the folk. The use made by the Kelto-Teutonic peoples of oxen, sheep, goats, swine, deer, geese, and fowls requires no explanation. A common victim was also the horse, which the Germans seem, up to a late date, to have kept in droves and used for food. The strong opposition of the Church to the sacrificial use of horse-flesh may possibly account for the prejudice against it as a food-stuff in modern Europe[1]. A similar prejudice, however, in the case of the hare, an animal of great importance in folk belief, already existed in the time of Caesar[2]. It is a little more puzzling to find distinct traces of sacrificial

---

[1] Grimm, i. 47 ; Golther, 565 ; Gummere, *G.O.*40,457. Gregory III wrote (†731) to Boniface (*P. L.*lxxxix. 577) 'inter cetera agrestem caballum aliquantos comedere adiunxisti plerosque et domesticum. hoc nequaquam fieri deinceps sinas,' cf. *Councils of Cealcythe and Pincanhale* (787), c. 19 (Haddan-Stubbs, iii. 458) 'equos etiam plerique in vobis comedunt, quod nullus Christianorum in Orientalibus facit.' The decking of horses is a familiar feature of May-day in London and elsewhere.

[2] C. J. Billson, *The Easter Hare*, in *F. L.* iii. 441.

customs in connexion with animals, such as the dog, cat, wolf, fox, squirrel, owl, wren, and so forth, which are not now food animals[1]. But they may once have been such, or the explanation may lie in an extension of the sacrificial practice after the first rationale of it was lost.

At every agricultural festival, then, animal sacrifice may be assumed as an element. The analogy of the relation between the fertilization spirit and his worshippers to the human blood bond makes it probable that originally the rite was always a bloody one[2]. Some of the blood was poured on the sacred tree. Some was sprinkled upon the worshippers, or smeared over their faces, or solemnly drunk by them[3]. Hides, horns, and entrails were also hung upon the tree[4], or worn as festival trappings[5]. The flesh was, of course, solemnly eaten in the sacrificial meal[6]. The crops, as well as their cultivators, must benefit by the rites; and therefore the fields, and doubtless also the cattle, had their sprinkling of blood, while heads or pieces of flesh were buried in the furrows, or at the threshold of the byre[7]. A fair notion of the whole proceeding may be obtained from the account of the similar Indian worship of the earth-goddess given in Appendix I. The intention of the ceremonies will be obvious by a comparison with those already explained. The wearing of the skins of the victims is precisely parallel to the wearing of the green vegetation, the sprinkling with blood to the sprinkling with lustral water, the burial in the fields of flesh and skulls to the burial of

[1] N. W. Thomas in *F. L.* xi. 227.

[2] Grimm, i. 55; Golther, 559, 575; Gummere, *G. O.* 456. The universal Teutonic term for sacrificing is *blôtan*.

[3] Frazer, *Pausanias*, iii. 20; Jevons, 130, 191. Does the modern huntsman know why he 'bloods' a novice?

[4] Grimm, i. 47, 57, 77; Jahn, 24; Gummere, *G. O.* 459. Hence the theriomorphic 'image.'

[5] Robertson Smith, 414, 448; Jevons, 102, 285; Frazer, ii. 448; Lang, *M. R. R.*[1] ii. 73, 80, 106, 214, 226; Grant Allen, 335; Du Méril, *Com.* i. 75. Hence the theriomor-phic *larva* or mask (Frazer, *Pausanias*, iv. 239).

[6] Grimm, i. 46, 57; Golther, 576; Frazer, ii. 318, 353; Jevons, 144; Grant Allen, 325. Savages believe that by eating an animal they will acquire its bodily and mental qualities.

[7] Jahn, 14, and for classical parallels Frazer, ii. 315; *Pausanias*, iii. 288; Jevons, *Plutarch*, lxix. 143. Grant Allen, 292, was told as a boy in Normandy that at certain lustrations 'a portion of the Host (stolen or concealed, I imagine) was sometimes buried in each field.'

brands from the festival-fire.   In each case the belief in the
necessity of direct physical contact to convey the beneficent
influence is at the bottom of the practice.   It need hardly be
said that of such physical contact the most complete example
is in the sacramental banquet itself.

It is entirely consistent with the view here taken of the
primitive nature of sacrifice, that the fertilization spirit was
sacrificed at the village festivals in its vegetable as well as in
its animal form.   There were bread-offerings as well as meat-
offerings [1].   Sacramental cakes were prepared with curious
rituals which attest their primitive character.   Like the
tcharnican or Beltane cakes, they were kneaded and moulded
by hand and not upon a board [2]; like the loaf in the Anglo-
Saxon charm, they were compounded of all sorts of grain
in order that they might be representative of every crop in
the field [3].   At the harvest they would naturally be made,
wholly or in part, of the last sheaf cut.   The use of them
corresponded closely to that made of the flesh of the sacrificial
victim.   Some were laid on a branch of the sacred tree [4];
others flung into the sacred well or the festival-fire; others
again buried in the furrows, or crumbled up and mingled with
the seed-corn [5].   And like the flesh they were solemnly eaten
by the worshippers themselves at the sacrificial banquet.
With the sacrificial cake went the sacrificial draught, also
made out of the fruits of the earth, in the southern lands wine,
but in the vineless north ale, or cider, or that mead which
Pytheas described the Britons as brewing out of honey and
wheat [6].   Of this, too, the trees and crops received their share,
while it filled the cup for those toasts or *minnes* to the dead and
to Odin and Freyja their rulers, which were afterwards transferred by Christian Germany to St. John and St. Gertrude [7].

The animal and the cereal sacrifices seem plausible enough,
but they do not exhaust the problem.   One has to face the
fact that human sacrifice, as Victor Hehn puts it, 'peers

[1] Frazer, ii. 318; Grant Allen,
337; Jevons, 206.
[2] *F. L.* vi. 1.
[3] Frazer, ii. 319; Jevons, 214;
cf. the πάνσπερμα at the Athenian
Pyanepsia.
[4] In the Beltane rite (*F. L.* vi.

2) a bit of the bannock is reserved
for the 'cuack' or cuckoo, here
doubtless the inheritor of the gods.
[5] Grimm, iii. 1240.
[6] Elton, 428.
[7] Grimm, i. 59; Gummere, *G. O.*
455.

uncannily forth from the dark past of every Aryan race[1]. So far as the Kelts and Teutons go, there is plenty of evidence to show, that up to the very moment of their contact with Roman civilization, in some branches even up to the very moment of their conversion to Christianity, it was not yet obsolete[2]. An explanation of it is therefore required, which shall fall in with the general theory of agricultural sacrifice. The subject is very difficult, but, on the whole, it seems probable that originally the slaying of a human being at an annually recurring festival was not of the nature of sacrifice at all. It is doubtful whether it was ever sacrifice in the sacramental sense, and although in time it came to be regarded as an oblation, this was not until the first meaning, both of the sacrifice and of the human death, had been lost. The essential facts bearing on the question have been gathered together by Dr. Frazer in *The Golden Bough*. He brings out the point that the victim in a human sacrifice was not originally merely a man, but a very important man, none other than the king, the priest-king of the tribe. In many communities, Aryan-speaking and other, it has been the principal function of such a priest-king to die, annually or at longer intervals, for the people. His place is taken, as a rule, by the tribesman who has slain him[3]. Dr. Frazer's own explanation of this custom is, that the head of the tribe was looked upon as possessed of great magical powers, as a big medicine man, and was in fact identified with the god himself. And his periodical death, says Dr. Frazer, was necessary, in order to renew the vitality of the god, who might decay and cease to exist, were he not from time to time reincarnated by being slain and passing into the body of his slayer and successor[4]. This is a highly ingenious

---

[1] V. Hehn, *Culturpflanzen*, 438.

[2] Grimm, i. 44, 48, 53 ; Golther, 561 ; Gummere, *G. O.* 459; Schräder, 422 ; Mogk, iii. 388 ; Meyer, 199, and for Keltic evidence Elton, 270. Many of these examples belong rather to the war than to the agricultural cult. The latest in the west are *Capit. de partib. Saxon.* 9 'Si quis hominem diabolo sacrificaverit et in hostiam, more paga-norum, daemonibus obtulerit' ; *Lex Frisionum,* additio sup. tit. 42 'qui fanum effregerit . . . immolatur diis, quorum templa violavit' ; *Epist. Greg. III,* 1 (*P. L.* lxxxix, 578) 'hoc quoque inter alia crimina agi in partibus illis dixisti, quod quidam ex fidelibus ad immolandum paganis sua venundent mancipia.'

[3] Frazer, ii. 1 ; Jevons, 279.

[4] Frazer, ii. 5, 59.

and fascinating theory, but unfortunately there are several difficulties in the way of accepting it. In the first place it is inconsistent with the explanation of the sacramental killing of the god arrived at by Professor Robertson Smith. According to this the sacrifice of the god is for the sake of his worshippers, that the blood-bond with them may be renewed; and we have seen that this view fits in admirably with the minor sacrificial rites, such as the eating and burying of the flesh, as the wearing of the horns and hides. Dr. Frazer, however, obliges us to hold that the god is also sacrificed for his own sake, and leaves us in the position of propounding two quite distinct and independent reasons for the same fact. Secondly, there is no evidence, at least amongst Aryan-speaking peoples, for that breaking down of the very real and obvious distinction between the god and his chief worshipper or priest, which Dr. Frazer's theory implies. And thirdly, if the human victim were slain as being the god, surely this slaughter should have replaced the slaughter of the animal victim previously slain for the same reason, which it did not, and should have been followed by a sacramental meal of a cannibal type, of which also, in western Europe, there is but the slightest trace[1].

Probably, therefore, the alternative explanation of Dr. Frazer's own facts given by Dr. Jevons is preferable. According to this the death of the human victim arises out of the circumstances of the animal sacrifice. The slaying of the divine animal is an act approached by the tribe with mingled feelings. It is necessary, in order to renew the all-essential blood-bond between the god and his worshippers. And at the same time it is an act of sacrilege; it is killing the god. There is some hesitation amongst the assembled worshippers. Who will dare the deed and face its consequences? 'The clansman,' says Dr. Jevons, 'whose religious conviction of the clan's need of communion with the god was deepest, would eventually and after long waiting be the one to strike, and take upon himself the issue, for the sake of

[1] Strabo, iv. 5. 4; Bastian, *Oestl. Asien*, v. 272. The Mexican evidence given by Frazer, iii. 134, does not necessarily represent a primitive notion of the nature of the rite.

his fellow men.' This issue would be twofold. The slayer would be exalted in the eyes of his fellows. He would naturally be the first to drink the shed blood of the god. A double portion of the divine spirit would enter into him. He would become, for a while, the leader, the priest-king, of the community. At the same time he would incur blood-guiltiness. And in a year's time, when his sanctity was exhausted, the penalty would have to be paid. His death would accompany the renewal of the bond by a fresh sacrifice, implying in its turn the self-devotion of a fresh annual king[1].

These theories belong to a region of somewhat shadowy conjecture. If Dr. Jevons is right, it would seem to follow that, as has already been suggested, the human death at an annual festival was not initially sacrifice. It accompanied, but did not replace the sacramental slaughter of a divine animal. But when the animal sacrifice had itself changed its character, and was looked upon, no longer as an act of communion with the god, but as an offering or bribe made to him, then a new conception of the human death also was required. When the animal ceased to be recognized as the god, the need of a punishment for slaying it disappeared. But the human death could not be left meaningless, and its meaning was assimilated to that of the animal sacrifice itself. It also became an oblation, the greatest that could be offered by the tribe to its protector and its judge. And no doubt this was the conscious view taken of the matter by Kelts and Teutons at the time when they appear in history. The human sacrifice was on the same footing as the animal sacrifice, but it was a more binding, a more potent, a more solemn appeal.

In whatever way human sacrifice originated, it was obviously destined, with the advance of civilization, to undergo modification. Not only would the growing moral sense of mankind learn to hold it a dark and terrible thing, but also to go on killing the leading man of the tribe, the king-priest, would have its obvious practical inconveniences. At first, indeed, these would not be great. The king-priest would be

---

[1] Jevons, 291 ; *Plutarch*, lxx. For traces of the blood-guiltiness incurred by sacrifice, cf. the βουφόνια at Athens and the *regifugium* at Rome (Frazer, ii. 294 ; Robertson Smith, i. 286).

little more than a rain-maker, a *rex sacrorum*, and one man might perform the ceremonial observances as well as another. But as time went on, and the tribe settled down to a comparatively civilized life, the serious functions of its leader would increase. He would become the arbiter of justice, the adviser in debate; above all, when war grew into importance, the captain in battle. And to spare and replace, year by year, the wisest councillor and the bravest warrior would grow into an intolerable burden. Under some such circumstances, one can hardly doubt, a process of substitution set in. Somebody had to die for the king. At first, perhaps, the substitute was an inferior member of the king's own house, or even an ordinary tribesman, chosen by lot. But the process, once begun, was sure to continue, and presently it was sufficient if a life of little value, that of a prisoner, a slave, a criminal, a stranger within the gates, was sacrificed[1]. The common belief in madness or imbecility as a sign of divine possession may perhaps have contributed to make the village fool or natural seem a particularly suitable victim. But to the very end of Teutonic and Keltic heathenism, the sense that the substitute was, after all, only a substitute can be traced. In times of great stress or danger, indeed, the king might still be called upon to suffer in person[2]. And always a certain pretence that the victim was the king was kept up. Even though a slave or criminal, he was for a few days preceding the sacrifice treated royally. He was a temporary king, was richly dressed and feasted, had a crown set on his head, and was permitted to hold revel with his fellows. The farce was played out in the sight of men and gods[3]. Ultimately, of course, the natural growth of the sanctity of human life in a progressive people, or in an unprogressive people the pressure of outside ideals[4], forbids the sacrifice of a man at all. Perhaps the temporary

[1] Frazer, ii. 15, 55, 232; Jevons, 280; Grant Allen, 242, 296, 329.

[2] In three successive years of famine the Swedes sacrificed first oxen, then men, finally their king Dômaldi himself (*Ynglingasaga*, c. 18).

[3] Frazer, ii. 24; Jevons, 280;

Grant Allen, 296.

[4] The British rule in India forbids human sacrifice, and the Khonds, a Dravidian race of Bengal, have substituted animal for human victims within the memory of man (Frazer, ii. 245).

king is still chosen, and even some symbolic mimicked slaying
of him takes place; but actually he does not die. An animal
takes his place upon the altar; or more strictly speaking, an
animal remains the last victim, as it had been the first, and in
myth is regarded as a substitute for the human victim which
for a time had shared its fate. Of such a myth the legends
of Abraham and Isaac and of Iphigeneia at Aulis are the
classical examples.

There is another group of myths for which, although they
lack this element of a substituted victim, mythologists find an
origin in a reformation of religious sentiment leading to the
abolition of human sacrifice. The classical legend of Perseus
and Andromeda, the hagiological legend of St. George and
the Dragon, the Teutonic legend of Beowulf and Grendel,
are only types of innumerable tales in which the hero puts
an end to the periodical death of a victim by slaying the
monster who has enforced and profited by it[1]. What is
such a story but the imaginative statement of the fact that
such sacrifices at one time were, and are not? It is, however, noticeable, that in the majority of these stories, although
not in all, the dragon or monster slain has his dwelling in
water, and this leads to the consideration of yet another
sophistication of the primitive notion of sacrifice. According
to this notion sacrifice was necessarily bloody; in the shedding of blood and in the sacrament of blood partaken of by
the worshippers, lay the whole gist of the rite: a bloodless
sacrifice would have no *raison d'être*. On the other hand,
the myths just referred to seem to imply a bloodless sacrifice
by drowning, and this notion is confirmed by an occasional
bit of ritual, and by the common superstition which represents the spirits of certain lakes and rivers as claiming
a periodical victim in the shape of a drowned person[2].
Similarly there are traces of sacrifices, which must have been
equally bloodless, by fire. At the Beltane festival, for
instance, one member of the party is chosen by lot to be

---

[1] Hartland, iii. 1; Frazer, *Pausanias*, iv. 197; v. 44, 143; Bérenger-Féraud, i. 207. Mr. Frazer enu-
merates forty-one versions of the
legend.

[2] Hartland, iii. 81; Grimm, ii.
494; Gummere, *G. O.* 396. The
slaves of Nerthus were drowned in
the same lake in which the goddess was dipped.

the 'victim,' is made to jump over the flames and is spoken of in jest as 'dead [1].' Various Roman writers, who apparently draw from the second-century B.C. Greek explorer Posidonius, ascribe to the Druids of Gaul a custom of burning human and other victims at quinquennial feasts in colossal images of hollow wickerwork; and squirrels, cats, snakes and other creatures are frequently burnt in modern festival-fires [2]. The constant practice, indeed, of burning bones in such fires has given them the specific name of bonfires, and it may be taken for granted that the bones are only representatives of more complete victims. I would suggest that such sacrifices by water and fire are really developments of the water- and fire-charms described in the last chapter; and that just as the original notion of sacrifice has been extended to give a new significance to the death of a human being at a religious festival, when the real reason for that death had been forgotten, so it has been still further extended to cover the primitive water- and fire-charms when they too had become meaningless. I mean that at a festival the victims, like the image and the worshippers, were doubtless habitually flung into water or passed through fire as part of the charm; and that, at a time when sacrifice had grown into mere oblation and the shedding of blood was therefore no longer essential, these rites were adapted and given new life as alternative methods of effecting the sacrifice.

It is not surprising that there should be but few direct and evident survivals of sacrifice in English village custom. For at the time of the conversion the rite must have borne the whole brunt of the missionary attack. The other elements of the festivals, the sacred garlands, the water- and fire-charms, had already lost much of their original significance. A judgement predisposed to toleration might plausibly look upon

---

[1] *F. L.* vi. I.

[2] Frazer, iii. 319; Gaidoz, 27; Cortet, 213; Simpson, 221; Bertrand, 68; *F. L.* xii. 315. The work of Posidonius does not exist, but was possibly used by Caesar, *B. G.* vi. 15; Strabo, iv. 4. 5; Diodorus, v. 32. Wicker 'giants' are still burnt in some French festival-fires. But elsewhere, as in the midsummer shows, such 'giants' seem to be images of the agricultural divinities, and it is not clear by what process they came to be burnt and so destroyed. Perhaps they were originally only smoked, just as they were dipped.

them as custom rather than worship. It was not so with sacrifice. This too had had its history, and in divers ways changed its character. But it was still essentially a liturgy. Oblation or sacrament, it could not possibly be dissociated from a recognition of the divine nature of the power in whose honour it took place. And therefore it must necessarily be renounced, as a condition of acceptance in the Church at all, by the most weak-kneed convert. What happened was precisely that to which Gregory the Great looked forward. The sacrificial banquet, the great chines of flesh, and the beakers of ale, cider, and mead, endured, but the central rite of the old festival, the ceremonial slaying of the animal, vanished. The exceptions, however, are not so rare as might at first sight be thought, and naturally they are of singular interest. It has already been pointed out that in times of stress and trouble, the thinly veneered heathenism of the country folk long tended to break out, and in particular that up to a very late date the primitive need-fire was occasionally revived to meet the exigencies of a cattle-plague. Under precisely similar circumstances, and sometimes in immediate connexion with the need-fire, cattle have been known, even during the present century, to be sacrificed [1]. Nor are such sporadic instances the only ones that can be adduced. Here and there sacrifice, in a more or less modified form, remains an incident in the village festival. The alleged custom of annually sacrificing a sheep on May-day at Andreas in the Isle of Man rests on slight evidence [2]; but there is a fairly well authenticated example in the 'ram feast' formerly held on the same day in the village of Holne in Devonshire. A ram was slain at a granite pillar or ancient altar in the village 'ploy-field,' and a struggle took place for slices which were supposed to bring luck [3].

---

[1] Gomme, *Ethnology*, 137; *F.L.* ii. 300; x. 101; xii. 217; Vaux, 287; Rhys, *C.F.* i. 306.

[2] *F.L.* ii. 302; Rhys, *C.F.* i. 307. In 1656, bulls were sacrificed near Dingwall (*F.L.* x. 353). A few additional examples, beyond those here given, are mentioned by N.W. Thomas, in *F.L.* xi. 247.

[3] 1 *N.Q.* vii. 353; Gomme, *Ethnology*, 32; *Village Community*, 113; Grant Allen, 290. The custom was extinct when it was first described in 1853, and some doubt has recently been thrown upon the 'altar,' the 'struggle' and other details; cf. *Trans. of Devonshire Assn.* xxviii. 99; *F.L.* viii. 287.

Still more degenerate survivals are afforded by the Whitsun feast at King's Teignton, also in Devonshire [1], and by the Whitsun 'lamb feast' at Kidlington [2], the Trinity 'lamb ale' at Kirtlington [3], and the 'Whit hunt' in Wychwood Forest [4], all three places lying close together in Oxfordshire. These five cases have been carefully recorded and studied; but they do not stand alone; for the folk-calendar affords numerous examples of days which are marked, either universally or locally, by the ceremonial hunting or killing of some wild or domestic animal, or by the consumption of a particular dish which readily betrays its sacrificial origin [5]. The appearance of animals in ecclesiastical processions in St. Paul's cathedral [6] and at Bury St. Edmunds [7] is especially significant; and it is natural to find an origin for the old English sport of bull-baiting rather in a survival of heathen ritual than in any reminiscence of the Roman amphitheatre [8]. Even where sacrifice itself has vanished, the minor rites which once accompanied it are still perpetuated in the superstitions or the festival customs of the peasantry. The heads and hides of horses or cattle, like the *exuviae* of the sacrificial victims, are worn or carried in dance, procession or *quête* [9]. The dead bodies of animals are suspended by shepherds or game-keepers upon tree and barn-door, from immemorial habit or from

---

[1] 1 *N. Q.* vii. 353; Gomme, *Ethnology*, 30; Vaux, 285.

[2] Blount, *Jocular Tenures* (ed. Beckwith), 281; Dyer, 297.

[3] Dunkin, *Hist. of Bicester* (1816), 268; P. Manning, in *F. L.* viii. 313.

[4] P. Manning, in *F. L.* viii. 310; Dyer, 282.

[5] N. W. Thomas, in *F. L.* xi. 227; Dyer, 285, 438, 470; Ditchfield, 85, 131.

[6] Certain lands were held of the chapter for which a fat buck was paid on the Conversion of St. Paul (January 25), and a fat doe on the Commemoration of St. Paul (June 30). They were offered, according to one writer, alive, at the high altar; the flesh was baked, the head and horns carried in festal procession. The custom dated from at least 1274 (Dyer, 49; W.

Sparrow Simpson, *St. Paul's Cath. and Old City Life*, 234).

[7] *F. L.* iv. 9; x. 355. White bulls are said to have been led to the shrine by women desirous of children. F. C. Conybeare, in *R. de l'Hist. des Religions*, xliv. 108, describes some survivals of sacrificial rites in the Armenian church which existed primitively in other Greek churches also.

[8] *F. L.* vii. 346. Bull-baiting often took place on festivals, and in several cases, as at Tutbury, the bull was driven into or over a river. Bear-baiting is possibly a later variant of the sport.

[9] Burton, 165; *Suffolk F. L.* 71; Ditchfield, 227; Dyer, 387; Pfannenschmidt, 279; cf. the Abbots Bromley Horn-dance (ch. viii).

some vague suspicion of the luck they will bring. Although inquiry will perhaps elicit the fallacious explanation that they are there *pour encourager les autres*[1]. In the following chapters an attempt will be made to show how widely sacrifice is represented in popular amusements and *ludi*. Here it will be sufficient to call attention to two personages who figure largely in innumerable village festivals. One is the 'hobby-horse,' not yet, though Shakespeare will have it so, 'forgot[2]': the other the 'fool' or 'squire,' a buffoon with a pendent cow's tail, who is in many places *de rigueur* in Maying or rushbearing[3]. Both of these grotesques seem to be at bottom nothing but worshippers careering in the skins of sacrificed animals.

The cereal or liquor sacrifice is of less importance. Sugar and water, which may be conjectured to represent mead, is occasionally drunk beside a sacred well, and in one instance, at least, bread and cheese are thrown into the depths. Sometimes also a ploughman carries bread and cheese in his pocket when he goes abroad to cut the first furrow[4]. But the original rite is probably most nearly preserved in the custom of 'youling' fruit-trees to secure a good crop. When this is done, at Christmas or Ascension-tide, ale or cider is poured on the roots of the trees, and a cake placed in a fork of the boughs. Here and there a cake is also hung on the horn of an ox in the stall[5]. Doubtless the 'feasten' cake, of traditional

---

[1] *F. L.* iv. 5. The custom of sacrifice at the foundation of a new building has also left traces: cf. Grant Allen, 248; *F. L.* xi. 322, 437; Speth, *Builders' Rites and Ceremonies.*

[2] Douce, 598, gives a cut of a hobby-horse, i.e. a man riding a pasteboard or wicker horse with his legs concealed beneath a footcloth. According to Du Méril, *Com.* i. 79, 421, the device is known throughout Europe. In France it is the *chevalet, cheval-mallet, cheval-fol,* &c.; in Germany the *Schimmel.*

[3] Dyer, 182, 266, 271; Ditchfield, 97; Burton, 40; *F. L.* viii. 309, 313, 317; cf. ch. ix on the

'fool' or 'squire' in the sword and morris dances, and ch. xvi on his court and literary congener. The folk-fool wears a cow's tail or fox's brush, or carries a stick with a tail at one end and a bladder and peas at the other. He often wears a mask or has his face blacked. In Lancashire he is sometimes merged with the 'woman' grotesque of the folk-festivals, and called 'owd Bet.'

[4] W. Gregor, *F. L. of N. E. Scotland,*181, says that bread and cheese were actually laid in the field, and in the plough when it was 'strykit.'

[5] Dyer, 20, 207, 447; Ditchfield, 46; *F. L.* vi. 93. Pirminius v. Reichenau, *Dicta* († 753), c. 22,

shape and composition, which pervades the country, is in its origin sacramental[1]. Commonly enough, it represents an animal or human being, and in such cases it may be held, while retaining its own character of a cereal sacrifice, to be also a substitute for the animal or human sacrifice with which it should by rights be associated[2].

An unauthenticated and somewhat incredible story has been brought from Italy to the effect that the mountaineers of the Abruzzi are still in the habit of offering up a human sacrifice in Holy week[3]. In these islands a reminiscence of the observance is preserved in the 'victim' of the Beltane festival[4], and a transformation of it in the whipping of lads when the bounds are beaten in the Rogations[5]. Some others, less obvious, will be suggested in the sequel. In any case one ceremony which, as has been seen, grew out of human sacrifice, has proved remarkably enduring. This is the election of the temporary king. Originally chosen out of the lowest of the people for death, and fêted as the equivalent or double of the real king-priest of the community, he has survived the tragic event which gave him birth, and plays a great part as the master of the ceremonies in many a village revel. The English 'May-king,' or 'summer-king,' or 'harvest-lord[6],' or 'mock-mayor[7],' is a very familiar personage, and can be even more abundantly paralleled

forbids 'effundere super truncum frugem et vinum.'

[1] F. L. Congress, 449, gives a list of about fifty 'feasten' cakes. Some are quite local; others, from the Shrove Tuesday pancake to the Good Friday hot cross bun, widespread.

[2] Grimm, i. 57; Frazer, ii. 344; Grant Allen, 339; Jevons, 215; Dyer, 165; Ditchfield, 81.

[3] F. L. vi. 57; viii. 354; ix. 362; x. 111.

[4] F. L. vi. 1.

[5] Ditchfield, 116, 227; Suffolk F. L. 108; Dyer, Old English Social Life, 197. The boys are now said to be whipped in order that they may remember the boundaries; but the custom, which

sometimes includes burying them, closely resembles the symbolical sacrifices of the harvest field (p. 158). Grant Allen, 270, suggests that the tears shed are a rain-charm. I hope he is joking.

[6] Brand, ii. 13; Suffolk F. L. 69, 71; Leicester F. L. 121. A 'harvest-lord' is probably meant by the 'Rex Autumnalis' mentioned in the Accounts of St. Michael's, Bath (ed. Somerset Arch. Soc. 88), in 1487, 1490, and 1492. A corona was hired by him from the parish. Often the reaper who cuts the last sheaf (i.e. slays the divinity) becomes harvest-lord.

[7] Gomme, Village Community, 107; Dyer, 339; Northall, 202; Gloucester F. L. 33.

from continental festivals[1]. To the May-king in particular we shall return. But in concluding this chapter it is worth while to point out and account for two variants of the custom under consideration. In many cases, probably in the majority of cases so far as the English May-day is concerned, the king is not a king, but a queen. Often, indeed, the part is played by a lad in woman's clothes, but this seems only to emphasize the fact that the temporary ruler is traditionally regarded as a female one[2]. It is probable that we have here no modern development, but a primitive element in the agricultural worship. Tacitus records the presence amongst the Germans of a male priest 'adorned as women use[3],' while the exchange of garments by the sexes is included amongst festival abuses in the ecclesiastical discipline-books[4]. Occasionally, moreover, the agricultural festivals, like those of the *Bona Dea* at Rome, are strictly feminine functions, from which all men are excluded[5]. Naturally I regard these facts as supporting my view of the origin of the agricultural worship in a women's cult, upon which the pastoral cult of the men was afterwards engrafted. And finally, there are cases in which not a king alone nor a queen alone is found, but a king and a queen[6]. This also would be a reasonable outcome of the merging of the two cults. Some districts know the May-queen as the May-bride, and it is possible that a symbolical wedding of a priest and priestess may have been one of the regular rites of the summer festivals. For this there seem to be some parallels in Greek and Roman custom, while the myth which

---

[1] Frazer, i. 216; E. Pabst, *Die Volksfeste des Maigrafen* (1865).

[2] Frazer, i. 219; Cortet, 160; Brand, i. 126; Dyer, 266; Ditchfield, 98.

[3] Tacitus, *Germ.* c. 43 'apud Nahanarvalos antiquae religionis lucus ostenditur. praesidet sacerdos muliebri ornatu.'

[4] *Conc. of Trullo* (692), c. 62 (Mansi, xi. 671) 'Nullus vir deinceps muliebri veste induatur, vel mulier veste viro conveniente'; *Conc. of Braga* (of doubtful date), c. 80 (Mansi, ix. 844) 'Si quis ballationes ante ecclesias sanctorum fecerit, seu quis faciem suam transformaverit

in habitu muliebri et mulier in habitu viri emendatione pollicita tres annos poeniteat.' The exchange of head-gear between men and women remains a familiar feature of the modern bankholiday. Some Greek parallels are collected by Frazer, *Pausanias*, iii. 197. E. Crawley, *The Mystic Rose* (1902), viii. 371, suggests another explanation, which would connect the custom with the amorous side of the primitive festivals.

[5] Frazer, ii. 93, 109.

[6] Ibid. i. 220; Brand, i. 157; Dyer, 217; Ditchfield, 97; Kelly, 62: cf. ch. viii.

represents the heaven as the fertilizing husband of the fruitful earth is of hoar antiquity amongst the Aryan-speaking peoples. The forces which make for the fertility of the fields were certainly identified in worship with those which make for human fertility. The waters of the sacred well or the blaze of the festival fire help the growth of the crops; they also help women in their desire for a lover and for motherhood. And it may be taken for granted that the summer festivals knew from the beginning that element of sexual licence which fourteen centuries of Christianity have not wholly been able to banish [1].

[1] Pearson, ii. 24, 407. Cf. the evidence for a primitive human pairing-season in Westermarck, 25.

CHAPTER VII

FESTIVAL PLAY

[*Bibliographical Note.*—A systematic revision of J. Strutt, *The Sports and Pastimes of the People of England* (1801, ed. W. Hone, 1830), is, as in the case of Brand's book, much needed. On the psychology of play should be consulted K. Groos, *Die Spiele der Thiere* (1896, transl. 1898), and *Die Spiele der Menschen* (1899, transl. 1901). Various anthropological aspects of play are discussed by A. C. Haddon, *The Study of Man* (1898), and the elaborate dictionary of *The Traditional Games of England, Scotland and Ireland* by Mrs. A. B. Gomme (1894–8) may be supplemented from W. W. Newell, *Games and Songs of American Children* (1884), H. C. Bolton, *The Counting-Out Rhymes of Children* (1888), E. W. B. Nicholson, *Golspie* (1897), and R. C. Maclagan, *The Games and Diversions of Argyleshire* (F.L.S. 1901). The *charivari* is treated by C. R. B. Barrett, *Riding Skimmington and Riding the Stang* in the *Journal of the British Archaeological Association*, N. S. i. 58, and C. Noirot, *L'Origine des Masques* (1609), reprinted with illustrative matter by C. Leber, *Dissertations relatives à l'Histoire de France*, vol. ix. The account of the Coventry Hox Tuesday Play given in *Robert Laneham's Letter* (1575) will be found in Appendix H.]

THE charms, the prayer, the sacrifice, make up that side of the agricultural festival which may properly be regarded as cult: they do not make up the whole of it. It is natural to ask whether, side by side with the observances of a natural religion, there were any of a more spiritual type; whether the village gods of our Keltic and Teutonic ancestors were approached on festival occasions solely as the givers of the good things of earth, or whether there was also any recognition of the higher character which in time they came to have as the guardians of morality, such as we can trace alike in the ritual of Eleusis and in the tribal mysteries of some existing savage peoples. It is not improbable that this was so; but it may be doubted whether there is much available evidence on the matter, and, in any case, it cannot be gone into here[1]. There is, however, a third element of

---

[1] Purity of life is sometimes required of those who are to kindle the new fire (Frazer, iii. 260, 302).

the village festival which does demand consideration, and that is the element of play. The day of sacrifice was also a day of cessation from the ordinary toil of the fields, a holiday as well as a holy day. Sacred and secular met in the amorous encounters smiled upon by the liberal wood-goddess, and in the sacramental banquet with its collops of flesh and spilth of ale and mead. But the experience of any bank holiday will show that, for those who labour, the suspension of their ordinary avocations does not mean quiescence. When the blood is heated with love and liquor, the nervous energies habitually devoted to wielding the goad and guiding the plough must find vent in new and for the nonce unprofitable activities. But such activities, self-sufficing, and primarily at least serving no end beyond themselves, are, from pushpin to poetry, exactly what is meant by play[1].

The instinct of play found a foothold at the village feast in the débris which ritual, in its gradual transformation, left behind. It has already been noted as a constant feature in the history of institutions that a survival does not always remain merely a survival; it may be its destiny, when it is emptied of its first significance, to be taken up into a different order of ideas, and to receive a new lease of vitality under a fresh interpretation. Sacrifice ceases to be sacrament and becomes oblation. Dipping and smoking customs, originally magical, grow to be regarded as modes of sacrificial death. Other such waifs of the past become the inheritance of play. As the old conception of sacrifice passed into the new one, the subsidiary rites, through which the sacramental influence had of old been distributed over the worshippers and their fields, although by no means disused, lost their primitive meaning. Similarly, when human sacrifice was abolished, that too left traces of itself, only imperfectly intelligible, in mock or symbolical deaths, or in the election of the temporary king. Thus, even before Christianity antiquated the whole structure of the village festivals, there were individual practices kept alive only by the conservatism of

[1] H. Spencer, *Principles of Psychology*, ii. 629; K. Groos, *Play of Man*, 361; Hirn, 25.

L 2

tradition, and available as material for the play instinct. These find room in the festivals side by side with other customs which the same instinct not only preserved but initiated. Of course, the antithesis between play and cult must not be pushed too far. The peasant mind is tenacious of acts and forgetful of explanations; and the chapters to come will afford examples of practices which, though they began in play, came in time to have a serious significance of quasi-ritual, and to share in the popular imagination the prestige as fertility charms of the older ceremonies of worship with which they were associated. The *ludi* to be immediately discussed, however, present themselves in the main as sheer play. Several of them have broken loose from the festivals altogether, or, if they still acknowledge their origin by making a special appearance on some fixed day, are also at the service of ordinary amusement, whenever the leisure or the whim of youth may so suggest.

To begin with, it is possible that athletic sports and horse-racing are largely an outcome of sacrificial festivals. Like the Greeks around the pyre of Patroclus, the Teutons cele-brated games at the tombs of their dead chieftains[1]. But games were a feature of seasonal, no less than funeral feasts. It will be remembered that the council of Clovesho took pains to forbid the keeping of the Rogation days with horse-races. A bit of wrestling or a bout of quarter-staff is still *de rigueur* at many a wake or rushbearing, while in parts of Germany the winner of a race or of a shooting-match at the popinjay is entitled to light the festival fire, or to hold the desired office of May-king[2]. The reforming bishops of the thirteenth century include public wrestling-bouts and contests for prizes amongst the *ludi* whose performance they condemn; and they lay particular stress upon a custom described as *arietum super ligna et rotas elevationes*. The object of these 'ram-raisings' seems to be explained by the fact that in the days of Chaucer a ram was the traditional reward proposed for a successful wrestler[3]; and this perhaps enables us to push the connexion

---

[1] Gummere, *G. O.* 331.
[2] Frazer, i. 217; iii. 258.
[3] Chaucer says of the Miller

(*C. T.* prol. 548):
'At wrastlynge he wolde have alwey the ram';

with the sacrificial rite a little further. I would suggest that the original object of the man who wrestled for a ram, or climbed a greasy pole for a leg of mutton, or shot for a popin-jay, was to win a sacrificial victim or a capital portion thereof, which buried in his field might bring him abundant crops. The orderly competition doubtless evolved itself from such an indiscriminate scrimmage for the fertilizing fragments as marks the rites of the earth-goddess in the Indian village feast[1]. Tug-of-war would seem to be capable of a similar explana-tion, though here the desired object is not a portion of the victim, but rather a straw rope made out of the corn divinity itself in the form of the harvest-May[2]. An even closer analogy with the Indian rite is afforded by such games as hockey and football. The ball is nothing else than the head of the sacrificial beast, and it is the endeavour of each player to get it into his own possession, or, if sides are taken, to get it over a particular boundary[3]. Originally, of course, this was the player's own boundary; it has come to be regarded as that of his opponents; but this inversion of the point of view is not one on which much stress can be laid. In proof of this theory it may be pointed out that in many places football is still played, traditionally, on certain days of the year. The most notable example is perhaps at Dorking, where the annual Shrove Tuesday scrimmage in the streets

and of Sir Thopas (*C. T.* 13670):
'Of wrastlynge was ther noon his
    peer,
Ther any ram shål stonde.'
Strutt, 82, figures a wrestling from *Royal MS.* 2, B. viii, with a cock set on a pole as the prize.

[1] Cf. Appendix I., and Frazer, ii. 316; Jevons, *Plutarch*, lxix. 143, on the struggle between two wards— the Sacred Way and the Subura— for the head of the October Horse at Rome.

[2] Haddon, 270. The tug-of-war reappears in Korea and Japan as a ceremony intended to secure a good harvest.

[3] Mrs. Gomme, s. vv. *Bandy-ball, Camp, Football, Hockey, Hood, Hurling, Shinty.* These games, in which the ball is fought for, are distinct from those already mentioned as having a ceremonial use, in which it is amicably tossed from player to player (cf. p. 128). If *Golf* belongs to the present category, it is a case in which the endeavour seems to be actually to bury the ball. It is tempting to compare the name *Hockey* with the *Hock-cart* of the harvest festival, and with *Hock-tide*; but it does not really seem to be anything but *Hookey*. The original of both the hockey-stick and the golf-club was probably the shepherd's crook. Mr. Pepys tried to cast stones with a shepherd's crook on those very Epsom downs where the stock-broker now foozles his tee shot.

of the town and the annual efforts of the local authorities to
suppress it furnish their regular paragraph to the newspapers.
There are several others, in most of which, as at Dorking,
the contest is between two wards or districts of the town[1].
This feature is repeated in the Shrove Tuesday tug-of-war
at Ludlow, and in annual faction-fights elsewhere[2]. It is
probably due to that συνοικισμός of village communities by
which towns often came into being. Here and there, moreover, there are to be found rude forms of football in which
the primitive character of the proceeding is far more evident
than in the sophisticated game. Two of these deserve especial mention. At Hallaton in Leicestershire a feast is held
on Easter Monday at a piece of high ground called Hare-pie
Bank. A hare—the sacrificial character of the hare has
already been dwelt upon—is carried in procession. 'Hare-
pies' are scrambled for; and then follows a sport known as
'bottle-kicking.' Hooped wooden field-bottles are thrown
down and a scrimmage ensues between the men of Hallaton
and the men of the adjoining village of Medbourne. Besides
the connexion with the hare sacrifice, it is noticeable that
each party tries to drive the bottle towards its own boundary,
and not that of its opponents[3]. More interesting still is the
Epiphany struggle for the 'Haxey hood' at Haxey in
Lincolnshire. The 'hood' is a roll of sacking or leather, and
it is the object of each of the players to carry it to a public-
house in his own village. The ceremony is connected with
the Plough Monday *quête*, and the 'plough-bullocks' or
'boggons' led by their 'lord duke' and their 'fool,' known
as 'Billy Buck,' are the presiding officials. On the following
day a festival-fire is lit, over which the fool is 'smoked.'

---

[1] *F. L.* vii. 345; M. Shearman,
Athletics and Football, 246; Haddon, 271; Gomme, *Vill. Comm.*
240; Ditchfield, 57, 64; W. Fitzstephen, *Vita S. Thomae* († 1170–
82) in *Mat. for Hist. of Becket*
(R. S.), iii. 9, speaks of the 'lusum
pilae celebrem' in London 'die
quae dicitur Carnilevaria.' Riley,
571, has a London proclamation
of 1409 forbidding the levy of
money for 'foteballe' and 'cok-
thresshyng.' At Chester the
annual Shrove Tuesday football on
the Roodee was commuted for races
in 1540 (*Hist. MSS.* viii. 1. 362).
At Dublin there was, in 1569, a
Shrove Tuesday 'riding' of the
'occupacions' each 'bearing balles'
(Gilbert, ii. 54).

[2] Haddon, *loc. cit.*; Gomme, *loc.
cit.*; *Gloucester F. L.* 38. Cf. the
conflictus described in ch. ix, and
the classical parallels in Frazer,
Pausanias, iii. 267.

[3] *F. L.* iii. 441; Ditchfield, 85.

The strongest support is given to my theory of the origin of this type of game, by an extraordinary speech which the fool delivers from the steps of an old cross. As usual, the cross has taken the place of a more primitive tree or shrine. The speech runs as follows: 'Now, good folks, this is Haxa' Hood. We've killed two bullocks and a half, *but the other half we had to leave running field*: we can fetch it if it's wanted. Remember it's

> 'Hoose agin hoose, toon agin toon,
> And if you meet a man, knock him doon.'

In this case then, the popular memory has actually preserved the tradition that the 'hood' or ball played with is the half of a bullock, the head that is to say, of the victim decapitated at a sacrifice [1].

Hockey and football and tug-of-war are lusty male sports, but the sacrificial survival recurs in some of the singing games played by girls and children. The most interesting of these is that known as 'Oranges and Lemons.' An arch is formed by two children with raised hands, and under this the rest of the players pass. Meanwhile rhymes are sung naming the bells of various parishes, and ending with some such formula as

> 'Here comes a chopper to chop off your head:
> The last, last, last, last man's head.'

As the last word is sung, the hands forming the arch are lowered, and the child who is then passing is caught, and falls in behind one of the leaders. When all in turn have been so caught, a tug-of-war, only without a rope, follows. The 'chopping' obviously suggests a sacrifice, in this case a human sacrifice. And the bell-rhymes show the connexion of the game with the parish contests just described. There exists indeed a precisely similar set of verses which has the title, *Song of the Bells of Derby on Football Morning*. The set ordinarily used in 'Oranges and Lemons' names London

---

[1] *F. L.* vii. 330 (a very full account); viii. 72, 173; Ditchfield, 50. There is a local aetiological myth about a lady who lost her hood on a windy day, and instituted the contest in memory of the event.

parishes, but here is a Northamptonshire variant, which is particularly valuable because it alludes to another rite of the agricultural festival, the sacramental cake buried in a furrow :

> ' Pancakes and fritters,
> Says the bells of St. Peter's :
> Where must we fry 'em ?
> Says the bells of Cold Higham :
> In yonder land thurrow (furrow)
> Says the bells of Wellingborough, &c. [1]

Other games of the same type are ' How many Miles to Babylon,' 'Through the Needle Eye,' and 'Tower of London.' These add an important incident to 'Oranges and Lemons,' in that a ' king ' is said to be passing through the arch. On the other hand, some of them omit the tug-of-war [2]. With all these singing games it is a little difficult to say whether they proceed from children's imitations of the more serious proceedings of their elders, or whether they were originally played at the festivals by grown men and maidens, and have gradually, like the May *quête* itself, fallen into the children's hands. The ' Oranges and Lemons ' group has its analogy to the tug-of-war ; the use of the arch formation also connects it with the festival ' country ' dances which will be mentioned in the next chapter.

The rude punishments by which the far from rigid code of village ethics vindicates itself against offenders, are on the border line between play and jurisprudence. These also appear to be in some cases survivals, diverted from their proper context, of festival usage. It has been pointed out that the ducking which was a form of rain-charm came to be used as a penalty for the churlish or dispirited person, who declined to throw up his work or to wear green on the festival day. In other places this same person has to ' ride the stang.' That is to say, he is set astride a pole and borne about with contumely, until he compounds for his misdemeanour by a fine in coin or liquor [3]. ' Riding the stang,' however, is

---

[1] Mrs. Gomme, s.v. *Oranges and Lemons*.
[2] Mrs. Gomme, s. vv.
[3] Dyer, 6, 481. ' Stang ' is a word, of Scandinavian origin, for ' pole ' or ' stake.' The Scandinavian *nîð-stöng* (scorn-stake) was a horse's head on a pole, with a written

a rural punishment of somewhat wide application[1]. It is common to England and to France, where it can be traced back, under the names of *charivari* and *chevauchée*, to the fifteenth century[2]. The French *sociétés joyeuses*, which will be described in a later chapter, made liberal use of it[3]. The offences to which it is appropriate are various. A miser, a henpecked husband or a wife-beater, especially in May, and, on the other hand, a shrew or an unchaste woman, are liable to visitation, as are the parties to a second or third marriage, or to one perilously long delayed, or one linking May to December. The precise ceremonial varies considerably. Sometimes the victim has to ride on a pole, sometimes on a hobby-horse[4], or on an ass with his face turned to the tail[5]. Sometimes, again, he does not appear at all, but is represented by an effigy or guy, or, in France, by his next-door neighbour[6]. This dramatic version is, according to Mr. Barrett, properly called a 'skimmington riding,' while the term 'riding the stang' is reserved for that in which the offender figures in person. The din of kettles, bones, and cleavers, so frequent an element in rustic ceremonies, is found here also,

curse and a likeness of the man to be ill-wished (Vigfusson, *Icel. Dict.* s.v. *nið*).

[1] Cf. with Mr. Barrett's account, Northall, 253; Ditchfield, 178; *Northern F. L.* 29; Julleville, *Les Com.* 205; also Thomas Hardy's *Mayor of Casterbridge*, and his *The Fire at Tranter Sweatley's* (*Wessex Poems*, 201). The penalty is used by schoolboys (*Northern F. L.* 29) as well as villagers.

[2] Grenier, 375; Ducange, s. v. *Charivarium*, which he defines as 'ludus turpis tinnitibus et clamoribus variis, quibus illudunt iis, qui ad secundas convolant nuptias.' He refers to the statutes of Melun cathedral (1365) in *Instrumenta Hist. Eccl. Melud.* ii. 503. Cf. *Conc. of Langres* (1404) 'ludo quod dicitur Chareuari, in quo utuntur larvis in figura daemonum, et horrenda ibidem committuntur'; *Conc. of Angers* (1448), c. 12 (Labbé, xiii. 1358) 'pulsatione patellarum, pelvium et campanarum, eorum oris

et manibus sibilatione, instrumento aeruginariorum, sive fabricantium, et aliarum rerum sonorosarum, vociferationibus tumultuosis et aliis ludibriis et irrisionibus, in illo damnabili actu (qui cariuarium, vulgariter *charivari*, nuncupatur) circa domos nubentium, et in ipsorum detestationem et opprobrium post eorum secundas nuptias fieri consuetum, &c.'

[3] Cf. ch. xvi, and Leber, ix. 148, 169; Julleville, *Les Com.* 205, 243. In 1579 a regular *jeu* was made by the Dijon *Mère-Folle* of the *chevauchée* of one M. Du Tillet. The text is preserved in *Bibl. Nat. MS.* 24039 and analysed by M. Petit de Julleville.

[4] In Berks a draped horse's head is carried, and the proceeding known as a Hooset Hunt (Ditchfield, 178).

[5] Ducange, s.v. *Asini caudam in manu tenens.*

[6] Julleville, *Les Com.* 207.

and in one locality at least the attendants are accustomed to blacken their faces[1]. It may perhaps be taken for granted that 'riding the stang' is an earlier form of the punishment than the more delicate and symbolical 'skimmington riding'; and it is probable that the rider represents a primitive village criminal haled off to become the literal victim at a sacrificial rite. The fine or forfeit by which in some cases the offence can be purged seems to create an analogy between the custom under consideration and other sacrificial survivals which must now be considered. These are perhaps best treated in connexion with Hock-tide and the curious play proper to that festival at Coventry[2]. This play was revived for the entertainment of Elizabeth when she visited the Earl of Leicester at Kenilworth in July, 1575, and there exists a description of it in a letter written by one Robert Laneham, who accompanied the court, to a friend in London[3]. The men of Coventry, led by one Captain Cox, who presented it called it an 'olld storiall sheaw,' with for argument the massacre of the Danes by Ethelred on Saint Brice's night 1002[4]. Laneham says that it was 'expressed in actionz and rymez,' and it appears from his account to have been a kind of sham fight or 'barriers' between two parties representing respectively Danish 'launsknights' and English, 'each with allder poll marcially in their hand[5].' In the end the Danes were defeated and 'many led captiue for triumph by our English wéemen.' The presenters also stated that the play was of 'an auncient beginning' and 'woont too bee plaid in oour Citee yeárely.' Of late, however, it had been 'laid dooun,' owing to the importunity of their preachers, and 'they woold make theyr humbl peticion vntoo her highnes, that they myght haue theyr playz vp agayn.' The records of

---

[1] So on Ilchester Meads, where the proceeding is known as Mommets or Mommicks (Barrett, 65).

[2] On Hock-tide and the Hock-play generally see Brand-Ellis, i. 107; Strutt, 349; Sharpe, 125; Dyer, 188; S. Denne, *Memoir on Hokeday* in *Archaeologia*, vii. 244.

[3] Cf. Appendix H. An allusion to the play by Sir R. Morrison (†1542) is quoted in chap. xxv.

[4] Laneham, or his informant, actually said, in error, 1012. On the historical event see Ramsay, i. 353.

[5] There were performers both on horse and on foot. Probably hobby-horses were used, for Jonson brings in Captain Cox 'in his Hobby-horse,' which was 'foaled in Queen Elizabeth's time' in the *Masque of Owls* (ed. Cunningham, iii. 188).

Coventry itself add but little to what Laneham gathered. The local *Annals*, not a very trustworthy chronicle, ascribe the invention of 'Hox Tuesday' to 1416–7, and perhaps confirm the *Letter* by noting that in 1575–6 the 'pageants on Hox Tuesday' were played after eight years[1]. We have seen that, according to the statement made at Kenilworth, the event commemorated by the performance was the Danish massacre of 1002. There was, however, another tradition, preserved by the fifteenth-century writer John Rous, which connected it rather with the sudden death of Hardicanute and the end of the Danish usurpation at the accession of Edward the Confessor[2]. It is, of course, possible that local *cantilenae* on either or both of these events may have existed, and may have been worked into the 'rymez' of the play. But I think it may be taken for granted that, as in the Lady Godiva procession, the historical element is comparatively a late one, which has been grafted upon already existing festival customs. One of these is perhaps the faction-fight just discussed. But it is to be noticed that the performance as described by Laneham ended with the Danes being led away captive by English women; and this episode seems to be clearly a dramatization of a characteristic Hock-tide *ludus* found in many places other than Coventry. On Hock-Monday, the women 'hocked' the men; that is to say, they went abroad with ropes, caught and bound any man they came across, and exacted a forfeit. On Hock-Tuesday, the men retaliated in similar fashion upon the women. Bishop Carpenter of Worcester forbade this practice in his diocese in 1450[3], but like some other festival customs it came

---

[1] Cf. *Representations*, s.v. Coventry.

[2] Rossius, *Hist. Regum Angliae* (ed. Hearne, 1716), 105 'in cuius signum usque hodie illa die vulgariter dicta Hox Tuisday ludunt in villis trahendo cordas partialiter cum aliis iocis.' Rous, who died 1491, is speaking of the death of Hardicanute. On the event see Ramsay, i. 434. Possibly both events were celebrated in the sixteenth century at Coventry. Two of the three plays proposed for municipal performance in 1591 were the 'Conquest of the Danes' and the 'History of Edward the Confessor.' These were to be upon the 'pagens,' and probably they were more regular dramas than the performance witnessed by Elizabeth in 1575 (*Representations*, s.v. Coventry).

[3] Leland, *Collectanea* (ed. Hearne), v. 298 'uno certo die heu usitato (*forsan* Hoc vocitato) hoc solempni festo paschatis transacto, mulieres

to be recognized as a source of parochial revenue, and the
'gaderyngs' at Hock-tide, of which the women's was always
the most productive, figure in many a churchwarden's budget
well into the seventeenth century[1]. At Shrewsbury in 1549
'hocking' led to a tragedy. Two men were 'smothered under
the Castle hill,' hiding themselves from maids, the hill falling
there on them[2].' 'Hockney day' is still kept at Hungerford,
and amongst the old-fashioned officers elected on this occasion, with the hay-ward and the ale-tasters, are the two
'tything men' or 'tutti men,' somewhat doubtfully said to be
so named from their poles wreathed with 'tutties' or nose-
gays, whose function it is to visit the commoners, and to claim
from every man a coin and from every woman a kiss[3]. The
derivation of the term Hock-tide has given rise to some wild
conjectures, and philologists have failed to come to a conclusion on the subject[4]. Hock-tide is properly the Monday
and Tuesday following the Second Sunday after Easter, and
'Hokedaie' or *Quindena Paschae* is a frequent term day in
leases and other legal documents from the thirteenth century
onwards[5].

'Hocking' can be closely paralleled from other customs of
the spring festivals. The household books of Edward I
record in 1290 a payment 'to seven ladies of the queen's
chamber who took the king in bed on the morrow of Easter,
and made him fine himself[6].' This was the *prisio* which at
a later date perturbed the peace of French ecclesiastics.
The council of Nantes, for instance, in 1431, complains that
clergy were hurried out of their beds on Easter Monday,
dragged into church, and sprinkled with water upon the
altar[7]. In this aggravated form the *prisio* hardly survived

homines, alioque die homines mulieres ligare, ac cetera media utinam
non inhonesta vel deteriora facere
moliantur et exercere, lucrum
ecclesiae fingentes, set dampnum
animae sub fucato colore lucrantes,
&c.' Riley, 561, 571, gives London
proclamations against 'hokkyng' of
1405 and 1409.
[1] Brand-Ellis, i. 113; Lysons,
Environs of London, i. 229; C.
Kerry, *Accts. of St. Lawrence, Read-*

ing; Hobhouse, 232; *N. E. D.* s. vv.
Hock, &c.
[2] Owen and Blakeway, *Hist. of
Shrewsbury*, i. 559.
[3] Dyer, 191; Ditchfield, 90.
[4] *N. E. D.* s. v. *Hock-day*.
[5] Brand-Ellis, i. 106.
[6] Ibid. i. 109.
[7] Ducange, s. v. *Prisio*; Barthélemy, iv. 463. On Innocents' Day,
the customs of taking in bed and
whipping were united (cf. ch. xii).

the frank manners of the Middle Ages. But it was essentially identical with the ceremonies in which a more modern usage has permitted the levying of forfeits at both Pasque and Pentecost. In the north of England, women were liable to have their shoes taken on one or other of these feasts, and must redeem them by payment. On the following day they were entitled to retaliate on the shoes of the men [1]. A more widely spread method of exacting the *droit* is that of 'heaving.' The unwary wanderer in some of the northern manufacturing towns on Easter Monday is still liable to find himself swung high in the air by the stalwart hands of factory girls, and will be lucky if he can purchase his liberty with nothing more costly than a kiss. If he likes, he may take his revenge on Easter Tuesday [2]. Another mediaeval custom described by Belethus in the twelfth century, which prescribed the whipping of husbands by wives on Easter Monday and of wives by husbands on Easter Tuesday, has also its modern parallel [3]. On Shrove Tuesday a hockey match was played at Leicester, and after it a number of young men took their stand with cart whips in the precincts of the Castle. Any passer-by who did not pay a forfeit was liable to lashes. The 'whipping Toms,' as they were called, were put down by a special Act of Parliament in 1847 [4]. The analogy of these customs with the requirement made of visitors to certain markets or to the roofs of houses in the building to 'pay their footing' is obvious [5].

In all these cases, even where the significant whipping or sprinkling is absent, the meaning is the same. The binding with ropes, the loss of the shoes, the lifting in the air, are

---

[1] *Northern F. L.* 84; Brand-Ellis, i. 94, 96; Vaux, 242; Ditchfield, 80; Dyer, 133.

[2] Brand-Ellis, i. 106; Owen and Blakeway, i. 559; Dyer, 173; Ditchfield, 90; Burne-Jackson, 336; *Northern F. L.* 84; Vaux, 242. A dignified H. M. I. is said to have made his first official visit to Warrington on Easter Monday, and to have suffered accordingly. Miss Burne describes sprinkling as an element in Shropshire heaving.

[3] Belethus, c. 120 'notandum quoque est in plerisque regionibus secundo die post Pascha mulieres maritos suos verberare ac vicissim viros eas tertio die.' The spiritually minded Belethus explains the custom as a warning to keep from carnal intercourse.

[4] Dyer, 79; Ditchfield, 83.

[5] Brand-Ellis, i. 114; Ditchfield, 252. Mr. W. Crooke has just studied this and analogous customs in *The Lifting of the Bride* (*F.L.* xiii. 226).

symbols of capture. And the capture is for the purposes of sacrifice, for which no more suitable victim, in substitution for the priest-king, than a stranger, could be found. This will, I think, be clear by comparison with some further parallels from the harvest field and the threshing-floor, in more than one of which the symbolism is such as actually to indicate the sacrifice itself, as well as the preliminary capture. In many parts of England a stranger, and sometimes even the farmer himself, when visiting a harvest field, is liable to be asked for 'largess'[1]. In Scotland, the tribute is called 'head-money,' and he who refuses is seized by the arms and feet and 'dumped' on the ground[2]. Similar customs prevail on the continent, in Germany, Norway, France; and the stranger is often, just as in the 'hocking' ceremony, caught with straw ropes, or swathed in a sheaf of corn. It is mainly in Germany that the still more elaborate rites survive. In various districts of Mecklenburg, and of Pomerania, the reapers form a ring round the stranger, and fiercely whet their scythes, sometimes with traditional rhymest which contain a threat to mow him down. In Schleswig, and again in Sweden, the stranger in a threshing-floor is 'taught the flail-dance' or 'the threshing-song.' The arms of a flail are put round his neck and pressed so tightly that he is nearly choked. When the madder-roots are being dug, a stranger passing the field is caught by the workers, and buried up to his middle in the soil[3].

The central incident of 'hocking' appears therefore to be nothing but a form of that symbolical capture of a human victim of which various other examples are afforded by the village festivals. The development of the custom into a play or mock-fight at Coventry may very well have taken place, as the town annals say, about the beginning of the fifteenth century. Whether it had previously been connected by local tradition with some event in the struggles of Danes and Saxons or not, is a question which one must be content to leave

---

[1] *Suffolk F. L.* 69; *F. L.* v. 167. The use of *largess*, a Norman-French word (*largitio*), is curious. It is also used for the subscriptions to Lancashire gyst-ales (Dyer, 182). [2] Ditchfield, 155. [3] Frazer, ii. 233; Pfannenschmidt, 93.

unsolved. A final word is due to the curious arrangement by which in the group of customs here considered the rôles of sacrificers and sacrificed are exchanged between men and women on the second day ; for it lends support to the theory already put forward that a certain stage in the evolution of the village worship was marked by the merging of previously independent sex-cults.

CHAPTER VIII

THE MAY-GAME

[*Bibliographical Note.*—The festal character of primitive dance and song is admirably brought out by R. Wallaschek, *Primitive Music* (1893); E. Grosse, *Die Anfänge der Kunst* (1894, French transl. 1902); Y. Hirn, *The Origins of Art* (1900); F. B. Gummere, *The Beginnings of Poetry* (1901). The popular element in French lyric is illustrated by A. Jeanroy, *Les Origines de la Poésie lyrique en France au Moyen Âge* (1889), and J. Tiersot, *Histoire de la Chanson populaire en France* (1889). Most of such English material as exists is collected in Mrs. Gomme's *Traditional Games* (1896-8) and G. F. Northall, *English Folk-Rhymes* (1892). For comparative study E. Martinengo-Cesaresco, *Essays in the Study of Folk-Songs* (1886), may be consulted. The notices of the May-game are scattered through the works mentioned in the bibliographical note to ch. vi and others.]

THE foregoing chapter has illustrated the remarkable variety of modes in which the instinct of play comes to find expression. But of all such the simplest and most primitive is undoubtedly the dance. Psychology discovers in the dance the most rudimentary and physical of the arts, and traces it to precisely that overflow of nervous energies shut off from their normal practical ends which constitutes play[1]. And the verdict of psychology is confirmed by philology; for in all the Germanic languages the same word signifies both 'dance' and 'play,' and in some of them it is even extended to the cognate ideas of 'sacrifice' or 'festival[2].' The dance must therefore

---

[1] Haddon, 335; Grosse, 167; Herbert Spencer in *Contemp. Review* (1895), 114; Groos, *Play of Man*, 88, 354. Evidence for the wide use of the dance at savage festivals is given by Wallaschek, 163, 187.

[2] Grimm, i. 39; Pearson, ii. 133; Müllenhoff, *Germania*, ch. 24, and *de antiq. Germ. poesi chorica*, 4; Kögel, i. 1. 8. The primitive word form should have been *laikaz*, whence Gothic *laiks*, O. N. *leikr*, O. H. G. *leih*, A.-S. *lâc*. The word has, says Müllenhoff, all the senses 'Spiel,

Tanz, Gesang, Opfer, Aufzug.' From the same root come probably *ludus*, and possibly, through the Celtic, the O. F. *lai*. The A.-S. *lâc* is glossed *ludus, sacrificium, victima, munus*. It occurs in the compounds *ecga-gelâc* and *sveorða-gelâc*, both meaning 'sword - dance,' *sige-lâc*, 'victory-dance,' *as-lâc*, 'god-dance,' *wine-lâc*, 'love-dance' (cf. p. 170), &c. An A.-S. synonym for *lâc* is *plega*, 'play,' which gives *sweord-plega* and *ecg-plega*. *Spil* is not A.-S. and *spilian* is a loan-word from O. H. G.

be thought of as an essential part of all the festivals with which we have to deal. And with the dance comes song: the rhythms of motion seem to have been invariably accompanied by the rhythms of musical instruments, or of the voice, or of both combined [1].

The dance had been from the beginning a subject of contention between Christianity and the Roman world [2]; but whereas the dances of the East and South, so obnoxious to the early Fathers, were mainly those of professional entertainers, upon the stage or at banquets, the missionaries of the West had to face the even more difficult problem of a folk-dance and folk-song which were amongst the most inveterate habits of the freshly converted peoples. As the old worship vanished, these tended to attach themselves to the new. Upon great feasts and wake-days, choruses of women invaded with wanton *cantica* and *ballationes* the precincts of the churches and even the sacred buildings themselves, a desecration against which generation after generation of ecclesiastical authorities was fain to protest [3]. Clerkly sentiment in the matter is repre-

[1] Gummere, *B. P.* 328; Kögel, i. 1. 6.

[2] S. Ambrose, *de Elia et Ieiunio*, c. 18 (*P. L.* xiv. 720), *de Poenitentia*, ii. 6 (*P. L.* xvi. 508); S. Augustine, *contra Parmenianum*, iii. 6 (*P. L.* xliii. 107); S. Chrysostom, *Hom.* 47 *in Iulian. mart.* p. 613; *Hom.* 23 *de Novilun.* p. 264; *C. of Laodicea* (†366), c. 53 (Mansi, ii. 571). Cf. *D. C. A.* s. v. Dancing, and ch. i. Barthélemy, ii. 438, and other writers have some rather doubtful theories as to liturgical dancing in early Christian worship; cf. Julian. *Dict. of Hymn.* 206.

[3] Du Méril, *Com.* 67; Pearson, ii. 17, 281; Gröber, ii. 1. 444; Kögel, i. 1. 25; *Indiculus Superstitionum* (ed. Saupe), 10 'de sacrilegiis per ecclesias.' Amongst the prohibitions are Caesarius of Arles (†542), *Sermo* xiii (*P. L.* xxxix. 2325) 'quam multi rustici et quam multae mulieres rusticanae cantica diabolica, amatoria et turpia memoriter retinent et ore decantant'; *Const. Childeberti* (c. 554) *de abol. relig. idololatriae* (Mansi, ix. 738) 'noctes

pervigiles cum ebrietate, scurrilitate, vel canticis, etiam in ipsis sacris diebus, pascha, natale Domini, et reliquis festivitatibus, vel adveniente die Dominico dansatrices per villas ambulare . . . nullatenus fieri permittimus'; *C. of Auxerre* (573–603), c. 9 (Maassen, i. 180) 'non licet in ecclesia choros secularium vel puellarum cantica exercere nec convivia in ecclesia praeparare'; *C. of Chalons* (639–54), c. 19 (Maassen, i. 212) 'Valde omnibus noscetur esse decretum, ne per dedicationes basilicarum aut festivitates martyrum ad ipsa solemnia confluentes obscoena et turpia cantica, dum orare debent aut clericos psallentes audire, cum choris foemineis, turpia quidem decantare videantur. unde convenit, ut sacerdotes loci illos a septa basilicarum vel porticus ipsarum basilicarum etiam et ab ipsis atriis vetare debeant et arcere.' *Sermo Eligii* (Grimm, iv. 1737) 'nullus in festivitate S. Ioannis vel quibuslibet sanctorum solemnitatibus solstitia aut valla-

sented by a pious legend, very popular in the Middle Ages, which told how some reprobate folk of Kölbigk in Anhalt disobeyed the command of a priest to cease their unholy revels before the church of Saint Magnus while he said mass on Christmas day, and for their punishment must dance there the year round without stopping [1]. The struggle was a long one, and in the end the Church never quite succeeded even in expelling the dance from its own doors. The chapter of Wells about 1338 forbade *choreae* and other *ludi* within the cathedral and the cloisters, chiefly on account of the damage

tiones vel saltationes aut caraulas aut cantica diabolica exerceat'; *Iudicium Clementis* († 693), c. 20 (Haddan-Stubbs, iii. 226) ' si quis in quacunque festivitate ad ecclesiam veniens pallat foris, aut saltat, aut cantat orationes amatorias . . . excommunicetur' (apparently a fragment of a penitential composed by Clement or Willibrord, an A.-S. missionary to Frisia, on whom see Bede, *H. E.* v. 9, and the only dance prohibition of possible A.-S. *provenance* of which I know); *Statuta Salisburensia* (Salzburg: † 800; Boretius, i. 229) 'Ut omnis populus . . . absque inlecebroso cantico et lusu saeculari cum laetaniis procedant'; *C. of Mainz* (813), c. 48 (Mansi, xiv. 74) 'canticum turpe atque luxuriosum circa ecclesias agere omnino contradicimus'; *C. of Rome* (826), c. 35 (Mansi, xiv. 1008) 'sunt quidam, et maxime mulieres, qui festis ac sacris diebus atque sanctorum natalitiis non pro eorum quibus debent delectantur desideriis advenire, sed ballando, verba turpia decantando, choros tenendo ac ducendo, similitudinem paganorum peragendo, advenire procurant'; cf. *Dicta abbatis Pirminii* (Caspari, *Kirchenhistorische Anecdota*, 188); *Penitentiale pseudo-Theodorianum* (Wasserschleben, 607); *Leonis IV Homilia* (847, Mansi, xiv. 895); Benedictus Levita, *Capitularia* († 850), vi. 96 (*M. G. H. Script.* iv. 2); and for Spain, *C. of Toledo* (589), c. 23 (Mansi, ix. 999), and the undated *C. of Braga*, c. 80 (quoted on p. 144). Cf. also the denunciations of the *Kalends* (ch. xi and Appendix N). Nearly four centuries after the *C. of Rome* we find the *C. of Avignon* (1209), c. 17 (Mansi, xxii. 791) 'statuimus, ut in sanctorum vigiliis in ecclesiis historicae saltationes, obscoeni motus, seu choreae non fiant, nec dicantur amatoria carmina, vel cantilenae ibidem . . .' Still later the *C. of Bayeux* (1300), c. 31 (Mansi, xxv. 66) 'ut dicit Augustinus, melius est festivis diebus fodere vel arare, quam choreas ducere'; and so on *ad infinitum*. The pseudo-Augustine *Sermo*, 265, *de Christiano nomine cum operibus non Christianis* (*P. L.* xxxix. 2237), which is possibly by Caesarius of Arles, asserts explicitly the pagan character of the custom: 'isti enim infelices et miseri homines, qui balationes et saltationes ante ipsas basilicas sanctorum exercere non metuunt nec erubescunt, etsi Christiani ad ecclesiam venerint, pagani de ecclesia revertuntur; quia ista consuetudo balandi de paganorum observatione remansit.' A mediaeval preacher (quoted by A. Lecoy de la Marche, *Chaire française au Moyen Âge*, 447, from *B. N. Lat. MS.* 17509, f. 146) declares, ' chorea enim circulus est cuius centrum est diabolus, et omnes vergunt ad sinistrum.'

[1] Tille, *D. W.* 301; G. Raynaud, in *Études dédiées à Gaston Paris*, 53; E. Schröder, *Die Tänzer von Kölbigk*, in *Z. f. Kirchengeschichte*, xvii. 94; G. Paris, in *Journal des Savants* (1899), 733.

too often done to its property[1]. A seventeenth-century French writer records that he had seen clergy and singing-boys dancing at Easter in the churches of Paris[2]; and even at the present day there are some astounding survivals. At Seville, as is well known, the six boys, called *los Seises*, dance with castanets before the Holy Sacrament in the presence of the archbishop at Shrovetide, and during the feasts of the Immaculate Conception and Corpus Christi[3]. At Echternach in Luxembourg there is an annual dance through the church of pilgrims to the shrine of St. Willibrord[4], while at Barjols in Provence a 'tripe-dance' is danced at mass on St. Marcel's day in honour of the patron[5].

Still less, of course, did dance and song cease to be important features of the secular side of the festivals. We have already seen how *cantilenae* on the great deeds of heroes had their vogue in the mouths of the *chori* of young men and maidens, as well as in those of the minstrels[6]. The *Carmina Burana*

---

[1] H. E. Reynolds, *Wells Cathedral*, 85 'cum ex choreis ludis et spectaculis et lapidum proiectionibus in praefata ecclesia et eius cemeteriis ac claustro dissentiones sanguinis effusiones et violentiae saepius oriantur et in hiis dicta Wellensis ecclesia multa dispendia patiatur.'

[2] Menestrier, *Des Ballets anciens et modernes* (1863), 4; on other French church dances, cf. Du Tilliot, 21; Barthélemy, iv. 447; Leber, ix. 420. The most famous are the *pilota* of Auxerre, which was accompanied with ball-play (cf. ch. vi) and the *bergeretta* of Besançon. Julian, *Dict. of Hymn.* 206, gives some English examples.

[3] Grove, 106. A full account of the ceremony at the feast of the Conception in 1901 is given in the *Church Times* for Jan. 17, 1902.

[4] Grove, 103; Bérenger-Féraud, iii. 430; *Mélusine* (1879), 39; *N. and Q.* for May 17, 1890. The dance is headed by the clergy, and proceeds to a traditional tune from the banks of the Sûre to the church, up sixty-two steps, along the north

aisle, round the altar *deasil*, and down the south aisle. It is curious that until the seventeenth century only *men* took part in it. St. Willibrord is famous for curing nervous diseases, and the pilgrimage is done by way of vow for such cures. The local legend asserts that the ceremony had its origin in an eighth-century cattle-plague, which ceased through an invocation of St. Willibrord: it is a little hard on the saint, whose prohibition of dances at the church-door has just been quoted.

[5] Bérenger-Féraud, iii. 409. A similarly named saint, St. Martial, was formerly honoured in the same way. Every psalm on his day ended, not with the *Gloria Patri*, but with a dance, and the chant, 'Saint-Marceau, pregas per nous, et nous epingaren per vous' (Du Méril, *La Com.* 68).

[6] Cf. p. 26. There were 'madinnis that dansit' before James IV of Scotland at Forres, Elgin and Dernway in 1504, but nothing is said of songs (*L. H. T. Accounts*, ii. 463).

describe the dances of girls upon the meadows as amongst
the pleasures of spring [1]. William Fitzstephen tells us that
such dances were to be seen in London in the twelfth century[2],
and we have found the University of Oxford solemnly forbidding them in the thirteenth. The *romans* and *pastourelles*
frequently mention *chansons* or *rondets de carole*, which appear
to have been the *chansons* used to accompany the choric
dances, and to have generally consisted of a series of couplets
sung by the leader, and a refrain with which the rest of the
band answered him. Occasionally the refrains are quoted [3].
The minstrels borrowed this type of folk *chanson*, and the
conjoint dance and song themselves found their way from the
village green to the courtly hall. In the twelfth century
ladies *carolent*, and more rarely even men condescend to take
a part [4]. Still later *carole*, like *tripudium*, seems to become a
term for popular rejoicing in general, not necessarily expressed
in rhythmical shape [5].

The customs of the village festival gave rise by natural
development to two types of dance [6]. There was the processional dance of the band of worshippers in progress round
their boundaries and from field to field, from house to house,

---

[1] *Carm. Bur.* 191 :
  'ludunt super gramina
    virgines decorae
    quarum nova carmina
      dulci sonant ore.'
Ibid. 195 :
  'ecce florescunt lilia,
    et virginum dant agmina
    summo deorum carmina.'
[2] W. Fitzstephen, *Descriptio
Londin.* (*Mat. for Hist. of Becket*,
R. S. iii. 11) 'puellarum Cytherea
ducit choros usque imminente luna,
et pede libero pulsatur tellus.'
[3] Jeanroy, 102, 387 ; Guy, 504 ;
Paris, *Journal des Savants* (1892),
407. M. Paris points out that
dances, other than professional,
first appear in the West after the
fall of the Empire. The French
terms for dancing—*baller, danser,
treschier, caroler*—are not Latin.
Caroler, however, he thinks to be
the Greek χοραυλεῖν, 'to accompany
a dance with a flute.' But the

French *carole* was always accompanied, not with a flute, but with a
sung *chanson*.
[4] Paris, *loc. cit.* 410 ; Jeanroy,
391. In Wace's description of
Arthur's wedding, the women *carolent* and the men *behourdent*. Cf.
Bartsch, *Romanzen und Pastourellen*, i. 13 :
  'Cez damoiseles i vont por
      caroler,
    cil escuier i vont por behorder,
    cil chevalier i vont por esgar-
      der.'
[5] On the return of Edward II
and Isabella of France in 1308, the
mayor and other dignitaries of
London went 'coram rege et regina
karolantes' (*Chronicles of Edward I and Edward II*, R. S. i.
152). On the birth of Prince Edward in 1312, they 'menerent la
karole' in church and street (Riley,
107).
[6] Kögel, i. 1. 6.

from well to well of the village. It is this that survives in the
dance of the Echternach pilgrims, or in the 'faddy-dance' in
and out the cottage doors at Helston wake. And it is probably this that is at the bottom of the interesting game of
'Thread the Needle.' This is something like 'Oranges and
Lemons,' the first part of which, indeed, seems to have been
adapted from it. There is, however, no sacrifice or 'tug-of-
war,' although there is sometimes a 'king,' or a 'king' and
his 'lady' or 'bride' in the accompanying rhymes, and in one
instance a 'pancake.' The players stand in two long lines.
Those at the end of each line form an arch with uplifted arms,
and the rest run in pairs beneath it. Then another pair form
an arch, and the process is repeated. In this way long strings
of lads and lasses stream up and down the streets or round
and about a meadow or green. In many parts of England
this game is played annually on Shrove Tuesday or Easter
Monday, and the peasants who play it at Châtre in central
France say that it is done 'to make the hemp grow.' Its
origin in connexion with the agricultural festivals can therefore hardly be doubtful[1]. It is probable that in the beginning
the players danced rather than ran under the 'arch'; and it
is obvious that the 'figure' of the game is practically identical
with one familiar in *Sir Roger de Coverley* and other old
English 'country' dances of the same type.

Just as the 'country' dance is derived from the processional
dance, so the other type of folk-dance, the *ronde* or 'round,' is
derived from the comparatively stationary dance of the group
of worshippers around the more especially sacred objects of
the festival, such as the tree or the fire[2]. The custom of
dancing round the May-pole has been more or less preserved
wherever the May-pole is known. But 'Thread the Needle'
itself often winds up with a circular dance or *ronde*, either
around one of the players, or, on festival occasions, around the
representative of the earlier home of the fertilization divinity,

[1] Mrs. Gomme, ii. 228; Haddon,
345.
[2] Cf. ch. vi on the motion *deasil*
round the sacred object. It is
curious that the modern round
dances go *withershins* round a
room. Grimm, i. 52, quotes Gregory the Great, *Dial*. iii. 28 on a
Lombard sacrifice, 'caput caprae,
hoc ei, per circuitum currentes,
carmine nefando dedicantes.'

the parish church. This custom is popularly known as
'clipping the church[1].'

Naturally the worshippers at a festival would dance in their
festival costume; that is to say, in the garb of leaves and
flowers worn for the sake of the beneficent influence of the
indwelling divinity, or in the hides and horns of sacrificial
animals which served a similar purpose. Travellers describe
elaborate and beautiful beast-dances amongst savage peoples,
and the Greeks had their own bear- and crane-dances, as well
as the dithyrambic goat-dance of the Dionysia. They had
also flower dances[2]. In England the village dancers wear
posies, but I do not know that they ever attempt a more
elaborate representation of flowers. But a good example of
the beast-dance is furnished by the 'horn-dance' at Abbots
Bromley in Staffordshire, held now at a September wake, and
formerly at Christmas. In this six of the performers wear sets
of horns. These are preserved from year to year in the church,
and according to local tradition the dance used at one time
to take place in the churchyard on a Sunday. The horns are
said to be those of the reindeer, and from this it may possibly
be inferred that they were brought to Abbots Bromley by
Scandinavian settlers. The remaining performers represent
a hobby-horse, a clown, a woman, and an archer, who makes
believe to shoot the horned men[3].

The *motifs* of the dances and their *chansons* must also at first
have been determined by the nature of the festivals at which
they took place. There were dances, no doubt, at such domestic

---

[1] At Bradford-on-Avon, Wilts
(which preserves its Anglo-Saxon
church), and at South Petherton,
Somerset, in both cases on Shrove
Tuesday (Mrs. Gomme, ii. 230); cf.
Vaux, 18. The church at Painswick,
Gloucester, is danced round on
wake-day (*F. L.* viii. 392). There
is a group of games, in which the
players wind and unwind in spirals
round a centre. Such are *Eller Tree,
Wind up the Bush Faggot,* and *Bulli-
heisle.* These Mrs. Gomme regards
as survivals of the ritual dance
round a sacred tree. Some obscure
references in the rhymes used to

'dumplings' and 'a bundle of rags'
perhaps connect themselves with
the cereal cake and the rags hung
on the tree for luck. In Cornwall
such a game is played under the
name of 'Snail's Creep' at certain
village feasts in June, and directed
by young men with leafy branches.
[2] Du Méril, *La Com.* 72; Haddon, 346; Grove, 50, 81; Haigh,
14; N. W. Thomas, *La Danse
totémique en Europe,* in *Actes d.
Cong. intern. d. Trad. pop.* (1900).
[3] Plot, *Hist. of Staffs.* (1686);
F. L. iv. 172; vii. 382 (with cuts of
properties); Ditchfield, 139.

festivals as weddings and funerals [1]. In Flanders it is still the custom to dance at the funeral of a young girl, and a very charming *chanson* is used [2]. The development of epic poetry from the *cantilenae* of the war-festival has been noted in a former chapter. At the agricultural festivals, the primary *motif* is, of course, the desire for the fertility of the crops and herds. The song becomes, as in the Anglo-Saxon charm, so often referred to, practically a prayer [3]. With this, and with the use of 'Thread the Needle' at Châtre 'to make the hemp grow,' may be compared the games known to modern children, as to Gargantua, in which the operations of the farmer's year, and in particular his prayer for his crops, are mimicked in a *ronde* [4]. Allusions to the process of the seasons, above all to the delight of the *renouveau* in spring, would naturally also find a place in the festival songs. The words of the famous thirteenth-century lyric were perhaps written to be sung to the twinkling feet of English girls in a round. It has the necessary refrain:

[1] The O. H. G. *hîleih*, originally meaning 'sex-dance,' comes to be 'wedding.' The root *hî*, like *wini* (cf. p. 170), has a sexual connotation (Pearson, ii. 132; Kögel, i. 1. 10).

[2] Coussemaker, *Chants populaires des Flamands de France*, 100:

'In den hemel is eenen dans:
   Alleluia.
Daer dansen all' de maegde-
      kens:
   Benedicamus Domino,
   Alleluia, Alleluia.
't is voor Amelia:
   Alleluia.
Wy dansen naer de maegde-
      kens:
   Benedicamus, etc.'

[3] Frazer, i. 35; Dyer, 7; Northall, 233. A Lancashire song is sung 'to draw you these cold winters away,' and wishes 'peace and plenty' to the household. A favourite French May *chanson* is

'Étrennez notre épousée,
   Voici le mois,
Le joli mois de Mai,
Étrennez notre épousée
   En bonne étrenne.

Voici le mois,
Le joli mois de Mai,
   Qu'on vous amène.'
If the *quêteurs* come on a churl, they have an ill-wishing variant. The following is characteristic of the French peasantry:

'J'vous souhaitons autant d'en-
      fants,
   Qu'y a des pierrettes dans les
      champs.'
Often more practical tokens of revenge are shown. The Plough Monday 'bullocks' in some places consider themselves licensed to plough up the ground before a house where they have been rebuffed.'

[4] Mrs. Gomme, ii. 1, 399; Haddon, 343; Du Méril, *La Com.* 81. Amongst the *jeux* of the young Gargantua (Rabelais, i. 22) was one 'à semer l'avoyne et au laboureur.' This probably resembled the games of *Oats and Beans and Barley*, and *Would you know how doth the Peasant?* which exist in English, French, Catalonian, and Italian versions. On the mimetic character of these games, cf. ch. viii.

'Sumer is icumen in,
 Lhude sing cuccu!
Groweth sed and bloweth med
 And springth the wdë nu,
    Sing cuccu!

'Awë bleteth after lomb,
 Lhouth after calvë cu.
Bulloc sterteth, buckë verteth,
 Murie sing cuccu!

'Cuccu, cuccu, wel singës thu, cuccu;
 Ne swik thu naver nu.
Sing cuccu nu. Sing cuccu.
 Sing cuccu. Sing cuccu nu!'[1]

The savour of the spring is still in the English May songs, the French *maierolles* or *calendes de mai* and the Italian *calen di maggio*. But for the rest they have either become little but mere *quête* songs, or else, under the influence of the priests, have taken on a Christian colouring[2]. At Oxford the 'merry ketches' sung by choristers on the top of Magdalen tower on May morning were replaced in the seventeenth century by the hymn now used[3]. Another very popular Mayers' song would seem to show that the Puritans, in despair of abolishing the festival, tried to reform it.

[1] Text from *Harl. MS.* 978 in H. E. Wooldridge, *Oxford Hist. of Music*, i. 326, with full account. The music, to which religious as well as the secular words are attached, is technically known as a *rota* or *rondel*. It is of the nature of polyphonic part-song, and of course more advanced than the typical mediaeval *rondet* can have been.

[2] On these songs in general, see Northall, 233; Martinengo-Cesaresco, 249; Cortet, 153; Tiersot, 191; Jeanroy, 88; Paris, *J. des Savants* (1891), 685, (1892), 155, 407.

[3] H. A. Wilson, *Hist. of Magd. Coll.* (1899), 50. Mr. Wilson discredits the tradition that the performance began as a mass for the obit of Henry VII. The hymn is printed in Dyer, 259; Ditchfield, 96. It has no relation to the summer festival, having been written in the seventeenth century by Thomas Smith and set by Benjamin Rogers as a grace. In other cases hymns have been attached to the village festivals. At Tissington the 'well-dressing,' on Ascension Day includes a clerical procession in which 'Rock of Ages' and 'A Living Stream' are sung (Ditchfield, 187). A special 'Rushbearers' Hymn' was written for the Grasmere Rushbearing in 1835, and a hymn for St. Oswald has been recently added (E. G. Fletcher, *The Rushbearing*, 13, 74).

'Remember us poor Mayers all,
    And thus we do begin
To lead our lives in righteousness,
    Or else we die in sin.

'We have been rambling all this night,
    And almost all this day:
And now returned back again,
    We have brought you a branch of May.

'A branch of May we have brought you,
    And at your door it stands;
It is but a sprout, but it's well budded out,
    By the work of our Lord's hands,' &c.[1]

Another religious element, besides prayer, may have entered
into the pre-Christian festival songs; and that is myth.
A stage in the evolution of drama from the Dionysiac dithyramb was the introduction of mythical narratives about the
wanderings and victories of the god, to be chanted or recited by
the *choragus.* The relation of the *choragus* to the *chorus* bears
a close analogy to that between the leader of the mediaeval
carole and his companions who sang the refrain. This leader
probably represents the Keltic or Teutonic priest at the head
of his band of worshippers; and one may suspect that in the
north and west of Europe, as in Greece, the pauses of the
festival dance provided the occasion on which the earliest
strata of stories about the gods, the hieratic as distinguished
from the literary myths, took shape. If so the development of
divine myth was very closely parallel to that of heroic myth[2].

After religion, the commonest *motif* of dance and song at
the village festivals must have been love. This is quite in
keeping with the amorous licence which was one of their
characteristics. The goddess of the fertility of earth was also
the goddess of the fertility of women. The ecclesiastical prohibitions lay particular stress upon the *orationes amatoriae* and
the *cantica turpia et luxuriosa* which the women sang at the
church doors, and only as love-songs can be interpreted the
winileodi forbidden to the inmates of convents by a capitulary

[1] Dyer, 240, from Hertfordshire. There are many other versions; cf.
Northall, 240.   [2] Kögel, i. 1. 32.

of 789 [1]. The love-interest continues to be prominent in the folk-song, or the minstrel song still in close relation to folk-song, of mediaeval and modern France. The beautiful wooing *chanson* of *Transformations*, which savants have found it difficult to believe not to be a *supercherie*, is sung by harvesters and by lace-makers at the pillow [2]. That of *Marion*, an ironic expression of wifely submission, belongs to Shrove Tuesday [3]. These are modern, but the following, from the *Chansonnier de St. Germain*, may be a genuine mediaeval folk-song of Limousin *provenance*:

> 'A l'entrada dal tems clar, eya,
> Per joja recomençar, eya,
> Et per jelos irritar, eya,
> Vol la regina mostrar
> Qu'el' es si amoroza.
> Alavi', alavia jelos,
> Laissaz nos, laissaz nos
> Ballar entre nos, entre nos [4].'

The 'queen' here is, of course, the festival queen or lady of the May, the *regina avrillosa* of the Latin writers, *la reine, la mariée, l'épousée, la trimousette* of popular custom [5]. The defiance of the *jelos*, and the desire of the queen and her maidens to dance alone, recall the conventional freedom of women from restraint in May, the month of their ancient sex-festival, and the month in which the mediaeval wife-beater still ran notable danger of a *chevauchée*.

[1] Pertz, *Leges*, i. 68 'nullatenus ibi uuinileodos scribere vel mittere praesumat.' Kögel, i. 1. 61: Goedeke, i. 11, quote other uses of the term from eighth-century glosses, e.g. 'uuiniliod, cantilenas saeculares, psalmos vulgares, seculares, plebeios psalmos, cantica rustica et inepta.' *Winiliod* is literally 'love-song,' from root *wini* (conn. with *Venus*). Kögel traces an earlier term O. H. G. *winileih*, A.-S. *winelác = hîleih*. On the erotic motive in savage dances, cf. Grosse, 165, 172; Hirn, 229.

[2] *Romania*, vii. 61; *Trad. Pop.* i. 98. Mr. Swinburne has adapted

the idea of this poem in *A Match* (*Poems and Ballads*, 1st Series, 116).

[3] *Romania*, ix. 568.

[4] K. Bartsch, *Chrest. Prov.* 111. A similar *chanson* is in G. Raynaud, *Motets*, i. 151, and another is described in the *roman* of *Flamenca* (ed. P. Meyer), 3244. It ends
'E, si parla, qu'il li responda:
Nom sones mot, faitz vos en lai,
Qu'entre mos bracs mos amics j'ai.
Kalenda maia. E vai s' en.'

[5] *Trimousette*, from *tri mâ câ*, an unexplained burden in some of the French *maierolles*.

The amorous note recurs in those types of minstrel song
which are most directly founded upon folk models. Such are
the *chansons à danser* with their refrains, the *chansons de mal-
mariées*, in which the '*jalous*' is often introduced, the *aubes*
and the *pastourelles*[1]. Common in all of these is the spring
setting proper to the *chansons* of our festivals, and of the
'queen' or 'king' there is from time to time mention. The
leading theme of the *pastourelles* is the wooing, successful or
the reverse, of a shepherdess by a knight. But the shepherdess
has generally also a lover of her own degree, and for this pair
the names of Robin and Marion seem to have been conven-
tionally appropriated. Robin was perhaps borrowed by the
pastourelles from the widely spread refrain

> 'Robins m'aime, Robins m'a :
> Robins m'a demandée : si m'ara[2].'

The borrowing may, of course, have been the other way round,
but the close relation of the *chanson à danser* with its refrain
to the dance suggests that this was the earliest type of lyric
minstrelsy to be evolved, as well as the closest to the folk-song
pattern. The *pastourelle* forms a link between folk-song and
drama, for towards the end of the thirteenth century Adan de
la Hale, known as ' le Bossu,' a minstrel of Arras, wrote a *Jeu de
Robin et Marion*, which is practically a *pastourelle par personnages*. The familiar theme is preserved. A knight woos
Marion, who is faithful to her Robin. Repulsed, he rides
away, but returns and beats Robin. All, however, ends
happily with dances and *jeux* amongst the peasants. Adan
de la Hale was one of the train of Count Robert of Artois in
Italy. The play may originally have been written about 1283
for the dejectation of the court of Robert's kinsman, Charles,
king of Naples, but the extant version was probably produced
about 1290 at Arras, when the poet was already dead.
Another hand has prefixed a dramatic prologue, the *Jeu du
Pèlerin*, glorifying Adan, and has also made some interpolations in the text designed to localize the action near Arras.

---

[1] Guy, 503.
[2] Tiersot, *Robin et Marion*; Guy,
506. See the refrain in Bartsch,
197, 295 ; Raynaud, *Rec. de Motets*,
i. 227.

The performers are not likely to have been villagers : they may have been the members of some *puy* or literary society, which had taken over the celebration of the summer festival. In any case the *Jeu de Robin et Marion* is the earliest and not the least charming of pastoral comedies [1].

It is impossible exactly to parallel from the history of English literature this interaction of folk-song and minstrelsy at the French *fête du mai*. For unfortunately no body of English mediaeval lyric exists. Even ' Sumer is icumen in ' only owes its preservation to the happy accident which led some priest to fit sacred words to the secular tune ; while the few pieces recovered from a Harleian manuscript of the reign of Edward I, beautiful as they are, read like adaptations less of English folk-song, than of French lyric itself [2]. Nevertheless, the village summer festival of England seems to have closely resembled that of France, and to have likewise taken in the long run a dramatic turn. A short sketch of it will not be without interest.

I have quoted at the beginning of this discussion of folk-customs the thirteenth-century condemnations of the *Inductio Maii* by Bishop Grosseteste of Lincoln and of the *ludi de Rege et Regina* by Bishop Chanteloup of Worcester. The *ludus de Rege et Regina* is not indeed necessarily to be identified with the *Inductio Maii*, for the harvest feast or *Inductio Autumni* of Bishop Grosseteste had also its ' king ' and ' queen,' and so too had some of the feasts in the winter cycle, notably Twelfth night [3]. It is, however, in the summer feast held usually on

---

[1] Langlois, *Robin et Marion* : *Romania*, xxiv. 437 ; H. Guy, *Adan de la Hale*, 177 ; J. Tiersot, *Sur le Jeu de Robin et Marion* (1897) ; Petit de Julleville, *La Comédie*, 27 ; *Rep. Com.* 21, 324. A *jeu* of *Robin et Marion* is recorded also as played at Angers in 1392, but there is no proof that this was Adan de la Hale's play, or a drama at all. There were folk going ' desguiziez, à un jeu que l'en dit Robin et Marion, ainsi qu'il est accoutumé de fere, chacun an, en les foiries de Penthecouste ' (Guy, 197). The best editions of *Robin et Marion* are those by E. Langlois (1896), and by Bartsch in *La Langue et la Littérature françaises* (1887), col. 523. E. de Coussemaker, *Œuvres de Adam de la Halle* (1872), 347, gives the music, and A. Rambeau, *Die dem Trouvère Adam de la Halle zugeschriebenen Dramen* (1886), facsimiles the text. On Adan de la Hale's earlier *sottie* of *La Feuillée*, see ch. xvi.

[2] Thomas Wright, *Lyrical Poems of the Reign of Edward I* (Percy Soc.).

[3] Cf. ch. xvii.

the first of May or at Whitsuntide [1], that these rustic dignitaries are more particularly prominent. Before the middle of the fifteenth century I have not come across many notices of them. That a summer king was familiar in Scotland is implied by the jest of Robert Bruce's wife after his coronation at Scone in 1306 [2]. In 1412 a 'somerkyng' received a reward from the bursar of Winchester College [3]. But from about 1450 onwards they begin to appear frequently in local records. The whole *ludus* is generally known as a 'May-play' or 'May-game,' or as a 'king-play [4],' 'king's revel [5],' or 'king-game [6].' The leading personages are indifferently the 'king' and 'queen,' or 'lord' and 'lady.' But sometimes the king is more specifically the 'somerkyng' or *rex aestivalis*. At other times he is the 'lord of misrule [7],' or takes a local title, such as that of the 'Abbot of Marham,' 'Mardall,' 'Marrall,' 'Marram,' 'Mayvole' or 'Mayvoll' at Shrewsbury [8], and the 'Abbot of Bon-Accord'

[1] The May-game is probably intended by the 'Whitsun pastorals' of *Winter's Tale*, iv. 4. 134, and the 'pageants of delight' at Pentecost, where a boy 'trimmed in Madam Julias gown' played 'the woman's part' (i.e. Maid Marian) of *Two Gentlemen of Verona*, iv. 4. 163. Cf. also W. Warner, *Albion's England*, v. 25 :
'At Paske began our Morrise, and
ere Penticost our May.'
[2] *Flores Historiarum* (R. S.), iii. 130 'aestimo quod rex aestivalis sis ; forsitan hyemalis non eris.'
[3] Cf. Appendix E.
[4] 'King-play' at Reading (*Reading St. Giles Accounts* in Brand-Hazlitt, i. 157 ; Kerry, *Hist. of St. Lawrence, Reading*, 226).
[5] 'King's revel' at Croscombe, Somerset (*Churchwardens' Accounts* in Hobhouse, 3).
[6] 'King's game' at Leicester (Kelly, 68) and 'King-game' at Kingston (Lysons, *Environs of London*, i. 225). On the other hand the King-game in church at Hascombe in 1578 (*Representations*, s. v. Hascombe), was probably a miracle-play of the Magi or Three Kings of Cologne. This belongs to Twelfth night (cf.

ch. xix), but curiously the accounts of St. Lawrence, Reading, contain a payment for the 'Kyngs of Colen' on *May day*, 1498 (Kerry, *loc. cit.*).
[7] Cf. ch. xvii. Local 'lords of misrule' in the *summer* occur at Montacute in 1447-8 (Hobhouse, 183 'in expensis Regis de Montagu apud Tyntenhull existentis tempore aestivali'), at Meriden in 1565 (Sharpe, 209), at Melton Mowbray in 1558 (Kelly, 65), at Tombland, near Norwich (*Norfolk Archaeology*, iii. 7 ; xi. 345), at Broseley, near Much Wenlock, as late as 1652 (Burne-Jackson, 480). See the attack on them in Stubbes, i. 146. The term 'lord of misrule' seems to have been borrowed from Christmas (ch. xvii). It does not appear whether the lords of misrule of Old Romney in 1525 (*Archaeologia Cantiana*, xiii. 216) and Braintree in 1531 (Pearson, ii. 413) were in winter or summer.
[8] Owen and Blakeway, i. 331 ; Jackson and Burne, 480 (cf. Appendix E). Miss Burne suggests several possible derivations of the name ; from *mar* 'make mischief,' from Mardoll or Marwell (St. Mary's Well), streets in Shrewsbury, or

at Aberdeen[1]. The use of an ecclesiastical term will be explained in a later chapter[2]. The queen appears to have been sometimes known as a 'whitepot' queen[3]. And finally the king and queen receive, in many widely separated places, the names of Robin Hood and Maid Marian, and are accompanied in their revels by Little John, Friar Tuck, and the whole joyous fellowship of Sherwood Forest[4]. This affiliation of the *ludus de Rege et Regina* to the Robin Hood legend is so curious as to deserve a moment's examination[5].

The earliest recorded mention of Robin Hood is in Langland's *Piers Plowman*, written about 1377. Here he is coupled with another great popular hero of the north as a subject of current songs:

> 'But I can rymes of Robyn hood, and Randolf erle of Chestre[6].'

In the following century his fame as a great outlaw spread far and wide, especially in the north and the midlands[7]. The Scottish chronicler Bower tells us in 1447 that whether for comedy or tragedy no other subject of romance and minstrelsy

from Muryvale or Meryvalle, a local hamlet. But the form 'Mayvoll' seems to point to 'Maypole.'

[1] *Representations*, s. v. Aberdeen. Here the lord of the summer feast seems to have acted also as presenter of the Corpus Christi plays.

[2] Cf. ch. xvii.

[3] Batman, *Golden Books of the Leaden Gods* (1577), f. 30. The Pope is said to be carried on the backs of four deacons, 'after the maner of carying whytepot queenes in Western May games.' A 'whitepot' is a kind of custard.

[4] Such phrases occur as 'the May-play called Robyn Hod' (Kerry, *Hist. of St. Lawrence, Reading*, 226, s. a. 1502), 'Robin Hood and May game' and 'Kynggam and Robyn Hode' (*Kingston Accounts*, 1505-36, in Lysons, *Environs of London*, i. 225). The accounts of St. Helen's, Abingdon, in 1566, have an entry 'for setting up Robin Hood's bower' (Brand-Hazlitt, i. 144). It is noticeable

that from 1553 Robin Hood succeeds the Abbot of Mayvole in the May-game at Shrewsbury (Appendix E). Similarly, in an Aberdeen order of 1508 we find 'Robert Huyid and Litile Johne, quhilk was callit, in yers bipast, Abbat and Prior of Bonacord' (*Representations*, s. v. Aberdeen). Robin Hood seems, therefore, to have come rather late into the May-games, but to have enjoyed a widening popularity.

[5] The material for the study of the Robin Hood legend is gathered together by S. Lee in *D. N. B.* s.v. Hood; Child, *Popular Ballads*, v. 39; Ritson, *Robin Hood* (1832); J.M. Gutch, *Robin Hood* (1847). Prof. Child gives a critical edition of all the ballads.

[6] *Piers Plowman*, B-text, passus v. 401.

[7] Fabian, *Chronicle*, 687, records in 1502 the capture of 'a felowe whych hadde renewed many of Robin Hode's pagentes, which named himselfe Greneleef.'

had such a hold upon the common folk[1]. The first of the extant ballads of the cycle, *A Gest of Robyn Hode*, was probably printed before 1500, and in composition may be at least a century earlier. A recent investigator of the legend, and a very able one, denies to Robin Hood any traceable historic origin. He is, says Dr. Child, 'absolutely a creation of the ballad muse.' However this may be, the version of the Elizabethan playwright Anthony Munday, who made him an earl of Huntingdon and the lover of Matilda the daughter of Lord Fitzwater, may be taken as merely a fabrication. And whether he is historical or not, it is difficult to see how he got, as by the sixteenth century he did get, into the May-game. One theory is that he was there from the beginning, and that he is in fact a mythological figure, whose name but faintly disguises either Woden in the aspect of a vegetation deity[2], or a minor wood-spirit Hode, who also survives in the Hodeken of German legend[3]. Against this it may be pointed out, firstly that Hood is not an uncommon English name, probably meaning nothing but 'à-Wood' or 'of the wood[4],' and secondly that we have seen no reason to suppose that the mock king, which is the part assigned to Robin Hood in the May-game, was ever regarded as an incarnation of the fertilization spirit at all. He is the priest of that spirit, slain at its festival, but nothing more. I venture to offer a more plausible explanation. It is noticeable that whereas in the May-game Robin Hood and Maid Marian are inseparable, in the early ballads Maid Marian has no part. She is barely mentioned in one or two of the latest ones[5]. Moreover Marian is not an English but a French name, and we have already seen that Robin and Marion are the typical shepherd and shepherdess of the French *pastourelles* and of Adan de

---

[1] Cf. p. 177.

[2] Kühn, in Haupt's *Zeitschrift*, v. 481.

[3] Ramsay, *F. E.* i. 168.

[4] In the Nottingham *Hall-books* (*Hist. MSS.* i. 105), the same locality seems to be described in 1548 as 'Robyn Wood's Well,' and in 1597 as 'Robyn Hood's Well.' Robin Hood is traditionally clad in green.

If he is mythological at all, may he not be a form of the 'wild-man' or 'wood-woz' of certain spring dramatic ceremonies, and the 'Green Knight' of romance? Cf. ch. ix.

[5] The earliest mention of her is (†1500) in A. Barclay, *Eclogue*, 5, 'some may fit of Maide Marian or else of Robin Hood.'

la Hale's dramatic *jeu* founded upon these. I suggest then, that the names were introduced by the minstrels into English and transferred from the French *fêtes du mai* to the 'lord' and 'lady' of the corresponding English May-game. Robin Hood grew up independently from heroic *cantilenae*, but owing to the similarity of name he was identified with the other Robin, and brought Little John, Friar Tuck and the rest with him into the May-game. On the other hand Maid Marian, who does not properly belong to the heroic legend, was in turn, naturally enough, adopted into the later ballads. This is an hypothesis, but not, I think, an unlikely hypothesis.

Of what, then, did the May-game, as it took shape in the fifteenth and sixteenth centuries, consist? Primarily, no doubt, of a *quête* or 'gaderyng.' In many places this became a parochial, or even a municipal, affair. In 1498 the corporation of Wells possessed moneys '*provenientes ante hoc tempus de Robynhode*[1].' Elsewhere the churchwardens paid the expenses of the feast and accounted for the receipts in the annual parish budget[2]. There are many entries concerning the May-game in the accounts of Kingston-on-Thames during some half a century. In 1506 it is recorded that 'Wylm. Kempe' was 'kenge' and 'Joan Whytebrede' was 'quen.' In 1513 and again in 1536 the game went to Croydon[3]. Similarly the accounts of New Romney note that in 1422 or thereabouts the men of Lydd 'came with their may and ours[4],' and those of Reading St. Lawrence that in 1505 came 'Robyn Hod of Handley and his company' and in 1507 'Robyn Hod and his company from ffynchamsted[5].' In contemporary Scotland James IV gave a present at mid-

<hr>

[1] *Hist. MSS.* i. 107, from *Convocation Book*, 'pecuniae ecclesiae ac communitatis Welliae... videlicet, provenientes ante hoc tempus de Robynhode, puellis tripudiantibus, communi cervisia ecclesiae, et huiusmodi.'

[2] The accounts of Croscombe, Somerset, contain yearly entries of receipts from 'Roben Hod's recones' from 1476 to 1510, and again in 1525 (Hobhouse, 1 sqq.). At Melton Mowbray the amount

raised by the 'lord' was set aside for mending the highways (Kelly, 65).

[3] Lysons, *Environs*, i. 225. Mention is made of 'Robin Hood,' 'the Lady,' 'Maid Marion,' 'Little John,' 'the Frere,' 'the Fool,' 'the Dysard,' 'the Morris-dance.'

[4] *Archaeologia Cantiana*, xiii. 216.

[5] C. Kerry, *History of St. Lawrence, Reading*, 226. 'Made Maryon,' 'the tree' and 'the morris-dance,' are mentioned.

summer in 1503 'to Robin Hude of Perth[1].' It would hardly have been worth while, however, to carry the May-game from one village or town to another, had it been nothing but a procession with a garland and a 'gaderyng'; and as a matter of fact we find that in England as in France dramatic performances came to be associated with the summer folk-festivals. The London 'Maying' included stage plays[2]. At Shrewsbury *lusores* under the Abbot of Marham acted interludes 'for the glee of the town' at Pentecost[3]. The guild of St. Luke at Norwich performed secular as well as miracle plays, and the guild of Holy Cross at Abingdon held its feast on May 3 with 'pageants, plays and May-games,' as early as 1445[4]. Some of these plays were doubtless miracles, but so far as they were secular, the subjects of them were naturally drawn, in the absence of *pastourelles*, from the ballads of the Robin Hood cycle[5]. Amongst the Paston letters is preserved one written in 1473, in which the writer laments the loss of a servant, whom he has kept 'thys iij yer to pleye Seynt Jorge and Robyn Hod and the Shryff off Nottyngham[6].' Moreover, some specimens of the plays themselves are still extant. One of them, unfortunately only a fragment, must be the very play referred to in the letter just quoted, for its subject is 'Robin Hood and the Sheriff of Nottingham,' and it is found on a scrap of paper formerly in the possession of Sir John Fenn, the first editor of the *Paston Letters*[7]. A second

---

[1] *L. H. T. Accounts*, ii. 377.

[2] Stowe, *Survey* (1598), 38. He is speaking mainly of the period before 1517, when there was a riot on 'Black' May-day, and afterwards the May-games were not 'so freely used as before.'

[3] Appendix E (vi).

[4] Cf. *Representations*.

[5] Bower († 1437), *Scotichronicon* (ed. Hearne), iii. 774 'ille famosissimus sicarius Robertus Hode et Litill-Iohanne cum eorum complicibus, de quibus stolidum vulgus hianter in comoediis et tragoediis prurienter festum faciunt, et, prae ceteris romanciis, mimos et bardanos cantitare delectantur.' On the ambiguity of 'comoediae' and 'tragoediae' in the fifteenth century, cf. ch. xxv.

[6] Gairdner, *Paston Letters*, iii. 89; Child, v. 90; 'W. Woode, whyche promysed . . . he wold never goo ffro me, and ther uppon I have kepyd hym thys iij yer to pleye Seynt Jorge and Robyn Hod and the Shryff off Nottyngham, and now, when I wolde have good horse, he is goon into Bernysdale, and I withowt a keeper.' The *Northumberland Household Book*, 60, makes provision for 'liveries for Robin Hood' in the Earl's household.

[7] Printed by Child, v. 90; Manly, i. 279. The MS. of the fragment probably dates before 1475.

play on 'Robin Hood and the Friar' and a fragment of a third on 'Robin Hood and the Potter' were printed by Copland in the edition of the *Gest of Robyn Hode* published by him about 1550 [1]. The Robin Hood plays are, of course, subsequent to the development of religious drama which will be discussed in the next volume. They are of the nature of interludes, and were doubtless written, like the plays of Adan de la Hale, by some clerk or minstrel for the delectation of the villagers. They are, therefore, in a less degree folk-drama, than the examples which we shall have to consider in the next chapter. But it is worthy of notice, that even in the heyday of the stage under Elizabeth and James I, the summer festival continued to supply motives to the dramatists. Anthony Munday's *Downfall and Death of Robert Earl of Huntingdon* [2], Chapman's *May-Day*, and Jonson's delightful fragment *The Sad Shepherd* form an interesting group of pastoral comedies, affinities to which may be traced in the *As You Like It* and *Winter's Tale* of Shakespeare himself.

As has been said, it is impossible to establish any direct affiliation between the Robin Hood plays and earlier *caroles* on the same theme, in the way in which this can be done for the *jeu* of Adan de la Hale, and the Robin and Marion of the *pastourelles*. The extant Robin Hood ballads are certainly not *caroles*; they are probably not folk-song at all, but minstrelsy of a somewhat debased type. The only actual trace of such *caroles* that has been come across is the mention of 'Robene hude' as the name of a dance in the *Complaynt of Scotland*

---

[1] Printed by Child, v. 114, 127; Manly, i. 281, 285. They were originally printed as one play by Copland (†1550).

[2] Printed in Dodsley-Hazlitt, vol. viii. These plays were written for Henslowe about February 1598. In November Chettle 'mended Roben hood for the corte' (*Henslowe's Diary*, 118–20, 139). At Christmas 1600, Henslowe had another play of 'Roben hoodes penerths' by William Haughton (*Diary*, 174–5). An earlier 'pastorall pleasant comedie of Robin Hood and Little John' was entered on the Stationers' Registers on May 18, 1594. These two are lost, as is *The May Lord* which Jonson wrote (*Conversations with Drummond*, 27). Robin Hood also appears in Peele's *Edward I* (†1590), and the anonymous *Look About You* (1600), and is the hero of Greene's *George a Greene the Pinner of Wakefield* (†1593). Anthony Munday introduced him again into his pageant of *Metropolis Coronata* (1615), and a comedy of *Robin Hood and his Crew of Soldiers*, acted at Nottingham on the day of the coronation of Charles II, was published in 1661. On all these plays, cf. F. E. Schelling, *The English Chronicle Play*, 156.

about 1548[1]. Dances, however, of one kind or another, there undoubtedly were at the May-games. The Wells corporation accounts mention *puellae tripudiantes* in close relation with *Robynhode*[2]. And particularly there was the morris-dance, which was so universally in use on May-day, that it borrowed, almost in permanence, for its leading character the name of Maid Marian. The morris-dance, however, is common to nearly all the village feasts, and its origin and nature will be matter for discussion' in the next chapter.

In many places, even during the Middle Ages, and still more afterwards, the summer feast dropped out or degenerated. It became a mere beer-swilling, an 'ale[3].' And so we find in the sixteenth century a 'king-ale[4]' or a 'Robin Hood's ale[5],' and in modern times a 'Whitsun-ale[6],' a 'lamb-ale[7]' or a 'gyst-ale[8]' beside the 'church-ales' and 'scot-ales' which the thirteenth-century bishops had already condemned[9]. On the other hand, the village festival found its way to court, and became a sumptuous pageant under the splendour-loving Tudors. For this, indeed, there was Arthurian precedent in the romance of Malory, who records how Guenever was taken

---

[1] Furnivall, *Robert Laneham's Letter*, clxiii. Chaucer, *Rom. of Rose*, 7455, has 'the daunce Joly Robin,' but this is from his French original 'li biaus Robins.'

[2] Cf. p. 176.

[3] Dyer, 278; Drake, 86; Brand-Ellis, i. 157; Cutts, *Parish Priests*, 317; *Archaeologia*, xii. 11; Stubbes, i. 150; *F. L.* x. 350. At an 'ale' a cask of home-brewed was broached for sale in the church or church-house, and the profits went to some public object; at a church-ale to the parish, at a clerk-ale to the clerk, at a bride-ale or bridal to the bride, at a bid-ale to some poor man in trouble. A love-ale was probably merely social.

[4] At Reading in 1557 (C. Kerry, *Hist. of St. Lawrence, Reading*, 226).

[5] At Tintinhull in 1513 (Hob-house, 200, 'Robine Hood's All').

[6] Brand-Ellis, i. 157; Dyer, 278. A carving on the church of St. John's, Chichester, represents a Whitsun-ale, with a 'lord' and 'lady.'

[7] Cf. p. 141.

[8] At Ashton-under-Lyne, from 1422 to a recent date (Dyer, 181). 'Gyst' appears to be either 'gist' (*gîte*) 'right of pasturage' or a corruption of 'guising'; cf. ch. xvii.

[9] Cf. p. 91. On *Scot-ale*, cf. Ducange, s. v. Scotallum; *Archaeologia*, xii. 11; H. T. Riley, *Munimenta Gildhallae Londin.* (R. S.), ii. 760. The term first appears as the name of a tax, as in a Northampton charter of 1189 (Markham-Cox, *Northampton Borough Records*, i. 26) 'concessimus quod sint quieti de . . . Brudtol et de Child-wite et de hieresgiue et de Scottale. ita quod Prepositus Northamptonie ut aliquis alius Ballivus scottale non faciat'; cf. the thirteenth-century examples quoted by Ducange. The *Council of Lambeth* (1206), c. 2, clearly defines the term as 'communes potationes,' and the primary sense is therefore probably that of an *ale* at which a *scot* or tax is raised.

by Sir Meliagraunce, when 'as the queen had mayed and all her knights, all were bedashed with herbs, mosses, and flowers, in the best manner and freshest [1].' The chronicler Hall tells of the Mayings of Henry VIII in 1510, 1511, and 1515. In the last of these some hundred and thirty persons took part. Henry was entertained by Robin Hood and the rest with shooting-matches and a collation of venison in a bower; and returning was met by a chariot in which rode the Lady May and the Lady Flora, while on the five horses sat the Ladies Humidity, Vert, Vegetave, Pleasaunce and Sweet Odour [2]. Obviously the pastime has here degenerated in another direction. It has become learned, allegorical, and pseudo-classic. At the Reformation the May-game and the May-pole were marks for Puritan onslaught. Latimer, in one of his sermons before Edward VI, complains how, when he had intended to preach in a certain country town on his way to London, he was told that he could not be heard, for 'it is Robyn hoodes daye. The parishe are gone a brode to gather for Robyn hoode [3].' Machyn's *Diary* mentions the breaking of a May-pole in Fenchurch by the lord mayor of 1552 [4], and the revival of elaborate and heterogeneous May-games throughout London during the brief span of Queen Mary [5]. The Elizabethan Puritans renewed the attack, but though something may have been done by reforming municipalities here and there to put down the festivals [6], the ecclesiastical authori-

---

[1] Malory, *Morte d'Arthur*, xix.1.2.

[2] Hall, 515, 520, 582; Brewer, *Letters and Papers of Henry VIII*, ii. 1504. In 1510, Henry and his courtiers visited the queen's chamber in the guise of Robin Hood and his men on the inappropriate date of January 18. In Scotland, about the same time, Dunbar wrote a 'cry' for a maying with Robin Hood; cf. *Texts*, s.v. Dunbar.

[3] Latimer, *Sermon vi before Edw. VI* (1549, ed. Arber, 173). Perhaps the town was Melton Mowbray, where Robin Hood was very popular, and where Latimer is shown by the churchwardens' accounts to have preached several years later in 1553 (Kelly, 67).

[4] Machyn, 20.

[5] Ibid. 89, 137, 196, 201, 283, 373. In 1559, e.g. 'the xxiiij of June ther was a May-game ... and Sant John Sacerys, with a gyant, and drumes and gunes [and the] ix wordes (worthies), with spechys, and a goodly pagant with a quen ... and dyvers odur, with spechys; and then Sant Gorge and the dragon, the mores dansse, and after Robyn Hode and lytyll John, and M[aid Marian] and frere Tuke, and they had spechys round a-bout London.'

[6] 'Mr. Tomkys publicke prechar' in Shrewsbury induced the bailiffs to 'reform' May-poles in 1588, and in 1591 some apprentices were com-

ties could not be induced to go much beyond forbidding them to take place in churchyards[1]. William Stafford, indeed, declared in 1581 that 'May-games, wakes, and revels' were 'now laid down[2],' but the violent abuse directed against them only two years later by Philip Stubbes, which may be taken as a fair sample of the Puritan polemic as a whole, shows that this was far from being really the case[3]. In Scotland the Parliament ordered, as early as 1555, that no one 'be chosen Robert Hude, nor Lytill Johne, Abbot of vnressoun, Quenis of Maij, nor vtherwyse, nouther in Burgh nor to landwart in ony tyme to cum[4].' But the prohibition was not very effective, for in 1577 and 1578 the General Assembly is found petitioning for its renewal[5]. And in England no similar action was taken until 1644 when the Long Parliament decreed the destruction of such May-poles as the municipalities had spared. Naturally this policy was reversed at the Restoration, and a new London pole was erected in the Strand, hard by Somerset House, which endured until 1717[6].

mitted for disobeying the order. A judicial decision was, however, given in favour of the 'tree' (Burne-Jackson, 358 ; Hibbert, *English Craft-Gilds*, 121). In London the Cornhill Maypole, which gave its name to St. Andrew Undershaft, was destroyed by persuasion of a preacher as early as 1549 (Dyer, 248) ; cf. also Stubbes, i. 306, and Morrison's advice to Henry VIII quoted in ch. xxv.

[1] Archbishop Grindal's *Visitation Articles* of 1576 (*Remains*, Parker Soc. 175), 'whether the minister and churchwardens have suffered any lords of misrule or summer lords or ladies, or any disguised persons, or others, in Christmas or at May-games, or any morris-dancers, or at any other times, to come unreverently into the church or churchyard, and there to dance, or play any unseemly parts, with scoffs, jests, wanton gestures, or ribald talk, namely in the time of Common Prayer.' Similarly worded *Injunctions* for Norwich (1569), York (1571), Lichfield (1584), London (1601) and Oxford

(1619) are quoted in the *Second Report* of the Ritual Commission ; cf. the eighty-eighth *Canon* of 1604. It is true that the *Visitation Articles* for St. Mary's, Shrewsbury, in 1584 inquire more generally 'whether there have been any lords of mysrule, or somer lords or ladies, or any disguised persons, as morice dancers, maskers, or mum'ers, or such lyke, within the parishe, ether in the nativititide or in som'er, or at any other tyme, and what be their names' ; but this church was a 'peculiar' and its 'official' the Puritan Tomkys mentioned in the last note (Owen and Blakeway, i. 333 ; Burne-Jackson, 481).

[2] Stafford, 16.

[3] Stubbes, i. 146 ; cf. the further quotations and references there given in the notes.

[4] 6 *Mary*, cap. 61.

[5] Child, v. 45 ; cf. *Representations*, s.v. Aberdeen, on the breaches of the statute there in 1562 and 1565.

[6] Dyer, 228 ; Drake, 85. At Cerne Abbas, Dorset, the May-pole was cut down in 1635 and made into a town ladder (*F. L.* x. 481).

CHAPTER IX

THE SWORD-DANCE

[*Bibliographical Note.*—The books mentioned in the bibliographical note to the last chapter should be consulted on the general tendency to μίμησις in festival dance and song. The symbolical dramatic ceremonies of the *renouveau* are collected by Dr. J. G. Frazer in *The Golden Bough*. The sword-dance has been the subject of two elaborate studies : K. Müllenhoff, *Ueber den Schwerttanz*, in *Festgaben für Gustav Homeyer* (1871), iii, with additions in *Zeitschrift für deutsches Alterthum*, xviii. 9, xx. 10 ; and F. A. Mayer, *Ein deutsches Schwerttanzspiel aus Ungarn* (with full bibliography), in *Zeitschrift für Völkerpsychologie* (1889), 204, 416. The best accounts of the morris-dance are in F. Douce, *Illustrations of Shakespeare* (1807, new ed. 1839), and A. Burton, *Rushbearing* (1891), 95.]

THE last two chapters have afforded more than one example of village festival customs ultimately taking shape as drama. But neither the English Robin Hood plays, nor the French *Jeu de Robin et Marion*, can be regarded as folk-drama in the proper sense of the word. They were written not by the folk themselves, but by *trouvères* or minstrels *for* the folk ; and at a period when the independent evolution of the religious play had already set a model of dramatic composition. Probably the same is true of the Hox Tuesday play in the form in which we may conjecture it to have been presented before Elizabeth late in the sixteenth century. Nevertheless it is possible to trace, apart from minstrel intervention and apart from imitation of miracles, the existence of certain embryonic dramatic tendencies in the village ceremonies themselves. Too much must not be made of these. Jacob Grimm was inclined to find in them the first vague beginnings of the whole of modern drama[1]. This is demonstrably wrong. Modern drama arose, by a fairly well defined line of evolution, from a threefold source, the ecclesiastical liturgy, the farce of the mimes, the classical revivals of humanism. Folk-drama contributed but the tiniest rill to the mighty stream. Such as

[1] Grimm, ii. 784 ; *Kleinere Schriften*, v. 281 ; Pearson, ii. 281.

it was, however, a couple of further chapters may be not unprofitably spent in its analysis.

The festival customs include a number of dramatic rites which appear to have been originally symbolical expressions of the facts of seasonal recurrence lying at the root of the festivals themselves. The antithesis of winter and summer, the *renouveau* of spring, are mimed in three or four distinct fashions. The first and the most important, as well as the most widespread of these, is the mock representation of a death or burial. Dr. Frazer has collected many instances of the ceremony known as the 'expulsion of Death[1].' This takes place at various dates in spring and early summer, but most often on the fourth Sunday in Lent, one of the many names of which is consequently *Todten-Sonntag*. An effigy is made, generally of straw, but in some cases of birch twigs, a beechen bough, or other such material. This is called Death, is treated with marks of fear, hatred or contempt, and is finally carried in procession, and thrust over the boundary of the village. Or it is torn in pieces, buried, burnt, or thrown into a river or pool. Sometimes the health or other welfare of the folk during the year is held to depend on the rite being duly performed. The fragments of Death have fertilizing efficacy for women and cattle ; they are put in the fields, the mangers, the hens' nests. Here and there women alone take part in the ceremony, but more often it is common to the whole village. The expulsion of Death is found in various parts of Teutonic Germany, but especially in districts such as Thuringia, Bohemia, Silesia, where the population is wholly or mainly Slavonic. A similar custom, known both in Slavonic districts and in Italy, France, and Spain, had the name of 'sawing the old woman.' At Florence, for instance, the effigy of an old woman was placed on a ladder. At Mid Lent it was sawn through, and the nuts and dried fruits with which it was stuffed scrambled for by the crowd. At Palermo there was a still more realistic representation with a real old woman, to whose neck a bladder of blood was fitted[2].

---

[1] Frazer, ii. 82 ; Grant Allen, 293, 315 ; Grimm, ii. 764 ; Pearson, ii. 283.

[2] Frazer, ii. 86 ; Martinengo-Cesaresco, 267. Cf. the use of the bladder of blood in the St. Thomas

The 'Death' of the German and Slavonic form of the custom has clearly come to be regarded as the personification of the forces of evil within the village ; and the ceremony of expulsion may be compared with other periodical rites, European and non-European, in which evil spirits are similarly expelled[1]. The effigy may even be regarded in the light of a scapegoat, bearing away the sins of the community[2]. But it is doubtful how far the notion of evil spirits warring against the good spirits which protect man and his crops is a European, or at any rate a primitive European one[3]; and it may perhaps be taken for granted that what was originally thought to be expelled in the rite was not so much either 'Death' or 'Sin' as winter. This view is confirmed by the evidence of an eighth-century homily, which speaks of the expulsion of winter in February as a relic of pagan belief[4]. Moreover, the expulsion of Death is often found in the closest relation to the more widespread custom of bringing summer, in the shape of green tree or bough, into the village. The procession which carries away the dead effigy brings back the summer tree ; and the rhymes used treat the two events as connected[5].

The homily just quoted suggests that the mock funeral or expulsion of winter was no new thing in the eighth century. On the other hand, it can hardly be supposed that customs which imply such abstract ideas as death, or even as summer and winter, belong to the earliest stages of the village festival. What has happened is what happens in other forms of festival play. The instinct of play, in this case finding vent in a dramatic representation of the succession of summer to

procession at Canterbury (*Representations*, s. v.).

[1] Frazer, iii. 70. Amongst such customs are the expulsion of Satan on New Year's day by the Finns, the expulsion of Kore at Easter in Albania, the expulsion of witches on March 1 in Calabria, and on May 1 in the Tyrol, the frightening of the wood-sprites Strudeli and Strätteli on Twelfth night at Brunnen in Switzerland. Such ceremonies are often accompanied with a horrible noise of horns, cleavers and the like. Horns are also used

at Oxford (Dyer, 261) and elsewhere on May 1, and I have heard it said that the object of the Oxford custom is to drive away evil spirits. Similar discords are *de rigueur* at Skimmington Ridings. I very much doubt whether they are anything but a degenerate survival of a barbaric type of music.

[2] Frazer, iii. 121.

[3] Tylor, *Anthropology*, 382.

[4] Caspari, 10 'qui in mense februario hibernum credit expellere... non christianus, sed gentilis est.'

[5] Frazer, ii. 91.

winter, has taken hold of and adapted to its own purposes
elements in the celebrations which, once significant, have
gradually come to be mere traditional survivals. Such are
the ceremonial burial in the ground, the ceremonial burning,
the ceremonial plunging into water, of the representative of
the fertilization spirit. In particular, the southern term ' the
old woman ' suggests that the effigy expelled or destroyed
is none other than the 'corn mother' or 'harvest-May,'
fashioned to represent the fertilization spirit out of the last
sheaf at harvest, and preserved until its place is taken by
a new and green representative in the spring.

There are, however, other versions of the mock death in
which the central figure of the little drama is not the representative of the fertilization spirit itself, but one of the worshippers.
In Bavaria the Whitsuntide *Pfingstl* is dressed in leaves and
water-plants with a cap of peonies. He is soused with water,
and then, in mimicry, has his head cut off. Similar customs
prevail in the Erzgebirge and elsewhere [1]. We have seen
this *Pfingstl* before. He is the Jack in the green, the worshipper clad in the god under whose protection he desires to
put himself [2]. But how can the killing of him symbolize the
spring, for obviously it is the coming summer, not the dying
winter, that the leaf-clad figure must represent ? The fact is
that the Bavarian drama is not complete. The full ceremony
is found in other parts of Germany. Thus in Saxony and
Thuringia a 'wild man' covered with leaves and moss is
hunted in a wood, caught, and executed. Then comes forward
a lad dressed as a doctor, who brings the victim to life again
by bleeding [3]. Even so annually the summer dies and has its
resurrection. In Swabia, again, on Shrove Tuesday, 'Dr.
Eisenbart' bleeds a man to death, and afterwards revives
him. This same Dr. Eisenbart appears also in the Swabian
Whitsuntide execution, although here too the actual resurrection seems to have dropped out of the ceremony [4]. It is

[1] Frazer, ii. 60.
[2] Sometimes the *Pfingstl* is called
a ' wild man.' Two ' myghty
woordwossys [cf. p. 392] or wyld
men' appeared in a revel at the court
of Henry VIII in 1513 (*Revels Account* in Brewer, ii. 1499), and

similar figures are not uncommon
in the sixteenth-century masques
and entertainments.
[3] Frazer, ii. 62.
[4] Ibid. ii. 61, 82 ; E. Meier,
*Deutsche Sagen, Sitten und Ge-
bräuche aus Schwaben*, 374, 409.

interesting to note that the green man of the peasantry, who dies and lives again, reappears as the Green Knight in one of the most famous divisions of Arthurian romance[1].

The mock death or burial type of folk-drama resolves itself, then, into two varieties. In one, it is winter whose passing is represented, and for this the discarded harvest-May serves as a nucleus. In the other, which is not really complete without a resurrection, it is summer, whose death is mimed merely as a preliminary to its joyful renewal; and this too is built up around a fragment of ancient cult in the person of the leaf-clad worshipper, who is, indeed, none other than the priest-king, once actually, and still in some sort and show, slain at the festival[2]. In the instances so far dealt with, the original significance of the rite is still fairly traceable. But there are others into which new meanings, due to the influence of Christian custom, have been read. In many parts of Germany customs closely analogous to those of the expulsion of winter or Death take place on Shrove Tuesday, and have suffered metamorphosis into 'burial of the Carnival[3].' England affords the 'Jack o' Lent' effigy which is taken to represent Judas Iscariot[4], the Lincoln 'funeral of Alleluia[5],' the Tenby

---

[1] *Syr Gawayne and the Grene Knyghte* (ed. Madden, Bannatyne Club, 1839); cf. J. L. Weston, *The Legend of Sir Gawain*, 85. Arthur was keeping New Year's Day, when a knight dressed in green, with a green beard, riding a green horse, and bearing a holly bough, and an axe of green steel, entered the hall. He challenged any man of the Round Table to deal him a buffet with the axe on condition of receiving one in return after the lapse of a year. Sir Gawain accepts. The stranger's head is cut off, but he picks it up and rides away with it. This is a close parallel to the resurrection of the slain 'wild man.'

[2] Frazer, ii. 105, 115, 163, 219; *Pausanias*, iii. 53; v. 259; Gardner, *New Chapters in Greek History*, 395, give Russian, Greek, and Asiatic parallels.

[3] Frazer, ii. 71; Pfannenschmidt, 302. The victim is sometimes known as the Carnival or Shrovetide 'Fool' or 'Bear.'

[4] Dyer, 93. The Jack o' Lent apparently stood as a cock-shy from Ash Wednesday to Good Friday, and was then burnt. Portuguese sailors in English docks thrash and duck an effigy of Judas Iscariot on Good Friday (Dyer, 155).

[5] Alleluia was not sung during Lent. Fosbrooke, *British Monachism*, 56, describes the Funeral of Alleluia by the choristers of an English cathedral on the Saturday before Septuagesima. A turf was carried in procession with howling to the cloisters. Probably this cathedral was Lincoln, whence Wordsworth, 105, quotes payments 'pro excludend' Alleluya' from 1452 to 1617. Leber, ix. 338; Barthélemy, iii. 481, give French examples of the custom; cf. the Alleluia top, p. 128.

'making Christ's bed[1],' the Monkton 'risin' and buryin' Peter[2].' The truth that the vitality of a folk custom is far greater than that of any single interpretation of it is admirably illustrated.

Two other symbolical representations of the phenomena of the *renouveau* must be very briefly treated. At Briançon in Dauphiné, instead of a death and resurrection, is used a pretty little May-day drama, in which the leaf-clad man falls into sleep upon the ground and is awakened by the kiss of a maiden[3]. Russia has a similar custom; and such a magic kiss, bringing summer with it, lies at the heart of the story of the Sleeping Beauty. Indeed, the marriage of heaven and earth seems to have been a myth very early invented by the Aryan mind to explain the fertility of crops beneath the rain, and it probably received dramatic form in religious ceremonies both in Greece and Italy[4]. Finally, there is a fairly widespread spring custom of holding a dramatic fight between two parties, one clad in green to represent summer, the other in straw or fur to represent winter. Waldron describes this in the Isle of Man[5]; Olaus Magnus in Sweden[6]. Grimm says that it is found in various districts on both sides of the middle Rhine[7]. Perhaps both this dramatic battle and that of the Coventry Hox Tuesday owe their origin to the struggle for the fertilizing head of a sacrificial animal, which also issued in football and similar games. Dr. Frazer quotes several instances from all parts of the world in which a mock fight, or an interchange of abuse and raillery taking the place of an actual fight, serves as a crop-charm[8]. The summer and winter battle gave to literature a famous type of neo-Latin and Romance *débat*[9]. In one of the most interesting forms of

---

[1] Dyer, 158. Reeds were woven on Good Friday into the shape of a crucifix and left in some hidden part of a field or garden.

[2] Dyer, 333. The village feast was on St. Peter's day, June 29. On the Saturday before an effigy was dug up from under a sycamore on Maypole hill; a week later it was buried again. In this case the order of events seems to have been inverted.

[3] Frazer, i. 221. The French May-queen is often called *la mariée* or *l'épouse*.

[4] Frazer, i. 225; Jevons, *Plutarch R. Q.* lxxxiii. 56.

[5] Waldron, *Hist. of Isle of Man*, 95; Dyer, 246.

[6] Olaus Magnus, *History of Swedes and Goths*, xv. 4, 8, 9; Grimm, ii. 774.

[7] Grimm, ii.765; Paul, *Grundriss* (ed. 1), i. 836.

[8] Frazer, *Pausanias*, iii. 267.

[9] Cf. ch. iv.

this, the eighth- or ninth-century *Conflictus Veris et Hiemis*, the subject of dispute is the cuckoo, which spring praises and winter chides, while the shepherds declare that he must be drowned or stolen away, because summer cometh not. The cuckoo is everywhere a characteristic bird of spring, and his coming was probably a primitive signal for the high summer festival[1].

The symbolical dramas of the seasons stand alone and independent, but it may safely be asserted that drama first arose at the village feasts in close relation to the dance. That dancing, like all the arts, tends to be mimetic is a fact which did not escape the attention of Aristotle[2]. The pantomimes of the decadent Roman stage are a case in point. Greek tragedy itself had grown out of the Dionysiac dithyramb, and travellers describe how readily the dances of the modern savage take shape as primitive dramas of war, hunting, love, religion, labour, or domestic life[3]. Doubtless this was the case also with the *caroles* of the European festivals. The types of *chanson* most immediately derived from these are full of dialogue, and already on the point of bursting into drama. That they did do this, with the aid of the minstrels, in the *Jeu de Robin et de Marion* we have seen[4]. A curious passage in the *Itinerarium Cambriae* of Giraldus Cambrensis († 1188) describes a dance of peasants in and

---

[1] Grimm, ii. 675, 763 ; Swainson, *Folk-lore of British Birds* (F. L.S.), 109; Hardy, *Popular History of the Cuckoo*, in *F. L. Record*, ii ; Mannhardt, in *Zeitschrift für deutsche Mythologie*, iii. 209. Cf. ch. v.

[2] Aristotle, *Poetics*, i. 5 αὐτῷ δὲ τῷ ῥυθμῷ [ποιεῖται τὴν μίμησιν] χωρὶς ἁρμονίας ἡ [τέχνη] τῶν ὀρχηστῶν, καὶ γὰρ οὗτοι διὰ τῶν σχηματιζομένων ῥυθμῶν μιμοῦνται καὶ ἤθη καὶ πάθη καὶ πράξεις. Cf. Lucian, *de Saltatione*, xv. 277. Du Méril, 65, puts the thing well : ' La danse n'a été l'invention de personne : elle s'est produite d'elle-même le jour que le corps a subi et dû refléter un état de l'âme ... On ne tarda pas cependant à la séparer de sa cause première et à la reproduire pour

elle-même ... en simulant la gaieté on parvenait réellement à la sentir.'

[3] Wallaschek, 216 ; Grosse, 165, 201 ; Hirn, 157, 182, 229, 259, 261 ; Du Méril, *Com.* 72 ; Haddon, 346 ; Grove, 52, 81 ; Mrs. Gomme, ii. 518 ; G. Catlin, *On Manners* . . . *of N. Amer. Indians* (1841), i. 128, 244. Lang, *M. R. R.* i. 272, dwells on the representation of myths in savage mystery-dances, and points out that Lucian (*loc. cit.*) says that the Greeks used to 'dance out' (ἐξορχεῖσθαι) their mysteries.

[4] The *chanson* of *Transformations* (cf. p. 170) is sung by peasant-girls as a semi-dramatic duet (*Romania*, vii. 62) ; and that of *Marion* was performed 'à deux personnages' on Shrove Tuesday in Lorraine (*Romania*, ix. 568).

about the church of St. Elined, near Brecknock on the Gwyl
Awst, in which the ordinary operations of the village life, such
as ploughing, sewing, spinning were mimetically represented[1].
Such dances seem to survive in some of the *rondes* or 'singing-
games,' so frequently dramatic, of children[2]. On the whole,
perhaps, these connect themselves rather with the domestic
than with the strictly agricultural element in village cult.
A large proportion of them are concerned with marriage.
But the domestic and the agricultural cannot be altogether
dissociated. The game of 'Nuts in May,' for instance, seems
to have as its kernel a reminiscence of marriage by capture ;
but the 'nuts ' or rather 'knots ' or 'posies ' 'in May ' certainly
suggest a setting at a seasonal festival. So too, with 'Round
the Mulberry Bush.' The mimicry here is of domestic operations, but the 'bush ' recalls the sacred tree, the natural centre
of the seasonal dances. The closest parallels to the dance
described by Giraldus Cambrensis are to be found in the
rondes of 'Oats and Beans and Barley ' and 'Would you know
how doth the Peasant ? ', in which the chief, though not always
the only, subjects of mimicry are ploughing, sowing and the
like, and which frequently contain a prayer or aspiration for
the welfare of the crops[3].

---

[1] Giraldus Cambrensis, *Itinerarium Cambriae*, i. 2 (*Opera*, R.S. vi.
32) 'Videas enim hic homines seu
puellas, nunc in ecclesia, nunc in
coemiterio, nunc in chorea, quae
circa coemiterium cum cantilena
circumfertur, subito in terram cor-
ruere, et primo tanquam in extasim
ductos et quietos ; deinde statim
tanquam in phrenesim raptos exsi-
lientes, opera quaecunque festis
diebus illicite perpetrare consue-
verant, tam manibus quam pedibus,
coram populo repraesentantes. videas hunc aratro manus aptare,
illum quasi stimulo boves excitare ;
et utrumque quasi laborem miti-
gando solitas barbarae modulatio-
nis voces efferre. videas hunc artem
sutoriam, illum pellipariam imitari.
item videas hanc quasi colum ba-
iulando, nunc filum manibus et
brachiis in longum extrahere, nunc

extractum occandum tanquam in
fusum revocare : istam deambu-
lando productis filis quasi telam
ordiri : illam sedendo quasi iam
orditam oppositis lanceolae iactibus
et alternis calamistrae cominus icti-
bus texere mireris. Demum vero
intra ecclesiam cum oblationibus ad
altare perductos tanquam experrec-
tos et ad se redeuntes obstupescas.'
[2] Cf. p. 151 with Mrs. Gomme's
Memoir (ii. 458) *passim*, and
Haddon, 328. Parallel savage
examples are in Wallaschek, 216 ;
Hirn, 157, 259.
[3] Mrs. Gomme, ii. 399, 494 and
s. vv. ; Haddon, 340. Similar
games are widespread on the continent ; cf. the Rabelais quotation on
p. 167. Haddon quotes a French
formula, ending
'Aveine, aveine, aveine,
Que le Bon Dieu t'amène.'

I have treated the mimetic element of budding drama in the agricultural festivals as being primarily a manifestation of the activities of play determined in its direction by the dominant interests of the occasion, and finding its material in the débris of ritual custom left over from forgotten stages of religious thought. It is possible also to hold that the *mimesis* is more closely interwoven with the religious and practical side of the festivals, and is in fact yet another example of that primitive magical notion of causation by the production of the similar, which is at the root of the rain- and sun-charms. Certainly the village dramas, like the other ceremonies which they accompany, are often regarded as influencing the luck of the farmer's year; just as the hunting- and war-dances of savages are often regarded not merely as amusement or as practice for actual war and hunting, but as charms to secure success in these pursuits[1]. But it does not seem clear to me that in this case the magical efficacy belongs to the drama from the beginning, and I incline to look upon it as merely part of the sanctity of the feast as a whole, which has attached itself in the course of time even to that side of it which began as play.

The evolution of folk-drama out of folk-dance may be most completely studied through a comparison of the various types of European sword-dance with the so-called 'mummers',' 'guisers',' or 'Pace-eggers'' play of Saint George. The history of the sword-dance has received a good deal of attention from German archaeologists, who, however, perhaps from imperfect acquaintance with the English data, have stopped short of the affiliation to it of the play[2]. The dance itself can boast a hoar antiquity. Tacitus describes it as the one form of *spectaculum* to be seen at the gatherings of the Germans with whom he was conversant. The dancers were young men who leapt with much agility amongst menacing

---

[1] Wallaschek, 273; Hirn, 285.

[2] The German data here used are chiefly collected by Müllenhoff and F. A. Mayer; cf. also Creizenach, i. 408; Michels, 84; J. J. Ammann, *Nachträge zum Schwerttanz*, in *Z. f. d. Alterthum* xxxiv (1890), 178; A. Hartmann, *Volksschauspiele* (1880), 130; F. M. Böhme, *Ge-schichte des Tanzes in Deutschland* (1886); Sepp, *Die Religion der alten Deutschen, und ihr Fortbestand in Volkssagen, Aufzügen und Fest-bräuchen bis zur Gegenwart* (1890), 91; O. Wittstock, *Ueber den Schwert-tanz der Siebenbürger Sachsen*, in *Philologische Studien: Festgabe für Eduard Sievers* (1896), 349.

spear-points and sword-blades[1]. Some centuries later the use of *sweorda-gelac* as a metaphor for battle in *Beowulf* shows that the term was known to the continental ancestors of the Anglo-Saxons[2]. Then follows a long gap in the record, bridged only by a doubtful reference in an eighth-century Frankish homily[3], and a possible representation in a ninth-century Latin and Anglo-Saxon manuscript[4]. The minstrels seem to have adopted the sword-dance into their repertory[5], but the earliest mediaeval notice of it as a popular *ludus* is at Nuremberg in 1350. From that date onwards until quite recent years it crops up frequently, alike at Shrovetide, Christmas and other folk festivals, and as an element in the revels at weddings, royal entries, and the like[6]. It is fairly widespread throughout Germany. It is found in Italy, where it is called the *mattaccino*[7], and in Spain (*matachin*), and under this name or that of the *danse des bouffons* it was known both in France and England at the Renaissance[8]. It is given by Paradin in his *Le Blason des Danses* and, with the music and cuts of the performers, by Tabourot in his *Orchésographie* (1588)[9]. These are the sophisticated versions of courtly halls. But about the same date Olaus Magnus describes it as a folk-dance, to the accompaniment of pipes or *cantilenae*, in Sweden[10]. In England, the main area of the

---

[1] Tacitus, *Germania*, 24 'genus spectaculorum unum atque in omni coetu idem. nudi iuvenes, quibus id ludicrum est, inter gladios se atque infestas frameas saltu iaciunt. exercitatio artem paravit, ars decorem, non in quaestum tamen aut mercedem ; quamvis audacis lasciviae pretium est voluptas spectantium.'

[2] *Beowulf*, 1042. It is in the hall of Hrothgar at Heorot,
'þæt wæs hilde - setl : heah-cyninges,
þonne sweorda - gelác : sunu Healfdenes
efnan wolde : næfre on óre læg
wíd - cúþes wíg : þonne walu féollon.'

[3] Appendix N, no. xxxix; 'arma in campo ostendit.'

[4] Strutt, 215. The tenth-century τὸ γοτθικόν at Byzantium seems to

have been a kind of sword-dance (cf. ch. xii *ad fin.*).

[5] Strutt, 260 ; Du Méril, *La Com.* 84.

[6] Mayer, 259.

[7] Müllenhoff, 145, quoting *Don Quixote*, ii. 20 ; *Z. f. d. A.* xviii. 11 ; Du Méril, *La Com.* 86.

[8] Webster, *The White Devil*, v. 6, 'a matachin, it seems by your drawn swords'; the 'buffons' is included in the list of dances in the *Complaynt of Scotland* (†1548); cf. Furnivall, *Laneham's Letter*, clxii.

[9] Tabourot, *Orchésographie*, 97, *Les Bouffons ou Mattachins*. The dancers held bucklers and swords which they clashed together. They also wore bells on their legs.

[10] Cf. Appendix J.

acknowledged sword-dance is in the north. It is found, according to Mr. Henderson, from the Humber to the Cheviots; and it extends as far south as Cheshire and Nottinghamshire [1]. Outlying examples are recorded from Winchester [2] and from Devonshire [3]. In Scotland Sir Walter Scott found it among the farthest Hebrides, and it has also been traced in Fifeshire [4].

The name of *danse des bouffons* sometimes given to the sword-dance may be explained by a very constant feature of the English examples, in which the dancers generally include or are accompanied by one or more comic or grotesque personages. The types of these grotesques are not kept very distinct in the descriptions, or, probably, in fact. But they appear to be fundamentally two. There is the 'Tommy' or 'fool,' who wears the skin and tail of a fox or some other animal, and there is the 'Bessy,' who is a man dressed in a woman's clothes. And they can be paralleled from outside England. A *Narr* or *Fasching* (carnival fool) is a figure in several German sword-dances, and in one from Bohemia he has his female counterpart in a *Mehlweib* [5].

With the *cantilenae* noticed by Olaus Magnus may be compared the sets of verses with which several modern sword-dances, both in these islands and in Germany, are provided. They are sung before or during part of the dances, and as a rule are little more than an introduction of the performers, to whom they give distinctive names. If they contain any

---

[1] Henderson, 67. The sword-dance is also mentioned by W. Hutchinson, *A View of Northumberland* (1778), ii *ad fin.* 18; by J. Wallis, *Hist. of Northumberland* (1779), ii. 28, who describes the leader as having 'a fox's skin, generally serving him for a covering and ornament to his head, the tail hanging down his back'; and as practised in the north Riding of Yorks. by a writer in the *Gentleman's Magazine* (1811), lxxxi. I. 423. Here it took place from St. Stephen's to New Year's Day. There were six lads, a fiddler, Bessy and a Doctor. At Whitby, six dancers went with the 'Plough Stots' on Plough Monday. The figures included the placing of a hexagon or rose of swords on the head of one of the performers. The dance was accompanied with 'Toms or *clowns*' masked or painted, and '*Madgies* or Madgy-Pegs' in women's clothes. Sometimes a farce, with a king, miller, clown and doctor was added (G. Young, *Hist. of Whitby* (1817), ii. 880).

[2] Cf. Appendix J.

[3] R. Bell, *Ancient Poems, Ballads and Songs of the Peasantry of England*, 175.

[4] Cf. Appendix J.

[5] Mayer, 230, 417.

incident, it is generally of the nature of a quarrel, in which one of the dancers or one of the grotesques is killed. To this point it will be necessary to return. The names given to the characters are sometimes extremely nondescript; sometimes, under a more or less literary influence, of an heroic order. Here and there a touch of something more primitive may be detected. Five sets of verses from the north of England are available in print. Two of these are of Durham *provenance*. One, from Houghton-le-Spring, has, besides the skin-clad ' Tommy ' and the ' Bessy,' five dancers. These are King George, a Squire's Son also called Alick or Alex, a King of Sicily, Little Foxey, and a Pitman[1]. The other Durham version has a captain called True Blue, a Squire's Son, Mr. Snip a tailor, a Prodigal Son (replaced in later years by a Sailor), a Skipper, a Jolly Dog. There is only one clown, who calls himself a ' fool,' and acts as treasurer. He is named Bessy, but wears a hairy cap with a fox's brush pendent[2]. Two other versions come from Yorkshire. At Wharfdale there are seven dancers, Thomas the clown, his son Tom, Captain Brown, Obadiah Trim a tailor, a Foppish Knight, Love-ale a vintner, and Bridget the clown's wife[3]. At Linton in Craven there are five, the clown, Nelson, Jack Tar, Tosspot, and Miser a woman[4]. The fifth version is of unnamed locality. It has two clowns, Tommy in skin and tail, and Bessy, and amongst the dancers are a Squire's Son

[1] Henderson, 67. The clown introduces each dancer in turn ; then there is a dance with raised swords which are tied in a ' knot.' Henderson speaks of a later set of verses also in use, which he does not print.

[2] R. Bell, *Ancient Poems, Ballads and Songs of the Peasantry of England*, 175 (from Sir C. Sharpe's *Bishoprick Garland*). A Christmas dance. The captain began the performance by drawing a circle with his sword. Then the Bessy introduced the captain, who called on the rest in turn, each walking round the circle to music. Then came an elaborate dance with careful formations, which degenerated into a fight. Bell mentions a similar set of verses from Devonshire.

[3] Bell, 172. A Christmas dance. The clown makes the preliminary circle with his sword, and calls on the other dancers.

[4] Bell, 181. The clown calls for ' a room,' after which one of the party introduces the rest. This also is a Christmas dance, but as the words ' we've come a pace-egging ' occur, it must have been transferred from Easter. Bell says that a somewhat similar performance is given at Easter in Coniston, and Halliwell, *Popular Rhymes and Nursery Tales*, 244, describes a similar set of rhymes as used near York for pace-egging.

and a Tailor[1]. Such a nomenclature will not repay much analysis. The 'Squire,' whose son figures amongst the dancers, is identical with the 'Tommy,' although why he should have a son I do not know. Similarly, the 'Bridget' at Wharfdale and the 'Miser' at Linton correspond to the 'Bessy' who appears elsewhere.

The Shetland dance, so far as the names go, is far more literary and less of a folk affair than any of the English examples. The grotesques are absent altogether, and the dancers belong wholly to that heroic category which is also represented in a degenerate form at Houghton-le-Spring. They are in fact those 'seven champions of Christendom'— St. George of England, St. James of Spain, St. Denys of France, St. David of Wales, St. Patrick of Ireland, St. Anthony of Italy, and St. Andrew of Scotland—whose legends were first brought together under that designation by Richard Johnson in 1596[2].

Precisely the same divergence between a popular and a literary or heroic type of nomenclature presents itself in such of the German sword-dance rhymes as are in print. Three very similar versions from Styria, Hungary, and Bohemia are traceable to a common 'Austro-Bavarian' archetype[3]. The names of these, so far as they are intelligible at all, appear to be due to the village imagination, working perhaps in one or two instances, such as 'Grünwald' or 'Wilder Waldmann,' upon stock figures of the folk festivals[4]. It is the heroic element, however, which predominates in the two other sets of verses which are available. One is from the Clausthal in the Harz mountains, and here the dancers represent the five kings of England, Saxony, Poland, Denmark, and Moorland, together with a serving-man, Hans, and one Schnortison, who acts as leader and treasurer of the

[1] Described by Müllenhoff, 138, from *Ausland* (1857), No. 4, f. 81. The clown gives the prologue, and introduces the rest.

[2] Cf. p. 221.

[3] Mayer prints and compares all three texts.

[4] Cf. p. 185. The original names seem to be best preserved in the Styrian verses: they are Obersteiner (the *Vortänzer*) or Hans Kanix, Fasching (the *Narr*), Obermayer, Jungesgsell, Grünwald, Edlesblut, Springesklee, Schellerfriedl, Wilder Waldmann, Handssupp, Rubendunst, Leberdarm, Rotwein, Höfenstreit.

party[1]. In the other, from Lübeck, the dancers are the 'worthies' Kaiser Karl, Josua, Hector, David, Alexander, and Judas Maccabaeus. They fight with one Sterkader, in whom Müllenhoff finds the Danish hero Stercatherus mentioned by Saxo Grammaticus; and to the Hans of the Clausthal corresponds a Klas Rugebart, who seems to be the red-bearded St. Nicholas[2].

In view of the wide range of the sword-dance in Germany, I do not think it is necessary to attach any importance to the theories advanced by Sir Walter Scott and others that it is, in England and Scotland, of Scandinavian origin. It is true that it appears to be found mainly in those parts of these islands where the influence of Danes and Northmen may be conjectured to have been strongest. But I believe that this is a matter of appearance merely, and that a type of folk-dance far more widely spread in the south of England than the sword-dance proper, is really identical with it. This is the morris-dance, the chief characteristic of which is that the performers wear bells which jingle at every step. Judging by the evidence of account-books, as well as by the allusions of contemporary writers, the morris was remarkably popular in the sixteenth and seventeenth centuries[3]. Frequently, but by no means always, it is mentioned in company with the May-game[4]. In a certain painted window at Betley in Staffordshire are represented six morris-dancers, together with a Maypole, a musician, a fool, a crowned man on a hobby-horse, a crowned lady with a pink in her hand, and a friar. The last three may reasonably be regarded as Robin Hood, Maid Marian, and Friar Tuck[5]. The closeness

---

[1] H. Pröhle, *Weltliche und geistliche Volkslieder und Volksschauspiele* (1855), 245.

[2] Müllenhoff, *Z. f. d. A.* xx. 10.

[3] Brand-Ellis, i. 142; Douce, 576; Burton, 95; Gutch, *Robin Hood*, i. 301; Drake, 76.

[4] Burton, 117; Warner, *Albion's England*, v. 25 'At Paske begun our Morrise, and ere Penticost our May.' The morris was familiar in the revels of Christmas. Laneham, 23, describes at the Bride-ale

shown before Elizabeth at Kenilworth 'a lively morrisdauns, according too the auncient manner: six daunserz, Mawdmarion, and the fool.'

[5] A good engraving of the window is in *Variorum Shakespeare*, xvi. 419, and small reproductions in Brand, i. 145; Burton, 103; Gutch, i. 349; Mr. Tollet's own account of the window, printed in the *Variorum, loc. cit.*, is interesting, but too ingenious. He dates the window

of the relation between the morris-dance and the May-game is, however, often exaggerated. The Betley figures only accompany the morris-dance ; they do not themselves wear the bells. And besides the window, the only trace of evidence that any member of the Robin Hood *cortège*, with the exception of Maid Marian, was essential to the morris-dance, is a passage in a masque of Ben Jonson's, which so seems to regard the friar[1]. The fact is that the morris-dance was a great deal older, as an element in the May-game, than Robin Hood, and that when Robin Hood's name was forgotten in this connexion, the morris-dance continued to be in vogue, not at May-games only, but at every form of rustic merry-making. On the other hand, it is true that the actual dancers were generally accompanied by grotesque personages, and that one of these was a woman, or a man dressed in woman's clothes, to whom literary writers at least continued to give the name of Maid Marian. The others have nothing whatever to do with Robin Hood. They were a clown or fool, and a hobby-horse, who, if the evidence of an Elizabethan song can be trusted, was already beginning to go out of fashion[2]. A rarer feature was a dragon, and it is possible

in the reign of Henry VIII ; Douce, 585, a better authority, ascribes it to that of Edward IV.

[1] Ben Jonson, *The Gipsies Metamorphosed* (ed. Cunningham, iii. 151) :

'*Clod*. They should be morris-dancers by their gingle, but they have no napkins.

'*Cockrel*. No, nor a hobby-horse.

'*Clod*. Oh, he's often forgotten, that's no rule ; but there is no Maid Marian nor Friar amongst them, which is the surer mark.

'*Cockrel*. Nor a fool that I see.'

[2] The lady, the fool, the hobby-horse are all in Tollet's window, and in a seventeenth-century printing by Vinkenboom from Richmond palace, engraved by Douce, 598 ; Burton, 105. Cf. the last note and other passages quoted by Douce, Brand, and Burton. In *Two Noble Kinsmen*, iii. 5, 125, a morris of six men and six women is thus presented by Gerrold, the

schoolmaster :

'I first appear . . .
The next, the Lord of May and Lady bright,
The Chambermaid and Serving-man, by night
That seek out silent hanging : then mine Host
And his fat Spouse, that welcomes to their cost
The galled traveller, and with a beck'ning
Informs the tapster to inflame the reck'ning :
Then the beast-eating Clown, and next the Fool,
The Bavian, with long tail and eke long tool ;
Cum multis aliis, that make a dance.'

Evidently some of these *dramatis personae* are not traditional ; the ingenuity of the presenter has been at work on them. 'Bavian' as a name for the fool, is the Dutch *baviaan*, 'baboon.' His 'tail' is to

that, when there was a dragon, the rider of the hobby-horse was supposed to personate St. George [1]. The morris-dance is by no means extinct, especially in the north and midlands. Accounts of it are available from Lancashire and Cheshire [2], Derbyshire [3], Shropshire [4], Leicestershire [5], and Oxford-

be noted; for the phallic shape sometimes given to the bladder which he carries, cf. Rigollot, 164. In the Betley window the fool has a bauble; in the Vinkenboom picture a staff with a bladder at one end, and a ladle (to gather money in) at the other. In the window the ladle is carried by the hobby-horse. ' The hobby-horse is forgot ' is a phrase occurring in *L. L. L.* iii. 1. 30; *Hamlet*, iii. 2. 144, and alluded to by Beaumont and Fletcher, *Women Pleased*, iv. 1, and Ben Jonson, in the masque quoted above, and in *The Satyr* (Cunningham, ii. 577). Apparently it is a line from a lost ballad.

[1] Stubbes, i. 147, of the ' devil's daunce ' in the train of the lord of misrule, evidently a morris, ' then haue they their Hobby-horses, dragons & other Antiques.' In W. Sampson's *Vow-breaker* (1636), one morris-dancer says ' I'll be a fiery dragon'; another, ' I'll be a thund'ring Saint George as ever rode on horseback.'

[2] Burton, 40, 43, 48, 49, 56, 59, 61, 65, 69, 75, 115, 117, 121, 123, cites many notices throughout the century, and gives several figures. The morris is in request at wakes and rushbearings. Both men and women dance, sometimes to the number of twenty or thirty. Gay dresses are worn, with white skirts, knee-breeches and ribbons. Handkerchiefs are carried or hung on the arm or wrist, or replaced by dangling streamers, cords, or skeins of cotton. Bells are not worn on the legs, but jingling horse-collars are sometimes carried on the body. There is generally a fool, described in one account as wearing ' a horrid mask.' He is, however, generally black, and is known as

'King Coffee' (Gorton), 'owd sooty-face,' ' dirty Bet,' and ' owd molly-coddle.' This last name, like the ' molly-dancers ' of Gorton, seems to be due to a linguistic corruption. In 1829 a writer describes the fool as ' a nondescript, made up of the ancient fool and Maid Marian.' At Heaton, in 1830, were two figures, said to represent Adam and Eve, as well as the fool. The masked fool, mentioned above, had as companion a shepherdess with lamb and crook.

[3] Burton, 115, from *Journal of Archaeol. Assoc.* vii. 201. The dancers went on Twelfth-night, without bells, but with a fool, a ' fool's wife ' and sometimes a hobby-horse.

[4] Jackson and Burne, 402, 410, 477. The morris-dance proper is mainly in south Shropshire and at Christmas. At Shrewsbury, in 1885, were ten dancers, with a fool. Five carried trowels and five short staves which they clashed. The fool had a black face, and a bell on his coat. No other bells are mentioned. Staves or wooden swords are used at other places in Shropshire, and at Brosely all the faces are black. The traditional music is a tabor and pipe. A 1652 account of the Brosely dance with six sword-bearers, a ' leader or lord of misrule ' and a ' vice ' (cf. ch. xxv) called the ' lord's son ' is quoted. In north-east Shropshire, the Christmas ' guisers ' are often called ' morris-dancers,' ' murry-dancers,' or ' merry-dancers.' In Shetland the name 'merry dancers' is given to the *aurora borealis* (J. Spence, *Shetland Folk-Lore,* 116).

[5] *Leicester F. L.* 93. The dance was on Plough Monday with paper

shire [1]; and there are many other counties in which it makes, or has recently made, an appearance [2]. The hobby-horse, it would seem, is now at last, except in Derbyshire, finally 'forgot'; but the two other traditional grotesques are still *de rigueur*. Few morris-dances are complete without the 'fool' or clown, amongst whose various names that of 'squire' in Oxfordshire and that of 'dirty Bet' in Lancashire are the most interesting. The woman is less invariable. Her Tudor name of Maid Marian is preserved in Leicestershire alone; elsewhere she appears as a shepherdess, or Eve, or 'the fool's wife'; and sometimes she is merged with the 'fool' into a single nondescript personage.

The morris-dance is by no means confined to England. There are records of it from Scotland [3], Germany [4], Flanders [5], Switzerland [6], Italy [7], Spain [8], and France [9]. In the last-named

masks, a plough, the bullocks, men in women's dresses, one called Maid Marian, Curly the fool, and Beelzebub. This is, I think, the only survival of the name Maid Marian, and it may be doubted if even this is really popular and not literary.

[1] P. Manning, *Oxfordshire Seasonal Festivals*, in *F. L.* viii. 317, summarizes accounts from fourteen villages, and gives illustrations. There are always six dancers. A broad garter of bells is worn below the knee. There are two sets of figures: in one handkerchiefs are carried, in the other short staves are swung and clashed. Sometimes the dancers sing to the air, which is that of an old country-dance. There is always a fool, who carries a stick with a bladder and cow's tail, and is called in two places 'Rodney,' elsewhere the 'squire.' The music is that of a pipe and tabor ('whittle' and 'dub') played by one man; a fiddle is now often used. At Bampton there was a solo dance between crossed tobacco-pipes. At Spelsbury and at Chipping Warden the dance used to be on the church-tower. At the Bampton Whit-feast and the Ducklington Whit-hunt, the dancers were accompanied by a sword-bearer, who impaled a cake. A

sword-bearer also appears in a list of Finstock dancers, given me by Mr. T. J. Carter, of Oxford. He also told me that the dance on Spelsbury church-tower, seventy years ago, was by women.

[2] Norfolk, Monmouthshire, Berkshire (Douce, 606); Worcestershire, Northamptonshire, Gloucestershire, Somersetshire, Wiltshire, Warwickshire, and around London (Burton, 114).

[3] *L. H. T. Accounts*, ii. 414; iii. 359, 381.

[4] Pfannenschmidt, 582; Michels, 84; Creizenach, i. 411. Burton, 102, reproduces, from *Art Journal* (1885), 121, cuts of ten morris-dancers carved in wood at Munich by Erasmus Schnitzer in 1480.

[5] Douce, 585, and Burton, 97, reproduce Israel von Mecheln's engraving (†1470) of a morris with a fool and a lady.

[6] Coquillart, *Œuvres* (†1470), 127.

[7] *Mémoires de Pétrarque*, ii. app. 3, 9; Petrarch danced 'en pourpoint une belle et vigoureuse moresque' to please the Roman ladies on the night of his coronation.

[8] *Somers Tracts*, ii. 81, 87. The Earl of Nottingham, when on an embassy from James I, saw morrice-dancers in a Corpus Christi procession.

[9] Douce, 480; Favine, *Theater*

country Tabourot described it about 1588 under the name
of *morisque*[1], and the earlier English writers call it the
morisce, morisk, or *morisco*[2]. This seems to imply a derivation of the name at least from the Spanish *morisco,* a Moor.
The dance itself has consequently been held to be of Moorish
origin, and the habit of blackening the face has been considered as a proof of this[3]. Such a theory seems to invert
the order of facts. The dance is too closely bound up with
English village custom to be lightly regarded as a foreign
importation; and I would suggest that the faces were not
blackened, because the dancers represented Moors, but rather
the dancers were thought to represent Moors, because their
faces were blackened. The blackened face is common
enough in the village festival. Hence, as we have seen,
May-day became proper to the chimney-sweeps, and we have
found a conjectural reason for the disguise in the primitive
custom of smearing the face with the beneficent ashes of the
festival fire[4]. Blackened faces are known in the sword-dance
as well as in the morris-dance[5]; and there are other reasons
which make it probable that the two are only variants of the

of Honor, 345: at a feast given by
Gaston de Foix at Vendôme, in
1458, 'foure young laddes and
a damosell, attired like savages,
daunced (by good direction) an
excellent *Morisco*, before the assembly.'

[1] Tabourot, *Orchésographie*, 94:
in his youth a lad used to come
after supper, with his face blackened, his forehead bound with
white or yellow taffeta, and bells
on his legs, and dance the morris
up and down the hall.

[2] Douce, 577; Burton, 95.

[3] A dance certainly of Moorish
origin is the fandango, in which
castanets were used; cf. the comedy
of *Variety* (1649) 'like a Baccha-
nalian, dancing the Spanish Morisco,
with knackers at his fingers' (Strutt,
223). This, however, seems to show
that the fandango was considered
a variety of morisco. Douce, 602;
Burton, 124, figure an African woman
from Fez dancing with bells on her
ankles. This is taken from Hans

Weigel's book of national costumes
published at Nuremberg in 1577.

[4] Tabourot's morris-dancing boy
had his face blackened, and Junius
(F. Du Jon), *Etymologicum Anglicanum* (1743), says of England
'faciem plerumque inficiunt fuligine,
et peregrinum vestium cultum as-
sumunt, qui ludicris talibus indul-
gent, ut Mauri esse videantur, aut
e longius remota patria credantur
advolasse, atque insolens recrea-
tionis genus advexisse.' In *Spousalls
of Princess Mary* (1508) 'morisks'
is rendered 'ludi Maurei quas
morescas dicunt.' In the modern
morris the black element is represented, except at Brosely, chiefly by
'owd sooty face,' the fool: in Leicestershire it gives rise to a distinct
figure, Beelzebub.

[5] Du Méril, *La Com.* 89, quotes
a sixteenth-century French sword-
dance of 'Mores, Sauvages, et
Satyres.' In parts of Yorkshire the
sword-dancers had black faces or
masks (Henderson, 70).

same performance. Tabourot, it is true, distinguishes *les bouffons*, or the sword-dance, and *le morisque*; but then Tabourot is dealing with the sophisticated versions of the folk-dances used in society, and Cotgrave, translating *les buffons*, can find no better English term than *morris* for the purpose [1]. The two dances appear at the same festivals, and they have the same grotesques; for the Tommy and Bessy of the English sword-dance, who occasionally merge in one, are obviously identical with the Maid Marian and the 'fool' of the morris-dance, who also nowadays similarly coalesce. There are traces, too, of an association of the hobby-horse with the sword-dance, as well as with the morris-dance [2]. Most conclusive of all, however, is the fact that in Oxfordshire and in Shropshire the morris-dancers still use swords or wooden staves which obviously represent swords, and that the performers of the elaborate Revesby sword-dance or play, to be hereafter described, are called in the eighteenth-century manuscript 'morrice dancers [3].' I do not think that the floating handkerchiefs of the morris-dance are found in its congener, nor do I know what, if any, significance they have. Probably, like the ribbons, they merely represent rustic notions of ornament. Müllenhoff lays stress on the white shirts or smocks which he finds almost universal in the sword-dance [4]. The morris-dancers are often described as dressed in white; but here too, if the ordinary work-a-day costume is a smock, the festal costume is naturally a clean white smock. Finally, there are the bells. These, though they have partially disappeared in the north, seem to be proper to the morris-

---

[1] Cotgrave, '*Dancer les Buffons*, To daunce a morris.' The term 'the madman's morris' appears as the name of the dance in *The Figure of Nine* (temp. Charles II); cf. Furnivall, *Laneham's Letter*, clxii. The *buffon* is presumably the 'fool'; cf. Cotgrave, '*Buffon*: m. A buffoon, jeaster, sycophant, merrie fool, sportfull companion: one that lives by making others merrie.'

[2] Henderson, 70. In Yorkshire the sword-dancers carried the image of a white horse; in Cheshire a horse's head and skin.

[3] Cf. ch. x; also Wise, *Enquiries concerning the Inhabitants, . . . of Europe*, 51 'the common people in many parts of England still practise what they call a Morisco dance, in a wild manner, and as it were in armour, at proper intervals striking upon one another's staves,' &c. Johnson's *Dictionary* (1755) calls the morris 'a dance in which bells are gingled, or staves or swords clashed.'

[4] Müllenhoff, 124; cf. Mayer, 236.

dance, and to differentiate it from the sword-dance[1]. But this is only so when the English examples are alone taken into consideration, for Müllenhoff quotes one Spanish and three German descriptions of sword-dances in which the bells are a feature[2]. Tabourot affords similar evidence for the French version[3]; while Olaus Magnus supplements his account of the Scandinavian sword-dance with one of a similar performance, in which the swords were replaced by bows, and bells were added[4]. The object of the bells was probably to increase or preserve the musical effect of the clashing swords. The performers known to Tacitus were *nudi*, and no bells are mentioned. One other point with regard to the morris-dance is worth noticing before we leave the subject. It is capable of use both as a stationary and a processional dance, and therefore illustrates both of the two types of dancing motion naturally evolved from the circumstances of the village festival[5].

Müllenhoff regards the sword-dance as primarily a rhythmic *Abbild* or mimic representation of war, subsequently modified in character by use at the village feasts[6]. It is true that the notice of Tacitus and the allusion in *Beowulf* suggest that it had a military character; and it may fairly be inferred that it formed part of that war-cult from which, as pointed out in a previous chapter, heroic poetry sprang. This is confirmed by the fact that some at least of the *dramatis personae* of the modern dances belong to the heroic category. Side by side with local types such as the Pitman or the Sailor, and with doublets of the grotesques such as Little Foxey or the

---

[1] Douce, 602; Burton, 123. The bells were usually fastened upon broad garters, as they are still worn in Oxfordshire. But they also appear as anklets or are hung on various parts of the dress. In a cut from Randle Holme's *Academie of Armorie*, iii. 109 (Douce, 603; Burton, 127), a morris-dancer holds a pair of bells in his hands. Sometimes the bells were harmonized. In *Pasquil and Marforius* (1589) Penry is described as 'the fore gallant of the Morrice with the treble bells'; cf. Rowley, *Witch of Edmonton*, i. 2.

[2] Müllenhoff, 123; Mayer, 235.

[3] Tabourot, *Orchésographie*, 97.

[4] Cf. Appendix J. A figure with a bow and arrow occurs in the Abbots Bromley horn-dance (p. 166).

[5] W. Kempe's *Nine Days Wonder* (ed. Dyce, Camden Soc.) describes his dancing of the morris in bell-shangles from London to Norwich in 1599.

[6] Müllenhoff, 114.

Squire's Son [1], appear the five kings of the Clausthal dance,
the 'worthies' of the Lübeck dance, and the 'champions of
Christendom' of the Shetland dance. These particular groups
betray a Renaissance rather than a mediaeval imagination; as
with the morris-dance of *The Two Noble Kinsmen*, the village
schoolmaster, Holophernes or another, has probably been at
work upon them [2]. Some of the heterogeneous English
dramatis personae, Nelson for instance, testify to a still later
origin. On the other hand, the Sterkader or Stercatherus
of the Lübeck dance suggests that genuine national heroes
were occasionally celebrated in this fashion. At the same
time I do not believe, with Müllenhoff, that the sword-dance
originated in the war-cult. Its essentially agricultural
character seems to be shown by the grotesques traditionally
associated with it, the man in woman's clothes, the skin or
tail-wearing clown and the hobby-horse, all of which seem
to find their natural explanation in the facts of agricultural
worship [3]. Again, the dance makes its appearance, not like
heroic poetry in general as part of the minstrel repertory, but
as a purely popular thing at the agricultural festivals. To
these festivals, therefore, we may reasonably suppose it to
have originally belonged, and to have been borrowed from
them by the young warriors who danced before the king.
They, however, perhaps gave it the heroic element which, in

[1] The 'Squire's Son' of the
Durham dances is probably the
clown's son of the Wharfdale
version; for the term 'squire' is
not an uncommon one for the rustic
fool. Cf. also the Revesby play
described in the next chapter. Why
the fool should have a son, I do not
know.

[2] The 'Nine Worthies' of *Love's
Labour's Lost*, v. 2, are a pageant
not a dance, and the two sets of
speeches quoted from Bodl. Tanner
MS. 407, by Ritson, *Remarks on
Shakespeare*, 38, one of which is
called by Ashton, 127, the earliest
mummers' play that he can find,
also probably belong to pageants.
The following, also quoted by Ritson
loc. cit. from *Harl. MS.* 1197, f. 101*

(sixteenth century), looks more like
a dance or play:
'I ame a knighte
  And menes to fight
    And armet well ame I
Lo here I stand
With swerd ine hand
    My manhoud for to try.

Thou marciall wite
That menes to fight
    And sete vppon me so
Lo heare J stand
With swrd in hand
    To dubbelle eurey blow.'

[3] Mayer, 230, 425, finds in the
dance a symbolical drama of the
death of winter; but he does not
seem to see the actual relic of a
sacrificial rite.

its turn, drifted into the popular versions. We have already seen that popular heroic *cantilenae* existed together with those of minstrelsy up to a late date. Nor does Müllenhoff's view find much support from the classical sword-dances which he adduces. As to the origin of the *lusus Troiae* or Pyrrhic dance which the Romans adopted from Doric Greece, I can say nothing [1]; but the native Italian dance of the *Salii* or priests of Mars in March and October is clearly agricultural. It belongs to the cult of Mars, not as war-god, but in his more primitive quality of a fertilization spirit [2].

Further, I believe that the use of swords in the dance was not martial at all ; their object was to suggest not a fight, but a mock or symbolical sacrifice. Several of the dances include figures in which the swords are brought together in a significant manner about the person of one or more of the dancers. Thus in the Scandinavian dance described by Olaus Magnus, a *quadrata rosa* of swords is placed on the head of each performer. A precisely similar figure occurs in the Shetland and in a variety of the Yorkshire dances [3]. In the Siebenbürgen dances there are two figures in which the performers pretend to cut at each other's heads or feet, and a third in which one of them has the swords put in a ring round his neck [4]. This latter evolution occurs also in a variety of the Yorkshire dance [5] and in a Spanish one described by Müllen-

---

[1] Müllenhoff, 114 ; Du Méril, *La Com.* 82 ; Plato, *Leges*, 815 ; Dion Cassius, lx. 23 ; Suetonius, *Julius*, 39, *Nero*, 12 ; Servius *ad Aen.* v. 602 ; cf. p. 7. A Thracian sword-dance, ending in a mimic death, and therefore closely parallel to the west European examples mentioned in the next chapter, is described by Xenophon, *Anabasis*, v. 9.

[2] Müllenhoff, 115 ; Frazer, iii. 122 ; W. W. Fowler, *The Roman Festivals*, 38, 44. The song of the *Salii* mentioned Saeturnus, god of sowing. It appears also to have been their function to expel the Mamurius Veturius in spring. Servius *ad Aen.* viii. 285, says that the *Salii* were founded by Morrius, king of Veii.

According to Frazer, Morrius is etymologically equivalent to Mamurius—Mars. He even suggests that Morris may possibly belong to the same group of words.

[3] Cf. Appendix J. In other dances a performer stands on a similar 'knot' or *Stern* of swords. Mayer, 230, suggests that this may represent the triumph of summer, which seems a little far-fetched.

[4] Mayer, 243 ; O. Wittstock, in *Sievers-Festgabe*, 349.

[5] Grimm, i. 304, gives the following as communicated to him by J. M. Kemble, from the mouth of an old Yorkshireman : 'In some parts of northern England, in Yorkshire, especially Hallamshire, popular customs show remnants of the

hoff after a seventeenth-century writer. And here the figure has the significant name of *la degollada*, 'the beheading [1].'

worship of Fricg. In the neighbourhood of Dent, at certain seasons of the year, especially autumn, the country folk hold a procession and perform old dances, one called the giant's dance : the leading giant they name *Woden*, and his wife *Frigga*, the principal action of the play consisting in two swords being swung and clashed together about the neck of a boy without hurting him.' There is nothing about this in the account of Teutonic mythology in J. M. Kemble's own *Saxons in England*. I do not believe that the names of Woden and Frigga were preserved in connexion with this custom continuously from heathen times. Probably some antiquary had introduced them ; and in error, for there is no reason to suppose that the 'clown' and 'woman' of the sword-dance were ever thought to represent gods. But the description of the business with the swords is interesting.

[1] Müllenhoff, *Z. f. d. A.* xviii. 11, quoting Covarubias, *Tesoro della lengua castellana* (1611), s.v. *Danza de Espadas* : 'una mudanza que llaman la degollada, porque cercan el cuello del que los guia con las espadas.' With these sword manœuvres should be compared the use of scythes and flails in the mock sacrifices of the harvest-field and threshing-floor (p. 158), the 'Chop off his head' of the 'Oranges and Lemons' game (p. 151), and the ancient tale of Wodan and the Mowers.

CHAPTER X

THE MUMMERS' PLAY

[*Bibliographical Note.*—The subject is treated by T. F. Ordish, *English Folk-Drama* in *Folk-Lore*, ii. 326, iv. 162. The Folk-Lore Society has in preparation a volume on Folk-Drama by Mr. Ordish (*F. L.* xiii. 296). The following is a list of the twenty-nine printed versions upon which the account of the St. George play in the present chapter is based. The Lutterworth play is given in Appendix K.

NORTHUMBERLAND.
　1. *Newcastle.* Chap-book—W. Sandys, *Christmastide*, 292, from *Alexander and the King of Egypt. A mock Play, as it is acted by the Mummers every Christmas.* Newcastle, 1788. (Divided into Acts and Scenes.)

CUMBERLAND.
　2. *Whitehaven.* Chap-book—Hone, *E. D. B.* ii. 1646. (Practically identical with (1).)

LANCASHIRE.
　3. *Manchester.* Chap-book—*The Peace Egg*, published by J. Wrigley, 30, Miller Street, Manchester. (Brit. Mus. 1077, *g*/27 (37): Acts and Scenes: a coloured cut of each character.)

SHROPSHIRE.
　4. *Newport.* Oral. Jackson and Burne, 484. (Called the Guisers' (gheez'u'rz) play.)

STAFFORDSHIRE.
　5. *Eccleshall.* Oral. *F. L. J.* iv. 350. (Guisers' play: practically identical with (4). I have not seen a version from Stone in W. W. Bladen, *Notes on the Folk-lore of North Staffs.*: cf. *F. L.* xiii. 107.)

LEICESTERSHIRE.
　6. *Lutterworth.* Oral. Kelly, 53; Manly, i. 292; *Leicester F. L.* 130.

WORCESTERSHIRE.
　7. *Leigh.* Oral. 2 *N. Q.* xi. 271.

WARWICKSHIRE.
　8. *Newbold.* Oral. *F. L.* x. 186 (with variants from a similar Rugby version).

OXFORDSHIRE.
　9. *Islip.* Oral. Ditchfield, 316.
　10. *Bampton.* Oral. Ditchfield, 320.
　11. *Thame.* Oral. 5 *N. Q.* ii. 503; Manly, i. 289.
　12. *Uncertain.* Oral. 6 *N. Q.* xii. 489; Ashton, 128.

BERKSHIRE.
　13. *Uncertain.* Oral. Ditchfield, 310.

MIDDLESEX.
　14. *Chiswick.* Oral. 2 *N. Q.* x. 466.

Sussex.
15. *Selmeston.* Oral. Parish, *Dict. of Sussex Dialect* (2nd ed. 1875), 136.
16. *Hollington.* Oral. 5 *N. Q.* x. 489.
17. *Steyning.* Oral. *F. L. J.* ii. 1. (The 'Tipteerers'' play.)

Hampshire.
18. *St. Mary Bourne.* Oral. Stevens, *Hist. of St. Mary Bourne,* 340.
19. *Uncertain.* Oral. 2 *N. Q.* xii. 492.

Dorsetshire.
20. (A) *Uncertain.* Oral. *F. L. R.* iii. 92 ; Ashton, 129.
21. (B) *Uncertain.* Oral. *F. L. R.* iii. 102.

Cornwall.
22. *Uncertain.* Oral. Sandys, *Christmastide,* 298. (Slightly different version in Sandys, *Christmas Carols,* 174; Du Méril, *La Com.* 428.)

Wales.
23. *Tenby.* Oral. Chambers, *Book of Days,* ii. 740, from *Tales and Traditions of Tenby.*

Ireland.
24. *Belfast.* Chap-book. 4 *N. Q.* x. 487. ('The Christmas Rhymes.')
25. *Ballybrennan, Wexford.* Oral. Kennedy, *The Banks of the Boro,* 226.

Uncertain Locality.
26. *Sharpe's London Magazine,* i. 154. Oral.
27. *Archaeologist,* i. 176. Chap-book. H. Sleight, *A Christmas Pageant Play or Mysterie of St. George, Alexander and the King of Egypt.* (Said to be 'compiled from and collated with several curious ancient black-letter editions.' I have never seen or heard of a 'black-letter' edition, and I take it the improbable title is Mr. Sleight's own.)
28. Halliwell. Oral. *Popular Rhymes,* 231. (Said to be the best of six versions.)
29. *F. L. J.* iv. 97. (Fragment, from 'old MS.')]

THE *degollada* figures of certain sword-dances preserve with some clearness the memory of an actual sacrifice, abolished and replaced by a mere symbolic dumb show. Even in these, and still more in the other dances, the symbolism is very slight. It is completely subordinated to the rhythmic evolutions of a choric figure. There is an advance, however, in the direction of drama, when in the course of the performance some one is represented as actually slain. In a few dances of the type discussed in the last chapter, such a dramatic episode precedes or follows the regular figures. It is recorded in three or four of the German examples[1]. A writer in the *Gentleman's Magazine* describes a Yorkshire dance in which 'the Bessy interferes while they are making a hexagon with their swords, and is killed.' Amongst the characters of this dance is

[1] Mayer, 229.

a Doctor, and although the writer does not say so, it may be inferred that the function of the Doctor is to bring the Bessy to life again [1]. It will be remembered that a precisely similar device is used in the German Shrove Tuesday plays to symbolize the resurrection of the year in spring after its death in winter. The Doctor reappears in one of the Durham dances, and here there is no doubt as to the part he plays. At a certain point the careful formations of the dance degenerate into a fight. The parish clergyman rushes in to separate the combatants. He is accidentally slain. There is general lamentation, but the Doctor comes forward, and revives the victim, and the dance proceeds [2].

It is but a step from such dramatic episodes to the more elaborate performances which remain to be considered in the present chapter, and which are properly to be called plays rather than dances. They belong to a stage in the evolution of drama from dance, in which the dance has been driven into the background and has sometimes disappeared altogether. But they have the same characters, and especially the same grotesques, as the dances, and the general continuity of the two sets of performances cannot be doubted. Moreover, though the plays differ in many respects, they have a common incident, which may reasonably be taken to be the central incident, in the death and revival, generally by a Doctor, of one of the characters. And in virtue of this central incident one is justified in classing them as forms of a folk-drama in which the resurrection of the year is symbolized.

I take first, on account of the large amount of dancing which remains in it, the play acted at the end of the eighteenth century by 'The Plow Boys or Morris Dancers' of Revesby in Lincolnshire [3]. There are seven dancers : six men, the Fool

---

[1] *Gentleman's Magazine*, lxxxi (1811), I. 423. The dance was given in the north Riding from St. Stephen's day to the New Year. Besides the Bessy and the Doctor there were six lads, one of whom acted king ' in a kind of farce which consists of singing and dancing.'

[2] Bell, 178 ; cf. p. 193. I do not feel sure whether the actual parish

clergyman took part, or whether a mere personage in the play is intended ; but see what Olaus Magnus (App. J (i)) says about the propriety of the sword-dances for *clerici*. It will be curious if the Christian priest has succeeded to the part of the heathen priest slain, first literally, and then in mimicry, at the festivals.

[3] Printed by Mr. T. F. Ordish in

and his five sons, Pickle Herring, Blue Breeches, Pepper Breeches, Ginger Breeches, and Mr. Allspice[1]; and one woman, Cicely. The somewhat incoherent incidents are as follows. The Fool acts as presenter and introduces the play. He fights successively a Hobby-horse and a 'Wild Worm' or dragon. The dancers 'lock their swords to make the glass,' which, after some jesting, is broken up again. The sons determine to kill the Fool. He kneels down and makes his will, with the swords round his neck[2]; is slain and revived by Pickle Herring stamping with his foot. This is repeated with variations. Hitherto, the dancers have 'footed it' round the room at intervals. Now follow a series of sword-dances. During and after these the Fool and his sons in turn woo Cicely, the Fool taking the name of 'Anthony[3],' Pickle Herring that of 'the Lord of Pool,' and Blue Breeches that of 'the Knight of Lee.' There is nothing particularly interesting about this part of the play, obviously written to 'work in' the woman grotesque. In the course of it a morris-dance is introduced, and a final sword-dance, with an obeisance to the master of the house, winds up the whole.

Secondly, there are the Plough Monday plays of the east Midlands[4]. These appear in Nottinghamshire, Northampton-

---

F.L.J. vii. 338, and again by Manly, i. 296. The MS. used appears to be headed 'October Ye 20, 1779'; but the performers are called 'The Plow Boys or Morris Dancers' and the prologue says that they 'takes delight in Christmas toys.' I do not doubt that the play belonged to Plough Monday, which only falls just outside the Christmas season.

[1] On the name Pickle Herring, see W. Creizenach, *Die Schauspiele der englischen Komödianten*, xciii. It does not occur in old English comedy, but was introduced into Anglo-German and German farce as a name for the 'fool' or 'clown' by Robert Reynolds, the 'comic lead' of a company of English actors who crossed to Germany in 1618. Probably it was Reynolds' invention, and suggested by the *sobriquet* 'Stockfish' taken by an earlier Anglo-German actor, John Spencer. The 'spicy' names of the other Revesby clowns are probably imitations of Pickle Herring.

[2] The lines (197-8)
'Our old Fool's bracelet is not made of gold
But it is made of iron and good steel'
suggest the vaunt of the champions in the St. George plays.

[3] Is 'Anthony' a reminiscence of the Seven Champions? The Fool says (ll. 247-9), like Beelzebub in the St. George plays,
'Here comes I that never come yet, . . .
I have a great head but little wit.'
He also jests (l. 229) on his 'tool'; cf. p. 196 n.

[4] Brand, i. 278; Dyer, 37; Ditchfield, 47; Drake, 65, Mrs. Chaworth

shire and Lincolnshire. Two printed versions are available. The first comes from Cropwell in Nottinghamshire [1]. The actors are 'the plough-bullocks.' The male characters are Tom the Fool, a Recruiting Sergeant, and a Ribboner or Recruit, three farm-servants, Threshing Blade, Hopper Joe [2], and the Ploughman, a Doctor, and Beelzebub [3]. There are two women, a young Lady and old Dame Jane. Tom Fool is presenter. The Ribboner, rejected by the young Lady, enlists as a recruit. The Lady is consoled by Tom Fool. Then enter successively the three farm-servants, each describing his function on the farm. Dame Jane tries to father a child on

Musters, *A Cavalier Stronghold*, 387. Plough Monday is the Monday after Twelfth night, when the field work begins. A plough is dragged round the village and a *quête* made. The survivals of the custom are mainly in the north, east and east midlands. In the city, a banquet marks the day. A Norfolk name is 'Plowlick Monday,' and a Hunts one 'Plough-Witching.' The plough is called the 'Fool Plough,' 'Fond Plough,' 'Stot Plough' or 'White Plough'; the latter name probably from the white shirts worn (cf. p. 200). At Cropwell, Notts, horses cut out in black or red adorn these. In Lincolnshire, bunches of corn were worn in the hats. Those who draw the plough are called 'Plough Bullocks,' 'Boggons' or 'Stots.' They sometimes dance a morris- or sword-dance, or act a play. At Haxey, they take a leading part in the Twelfth day 'Hood-game' (p. 150). In Northants their faces are blackened or reddled. The plough is generally accompanied by the now familiar grotesques, 'Bessy' and the Fool or 'Captain Cauf-Tail.' In Northants there are two of each; the Fools have humps, and are known as 'Red Jacks'; there is also a 'Master.' In Lincolnshire, reapers, threshers, and carters joined the procession. A contribution to the *quête* is greeted with the cry of 'Largess!' and a churl is liable to have the ground before his door ploughed up. Of old the profits of the *quête* or 'plow-gadrin' went into the parish chest, or as in Norfolk kept a 'plow-light' burning in the church. A sixteenth century pamphlet speaks of the 'sensing the Ploughess' on Plough Monday. Jevons, 247, calls the rite a 'worship of the plough'; probably it rather represents an early spring perambulation of the fields in which the divinity rode upon a plough, as elsewhere upon a ship. A plough-ing custom of putting a loaf in the furrow has been noted. Plough Monday has also its water rite. The returning ploughman was liable to be soused by the women, like the bearer of the 'neck' at harvest. Elsewhere, the women must get the kettle on before the ploughman can reach the hearth, or pay for-feit.

[1] Printed by Mrs. Chaworth Musters in *A Cavalier Stronghold* (1890), 388, and in a French transla-tion by Mrs. H. G. M. Murray-Aynsley, in *R. d. T. P.* iv. 605.

[2] 'Hopper Joe' also calls himself 'old Sanky-Benny,' which invites interpretation. Is it 'Saint Bennet' or 'Benedict'?

[3] 'In comes I, Beelzebub,
    On my shoulder I carry my club,
    In my hand a wet leather frying-pan;
    Don't you think I'm a funny old man?'
Cf. the St. George play (p. 214).

Tom Fool. Beelzebub knocks her down [1], and kills her. The Doctor comes in, and after some comic business about his travels, his qualifications and his remedies [2], declares Dame Jane to be only in a trance, and raises her up. A country dance and songs follow, and the performance ends with a *quête*. The second version, from Lincolnshire, is very similar [3]. But there are no farm-servants, and instead of Beelzebub is a personage called 'old Esem Esquesem,' who carries a broom. It is he, not an old woman, who is killed and brought to life. There are several dancers, besides the performers; and these include 'Bessy,' a man dressed as a woman, with a cow's tail.

The distinction between a popular and a literary or heroic type of personification which was noticeable in the sword-dances persists in the folk-plays founded upon them. Both in the Revesby play and in the Plough Monday plays, the drama is carried on by personages resembling the 'grotesques' of the sword- and morris-dances [4]. There are no heroic characters. The death is of the nature of an accident or an execution. On the other hand, in the 'mummers' play' of St. George, the heroes take once more the leading part, and the death, or at least one of the deaths, is caused by a fight amongst them. This play is far more widely spread than its rivals. It is found in all parts of England, in Wales, and in Ireland; in Scotland it occurs also, but here some other hero is generally substituted as protagonist for St. George [5]. The

---

[1] 'Dame Jane' says,
'My head is made of iron,
My body made of steel,
My hands and feet of knuckle-
bone,
I think nobody can make me
feel.'
In the Lincolnshire play Beelzebub has this vaunt. Cf. the St. George play (p. 220).

[2] The Doctor can cure 'the hipsy-pipsy, palsy, and the gout'; cf. the St. George play (p. 213).

[3] Printed in French by Mrs. Murray Aynsley in *R. d. T. P.* iv. 609.

[4] The farce recorded as occasionally introduced at Whitby (cf. p. 192,

n. 1) but not described, probably belonged to the 'popular' type.

[5] Chambers, *Popular Rhymes of Scotland*, 169, prints a Peebles version. Instead of George, a hero called Galatian fights the Black Knight. Judas, with his bag, replaces Beelzebub. But it is the same play. Versions or fragments of it are found all over the Lowlands. The performers are invariably called 'guizards.' In a Falkirk version the hero is Prince George of Ville. Hone, *E. D. B.*, says that the hero is sometimes Galacheus or St. Lawrence. But in another Falkirk version, part of which he prints, the name is Galgacus, and of this

following account is based on the twenty-nine versions, drawn from chap-books or from oral tradition, enumerated in the bibliographical note. The list might, doubtless, be almost indefinitely extended. As will soon be seen, the local variations of the play are numerous. In order to make them intelligible, I have given in full in an appendix a version from Lutterworth in Leicestershire. This is chosen, not as a particularly interesting variant, for that it is not, but on the contrary as being comparatively colourless. It shows very clearly and briefly the normal structure of the play, and may be regarded as the type from which the other versions diverge [1].

The whole performance may be divided, for convenience of analysis, into three parts, the Presentation, the Drama, the *Quête*. In the first somebody speaks a prologue, claiming a welcome from the spectators [2], and then the leading characters are in turn introduced. The second consists of a fight followed by the intervention of a doctor to revive the slain. In the third some supernumerary characters enter, and there is a collection. It is the dramatic nucleus that first requires consideration. The leading fighter is generally St. George, who alone appears in all the versions. Instead of ' St. George,' he is sometimes called ' Sir George,' and more often ' Prince George ' or 'King George,' modifications which one may reasonably suppose to be no older than the present Hanoverian dynasty. At Whitehaven and at Falkirk he is ' Prince George of Ville.' George's chief opponent is usually one of two per-

both Galacheus and Galatian are probably corruptions, for Galgacus or Calgacus was the leader of the Picts in their battle with Agricola at the Mons Graupius (A. D. 84; Tacitus, *Agricola*, 29).

[1] Appendix K. Other versions may be conveniently compared in Manly, i. 289; Ditchfield, 310. The best discussions of the St. George plays in general, besides Mr. Ordish's, are J. S. Udall, *Christmas Mummers in Dorsetshire* (*F. L. R.* iii. 1. 87); Jackson and Burne, 482; G. L. Gomme, *Christmas Mummers* (*Nature*, Dec. 23, 1897). The notes and introductions to the versions tabulated above give many useful data.

[2] In *F. L.* x. 351, Miss Florence Grove describes some Christmas mummers seen at Mullion, Cornwall, in 1890-1. 'Every one naturally knows who the actors are, since there are not more than a few hundred persons within several miles ; but no one is supposed to know who they are or where they come from, nor must any one speak to them, nor they to those in the houses they visit. As far as I can remember the performance is silent and dramatic ; I have no recollection of reciting.' The dumb show is rare and probably a sign of decadence, but the bit of rural etiquette is archaic, and recurs in savage drama.

sonages, who are not absolutely distinct from each other [1]. One is the ' Turkish Knight,' of whom a variant appears to be the ' Prince of Paradine' (Manchester), or ' Paradise' (Newport, Eccleshall), perhaps originally ' Palestine.' He is sometimes represented with a blackened face [2]. The other is variously called ' Slasher,' ' Captain Slasher,' ' Bold Slasher,' or, by an obvious corruption, ' Beau Slasher.' Rarer names for him are ' Bold Slaughterer' (Bampton), 'Captain Bluster' (Dorset [A]), and ' Swiff, Swash, and Swagger' (Chiswick). His names fairly express his vaunting disposition, which, however, is largely shared by the other characters in the play. In the place of, or as minor fighters by the side of George, the Turkish Knight and Bold Slasher, there appear, in one version or another, a bewildering variety of personages, of whom only a rough classification can be attempted. Some belong to the heroic cycles. Such are ' Alexander' (Newcastle, Whitehaven), ' Hector' (Manchester), ' St. Guy' (Newport), ' St. Giles' (Eccleshall) [3], ' St. Patrick' (Dorset [A], Wexford), ' King Alfred' and ' King Cole' (Brill), ' Giant Blunderbore' (Brill), ' Giant Turpin' (Cornwall). Others again are moderns who have caught the popular imagination : ' Bold Bonaparte' (Leigh) [4], and ' King of Prussia' (Bampton, Oxford) [5], ' King William' (Brill), the ' Duke of Cumberland' (Oxford) and the ' Duke of Northumberland' (Islip), ' Lord Nelson' (Stoke Gabriel, Devon) [6], ' Wolfe' and ' Wellington' (Cornwall) [7], even the ' Prince Imperial' (Wilts) [8], all have been pressed into the service. In some cases characters have lost their personal names, if they ever had any, and figure merely as ' Knight,' ' Soldier,' ' Valiant Soldier,' ' Noble Captain,' ' Bold Prince,' ' Gracious King.' Others bear names which defy explanation, ' Alonso' (Chiswick), ' Hy Gwyer' (Hollington),

---

[1] In Berkshire and at Eccleshall, Slasher is ' come from Turkish land.' On the other hand, the two often appear in the same version, and even, as at Leigh, fight together.

[2] Burne-Jackson, 483.

[3] Ibid. 483. He appears in the MSS. written by the actors as ' Singuy' or ' Singhiles.' Professor Skeat points out that, as he ' sprang from English ground,' St. Guy (of Warwick) was probably the original form, and St. Giles a corruption.

[4] Here may be traced the influence of the Napoleonic wars. In Berkshire, Slasher is a ' French officer.'

[5] *F. L.* v. 88.

[6] Ditchfield, 12.

[7] Sandys, 153.

[8] P. Tennant, *Village Notes*, 179.

'Marshalee' and 'Cutting Star' (Dorset [B]). The significance of 'General Valentine' and 'Colonel Spring' (Dorset
[A]) will be considered presently; and 'Room' (Dorset [B]),
'Little Jack,' the 'Bride' and the 'Fool' (Brill), and the 'King
of Egypt' (Newcastle, Whitehaven) have strayed in amongst
the fighters from the presenters. The fighting generally takes
the form of a duel, or a succession of duels. In the latter case,
George may fight all comers, or he may intervene to subdue
a previously successful champion. But an important point is
that he is not always victorious. On the contrary, the versions
in which he slays and those in which he is slain are about
equal in number. In two versions (Brill, Steyning) the fighting is not a duel or a series of duels, but a *mêlée*. The Brill
play, in particular, is quite unlike the usual type. A prominent
part is taken by the Dragon, with whom fight, all at once,
St. George and a heterogeneous company made up of King
Alfred and his Bride, King Cole, King William, Giant Blunderbore, Little Jack and a morris-dance Fool.

Whatever the nature of the fight, the result is always the
same. One or more of the champions falls, and then appears
upon the scene a Doctor, who brings the dead to life again.
The Doctor is a comic character. He enters, boasting his
universa skill, and works his cure by exhibiting a bolus, or by
drawing out a tooth with a mighty pair of pliers. At Newbold he is 'Dr. Brown,' at Islip 'Dr. Good' (also called 'Jack
Spinney'), at Brill 'Dr. Ball'; in Dorsetshire (A) he is an
Irishman, 'Mr. Martin' (perhaps originally 'Martyr') 'Dennis.'
More often he is nameless. Frequently the revival scene is
duplicated; either the Doctor is called in twice, or one cure
is left to him, and another is effected by some other performer, such as St. George (Dorset [B]), 'Father Christmas'
(Newbold, Steyning), or the Fool (Bampton).

The central action of the play consists, then, in these two
episodes of the fight and the resurrection; and the protagonists, so to speak, are the heroes—a ragged troop of heroes,
certainly—and the Doctor. But just as in the sword-dances,
so in the plays, we find introduced, besides the protagonists,
a number of supernumerary figures. The nature of these, and
the part they take, must now be considered. Some of them

are by this time familiar. They are none other than the grotesques that have haunted this discussion of the village festivals from the very beginning, and that I have attempted to trace to their origin in magical or sacrificial custom. There are the woman, or lad dressed in woman's clothes, the hobby-horse, the fool, and the black-faced man. The woman and the hobby-horse are unmistakable ; the other two are a little more Protean in their modern appearance. The 'Fool' is so called only at Manchester and at Brill, where he brings his morris-dance with him. At Lutterworth he is the 'Clown'; in Cornwall, 'Old Squire'; at Newbold, 'Big Head and Little Wits.' But I think that we may also recognize him in the very commonly occurring figure 'Beelzebub,' also known in Cornwall as 'Hub Bub' and at Chiswick as 'Lord Grubb.' The key to this identification is the fact that in several cases Beelzebub uses the description 'big head and little wit' to announce himself on his arrival. Occasionally, however, the personality of the Fool has been duplicated. At Lutterworth Beelzebub and the Clown, at Newbold Beelzebub and Big Head and Little Wits appear in the same play [1]. The black-faced man has in some cases lost his black face, but he keeps it at Bampton, where he is 'Tom the Tinker,' at Rugby, where he is 'Little Johnny Sweep,' and in a Sussex version, where he is also a sweep [2]. The analogy of the May-day chimney-sweeps is an obvious one. A black face was a feature in the mediaeval representation of devils, and the sweep of some plays is probably in origin identical with the devil, black-faced or not, of others. This is all the more so,

---

[1] Beelzebub appears also in the Cropwell Plough Monday play ; cf. p. 209. Doubtless he once wore a calf-skin, like other rural 'Fools,' but, as far as I know, this feature has dropped out. Sandys, 154, however, quotes 'Captain Calf-tail' as the name of the 'Fool' in an eighteenth-century Scotch version, and Mr. Gomme (*Nature*, Dec. 23, 1897), says 'some of the mummers, or maskers as the name implies, formerly disguised themselves as animals—goats, oxen, deer, foxes and horses being represented at different places where details of the mumming play have been recorded.' Nowadays, Beelzebub generally carries a club and a ladle or frying-pan, with which he makes the *quête*. At Newport and Eccleshall he has a bell fastened on his back ; at Newbold he has a black face. The 'Fool' figured in the Manchester chap-book resembles Punch.

[2] See notes to Steyning play in *F. L. J.* ii. 1.

as the devil, like the sweep, usually carries a besom [1]. One
would expect *his* name, and not the Fool's, to be Beelzebub.
He is, however, ' Little Devil Dout' or ' Doubt,' ' Little Jack
Doubt ' or ' Jack Devil Doubt.'   At Leigh Little Devil Doubt
also calls himself ' Jack,'

> ' With my wife and family on my back';

and perhaps we may therefore trace a further avatar of this
same personage in the 'John' or 'Johnny Jack' who at
Salisbury gives a name to the whole performance [2].   He is
also ' Little Jack' (Brill, St. Mary Bourne), 'Fat Jack ' (Islip),
'Happy Jack' (Berkshire, Hollington), 'Humpty Jack' (Newbold). He generally makes the remark about his wife and
family.   What he does carry upon his back is sometimes
a hump, sometimes a number of rag-dolls.   I take it that the
hump came first, and that the dolls arose out of Jack's jocular
explanation of his own deformity.   But why the hump?
Was it originally a bag of soot?   Or the *saccus* with which
the German *Knechte Ruperte* wander in the Twelve nights? [3]
At Hollington and in a Hampshire version Jack has been
somewhat incongruously turned into a press-gang.   In this
capacity he gets at Hollington the additional name of
' Tommy Twing-twang.'

Having got these grotesques, traditional accompaniments
of the play, to dispose of somehow, what do the playwrights
do with them?   The simplest and most primitive method is
just to bring them in, to show them to the spectators when
the fighting is over.   Thus Beelzebub, like the Fool at one
point in the Revesby play, often comes in with

> ' Here come I ; ain't been yit,
>   Big head and little wit.'

' Ain't been yit!'   Could a more naïve explanation of the
presence of a 'stock' character on the stage be imagined?

---

[1] Mr. Gomme, in *Nature* for
Dec. 23, 1897, finds in this broom
'the magic weapon of the witch'
discussed by Pearson, ii. 29.   Probably, however, it was introduced
into the plays for the purposes of
the *quête*; cf. p. 217.   It is used
also to make a circle for the players,
but here it may have merely taken
the place of a sword.

[2] Parish, *Dict. of Sussex Dialect*,
136.   The mummers are called
'John Jacks.'

[3] Cf. p. 268, n. 4.

Similarly in Cornwall the woman is worked in by making 'Sabra,' a *persona muta*, come forward to join St. George[1]. In the play printed in *Sharpe's London Magazine* the 'Hobby-horse' is led in. Obviously personages other than the traditional four can be introduced in the same way, at the bidding of the rustic fancy. Thus at Bampton 'Robin Hood' and 'Little John' briefly appear, in both the Irish plays and at Tenby 'Oliver Cromwell,' at Belfast 'St. Patrick,' at Steyning the 'Prince of Peace.'

Secondly, the supernumeraries may be utilized, either as presenters of the main characters or for the purposes of the *quête* at the end. Thus at Leigh the performance is begun by Little Devil Doubt, who enters with his broom and sweeps a 'room' or 'hall' for the actors, just as in the sword-dances a preliminary circle is made with a sword upon the ground[2]. In the Midlands this is the task of the woman, called at Islip and in Berkshire 'Molly,' and at Bright-Walton 'Queen Mary[3].' Elsewhere the business with the broom is omitted; but there is nearly always a short prologue in which an appeal is made to the spectators for 'room.' This prologue may be spoken, as at Manchester by the Fool, or as at Lutterworth by one of the fighters. The commonest presenter, however, is a personification of the festal season at which the plays are usually performed, 'Old Father Christmas.'

'Here comes I, Father Christmas, welcome or welcome not,
I hope Old Father Christmas will never be forgot.'

At St. Mary Bourne Christmas is accompanied by 'Mince-Pie,' and in both the Dorset versions, instead of calling for 'room,' he introduces 'Room' as an actual personage. Similarly, at Newport and Eccleshall, the prologue speaker receives the curious soubriquet of 'Open-the-Door.' After the pro-

---

[1] Sandys, 301.

[2] Cf. Capulet, in *Romeo and Juliet*, i. 5. 28 'A hall, a hall! give room! and foot it, girls'; and Puck who precedes the dance of fairies in *Midsummer Night's Dream*, v. 1. 396
'I am sent with broom before,
To sweep the dust behind the door.'

[3] Ditchfield, 315. 'The play in this village is performed in most approved fashion, as the Rector has taken the matter in hand, coached the actors in their parts, and taught them some elocution.' This sort of thing, of course, is soon fatal to folk-drama.

logue, the fighters are introduced. They stand in a clump outside the circle, and in turns step forward and strut round it [1]. Each is announced, by himself or by his predecessor or by the presenter, with a set of rhymes closely parallel to those used in the sword-dances. With the fighters generally comes the 'King of Egypt' (occasionally corrupted into the 'King of England'), and the description of St. George often contains an allusion to his fight with the dragon and the rescue of Sabra, the King of Egypt's daughter. In one or two of the northern versions (Newcastle, Whitehaven) the King of Egypt is a fighter; generally he stands by. In one of the Dorset versions (A) he is called 'Anthony.' Sabra appears only in Cornwall, and keeps silence. The Dragon fights with St. George in Cornwall, and also, as we have seen, in the curious Brill *mêlée*.

The performance, naturally, ends with a *quête*. This takes various forms. Sometimes the presenter, or the whole body of actors, comes forward, and wishes prosperity to the household. Beelzebub, with his frying-pan or ladle, goes round to gather in the contributions. In the version preserved in *Sharpe's London Magazine*, this is the function of a special personage, 'Boxholder.' In a considerable number of cases, however, the *quête* is preceded by a singular action on the part of Little Devil Dout. He enters with his broom, and threatens to sweep the whole party out, or 'into their graves,' if money is not given. In Shropshire and Staffordshire he sweeps up the hearth, and the custom is probably connected with the superstition that it is unlucky to remove fire or ashes from the house on Christmas Day. 'Dout' appears to be a corruption of 'Do out [2].'

Another way of working in the grotesques and other supernumeraries is to give them minor parts in the drama itself. Father Christmas or the King of Egypt is utilized as a sort

[1] Burne-Jackson, 484; Manly, i. 289.

[2] Burne-Jackson, 402, 410; *F. L.* iv. 162; Dyer, 504. The broom is used in Christmas and New Year *quêtes* in Scotland and Yorkshire, even when there is no drama. Northall 205, gives a Lancashire Christmas song, sung by 'Little David Doubt' with black face, skin coat and broom. At Bradford they 'sweep out the Old Year'; at Wakefield they sweep up dirty hearths. In these cases the notion of threatening to do the unlucky thing has gone.

of chorus, to cheer on the fighters, lament the vanquished, and summon the Doctor. At Newbold the woman, called ' Moll Finney,' plays a similar part, as mother of the Turkish Knight. At Stoke Gabriel, Devon, the woman is the Doctor's wife[1]. Finally, in three cases, a complete subordinate dramatic episode is introduced for their sake. At Islip, after the main drama is concluded, the presenter Molly suddenly becomes King George's wife 'Susannah.' She falls ill, and the Doctor's services are requisitioned to cure her. The Doctor rides in, not on a hobby-horse, but on one of the disengaged characters who plays the part of a horse. In Dorsetshire the secondary drama is quite elaborate. In the ' A ' version ' Old Bet ' calls herself ' Dame Dorothy,' and is the wife of Father Christmas, named, for the nonce, ' Jan.' They quarrel about a Jack hare, which he wants fried and she wants roasted. He kills her, and at the happy moment the Doctor is passing by, and brings her to life again. Version ' B ' is very similar, except that the performance closes by Old Bet bringing in the hobby-horse for Father Christmas to mount.

I do not think that I need further labour the affiliation of the St. George plays to the sword-dances. Placed in a series, as I have placed them in these chapters, the two sets of performances show a sufficiently obvious continuity. They are held together by the use of the swords, by their common grotesques, and by the episode of the Doctor, which connects them also with the German Shrovetide and Whitsun folkceremonies. They are properly called folk-drama, because they are derived, with the minimum of literary intervention, from the dramatic tendencies latent in folk-festivals of a very primitive type. They are the outcome of the instinct of play, manipulating for its own purposes the mock sacrifice and other débris of extinct ritual. Their central incident symbolizes the *renouveau*, the annual death of the year or the fertilization spirit and its annual resurrection in spring[2]. To this

---

[1] Ditchfield, 12. An ' Old Bet ' is mentioned in 5 *N. Q.* iv. 511, as belonging to a Belper version. The woman is worked in with various ingenuity, but several versions have lost her. The prologue to the New-

castle chap-book promises a ' Dives ' who never appears. Was this the woman ? In the Linton in Craven sword-dance, she has the similar name of ' Miser.'

[2] I hardly like to trace a remi-

have become attached some of those heroic *cantilenae* which, as the early mediaeval chroniclers tell us, existed in the mouths of the *chori iuvenum* side by side with the *cantilenae* of the minstrels. The symbolism of the *renouveau* is preserved unmistakably enough in the episode of the Doctor, but the *cantilenae* have been to some extent modified by the comparatively late literary element, due perhaps to that universal go-between of literature and the folk, the village schoolmaster. The genuine national heroes, a Stercatherus or a Galgacus, have given way to the 'worthies' and the 'champions of Christendom,' dear to Holophernes. The literary tradition has also perhaps contributed to the transformation of the *chorus* or semi-dramatic dance into drama pure and simple. In the St. George plays dancing holds a very subordinate place, far more so than in the 'Plow-boys' play of Revesby. Dances and songs are occasionally introduced before the *quête*, but rarely during the main performance. In the eccentric Brill version, however, a complete morris-dance appears. And of course it must be borne in mind that the fighting itself, with its gestures and pacings round the circle and clashing of swords, has much more the effect of a sword-dance than of a regular fight. So far as it is a fight, the question arises whether we ought to see in it, besides the heroic element introduced by the *cantilenae*, any trace of the mimic contest between winter and summer, which is found here and there, alternating with the resurrection drama, as

niscence of the connexion with the *renouveau* in the 'General Valentine' and 'Colonel Spring' who fight and are slain in the Dorset (A) version; but there the names are. Mr. Gomme (*Nature* for Dec. 23, 1897) finds in certain mumming costumes preserved in the Anthropological Museum at Cambridge and made of paper scales, a representation of leaves of trees. Mr. Ordish, I believe, finds in them the scales of the dragon (*F. L.* iv. 163). Some scepticism may be permitted as to these conjectures. In most places the dress represents little but rustic notions of the ornamental.

Cf. Thomas Hardy, *The Return of the Native*, bk. ii. ch. 3 : ' The girls could never be brought to respect tradition in designing and decorating the armour : they insisted on attaching loops and bows of silk and velvet in any situation pleasing to their taste. Gorget, gusset, bassinet, cuirass, gauntlet, sleeve, all alike in the view of these feminine eyes were practicable spaces whereon to sew scraps of fluttering colour.' The usual costume of the sword-dancers, as we have seen (p. 200), was a clean white smock, and probably that of the mummers is based upon this.

a symbolical representation of the *renouveau*. The fight does not, of course, in itself stand in any need of such an explanation; but it is suggested by a singular passage which in several versions is put in the mouth of one or other of the heroes. St. George, or the Slasher, or the Turkish Knight, is made to boast something as follows:

'My arms are made of iron, my body's made of steel,
　My head is made of beaten brass, no man can make me feel.'

It does not much matter who speaks these words in the versions of Holophernes, but there are those who think that they originally belonged to the representative of winter, and contained an allusion to the hardness of the frost-bound earth[1]. Personally I do not see why they should refer to anything but the armour which a champion might reasonably be supposed to wear.

A curious thing about the St. George play is the width of its range. All the versions, with the possible exception of that found at Brill, seem to be derived from a common type. They are spread over England, Wales, Scotland and Ireland, and only in the eastern counties do they give way to the partly, though not wholly, independent Plough Monday type. Unfortunately, the degeneracy of the texts is such that any closer investigation into their inter-relations or into the origin and transmission of the archetype would probably be futile. Something, however, must be said as to the prominence, at any rate outside Scotland, of the character of St. George. As far as I can see, the play owes nothing at all to John Kirke's stage-play of *The Seven Champions of Christendom*, printed in 1638[2]. It is possible, however, that it may be a development of a sword-dance in which, as in the Shetland dance, the 'seven champions' had usurped the place of more primitive heroes. If so the six champions, other than St. George, have

---

[1] T. F. Ordish, in *F. L.* iv. 158.
[2] Printed in *The Old English Drama* (1830), vol. iii. Burne-Jackson, 490, think that 'the masque owes something to the play,' but the resemblances they trace are infinitesimal. A play of *St. George for England*, by William or Went-worth Smith, was amongst the manuscripts destroyed by Warburton's cook, and a Bartholomew Fair 'droll' of *St. George and the Dragon* is alluded to in the *Theatre of Compliments*, 1688 (Fleay, *C. H.* ii. 251; Hazlitt, *Manual*, 201).

singularly vanished[1]. In any case, there can have been no 'seven champions,' either in sword-dance or mummers' play, before Richard Johnson brought together the scattered legends of the national heroes in his *History of the Seven Champions* in 1596[2]. This fact presents no difficulty, for the archetype of our texts need certainly not be earlier than the seventeenth century[3]. By this time the literary dramatic tradition was fully established, even in the provinces, and it may well have occurred to Holophernes to convert the sword-dance into the semblance of a regular play.

On the other hand, the mediaeval period had its dramatic or semi-dramatic performances in which St. George figured, and possibly it is to these, and not to the 'seven champions,' that his introduction into the sword-dance is due. These performances generally took the form of a 'riding' or proces-

[1] In the Dorset (A) version, the king of Egypt is 'Anthony' and the doctor 'Mr. Martin Dennis.' Conceivably these are reminiscences of St. Anthony of Padua and St. Denys of France. The Revesby Plough Monday play (cf. p. 208) has also an 'Anthony.' The 'Seven Champions' do not appear in the English sword-dances described in ch. ix, but the morris-dancers at Edgemond wake used to take that name (Burne-Jackson, 491). Mrs. Nina Sharp writes in *F. L. R.* iii. 1. 113: 'I was staying at Minety, near Malmesbury, in Wilts (my cousin is the vicar), when the mummers came round (1876). They went through a dancing fight in two lines opposed to each other—performed by the Seven Champions of Christendom. There was no St. George, and they did not appear to have heard of the Dragon. When I inquired for him, they went through the performance of drawing a tooth—the tooth produced, after great agony, being a horse's. The mummers then carried into the hall a bush gaily decorated with coloured ribbons . . . [They] were all in white smock frocks and masks. At Acomb, near York, I saw very similar mummers a few years ago, but they distinguished St. George, and the Dragon was a prominent person. There was the same tooth-drawing, and I think the Dragon was the patient, and was brought back to life by the operation.' I wonder whether the 'Seven Champions' were *named* or whether Mrs. Sharp *inferred them*. Anyhow, there could not have been *seven* at Minety, without St. George. The 'bush' is an interesting feature. According to C. R. Smith, *Isle of Wight Words* (*Eng. Dial. Soc.* xxxii. 63) the mummers are known in Kent as the 'Seven Champions.'

[2] Entered on the *Stationers' Registers* in 1596. The first extant edition is dated 1597. Johnson first introduced Sabra, princess of Egypt, into the story; in the mediaeval versions, the heroine is an unnamed princess of Silena in Libya. The mummers' play follows Johnson, and makes it Egypt. On Johnson was based Heylin's *History of St. George* (1631 and 1633), and on one or both of these Kirke's play.

[3] Jackson and Burne, 489: 'Miss L. Toulmin Smith . . . considers that the diction and composition of the [Shropshire] piece, as we now have it, date mainly from the seventeenth century.'

sion on St. George's day, April 23. Such ridings may, of
course, have originally, like the Godiva processions or the
midsummer shows, have preserved the memory of the pre-
Christian perambulations of the fields in spring, but during
the period for which records are available they were rather
municipal celebrations of a semi-ecclesiastical type. St. George
was the patron saint of England, and his day was honoured
as one of the greater feasts, notably at court, where the
chivalric order of the Garter was under his protection [1]. The
conduct of the ridings was generally, from the end of the
fourteenth century onwards, in the hands of a guild, founded
not as a trade guild, but as a half social, half religious fraternity,
for the worship of the saint, and the mutual aid and good
fellowship of its members. The fullest accounts preserved
are from Norwich, where the guild or company of St. George
was founded in 1385, received a charter from Henry V in 1416,
and by 1451 had obtained a predominant share in the government of the city [2]. The records of this guild throw a good
deal of light on the riding. The brethren and 'sustren' had
a chapel in the choir of the cathedral, and after the Reformation held their feasts in a chapel of the common hall of the
city, which had formerly been the church of a Dominican
convent. The riding was already established by 1408 when
the court of the guild ordered that 'the George shall go in
procession and make a conflict with the Dragon and keep his
estate both days.' The George was a man in 'coat armour
beaten with silver,' and had his club-bearer, henchmen, minstrels and banners. He was accompanied by the Dragon, the
guild-priest, and the court and brethren of the guild in red
and white capes and gowns. The procession went to 'the
wood' outside the city, and here doubtless the conflict with
the dragon took place. By 1537 there had been added to the

---

[1] Dyer, 193; Anstis, *Register of the Garter* (1724), ii. 38; E. Ashmole, *Hist. of the Garter* (ed. 1672), 188, 467; (ed. 1715), 130, 410.

[2] F. Blomefield, *Hist. of Norfolk* (1805), iv. 6, 347; Mackerell, MS. *Hist. of Norfolk* (1737), quoted in *Norfolk Archaeology*, iii. 315; *No-*

tices Illustrative of Municipal Pageants and Processions (with plates, publ. C. Muskett, Norwich, 1850); Toulmin Smith, *English Gilds* (E. E. T. S.), 17, 443; Kelly, 48. Hudson and Tingey, *Cal. of Records of Norwich* (1898), calendar many documents of the guild.

dramatis personae St. Margaret, also called 'the lady,' who apparently aided St. George in his enterprise[1]. Strange to say, the guild survived the Reformation. In 1552, the court ordered, 'there shall be neither George nor Margaret, but for pastime the dragon to come and show himself, as in other years.' But the feast continued, and in spite of an attempt to get rid of him under the Long Parliament, the Dragon endured until 1732 when the guild was dissolved. Eighteenth-century witnesses describe the procession as it then existed. The Dragon was carried by a man concealed in its body. It was of basket work and painted cloth, and could move or spread its wings, and distend or contract its head. The ranks were kept by 'whifflers' who juggled with their swords, and by 'Dick Fools,' in motley and decked with cats' tails and small bells. There is one more point of interest about the Norwich guild. In the fifteenth century it included many persons of distinction in Norfolk. Sir John Fastolf gave it an 'angell silver and guylt.' And amongst the members in 1496 was Sir John Paston. I have already quoted the lament in the *Paston Letters* over William Woode, the keeper, whom the writer 'kepyd thys iij yer to pleye Seynt Jorge and Robyn Hod and the Shryff off Nottyngham,' and who at a critical moment went off to Bernysdale and left his master in the lurch[2]. I have also identified his Robin Hood play, and now it becomes apparent where he played 'Seynt Jorge.' It is curious how the fragments of the wreckage of time fit into one another. The riding of the George is not peculiar to Norwich. We find it at Leicester[3], at Coventry[4], at Strat-

---

[1] Hartland, iii. 58, citing Jacobus à Voragine, *Legenda Aurea*, xciii, gives the story of St. Margaret, and the appearance of the devil to her in the shape of a dragon. She was in his mouth, but made the sign of the cross, and he burst asunder.

[2] Cf. p. 177.

[3] Kelly, 37. The 'dressyng of the dragon' appears in the town accounts for 1536. The guild had dropped the riding, even before the Reformation.

[4] Harris, 97, 190, 277; Kelly, 41. The guild was formed by journey-men in 1424. Probably there was a riding. In any case, at the visit of Prince Edward in 1474, there was a pageant or *mystère mimé* 'upon the Conddite in the Crosse Chepyng' of 'seint George armed and Kynges dought[r] knelyng afore hym w[t] a lambe and the fader and the moder beyng in a toure a boven beholdyng seint George savyng their dought[r] from the dragon.' There was a similar pageant at the visit of Prince Arthur in 1498.

ford [1], at Chester [2], at York, at Dublin [3]. An elaborate programme for the Dublin procession is preserved. It included
an emperor and empress with their train, St. George on horseback, the dragon led by a line and the king and queen of·Dele.
But no princess is mentioned. The ' may ' or maiden figured
at York, however, and there was also a St. Christopher. At
other places, such as Reading, Aston [4] and Louth [5], an equestrian figure, called a ' George,' is known to have stood on
a ' loft ' in the church, and here, too, an annual ' riding ' may
be presumed.

There is no proof that the dramatic element in these
' ridings ' was anything more than a *mystère mimé*, or
pageant in dumb show. On the other hand, there were places
where the performance on St. George's day took the form
of a regular miracle-play. The performance described by
Collier as taking place before Henry V and the Emperor
Sigismund at Windsor in 1416 turns out on examination of
Collier's authority to be really a ' soteltie,' a cake or raised
pie of elaborate form. But the town of Lydd had its
St. George play in 1456, and probably throughout the
century ; while in 1490 the chaplain of the guild of St. George
at New Romney went to see this Lydd play with a view to
reproducing it at the sister town. In 1511 again a play of
St. George is recorded to have been held at Bassingbourne in
Cambridgeshire, not on St. George's, but on St. Margaret's day [6].

Obviously the subject-matter of all these pageants and
miracles was provided by the familiar ecclesiastical legend of

---

[1] Kelly, 42.

[2] Morris, 139, 168; Fenwick,
Hist. of Chester, 372 ; Dyer, 195.
The Fraternity of St. George was
founded for the encouragement of
shooting in 1537. They had a chapel with a George in the choir of
St. Peter's. St. George's was the
great day for races on the Rood-
dee. In 1610 was a famous show,
wherein St. George was attended by
Fame, Mercury, and various allegorical figures.

[3] Cf. *Representations*, s. v. York,
Dublin.

[4] Dyer, 194, gives from Coates,

Hist. of Reading, 221, the account
for setting-up a ' George' in 1536.
Dugdale, *Hist. of Warwickshire*,
928, has a notice of a legacy
in 1526 by John Arden to Aston
church of his ' white harneis ... for
a George to were it, and to stand
on his pewe, a place made for it.'

[5] R. W. Goulding, *Louth Records*,
quotes from the churchwardens' accounts for 1538 payments for taking
down the image of St. George and
his horse.

[6] *Representations*, s. v. Windsor,
Lydd, New Romney, Bassingbourne.

St. George the dragon-slayer, with which was occasionally interwoven the parallel legend of St. Margaret[1]. Similar performances can be traced on the continent. There was one at Mons called *le lumeçon*[2]. Rabelais describes one at Metz, of which, however, the hero was not St. George, but yet another dragon-slayer, St. Clement[3]. There is no need to ascribe to them a folk origin, although the dragon-slaying champion is a common personage in folk-tale[4]. They belong to the cycle of religious drama, which is dealt with in the second volume of this book. And although in Shropshire at least they seem to have been preserved in a village stage-

[1] For the legend, see *Acta Sanctorum, April*, iii. 101; Jacobus à Voragine, *Legenda Aurea* (1280), lviii; E. A. W. Budge, *The Martyrdom and Miracles of St. George of Cappadocia: the Coptic Texts* (Oriental Text Series, 1888). In Rudder, *Hist. of Gloucestershire*, 461, and *Gloucester F. L.* 47, is printed an English version of the legend, apparently used for reading in church on the Sunday preceding St. George's day, April 23. Cf. also Gibbon (ed. Bury), ii. 472, 568; Hartland, *Perseus*, iii. 38; Baring-Gould, *Curious Myths of the Middle Ages*, 266; Zöckler, s.v. St. Georg, in Herzog and Plitt's *Encyclopedia*; F. Görres, *Ritter St. Georg in Geschichte, Legende und Kunst*, in *Zeitschrift für wissenschaftliche Theologie*, xxx (1887), 54; F. Vetter, *Introduction* to Reimbot von Durne's *Der heilige Georg* (1896). Gibbon identified St. George with the Arian bishop George of Cappadocia, and the dragon with Athanasius. This view has been recently revived with much learning by J. Friedrich in *Sitzb. Akad. Wiss. München (phil.-hist.Kl.)*, 1899, ii. 2. Pope Gelasius (†495) condemned the *Passio* as apocryphal and heretical, but he admits the historical existence of the saint, whose cult indeed was well established both in East and West in the fifth century. Budge tries to find an historical basis for him in a young man at Nicomedia who tore down an edict during the persecution of Diocletian (†303), and identifies his torturer Dadianus with the co-emperor Galerius.

[2] Du Méril, *La Com.* 98. He quotes Novidius, *Sacri Fasti* (ed. 1559), bk. vi. f. 48vo:
'perque annos duci monet [rex]
    in spectacula casum
    unde datur multis annua
        scena locis.'
A fifteenth-century Augsburg miracle-play of St. George is printed by Keller, *Fastnachtsspiele*, No. 125; for other Continental data cf. Creizenach, i. 231, 246; Julleville, *Les Myst.* ii. 10, 644; D'Ancona, i. 104.

[3] Rabelais, *Gargantua*, iv. 59. The dragon was called Graoully, and snapped its jaws, like the Norwich 'snap-dragons' and the English hobby-horse.

[4] Cf. p. 138. The myth has attached itself to other undoubtedly historical persons besides St. George (Bury, *Gibbon*, ii. 569). In his case it is possibly due to a misunderstood bit of rhetoric. In the Coptic version of the legend edited by Budge (p. 223), Dadianus is called 'the dragon of the abyss.' There is no literal dragon in this version: the princess is perhaps represented by Alexandra, the wife of Dadianus, whom George converts. Cf. Hartland, *Perseus*, iii. 44.

play up to quite a recent date [1], they obviously do not directly survive in the folk-play with which we are concerned. As far as I know, that nowhere takes place on St. George's day. The Dragon is very rarely a character, and though St. George's traditional exploit is generally mentioned, it is, as that very mention shows, not the motive of the action. On the other hand the legend, in its mediaeval form, has no room for the episode of the Doctor [2]. At the same time the Dragon does sometimes occur, and the traditional exploit is mentioned, and therefore if any one chooses to say that the fame of St. George in the guild celebrations as well as the fame of the 'seven champions' romance determined his choice as the hero of the later sword-dance rhymes, I do not see that there is much to urge against the view [3].

With regard to the main drift of this chapter, the criticism presents itself; if the folk-plays are essentially a celebration of the *renouveau* of spring, how is it that the performances generally take place in mid-winter at Christmas? The answer is that, as will be shown in the next chapter, none of the Christmas folk-customs are proper to mid-winter. They have been attracted by the ecclesiastical feast from the seasons which in the old European calendar preceded and followed it, from the beginning of winter and the beginning of summer or spring. The folk-play has come with the rest. But the transference has not invariably taken place. The Norfolk versions belong not to Christmas but to Plough Monday, which lies immediately outside the Christmas season proper, and is indeed, though probably dislocated from its primitive date, the earliest of the spring feasts. The St. George play itself is occasionally performed at Easter, and even perhaps on May-day, whilst versions, which in their present form contain clear allusions to Christmas, yet betray another origin by the title which they bear of the 'Pace-eggers'' or 'Pasque-eggers''

---

[1] Cf. ch. xxiv, as to these plays.

[2] I ought perhaps to say that in one of the Coptic versions of the legend St. George is periodically slain and brought back to life by a miracle during the space of seven years. But I do not think that this episode occurs in any of the European versions of the legend.

[3] 'Sant George and the dragon' are introduced into a London May-game in 1559 (ch. viii).

play[1]. Christmas, however, has given to the play the characteristic figure of Old Father Christmas. And the players are known as ' mummers ' and 'guisers,' or, in Cornwall, ' geesedancers,' because their performance was regarded as a variety of the ' mumming' or ' disguising' which, as we shall see, became a regular name for the Christmas revel or *quête* [2].

[1] See the Manchester *Peace Egg* chap-book. At Manchester, Langdale, and, I believe, Coniston, the play is performed at Easter: cf. Halliwell, *Popular Rhymes*, 231. The Steyning play is believed to have been given at May-day as well as Christmas. Of course, so far as this goes, the transference might have been from Christmas, not to Christmas, but the German analogies point the other way. The Cheshire performance on All Souls' Day (Nov. 2), mentioned by Child, v. 291, is, so far as I know, exceptional.

[2] Cf. ch. xvii: In the Isle of Wight the performers are called the ' Christmas Boys' (C. R. Smith, *Isle of Wight Words*, in *E. D. S.* xxxii. 63). The terms ' Seven Champions' (Kent) and ' John Jacks' (Salisbury) have already been explained. The Steyning ' Tipteers' or ' Tipteerers' may be named from the 'tips' collected in the *quête*. The ' Guisers' of Staffordshire become on the Shropshire border ' Morris-dancers,' ' Murry-dancers,' or ' Merry-dancers' — a further proof of the essential identity of the morris- or sword-dance with the play.

CHAPTER XI

THE BEGINNING OF WINTER

[*Bibliographical Note.*—I have largely followed the conclusions of A. Tille, *Deutsche Weihnacht* (1893) and *Yule and Christmas* (1899). The Roman winter feasts are well treated by J. Marquardt and T. Mommsen, *Handbuch der römischen Alterthümer* (3rd ed. 1881–8), vol. vii; W. W. Fowler, *The Roman Festivals of the Period of the Republic* (1899); G. Wissowa, *Religion und Kultus der Römer* (1902); and the Christian feasts by L. Duchesne, *Origines du Culte chrétien* (2nd ed. 1898). On the history of Christmas, H. Usener, *Das Weihnachtsfest*, in *Religionsgeschichtliche Untersuchungen*, vol. i (1889), and F. C. Conybeare's introduction to *The Key of Truth* (1898) should also be consulted. Much information on the Kalends customs is collected by M. Lipenius, *Strenarum Historia*, in J. G. Graevius, *Thesaurus Antiquitatum Romanarum* (1699), vol. xii. I have brought together a number of ecclesiastical references to the Kalends, from the third to the eleventh century, in Appendix N.]

So far this study has concerned itself, on the one hand with the general character of the peasant festivals, on the other with the special history of such of these as fall within the summer cycle of the agricultural year, from ploughing to harvest. The remaining chapters will approach the corresponding festivals, centring around Christmas, of winter. These present a somewhat more difficult problem, partly because their elements are not quite so plainly agricultural, partly ·because of the remarkable dislocations which the development and clash of civilizations have brought about.

It must, I think, be taken as established that the Germano-Keltic tribes had no primitive mid-winter feast, corresponding directly to the modern Christmas[1]. They had no solstitial feast, for they knew nothing of the solstices. And although they had a winter feast of the dead, belonging rather to the domestic than to the elemental side of cult, this probably fell not at the middle, but at the beginning of the season. It was an aspect in the great feast with which not the winter only but the Germano-Keltic year began. This took place

[1] Tille, *Y. and C.* 78, 107; Rhys, *C. H.* 519: cf. ch. v.

when the advance of snow and frost drove the warriors back from foray and the cattle from the pastures. The scarcity of fodder made the stall-feeding of the whole herd an impossibility, and there was therefore an economic reason for a great slaughtering. This in its turn led to a great banquet on the fresh meat, and to a great sacrifice, accompanied with the usual perambulations, water-rites and fire-rites which sacrifice to the deities of field and flock entailed[1]. The vegetation spirit would again be abroad, no longer, as in spring or summer, in the form of flowers and fresh green boughs, but in that of the last sheaf or 'kern-baby' saved from harvest, or in that of such evergreens or rarer blossoms as might chance to brave the snows. The particular 'intention' of the festival would be to secure the bounty of the divine powers for the coming year, and a natural superstition would find omens for the whole period in the events of the initial day. The feast, however, would be domestic, as well as seasonal. The fire on the hearth was made 'new,' and beside it the fathers, resting from the toils of war, or herding or tillage, held jollification with their children. Nor were the dead forgotten. *Minni* were drunk in honour of ancestors and ancestral deities; and a share of the banquet was laid out for such of these as might be expected, in the whirl of the wintry storm, to revisit the familiar house-place.

Originally, no doubt, the time of the feast was determined by the actual closing of the war-ways and the pastures. Just as the first violet or some migratory bird of March was hailed for the herald of summer, so the first fall of snow gave the signal that winter was at hand[2]. In the continental home of the Germano-Keltic tribes amongst the forests of central Europe this would take place with some regularity about the middle of November[3]. A fixed date for the feast could only arise when, at some undefined time, the first calendar, the 'three-score-day-tide' calendar of unknown origin, was intro-

---

[1] Tille, *Y. and C.* 18; *D. W.* 6. Bede, *D. T. R.* 15, gives Blot-monath as the Anglo-Saxon name for November, and explains it as 'mensis immolationum, quia in ea pecora quae occisuri erant, Diis suis voverent.'

[2] Burton, 15, notes a tradition at Disley, in Cheshire, that the local wake was formerly held after the first fall of snow.

[3] Tille, *Y. and C.* 18.

duced[1]. Probably it was thenceforward held regularly upon a
day corresponding to either November the 11th or the 12th in
our reckoning. If it is accurately represented by St. Martin's
day, it was the 11th[2], if by the Manx *Samhain*, the 12th[3].
It continued to begin the year, and also the first of the six
tides into which that year was divided. As good fortune will
have it, the name of that tide is preserved to us in the Gothic
term *Iuleis* for November and December[4], in the Anglo-
Saxon *Giuli* or *Geola* which, according to Bede, applied both to
December and to January[5], and in *Yule*, the popular designation, both in England and Scandinavia, of Christmas itself[6].
The meaning of this name is, however, more doubtful. The
older philology, with solstices running in its brain, supposed
that it applied primarily to a mid-winter feast, and connected it with the Anglo-Saxon *hwéol*, a wheel[7]. Bede
himself, learned in Roman lore, seems to hint at such an
explanation[8]. The current modern explanation derives the

---

[1] Mogk, iii. 391; Tille, *Y. and C.*
24, find the winter feast in the festival
of Tanfana which the Marsi were
celebrating when Germanicus attacked them in A.D. 14 (Tacitus,
Ann. i. 51). Winter, though immi-
nent, had not yet actually set in,
but this might be the case in any
year after the festival had come to
be determined by a fixed calendar.

[2] Tille, *Y. and C.* 57.

[3] Rhys, *C. H.* 513, says that the
Samhain fell on Nov. 1. The preceding night was known as *Nos
Galan-geaf*, the 'night of winter
calends,' and that following as *Dy'
gwyl y Meirw*, 'the feast of the
Dead.' In *F. L.* ii. 308 he gives
the date of the Manx *Samhain* as
Nov. 12, and explains this as being
Nov. 1, O.S. But is it not really
the original date of the feast which
has been shifted elsewhere to the
beginning of the month?

[4] Tille, *Y. and C.* 12, citing M.
Heyne, *Ulfilas*, 226: 'In a Gothic
calendarium of the sixth century
November, or *Naubaimbair*, is called
fruma Iuleis, which presupposes
that December was called **aftuma
Iuleis*.'

[5] Bede, *de temp. rat.* c. 15. Tille,
Y. and C. 20, points out that the
application of the old tide-name to
fit November and December by the
Goths and December and January
by the Anglo-Saxons is fair evidence
for the belief that the tide itself
corresponded to a period from mid-
November to mid-January.

[6] Tille, *Y. and C.* 147. The terms
gehhol, geóhel, geól, giúl, iúl, &c.
signify the Christmas festival season
from the ninth century onwards, and
from the eleventh also Christmas
Day itself. The fifteenth-century
forms are *Yule, Ywle, Yole, Yowle*.
In the A.-S. Chronicle the terms
used for Christmas are 'midewinter,'
'Cristes mæssa,' 'Cristes tyde,'
'Natiuitedh.' As a single word
'Cristesmesse' appears first in 1131
(Tille, *Y. and C.* 159). The German
'Weihnacht' (M.H.G. *wich*, 'holy')
appears † 1000 (Tille, *D. W.* 22).

[7] Pfannenschmidt, 238, 512.

[8] The notion is of a circular course
of the sun, passing through the four
turning- or wheeling-points of the
solstices and equinoxes. Cf. ch. vi
for the use of the wheel as a solar
symbol.

word from a supposed Germanic *jehwela*, equivalent to the
Latin *ioculus* [1]. It would thus mean simply a 'feast' or
'rejoicing,' and some support seems to be lent to this de-
rivation by the occasional use of the English '*yule*' and the
Keltic *gwyl* to denote feasts other than that of winter [2].
Other good authorities, however, prefer to trace it to a
Germanic root *jeula-* from which is derived the Old Norse *él*,
'a snowstorm'; and this also, so far as its application to the
feast and tide of winter is concerned, seems plausible enough [3].
It is possible that to the winter feast originally belonged the
term applied by Bede to December 24 of *Modranicht* or
Modraneht [4]. It would be tempting to interpret this as 'the
night which gives birth to the year'; but philologists say
that it can only mean 'night of mothers,' and we must therefore explain it as due to some cult of the *Matres* or triad of
mother-goddesses, which took place at the feast [5].

[1] Mogk, iii. 391, quoting Kluge,
Englische Studien, ix. 311, and
Bugge, *Ark. f. nord. Filolog.* iv. 135.
Tille, *Y. and C.* 8, 148, desirous to
establish an Oriental origin for the
Three Score Day tides, doubts the
equation *jehwela = ioculus*, and
suggests a connexion between the
Teutonic terms and the old Cypriote
names ἰλαῖος, ἰουλαῖος, ἰουλίηος, ἰούλιος
for the period Dec. 22 to Jan. 23 (K.
F. Hermann, *Über griech. Monats-
kunde*, 64), and, more hesitatingly,
with the Greek Ἴουλος or hymn to
Ceres. Weinhold, *Deutsche Monatsnamen*, 4; *Deutsche Jahrteilung*, 15,
thinks that both the Teutonic and
Cypriote names are the Roman
Julius transferred from mid-summer
to mid-winter. Northall, 208, makes
yule = ol, oel, a feast or 'ale,' for
which I suppose there is nothing to
be said. Skeat, *Etym. Dict.* s. v.,
makes it 'a time of revelry,' and
connects with M.E. *youlen, yollen*,
to 'yawl' or 'yell,' and with A.-S.
gýlan, Dutch *joelen*, to make merry,
G. *jolen, jodeln*, to sing out. He
thus gets in a different way much
the sense given in the text.
[2] At a Cotswold Whitsun ale a
lord and lady 'of yule' were chosen
(*Gloucester F. L.* 56). Rhys, *C. H.*

412, 421, 515, and in *F. L.* ii. 305,
gives *Gwyl* as a Welsh term for
'feast' in general, and in particular
mentions, besides the *Gwyl y Meirw*
at the *Samhain*, the *Gwyl Aust*
(Aug. 1, Lammas or Lugnassad
Day). This also appears in Latin
as the *Gula Augusti* (Ducange, s. v.
temp. Edw. III), and in English as
'the Gule of August' (Hearne, *Robert
of Gloucester's Chron.* 679). Tille,
Y. and C. 56, declares that *Gula*
here is only a mutilation of *Vincula*,
Aug. 1 being in the ecclesiastical
calendar the feast of St. Peter *ad
Vincula*.
[3] Kluge and Lutz, *English Etymology*, s. v. Yule.
[4] Bede, *D. T. R.* c. 15 'ipsam
noctem nobis sacrosanctam, tunc
gentili vocabulo *Modranicht* [v.l.
Modraneht], id est, matrum noctem
appellabant; ob causam ut suspi-
camur ceremoniarum, quas in ea
pervigiles agebant.'
[5] Mogk, iii. 391. Tille, *Y. and C.*
152, gives some earlier explanations, criticizes that of Mogk, and
offers as his own a reference to a
custom of baking a cake (*placenta*)
to represent the physical motherhood of the Virgin. The practice
doubtless existed and was con-

The subsequent history of the winter feast consists in its gradual dislocation from the original mid-November position, and dispersion over a large number of dates covering roughly the whole period between Michaelmas and Twelfth night. For this process a variety of causes are responsible. Some of these are economic. As civilization progressed, mid-November came to be, less than of old, a signal turning-point in the year. In certain districts to which the Germano-Keltic tribes penetrated, in Gaul, for instance, or in Britain with its insular climate, the winter tarried, and the regular central European closing of the pastures was no longer a law. Then again tillage came gradually to equal or outstrip pasturage in importance, and the year of tillage closed, even in Germany, at the end of September rather than in mid-November. The harvest feast began to throw the winter feast rather into the shade as a wind-up of the year's agricultural labours. This same development of tillage, together with the more scientific management of pasturage itself, did more. It provided a supply of fodder for the cattle, and by making stall-feeding possible put off further and further into the winter the necessity of the great annual slaughter. The importance in Germany, side by side with St. Martin's day (November 11), of St. Andrew's day (November 30), and still more St. Nicholas' day (December 6)[1], as folk-feasts, seems to suggest a consequent tendency to a gradual shifting of the winter festival.

These economic causes came gradually into operation throughout a number of centuries. In displacing the November feast, they prepared the way for and assisted the action of one still more important. This was the influence of Roman usage. When the Germano-Keltic tribes first came into

demned by Pope Hormisdas (514–23), by the Lateran Council of 649, the Council of Hatfield (680), and the Trullan Council (692). But Bede must have known this as a Christian abuse, and he is quite plainly speaking of a pre-Christian custom. J. M. Neale, *Essays in Liturgiology* (1867), 511, says, ' In most Celtic languages Christmas eve is called the night of Mary,' the Virgin, here as elsewhere, taking over the cult of the mother-goddesses.

[1] Tille, *Y. and C.* 65. In his earlier book *D. W.* 7, 29, Dr. Tille held the view that there had always been a second winter feast about three weeks after the first, when the males held over for breeding were slain.

contact with the Roman world, the beginning of the Roman year was still, nominally at least, upon the Kalends, or first of March. This did not, so far as I know, leave any traces upon the practice of the barbarians [1]. In 45 B.C. the Julian calendar replaced the Kalends of March by those of January. During the century and a half that followed, Gaul became largely and Britain partially Romanized, while there was a steady infiltration of Roman customs and ideas amongst the German tribes about and even far beyond the Rhine. With other elements of the southern civilization came the Roman calendar which largely replaced the older Germanic calendar of three-score-day-tides. The old winter festival fell in the middle of a Roman month, and a tendency set in to transfer the whole or a part of its customs either to the beginning of this month [2] or, more usually, to the beginning of the Roman year, a month and a half later. This process was doubtless helped by the fact that the Roman New Year customs were not in their origin, or even at the period of contact, essentially different from those of their more northerly cousins. It remained, of course, a partial and incomplete one. In Gaul, where the Roman influence was strongest, it probably reached its maximum. But in Germany the days of St. Martin [3] and St. Nicholas [4] have fully maintained their position as folk-feasts by the side of New Year's day, and even Christmas itself; while St. Martin's day at least has never been quite forgotten in our islands [5]. The state of transition is represented by the

---

[1] According to Bede, *D. T. R.* c. 15, the Anglo-Saxons had adopted the system of intercalary months which belongs to the pre-Julian and not the Julian Roman calendar. But Bede's chapter is full of confusions : cf. Tille, *Y. and C.* 145.

[2] All Saints' day or Hallowmas (November 1) and All Souls' day (November 2) have largely, though not wholly, absorbed the November feast of the Dead.

[3] Pfannenschmidt, 203; Jahn, 229; Tille, *Y. and C.* 21, 28, 36, 42, 57; *D. W.* 23.

[4] Tille, *D. W.* 29; Müller, 239, 248. According to Tille, *D. W.* 63,

Christmas only replaced the days of St. Martin and St. Nicholas as a German children's festival in the sixteenth century.

[5] Tille, *Y. and C.* 34, 65; Pfannenschmidt, 206; Dyer, 418; N. Drake, *Shakespeare and his Times* (1838), 93. Martinmas was a favourite Anglo-Saxon and mediaeval legal term. It survived also as a traditional 'tyme of slaughter' for cattle. 'Martlemas beef' was a common term for salt beef. In Scotland a Mart is a fat cow or bullock, but the derivation of this appears to be from a Celtic word *Mart* = cow.

isolated Keltic district known as the Isle of Man. Here, according to Professor Rhys, the old *Samhain* or Hollantide day of November 12 is still regarded by many of the inhabitants as the beginning of the year. Others accept January 1; and there is considerable division of opinion as to which is the day whereon the traditional New Year observances should properly be held [1].

A final factor in the dislocation of the winter feast was the introduction of Christianity, and in especial the establishment of the great ecclesiastical celebration of Christmas. When Christianity first began to claim the allegiance of the Roman world, the rulers of the Church were confronted by a series of southern winter feasts which together made the latter half of December and the beginning of January into one continuous carnival. The nature and position of these feasts claim a brief attention.

To begin with, there were the feasts of the Sun. The *Bruma* (*brevissima*) or *Brumalia* was held on November 24, as the day which ushered in the period of the year during which the sun's light is diminished. This seems to have been a beginning of winter feast, adopted by Rome from Thrace [2]. The term *bruma* was also sometimes applied to the whole period between November 24 and the solstice, and ultimately even to the solstitial day itself, fixed somewhat incorrectly by the Julian calendar on December 25 [3]. On this day also came a festival, which probably owed its origin to the Emperor Aurelian (270-75), whose mother was a semi-Oriental priestess of the Sun, in one of his Syrian forms as Baal or Belus [4], and who instituted an official cult of this divinity at Rome with a temple on the Quirinal, a *collegium* of *pontifices*, and *ludi circenses* held every fourth year [5]. These fell on the day of the solstice, which from the lengthening of the sun's

[1] Rhys, in *F. L.* ii. 308.
[2] Mommsen, *C. I. L.* i². 287; Pauly-Wissowa, *Real-Encycl.* s. v. *Bruma*; Tomaschek, in *Sitzb. Akad. Wiss. Wien*, lx (1869), 358.
[3] Ovid, *Fasti*, i. 163 'bruma novi prima est veterisque novissima solis.'

[4] Cf. p. 112.
[5] Preller, ii. 408; P. Allard, *Julien l'Apostat*, i. 16; J. Réville, *La Religion à Rome sous les Sévères* (1885); Wissowa, 306. An earlier cult of the same type introduced by Elagabalus did not survive its founder.

course was known as the 'birthday' of *Sol Novus* or *Sol Invictus*[1]. This cult was practised by Diocletian and by Constantine before his conversion, and was the rallying-point of Julian in his reaction against Christianity[2]. Moreover, the *Sol Invictus* was identified with the central figure of that curious half-Oriental, half-philosophical worship of Mithra, which at one time threatened to become a serious rival to Christianity as the religion of the thinking portion of the Roman world[3]. That an important Mithraic feast also fell on December 25 can hardly be doubted, although there is no direct evidence of the fact[4].

The cult of the *Sol Invictus* was not a part of the ancient Roman religion, and, like the *Brumalia*, the solstitial festival in his honour, however important to the educated and official classes of the empire, was not a folk-festival. It lay, however, exactly between two such festivals. The *Saturnalia* imme-

---

[1] The earliest reference is probably that in the calendar of the Greek astronomer, of uncertain date, Antiochus, Ἡλίου γενέθλιον· αὔξει φῶς (Cumont, i. 342, from *Cod. Monac. gr.* 287, f. 132). The *Fasti* of Furius Dionysius Philocalus (A.D. 354) have VIII. KAL. IAN. N[atalis] INVICTI C[ircenses] M[issus] XXX' (*C. I. L.* i². 278, 338). Cf. Julian, *Orat.* 4 (p. 156 ed. Spanheim) εὐθέως μετὰ τὸν τελευταῖον τοῦ Κρόνου μῆνα ποιοῦμεν ἡλίῳ τὸν περιφανέστατον ἀγῶνα, τὴν ἑορτὴν Ἡλίῳ καταφημίσαντες Ἀνικήτῳ; Corippus, *de laud. Iust. min.* i. 314 'Solis honore novi grati spectacula circi'; cf. the Christian references on p. 242. Mommsen's *Scriptor Syrus* quoted *C. I. L.* i². 338 tells us that lights were used; 'accenderunt lumina festivitatis causa.'

[2] Preller, ii. 410; Gibbon, ii. 446.

[3] On Mithraicism, cf. F. Cumont, *Textes et Monuments relatifs aux Mystères de Mithra* (1896-9); also the art. by the same writer in Roscher's *Lexicon*, ii. 3028, and A. Gasquet, *Le Culte de Mithra* (*Revue des Deux Mondes* for April 1, 1899); J. Réville, *La Religion à Rome sous les Sévères*, 77; Wis-

sowa, 307; Preller, ii. 410; A. Gardner, *Julian the Apostate*, 175; P. Allard, *Julien l'Apostat*, i. 18; ii. 232; G. Zippel, *Le Taurobolium*, in *Festschrift f. L. Friedländer* (1895), 498. Mithra was originally a form of the Aryan Sun-god, who though subordinated in the Mazdean system to Ahoura Mazda continued to be worshipped by the Persian folk. His cult made its appearance in Rome about 70 B.C., and was developed during the third and fourth centuries A.D. under philosophic influences. Mithra was regarded as the fount of all life, and the yearly obscuration of the sun's forces in winter became a hint and promise of immortality to his worshippers: cf. *Carm. adv. paganos*, 47 'qui hibernum docuit sub terra quaerere solem.' Mithraic votive stones have been found in all parts of the empire, Britain included. They are inscribed 'Soli Invicto,' 'Deo Soli Invicto Mithrae,' 'Numini Invicto Soli Mithrae,' and the like.

[4] Cumont, *Textes et Mon.* i. 325; ii. 66, and in Roscher's *Lexicon*, ii. 3065; Lichtenberger, *Encycl. des Sciences religieuses*, s. v. Mithra.

diately preceded it; a few days later followed the January
Kalends.

The *Saturnalia*, so far as the religious feast of Saturn was
concerned, took place on December 17. Augustus, however,
added two days to the *feriae iudiciariae*, during which the
law-courts were shut, and popular usage extended the festival
to seven. Amongst the customs practised was that of the
sigillariorum celebritas, a kind of fair, at which the *sigillaria*,
little clay dolls or *oscilla*, were bought and given as presents.
Originally, perhaps, these *oscilla* were like some of our feasten
cakes, figures of dough. Candles (*cerei* or *candelae*) appear
also to have been given. On the second and third days it
was customary to bathe in the early morning[1]. But the chief
characteristic of the feast was the licence allowed to the lower
classes, to freedmen and to slaves. During the *libertas
Decembris* both moral and social restraints were thrown off[2].
Masters made merry with their servants, and consented for
the time to be on a footing of strict equality with them[3].
A *rex Saturnalitius*, chosen by lot, led the revels, and was
entitled to claim obedience for the most ludicrous commands[4].

[1] Preller, *R. M.* ii. 15; Mommsen, in *C. I. L.* i[2]. 337; Marquardt
and Mommsen, *Handbuch der römischen Alterthümer*, vi. 562; *Dict.
of Cl. A.* s. v. Saturnalia; Tille,
Y. and C. 85; Frazer, iii. 138;
W. W. Fowler, 268; C. Dezobry,
Rome au Siècle d'Auguste (ed. 4,
1875), iii. 140.

[2] Horace, *Satires*, ii. 7. 4:
'age, libertate Decembri,
quando ita maiores voluerunt,
utere; narra.'

[3] The democratic character of
the feast is brought out in the νόμοι
put by Lucian (Luc. *Opp.* ed.
Jacobitz, iii. 307; *Saturnalia*, p. 393)
in the mouth of the divinely in-
structed νομοθέτης, Chronosolon,
and in the 'Letters of Saturn' that
follow.

[4] According to Tacitus, *Ann.*
xiii. 15, Nero was king of the
Saturnalia at the time of the murder
of Britannicus. On the nature of
this sovereignty, cf. Arrian, *Epi-
ctetus*, i. 25; Martial, xi. 6:

'unctis falciferi senis diebus,
regnator quibus imperat fritil-
lus.'
Lucian, *Saturnalia*, p. 385, introduces a dialogue between Saturn
and his priests. Saturn says ἑπτὰ
μὲν ἡμερῶν ἡ πᾶσα βασιλεία, καὶ ἢν
ἐκπρόθεσμος τούτων γένωμαι, ἰδιώτης
εὐθύς εἰμι, καὶ τοῦ πολλοῦ δήμου εἷς·
ἐν αὐταῖς δὲ ταῖς ἑπτὰ σπουδαῖον
μὲν οὐδὲν οὐδὲ ἀγοραῖον διοικήσασθαί
μοι συγκεχώρηται, πίνειν δὲ καὶ με-
θύειν καὶ βοᾶν καὶ παίζειν καὶ κυ-
βεύειν καὶ ἄρχοντας καθίσταναι καὶ
τοὺς οἰκέτας εὐωχεῖν καὶ γυμνὸν ᾄδειν
καὶ κροτεῖν ὑποτρέμοντα, ἐνίοτε δὲ καὶ
ἐς ὕδωρ ψυχρὸν ἐπὶ κεφαλὴν ὠθεῖσθαι
ἀσβόλῳ κεχρισμένον τὸ πρόσωπον,
ταῦτα ἐφεῖταί μοι ποιεῖν; and again:
εὐωχώμεθα δὲ ἤδη καὶ κροτῶμεν καὶ
ἐπὶ τῇ ἑορτῇ ἐλευθεριάζωμεν, εἶτα
πεττεύωμεν ἐς τὸ ἀρχαῖον ἐπὶ καρύων
καὶ βασιλέας χειροτονῶμεν καὶ πειθαρ-
χῶμεν αὐτοῖς· οὕτω γὰρ ἂν τὴν παροι-
μίαν ἐπαληθεύσαιμι, ἥ φησι, παλίμπαι-
δας τοὺς γέροντας γίγνεσθαι. The
ducking is curiously suggestive of

The similarity of the *Saturnalia* to the folk-feasts of western Europe will be at once apparent. The name *Saturnus* seems to point to a ploughing and sowing festival, although how such a festival came to be held in mid-December must be matter of conjecture[1]. The *Kalends*, on the other hand, are clearly a New Year festival. They began on January 1, with the solemn induction of the new consuls into office. As in the case of the *Saturnalia*, the *feriae* lasted for more than one day, covering at least a *triduum*. The third day was the day of *vota* or solemn wishes of prosperity for the New Year to the emperor. The houses were decked with lights and greenery, and once more the masters drank and played dice with their slaves. The resemblance in this respect between the *Kalends* and the *Saturnalia* was recognized by a myth which told how when Saturn came bringing the gifts of civilization to Italy he was hospitably received by Janus, who then reigned in the land[2]. Another Kalends custom, the knowledge of which we owe to the denunciations of the Fathers, was the parading of the city by bands of revellers

western festival customs, but I do not feel sure whether it was the image of Saturn that was ducked or the *rex* with whom he appears to half, and only half, identify himself. Frazer, iii. 140, lays stress on the primitive sacrificial character of the 'rex,' who is said still to have been annually slain in Lower Moesia at the beginning of the fourth century A.D.; cf. *Acta S. Dasii*, in *Acta Bollandiana*, xvi. (1897), 5; Parmentier et Cumont, *Le Roi des Saturnales*, in *R. de Philologie*, xxi (1897), 143.

[1] Frazer, iii. 144, suggests that the *Saturnalia* may once have been in February, and have left a trace of themselves in the similar festival of the female slaves, the *Matronalia*, on March 1, which, like the winter feasts, came in for Christian censure; cf. Appendix N. No. (i).

[2] Preller, *R. M.* i. 64, 178; ii. 13; C. Dezobry, *Rome au Siècle d'Auguste* (ed. 4, 1875), ii. 169; Mommsen and Marquardt, vi. 545;

vii. 245; Roscher, *Lexicon*, ii. 37; W. W. Fowler, 278; Tille, *Y. and C.* 84; M. Lipenius, *Strenarum Historia* in J. G. Graevius, *Thesaurus Antiq. Rom.* (1699), xii. 409. The last-named treatise contains a quantity of information set out with some obsolete learning. The most important contemporary account is that of Libanius (314–†95) in his εἰς τὰς καλάνδας and his καλανδῶν ἔκφρασις (ed. Reiske, i. 256; iv. 1053; cf. Sievers, *Das Leben der Libanius*, 170, 204). In the former speech he says ταύτην τὴν ἑορτὴν εὕροι τ' ἂν τεταμένην ἐφ' ἅπαν, ὅσον ἡ Ῥωμαίων ἀρχὴ τέταται, in the latter, μίαν δὲ οἶδα κοινὴν ἁπάντων ὁπόσοι ζῶσιν ὑπὸ τὴν Ῥωμαίων ἀρχήν. Under the emperors, who made much of the *strenae* and *vota*, the importance of the Kalends grew, probably at the expense of the Saturnalia; cf. Macrobius, *Saturnalia*, i. 2. 1 'adsunt feriae quas indulget magna pars mensis Iano dicati.'

dressed in women's clothes or in the skins of animals. And, finally, a series of superstitious observances testified to the belief that the events of the first day of the year were ominous for those of the year itself. A table loaded all night long with viands was to ensure abundance of food; such necessaries of life as iron and fire must not be given or lent out of the house, lest the future supply of them should fail. To this order of ideas belonged, ultimately at least, if not originally, the central feature of the whole feast, the *strenae* or presents so freely exchanged between all classes of society on the Kalends. Once, so tradition had it, the *strenae* were nothing more than twigs plucked from the grove of the goddess Strenia, associated with Janus in the feast[1]; but in imperial times men gave honeyed things, that the year of the recipient might be full of sweetness, lamps that it might be full of light, copper and silver and gold that wealth might flow in amain[2].

Naturally, the Fathers were not slow to protest against these feasts, and, in particular, against the participation in them of professing Christians. Tertullian is, as usual, explicit and emphatic in his condemnation[3]. The position was aggravated when, probably in the fourth century, the Christian feast of the Birthday of Christ came to be fixed upon December 25, in the very heart of the pagan rejoicings and upon the actual day hitherto sacred to *Sol Invictus*. The origin of Christmas is wrapped in some obscurity[4]. The earliest notices of a

---

[1] Preller, i. 180; Mommsen and Marquardt, vi. 14; vii. 245; W.W. Fowler, 278; Tille, *Y. and C.* 84, 104. *Strenia* was interpreted in the sense of 'strenuous'; cf. Symmachus, *Epist.* x. 15 'ab exortu paene urbis Martiae strenarum usus adolevit auctore Tatio rege, qui verbenas felicis arboris ex luco Streniae anni novi auspices primus accepit. . . . Nomen indicio est viris strenuis haec convenire virtute.' Preller calls Strenia a Sabine *Segensgöttin*.

[2] Mommsen and Marquardt, vii. 245; Lipenius, 489. The gifts were often inscribed 'anno novo faustum felix tibi.' It is probable

that the sweet cakes and the lamps like the *verbenae* had originally a closer connexion with the rites of the feast than that of mere omens. The emperors expected liberal *strenae*, and from them the custom passed into mediaeval and Renaissance courts. Queen Elizabeth received sumptuous new year gifts from her subjects. For a money payment the later empire used the term καλανδικόν or *kalendaticum*. *Strenae* survives in the French *étrennes* (Müller, 150, 504).

[3] Appendix N, Nos. (i), (ii).

[4] The most recent authorities are Tille, *Y. and C.* 119; H. Usener, *Religionsgeschichtliche Untersuch-*

celebration of the birth of Christ in the eastern Church attach it to that of his baptism on the Epiphany. This feast is as old as the second century. By the fourth it was widespread in the East, and was known also in Gaul and probably in northern Italy [1]. At Rome it cannot be traced so early; but it was generally adopted there by the beginning of the fifth, and Augustine blames the Donatists for rejecting it, and so cutting themselves off from fellowship with the East [2]. Christmas, on the other hand, made its appearance first at Rome, and the East only gradually and somewhat grudgingly accepted it. The Paulician Christians of Armenia to this day continue to feast the birth and the baptism together on January 6, and to regard the normal Christian practice as heretical. An exact date for the establishment of the Roman feast cannot be given, for the theory which ascribed it to Pope Liberius in 353 has been shown to be baseless [3]. But it appears from a document of 336 that the beginning of the liturgical year then already fell between December 8 and

ungen, i, *Das Weihnachtsfest* (1889); L. Duchesne, *Origines du Culte chrétien* (ed. 2, 1898), 247, and in *Bulletin critique* (1890), 41; F. C. Conybeare, *The History of Christmas*, in *American Journal of Theology* (1899), iii. 1, and *Introduction* to *The Key of Truth* (1898); F. Cumont, *Textes et Monuments mithraïques*, i (1899), 342, 355. I have not been able to see an article praised by Mr. Conybeare, in P. de Lagarde, *Mittheilungen* (1890), iv. 241.

[1] Conybeare, *Am. J. Th.* iii. 7, cites, without giving exact references, two 'north Italian homilies' of the fourth century, which seem to show this.

[2] *Sermo* ccii (*P.L.* xxxviii. 1033).

[3] The *depositio martyrum*, attached to the *Fasti* of Philocalus drawn up in 354, opens with the entry 'viii kl. ianu. natus Christus in Bethleem Iudeae.' December 25 was therefore kept as the birthday at least as early as 353. Usener, i. 267, argued that the change must have taken place in this very year, because Liberius, while veiling Mar-

cellina, the sister of St. Ambrose, on the Epiphany, spoke of the day as 'natalem Sponsi tui' (*de Virginibus*, iii. 1, in *P.L.* xvi. 219). But it is not proved either that this event took place in 363, or that it was on Epiphany rather than Christmas day. Liberius refers to the Marriage at Cana and the Feeding of the Five Thousand. But the first allusion is directly led up to by the *sponsalia* of Marcellina, and both events, although at a later date commemorated at Epiphany, may have belonged to Christmas at Rome, before Epiphany made its appearance (Duchesne, *Bulletin critique* (1890), 41). Usener adds that Liberius built the *Basilica Liberii*, also known as *Sta. Maria ad Praesepe* or *Sta. Maria Maggiore*, which is still a great station for the Christmas ceremonies, in honour of the new feast. But Duchesne shows that the dedication to St. Mary only dates from a rebuilding in the fifth century, that the *praesepe* cannot be traced there before the seventh, and that the original Christmas *statio* was at St. Peter's.

27 [1]. Christmas may, therefore, be assumed to have been in existence at least by 336.

It would seem, then, that the fourth century witnessed the establishment, both at Rome and elsewhere, of Christmas and Epiphany as two distinct feasts, whereas only one, although probably not everywhere the same one, had been known before. This fact is hardly to be explained by a mere attempt to accommodate varying local uses. The tradition of the Armenian doctors, who stood out against Christmas, asserts that their opponents removed the birthday of Christ from January 6 out of 'disobedience [2].' This points to a doctrinal reason for the separate celebration of the birth and the baptism. And such a reason may perhaps be found in the Adoptionist controversies. The joint feast appeared to lend credence to the view, considered a heresy, but still adhered to by the Armenian Church, that Christ was God, not from his mother's womb, but only from his adoption or spiritual birth at the baptism in Jordan. It was needful that orthodox Christians should celebrate him as divine from the very moment of his carnal birth [3].

The choice of December 25 as the day for the Roman feast cannot be supposed to rest upon any authentic tradition as to the historic date of the Nativity. It is one of several early

---

[1] Duchesne, *Bulletin critique* (1890), 44. This document also belongs to the collection of Philocalus.

[2] Conybeare, *Key of Truth*, clii–clvii, quoting an Armenian bishop Hippolytus in *Bodl. Armen. Marsh* 467, f. 338ᵃ, 'as many as were disobedient have divided the two feasts.' According to the *Catechism of the Syrian Doctors* in the same MS., Sahak asked Afrem why the churches feast Dec. 25: the teacher replied, 'The Roman world does so from idolatry, because of the worship of the Sun. And on the 25th of Dec., which is the first of Qanûn; when the day made a beginning out of the darkness they feasted the Sun with great joy, and declared that day to be the nuptials [? 'natals,' but cf. p. 241, n. 1] of the

Sun. However, when the Son of God was born of the Virgin, they celebrated the same feast, although they had turned from their idols to God. And when their bishops (*or* primates) saw this, they proceeded to take the Feast of the Birth of Christ, which was on the sixth of January, and placed it there (viz. on Dec. 25). And they abrogated the feast of the Sun, because it (the Sun) was nothing, as we said before.' Mommsen, *C. I. L.* i². 338, quotes to the same effect another *Scriptor Syrus* (in Assemanus, *Bibl. Orient.* ii. 164): cf. p. 235. The early apologists (Tertullian, *Apol.* 16; *ad Nationes*, i. 13; Origen, *contra Celsum*, viii. 67) defend Christianity against pagan charges of Sun-worship.

[3] Conybeare, *J. Am. Th.* iii. 8.

patristic guesses on the subject. It is not at all improbable that it was determined by an attempt to adopt some of the principal Christian festivals to the solstices and equinoxes of the Roman calendar[1]. The enemies of Roman orthodoxy were not slow to assert that it merely continued under another name the pagan celebration of the birthday of *Sol Invictus*[2]. Nor was the suggestion entirely an empty one.

[1] Most of these dates were in the spring (Duchesne, 247). As late as †243 the Pseudo-Cyprianic *de Pascha computus* gives March 28. On the other hand, December 25 is given early in the third century by Hippolytus, *Comm. super Danielem*, iv. 23 (p. 243, ed. Bonwetsch, 1897), although the text has been suspected of interpolation (Hilgenfeld, in *Berlin. phil. Wochenschrift*, 1897, p. 1324, s.). Ananias of Shirak (†600–50), *Hom. de Nat.* (transl. in *Expositor*, Nov. 1890), says that the followers of Cerinthus first separated the birth and baptism: cf. Conybeare, *Key of Truth*, cliv. This is further explained by Paul of Taron (ob. 1123), *adv. Theopistum*, 222 (quoted Conybeare, clvi), who says that Artemon calculated the dates of the Annunciation as March 25 and the Birth as December 25, 'the birth, not however of the Divine Being, but only of the mere man.' Both Cerinthus (end of 1st cent.) and Artemon (†202–17) appear to have held Adoptionist tenets: cf. Schaff, iv. 465, 574. Paul adds that Artemon calculated the dates from those for the conception and nativity of John the Baptist. This implies that St. John Baptist's day was already June 24 by †200. It was traditional on that day by St. Augustine's time, 'Hoc maiorum traditione suscepimus' (*Sermo* ccxcii. 1, in Migne, *P. L.* xxxviii. 1320). The six months' interval between the two nativities may be inferred from *St. Luke* i. 26. St. Augustine refers to the symbolism of their relation to each other, and quotes with regard to their position on the solstices the words ascribed to the Baptist in

St. John iii. 30 'illum oportet crescere, me autem minui' (*Sermo* cxciv. 2; cclxxxvii. 3; cclxxxviii. 5; Migne, *P. L.* xxxviii. 1016, 1302, 1306). Duchesne, 250, conjectures that the varying dates of West (Dec. 25) and East (Jan. 6) depended on a similar variation in the date assigned to the Passion, it being assumed in each case that the life of Christ must have been a complete circle, and that therefore he must have died on the anniversary of his conception in the womb. Thus St. Augustine (*in Heptat.* ii. 90) upbraids the Jews, 'non coques agnum in lacte matris suae.' March 25 was widely accepted for the Passion from Tertullian onwards, and certain Montanists held to the date of April 6. Astronomy makes it impossible that March 25 can be historically correct, and therefore the whole calculation, if Duchesne is right, probably started from an arbitrary identification of a Christian date with the spring equinox, just as, if Ananias of Shirak is right, it started from a similar identification of another such date with the summer solstice. But it seems just as likely that the birth was fixed first, and the Annunciation and St. John Baptist's day calculated back from that. If the Passion had been the starting-point, would not the feast of Christmas, as distinct from the traditional date for the event, have become a movable one?

[2] The Armenian criticism just quoted only re-echoes that put by St. Augustine in the mouth of the Manichaeans in *Contra Faustum*, xx. 4 (*Corp. Script. Eccl.* xxv) 'Faustus dixit... solemnes gentium

The worshippers of *Sol Invictus*, and in particular the Mithraic sect, were not quite on the level of the ordinary pagans by tradition. Mithraism had claims to be a serious and reasonable rival to Christianity, and if its adherents could be induced by argument to merge their worship of the physical sun in that of the 'Sun of Righteousness,' they were well worth winning[1]. On the other hand there were obvious dangers in the Roman policy which were not wholly averted, and we find Leo the Great condemning certain superstitious customs amongst his flock which it is difficult to distinguish from the sun-worship practised alike by pagans and by Saint Augustine's heretical opponents, the Manichaeans[2].

dies cum ipsis celebratis ut Kalendas et solstitia.' Augustine answers other criticisms of the same order in the course of the book, but he does not take up this one.

[1] Augustine, in his sermons, uses a solar symbolism in two ways, besides drawing the parallel with St. John already quoted. Christ is *lux e tenebris*: 'quoniam ipsa infidelitas quae totum mundum vice noctis obtexerat, minuenda fuerat fide crescente; ideo die Natalis Domini nostri Iesu Christi, et nox incipit perpeti detrimenta, et dies sumere augmenta' (*Sermo* cxc. 1 in *P. L.* xxxviii. 1007). He is also *sponsus procedens de thalamo suo* (*Sermo* cxcii. 3; cxcv. 3, in *P. L.* xxxviii. 1013, 1018). Following this Caesarius or another calls Christmas the *dies nuptialis Christi*, on which 'sponsae suae Ecclesiae adiunctus est' (*Serm. Pseudo-Aug.* cxvi. 2, in *P. L.* xxxix. 1975). Cumont, i. 355, gives other examples of *Le Soleil Symbole du Christ* from an early date, and especially of the use of the phrase *Sol Iustitiae* from *Malachi*, iv. 2.

[2] Pseudo-Chrysostom (Italian, 4th cent.), *de solstitiis et aequinoctiis* (*Op.* Chrys. ed. 1588, ii. 118) 'Sed et dominus nascitur mense Decembri, hiemis tempore, viii kal. Ianuarias . . . Sed et invicti natalem appellant. Quis utique tam invictus nisi dominus noster qui Mortem subactam devicit? vel quod dicant Solis esse natalem, ipse est Sol iustitiae de quo Malachias propheta dixit'; St. Augustine, *Sermo* cxc. 1 (*P. L.* xxxviii. 1007) 'habeamus, igitur, fratres, solemnem istum diem; non sicut infideles propter hunc solem, sed propter eum qui fecit hunc solem'; *Tract. in Iohann.* xxxiv. 2 (*P. L.* xxxv. 1652) 'numquid forte Dominus Christus est Sol iste qui ortu et occasu peragit diem? Non enim defuerunt heretici qui ita senserunt . . . (c. 4) ne quis carnaliter sapiens solem istum intelligendum putaret'; Pseudo-Ambrose (perhaps Maximus of Turin, †412–65), *Sermo* vi. (*P. L.* xvii. 614) 'bene quodammodo sanctum hunc diem natalis Domini solem novum vulgus appellat . . . quod libenter nobis amplectendum est; quia oriente Salvatore non solum humani generis salus, sed etiam solis ipsius claritas innovatur'; Leo Magnus, *Sermo* xxii, *in Nativ. Dom.* (*P. L.* liv. 198) 'Ne idem ille tentator, cuius iam a vobis dominationem Christus exclusit, aliquibus vos iterum seducat insidiis, et haec ipsa praesentis diei gaudia suae fallaciae arte corrumpat, illudens simplicioribus animis de quorumdam persuasione pestifera, quibus haec dies solemnitatis nostrae

From Rome the Christmas feast gradually made its way over East and West. It does not seem to have reached Jerusalem until at least the sixth century, and, as we have seen, the outlying Church of Armenia never adopted it. But it was established at Antioch about 375 and at Alexandria about 430 [1]. At Constantinople an edict of 400 included it in the list of holy days upon which *ludi* must not be held [2]. In 506 the council of Agatha recognized the Nativity as one of the great days of the Christian year [3], while fasting on that day was forbidden by the council of Braga in 561 as savouring of Priscillianist heresy [4]. The feast of the Epiphany, meanwhile, was relegated to a secondary place; but it was not forgotten, and served as a celebration, in addition to the baptism, of a number of events in the life of Christ, which included the marriage at Cana and the feeding of the five

non tam de nativitate Christi quam de novi, ut dicunt, solis ortu honorabilis videatur'; *Sermo* xxvii, *in Nat. Dom.* (*P. L.* liv. 218) 'De talibus institutis etiam illa generatur impietas ut sol in inchoatione diurnae lucis exsurgens a quibusdam insipientioribus de locis eminentioribus adoretur; quod nonnulli etiam Christiani adeo se religiose facere putant, ut priusquam ad B. Petri apostoli basilicam, quae uni Deo vivo et vero est dedicata, perveniant, superatis gradibus quibus ad suggestum areae superioris ascenditur, converso corpore ad nascentem se solem reflectant, et curvatis cervicibus, in honorem se splendidi orbis inclinent. Quod fieri partim ignorantiae vitio, partim paganitatis spiritu, multum tabescimus et dolemus.' Eusebius, *Sermo* xxii. περὶ ἀστρονόμων (*P. G.* lxxxvi. 453), also refers to the adoration of the sun by professing Christians. The 'tentator' of Leo and the 'heretici' of Augustine are probably Manichaeus and his followers, against whose sun-worship Augustine argues at length in *Contra Faustum*, xx (*Corp. Script. Eccl.* xxv).

[1] Duchesne, 248.
[2] Cf. p. 14.

[3] *C. Agathense*, c. 21 (Mansi, viii. 328) 'Pascha vero, natale domini, epiphania, ascensionem domini, pentecostem, et natalem S. Ioannis Baptistae, vel si qui maximi dies in festivitatibus habentur, non nisi in civitatibus aut in parochiis teneant.'
[4] *Conc. Bracarense* (†560), Prop. 4 (Mansi, ix. 775) 'Si quis natalem Christi secundum carnem non bene honorat, sed honorare se simulat, ieiunans in eodem die, et in dominico; quia Christum in vera hominis natura natum esse non credit, sicut Cerdon, Marcion, Manichaeus, et Priscillianus, anathema sit.' A similar prohibition is given by Gregory II (†725), *Capitulare*, c. 10 (*P. L.* lxxxix. 534). To failings in the opposite direction the Church was more tender: cf. *Penitentiale Theodori* (Haddan and Stubbs, iii. 177), *de Crapula et Ebrietate* 'Si vero pro infirmitate aut quia longo tempore se abstinuerit, et in consuetudine non erit ei multum bibere vel manducare, aut pro gaudio in Natale Domini aut in Pascha aut pro alicuius Sanctorum commemoratione faciebat, et tunc plus non accipit quam decretum est a senioribus, nihil nocet. Si episcopus iuberit, non nocet illi, nisi ipse similiter faciat.'

thousand, and of which the visit of the *Magi* gradually became the leading feature. The *Dodecahemeron*, or period of twelve days, linking together Christmas and Epiphany, was already known to Ephraim Syrus as a festal tide at the end of the fourth century [1], and was declared to be such by the council of Tours in 567 [2].

To these islands Christmas came, if not with the Keltic Church, at least with St. Augustine in 592. On Christmas day, 598, more than ten thousand English converts were baptized [3], and by the time of Bede († 734) Christmas was established, with Epiphany and Easter, as one of the three leading festivals of the year [4]. The *Laws* of Ethelred (991–1016) and of Edward the Confessor ordain it a holy tide of peace and concord [5]. Continental Germany received it from the synod of Mainz in 813 [6], while Norway owed it to King Hakon the Good in the middle of the tenth century [7].

Side by side with the establishment of Christmas proceeded the ecclesiastical denunciation of those pagan festivals whose place it was to take. Little is heard in Christian times of the *Saturnalia*, which do not seem to have shared the popularity of the Kalends outside the limits of Rome itself. But these latter, and especially the Kalends, are the subject of attack in every corner of the empire. Jerome of Rome, Ambrose of Milan, Maximus of Turin, Chrysologus of Ravenna, assail them in Italy; Augustine in Africa; Chrysostom and Asterius and the Trullan council in the East. In Spain, Bishop Pacian of Barcelona made a treatise upon one of the most objectionable features of the festival which, as he says with some humour, probably tended to increase its vogue. In Gaul, Caesarius of Arles initiated a vigorous campaign. To cite all the ecclesiastical pro-

[1] Tille, *Y. and C.* 122.

[2] Cf. Appendix N, No. xxii.

[3] *Epist. Gregorii ad Eulogium* (Haddan and Stubbs, iii. 12).

[4] *Epist. Bedae ad Egbertum* (Haddan and Stubbs, iii. 323).

[5] *Leges Ethelredi* (Thorpe, *Ancient Laws*, i. 309) 'Ordâl and âdhar sindon tocweden . . . fram Adventum Domini odh octavas Epiphanie. . . . And beo tham hâl-gum tîdan eal swa hit riht is, eallum cristenum mannum sib and sôm gemæne, and ælc sacu getwæmed.' Cf. *Leges Edwardi* (Thorpe, i. 443).

[6] *C. Moguntiacum*, c. 36 (Mansi, xiv. 73) 'In natali Domini dies quatuor, octavas Domini, epiphaniam Domini.'

[7] Tille, *Y. and C.* 203.

nouncements on the subject would be tedious. Homily
followed homily, canon followed canon, capitulary followed
capitulary, penitential followed penitential, for half a thousand
years. But the Kalends died hard. When Boniface was
tackling them amongst the Franks in the middle of the
eighth century, he was sorely hampered by the bad example
of their continued prevalence at the very gates of the Vatican;
and when Burchardus was making his collection of heathen
observances in the eleventh century, those of the Kalends
were still to be included. In England there is not much heard
of them, but a reference in the so-called *Penitential of Egbert*
about 766 proves that they were not unknown. It need hardly
be said that all formal religious celebration of the Kalends
disappeared with the official victory of Christianity. But this
element had never been of great importance in the feast; and
the terms in which the ecclesiastical references from beginning
to end are couched prove that they relate mainly to popular
New Year customs common to the Germanic and the more
completely Latinized populations[1].

It appears from a decree of the council of Tours in 567 that,
ad calcandam Gentilium consuetudinem, the fourth-century
Fathers established on the first three days of January a
triduum ieiunii, with litanies, in spite of the fact that these
days fell in the very midst of the festal period of the
Dodecahemeron[2]. At the same time January 1 was kept
as the octave of Christmas, and the early Roman ritual-
books show two masses for that day, one *in octavis Domini*,
the other *ad prohibendum ab idolis*. The Jewish custom by
which circumcision took place eight days after birth made it
almost inevitable that there should be some celebration of the
circumcision of Christ upon the octave of his Nativity. This
was the case from the sixth century, and ultimately, about
the eighth, the attempt to keep up a fast on January 1 was
surrendered, and the festival of the Circumcision took its
place[3].

Some tendency was shown by the Church not merely to

[1] Cf. the collection of prohibitions in Appendix N.
[2] *C. of Tours*, c. 18 (Appendix

N, No. xxii).
[3] R. Sinker, in *D. C. A.* s. v.
Circumcision.

set up Christmas as a rival to the pagan winter feasts, but also to substitute it for the Kalends of January as the beginning of the year. But the innovation never affected the civil year, and was not maintained even by ecclesiastical writers with any consistency, for even they prefer in many cases a year dating from the Annunciation, or more rarely from Easter. The so-called Annunciation style found favour even for many civil purposes in Great Britain, and was not finally abandoned until 1753[1]. But although Christmas cannot be said to have ever become a popular New Year's day, yet its festal importance and its propinquity to January 1 naturally led to a result undesired and possibly undreamt of by its founders, namely, the further transference to it of many of the long-suffering Germano-Keltic folk-customs, which had already travelled under Roman influence from the middle of November to the beginning of January[2]. Already in the sixth century it had become necessary to forbid the abuses which had gathered around the celebration of Christmas eve[3]; and the Christmas customs of to-day, even where their name does not testify to their original connexion with the Kalends[4], are in a large number of

---

[1] On this difficult subject see Tille, *Y. and C.* 134; H. Grotefend, *Taschenbuch der Zeitrechnung* (1898), 11; F. Ruhl, *Chronologie des Mittelalters und der Neuzeit* (1897), 23; C. Plummer, *Anglo-Saxon Chronicle*, ii. cxxix; R. L. Poole, in *Eng. Hist. Review* (1901), 719.

[2] The position of Christmas would have made it natural that it should attract observances from the spring festivals also, and, in fact, it did attract the Mummers' play: cf. p. 226. It cannot of course be positively said whether the Epiphany fires and some of the other agricultural rites to be presently mentioned (ch. xii) came from the November or the ploughing festival.

[3] C. of Auxerre (573–603), c. 11 (Appendix N. No. xxv).

[4] In the south of France Christmas is *Chalendes*, in Provence *Calendas* or *Calenos*. The log is *calignau*, *chalendau*, *chalendal*, *calignaon*, or *culenos*, and the peasants sang round it 'Calène vient' (Tille, *D. W.* 286; Müller, 475, 478). Thiers, i. 264, speaks of 'le pain de Calende.' Christmas songs used to be known in Silesia as *Kolendelieder* (Tille, *D. W.* 287). The Lithuanian term for Christmas is *Kalledos* and the Czechic *Koleda* (Polish *Kolenda*, Russian *Koljada*). A verb *colendisare* appears as a Bohemian law term (Tille, *Y. and C.* 84); while in the fourteenth century the Christmas *quête* at Prague was known as the *Koledasammeln* (Tille, *D. W.* 112). The Bohemian Christmas procession described by Alsso (cf. ch. xii) was called *Calendizatio*, and according to tradition St Adalbert (tenth century) transferred it from the Kalends to Christmas, and called it *colendizatio* '*a colendo*.'

cases, so far of course as they are not simply ecclesiastical, merely doublets of those of the New Year.

What is true of Christmas is true also of Epiphany or Twelfth night ; and the history of the other modern festivals of the winter cycle is closely parallel. The old Germanic New Year's day on November 11 became the day of St. Martin, a fourth-century bishop of Tours, and the *pervigiliae* of St. Martin, like those of the Nativity itself, already caused a scandal in the sixth century [1]. The observances of the deferred days of slaughter clustered round the feasts of St. Andrew on November 30, and more especially St. Nicholas on December 6. The *Todtenfest*, which had strayed to the beginning of November, was continued in the feasts of All Saints or Hallowmas, the French *Toussaint*, on November 1, and its charitable supplement of All Souls, on November 2. That which had strayed still further to the time of harvest became the *Gemeinwoche* or week-wake, and ultimately St. Michael and All Angels. Nor is this all. Very similar customs attached themselves to the minor feasts of the *Dodecahemeron*, St. Stephen's, St. John the Evangelist's, Innocents' days, to the numerous dedication wakes that fell on days, such as St. Luke's [2], in autumn or early winter, or to the miscellaneous feasts closely approaching the Christmas season, St. Clement's, St. Catherine's, St. Thomas's, with which indeed in many localities that season is popularly supposed to begin [3]. Nor was this process sensibly affected by the establishment in the sixth century of the *ieiunium* known as Advent, which stretched for a *Quadragesima*, or period

[1] *C. of Auxerre* (573–603), c. 5 (Appendix N, No. xxv). Pfannenschmidt, 498, has collected a number of notices of *Martinalia* from the tenth century onwards.

[2] Pfannenschmidt, 279; Dyer, 386, describe the 'Horn Fair' at Charlton, Kent, on St. Luke's Day, Oct. 18. A king and queen were chosen, who went in procession to the church, wearing horns. The visitors wore masks or women's clothes, and played practical jokes with water. Rams' horns were sold at the fair, which lasted three days,

and the gilt on the gingerbread took the same shape. It will be remembered that the symbol of St. Luke in Christian art is a horned ox.

[3] Cf. p. 114. According to Spence, 196, the Shetland Christmas begins on St. Thomas's Day and ends on Jan. 18, known as 'Four and Twenty Day.' Candlemas (Feb. 2) is also often regarded as the end of the Christmas season. The Anglo-Saxon Christmas feast lasted to the Octave of Epiphany (Tille, *Y and C.* 165).

of forty days, from Martinmas onwards. And finally, just as in May village dipping customs attached themselves in the seventeenth century to Royal Oak day, so in the same century we find the winter festival fires turned to new account in the celebration of the escape of King and Parliament from the nefarious machinations of Guy Fawkes.

CHAPTER XII

NEW YEAR CUSTOMS

[*Bibliographical Note.*—The two works of Dr. Tille remain of importance. The compilations specially devoted to the usages of the Christmas season are chiefly of a popular character; W. Sandys, *Christmas Tide* (n.d.), J. Ashton, *A Righte Merrie Christmasse!!!*(n. d.), and, for French data, E. Müller, *Le Jour de l'An* (n. d.), may be mentioned; H. Usener, *Religionsgeschichtliche Untersuchungen*, vol. ii (1889), prints various documents, including the *Largum Sero* of a Bohemian priest named Alsso, on early fifteenth-century Christmas eve customs. Most of the books named in the bibliographical note to chap. v also cover the subject. A *Bibliography of Christmas* runs through *Notes and Queries*, 6th series, vi. 506, viii. 491, x. 492, xii. 489; 7th series, ii. 502, iii. 152, iv. 502, vi. 483, x. 502, xii. 483; 8th series, ii. 505, iv. 502, vi. 483, viii. 483, x. 512, xii. 502; 9th series, ii. 505, iv. 515, vi. 485.]

IT is the outcome of the last chapter that all the folk-customs of the winter half of the year, from Michaelmas to Plough Monday, must be regarded as the flotsam and jetsam of a single original feast. This was a New Year's feast, held by the Germano-Keltic tribes at the beginning of the central European winter when the first snows fell about the middle of November, and subsequently dislocated and dispersed by the successive clash of Germano-Keltic civilization with the rival schemes of Rome and of Christianity. A brief summary of the customs in question will show clearly their common character. For purposes of classification they may be divided into several groups. There are such customs belonging to the agricultural side of the old winter feast as have not been transferred with the growing importance of tillage to the feast of harvest. There are the customs of its domestic side, as a feast of the family hearth and of the dead ancestors. There are the distinctively New Year customs of omen and prognostication for the approaching twelve months. There are the customs of play, common more or less to all the village festivals. And, finally, there are a small number of customs, or perhaps it would be truer to say legends, which appear to owe their origin not merely to heathenism transformed by Christianity, but to Christianity itself. Each of these groups may well claim a more thoroughgoing consideration than can here be given to any one of them.

The agricultural customs are just those of the summer feasts over again. Once more the fertilization spirit is abroad in the land. The embodiment of it in vegetation takes several forms. Obviously the last foliage and burgeoning flowers of spring and summer are no longer available. But there is, to begin with, the sheaf of corn or 'harvest-May' in which the spirit appeared at harvest, and which is called upon once more to play its part in the winter rites. This, however, is not a very marked part. A Yorkshire custom of hanging a sheaf on the church door at Christmas is of dubious origin[1]. But Swedish and Danish peasants use the grain of the 'last sheaf' to bake the Christmas cake, and both in Scandinavia and Germany the 'Yule straw' serves various superstitious purposes. It is scattered on barren fields to make them productive. It is strewed, instead of rushes, upon the house floor and the church floor. It is laid in the mangers of the cattle. Fruit-trees are tied together with straw ropes, that they may bear well and are said to be 'married[2].'

More naturally the fertilization spirit may be discerned at the approach of winter in such exceptional forms of vegetation as endure the season. In November the apples and the nuts still hang upon their boughs, and these are traditional features in the winter celebrations. Then there are the evergreens. Libanius, Tertullian, and Chrysostom tell how on the Kalends the doors of houses throughout the Roman empire were crowned with bay. Martin of Braga forbade the 'pagan observance' in a degree which found its way into the canon law. The original *strena* which men gave one another on the same day for luck was nothing but a twig plucked from a sacred grove; and still in the fifth century men

---

[1] Dyer, 451; Ashton, 118, where the custom is said to have been 'started by the Rev. J. Kenworthy, Rector of Ackworth, in Yorkshire, ... for the special benefit of the birds.'

[2] Frazer, i. 177, ii. 172, 286; Grimm, iv. 1783; Tille, *D. W.* 50, 178; Alsso, in Usener, ii. 61, 65.

returned from their new year auguries laden with *ramusculi*
that they might thereafter be laden with wealth[1]. It is not
necessary to dwell upon the surviving use of evergreens in
the decoration at Christmas of houses and churches[2]. The
sacredness of these is reflected in the taboo which enjoins
that they shall not be cast out upon the dust-heap, but shall,
when some appropriate day, such as Candlemas, arrives, be
solemnly committed to the flames[3]. Obviously amongst
other evergreens the holly and the ivy, with their clustering
pseudo-blossoms of coral and of jet, are the more adequate
representatives of the fertilization spirit[4]; most of all the
mistletoe, perched an alien visitant, faintly green and white,
amongst the bared branches of apple or of oak. The mistletoe has its especial place in Scandinavian myth[5]: Pliny
records the ritual use of it by the Druids[6]; it is essential to
the winter revels in their amorous aspect; and its vanished
dignities still serve, here to bar it from, there to make it imperative in, the edifices of Christian worship[7]. A more artificial
embodiment of the fertilization spirit is the 'Christmas tree'

[1] Lipenius, 423; cf. Appendix N, Nos. i, vi, xiii, xxiv.

[2] Tille, *Y. and C.* 103, 174; Philpot, 164; Jackson and Burne, 397; Dyer, 457; Stow, *Survey of London* (ed. 1618), 149 'Against the feast of Christmas, euery mans house, as also their parish Churches, were decked with Holm, Iuy, Bayes, and whatsoever the season of the yeere aforded to be greene. The Conduits and Standards in the streetes were, likewise, garnished.' He gives an example from 1444.

[3] Burne-Jackson, 245, 397, 411; Ashton, 95. Customs vary: here the evergreens must be burnt; there given to the cattle. They should not touch the ground (Grimm, iii. 1207). With this taboo compare that described by ancient writers, probably on the authority of Posidonius, as existing in a cult of a god identified with Dionysus amongst the Namnites on the west coast of Gaul. A temple on an island was unroofed and reroofed by the priestesses annually. Did

one of them drop her materials on the ground, she was torn to pieces by her companions (Rhys, *C. H.* 196). They are replaced on Candlemas by snowdrops, or, according to Herrick, 'the greener box.' In Shropshire a garland made of blackthorn is left hanging from New Year to New Year, and then burnt in a festival fire (*F. L.* x. 489; xii. 349).

[4] The Christmas rivalry between holly and ivy is the subject of carols, some dating from the fifteenth century; cf. Ashton, 92; Burne-Jackson, 245.

[5] Grimm, iii. 1205.

[6] Pliny, *Nat. Hist.* xxi. 95.

[7] Ashton, 81, 92; Ditchfield, 18; Brand, i. 285; Dyer, 458; Philpot, 164. Mistletoe is the chief ingredient of the 'kissing-bunch,' sometimes a very elaborate affair, with apples and dolls hung in it. The ecclesiastical taboo is not universal; in York Minster, e.g., mistletoe was laid on the altar.

par excellence, adorned with lights and apples, and often with
a doll or image upon the topmost sprig. The first recorded
Christmas tree is at Strassburg in 1604. The custom is
familiar enough in modern England, but there can be little
doubt that here it is of recent introduction, and came in, in
fact, with the Hanoverians [1].

Finally, there can be little wonder that the popular
imagination found a special manifestation of the fertilization spirit in the unusual blossoming of particular trees or
species of trees in the depths of winter. In mild seasons
a crab or cherry might well adorn the old winter feast
in November. A favourable climate permits such a thing
even at mid-winter. Legend, at any rate, has no doubt of
the matter, and connects the event definitely with Christmas.
A tenth-century Arabian geographer relates how all the trees
of the forest stand in full bloom on the holy night. In the
thirteenth-century *Vita* of St. Hadwigis the story is told of
a cherry-tree. A fifteenth-century bishop of Bamberg tells
it of two apple-trees, and to apple-trees the miracle belongs,
in German folk-belief, to this day [2]. In England the stories
of Christmas-flowering hawthorns or blackthorns are specific
and probably not altogether baseless [3]. The belief found a

---

[1] Tille, *Y. and C.* 174; *D. W.*
256, and in *F. L.* iii. 166; Philpot,
164; Ashton, 189; Kempe, *Loseley
MSS.* 75. The earliest English
mention is in 1789.

[2] Tille, *Y. and C.* 170.

[3] Ibid. 172; Ashton, 105, quoting
Aubrey, *Natural Hist. of Wilts*,
'Mr. Anthony Hinton, one of the
officers of the Earle of Pembroke,
did inoculate, not long before the
late civill warres (ten yeares or
more), a bud of Glastonbury Thorne,
on a thorne, at his farm house, at
Wilton, which blossoms at Christmas, as the other did. My mother
has had branches of them for a
flower-pott, several Christmasses,
which I have seen. Elias Ashmole,
Esq., in his notes upon *Theatrum
Chymicum*, saies that in the churchyard at Glastonbury grew a walnutt
tree, that did putt out young leaves
at Christmas, as doth the King's

Oake in the New Forest. In Par-
ham Park, in Suffolk (Mr. Bou-
tele's), is a pretty ancient thorne,
that blossomes like that at Glastonbury; the people flock hither to see
it on Christmas day. But in the
rode that leades from Worcester to
Droitwiche is a black thorne hedge
at Clayes, half a mile long or more,
that blossoms about Christmas-day
for a week or more together. Dr.
Ezerel Tong sayd that about
Rumly-Marsh in Kent, are thornes
naturally like that near Glastonbury. The Soldiers did cutt downe
that near Glastonbury: the stump
remaines.' Specimens are still found
about Glastonbury of *Crataegus
oxyacantha praecox*, a winter-
flowering variety of hawthorn: some
of the alleged slips from the Glastonbury thorn appear, however, to
be *Prunus communis*, or blackthorn. A writer in the *Gentleman's*

special location at Glastonbury, where the famous thorn is said by William of Malmesbury and other writers to have budded from the staff of Joseph of Arimathea, who there ended his wanderings with the Holy Grail. Where winter-flowering trees are not found, a custom sometimes exists of putting a branch of cherry or of hawthorn in water some weeks before Christmas in order that it may blossom and serve as a substitute [1].

It may fairly be conjectured that at the winter, as at the summer feast, the fertilization spirit, in the form of bush or idol, was borne about the fields. The fifteenth-century writer, Alsso, records the *calendisationes* of the god Bel in Bohemia, suppressed by St. Adalbert [2]. In modern England, a 'holly-bough' or 'wesley-bob,' with or without an image or doll, occasionally goes its rounds [3]. But a definite lustration of the bounds is rare [4], and, for the most part, the winter procession either is merely riotous or else, like too many of the summer processions themselves, has been converted, under the successive influence of the *strenae* and the cash nexus, into little more than a *quête*. Thus children and the poor go 'souling' for apples and 'soul-cakes' on All Souls' day; on November 5 they collect for the 'guy'; on November 11 in Germany, if not in England, for St. Martin; on St. Clement's day (November 23) they go 'clemencing'; on St. Catherine's (November 25) 'catherning.' Wheat is the coveted boon on St. Thomas's day (December 21) or 'doling day,' and the *quête* is variously known as 'thomasing,' 'mumping,' 'corn-ing,' 'gooding,' 'hodening,' or 'hooding [5].' Christmas brings

---

Magazine for 1753 reports that the opponents of the 'New Style' introduced in 1752 were encouraged by the refusal of the thorns at Glastonbury and Quainton in Buckinghamshire to flower before Old Christmas day. A Somerset woman told a writer in 3 *N. Q.* ix. 33 that the buds of the thorns burst into flower at midnight on Christmas Eve, 'As they comed out, you could hear 'um haffer.'

[1] Tille, *Y. and C.* 175.

[2] Usener, ii. 61. Alsso says that St. Adalbert substituted a crucifix

for the idol, and the cry of 'Vele, Vele,' for that of 'Bely, Bely.'

[3] Ashton, 244; Dyer, 483; Ditchfield, 15. The dolls sometimes represent the Virgin and Child. 'Wesley-bob' and the alternative 'vessel-cup' appear to be corruptions of 'wassail.'

[4] Cf., however, the Burghead ceremony (p. 256).

[5] Brand, i. 217; Burne-Jackson, 381; Dyer, 405; Ditchfield, 25, 161; Northall, 216; Henderson, 66; Haddon, 476; Pfannenschmidt, 206. The *N. E. D.* plausibly ex-

'wassailing' with its bowl of lamb's-wool and its bobbing apple, and this is repeated on New Year's day or eve[1]. The New Year *quête* is probably the most widespread and popular of all. Ducange records it at Rome[2]. In France it is known as *l'Aguilaneuf*[3], in Scotland and the north of England as Hogmanay, terms in which the philologists meet problems still unsolved[4]. Other forms of the winter *quête*

plains 'gooding,' which seems to be used of any of these *quêtes* as 'wishing good,' and 'hooding' may be a corruption of this.

[1] Brand, i. 1; Dyer, 501; Ditchfield, 42; Northall, 183. Skeat derives *wassail*, M.E. *wasseyl*, 'a health-drinking,' from N.E. *wæs hǽl*, A.-S. *wes hál*, 'be whole.'

[2] Ducange, *Gloss.* s. v. Kalendae Ianuarii, quoting *Cerem. Rom. ad calcem Cod. MS. eccl. Camerac.* 'Hii sunt ludi Romani communes in Kalendis Ianuarii. In vigilia Kalendarum in sero surgunt pueri, et portant scutum. Quidam eorum est larvatus cum maza in collo; sibilando sonant timpanum, eunt per domos, circumdant scutum, timpanum sonat, larva sibilat. Quo ludo finito, accipiunt munus a domino domus, secundum quod placet ei. Sic faciunt per unamquamque domum. Eo die de omnibus leguminibus comedunt. Mane autem surgunt duo pueri ex illis, accipiunt ramos olivae et sal, et intrant per domos, salutant domum : Gaudium et laetitia sit in hac domo; tot filii, tot porcelli, tot agni, et de omnibus bonis optant, et antequam sol oriatur, comedunt vel favum mellis, vel aliquid dulce, ut totus annus procedat eis dulcis, sine lite et labore magno.'

[3] Du Tilliot, 67, quoting J. B. Thiers, *Traité des jeux et des divertissemens*, 452; Müller, 103. There are some Guillaneu songs in Bujeaud, ii. 153. The *quête* was prohibited by two synods of Angers in 1595 and 1668.

[4] Brand, i. 247; Dyer, 505; Ditchfield, 44; Ashton, 217; Northall, 181; Henderson, 76; Tille, *Y. and C.* 204; Nicholson, *Gol-*

spie, 100; Rhys, in *F. L.* ii. 308. Properly speaking, ' Hogmanay' is the gift of an oaten farl asked for in the *quête*. It is also applied to the day on which the *quête* takes place, which is in Scotland generally New Year's Eve. Besides the *quête*, Hogmanay night, like Halloween elsewhere, is the night for horse-play and practical joking. The name appears in many forms, ' Hogmana,' ' Hogomanay,' ' Nog-money ' (Scotland), ' Hogmina ' (Cumberland), ' Hagmena ' (Northumberland), ' Hagman heigh !' ' Hagman ha!' (Yorkshire), ' Agganow ' (Lancashire), ' Hob dy naa,' ' Hob ju naa' (Isle of Man). It is generally accepted as equivalent to the French *aguilanneuf, aguilanleu, guillaneu, hagui men lo, hoquinano*, &c., ad infin., the earliest form being *aguilanleu* (1353). With the Scotch

> ' Hogmanay,
> Trollolay,
> Give us of your white bread and
>   none of your grey'!

may be compared the French,

> ' Tire lire,
> Maint de blanc, et point du bis.'

On no word has amateur philology been more riotous. It has been derived from ' au gui menez,' ' à gui l'an neuf,' ' au gueux menez,' ' Hálig monath,' ἁγία μήνη, ' Homme est né,' and the like. Tille thinks that the whole of December was formerly Hogmanay, and derives from *monâth* and either **hoggva*, ' hew,' *hag*, ' witch,' or *hog*, ' pig.' Nicholson tries the other end, and traces *auguilanleu* to the Spanish *aguinaldo* or *aguilando*, ' a New Year's gift.' This in turn he makes the gerund of **aguilar*, an assumed corruption of *alquilar*, ' to hire one-will crop up presently, and the visits of the guisers with their play or song, the carol singers and the waits may be expected at any time during the Christmas season. As at the summer *quêtes*, some reminiscence of the primitive character of the processions is to be found in the songs sung, with their wish of prosperity to the liberal household and their ill-will to the churl [1].

In the summer festivals both water-rites and fire-rites frequently occur. In those of winter, water-rites are comparatively rare, as might naturally be expected at a season when snow and ice prevail. There is some trace, however, of a custom of drawing 'new' water, as of making 'new' fire, for the new year [2]. Festival fires, on the other hand, are widely distributed, and agree in general features with those of summer. Their relation to the fertility of crop and herd is often plainly enough marked. They are perhaps most familiar to-day in the comparatively modern form of the Guy Fawkes celebration on November 5 [3], but they are known

self out.' Hogmanay will thus mean properly 'handsel' or 'hiring-money,' and the first Monday in the New Year is actually called in Scotland 'Handsel Monday.' This is plausible, but, although no philologist, I think a case might be made out for regarding the terms as corruptions of the Celtic *Nos Galan-gaeaf*, 'the night of the winter Calends' (Rhys, 514). This is All Saints' eve, while the Manx 'Hob dy naa' *quête* is on Hollantide (November 12 ; cf. p. 230).

[1] A Gloucestershire wassail song in Dixon, *Ancient Poems*, 199, ends, 'Come, butler, come bring us a bowl of the best :
I hope your soul in heaven will rest ;
But if you do bring us a bowl of the small,
Then down fall butler, bowl and all.'

[2] In Herefordshire and the south of Scotland it is lucky to draw 'the cream of the well' or 'the flower of the well,' i.e. the first pail of water after midnight on New Year's eve (Dyer, 7, 17). In Germany

Heilwag similarly drawn at Christmas is medicinal (Grimm, iv. 1810). Pembroke folk sprinkle each other on New Year's Day (*F. L.* iii. 263). St. Martin of Braga condemns amongst Kalends customs 'panem in fontem mittere (Appendix N, No. xxiii), and this form of well-cult survives at Christmas in the Tyrol (Jahn, 283) and in France (Müller, 500). Tertullian chaffs the custom of early bathing at the *Saturnalia* (Appendix N, No. ii). Gervase of Tilbury (ed. Liebrecht, ii. 12) mentions an English belief (†1200) in a wonder-working Christmas dew. This Tille (*Y. and C.* 168) thinks an outgrowth from the Advent chant *Rorate coeli*, but it seems closely parallel to the folk belief in May-dew.

[3] Burne-Jackson, 388; Simpson, 202; *F. L.* v. 38; Dyer, 410. The festival in its present form can only date from the reign of James I, but the Pope used to be burned in bonfires as early as 1570 upon the accession day of Elizabeth, Nov. 17 (Dyer, 422).

also on St. Crispin's day (October 25)[1], Hallow e'en[2], St. Martin's day[3], St. Thomas's day[4], Christmas eve[5], New Year[6], and Twelfth night[7]. An elaborate and typical example is the 'burning of the clavie' at the little fishing village of Burghead on the Moray Firth[8]. This takes place on New Year's eve, or, according to another account[9], Christmas eve (O.S.). Strangers to the village are excluded from any share in the ritual. The 'clavie' is a blazing tar-barrel hoisted on a pole. In making it, a stone must be used instead of a hammer, and must then be thrown away. Similarly, the barrel must be lit with a blazing peat, and not with lucifer matches. The bearers are honoured, and the bridegroom of the year gets the 'first lift.' Should a bearer stumble, it portends death to himself during the year and ill-luck to the town. The procession passes round the boundaries of Burghead, and formerly visited every boat in the harbour. Then it is carried to the top of a hillock called the 'Doorie,' down the sides of which it is finally rolled. Blazing brands are used to kindle the house fires, and the embers are preserved as charms.

The central heathen rite of sacrifice has also left its abundant traces upon winter custom. Bede records the significant name of *blôt-monath*, given to November by the still unconverted Anglo-Saxons[10]. The tradition of solemn slaughter hangs around both Martinmas and Christmas. 'Martlemas beef' in England, St. Martin's swine, hens, and geese in Germany, mark the former day[11]. At Christmas

---

[1] Dyer, 389 (Sussex).

[2] Brand, i. 210, 215 (Buchan, Perthshire, Aberdeenshire, North Wales).

[3] Pfannenschmidt, 207; Jahn, 240.

[4] Ashton, 47 (Isle of Man, where the day is called 'Fingan's Eve').

[5] Jahn, 253.

[6] *F. L.* xii. 349; W. Gregor, *Brit. Ass. Rept.* (1896), 620 (Minnigaff, Galloway; bones being saved up for this fire); Gomme, *Brit. Ass. Rept.* (1896), 633 (Biggar, Lanarkshire).

[7] Brand, i. 14; Dyer, 22 (Gloucestershire, Herefordshire). Twelve

small fires and one large one are made out in the wheat-fields.

[8] Dyer, 507; Ashton, 218; Simpson, 205; Gomme, *Brit. Ass. Rept.* (1896), 631; *F.L.J.* vii. 12; *Trans. Soc. Antiq. Scot.* x. 649.

[9] Simpson, 205, quoting Gordon Cumming, *From the Hebrides to the Himalayas*, i. 245.

[10] Bede, *D. T. R.* c. 17: cf. the A.-S. passage quoted by Pfannenschmidt, 495; Jahn, 252. Other Germanic names for the winter months are 'Schlachtmonat,' 'Gormânaða': cf. Weinhold, *Die deutschen Monatsnamen*, 54.

[11] Jahn, 229; Tille, *Y. and C.*

the outstanding victim seems to be the boar. *Caput apri defero : reddens laudem Domino*, sings the taberdar at Queen's College, Oxford, as the manciple bears in the boar's head to the Christmas banquet. So it was sung in many another mediaeval and Elizabethan hall[1], while the gentlemen of the Inner Temple broke their Christmas fast on ' brawn, mustard, and malmsey[2],' and in the far-off Orkneys each householder of Sandwick must slay his sow on St. Ignace's or ' Sow ' day, December 17[3]. The older mythologists, with the fear of solstices before their eyes, are accustomed to connect the Christmas boar with the light-god, Freyr[4]. If the cult of any one divinity is alone concerned, the analogous use of the pig in the Eleusinian mysteries of Demeter would make the earth-goddess a more probable guess[5]. A few more recondite customs associated with particular winter anniversaries may be briefly named. St. Thomas's day is at Wokingham the day for bull-baiting[6]. On St. Stephen's day, both in England and Germany, horses are let blood[7]. On or about Christmas, boys are accustomed to set on foot a hunt of victims not ordinarily destined to such a fate[8]; owls and squirrels, and especially wrens, the last, be it noted, creatures which at other times of the year a taboo protects. The wren-hunt is found on various dates in France, England, Ireland, and the Isle of Man, and is carried out with various curious rituals. Often the body is borne in a *quête*, and in the Isle of Man the *quêteurs* give a feather as an amulet in return for hospitality. There are other examples of winter *quêtes*, in which the representation of a sacrificial victim is carried round[9]. 'Hoodening' in Kent and other parts of England

28, 65; Pfannenschmidt, 206, 217, 228.

[1] Dyer, 456, 470, 474, 477; Ashton, 171; Karl Blind, *The Boar's Head Dinner at Oxford and an Old Teutonic Sun-God*, in *Saga Book* of Viking Club for 1895.

[2] Dyer, 473.

[3] Hampson, i. 82.

[4] Gummere, *G. O.* 433.

[5] Tacitus, *Germ.* 45, of the Aestii, ' matrem deum venerantur. insigne superstitionis formas aprorum ges-

tant: id pro armis omnique tutela securum deae cultorem etiam inter hostis praestat.'

[6] Dyer, 439.

[7] Dyer, 492; Ashton, 204; Grimm, iv. 1816.

[8] Dyer, 481; N. W. Thomas, in *F. L.* xi. 250. Cf. ch. xvii for the hunt of a cat and a fox at the ' grand Christmas ' of the Inner Temple.

[9] Dyer, 494, 497; Frazer, ii. 442; Northall, 229.

is accompanied by a horse's head or hobby-horse[1]. The Welsh 'Mari Lwyd' is a similar feature[2], while at Kingscote, in Gloucestershire, the wassailers drink to a bull's head called 'the Broad[3].'

The hobby-horse is an example of an apparently grotesque element which is found widespread in folk-processions, and which a previous chapter has traced to its ritual origin. The man clad in a beast-skin is the worshipper putting himself by personal contact under the influence and protection of the sacrificed god. The rite is not a very salient one in modern winter processions, although it has its examples, but its historical importance is great. A glance at the ecclesiastical denunciations of the Kalends collected in an appendix will disclose numerous references to it. These are co-extensive with the western area of the Kalends celebrations. In Italy, in Gaul, in southern Germany, apparently also in Spain and in England, men decked themselves for riot in the heads and skins of cattle and the beasts of the chase, blackened their faces or bedaubed them with filth, or wore masks fit to terrify the demons themselves. The accounts of these proceedings are naturally allusive rather than descriptive; the fullest are given by a certain Severian, whose locality and date are unknown, but who may be conjectured to speak for Italy, by Maximus of Turin and Chrysologus of Ravenna in the fifth century, and by Caesarius of Arles in the beginning of the sixth. Amongst the *portenta* denounced is a certain *cervulus*, which lingers in the *Penitentials* right up to the tenth century, and with which are sometimes associated a *vitula* or *iuvenca*. Caesarius adds a *hinnicula*, and St. Eadhelm, who is my only authority for the presence of the *cervulus* in England, an *ermulus*. These seem to be precisely of the nature of 'hobby-horses.' Men are said *cervulum ambulare, cervulum facere, in cervulo vadere*, and Christians are forbidden to allow these *portenta* to come before their houses. The *Penitential* of the Pseudo-Theodore tells us that the performers were those who wore the skins

---

[1] Ashton, 114 (Reculver); Dyer, 472 (Ramsgate); Ditchfield, 27 (Walmer), 28 (Cheshire: All Souls' day).
[2] Dyer, 486.   [3] Ditchfield, 28.

and heads of beasts. Maximus of Turin, and several writers after him, put the objection to the beast-mimicry of the Kalends largely on the ground that man made in the image of God must not transform himself into the image of a beast. But it is clear that the real reason for condemning it was its unforgettable connexion with heathen cult. Caesarius warns the culprit that he is making himself into a *sacrificium daemonum*, and the disguised reveller is more than once spoken of as a living image of the heathen god or demon itself. There is some confusion of thought here, and it must be remembered that the initial significance of the skin-wearing rite was probably buried in oblivion, both for those who practised it and for those who reprobated. But it is obvious that the worshipper wearing a sacrificial skin would bear a close resemblance to the theriomorphic or semi-theriomorphic image developed out of the sacrificial skin nailed on a tree-trunk; and it is impossible not to connect the fact that in the prohibitions a *cervulus* or 'hobby-buck' rather than a 'hobby-horse' is prominent with the widespread worship throughout the districts whence many of these notices come of the mysterious stag-horned deity, the *Cernunnos* of the Gaulish altars[1]. On the whole I incline to think that at least amongst the Germano-Keltic peoples the agricultural gods were not mimed in procession by human representatives. It is true that in the mediaeval German processions which sprang out of those of the Kalends St. Nicholas plays a part, and that the presence of St. Nicholas may be thought to imply that of some heathen precursor. It will, however, be seen shortly that St. Nicholas may have got into these processions through a different train of ideas, equally connected with the Kalends, but not with the strictly agricultural aspect of that festival. But of the continuity of the beast-masks and other horrors of these Christmas processions with those condemned in the prohibitions, there can be no doubt[2]. A few other survivals of the *cervulus* and its revel can be traced in various parts of Europe[3].

---

[1] Bertrand, 314; Arbois de Jubainville, *Cycl. myth.* 385; Rhys, *C. H.* 77.

[2] Tille, *D. W.* 109.

[3] C. de Berger (1723), *Commentatio de personis vulgo larvis seu*

The sacrifices of cereals and of the juice of the vine or the barley are exemplified, the one by the traditional furmenty, plum-porridge, mince-pie, souling-cake, Yule-dough, Twelfth night cake, *pain de calende*, and other forms of 'feasten' cake[1]; the other by the wassail-bowl with its bobbing apple[2]. The summer 'youling' or 'tree-wassailing' is repeated in the orchard[3], and a curious Herefordshire custom represents an extension of the same principle to the ox-byre[4]. A German hen-yard custom requires mixed corn, for the familiar reason that every kind of crop must be included in the sacrifice[5].

Human sacrifice has been preserved in the whipping of boys on Innocents' day, because it could be turned into the symbol of a Christian myth[6]. It is preserved also, as throughout the summer, in the custom, Roman as well as Germano-Keltic, of electing a mock or temporary king. Of such the Epiphany king or 'king of the bean' is, especially in France, the best known[7]. Here again, the association with

---

mascharis, 218 'Vecolo aut cervolo facere; hoc est sub forma vitulae aut cervuli per plateas discurrere, ut apud nos in festis Bacchanalibus vulgo dicitur *correr la tora*'; J. Ihre (†1769), *Gloss. Suio-Gothicum*, s.v. Jul. 'Julbock est ludicrum, quo tempore hoc pellem et formam arietis induunt adolescentuli et ita adstantibus incursant. Credo idem hoc esse quod exteri scriptores cervulum appellant.' In the *Life of Bishop Arni* (nat. 1237) it is recorded how in his youth he once joined in a *scinnleic* or 'hide-play' (*C. P. B.* ii. 385). Frazer, ii. 447, describes the New Year custom of *colluinn* in Scotland and St. Kilda. A man clad in a cowhide is driven *deasil* round each house to bless it. Bits of hide are also burnt for amulets. Probably the favourite Christmas game of Blind Man's Buff was originally a *scinnleic* (N. W. Thomas, in *F. L.* xi. 262).

[1] Brand, i. 210, 217; Jackson and Burne, 381, 392, 407; Ashton, 178; Jahn, 487, 500; Müller, 487, 500. Scandinavian countries bake the Christmas 'Yule-boar.' Often this is made from the last sheaf and

the crumbs mixed with the seed-corn (Frazer, ii. 29). Germany has its *Martinshörner* (Jahn, 250; Pfannenschmidt, 215).

[2] Dyer, 501; Ashton, 214.

[3] Brand, i. 19; Dyer, 21, 447; Ashton, 86, 233. Brand, i. 210, describes a Hallow-e'en custom in the Isle of Lewis of pouring a cup of ale in the sea to 'Shony,' a sea god.

[4] Brand, i. 14; Dyer, 22, 448; Northall, 187. A cake with a hole in the middle is hung on the horn of the leading ox.

[5] Grimm, iv. 1808. Hens are fed on New Year's day with mixed corn to make them lay well.

[6] Gregory, *Posthuma*, 113 'It hath been a Custom, and yet is elsewhere, to whip up the Children upon Innocents-Day morning, that the memory of this Murther might stick the closer, and in a moderate proportion to act over the cruelty again in kind.' In Germany, adults are beaten (Grimm, iv. 1820). In mediaeval France 'innocenter,' 'donner les innocents,' was a custom exactly parallel to the Easter *prisio* (Rigollot, 138, 173).

[7] Dyer, 24; Cortet, 32; Frazer,

the three kings or *Magi* has doubtless prolonged his sway. But he is not unparalleled. The *rex autumnalis* of Bath is perhaps a harvest rather than a beginning of winter king[1]. But the shoemakers choose their King Crispin on October 25, the day of their patron saints, Crispin and Crispinian; on St. Clement's (November 23) the Woolwich blacksmiths have their King Clem, and the maidens of Peterborough and elsewhere a queen on St. Catherine's (November 25). Tenby, again, elects its Christmas mock mayor[2]. At York, the proclaiming of Yule by 'Yule' and 'Yule's wife' on St. Thomas's day was once a notable pageant[3]. At Norwich, the riding of a 'kyng of Crestemesse' was the occasion of a serious riot in 1443[4]. These may be regarded as 'folk' versions of the

iii. 143; Deslyons, *Traités contre le Paganisme du Roi boit* (2nd ed. 1670). The accounts of Edward II record a gift to the *rex fabae* on January 1, 1316 (*Archaeologia*, xxvi. 342). Payments to the 'King of Bene' and 'for furnissing his graith' were made by James IV of Scotland between 1490 and 1503 (*L. H. T. Accounts*, I. ccxliii; II. xxiv, xxxi, &c.). The familiar mode of choosing the king is thus described at Mont St. Michel 'In vigilia Epyphaniae ad prandium habeant fratres gastellos et ponatur faba in uno; et frater qui inveniet fabam, vocabitur rex et sedebit ad magnam mensam, et scilicet sedebit ad vesperas et matutinam et ad magnam missam in cathedra parata' (Gasté, 53). The pre-eminence of the bean, largest of cereals, in the mixed cereal cake (cf. ch. vi) presents no great difficulty; on the religious significance attached to it in South Europe, cf. W. W. Fowler, 94, 110, 130. Lady Jane Grey was scornfully dubbed a Twelfth-day queen by Noailles (Froude, v. 206), just as the Bruce's wife held her lord a summer king (ch. viii).

[1] *Accts. of St. Michael's, Bath*, s. ann. 1487, 1490, 1492 (*Somerset Arch. Soc. Trans.* 1878, 1879, 1883). One entry is 'pro corona conducta Regi Attumnali.' The learned editor explains this as 'a quest conducted by the King's Attorney'!

[2] Ashton, 119; Dyer, 388, 423, 427.

[3] Brand, i. 261, prints from Leland, *Itinerary* (ed. 1769), iv. 182, a description of the proclamation of Youle by the sheriffs at the 'Youle-Girth' and throughout the city. In Davies, 270, is a letter from Archbp. Grindal and other ecclesiastical commissioners to the Lord Mayor, dated November 13, 1572, blaming 'a very rude and barbarouse custome maynteyned in this citie and in no other citie or towne of this realme to our knowledge, that yerely upon St. Thomas day before Christmas twoo disguysed persons, called Yule and Yule's wife, shoulde ryde throughe the citie very undecently and uncomely ...' Hereupon the council suppressed the riding. Drake, *Eboracum* (1736), 217, says that originally a friar rode backwards and 'painted like a Jew.' He gives an historical legend to account for the origin of the custom. Religious interludes were played on the same day: cf. *Representations*. The 'Yule' of York was perhaps less a 'king' than a symbolical personage like the modern 'Old Father Christmas.'

[4] Ramsay, *Y. and L.* ii. 52; Blomefield, *Hist. of Norfolk*, iii.

mock king. Others, in which the folk were less concerned, will be the subject of chapters to follow.

Before passing to a fresh group of Christmas customs, I must note the presence of one more bit of ritual closely related to sacrificial survivals. That is, the man masquerading in woman's clothes, in whom we have found a last faint reminiscence of the once exclusive supremacy of women in the conduct of agricultural worship. At Rome, musicians dressed as women paraded the city, not on the Kalends, but on the Ides of January[1]. The Fathers, however, know such disguising as a Kalends custom, and a condemnation of it often accompanies that of beast-mimicry, from the fourth to the eighth century[2].

The winter festival is thus, like the summer festivals, a moment in the cycle of agricultural ritual, and is therefore shared in by the whole village in common. It is also, and from the time of the institution of harvest perhaps pre-eminently, a festival of the family and the homestead. This side of it finds various manifestations. There is the solemn renewal of the undying fire upon the hearth, the central symbol and almost condition of the existence of the family as such. This survives in the institution of the 'Yule-log,' which throughout the Germano-Keltic area is lighted on Christmas or more rarely New Year's eve, and must burn,

149. The riot was against the Abbot of St. Benet's Holm, and the monks declared that one John Gladman was set up as a king, an act of treason against Henry VI. The city was fined 1,000 marks. In 1448 they set forth their wrongs in a 'Bill' and explained that Gladman 'who was ever, and at thys our is, a man of sad disposition, and trewe and feythfull to God and to the Kyng, of disporte as hath ben acustomed in ony cite or burgh thorowe alle this realme, on Tuesday in the last ende of Cristemesse, viz. Fastyngonge Tuesday, made a disport with hys neyghbours, havyng his hors trappyd with tynnsoyle and other nyse disgisy things, coronned as kyng of Crestemesse, in tokyn that seson should end with the twelve monethes of the yere, aforn hym yche moneth disguysed after the seson requiryd, and Lenton clad in whyte and red heryngs skinns, and his hors trapped with oystyr-shells after him, in token that sadnesse shuld folowe, and an holy tyme, and so rode in diverse stretis of the cite, with other people, with hym disguysed makyng myrth, disportes and plays.'

[1] Jevons, *Plutarch's Romane Questions*, 86. The Ides (Jan. 9) must have practically been included in the Kalends festival. The Agonium, probably a sacrifice to Janus, was on that day (W. W. Fowler, 282).

[2] Appendix N, Nos. ix, xi, xiv, xvii, xviii, xxviii, xxxvi.

as local custom may exact, either until midnight, or for three days, or during the whole of the Twelve-night period, from Christmas to Epiphany[1]. Dr. Tille, intent on magnifying the Roman element in western winter customs, denies any Germano-Keltic origin to the Christmas blaze, and traces it to the Roman practice of hanging lamps upon the house-doors during the *Saturnalia* and the Kalends[2]. It is true that the Yule-log is sometimes supplemented or even replaced by the Christmas candle[3], but I do not think that there can be any doubt which is the primitive form of rite. And the Yule-log enters closely into the Germano-Keltic scheme of festival ideas. The preservation of its brands or ashes to be placed in the mangers or mingled with the seed-corn suggests many and familiar analogies. Moreover, it is essentially con-nected with the festival fire of the village, from which it is still sometimes, and once no doubt was invariably, lit, afford-ing thus an exact parallel to the Germano-Keltic practice on the occasion of summer festival fires, or of those built to stay an epidemic.

Another aspect of the domestic character of the winter festival is to be found in the prominent part which children take in it. As *quêteurs*, they have no doubt gradually replaced the elder folk, during the process through which, even within the historical purview, ritual has been trans-formed into play. But St. Nicholas, the chief mythical figure of the festival, is their patron saint; for their benefit especially, the *strenae* or Christmas and New Year's gifts are main-tained; and in one or two places it is their privilege, on some fixed day during the season, to 'bar out' their parents or masters[4].

Thirdly, the winter festival included a commemoration of

---

[1] G. L. Gomme, in *Brit. Ass. Rep.* (1896), 616 sqq.; Tille, *D. W.* 11, *Y. and C.* 90; Jahn, 253; Dyer, 446, 466; Ashton, 76, 219; Grimm, iv. 1793, 1798, 1812, 1826, 1839, 1841; Bertrand, 111, 404; Müller, 478.

[2] Tille, *Y. and C.* 95.

[3] Dyer, 456; Ashton, 125, 188. A Lombard *Capitulary* (App. N,

No. xxxviii) forbids a Christmas candle to be burnt beneath the kneading-trough.

[4] Müller, 236; Dyer, 430; Ashton, 54; Rigollot, 173; *Records of Aberdeen* (Spalding Club), ii. 39, 45, 66. In Belgium the household keys are entrusted to the youngest child on Innocents' day (Durr, 73).

ancestors. It was a feast, not only of riotous life, but of the dead. For, to the thinking of the Germano-Keltic peoples, the dead kinsmen were not altogether outside the range of human fellowship. They shared with the living in banquets upon the tomb. They could even at times return to the visible world and hover round the familiar precincts of their ôwn domestic hearth. The Germans, at least, heard them in the gusts of the storm, and imagined for them a leader who became Odin. From another point of view they were naturally regarded as under the keeping of earth, and the earth-mother, in one aspect a goddess of fertility, was in another the goddess of the dead. As such she was worshipped under various names and forms, amongst others in the triad of the *Matres* or *Matronae*. In mediaeval superstition she is represented by Frau Perchte, Frau Holda and similar personages, by Diana, by Herodias, by St. Gertrude, just as the functions of Odin are transferred to St. Martin, St. Nicholas, St. John, Hellequin. It was not unnatural that the return of the spirits, in the 'wild hunt' or otherwise, to earth should be held to take place especially at the two primitive festivals which respectively began the winter and the summer. Of the summer or spring commemoration but scant traces are to be recovered [1]; that of winter survives, in a dislocated form, in more than one important anniversary. Its observances have been transferred with those of the agricultural side of the feast to the *Gemeinwoche* of harvest [2];

---

[1] Saupe, 9; Tille, *Y. and C.* 118; Duchesne, 267. A custom of feasting on the tombs of the dead on the day of St. Peter de Cathedra (Feb. 22) is condemned by the *Council of Tours* (567), c. 23 (Maassen, i. 133) 'sunt etiam qui in festivitate cathedrae domui Petri apostoli cibos mortuis offerunt, et post missas redeuntes ad domos proprias, ad gentilium revertuntur errores, et post corpus Domini, sacratas daemoni escas accipiunt.' I do not doubt that the Germano-Keltic tribes had their spring *Todtenfest*, but the date Feb. 22 seems determined by the Roman *Parentalia* extending from Feb. 13 to either Feb. 21 (*Feralia*) or Feb. 22 (*Cara Cognatio*): cf. Fowler, 306. The 'cibi' mentioned by the council of Tours seem to have been offered in the house, like the winter offerings described below; but there is also evidence for similar Germano-Keltic offerings on the tomb or howe itself; and these were often accompanied by *dadsisas* or dirges; cf. Saupe, *Indiculus*, 5–9. Saupe considers the *spurcalia in Februario*, explained above (p. 114) as a ploughing rite, to be funereal.

[2] Pfannenschmidt, 123, 165, 435; Saupe, 9; Golther, 586; *C. P. B.* i. 43; Jahn, 251. The chronicler Widukind, *Res gestae Sax.* (Pertz,

but they are also retained, at or about their original date, on
All Saints' and All Souls' days [1]; and, as I proceed to show,
they form a marked and interesting part of the Christmas
and New Year ritual. I do not, indeed, agree with Dr. Mogk,
who thinks that the Germans held their primitive feast of the
dead in the blackest time of winter, for it seems to me more
economical to suppose that the observances in question have
been shifted like others from November to the Kalends. But I
still less share the view of Dr. Tille, who denies that any relics of
a feast of the dead can be traced in the Christmas season at all [2].

Bede makes the statement that the heathen Anglo-Saxons
gave to the eve of the Nativity the name of *Modranicht* or
'night of mothers,' and in it practised certain ceremonies [3].
It is a difficult passage, but the most plausible of various
explanations seems to be that which identifies these ceremonies with the cult of 'those *Matres* or *Matronae*, corresponding with the Scandinavian *disar*, whom we seem justified
in regarding as guardians and representatives of the dead.
Nor is there any particular difficulty in guessing at the nature
of the ceremonies referred to. Amongst all peoples the cult
of the dead consists in feeding them; and there is a long
catena of evidence for the persistent survival in the Germano-
Keltic area of a Christmas and New Year custom closely
parallel to the *alfablót* and *disablót* of the northern *jul*. When
the household went to bed after the New Year revel, a portion
of the banquet was left spread upon the table in the firm
belief that during the night the ancestral spirits and their
leaders would come and partake thereof. The practice,
which was also known on the Mediterranean, does not escape

Mon. SS. iii. 423), describes a
Saxon three-days' feast in honour
of a victory over the Thuringi in
534. He adds 'acta sunt autem
haec omnia, ut maiorum memoria
prodit, die Kal. Octobris, qui dies
erroris, religiosorum sanctione virorum mutati sunt in ieiunia et orationes, oblationes quoque omnium
nos praecedentium christianorum.'
This is probably a myth to account
for the harvest *Todtenfest*, which
may more naturally be thought of
as transferred with the agricultural
rites from November. For the
mediaeval *Gemeinwoche*, beginning
on the Sunday after Michaelmas,
was common to Germany, and not
confined to Saxony. Michaelmas,
the feast of angels, known at Rome
in the sixth century, and in Germany
by the ninth, also adapts itself to
the notion of a *Todtenfest*.

[1] Pfannenschmidt, 168, 443.
[2] Mogk, in Paul, iii. 260; Tille,
Y. and C. 107.
[3] Cf. p. 231.

the animadversion of the ecclesiastical prohibitions. The earlier writers who speak of it, Jerome, Caesarius, Eligius, Boniface, Zacharias, the author of the *Homilia de Sacrilegiis*, if they give any explanation at all, treat it as a kind of charm[1]. The laden table, like the human over-eating and over-drinking, is to prognosticate or cause a year of plentiful fare. The preachers were more anxious to eradicate heathenism than to study its antiquities. Burchardus, however, had a touch of the anthropologist, and Burchardus says definitely that food, drink, and three knives were laid on the Kalends table for the three *Parcae*, figures of Roman mythology with whom the western *Matres* or 'weird sisters' were identified[2]. Mediaeval notices confirm the statement of Burchardus. Martin of Amberg[3], the *Thesaurus Pauperum*[4] and the Kloster Scheyern manuscript[5] make the recipient of the bounty Frau Perchte. In Alsso's *Largum Sero* it is for the heathen gods or demons[6]; in *Dives and Pauper* for 'Atholde or Gobelyn[7].' In modern survivals it is still often Frau Perchte or the Perchten or Persteln for whom fragments of food are left; in other cases the custom has taken on a Christian colouring, and the ancestors' bit becomes the portion of *le bon Dieu* or the Virgin or Christ or the *Magi*, and is actually given to *quêteurs* or the poor[8].

---

[1] Appendix N, Nos. xii, xvii, xxvii, xxxiii, xxxv, xxxix.

[2] Appendix N, No. xlii.

[3] Martin of Amberg, *Gewissensspiegel* (thirteenth century, quoted Jahn, 282), the food and drink are left for ' Percht mit der eisnen nasen.'

[4] *Thes. Paup.* s. v. Superstitio (fifteenth century, quoted Jahn, 282) ' multi credunt sacris noctibus inter natalem diem Christi et noctem Epiphaniae evenire ad domos suas quasdam mulieres, quibus praeest domina Perchta ... multi in domibus in noctibus praedictis post coenam dimittunt panem et caseum, lac, carnes, ova, vinum, et aquam et huiusmodi super mensas et coclearea, discos, ciphos, cultellos et similia propter visitationem Perhtae cum cohorte sua, ut eis complaceant

... ut inde sint eis propitii ad prosperitatem domus et negotiorum rerum temporalium.'

[5] Usener, ii. 84 'Qui preparant mensam dominae Perthae'(fifteenth century). Schmeller, *Bairisch. Wörterb.* i. 270, gives other references for Perchte in this connexion.

[6] Usener, ii. 58.

[7] *Dives and Pauper* (Pynson, 1493) 'Alle that ... use nyce observances in the . . . new yere, as setting of mete or drynke, by nighte on the benche, to fede Atholde or Gobelyn.' In English folk-custom, food is left for the house-spirit or ' brownie' on ordinary as well as festal days; cf. my 'Warwick' edition of *Midsummer Night's Dream*, 145.

[8] Jahn, 283; Brand, i. 18; Bertrand, 405; Cortet, 33, 45.

It is the ancestors, perhaps, who are really had in mind when libations are made upon the Yule-log, an observance known to Martin of Braga in the sixth century[1], and still in use in France[2]. Nor can it be doubted that the healths drunk to them, and to the first of them, Odin, lived on in the St. John's *minnes*, no less than in the St. Martin's *minnes*, of Germany[3]. Apart from eating and drinking, numerous folk-beliefs testify to the presence of the spirits of the dead on earth in the Twelve nights of Christmas. During these days, or some one of them, Frau Holle and Frau Perchte are abroad[4]. So is the 'wild hunt[5].' Dreams then dreamt come true[6], and children then born see ghosts[7]. The wer-wolf, possessed by a human spirit, is to be dreaded[8]. The devil and his company dance in the Isle of Man[9]: in Brittany the *korrigans* are unloosed, and the dolmens and menhirs disclose their hidden treasures[10]. Marcellus in *Hamlet* declares:

'Some say that ever 'gainst that season comes
Wherein our Saviour's birth is celebrated,
The bird of dawning singeth all night long;
And then, they say, no spirit dare stir abroad;
The nights are wholesome; then no planets strike,
No fairy takes, nor witch hath power to charm,
So hallow'd and so gracious is the time[11].'

The folk-lorist can only reply, 'So have I heard, and do not in the least believe it.'

[1] Appendix N, No. xxiii. If the words 'in foco' are not part of the text, 'youling' (cf. pp. 142, 260) may be intended.

[2] Bertrand, 111, 404.

[3] Jahn, 120, 244, 269: the *Gertruden-minnes* on St. Gertrude's day (March 17) perhaps preserve another fragment of the spring *Todtenfest*, St. Gertrude here replacing the mother-goddess; cf. Grimm, iii. xxxviii.

[4] Grimm, i. 268, 273, 281; Mogk, in Paul, iii. 279. The especial day of Frau Perchte is Epiphany.

[5] Mogk, in Paul, iii. 260; Tille, *D. W.* 173.

[6] Grimm, iv. 1798.

[7] Ibid. iv. 1814.

[8] Tille, *D. W.* 163; Grimm, iv. 1782.

[9] Ashton, 104.

[10] Müller, 496.

[11] *Hamlet*, i. 1. 158. I do not know where Shakespeare got the idea, of which I find no confirmation; but its origin is probably an ecclesiastical attempt to parry folk-belief. Other Kalends notions have taken on a Christian colouring. The miraculous events of Christmas night are rooted in the conception that the Kalends must abound in all good things, in order that the

The wanderings of Odin in the winter nights must be at the bottom of the nursery myth that the Christian representatives of this divinity, Saints Martin and Nicholas (the Santa Claus of modern legend), are the nocturnal givers of *strenae* to children. In Italy, the fairy Befana (Epiphania), an equivalent of Diana, has a similar function [1]. It was but a step to the actual representation of such personages for the greater delight of the children. In Anspach the skin-clad *Pelzmarten*, in Holland St. Martin in bishop's robes, make their rounds on St. Martin's day with nuts, apples, and suchlike [2]. St. Nicholas does the same on St. Nicholas' day, in Holland and Alsace-Lorraine, at Christmas in Germany [3]. The beneficent saints were incorporated into the Kalends processions already described, which in the sixteenth-century Germany included two distinct groups, a dark one of devils and beast-masks, terrible to children, and a white or kindly one, in which sometimes appeared the *Jesus-Kind* himself [4].

coming year may do so. But allusions to Christian legend have been worked into and have transformed them. On Christmas night bees sing (Brand, i. 3), and water is turned into wine (Grimm, iv. 1779, 1809). While the genealogy is sung at the midnight mass, hidden treasures are revealed (Grimm, iv. 1840). Similarly, the cattle of heathen masters naturally shared in the Kalends good cheer; whence a Christian notion that they, and in particular the ox and the ass, witnesses of the Nativity, can speak on that night, and bear testimony to the good or ill-treatment of the farmers (Grimm, iv. 1809, 1840); cf. the *Speculum Perfectionis*, c. 114, ed. Sabatier, 225 'quod volebat [S. Franciscus] suadere imperatori ut faceret specialem legem quod in Nativitate Domini homines bene providerent avibus et bovi et asino et pauperibus': also p. 250, n. 1.— Ten minutes after writing the above note, I have come on the following passage in Tolstoi, *Résurrection* (trad. franç.), i. 297 'Un proverbe dit que les coqs chantent de bonne heure dans les nuits joyeuses.'

[1] Müller, 272.
[2] Pfannenschmidt, 207.
[3] Müller, 235, 239, 248.
[4] Tille, *D. W.* 107; *Y. and C.* 116; Saupe, 28; Io. Iac. Reiske, *Comm. ad Const. Porph., de Caeremoniis,* ii. 357 (*Corp. Script. Byz.* 1830) 'Vidi puerulus et horrui robustos iuvenes pelliceis indutos, cornutos in fronte, vultus fuligine atratos, intra dentes carbones vivos tenentes, quos reciprocato spiritu animabant, et scintillis quaquaversum sparsis ignem quasi vomebant, cum saccis cursitantes, in quos abdere puerulos occursantes minitabantur, appensis cymbalis et insano clamore frementes.' He calls them 'die Knecht Ruperte,' and says that they performed in the Twelve nights. The *sacci* are interesting, for English nurses frighten children with a threat that the chimney-sweep (here as in the May-game inheriting the tradition on account of his black face) will put them in his sack. The *beneficent* Christmas wanderers use the sack to bring presents in ; cf. the development of the sack in the Mummers' play (p. 215).

It is perhaps a relic of the same merging which gives the German and Flemish St. Nicholas a black Moor as companion in his nightly peregrinations [1].

Besides the customs which form part of the agricultural or the domestic observances of the winter feasts, there are others which belong to these in their quality as feasts of the New Year. To the primitive mind the first night and day of the year are full of omen for the nights and days that follow. Their events must be observed as foretelling, nay more, they must as far as possible be regulated as determining, those of the larger period. The eves and days of All Saints, Christmas, and the New Year itself, as well as in some degree the minor feasts, preserve in modern folk-lore this prophetic character. It is but an extension and systematization of the same notion that ascribes to each of the twelve days between Christmas and Epiphany a special influence upon one of the twelve months of the year [2]. This group of customs I can only touch most cursorily. The most interesting are those which, as I have just said, attempt to go beyond foretelling and to determine the arrival of good fortune. Their method is symbolic. In order that the house may be prosperous during the year, wealth during the critical day must flow in and not flow out. Hence the taboos which forbid the carrying out in particular of those two central elements of early civilization, fire [3] and iron [4]. Hence too the belief that a job of work begun on the feast day will succeed, which

---

[1] Müller, 235, 248.

[2] A mince-pie eaten in a different house on each night of the Twelves (*not* twelve mince-pies eaten *before* Christmas) ensures twelve lucky months. The weather of each day in the Twelves determines that of a month (Harland, 99; Jackson and Burne, 408). I have heard of a custom of leaping over twelve lighted candles on New Year's eve. Each that goes out means ill-luck in a corresponding month.

[3] Caesarius; Boniface (App. N, Nos. xvii, xviii, xxxiii); Alsso, in Usener, ii. 65; *F. L.* iii. 253; Jackson and Burne, 400; Ashton, 111; *Brit. Ass. Report* (1896), 620. In some of the cases quoted under the last reference and elsewhere, *nothing* may be taken out of the house on New Year's Day. Ashes and other refuse which would naturally be taken out in the morning were removed the night before. Ashes, of course, share the sanctity of the fire. Cf. the maskers' threat (p. 217).

[4] Boniface (App. N, No. xxxiii); cf. the Kloster Scheyern (Usener, ii. 84) condemnation of those 'qui vomerem ponunt sub mensa tempore nativitatis Christi.' For other uses of iron as a potent agricultural charm, cf. Grimm, iv. 1795, 1798, 1807, 1816; Burne-Jackson, 164.

conflicts rather curiously in practice with the universal rustic sentiment that to work or make others work on holidays is the act of a churl[1]. Nothing, again, is more important to the welfare of the household during the coming year than the character of the first visitor who may enter the house on New Year's day. The precise requirements of a 'first foot' vary in different localities; but as a rule he must be a boy or man, and not a girl or woman, and he must be dark-haired and not splay-footed[2]. An ingenious conjecture has connected the latter requirements with the racial antagonism of the high-instepped dark pre-Aryan to the flat-footed blonde or red-haired invading Kelt[3]. A Bohemian parallel enables me to explain that of masculinity by the belief in the influence of the sex of the 'first foot' upon that of the cattle to be born during the year[4]. I regret to add that there are traces also of a requirement that the 'first foot' should not be a priest, possibly because in that event the shadow of celibacy would make any births at all improbable[5].

Some of the New Year observances are but prophetic by second intention, having been originally elements of cult. An example is afforded by the all-night table for the leaders of the dead, which, as has been pointed out, was regarded by

[1] Cf. Burchardus (App. N, No. xlii); Grimm, iv. 1793, with many other superstitions in the same appendix to Grimm; Brand, i. 9; Ashton, 222; Jackson and Burne, 403. The practical outcome is to begin jobs for form's sake and then stop. The same is done on Saint Distaff's day, January 7; cf. Brand, i. 15.

[2] Harland, 117; Jackson and Burne, 314; *Brit. Ass. Rep.* (1896), 620; Dyer, 483; Ashton, 112, 119, 224. There is a long discussion in *F. L.* iii. 78, 253. I am tempted to find a very early notice of the 'first foot' in the prohibition 'pedem observare' of Martin of Braga (App. N, No. xxiii).

[3] *F. L.* iii. 253.

[4] *Kloster Scheyern MS.* (fifteenth century) in Usener, ii. 84 'Qui credunt, quando masculi primi intrant domum in die nativitatis, quod omnes vaccae generent masculos et e converso.'

[5] Müller, 269 (Italy). Grimm, iv. 1784, notes 'If the first person you meet in the morning be a virgin or a priest, 'tis a sign of bad luck; if a harlot, of good': cf. Caspari, *Hom. de Sacrilegiis*, § 11 'qui clericum vel monachum de mane aut quacumque hora videns aut o[b]vians, abominosum sibi esse credet, iste non solum paganus, sed demoniacus est, qui christi militem abominatur.' These German examples have no special relation to the New Year, and the 'first foot' superstition is indeed only the ordinary belief in the ominous character of the first thing seen on leaving the house, intensified by the critical season.

the Fathers who condemned it as merely a device, with the festal banquet itself, to ensure carnal well-being. Another is the habit of giving presents. This, though widespread, is apparently of Italian and not Germano-Keltic origin [1]. It has gone through three phases. The original *strena* played a part in the cult of the wood-goddess. It was a twig from a sacred tree and the channel of the divine influence upon the personality of him who held or wore it. The later *strena* had clearly become an omen, as is shown by the tradition which required it to be honeyed or light-bearing or golden [2]. To-day even this notion may be said to have disappeared, and the Christmas-box or *étrenne* is merely a token of goodwill, an amusement for children, or a blackmail levied by satellites.

The number of minor omens by which the curiosity, chiefly of women, strives on the winter nights to get a peep into futurity is legion [3]. Many of them arise out of the ordinary incidents of the festivities, the baking of the Christmas cakes [4], the roasting of the nuts in the Hallow-e'en fire [5]. Some of them preserve ideas of extreme antiquity, as when a girl takes off her shift and sits naked in the belief that the vision of her future husband will restore it to her. Others are based upon the most naïve symbolism, as when the same girl pulls a stick out of the wood-pile to see if her husband will be straight or crooked [6]. But however diversified the methods, the objects of the omens are few and unvarying. What will be the weather and what his crops? How shall he fare in love and the begetting of children? What are his chances of escaping for yet another year the summons of the lord of shadows? Such are the simple questions to which the rustic claims from his gods an answer.

---

[1] Tille, *D. W.* 189; *Y. and C.* 84, 95, 104.

[2] Cf. p. 238.

[3] Brand, i. 3, 209, 226, 257; Spence, *Shetland Folk-Lore*, 189; Grimm, iv. 1777–1848 *passim*; Jackson and Burne, 176, 380, &c., &c. Burchardus (App. N, No. xlii) mentions that the Germans took New Year omens sitting girt with a sword on the housetop or upon a [sacrificial] skin at the crossways. This was called *liodor-sâza*, a term which a *glossator* also uses for the kindred custom of *cervulus* (Tille, *Y. and C.* 96). Is the man in *Hom. de Sacr.* (App. N, No. xxxix) 'qui arma in campo ostendit' taking omens like the man on the housetop, or is he conducting a sword-dance?

[4] Burchardus (App. N, No. xlii).

[5] Brand, i. 209.

[6] Grimm, iv. 1781, 1797, 1818.

Finally, the instinct of play proved no less enduring in the Germano-Keltic winter feasts than in those of summer. The priestly protests against the invasion of the churches by folk-dance and folk-song apply just as much to Christmas as to any other festal period. It is, indeed, to Christmas that the monitory legend of the dancers of Kölbigk attaches itself. A similar pious narrative is that in the thirteenth-century *Bonum Universale de Apibus* of Thomas of Cantimpré, which tells how a devil made a famous song of St. Martin, and spread it abroad over France and Germany[1]. Yet a third is solemnly retailed by a fifteenth-century English theologian, who professes to have known a man who once heard an indecent song at Christmas, and not long after died of a melancholy[2]. During the seventeenth century folk still danced and cried 'Yole' in Yorkshire churches after the Christmas services[3]. Hopeless of abolishing such customs, the clergy tried to capture them. The Christmas crib was rocked to the rhythms of a dance, and such great Latin hymns as the *Hic iacet in cunabulis* and the *Resonat in laudibus* became the parents of a long series of festival songs, half sacred, half profane[4]. In Germany these were known as *Wiegenlieder*, in France as *noëls*, in England as carols; and the latter name makes it clear that they are but a specialized development of those *caroles* or *rondes* which of all mediaeval *chansons* came nearest to the type of Germano-Keltic folk-song. A single passage in a Byzantine

---

[1] Quoted Pfannenschmidt, 489 'quod autem obscoena carmina finguntur a daemonibus et perditorum mentibus immittuntur, quidam daemon nequissimus, qui in Nivella urbe Brabantiae puellam nobilem anno domini 1216 prosequebatur, manifeste populis audientibus dixit : cantum hunc celebrem de Martino ego cum collega meo composui et per diversas terras Galliae et Theutoniae promulgavi. Erat autem cantus ille turpissimus et plenus luxuriosis plausibus.' On *Martinslieder* in general cf. Pfannenschmidt, 468, 613.

[2] T. Gascoigne, *Loci e Libro Veritatum* (1403-58), ed. Rogers, 144.

[3] Aubrey, *Gentilisme and Judaisme (F. L. S.)*, 1.

[4] Tille, *D. W.* 55; K. Simrock, *Deutsche Weihnachtslieder* (1854); Cortet, 246; Grove, *Dict. of Music*, s. v. Noël; Julian, *Dict. of Hymn.* s. v. Carol; A. H. Bullen, *Carols and Poems*, 1885; Helmore, *Carols for Christmastide*. The cry 'Noel' appears in the fifteenth century both in France and England as one of general rejoicing without relation to Christmas. It greeted Henry V in London in 1415 and the Marquis of Suffolk in Rouen in 1446 (Ramsay, *Lancaster and York*, i. 226; ii. 60).

writer gives a tantalizing glimpse of such a folk-revel or *laiks* at a much earlier stage. Constantine Porphyrogennetos describes amongst the New Year sports and ceremonies of the court of Byzantium in the tenth century one known as τὸ Γοτθικόν. In this the courtiers were led by two 'Goths' wearing skins and masks, and carrying staves and shields which they clashed together. An intricate dance took place about the hall, which naturally recalls the sword-dance of western Europe. A song followed, of which the words are preserved. They are only partly intelligible, and seem to contain allusions to the sacrificial boar and to the Gothic names of certain deities. From the fact that they are in Latin, the scholars who have studied them infer that the Γοτθικόν drifted to Byzantium from the court of the great sixth-century Ostrogoth, Theodoric [1].

[1] Constantinus Porphyrogenitus, *de Caeremoniis Aulae Byzantinae*, Bk. i. c. 83 (ed. Reiske, in *Corp. Script. Hist. Byz.* i. 381) ; cf. Bury-Gibbon, vi. 516 ; Kögel, i. 34 ; D. Bieliaiev, *Byzantina*, vol. ii ; Haupt's *Zeitschrift*, i. 368 ; C. Kraus, *Gotisches Weihnachtsspiel*, in *Beitr. z. Gesch. d. deutschen Sprache und Litteratur*, xx (1895), 223.

CHAPTER XIII

THE FEAST OF FOOLS

[*Bibliographical Note.*—The best recent accounts of the Feast of Fools as a whole are those of G. M. Dreves in *Stimmen aus Maria-Laach* (1894), xlvii. 571, and Heuser in Wetzer and Welte, *Kirchenlexicon* (ed. 2), iv. 1402, s. v. *Feste* (2), and an article in *Zeitschrift für Philosophie und katholische Theologie* (Bonn, 1850), N. F. xi. 2. 161. There is also a summary by F. Loliée in *Revue des Revues*, xxv (1898), 400. The articles by L. J. B. Bérenger-Féraud in *Superstitions et Survivances* (1896), vol. iv, and in *La Tradition*, viii. 153 ; ix. 1 are unscholarly compilations. A pamphlet by J. X. Carré de Busserolle, published in 1859, I have not been able to see ; another, or a reprint of the same, was promised in his series of *Usages singuliers de Touraine*, but as far as I know never appeared. Of the older learning the interest is mainly polemical in J. Deslyons, *Traitez singuliers et nouveaux contre le Paganisme du Roy-boit* (1670) ; J. B. Thiers, *De Festorum Dierum Imminutione* (1668), c. 48 ; *Traité des Jeux et des Divertissemens* (1686), c. 33 ; and historical in Du Tilliot, *Mémoires pour servir à l'Histoire de la Fête des Foux* (1741 and 1751) ; F. Douce, in *Archaeologia*, xv. 225 ; M. J. R[igollot] et C. L[eber], *Monnaies inconnues des Évêques des Innocens, des Fous, &c.* (1837). Vols. ix and x of C. Leber, *Collection des meilleurs Dissertations, &c., relatifs à l'Histoire de France* (1826 and 1838), contain various treatises on the subject, some of them, by the Abbé Lebeuf and others, from the *Mercure de France*. A. de Martonne, *La Piété du Moyen Age* (1855), 202, gives a useful bibliographical list. The collection of material in Ducange's *Glossary*, s.vv. *Deposuit, Festum Asini, Kalendae,* &c., is invaluable. Authorities of less general range are quoted in the footnotes to this chapter : the most important is A. Chérest's account of the Sens feast in *Bulletin de la Soc. des Sciences de l'Yonne* (1853), vol. vii. Chérest used a collection of notes by E. Baluze (1630–1718) which are in *MS. Bibl. Nat.* 1351 (cf. *Bibl. de l'École des Chartes*, xxxv. 267). Dom. Grenier (1725–89) wrote an account of the Picardy feasts, in his *Introduction à l'Histoire de Picardie (Soc. des Antiquaires de Picardie, Documens inédits* (1856), iii. 352). But many of his *probata* remain in his *MSS. Picardie* in the *Bibl. Nat.* (cf. *Bibl. de l'École des Chartes*, xxxii. 275). Some of this material was used by Rigollot for the book named above.]

THE New Year customs, all too briefly summed up in the last chapter, are essentially folk customs. They belong to the ritual of that village community whose primitive organization still, though obscurely, underlies the complex society of western Europe. The remaining chapters of the present volume will deal with certain modifications and developments introduced into those customs by new social classes which gradually differentiated themselves during the Middle Ages from the village folk. The churchman, the *bourgeois*, the courtier, celebrated the New Year, even as the peasant did. But they put their own temper into the observances ; and it is worth while to accord a separate treatment to the shapes which these took in such hands, and to the resulting influence upon the dramatic conditions of the sixteenth century.

The discussion must begin with the somewhat startling New Year revels held by the inferior clergy in mediaeval cathedrals and collegiate churches, which may be known generically as the ' Feast of Fools.' Actually, the feast has different names in different localities. Most commonly it is the *festum stultorum, fatuorum* or *follorum* ; but it is also called the *festum subdiaconorum* from the highest of the *minores ordines* who, originally at least, conducted it, and the *festum baculi* from one of its most characteristic and symbolical ceremonies ; while it shares with certain other rites the suggestive title of the ' Feast of Asses,' *asinaria festa*.

The main area of the feast is in France, and it is in France that it must first of all be considered. I do not find a clear notice of it until the end of the twelfth century[1]. It is mentioned, however, in the *Rationale Divinorum Officium* († 1182–90) of Joannes Belethus, rector of Theology at Paris, and afterwards a cathedral dignitary at Amiens. ' There are four *tripudia*,' Belethus tells us, ' after Christmas. They are those of the deacons, priests, and choir-children, and finally that of the subdeacons, *quod vocamus stultorum*, which is held according to varying uses, on the Circumcision, or on Epiphany, or on the octave of Epiphany[2].' Almost simultaneously the feast can

---

[1] Fouquier-Cholet, *Hist. des Comtes de Vermandois*, 159, says that Heribert IV (ob. †1081) persuaded the clergy of the Vermandois to suppress the *fête de l'âne*. This would have been a century before Belethus wrote. But he does not give his *probatum*, and I suspect he misread it.

[2] Belethus, c. 72 ' Festum hypodiaconorum, quod vocamus stultorum, a quibusdam perficitur in Circumcisione, a quibusdam vero in Epiphania, vel in eius octavis. Fiunt autem quatuor tripudia post Nativitatem Domini in Ecclesia, levitarum scilicet, sacerdotum, puerorum, id est minorum aetate et ordine, et hypodiaconorum, qui ordo incertus est. Unde fit ut ille quandoque annumeretur inter sacros ordines, quandoque non, quod expresse ex eo intelligitur quod certum tempus non habeat,

be traced in the cathedral of Notre-Dame at Paris, through an epigram written by one Leonius, a canon of the cathedral, to a friend who was about to pay him a visit for the *festum baculi* at the New Year [1]. The *baculus* was the staff used by the precentor of a cathedral, or whoever might be conducting the choir in his place [2]. Its function in the Feast of Fools may be illustrated from an order for the reformation of the Notre-Dame ceremony issued in 1199. This order was made by Eudes de Sully, bishop of Paris, together with the dean and other chapter officers [3]. It recites a mandate sent to them by cardinal Peter of Capua, then legate in France. The legate had been informed of the improprieties and disorders, even to shedding of blood, which had given to the feast of the Circumcision in the cathedral the appropriate name of the *festum fatuorum*. It was not a time for mirth, for the fourth crusade had failed, and Pope Innocent III was preaching the fifth. Nor could such *spurcitia* be allowed in the sanctuary of God. The bishop

et officio celebretur confuso.' Cf. ch. xv on the three other *tripudia*.

[1] Lebeuf, *Hist. de Paris* (1741), ii. 277 ; Grenier, 365 :

Ad amicum venturum ad festum Baculi.

Festa dies aliis Baculus venit et novus annus,

Qua venies, veniet haec mihi festa dies.

Leonius is named as canon of N.-D. in the *Obituary* of the church Guérard, *Cartulaire de N.-D.* in (*Doc. inédits sur l'Hist. de France*, iv. 34), but unfortunately the year of his death is not given.

[2] During the fifteenth century the *Chantre* of N.-D. 'porta le baston' at the chief feasts as ruler of the choir (F. L. Chartier, *L'ancien Chapitre de N.-D. de Paris* (1897), 176). This *baculus* must be distinguished from the *baculus pastoralis* or *episcopi*.

[3] Guérard, *Cartulaire de N.-D.* (*Doc. inéd. sur l'Hist. de France*), i. 73; also printed by Ducange, s. v. *Kalendae* ; *P. L.* ccxii. 70. The *charta*, dated 1198, runs in the

names of 'Odo [de Soliaco] episcopus, H. decanus, R. cantor, Mauricius, Heimericus et Odo archidiaconi, Galo, succentor, magister Petrus cancellarius, et magister Petrus de Corbolio, canonicus Parisiensis.' Possibly the real moving spirit in the reform was the dean H[ugo Clemens], to whom the Paris *Obituary* (Guérard, *loc. cit.* iv. 61) assigns a similar reform of the feast of St. John the Evangelist. Petrus de Corbolio we shall meet again. Eudes de Sully was bishop 1196-1208. His *Constitutions* (*P. L.* ccxii. 66) contain a prohibition of ' choreae . . . in ecclesiis, in coemeteriis et in processionibus.' In a second decree of 1199 (*P. L.* ccxii. 72) he provided a *solatium* for the loss of the Feast of Fools in a payment of three *deniers* to each clerk below the degree of canon, and two *deniers* to each boy present at Matins on the Circumcision. Should the abuses recur, the payment was to lapse. This donation was confirmed in 1208 by his successor Petrus de Nemore (*P.L.* ccxii. 92).

and his fellows must at once take order for the pruning of
the feast. In obedience to the legate they decree as follows.
The bells for first Vespers on the eve of the Circumcision are
to be rung in the usual way. There are to be no *chansons*,
no masks, and no hearse lights, except on the iron wheels or
on the *penna* at the will of the functionary who is to surrender
the cope [1]. The lord of the feast is not to be led in procession or with singing to the cathedral or back to his house.
He is to put on his cope in the choir, and with the precentor's
baculus in his hand to start the singing of the prose *Laetemur
gaudiis* [2]. Vespers, Compline, Matins and Mass are to be
sung in the usual festal manner. Certain small functions are
reserved for the sub-deacons, and the Epistle at Mass is to
be 'farced [3].' At second Vespers *Laetemur gaudiis* is to
be again sung, and also *Laetabundus* [4]. Then comes an
interesting direction. *Deposuit* is to be sung where it occurs
five times at most, and 'if the *baculus* has been taken,' Vespers
are to be closed by the ordinary officiant after a *Te Deum*.
Throughout the feast canons and clerks are to remain
properly in their stalls [5]. The abuses which it was intended

[1] A 'hearse' was a framework of
wood or iron bearing spikes for
tapers (Wordsworth, *Mediaeval
Services*, 156). The *penna* was also
a stand for candles (Ducange, s.v.).

[2] A *prosa* is a term given in
French liturgies to an additional
chant inserted on festal occasions
as a gloss upon or interpolation in
the text of the office or mass. It
covers nearly, though not quite, the
same ground as *Sequentia*, and
comes under the general head of
Tropus (ch. xviii). For a more
exact differentiation cf. Frere,
Winchester Troper, ix. *Laetemur
gaudiis* is a prose ascribed to Not-
ker Balbulus of St. Gall.

[3] *cum farsia :* a *farsia, farsa,*
or *farsura* (Lat. *farcire*, 'to stuff'), is
a *Tropus* interpolated into the text
of certain portions of the office or
mass, especially the *Kyrie*, the
Lectiones and the *Epistola*. Such
farces were generally in Latin, but
occasionally, especially in the

Epistle, in the vernacular (Frere,
Winchester Troper, ix, xvi).

[4] *Laetabundus :* i.e. St. Bernard's
prose beginning *Laetabundus exul-
tet fidelis chorus; Alleluia* (Daniel,
Thesaurus Hymnologicus, ii. 61),
which was widely used in the feasts
of the Christmas season.

[5] The document is too long to
quote in full. These are the essential passages. The legate says:
The Church of Paris is famous,
therefore diligence must be used
'ad exstirpandum penitus quod
ibidem sub praetextu pravae con-
suetudinis inolevit . . . Didicimus
quod in festo Circumcisionis Dominicae . . . tot consueverunt enor-
mitates et opera flagitiosa committi,
quod locum sanctum . . . non solum
foeditate verborum, verum etiam
sanguinis effusione plerumque con-
tingit inquinari, et . . . ut sacratis-
sima dies . . . festum fatuorum nec
immerito generaliter consueverit
appellari.' Odo and the rest order:

to eliminate from the feast are implied rather than stated ;
but the general character of the ceremony is clear. It consisted in the predominance throughout the services, for this
one day in the year, of the despised sub-deacons. Probably
they had been accustomed to take the canons' stalls. This
Eudes de Sully forbids, but even in the feast as he left it the
importance of the *dominus festi*, the sub-deacons' representative, is marked by the transfer to him of the *baculus*, and
with it the precentor's control. *Deposuit potentes de sede : et
exaltavit humiles* occurs in the *Magnificat*, which is sung at
Vespers ; and the symbolical phrase, during which probably
the *baculus* was handed over from the *dominus* of one year
to the *dominus* of the next, became the keynote of the feast,
and was hailed with inordinate repetition by the delighted
throng of inferior clergy[1].

' In vigilia festivitatis ad Vesperas
campanae ordinate sicut in duplo
simplici pulsabuntur. Cantor faciet
matriculam (the roll of clergy for
the day's services) in omnibus
ordinate ; rimos, personas, lumi-
naria herciarum nisi tantum in
rotis ferreis, et in penna, si tamen
voluerit ille qui capam redditurus
est, fieri prohibemus ; statuimus
etiam ne dominus festi cum processione vel cantu ad ecclesiam addu-
catur, vel ad domum suam ab
ecclesia reducatur. In choro autem
induet capam suam, assistentibus
ei duobus canonicis subdiaconis, et
tenens baculum cantoris, antequam
incipiantur Vesperae, incipiet pro-
sam *Laetemur gaudiis* : qua finita
episcopus, si praesens fuerit . . . incipiet Vesperas ordinate et solemniter celebrandas ; . . . a quatuor
subdiaconis indutis capis sericis
Responsorium cantabitur. . . . Missa
similiter cum horis ordinate cele-
brabitur ab aliquo praedictorum,
hoc addito quod Epistola cum farsia
dicetur a duobus in capis sericis,
et postmodum a subdiacono . . .
Vesperae sequentes sicut priores
a *Laetemur gaudiis* habebunt ini-
tium : et cantabitur *Laetabundus*,
loco hymni. *Deposuit* quinquies
ad plus dicetur loco suo ; et si

captus fuerit baculus, finito *Te
Deum laudamus*, consummabuntur
Vesperae ab eo quo fuerint in-
choatae. . . . Per totum festum in
omnibus horis canonici et clerici
in stallis suis ordinate et regulariter
se habebunt.'

[1] The feast lasted from Vespers
on the vigil to Vespers on the day
of the Circumcision. The *Haupt-
moment* was evidently the *Magnificat* in the second Vespers. But
what exactly took place then ? Did
the cathedral precentor hand over
the *baculus* to the *dominus festi*, or
was it last year's *dominus festi*,
who now handed it over to his
newly-chosen successor ? Probably
the latter. The *dominus festi* is
called at first Vespers 'capam redditurus' : doubtless the cope and
baculus went together. The *dominus festi* may have, as elsewhere,
exercised disciplinary and representative functions amongst the inferior clergy during the year. His
title I take to have been, as at Sens,
precentor stultorum. The order
says, ' si captus fuerit baculus ';
probably it was left to the chapter
to decide whether the formal instal-
lation of the *precentor* in church
should take place in any particular
year.

Shortly after the Paris reformation a greater than Eudes de Sully and a greater than Peter de Capua was stirred into action by the scandal of the Feast of Fools and the cognate *tripudia*. In 1207, Pope Innocent III issued a decretal to the archbishop and bishops of the province of Gnesen in Poland, in which he called attention to the introduction, especially during the Christmas feasts held by deacons, priests and sub-deacons, of *larvae* or masks and *theatrales ludi* into churches, and directed the discontinuance of the practice [1]. This decretal was included as part of the permanent canon law in the *Decretales* of Gregory IX in 1234 [2]. But some years before this it found support, so far as France was concerned, in a national council held at Paris by the legate Robert de Courçon in 1212, at which both regular and secular clergy were directed to abstain from the *festa follorum, ubi baculus accipitur* [3].

It was now time for other cathedral chapters besides that of Paris to set their houses in order, and good fortune has preserved to us a singular monument of the attempts which they made to do so. The so-called *Missel des Fous* of Sens may be seen in the municipal library of that city [4]. It is enshrined in a Byzantine ivory diptych of much older date

[1] *P. L.* ccxv. 1070 'Interdum ludi fiunt in eisdem ecclesiis theatrales, et non solum ad ludibriorum spectacula introducuntur in eas monstra larvarum, verum etiam in tribus anni festivitatibus, quae continue Natalem Christi sequuntur, diaconi, presbiteri ac subdiaconi vicissim insaniae suae ludibria exercentes, per gesticulationum suarum debacchationes obscoenas in conspectu populi decus faciunt clericale vilescere. . . . Fraternitati vestrae . . . mandamus, quatenus . . . praelibatam vero ludibriorum consuetudinem vel potius corruptelam curetis e vestris ecclesiis . . . exstirpare.' As to the scope of this decretal and the glosses of the canonists upon it, cf. the account of miracle plays (ch. xx).

[2] *Decretales Greg. IX,* lib. iii.tit. i. cap. 12 (*C. I. Can.* ed. Friedberg. ii.

452). I cannot verify an alleged confirmation of the decretal by Innocent IV in 1246.

[3] *C. of Paris* (1212), pars iv. c. 16 (Mansi, xxii. 842) 'A festis vero follorum, ubi baculus accipitur, omnino abstineatur. Idem fortius monachis et monialibus prohibemus.' Can. 18 is a prohibition against 'choreae,' similar to that of Eudes de Sully already referred to. Such general prohibitions are as common during the mediaeval period as during that of the conversion (cf. ch. viii), and probably covered the Feast of Fools. See e.g. *C. of Avignon* (1209), c. 17 (Mansi, xxii. 791), *C. of Rouen* (1231), c. 14 (Mansi, xxiii. 216), *C. of Bayeux* (1300), c. 31 (Mansi, xxv. 66).

[4] *Codex Senonen.* 46 A. There are two copies in the *Bibl. Nat.,* (i) *Cod. Parisin.* 10520 B, con-

than itself[1]. It is not a missal at all. It is headed *Officium Circumcisionis in usum urbis Senonensis*, and is a choir-book containing the words and music of the *Propria* or special chants used in the Hours and Mass at the feast[2]. Local tradition at Sens, as far back as the early sixteenth century, ascribed the compilation of this office to that very Petrus de

taining the text only, dated 1667; (ii) *Cod. Parisin.* 1351 C, containing text and music, made for Baluze (1630–1718). The *Officium* has been printed by F. Bourquelot in *Bulletin de la Soc. arch. de Sens* (1858), vi. 79, and by Clément, 125 sqq. The metrical portions are also in Dreves, *Analecta Hymnica Medii Aevi*, xx. 217, who cites other *Quellen* for many of them. See further on the MS., Dreves, *Stimmen aus Maria-Laach*, xlvii. 575; Desjardins, 126; Chérest, 14; A.L. Millin, *Monuments antiques inédits* (1802–6), ii. 336´; Du Tilliot, 13; J. A. Dulaure, *Environs de Paris* (1825), vii. 576; Nisard, in *Archives des Missions scientifiques et littéraires* (1851), 187; Leber, ix. 344 (l'Abbé Lebeuf). Before the *Officium* proper, on f. 1ᵛᵒ of the MS. a fifteenth-century hand (Chérest, 18) has written the following quatrain:

'Festum stultorum de consuetudine morum
omnibus urbs Senonis festivat nobilis annis,
quo gaudet precentor, sed tamen omnis honor
sit Christo circumciso nunc semper et almo':

and the following couplet:

'Tartara Bacchorum non pocula sunt fatuorum,
tartara vincentes sic fiunt ut sapientes.'

Millin, *loc. cit.* 344, cites a MS. dissertation of one Père Laire, which ascribes these lines to one Lubin, an official at Chartres. The last eight pages of the MS. contain epistles for the feasts of St. Stephen,

St. John the Evangelist, and the Innocents.

[1] Chérest, 14; Millin, *op. cit.* ii. 336 (plates), and *Voyage dans le Midi*, i. 60 (plates); Clément, 122, 162; Bourquelot, *op. cit.* vi. 79 (plates); A. de Montaiglon, in *Gazette des Beaux-arts* (1880), i. 24 (plates); E. Molinier, *Hist. générale des Arts appliqués*, i; *Les Ivoires* (1896), 47 (plate); A. M. Cust, *Ivory Workers of the Middle Ages* (1902), 34. This last writer says that the diptych is now in the Bibl. Nationale. The leaves of the diptych represent a Triumph of Bacchus, and a Triumph of Artemis or Aphrodite. It has nothing to do with the Feast of Fools, and is of sixth-century workmanship.

[2] Dreves, 575, thinks the MS. was 'für eine Geckenbruderschaft,' as the chants are not in the contemporary Missals, Breviaries, Graduals, and Antiphonals of the church. But if they were, a separate *Officium* book would be superfluous. Such special *festorum libri* were in use elsewhere, e.g. at Amiens. Nisard, *op. cit.*, thinks the *Officium* was an imitation one written by 'notaires' to amuse the choir-boys, and cites a paper of M. Carlier, canon of Sens, before the Historic Congress held at Sens in 1850 in support of this view. Doubtless the *goliardi* wrote such imitations (cf. the *missa lusorum* in Schmeller, *Carmina Burana*, 248; the *missa de potatoribus* in Wright-Halliwell, *Reliquiae Antiquae*, ii. 208; and the *missa potatorum* in F. Novati, *La Parodia sacra nelle Letterature moderne* (*Studi critici e letterari*, 289)); but this is too long to be one, and is not a burlesque at all.

Corbolio who was associated with Eudes de Sully in the Paris reformation [1]. Pierre de Corbeil, whom scholastics called *doctor opinatissimus* and his epitaph *flos et honor cleri,* had a varied ecclesiastical career. As canon of Notre-Dame and reader in the Paris School of Theology he counted amongst his pupils one no less distinguished than the future Pope Innocent III himself. He became archdeacon of Evreux, coadjutor of Lincoln (a fact of some interest in connexion with the scanty traces of the Feast of Fools in England), bishop of Cambrai, and finally archbishop of Sens, where he died in 1222. There is really no reason to doubt his connexion with the *Officium.* The handwriting of the manuscript and the character of the music are consistent with a date early in the thirteenth century [2]. Elaborate and interpolated offices were then still in vogue, and the good bishop enjoyed some reputation for literature as well as for learning. He composed an office for the Assumption, and is even suspected of contributions in his youth to goliardic song [3]. It is unlikely that he actually wrote much of the text of the *Officium Circumcisionis,* very little of which is peculiar to Sens. But he may well have compiled or revised it for his own cathedral, with the intention of pruning the abuses of the feast ; and, in so doing, he evidently admitted proses and *farsurae* with a far more liberal hand than did Eudes de Sully. The whole office, which is quite serious and not in the least burlesque, well repays study. I can only dwell on those parts of it which throw light on the general character of the celebration for which it was intended.

The first Vespers on the eve of the Circumcision are preceded by four lines sung *in ianuis ecclesiae:*

[1] Cf. the chapter decree of 1524 'festum Circumcisionis a defuncto Corbolio institutum,' which is doubtless the authority for the statements of Taveau, *Hist. archiep. Senonen.* (1608), 94 ; Saint-Marthe, *Gallia Christiana* (1770), xii. 60 ; Baluze, note in *B. N. Cod. Parisin.* 1351 C. (quoted Nisard, *op. cit.*).

[2] Dreves, 575 ; Chérest, 15, who quotes an elaborate opinion of M.

Quantin, 'archiviste de l'Yonne.' M. Quantin believes that the hand is that of a charter of Pierre de Corbeil, dated 1201, in the Yonne archives. On the other hand Nisard, *op. cit.,* and Danjou, *Revue de musique religieuse* (1847), 287, think that the MS. is of the fourteenth century.

[3] Chérest, 35 ; Dreves, 576.

'Lux hodie, lux laetitiae, me iudice tristis
quisquis erit, removendus erit solemnibus istis,
sint hodie procul invidiae, procul omnia maesta,
laeta volunt, quicunque colunt asinaria festa.'

These lines are interesting, because they show that the thirteenth-century name for the feast at Sens was the *asinaria festa*, the 'Feast of the Ass.' They are followed by what is popularly known as the 'Prose of the Ass,' but is headed in the manuscript *Conductus ad tabulam*. A *conductus* is a chant sung while the officiant is conducted from one station to another in the church[1], and the *tabula* is the *rota* of names and duties *pro cantu et lectura*, with the reading of which the Vespers began[2]. The text of the Prose of the Ass, as used at Sens and elsewhere, is given in an appendix[3]. Next come a trope and a farsed Alleluia, a long interpolation dividing 'Alle-' and '-luia,' and then another passage which has given a wrong impression of the nature of the office:

'*Quatuor vel quinque in falso retro altare:*
Haec est clara dies, clararum clara dierum,
haec est festa dies, festarum festa dierum,
nobile nobilium rutilans diadema dierum.

Duo vel tres in voce retro altare:
Salve festa dies, toto venerabilis aevo,
qua Deus est ortus virginis ex utero[4].'

[1] Liturgically a *conductus* is a form of *Cantio*, that is, an interpolation in the mass or office, which stands as an independent unit, and not, like the Tropes, Proses and Sequences, as an extension of the proper liturgical texts. The *Cantiones* are, however, only a further step in the process which began with Tropes (Nisard, *op. cit.* 191; Dreves, *Anal. Hymn.* xx. 6). From the point of view of musical science H. E. Wooldridge, *Oxford Hist. of Music*, i. 308, defines a *conductus* as 'a composition of equally free and flowing melodies in all the parts, in which the words are metri-cal and given to the lower voice only.' The term is several times used in the *Officium*. Clément, 163, falls foul of Dulaure for taking it as an adjective throughout, with *asinus* understood.

[2] Wordsworth, *Mediaeval Services*, 289; Clément, 126, 163. Dulaure seems to have taken the *tabula* for the altar. The English name for the *tabula* was *wax-brede*. An example († 1500) is printed by H. E. Reynolds, *Use of Exeter Cathedral*, 73.

[3] Appendix L; where the various versions of the 'Prose' are collated.

[4] There are many hymns begin-

The phrase *in falso* does not really mean 'out of tune.' It means, 'with the harmonized accompaniment known as *en faux bourdon,*' and is opposed to *in voce,* 'in unison [1].' The Vespers, with many further interpolations, then continue, and after them follow Compline, Matins, Lauds [2], Prime, Tierce, the Mass, Sext, and second Vespers. These end with three further pieces of particular interest from our point of view. The first is a *Conductus ad Bacularium,* the name *Bacularius* being doubtless that given at Sens to the *dominus festi* [3]. This opens in a marked festal strain:

> 'Novus annus hodie
> monet nos laetitiae
> laudes inchoare,
> felix est principium,
> finem cuius gaudium
> solet terminare.
> celebremus igitur
> festum annuale,
> quo peccati solvitur
> vinculum mortale
> et infirmis proponitur
> poculum vitale ;
> adhuc sanat aegrotantes
> hoc medicinale,

ning *Salve, festa dies.* The model is a couplet of Venantius Fortunatus, *Carmina,* iii. 9, *Ad Felicem episcopum de Pascha,* 39 (M. G. H. *Auct. Antiquiss.* iv. 1. 60):

'Salve, festa dies, toto venerabilis aevo,
  qua Deus infernum vicit et astra tenet.'

[1] Clément, 127, correcting an error of Lebeuf. A still more curious slip is that of M. Bourquelot, who found in the word *euouae,* which occurs frequently in the *Officium,* an echo of the Bacchic cry *évohé.* Now *euouae* represents the vowels of the words *Seculorum amen,* and is noted at the ends of antiphons in

most choir-books to give the tone for the following psalm (Clément, 164).

[2] Clément, 138, reads *Conductus ad Ludos,* and inserts before *In Laudibus* the word *Ludarius.* Dreves, *Anal. Hymn.* xx. 221, reads *Conductus ad Laudes.* The section *In Laudibus,* not being metrical, is not printed by him, so I do not know what he makes of *Ludarius.* If Clément is right, I suppose a secular revel divided Matins and Lauds, which seems unlikely.

[3] I follow Dreves, *Anal. Hymn.* xx. 228. Clément, 151, has again *Ludarium.*

  unde psallimus laetantes
  ad memoriale.
  ha, ha, ha,
  qui vult vere psallere,
  trino psallat munere,
  corde, ore, opere
   debet laborare,
  ut sic Deum colere
   possit et placare.'

The *Bacularius* is then, one may assume, led out of the church, with the *Conductus ad Poculum*, which begins,

  ' Kalendas Ianuarias
  solemnes, Christe, facias,
  et nos ad tuas nuptias
  vocatus rex suscipias.'

The manuscript ends, so far as the Feast of the Circumcision is concerned, with some *Versus ad Prandium*, to be sung in the refectory, taken from a hymn of Prudentius [1].

  The Sens *Missel des Fous* has been described again and again. Less well known, however, is the very similar *Officium* of Beauvais, and for the simple reason that although recent writers on the Feast of Fools have been aware of its existence, they have not been aware of its *habitat*. I have been fortunate enough to find it in the British Museum, and only regret that I am not sufficiently acquainted with textual and musical palaeography to print it *in extenso* as an appendix to this chapter [2]. The date of the manuscript is probably

[1] Prudentius, *Cathemerinon*, iii.

[2] *Egerton MS.* 2615 (*Catalogue of Additions to MSS. in B. M. 1882–87*, p. 336). On the last page is written ' Iste liber est beati petri beluacensis.' On ff. 78, 110^v are book-plates of the chapter of Beauvais, the former signed ' Vollet f[ecit].' The MS. was bought by the British Museum in 1883, and formerly belonged to Signor Pachiarotti of Padua. It was described and a facsimile of the harmonized Prose of the Ass given in *Annales* *archéologiques* (1856), xvi. 259, 300. Dreves, *Anal. Hymn.* xx. 230 (1895), speaks of it as 'vielleicht noch in Italien in Privatbesitz.' This, and not the MS. used by Ducange's editors, is the MS. whose description Desjardins, 127, 168, gives from a 1464 Beauvais inventory: ' N°. 76. Item ung petit volume entre deux ais sans cuir l'ung d'icelx ais rompu à demy contenant plusieurs proses antiennes et commencemens des messes avec oraisons commençant au ii° feuillet

1227–34 [1]. Like that of Sens it contains the *Propria* for the Feast of the Circumcision from Vespers to Vespers. Unluckily, there is a lacuna of several pages in the middle [2]. The office resembles that of Sens in general character, but is much longer. There are two lines of opening rubric, of which all that remains legible is . . . *medio stantes incipit cantor.* Then comes the quatrain *Lux hodie* similarly used at Sens, but with the notable variant of *praesentia festa* for *asinaria festa.* Then, under the rubric, also barely legible, *Conductus, quando asinus adducitur* [3], comes the 'Prose of the Ass.' At the end of Lauds is the following rubric: *Postea omnes eant ante ianuas ecclesiae clausas. Et quatuor stent foris tenentes singli urnas vino plenas cum cyfis vitreis. Quorum unus canonicus incipiat* Kalendas Ianuarias. *Tunc aperiantur ianuae.* Here comes the lacuna in the manuscript, which begins again in the Mass. Shortly before the prayer for the pope is a rubric *Quod dicitur, ubi apponatur baculus,* which appears to be a direction for a ceremony not fully described in the *Officium.* The 'Prose of the Ass' occurs a second time as the *Conductus Subdiaconi ad Epistolam,* and on this occasion the musical accompaniment is harmonized in three parts [4]. I can find nothing about a *Bacularius* at second Vespers, but the office ends with a series of *conductus* and hymns, some of which are also harmonized in parts. The *Officium* is followed in the manuscript by a Latin cloister play of *Daniel* [5].

An earlier manuscript than that just described was formerly preserved in the Beauvais cathedral library. It dated from 1160–80 [6]. It was known to Pierre Louvet, the seventeenth-century historian of Beauvais [7], and apparently to Dom

---

Bellebouche et au pénultième *coopertum stolla candida.*' The broken board was mended, after 420 years, by the British Museum in 1884.

[1] *B. M. Catalogue, loc. cit.,* 'Written in the xiii[th] cent., probably during the pontificate of Gregory IX (1227–41) and before the marriage of Louis IX to Marguerite of Provence in 1234.' There are prayers for Gregorius Papa and Ludovicus Rex on ff. 42, 42[v], but none for any queen of France.

[2] Between ff. 40vo and 41.

[3] So *B. M. Catalogue, loc. cit.* To me it reads like ' Conductus asi . . . adducitur.'

[4] F. 43.

[5] Cf. ch. xix.

[6] Louis VII married Adèle de Champagne in 1160 and died in 1180.

[7] Pierre Louvet, *Hist. du Dioc. de Beauvais* (1635), ii. 299, quoted

Grenier, who died in 1789 [1]. According to Grenier's account it must have closely resembled that in the British Museum.

'Aux premières vêpres, le chantre commençait par entonner au milieu de la nef : *Lux hodie, lux laetitiae*, etc. . . . À laudes rien de particulier que le *Benedictus* et son répons farcis. Les laudes finies on sortait de l'église pour aller trouver l'âne qui attendait à la grande porte. Elle était fermée. Là, chacun des chanoines s'y trouvant la bouteille et le verre à la main, le chantre entonnait la prose : *Kalendas ianuarias solemne Christe facias.* Voici ce que porte l'ancien cérémonial : *dominus cantor et canonici ante ianuas ecclesiae clausas stent foris tenentes singuli urnas vini plenas cum cyfis vitreis, quorum unus cantor incipiat : Kalendas ianuarias*, etc. Les battants de la porte ouverts, on introduisait l'âne dans l'église, en chantant la prose : *Orientis partibus.* Ici est une lacune dans le manuscrit jusque vers le milieu du *Gloria in excelsis.* . . . On chantait la litanie : *Christus vincit, Christus regnat*, dans laquelle on priait pour le pape Alexandre III, pour Henri de France, évêque de Beauvais, pour le roi Louis VII et pour Alixe ou Adèle de Champagne qui était devenue reine en 1160 ; par quoi on peut juger de l'antiquité de ce cérémonial. L'Évangile était précédé d'une prose et suivi d'une autre. Il est marqué dans le cérémonial de cinq cents ans que les encensements du jour de cette fête se feront avec le boudin et la saucisse : *hac die incensabitur cum boudino et saucita.*'

by Desjardins, 124. I am sorry not to have been able to get hold of the original. Nor can I find E. Charvet, *Rech. sur les anciens théâtres de Beauvais* (1881).

[1] Grenier, 362. He says the 'cérémonial' is 'tiré d'un ms. de la cathédrale de Beauvais,' and gives the footnote 'Preuv. part 1, n°. .' On the prose *Kalendas Ianuarias* and the censing his footnotes refer to Ducange, s. v. *Kalendae.* The 'Preuves' for his history are scattered through the *MSS. Picardie* in the *Bibl. Nat.* No doubt the reference here is to MSS. 14 and 158 which are copies of the Beauvais office (Dreves, in *Stimmen aus Maria-Laach*, xlvii. 575). These,

or parts of them, are printed by F. Bourquelot, in *Bulletin de la Soc. arch. de Sens* (1854), vi. 171 (which also, unfortunately, I have not seen), and chants from them are in Dreves, *Anal. Hymn.* xx. 229. But here Dreves seems to speak of them as copies of Pacchiarotti's MS. (*Egerton MS.* 2615). And Desjardins, 124, says that Grenier and Bourquelot used extracts from eighteenth-century copies of Pacchiarotti's MS. in the library of M. Borel de Brétizel. Are these writers mistaken, or did Grenier only see the copies, and take his description from Louvet ? And what has become of the twelfth-century MS. ?

Dom Grenier gives as the authority for his last sentence, not the *Officium*, but the *Glossary* of Ducange, or rather the additions thereto made by certain Benedictine editors in 1733-6. They quote the pudding and sausage rubric together with that as to the drinking-bout, which occurs in both the *Officia*, as from a Beauvais manuscript. This they describe as a *codex ann. circiter* 500 [1]. It seems probable that this was not an *Officium* at all, but something of the nature of a Processional, and that it was identical with the *codex* 500 *annorum* from which the same Benedictines derived their amazing account of a Beauvais ceremony which took place not on January 1 but on January 14 [2]. A pretty girl, with a child in her arms, was set upon an ass, to represent the Flight into Egypt. There was a procession from the cathedral to the church of St. Stephen. The ass and its riders were stationed on the gospel side of the altar. A solemn mass was sung, in which *Introit, Kyrie, Gloria* and *Credo* ended with a bray. To crown all, the rubrics direct that the celebrant, instead of saying *Ite, missa est*, shall bray three times (*ter hinhannabit*) and that the people shall respond in similar fashion. At this ceremony also the 'Prose of the Ass' was used, and the version preserved in the *Glossary* is longer and more ludicrous than that of either the Sens or the Beauvais *Officium*.

On a review of all the facts it would seem that the Beauvais documents represent a stage of the feast unaffected by any such reform as that carried out by Pierre de Corbeil at Sens. And the nature of that reform is fairly clear. Pierre de

---

[1] Ducange, s. v. *Kalendae*, 'MS. codice Bellovac. ann. circiter 500, ubi 1ª haec occurrit rubrica *Dominus ... ianuae.* Et alibi *Hac ... saucita.*'

[2] Ducange,s. v.*Festum Asinorum.* Desjardins and other writers give the date of the 'codex' as twelfth century. But 500 years from 1733-6 only bring it to the thirteenth century. The mistake is due to the fact that the *first* edition of Ducange, in which the 'codex' is not mentioned, is of 1678. Clément,

158, appears to have no knowledge of the MS. but what he read in Ducange; and it is not quite clear what he means when he says that it 'd'après nos renseignements, ne renferme pas un office, mais une sorte de *mystère* postérieur d'un siècle au moins à l'office de Sens, et n'ayant aucune autorité historique et encore bien moins religieuse.' The MS. was contemporary with the Sens *Officium*,and although certainly influenced by the religious drama was still liturgic (cf. ch. xx).

Corbeil provided a text of the *Officium* based either on that of Beauvais or on an earlier version already existing at Sens. He probably added very little of his own, for the Sens manuscript only contains a few short passages not to be found in that of Beauvais. And as the twelfth-century Beauvais manuscript seems to have closely resembled the thirteenth-century one still extant, Beauvais cannot well have borrowed from him. At the same time he doubtless suppressed whatever burlesque ceremonies, similar to the Beauvais drinking-bout in the porch and censing with pudding and sausage, may have been in use at Sens. One of these was possibly the actual introduction of an ass into the church. But it must be remembered that the most extravagant of such ceremonies would not be likely at either place to get into the formal service-books[1]. As the Sens *Officium* only includes the actual service of January 1 itself, it is impossible to compare the way in which the semi-dramatic extension of the feast was treated in the two neighbouring cathedrals. But Sens probably had this extension, for as late as 1634 there was an annual procession, in which the leading figures were the Virgin Mary mounted on an ass and a *cortège* of the twelve Apostles. This did not, however, at that time take part in the Mass[2].

The full records of the Feast of Fools at Sens do not begin until the best part of a century after the probable date of its *Officium*. But one isolated notice breaks the interval, and shows that the efforts of Pierre de Corbeil were not for long successful in purging the revel of its abuses. This is a letter written to the chapter in 1245 by Odo, cardinal of Tusculum, who was then papal legate in France. He calls attention to the *antiqua ludibria* of the feasts of Christmas week and of the Circumcision, and requires these

---

[1] Cf. Appendix L, on an *Officium* (1553) for Jan. 1, without *stulti* or *asinus*, from Puy.

Leber, ix. 238. This is a note by J. B. Salques to the reprint of D'Artigny's memoir on the *Fête des Fous*. The writer calls the ceremony the 'fête des apôtres,' and says that it was held at the same time as the 'fête de l'âne.'

He describes a Rabelaisian *contre-temps*, which is said to have put an end to the procession in 1634. No authority is given for this account, which I believe to be the source of all later notices. I may add that Ducange gives the name *Festum Apostolorum* to the feast of St. Philip and St. James on May 1.

to be celebrated, not *iuxta pristinum modum*, but with the proper ecclesiastical ceremonies. He specifically reprobates the use of unclerical dress and the wearing of wreaths of flowers [1].

A little later in date than either the Sens or the Beauvais *Officium* is a *Ritual* of St. Omer, which throws some light on the Feast of Fools as it was celebrated in the northern town on the day of the Circumcision about 1264. It was the feast of the vicars and the choir. A 'bishop' and a 'dean' of Fools took part in the services. The latter was censed in burlesque fashion, and the whole office was recited at the pitch of the voice, and even with howls. There cannot have been much of a reformation here [2].

A few other scattered notices of thirteenth-century Feasts of Fools may be gathered together. The *Roman de Renard* is witness to the existence of such a feast, with *jeux* and tippling, at Bayeux, about 1200 [3]. At Autun, the chapter forbade the *baculus anni novi* in 1230 [4]. Feasts of Fools

[1] *Cod. Senonens.* G. 133, printed by Chérest, 47; Quantin, *Recueil de pièces pour faire suite au Cartulaire général de l'Yonne* (1873), 235 (Nº. 504) 'mandamus, quatenus illa festorum antiqua ludibria, quae in contemptum Dei, opprobrium cleri, et derisum populi non est dubium exerceri, videlicet, in festis Sancti Ioannis Evangelistae, Innocentium, et Circumcisionis Domini, iuxta pristinum modum nullatenus faciatis aut fieri permittatis, sed iuxta formam et cultum aliarum festivitatum quae per anni circulum celebrantur, ita volumus et praecipimus celebrari. Ita quod ipso facto sententiam suspensionis incurrat quicumque in mutatione habitus aut in sertis de floribus seu aliis dissolutionibus iuxta praedictum ritum reprobatum adeo in praedictis festivitatibus seu aliis a modo praesumpserit se habere.'

[2] L. Deschamps de Pas, *Les Cérémonies religieuses dans la Collégiale de Saint-Omer au xiiiᵉ Siècle* (*Mém. de la Soc. de la Morinie*, xx. 147). The directions for Jan. 1 are fragmentary: 'In quo vicarii ceterique clerici chorum frequentantes et eorum episcopus se habeant in cantando et officiando sicut superius dictum est in festo Sanctorum Innocentium (cf. p. 370), hoc tamen excepto quod omnia quae ista die fiunt officiando quando est festum fatuorum pro posse fiunt et etiam ullulando ... domino decano fatuorum ferunt incensum sed prepostere ut dictum est.' *Ululatus* is, however, sometimes a technical term in church music; cf. vol. ii. p. 7.

[3] *R. de Renard*, xii. 469 (ed. Martin, vol. ii. 14):

'Dan prestre, il est la feste as fox.
Si fera len demein des chox
Et grant departie a Baieus:
Ales i, si verres les jeus.'

Branch xii of the *Roman* is the composition of Richart de Lison, who, according to Martin, suppl. 72, wrote in Normandy † 1200. The phrase 'faire les choux' = 'get drunk,' cabbages being regarded as prophylactic of the ill effects of liquor.

[4] *Hist. de l'Église d'Autun* (1774), 469, 631 'Item innovamus,

on Innocents' and New Year's days are forbidden by the statutes of Nevers cathedral in 1246 [1]. At Romans, in Dauphiné, an agreement was come to in 1274 between the chapter, the archbishop of Vienne and the municipal authorities, that the choice of an abbot by the cathedral clerks known as *esclaffardi* should cease, on account of the disturbances and scandals to which it had given rise [2]. The earliest mention of the feast at Laon is about 1280 [3]; while it is provided for as the sub-deacons' feast by an Amiens *Ordinarium* of 1291 [4]. Nor are the ecclesiastical writers oblivious of it. William of Auxerre opens an era of learned speculation in his *De Officiis Ecclesiasticis*, by explaining it as a Christian substitute for the *Parentalia* of the pagans [5]. Towards the end of the century, Durandus, bishop of Mende, who drew upon both William of Auxerre and Belethus for

quod ille qui de caetero capiet baculum anni novi nihil penitus habebit de bursa Capituli' (*Registr. Capit.* s. a. 1230).

[1] Martene and Durand, *Thesaurus Anecdotorum*, iv. 1070 'in festo stultorum, scilicet Innocentium et anni novi ... multa fiunt inhonesta ... ne talia festa irrisoria de cetero facere praesumant.'

[2] Ducange, s. v. *abbas esclaffardorum*, quoting *Hist. Delphin.* i. 132; J. J. A. Pilot de Thorey, *Usages, Fêtes et Coutumes en Dauphiné*, i. 182. The latter writer says that there was also an *episcopus*, who was not suppressed, that the canons did reverence to him, and that the singing of the *Magnificat* was part of the feast.

[3] C. Hidé, *Bull. de la Soc. acad. de Laon* (1863), xiii. 115.

[4] Grenier, 361 'Si hoc dicitur festum stultorum a subdiaconis fiat, et dominica eveniat, ab ipsis fiat festum in cappis sericis, sicut in libris festorum continetur.' These *libri* possibly resembled those of Sens and Beauvais.

[5] *Summa Gulielmi Autissiodorensis de Off. Eccles.* (quoted by Chérest, 44, from *Bibl. Nat. MS.* 1411) 'Quaeritur quare in hac die fit festum stultorum. ... Ante ad-

ventum Domini celebrabant festa quae vocabant Parentalia; et in illa die spem ponebant credentes quod si in illa die bene eis accideret, quod similiter in toto anno. Hoc festum voluit removere Ecclesia quod contra fidem est. Et quia extirpare omnino non potuit, festum illud permittit et celebrat illud festum celeberrimum ut aliud demittatur: et ideo in matutinali officio leguntur lectiones quae dehortantur ab huiusmodi quae sunt contra fidem (cf. p. 245). Et si ista die ab ecclesia quaedam fiunt praeter fidem, nulla tamen contra fidem. Et ideo ludos qui sunt contra fidem permutavit in ludos qui non sunt contra fidem.' There is clearly a confusion here between the Roman *Parentalia* (Feb. 13–22) and *Kalendae* (Jan. 1). On William of Auxerre, whose work remains in MS., cf. Lebeuf, in P. Desmolets, *Mémoires*, iii. 339; *Nouvelle Biographie universelle*, s. n. He was bishop of Auxerre, translated to Paris in 1220, ob. 1223. He must be distinguished from another William of Auxerre, who was archdeacon of Beauvais (†1230), and wrote a comment on Petrus Lombardus, printed at Paris in 1500 (Gröber, *Grundriss der röm. Philologie*, ii. 1. 239).

his *Rationale Divinorum Officiorum*, gave an account of it which agrees closely with that of Belethus[1]. Neither William of Auxerre nor Durandus shows himself hostile to the Feast of Fools. Its abuses are, however, condemned in more than one contemporary collection of sermons[2].

With the fourteenth century the records of the Feast of Fools become more frequent. In particular, the account-books of the chapter of Sens throw some light on the organization of the feast in that cathedral[3]. The *Compotus Camerarii* has, from 1345 onwards, a yearly entry *pro vino praesentato vicariis ecclesiae die Circumcisionis Domini*. Sometimes the formula is varied to *die festi fatuorum*. In course of time the whole expenses of the feast come to be a charge on the chapter, and in particular, it would appear, upon the sub-deacon canons[4]. In 1376 is mentioned, for the first time, the *dominus festi*, to whom under the title of *precentor et provisor festi stultorum* a payment is made. The *Compotus Nemorum* shows that by 1374 a prebend in the chapter woods had been appropriated to the vicars *pro festo fatuorum*. Similar entries occur to the end of the

[1] Gulielmus Durandus, *Rationale Div. Off.* (Antwerp, 1614), vi. 15, *de Circumcisione*, 'In quibusdam ecclesiis subdiaconi fortes et iuvenes faciunt hodie festum ad significandum quod in octava resurgentium, quae significatur per octavam diem, qua circumcisio fiebat, nulla erit debilis aetas, non senectus, non senium, non impotens pueritia ... &c.' A reference to the heathen Kalends follows; cf. also vii. 42, *de festis SS. Stephani, Ioannis Evang. et Innocentium*, '. . . subdiaconi vero faciunt festum in quibusdam ecclesiis in festo circumcisionis, ut ibi dictum est : in aliis in Epiphania et etiam in aliis in octava Epiphaniae, quod vocant festum stultorum. Quia enim ordo ille antiquitus incertus erat, nam in canonibus antiquis (extra de aetate et qualitate) multis quandoque vocatur sacer et quandoque non, ideo subdiaconi certum ad festandum non habent diem, et eorum festum officio cele-

bratur confuso.' On Durandus cf. the translation of his work by C. Barthélemy (1854). He was born at Puymisson in the diocese of Béziers (1230), finished the *Rationale* (1284), became bishop of Mende (1285), and ob. (1296).

[2] A. Lecoy de la Marche, *La Chaire française au M. A.* 368, citing *Bibl. Nat. MSS. fr.* 13314, f. 18; 16481, N°. 93. The latter MS., which is analysed by Echard, *Script. Ord. Predicatorum*, i. 269, contains Dominican sermons delivered in Paris, 1272-3.

[3] Chérest, 49 sqq., from Sens *Chapter Accounts* in *Archives de l'Yonne*, at Auxerre. The *Compotus Camerarii* begins in 1295-6. The *Chapter Register* is missing before 1662 : some of Baluze's extracts from it are in *Bibl. Nat. Cod. Parisin.* 1351.

[4] Chérest, 55 ' pro servitio faciendo die dicti festi quatenus tangit canonicos subdiaconos in ecclesia.'

fourteenth century and during the first quarter of the fifteenth[1]. Then came the war to disturb everything, and from 1420 the account-books rarely show any traces of the feast. Nor were civil commotions alone against it. As in the twelfth and thirteenth centuries, so in the fourteenth and fifteenth the abuses which clung about the Feasts of Fools rendered them everywhere a mark for the eloquence of ecclesiastical reformers. About 1400 the famous theologian and rector of Paris University, Jean-Charlier de Gerson, put himself at the head of a crusade against the *ritus ille impiissimus et insanus qui regnat per totam Franciam*, and denounced it roundly in sermons and *conclusiones*. The indecencies of the feast, he declares, would shame a kitchen or a tavern. The chapters will do nothing to stop them, and if the bishops protest, they are flouted and defied. The scandal can only be ended by the interposition of royal authority[2]. According

---

[1] Towards the end of this period the accounts are in French : 'le précentre de la feste aux fols.'

[2] *Epistola de Reformatione Theologiae* (Gerson, *Opera Omnia*, i. 121), from Bruges, 1st Jan. 1400 'ex sacrilegis paganorum idololatrarumque ritibus reliquiae,' &c. ; *Solemnis oratio ex parte Universitatis Paris. in praesentia Regis Caroli Sexti* (1405, *Opera* iv. 620 ; cf. French version in *Bibl. Nat. anc. f. fr.* 7275, described P. Paris, *Manus. franç. de la Bibl. du Roi*, vii. 266) 'hic commendari potest bona Regis fides et vestrum omnium Dominorum variis modis religiosorum, . . . in hoc quod iam dudum litteras dedistis contra abominabiles maledictiones et quasi idolatrias, quae in Francorum fiunt ecclesiis sub umbra Festi fatuorum. Fatui sunt ipsi, et perniciosi fatui, nec sustinendi, opus est executione'; *Rememoratio quorumdam quae per Praelatum quemlibet pro parte sua nunc agenda viderentur* (1407-8, *Opera*, ii. 109) 'sciatur quomodo ritus ille impiissimus et insanus qui regnat per totam Franciam poterit evelli aut saltem temperari. De hoc scilicet quod ecclesiastici faciunt, vel in die Innocentium, vel in die Circumcisionis, vel in Epiphania Domini, vel in Carnisprivio per Ecclesias suas, ubi fit irrisio detestabilis Servitii Domini et Sacramentorum : ubi plura fiunt impudenter et execrabiliter quam fieri deberent, in tabernis vel prostibulis, vel apud Saracenos et Iudaeos ; sciunt qui viderunt, quod non sufficit.censura Ecclesiastica ; quaeratur auxilium potestatis Regiae per edicta sua vehementer urgentia'; *Quinque conclusiones super ludo stultorum communiter fieri solito* (*Opera* iii. 309) 'qui per Regnum Franciae in diversis fiunt Ecclesiis et Abbatiis monachorum et monialium . . . hae enim insolentiae non dicerentur cocis in eorum culina absque dedecore aut reprehensione, quae ibi fiunt in Ecclesiis Sacrosanctis, in loco orationis, in praesentia Sancti Sacramenti Altaris, dum divinum cantatur servitium, toto populo Christiano spectante et interdum Iudaeis . . . adhuc peius est dicere, festum hoc adeo approbatum esse sicut festum Conceptionis Virginis Mariae, quod paulo ante asseruit quidam in urbe Altissiodorensi secundum quod dicitur et narrari solet, &c.'

to Gerson, Charles the Sixth did on one occasion issue letters
against the feast; and the view of the reformers found
support in the diocesan council of Langres in 1404 [1], and
the provincial council of Tours, held at Nantes in 1431 [2].
It was a more serious matter when, some years after Gerson's
death, the great council of Basle included a prohibition of
the feast in its reformatory decrees of 1435 [3]. By the
Pragmatic Sanction issued by Charles VII at the national
council of Bourges in 1438, these decrees became ecclesiastical law in France [4], and it was competent for the *Parlements* to put them into execution [5]. But the chapters were
obstinate; the feasts were popular, not only with the inferior clergy themselves, but with the *spectacle*-loving *bourgeois* of the cathedral towns; and it was only gradually that
they died out during the course of the next century and
a half. The failure of the Pragmatic Sanction to secure
immediate obedience in this matter roused the University of
Paris, still possessed with the spirit of Gerson, to fresh action.
On March 12, 1445, the Faculty of Theology, acting through
its dean, Eustace de Mesnil, addressed to the bishops and

[1] *Council of Langres* (1404)
'prohibemus clericis . . . ne intersint . . . in ludis illis inhonestis
quae solent fieri in aliquibus Ecclesiis in festo Fatuorum quod
faciunt in festivitatibus Natalis
Domini.'

[2] *Council of Nantes* (1431), c. 13
(J. Maan, *Sancta et Metrop. Eccl.
Turonensis*, ii. 101) 'quia in talibus
Ecclesiis Provinciae Turonensis
inolevit et servatur usus, . . . quod
festis Nativitatis Domini, Sanctorum Stephani, Ioannis et Innocentium, nonnulli Papam, nonnulli
Episcopum, alii Ducem vel Comitem
aut Principem in suis Ecclesiis ex
novitiis praecipuis faciunt et or-
dinant . . . Et talia . . . vulgari eloquio festum stultorum nuncupatur,
quod de residuis Kalendis Ianuariis
a multo tempore ortum fuisse cre-
datur.'

[3] *Council of Basle*, sessio xxi (June
9, 1435), can. xi (Mansi, xxix. 108)
'Turpem etiam illum abusum in

quibusdam frequentatum Ecclesiis,
quo certis anni celebritatibus nonnullis cum mitra, baculo ac vestibus
pontificalibus more episcoporum
benedicunt, alii ut reges ac duces
induti quod festum Fatuorum, vel
Innocentum seu Puerorum in quibusdam regionibus nuncupatur, alii
larvales et theatrales iocos, alii
choreas et tripudia marium et mulierum facientes homines ad spectacula et cachinnationes movent, alii
comessationes et convivia ibidem
praeparant.'

[4] *Council of Bourges*, July 7, 1438
(*Ordonnances des Rois de France de
la Troisième Race*, xiii. 287) 'Item.
Accepta Decretum de spectaculis
in Ecclesia non faciendis, quod
incipit: *Turpem*, &c.'

[5] F. Aubert, *Le Parlement de
Paris, sa Compétence, ses Attribu-
tions*, 1314-1422 (1890), 182 ; *Hist.
du Parlement de Paris*, 1250-1515
(1894), i. 163.

chapters of France a letter which, from the minuteness of its indictment, is perhaps the most curious of the many curious documents concerning the feast[1]. It consists of a preamble and no less than fourteen *conclusiones*, some of which are further complicated by *qualificationes*. The preamble sets forth the facts concerning the *festum fatuorum*. It has its clear origin, say the theologians, in the rites of paganism, amongst which this Janus-worship of the Kalends has alone been allowed to survive. They then describe the customs of the feast in a passage which I must translate:

'Priests and clerks may be seen wearing masks and monstrous visages at the hours of office. They dance in the choir dressed as women, panders or minstrels. They sing wanton songs. They eat black puddings at the horn of the altar while the celebrant is saying mass. They play at dice there. They cense with stinking smoke from the soles of old shoes. They run and leap through the church, without a blush at their own shame. Finally they drive about the town and its theatres in shabby traps and carts; and rouse the laughter of their fellows and the bystanders in infamous performances, with indecent gestures and verses scurrilous and unchaste[2].'

There follows a refutation of the argument that such *ludi* are but the relaxation of the bent bow in a fashion sanctioned by antiquity. On the contrary, they are due to original sin, and the snares of devils. The bishops are besought to follow the example of St. Paul and St. Augustine, of bishops Martin,

---

[1] *Epistola et xiv. conclusiones facultatis theologiae Parisiensis ad ecclesiarum praelatos contra festum fatuorum in Octavis Nativitatis Domini vel prima Ianuarii in quibusdam Ecclesiis celebratum* (H. Denifle, *Chartularium Univ. Paris.* iv. 652; *P. L.* ccvii. 1169). The document is too long and too scholastic to quote in full. The date is March 12, 1444⅘.

[2] 'Quis, quaeso, Christianorum sensatus non diceret malos illos sacerdotes et clericos, quos divini officii tempore videret larvatos, monstruosis vultibus, aut in vestibus mulierum, aut lenonum, vel histrionum choreas ducere in choro, cantilenas inhonestas cantare, offas pingues supra cornu altaris iuxta celebrantem missam comedere, ludum taxillorum ibidem exercere, thurificare de fumo fetido ex corio veterum sotularium, et per totam ecclesiam currere, saltare, turpitudinem suam non erubescere, ac deinde per villam et theatra in curribus et vehiculis sordidis duci ad infamia spectacula, pro risu astantium et concurrentium turpes gesticulationes sui corporis faciendo, et verba impudicissima ac scurrilia proferendo?'

Hilarius, Chrysostom, Nicholas and Germanus of Auxerre, all of whom made war on sacrilegious practices, not to speak of the canons of popes and general councils, and to stamp out the *ludibria*. It rests with them, for the clergy will not be so besotted as to face the Inquisition and the secular arm[1].

The *conclusiones* thus introduced yield a few further data as to the ceremonies of the feast. It seems to be indifferently called *festum stultorum* and *festum fatuorum*. It takes place in cathedrals and collegiate churches, on Innocents' day, on St. Stephen's, on the Circumcision, or on other dates. 'Bishops' or 'archbishops' of Fools are chosen, who wear mitres and pastoral staffs, and have crosses borne before them, as if they were on visitation. They take the Office, and give Benedictions to the readers of the lessons at Matins, and to the congregations. In exempt churches, subject only to the Holy See, a 'pope' of Fools is naturally chosen instead of a 'bishop' or an 'archbishop.' The clergy wear the garments of the laity or of fools, and the laity put on priestly or monastic robes. *Ludi theatrales* and *personagiorum ludi* are performed.

The manifesto of the Theological Faculty helped in at least one town to bring matters to a crisis. At Troyes the Feast of Fools appears to have been celebrated on the Circumcision in the three great collegiate churches of St. Peter, St. Stephen, and St. Urban, and on Epiphany in the abbey of St. Loup. The earliest records are from St. Peter's. In 1372 the chapter forbade the vicars to celebrate the feast without leave. In 1380 and 1381 there are significant entries of payments for damage done: in the former year Marie-la-Folle broke a *candelabrum*; in the latter a cross had to be repaired and gilded. In 1436, the year after the council of Basle, leave was given to hold the feast without irreverence. In 1439, the year after the Pragmatic Sanction, it was forbidden. In

---

[1] ' Concludimus, quod a vobis praelatis pendet continuatio vel abolitio huius pestiferi ritus; nam ipsos ecclesiasticos ita dementes esse et obstinatos in hac furia non est verisimile, quod si faciem praelati reperirent rigidam et nullatenus flexibilem a punitione cum assistentia inquisitorum fidei, et auxilio brachii saecularis, quam illico cederent aut frangerentur. Timerent namque carceres, timerent perdere beneficia, perdere famam et ab altaribus sacris repelli.'

1443, it was again permitted. But it must be outside the
church. The 'archbishop' might wear a rochet, but the
supper must take place in the house of one of the canons,
and not at a tavern. The experiment was not altogether
a success, for a canon had to be fined twenty sous *pour les
grandes sottises et les gestes extravagants qu'il s'était permis
à la fête des fols*[1]. Towards the end of 1444, when it was
proposed to renew the feast, the bishop of Troyes, Jean
Leguisé, intervened. The clergy of St. Peter's were apparently willing to submit, but those of St. Stephen's stood out.
They told the bishop that they were exempt from his jurisdiction, and subject only to his metropolitan, the archbishop
of Sens; and they held an elaborate revel with even more
than the usual insolence and riot. On the Sunday before
Christmas they publicly consecrated their 'archbishop' in the
most public place of the town with a *jeu de personnages* called
le jeu du sacre de leur arcevesque, which was a burlesque of
the *saint mistère de consécration pontificale*. The feast itself
took place in St. Stephen's Church. The vicar who was
chosen 'archbishop' performed the service on the eve and
day of the Circumcision *in pontificalibus*, gave the Benediction
to the people, and went in procession through the town.
Finally, on Sunday, January 3, the clergy of all three churches
joined in another *jeu de personnages*, in which, under the
names of *Hypocrisie, Faintise* and *Faux-semblant*, the bishop
and two canons who had been most active in opposing the
feast, were held up to ridicule. Jean Leguisé was not a man
to be defied with impunity. On January 23 he wrote a letter
to the archbishop of Sens, Louis de Melun, calling his
attention to the fact that the rebellious clerks had claimed
his authority for their action. He also lodged a complaint
with the king himself, and probably incited the Faculty of
Theology at Paris to back him up with the protest already
described. The upshot of it all was a sharp letter from

---

[1] T. Boutiot, *Hist. de la Ville de
Troyes* (1870–80), ii. 264; iii. 19.
A chapter decree of 1437 lays down
that a vicar who has served as
'archbishop' and has subsequently
left the cathedral and returned
again, need not serve a second
time. It was doubtless an expen-
sive dignity.

Charles VII to the *bailly* and *prévost* of Troyes, setting
forth what had taken place, and requiring them to see that
no repetition of the scandalous *jeux* was allowed [1]. Shortly
afterwards the chapter of St. Peter's sent for their *Ordinarium*,
and solemnly erased all that was derogatory to religion and
the good name of the clergy in the directions for the feast.
What the chapter of St. Stephen's did, we do not know.
The canons mainly to blame had already apologized to the
bishop. Probably it was thought best to say nothing, and
let it blow over. At any rate, it is interesting to note that
in 1595, a century and a half later, St. Stephen's was still
electing its *archevesque des saulx*, and that *droits* were
paid on account of the vicars' feast until all *droits* tumbled
in 1789 [2].

The proceedings at Troyes seem to have reacted upon the
feast at Sens. In December, 1444, the chapter had issued
an elaborate order for the regulation of the ceremony, in
which they somewhat pointedly avoided any reference to
the council of Basle or the Pragmatic Sanction, and cited only
the legatine statute of Odo of Tusculum in 1245. The order
requires that divine service shall be devoutly and decently
performed, *prout iacet in libro ipsius servitii*. By this is
doubtless meant the *Officium* already described. There must

---

[1] Boutiot, *op. cit.* iii. 20; A. de
Jubainville, *Inventaire sommaire
des Archives départementales de
l'Aube*, i. 244 (G. 1275); P. de
Julleville, *Les Com.* 35, *Rép. Com.*
330; A. Vallet de Viriville, in *Bibl.
de l'École des Chartes*, iii. 448. The
letter of Jean Leguisé to Louis de
Melun is printed in *Annales archéologiques*, iv. 209; *Revue des Soc.
Savantes* (2nd series), vi. 94;
Journal de Verdun, Oct. 1751, and
partly by Rigollot, 153. It is dated
only Jan. 23, but clearly refers to
the events of 1444-5. The *Ordon-
nance* of Charles VII is in Martene
and Durand, *Thesaurus Novus
Anecdotorum*, i. 1804; H. Denifle,
Chartularium Univ. Paris. iv. 657.
Extracts are given by Ducange,
s.v. *Kalendae*. The king speaks
of the Troyes affair as leading to

the Theological Faculty's letter. It
is permissible to conjecture that he
was moved, no doubt by the abstract rights and wrongs of the case,
but also by a rumour spread at
Troyes that he had revoked the
Pragmatic Sanction. For, as a
matter of fact, Peter of Brescia,
the papal legate, was trying hard
to get him to revoke it.

[2] Boutiot, *op. cit.* i. 494, iii. 20.
The chapters of St. Stephen's and
St. Urban's and the abbey of St.
Loup all continued to make payments for their feasts after 1445.
They may have been pruned of
abuses. In the sixteenth century
the Comte of Champagne pays five
sous to the 'archevesque des Saulx'
at St. Stephen's, and this appears
to be the *droit* charged upon the
royal demesne up to 1789.

be no mockery or impropriety, no unclerical costume, no dissonant singing. Then comes what, considering that this is a reform, appears a sufficiently remarkable direction. Not more than three buckets of water at most must be poured over the *precentor stultorum* at Vespers. The custom of ducking on St. John's eve, apparently the occasion when the precentor was elected, is also pruned, and a final clause provides that if nobody's rights are infringed the *stulti* may do what they like outside the church [1]. Under these straitened conditions the feast was probably held in 1445. There was, however, the archbishop as well as the chapter to be reckoned with. It was difficult for Louis de Melun, after the direct appeal made to him by his suffragan at Troyes, to avoid taking some action, and in certain statutes promulgated in November, 1445, he required the suppression of the whole *consuetudo* and ordered the directions for it to be erased from the chant-books [2]. There is now no mention of the feast until 1486, from which date an occasional payment for *la*

---

[1] Chérest, 66, from *Acta Capitularia* (Dec. 4, 1444) in *Bibl. Nat. Cod. Paris.* 1014 and 1351 'De servitio dominicae circumcisionis, viso super hoc statuto per quemdam legatum edito, et consideratis aliis circa hoc considerandis, et ad evitandum scandala, quae super hoc possent exoriri, ordinatum fuit unanimiter et concorditer, nemine discrepante, quod de caetero dictum servitium fiet, prout iacet in libro ipsius servitii, devote et cum reverentia; absque aliqua derisione, tumultu aut turpitudine, prout fiunt alia servitia in aliis festis, in habitibus per dictum statutum ordinatis, et non alias, et voce modulosa, absque dissonantia, et assistant in huiusmodi servitio omnes qui tenentur in eo interesse, et faciant debitum suum absque discursu aut turbatione servitii, potissime in ecclesia; nec proiiciatur aqua in vesperis super praecentorem stultorum ultra quantitatem trium sitularum ad plus; nec adducantur nudi in crastino festi dominicae nativitatis, sine brachis verenda tegentibus, nec etiam adducantur in ecclesia, sed ducantur ad puteum claustri, non hora servitii sed alia, et ibi rigentur sola situla aquae sine lesione. Qui contrarium fecerit occurrit ipso facto suspensionis censuram per dictum statutum latam; attamen extra ecclesiam permissum est quod stulti faciant alias ceremonias sine damno aut iniuria cuiusquam.' The proceedings on the day after the Nativity are probably explained by the election of the precentor on that day (after Vespers). The victims ducked may have failed to be present at the election; but cf. the Easter *prisio* (ch. vii).

[2] Saint-Marthe, *Gallia Christiana*, xii. 96, partly quoted by Ducange, s. v. *Kalendae*. The bishop describes the feast almost in the *ipsissima verba* of the Paris Theologians, but in one passage ('nudos homines sine verendorum tegmine inverecunde ducendo per villam et theatra in curribus et vehiculis sordidis, &c.') he adds a trait from the Sens chapter act just quoted.

feste du premier jour de l'an begins to appear again in the chapter account-books [1]. In 1511, the *servitium divinum* after the old custom is back in the church. But the chapter draws a distinction between the *servitium* and the *festum stultorum*, which is forbidden. The performance of *jeux de personnages* and the public shaving of the precentor's beard on a stage are especially reprobated [2]. The *servitium* was again allowed in 1514, 1516, 1517, and in 1520 with a provision that the *lucerna precentoris fatuorum* must not be brought into the church [3]. In 1522, both *servitium* and *festum* were forbidden on account of the war with Spain; the shaving of the precentor and the ceremony of his election on the feast of St. John the Evangelist again coming in for express prohibition [4]. In 1523 the *servitium* was allowed upon a protest by the vicars, but only with the strict exclusion of the popular elements [5]. In 1524 even the *servitium* was withheld, and though sanctioned again in 1535, 1539 and 1543, it was finally suppressed in 1547 [6]. Some feast, however, would still seem to have been held, probably outside the church, until 1614 [7], and even as late as 1634 there was a trace of it in the annual procession of the Virgin Mary and the Apostles, already referred to.

This later history of the feast at Sens is fairly typical, as the following chapter will show, of what took place all over France. The chapters by no means showed themselves

---

[1] Chérest, 68. The councils of Sens in 1460 and 1485 (p. 300) are for the province. That of 1528 (sometimes called of Sens, but properly of Paris) is national. They are not evidence for the feast at Sens itself.

[2] Ibid. 72 'Insolentias, tam de die quam de nocte, faciendo tondere barbam parte, ut fieri consuevit, in theatro . . . ac ludere personagia, die scilicet circumcisionis Domini.' The shaven face was characteristic of the mediaeval fool, minstrel, or actor (cf. ch. ii). Dreves, 586, adds that Tallinus Bissart, the precentor of this year, was threatened with excommunication.

[3] Ibid. 75.

[4] Ibid. 76 'prohibitum vicariis ne attentent, ultima die anni, in theatro tabulato ante valvas ecclesiae aut alibi in civitate Senonensi, publice barbam illius qui se praecentorem fatuorum nominat, aut alterius, radere, radifacere, permittere, aut procurare; et ne ad electionem dicti praecentoris die festo Sancti Iohannis Evangelistae sub poenis excommunicationis.

[5] Ibid. 77 'honeste, ac devote, sine laternis, sine precentore, sine delatione baculi domini precentoris, nec poterunt facere rasuram in theatro ante ecclesiam.'

[6] Ibid. 78.

[7] Dreves, 586.

universally willing to submit to the decree promulgated in the Pragmatic Sanction. In many of them the struggle between the conservative and the reforming parties was spread over a number of years. Councils, national, provincial and diocesan, continued to find it necessary to condemn the feast, mentioning it either by name or in a common category with other *ludi, spectacula, choreae, tripudia* and *larvationes*[1]. In one or two instances the authority of the *Parlements* was invoked. But in the majority of cases the feast either gradually disappeared, or else passed, first from the churches into the streets, and then from the clerks to the *bourgeois*, often to receive a new life under quite altered circumstances at the hands of some witty and popular *compagnie des fous*[2].

---

[1] *Prov. C. of Rouen* (1445), c. 11 (Labbé, xiii. 1304) ' prohibet haec sancta synodus ludos qui fatuorum vulgariter nuncupantur cum larvatis faciebus et alias inhoneste fieri in ecclesiis aut cemeteriis'; *Prov. C. of Sens* (1485, repeats decrees of earlier council of 1460), c. 3 (Labbé, xiii. 1728), quoting and adopting Basle decree, with careful exception for *consuetudines* of Nativity and Resurrection; cf. ch. xx; *Dioc. C. of Chartres* (1526, apparently repeated 1550, tit. 16; cf. Du Tilliot, 62) quoted Bochellus, iv. 7. 46 'denique ab Ecclesia eiiciantur vestes fatuorum personas scenicas agentium'; *Nat. C. of Paris* (1528, held by Abp. of Sens as primate), *Decr. Morum*, c. 16 (Labbé, xiv. 471) 'prohibemus ne fiat deinceps festum fatuorum aut innocentium, neque erigatur decanatus patellae.' The *Prov. C. of Rheims* (1456, held at Soissons) in Labbé, xiii. 1397, mentions only ' larvales et theatrales ioci,' ' choreae,' ' tripudia,' but refers explicitly to the Pragmatic Sanction. This, it may be observed, was suspended for a while in 1461 and finally annulled in 1516. Still more general are the terms of the *C. of Orleans* (1525, repeated 1587; Du Tilliot, 61); *C. of Narbonne* (1551), c. 46 (Labbé, xv. 26); *C. of Beauvais* (1554; E. Fleury, *Cinquante Ans de Laon*, 53); *C. of Cambrai* (1565), vi. 11 (Labbé, xv. 160); *C. of Rheims* (1583), c. 5 (Labbé, xv. 889); *C. of Tours* (1583, quoted Bochellus, iv. 7. 40). See also the councils quoted as to the Boy Bishop, in ch. xv. Finally, the *C. of Trent*, although in its 22nd session (1562) it renewed the decrees of popes and councils ' de choreis, aleis, lusibus' (*Decr. de Reformatione*, c. 1), made no specific mention of ' fatui' (*Can. et Decr. Sacros. Oec. Conc. Tridentini*, (Romae, 1845), 127). Probably the range of the feast was by this time insignificant.

[2] Cf. ch. xvi.

CHAPTER XIV

THE FEAST OF FOOLS (*continued*)

THE history of the Feast of Fools has been so imperfectly written, that it is perhaps worth while to bring together the records of its occurrence, elsewhere than in Troyes and Sens, from the fourteenth century onwards. They could probably be somewhat increased by an exhaustive research amongst French local histories, archives, and the transactions of learned societies. Of the feast in Notre-Dame at Paris nothing is heard after the reformation carried out in 1198 by Eudes de Sully [1]. The *bourgeois* of Tournai were, indeed, able to quote a Paris precedent for the feast of their own city in 1499 ; but this may have been merely the feast of some minor collegiate body, such as that founded in 1303 by cardinal Le Moine [2] ; or of the scholars of the University, or of the *compagnie joyeuse* of the *Enfants-sans-Souci*. At Beauvais, too, there are only the faintest traces of the feast outside the actual twelfth- and thirteenth-century service-books [3]. But there are several other towns in the provinces immediately north and east of the capital, Île de France, Picardy, Champagne, where it is recorded. The provision made for it in the Amiens *Ordinarium* of 1291 has been already quoted. Shortly after this,

---

[1] But there was another revel on Aug. 28. F. L. Chartier, *L'ancien Chapitre de N.-D. de Paris*, 175, quotes *Archives Nationales*, LL. 288, p. 219 'iniunctum est clericis matutinalibus, ne in festo S. Augustini faciant dissolutiones quas facere assueverant annis praeteritis.'

[2] Dulaure, *Hist. de Paris*, iii. 81 ;

Grenier, 370. A 'cardinal' was chosen on Jan. 13, and took part in the office.

[3] Grenier, 362. A model account form has the heading 'in die Circumcisionis, si fiat festum stultorum.' The 'rubriques du luminaire' provide for a distribution of wax to the sub-deacons and choir-clerks.'

bishop William de Maçon, who died in 1303, left his own
pontificalia for the use of the 'bishop of Fools[1].' When,
however, the feast reappears in the fifteenth century the
dominus festi is no longer a 'bishop,' but a 'pope.' In 1438
there was an endowment consisting of a share in the profits
of some lead left by one John le Caron, who had himself been
'pope[2].' In 1520 the feast was held, but no bells were to be
jangled[3]. It was repeated in 1538. Later in the year the
customary election of the 'pope' on the anniversary of Easter
was forbidden, but the canons afterwards repented of their
severity[4]. In 1540 the chapter paid a subsidy towards the
amusements of the 'pope' and his 'cardinals' on the Sunday
called *brioris*[5]. In 1548 the feast was suppressed[6]. At
Noyon the vicars chose a 'king of Fools' on Epiphany eve.
The custom is mentioned in 1366 as '*le gieu des roys.*' By
1419 it was forbidden, and canon John de Gribauval was
punished for an attempt to renew it by taking the sceptre off
the high altar at Compline on Epiphany. In 1497, 1499,
and 1505 it was permitted again, with certain restrictions.
The cavalcade must be over before Nones; there must be no

---

[1] Martonne, 49, giving no authority.

[2] Grenier, 361; Dreves, 583;
Rigollot, 15, quoting *Actum Capit.*
Leave was given to John Cornet,
of St. Michael's, John de Nœux of
St. Maurice's, rectors, and Everard
Duirech, *capellanus* of the cathedral, 'pridem electi, instituti et
assumpti in papatum stultorum
villae Ambianensis ... quod dictus
Cornet ... et sui praedecessores in
ipso papatu ordinati superstites die
circumcisionis Domini ... facerent
prandium in quo beneficiati ipsius
villae convocarentur ... ut inibi
eligere instituere et ordinare valerent papam ac papatum relevarent
absque tamen praeiudicio in aliquo
tangendo servitium divinum ...
faciendum.' Apparently the parochial clergy of Amiens joined with
the cathedral vicars and chaplains
in the feast.

[3] Grenier, 362; Rigollot, 15 'Servitium divinum facient honeste in
choro ecclesiae solemne, absque
faciendo insolentias aut aliquas
irrisiones, nec deferendo aliquas
campanas in dicta ecclesia, aut
alibi, et si dicti vicarii facere voluerint aliqua convivia, erit eorum
sumptibus et non sumptibus Dominorum canonicorum.'

[4] Rigollot, 16 'inhibuerunt capellanis et vicariis ... facere recreationes solitas in pascha annotino,
etiam facere electionem de Papa
Stultorum.' Later in the year the
'iocalia Papae, videlicet annulus
aureus, tassara (*sic*) argentea et
sigillum' were put in charge of the
'canonicus vicarialis.'

[5] Rigollot, 17 'licentiam dederunt
... ludere die dominica proxima
brioris.' Rigollot and Leber think
that 'brioris' may be for 'burarum,'
the feast of 'buras' or 'brandons'
on the first Sunday in Lent. Can
it be the same as the 'fête des
Braies' of Laon?

[6] Grenier, 414; Rigollot, 17.

licentious or scurrilous *chansons*, no dance before the great doors; the 'king' must wear ecclesiastical dress in the choir. In 1520, however, he was allowed to wear his crown *more antiquo*. The feast finally perished in 1721, owing to *la cherté des vivres*[1]. At Soissons, the feast was held on January 1, with masquing[2]. At Senlis, the *dominus festi* was a 'pope.' In 1403 there was much division of opinion amongst the chapter as to the continuance of the feast, and it was finally decided that it must take place outside the church. In 1523 it came to an end. The vicars of the chapter of Saint-Rieul had in 1501 their separate feast on January 1, with a 'prelate of Fools' and *jeux* in the churchyard[3]. From Laon fuller records are available[4]. A 'patriarch of Fools' was chosen with his 'consorts' on Epiphany eve after Prime, by the vicars, chaplains and choir-clerks. There was a cavalcade through the city and a procession called the *Rabardiaux*, of which the nature is not stated[5]. The chapter bore the expenses of the banquet and the masks. The first notice is about 1280. In 1307 one Pierre Caput was 'patriarch.' In 1454 the bishop upheld the feast against the dean, but it was decided that it should take place outside the church. A similar regulation was

---

[1] L. Mazière, *Noyon Religieux* in *Comptes-Rendus et Mémoires* of the *Comité arch. et hist. de Noyon* (1895), xi. 92; Grenier, 370, 413; Rigollot, 28, quoting *Actum Capit.* of 1497 'cavere a cantu carminum infamium et scandalosorum, nec non similiter carminibus indecoris et impudicis verbis in ultimo festo Innocentium per eos fetide decantatis; et si vicarii cum rege vadant ad equitatum solito, nequaquam fiet chorea et tripudia ante magnum portale, saltem ita impudice ut fieri solet.'

[2] Grenier, 365; Rigollot, 29, quoting, I think, a ceremonial (1350) of the collegiate church of Saint-Pierre-au-Parvis. The masquers obtained permission from some canons seated on a theatre near the house called *Grosse-Tête*.

[3] Grenier, 365; Rigollot, 26;

Dreves, 584, quoting cathedral *Actum Capit.* of 19 Dec. 1403, from Grenier's *MS. Picardie*, 158. Five canons said 'quod papa fieret in ecclesia, sed nulla elevatio, et quod, qui vellet venire, in habitu saeculari honesto veniret, et quod nulla dansio ibi fieret'; but the casting-vote of the dean was against them, 'sed extra possent facere capellani et alii quidquid vellent.'

[4] Grenier, 370; Rigollot, 22; E. Fleury, *Cinquante Ans de Laon*, 16; C. Hidé, in *Bull. de la Soc. académique de Laon* (1863), xiii. 111.

[5] Hidé, *op. cit.* 116, thinks that the Patriarch used *jetons de présence*, similar to those used by the Boy Bishop at Amiens and elsewhere (ch. xv). He figures some, but they may belong to the period of the *confrérie*.

made in 1455, 1456, 1459. In 1462 the *servitium* was allowed, and the *jeu* was to be submitted to censorship. In 1464 and 1465 mysteries were acted before the *Rabardiaux*. In 1486 the *jeu* was given before the church of St.-Martin-au-Parvis. In 1490 the *jeux* and cavalcade were forbidden, and the banquet only allowed. In 1500 a chaplain, Jean Hubreland, was fined for not taking part in the ceremony. In 1518 the worse fate of imprisonment befell Albert Gosselin, another chaplain, who flung fire from above the porch upon the 'patriarch' and his 'consorts.' By 1521 the *servitium* seems to have been conducted by the *curés* of the Laon churches, and the vicars and chaplains merely assisted. The expense now fell on the *curés*, and the chapter subsidy was cut down. In 1522 and 1525 the perquisites of the 'patriarch' were still further reduced by the refusal of a donation from the chapter as well as of the fines formerly imposed on absentees. In 1527 a protest of Laurent Brayart, 'patriarch,' demanding either leave to celebrate the feast *more antiquo* or a dispensation from assisting at the election of his successor, was referred to the ex-'patriarch.' In this same year canons, vicars, chaplains and *habitués* of the cathedral were forbidden to appear at the farces of the *fête des ânes*[1]. In 1531 the 'patriarch' Théobald Bucquet, recovered the right to play comedies and *jeux* and to take the absentee fines; but in 1541 Absalon Bourgeois was refused leave *pour faire semblant de dire la messe à liesse*. The feast was cut down to the bare election of the 'patriarch' in 1560, and seems to have passed into the hands of a *confrérie*; all that was retained in the cathedral being the *Primes folles* on Epiphany eve, in which the laity occupied the high stalls, and all present wore crowns of green leaves.

At Rheims, a Feast of Fools in 1490 was the occasion for a satirical attack by the vicars and choir-boys on the fashion of the hoods worn by the *bourgeoises*. This led to reprisals in the form of some anti-ecclesiastical farces played on the following *dimanche des Brandons* by the law clerks of the

---

[1] *MS. Hist.* of Dom. Bugniatre (eighteenth century) quoted Fleury, *op. cit.* 16. I do not feel sure that the term 'fête des ânes' was really used at Laon.

Rheims *Basoche*[1]. At Châlons-sur-Marne a detailed and
curious account is preserved of the way in which the Feast
of Fools was celebrated in 1570[2]. It took place on
St. Stephen's day. The chapter provided a banquet on
a theatre in front of the great porch. To this the 'bishop
of Fools' was conducted in procession from the *maîtrise des
fous*, with bells and music upon a gaily trapped ass. He was
then vested in cope, mitre, pectoral cross, gloves and crozier,
and enjoyed a banquet with the canons who formed his
'household.' Meanwhile some of the inferior clergy entered
the cathedral, sang gibberish, grimaced and made contortions.
After the banquet, Vespers were precipitately sung, followed
by a *motet*[3]. Then came a musical cavalcade round the
cathedral and through the streets. A game of *la paume*
took place in the market; then dancing and further cavalcades.
Finally a band gathered before the cathedral, howled and
clanged kettles and saucepans, while the bells were rung
and the clergy appeared in grotesque costumes.

Flanders also had its Feasts of Fools. That of St. Omer,
which existed in the twelfth century, lasted to the sixteenth[4].
An attempt was made to stop it in 1407, when the chapter
forbade any one to take the name of 'bishop' or 'abbot'
of Fools. But Seraphin Cotinet was 'bishop' of Fools in
1431, and led the *gaude* on St. Nicholas' eve[5]. The 'bishop'
is again mentioned in 1490, but in 1515 the feast was suppressed by Francis de Melun, bishop of Arras and provost of
St. Omer[6]. Some payments made by the chapter of Béthune

[1] Julleville, *Les Com.* 36; *Rép.
Com.* 348.; L. Paris, *Remensiana*,
32, *Le Théâtre à Reims*, 30;
Coquillart, *Œuvres* (Bibl. Elzév.), i.
cxxxv. Coquillart is said to have
written verses for the Basoche on
this occasion.

[2] Rigollot, 211, from A. Hugo,
La France pittoresque, ii. 226, on
the authority of a register of 1570
in the cathedral archives.

[3] It begins 'Cantemus ad honorem, gloriam et laudem Sancti
Stephani.'

[4] L. Deschamps de Pas, in *Mém.
de la Soc. des Antiq. de la Morinie*,
xx. 104, 107, 133; O. Bled, in *Bull.*

Hist., de la même Soc. (1887), 62.

[5] Deschamps de Pas, *op. cit.* 133
'solitum est fieri gaude in cena ob
reverentiam ipsius sancti.'

[6] Ibid. *op. cit.* 107. Grenier,
414, citing Sammarthanus, *Gallia
Christiana*, x. 1510, calls Francis
de Melun 'bishop of Terouanne.'
An earlier reform of the feast seems
implied by the undated Chapter
Statute in Ducange, s. v. *Episcopus
Fatuorum* 'quia temporibus retro-
actis multi defectus et plura scandala,
deordinationes et mala, occasione
Episcopi Fatuorum et suorum eve-
nerint, statuimus et ordinamus quod
de caetero in festo Circumcisionis

in 1445 and 1474 leave it doubtful how far the feast was really established in that cathedral [1]. At Lille the feast was forbidden by the chapter statutes of 1323 and 1328 [2]. But at the end of the fourteenth century it was in full swing, lasting under its ' bishop ' or ' prelate ' from the vigil to the octave of Epiphany. Amongst the payments made by the chapter on account of it is one to replace a tin can (*kanne stannee*) lost at the banquet. The ' bishop ' was chosen, as elsewhere, by the inferior clergy of the cathedral ; but he also stood in some relation to the municipality of Lille, and superintended the miracle plays performed at the procession of the Holy Sacrament and upon other occasions. In 1393 he received a payment from the duke of Burgundy for the *fête* of the *Trois Rois*. Municipal subsidies were paid to him in the fifteenth century ; he collected additional funds from private sources and offered prizes, by proclamation *soubz nostre seel de fatuité*, for pageants and *histoires de la Sainte Escripture* ; was, in fact, a sort of Master of the Revels for Lille. He was active in 1468, but in 1469 the town itself gave the prizes, in place *de l'evesque des folz, qui à présent est rué jus*. The chapter accounts show that he was re-appointed in 1485 *hoc anno, de gratia speciali*. In 1492 and 1493 the chapter payments were not to him but *sociis domus clericorum*, and from this year onwards he appears neither in the chapter accounts nor in those of the municipality [3]. Nevertheless, he did not yet cease to exist, for a statute was passed by the chapter for his extinction, together with that of the *ludus, quem Deposuit vocant*, in 1531 [4]. Five years before

Domini Vicarii caeterique chorum frequentantes et eorum Episcopus se habeant honeste, cantando et officiando sicut continetur plenius in Ordinario Ecclesiae.'

[1] De la Fons-Melicocq, *Cérémonies dramatiques et Anciens Usages dans les Églises du Nord de la France* (1850), 4. In 1445 is a payment to the 'évêque des fous de Saint-Aldegonde' for a ' jeu '; in 1474, one for the chapter's share of ' le feste du vesque des asnes, par dessus tout ce que ly cœurz paya.'

[2] E. Hautcœur, *Hist. de l'Église collégiale de Saint-Pierre de Lille* (1896–9), ii. 30 ; Id. *Cartulaire de l'Église*, &c. ii. 630, 651 (*Stat. Capit.* of July 7, 1323, confirmed June 23, 1328); 'item volumus festum folorum penitus anullari.'

[3] Hautcœur, *Hist.* ii. 215 ; De la Fons-Melicocq, *Archives hist. et litt. du Nord de France* (3rd series), v. 374 ; Flammermont, *Album paléographique du Nord de la France* (1896), No. 45.

[4] Ducange, s. v. *Deposuit* (*Stat. Capit. S. Petri Insul.* July 13, 1531,

this the canons and vicars were still wearing masks and playing comedies in public[1]. The history of the feast at Tournai is only known to me through certain legal proceedings which took place before the *Parlement* of Paris in 1499. It appears that the young *bourgeois* of Tournai were accustomed to require the vicars of Notre-Dame to choose an *évesque des sotz* from amongst themselves on Innocents' day. In 1489 they took one Matthieu de Porta and insulted him in the church itself. The chapter brought an action in the local court against the *prévost et jurez* of the town; and in the meantime obtained provisional letters inhibitory from Charles VIII, forbidding the vicars to hold the feast or the *bourgeois* to enforce it. All went well for some years, but in 1497 the *bourgeois* grumbled greatly, and in 1498, with the connivance of the municipal authorities themselves, they broke out. On the eve of the Holy Innocents, between nine and ten o'clock, Jacques de l'Arcq, mayor of the *Edwardeurs*, and others got into the house of Messire Pasquier le Pamê, a chaplain, and dragged him half naked, through snow and frost, to a *cabaret*. Seven or eight other vicars, one of whom was found saying his Hours in a churchyard, were similarly treated, and as none of them would be made *évesque des sotz* they were all kept prisoners. The chapter protested to the *prévost et jurez*, but in vain. On the following day the *bourgeois* chose one of the vicars *évesque*, baptized him by torchlight with three buckets of water at a fountain, led him about for three days in a surplice, and played scurrilous farces. They then dismissed the vicar,

ex Reg. k.) 'Scandala et ludibria quae sub Fatuitatis praetextu per beneficiatos et habituatos dictae nostrae ecclesiae a vigilia usque ad completas octavas Epiphaniae fieri et exerceri consueverunt . . . deinceps nullus nominetur, assumatur et creetur praelatus follorum, nec ludus, quem Deposuit vocant, in dicta vigilia, aut alio quocumque tempore, ludatur, exerceatur, aut fiat.' Probably to this date belongs the very similarly worded but undated memorandum in Delobel, *Collectanea*, f. 76, which Hautcœur,

Hist. ii. 220, 224, assigns to 1490. This adds ' de non . . . faciendo officio . . . per vicarios in octava Epiphaniae.' The municipal duties of the *praelatus* fell to the *confrérie* of the Prince des Foux, afterwards Prince d'Amour, which held revels in 1547 (Du Tilliot, 87), and still later to the 'fou de la ville' who led the procession of the Holy Sacrament, and flung water at the people in the eighteenth century (Leber, ix. 265).

[1] Rigollot, 14.

and elected as *évesque* a clerk from the diocese of Cambrai,
who defied the chapter. They drove Jean Parisiz, the *curé* of
La Madeleine, who had displeased them, from his church
in the midst of Vespers, and on Epiphany day made him too
a prisoner. In the following March the chapter and Messire
Jean Parisiz brought a joint action before the High Court
at Paris against the delinquents and the municipal authorities,
who had backed them up. The case came on for hearing
in November, when it was pleaded that the custom of electing
an *évesque des sotz* upon Innocents' day was an ancient one.
The ceremony took place upon a scaffold near the church
door; there were *jeux* in the streets for seven or eight days,
and a final *convici* in which the canons and others of the town
were satirized. The chapter and some of the citizens sent
bread and wine. The same thing was done in many dioceses
of Picardy, and even in Paris. It was all *ad solacium populi*,
and divine service was not disturbed, for nobody entered the
church. The vicar who had been chosen *évesque* thought it
a great and unexpected honour. There would have been
no trouble had not the *évesque* when distributing hoods with
ears at the end of the *jeux* unfortunately included certain
persons who would rather have been left out, and who consequently stirred up the chapter to take action. The court
adjourned the case, and ultimately it appears to have been
settled, for one of the documents preserved is endorsed with
a note of a *concordat* between the chapter and the town, by
which the feast was abolished in 1500 [1].

Of the Feast of Fools in central France I can say but
little. At Chartres, the *Papi-Fol* and his cardinals committed
many insolences during the first four days of the year, and
exacted *droits* from passers-by. They were suppressed in

---

[1] Two documents are preserved,
each giving a full account of the
event : (*a*) summons of the delinquents before the Parlement,
dated March 16, 1498 (J. F. Foppens,
Supplément (1748), to A. Miraeus,
Opera Diplomatica, iv. 295). This
is endorsed with some notes of
further proceedings; (*b*) official
notes of the hearing on Nov. 18,
1499 (*Bibl. de l'École des Chartes*,
iii. 568); cf. Julleville, *Rép. com.*
355; Cousin, *Hist. de Tournay*,
Bk. iv. 261. The Synod of Tournai
in 1520 still found it necessary to
forbid students to appear in church
'en habits de fous, en représentant
des personnages de comédie' on
St. Nicholas' day, Innocents' day,
or 'la fête de l'évêque' (E. Fleury,
Cinquante Ans de Laon, 54).

1479 and again in 1504 [1]. At Tours a *Ritual* of the four-teenth century contains elaborate directions for the *festum novi anni, quod non debet remanere, nisi corpora sint humi.* This is clearly a reformed feast, of which the chief features are the dramatic procession of the *Prophetae,* including doubtless Balaam on his ass, in church, and a *miraculum* in the cloister [2]. The 'Boy Bishop' gives the benediction at Tierce, and before Vespers there are *chori* (carols, I sup-pose) also in the cloisters. At Vespers *Deposuit* is sung three times, and the *baculus* may be taken. If so, the *thesaurarius* is beaten with *baculi* by the clergy at Compline, and the new *cantor* is led home with beating of *baculi* on the walls [3]. At Bourges, the use of the 'Prose of the Ass' in Notre-Dame de Sales seems to imply the existence of the feast, but I know no details [4]. At Avallon the *dominus festi* seems to have been, as at Laon, a 'patriarch,' and to have officiated on Innocents' day. A chapter statute regu-lated the proceedings in 1453, and another abolished them in 1510 [5]. At Auxerre, full accounts of a long chapter wrangle are preserved in the register [6]. It began in 1395 with an order requiring the decent performance of the *servitium,* and imposing a fee upon newly admitted canons

---

[1] Rigollot, 19, 157.

[2] Cf. ch. xix.

[3] Martene, iii. 41 '[at second Ves-pers] Cantor ... dicit ter *Deposuit* baculum tenens, et si baculus capi-tur, *Te Deum Laudamus* incipietur ... [at Compline] ascendunt duo clerici super formam thesaurarii et cantant *Haec est sancta dies,* &c. et post *Conserva Deus,* et dum canitur verberant eum clerici ba-culis, et ante eos cantores festi et erupitores ... Post incipit cantor novus *Verbum caro factum est,* et hoc cantando ducunt eum in domum suam per parietes cum baculis feriendo. Si autem baculus non accipitur, nihil de iis dicitur, sed vadunt, et extinguitur luminare.'

[4] Cf. Appendix L.

[5] Chérest, 9, 55, quoting *Acta Capit.* (1453) 'item circa festum In-nocentium ordinatum est quod in

ecclesia nullae fient insolenciae seu derisiones potissime tempore divini servitii et quod pulsentur matutinae non ante quartam horam. Permit-timus tamen quod reverenter et in habitu ecclesiastico per Innocentes et alios iuvenes de sedibus inferiori-bus dictum fiat officium, saltem circa ea quae sine sacris ordinibus possunt exerceri'; (1510) 'item turpem illum abusum festi fatuorum in nostra hactenus ecclesia, proh dolor, frequentatum quo in celebri-tate sanctorum Innocentium quidam sub nomine patriarchali divinum celebrant officium, penitus detesta-mus, abolemus et interdicimus.'

[6] Lebeuf, *Mém. concernant l'His-toire ... d'Auxerre* (ed. Challe et Quantin, 1848–55), ii. 30 ; iv. 232 (quoting *Acta Capit.* partly ex-tracted by Ducange, s.v. *Kalendae*); and in Leber, ix. 358, 375, 385.

towards the feast. In 1396 the feast was not held, owing to the recent defeat of Sigismund of Hungary and the count of Nevers by Bajazet and his Ottomans at Nicopolis [1]. In 1398 the dean entered a protest against a grant of wine made by the chapter to the thirsty revellers. In 1400 a further order was passed to check various abuses, the excessive ringing of bells, the licence of the *sermones fatui*, the impounding of copes in pledge for contributions, the beating of men and women through the streets, and all *derisiones* likely to bring discredit on the church [2]. In the following January, the bishop of Auxerre, Michel de Crency, intervened, forbidding the *fatui* to form a 'chapter,' or to appoint 'proctors,' or *clamare la fête aux fous* after the singing of the Hours in the church. This led to a storm. The bishop brought an action in the secular court, and the chapter appealed to the ecclesiastical court of the Sens province. In June, however, it was agreed as part of a general *concordat* between the parties, that all these proceedings should be *non avenu* [3]. It seems, however, to have been understood that the chapter would reform the feast. On December 2, the abbot of Pontigny preached a sermon before the chapter in favour of the abolition of the feast, and on the following day the dean came down and warned the canons that it was the intention of the University of Paris to take action, even if necessary, by calling in the secular arm [4]. It was better to

[1] 'Cum domini nostri rex et alii regales Franciae sint valde dolorosi, propter nova armaturae factae in partibus Ungariae contra Saracenos et inimicos fidei'; cf. Bury-Gibbon, vii. 35.

[2] 'Ordinavit quod de caetero omnes, qui de festo fatuorum fuerint, non pulsent campanam capituli sui post prandium, dempta prima die in qua suum episcopum eligent, et etiam quod in suis sermonibus fatuis non ponant seu dicant aliqua opprobria in vituperium alicuius personae.'

[3] Lebeuf, *Hist. d'Auxerre*, ii. 30.

[4] I suppose the intended action took shape in the *Quinque Conclusiones* of Gerson (p. 292), in which he quotes the dictum of an Auxerre preacher that the feast of Fools was as *approbatum* as that of the Conception. To this there seems to be a reference in the account of the Abbot of Pontigny's sermon in the *Acta Capit.* 'praedicavit ... quod dictum festum non erat, nec unquam fuerat a Deo nec Ecclesia approbandum seu approbatum.' Lebeuf, in Leber, ix. 385, points out that Gerson was intimate with one member of the Auxerre chapter This was Nicolas de Clamengis, whose *Opera*, 151 (ed. Lydius, 1613), include a treatise *De novis celebritatibus non instituendis*, in which the suppression of feasts in his diocese by Michael of Auxerre is alluded to.

reform themselves than to be reformed. It was then agreed to suppress the abuses of the feast, the sermons and the wearing of unecclesiastical garb, and to hold nothing but a *festum subdiaconorum* on the day of the Circumcision. Outside the church, however, the clergy might dance and promenade (*chorizare ... et ... spatiare*) on the *place* of St. Stephen's. These regulations were disregarded, on the plea that they were intended to apply only to the year in which they were made. In 1407 the chapter declared that they were to be permanent, but strong opposition was offered to this decision by three canons, Jean Piqueron, himself a sub-deacon, Jean Bonat, and Jean Berthome, who maintained that the *concordat* with the bishop was for reform, not for abolition. The matter was before the chapter for the last time, so far as the extant documents go, in 1411. On January 2, the dean reported that in spite of the prohibition certain *canonici tortrarii*[1], chaplains and choir-clerks had held the feast. A committee of investigation was appointed, and in December the prohibition was renewed. Jean Piqueron was once more a protestant, and on this occasion obtained the support of five colleagues[2]. It may be added that in the sixteenth century an *abbas stultorum* was still annually elected on July 18, beneath a great elm at the porch of Auxerre cathedral. He was charged with the maintenance of certain small points of choir discipline[3].

In Franche Comté and Burgundy, the Feast of Fools is also found. At Besançon it was celebrated by all the four great churches. In the cathedrals of St. John and St. Stephen, 'cardinals' were chosen on St. Stephen's day by the deacons

---

[1] These were canons of inferior rank at Auxerre (Ducange, s. v. *tortarius*).

[2] Canons J. Boileaue, Devisco, Pavionis, Viandi and H. Desnoes. Was Viandi the canon John Vivien who, according to Lebeuf, *Hist. d'Auxerre*, iv. 234, noted on his Breviary (now *Bibl. Nat. Cod. Colbert.* 4227) that at first Vespers on the Circumcision, *Hodie Christus* was sung after each Psalm, 'quia Festum Circumcisionis vocatur in diversis ecclesiis festum Fatuorum'?

[3] Chérest, 76; Julleville, *Les Com.* 234; Lebeuf, in Leber, ix. 358, 373, quoting a *Cry pour l'abbé de l'église d'Ausserre et ses supposts*, from the *Œuvres* of Roger de Collerye (1536). This resembles the productions of the *confréries des fous* (cf. ch. xvi) and begins,

'Sortez, saillez, venez de toutes parts,
Sottes et sots plus prompts que liépars.'

and sub-deacons, on St. John's day by the priests, on the
Holy Innocents' day by the choir-clerks and choir-boys. In
the collegiate churches of St. Paul and St. Mary Magdalen,
'bishops' or 'abbots' were similarly chosen. All these
domini festorum seem to have had the generic title of *rois
des fous*, and on the choir-feast four cavalcades went about
the streets and exchanged railleries (*se chantaient pouille*) when
they met. In 1387 the *Statutes* of cardinal Thomas of
Naples ordered that the feasts should be held jointly in each
church in turn ; and in 1518 the cavalcades were suppressed,
owing to a conflict upon the bridge which had a fatal ending.
Up to 1710, however, *reges* were still elected in St. Mary
Magdalen's ; not, indeed, those for the three feasts of Christmas week, but a *rex capellanorum* and a *rex canonicorum*,
who officiated respectively on the Circumcision and on
Epiphany [1]. At Autun the feast of the *baculus* in the
thirteenth century has already been recorded. In the fifteenth
and sixteenth centuries some interesting notices are available
in the chapter registers [2]. In 1411 the feast required reforming.
The canons were ordered to attend in decent clothes as on
the Nativity ; and the custom of leading an ass in procession
and singing a *cantilena* thereon was suppressed [3]. In 1412 the
abolition of the feast was decreed [4]. But in 1484 it was sanctioned again, and licence was given to punish those who failed
to put in an appearance at the Hours by burning at the well [5].

[1] Dunot de Charnage, *Hist. de
Besançon*, i. 227 ; Rigollot, 47 ;
Leber, ix. 434 ; x. 40.

[2] The anonymous author of the
Histoire de l'Église d'Autun (1774),
462, 628, gives *probata* from the
Acta Capitularia for some, but not
all of his statements. Du Tilliot,
24 and possibly Ducange, s. v. *Festum Asinorum* appear also to have
seen at least one register kept by
the *rotarius* which covered the
period 1411 to 1416.

[3] Deliberaverunt super festo folorum quod fieri consuevit anno quolibet in festo Circumcisionis Domini,
ad resecandum superfluitates et
derisiones quae fieri consueverunt
... item quod amodo non adduca-
tur asinus ad processionem dictae
diei, ut fuit solitum fieri, nec dica-
tur cantilena quae dici solebat super
dictum asinum, et supra officio
quod fieri consuetum est dicta die
in Ecclesia dicti Domini postea
providebunt.' Ducange says that
the ass had a golden foot-cloth of
which four of the principal canons
held the corners. On the *cantilena*
cf. Appendix L.

[4] 'Ordinaverunt quod festum folorum penitus cesset.'

[5] 'Concluserunt ad requestum
stultorum quod hoc anno fiat festum
folorum ... cum solemnitatibus in
dicto festo requisitis in libris dicti
festi descriptis ... qui defecerit in
matutinis et aliis horis statutis
comburatur in fonte.'

This custom, however, was forbidden in 1498[1]. Nothing
more is heard of the *asinus*, but it is possible that he
figured in the play of *Herod* which was undoubtedly performed at the feast, and which gave a name to the *dominus
festi*[2]. Under the general name of *festa fatuorum* was included at Autun, besides the feast of the Circumcision, also
that of the 'bishop' and 'dean' of Innocents, and a *missa
fatuorum* was sung *ex ore infantium* from the Innocents' day
to Epiphany[3]. In 1499 Jean Rolin, abbot of St. Martin's
and dean of Autun, led a renewed attack upon the feast.
He had armed himself with a letter from Louis XI, and
induced the chapter, in virtue of the Basle decree, to suppress
both Herod and the 'bishop' of Innocents[4]. In 1514 and
1515 the play of *Herod* was performed ; but in 1518, when
application was made to the chapter to sanction the election
of both a ' Herod ' and the 'bishop' and 'dean' of Innocents,
they applied to the king's official for leave, and failed to get
it. Finally in 1535 the chapter recurred to the Basle decree,
and again forbade the feast, particularly specifying under the
name of *Gaigizons* the obnoxious ceremony of 'ducking.[5]'
The feast held in the ducal, afterwards royal chapel of Dijon
yields documents which are unique, because they are in
French verse. The first is a *mandement* of Philip the Good,
duke of Burgundy, in 1454, confirming, on the request of the
haut-Bâtonnier, the privilege of the fête, against those who
would abolish it. He declares

> ' Que cette Fête célébrée
> Soit à jamais un jour l'année,

---

[1] 'In fine Matutinarum nonnulli
larvati alii inordinate vestiti choreas,
tripudia et saltus in eadem ecclesia
faciunt . . . [aliquos] ad fontem de-
ferunt et ibi aqua intinguntur.'

[2] Cf. ch. xix. A representation of
the ' Flight into Egypt' might well
come into a play of Herod. The
Hist. d'Autun, 462, says that, before
the reform of 1411, the ass appeared
as Balaam's ass in connexion with
a *Prophetae* on a stage at the church
door. There was a procession to
church, and the Prose. The *rex*

received a cheese from the chapter.

[3] Cf. ch. xv.

[4] 'Regna Herodis et Episcopatus
Innocentium, seu fatuorum festa
hactenus . . . fieri solita . . . abo-
lentes.'

[5] 'Quod vulgo dicitur *Les Gaigizons* . . . amplius neminem balneare
aut . . . pignus aufferre.' It is here
only the choice of 'bishop' and
' dean' of Innocents, 'quod festum
fatuorum a nonnullis nuncupatur'
that is forbidden. Apparently
'Herod' had died out.

Le premier du mois de Janvier;
Et que joyeux Fous sans dangier,
De l'habit de notre Chapelle,
Fassent la Fête bonne et belle,
Sans outrage ni derision.'

In 1477 Louis XI seized Burgundy, and in 1482 his representatives, Jean d'Amboise, bishop and duke of Langres, lieutenant of the duchy, and Baudricourt the governor, accorded to Guy Baroset

'Protonotaire et Procureur des Foux,'

a fresh confirmation for the privilege of the feast held by

'Le Bâtonnier et tous ses vrais suppôts[1].'

There was a second feast in Dijon at the church of St. Stephen. In 1494 it was the custom here, as at Sens, to shave the 'precentor' of Fools upon a stage before the church. In 1621 the vicars still paraded the streets with music and lanterns in honour of their 'precentor[2].' In 1552, however, the Feasts of Fools throughout Burgundy had been prohibited by an *arrêt* of the *Parlement* of Dijon. This was immediately provoked by the desire of the chapter of St. Vincent's at Châlons-sur-Saône to end the scandal of the feast under their jurisdiction. It was, however, general in its terms, and probably put an end to the *Chapelle* feast at Dijon, since to about this period may be traced the origin of the famous *compagnie* of the *Mère-Folle* in that city[3].

In Dauphiné there was a *rex et festum fatuorum* at St. Apollinaire's in Valence, but I cannot give the date[4]. At Vienne the *Statutes* of St. Maurice, passed in 1385, forbid the *abbas stultorum seu sociorum*, but apparently allow *rois*

[1] Du Tilliot, 100; Petit de Julleville, *Les Com.* 194. Amongst Du Tilliot's woodcuts is one of a *bâton* (No. 4) bearing this date 1482. It represents a nest of fools.

[2] Ibid. 21.

[3] Ibid. 74 'Icelle cour a ordonné et ordonne, que defenses seront faites aux Choriaux et habitués de ladite Église Saint-Vincent et de toutes autres Églises de son Ressort, et dorésnavant le jour de la Fête des Innocens, et autres jours faire aucunes insolences et tumultes esdites Églises, vacquer en icelles, et courir parmi les villes avec danses et habits indécens à leur état ecclésiastique.'

[4] Pilot de Thorey, i. 177.

on the Circumcision and Epiphany, as well as in the three post-Nativity feasts. They also forbid certain *ludibria*. No *pasquinades* are to be recited, and no one is to be carried *in Rost* or to have his property put in pawn[1]. More can be said of the feast at Viviers. A *Ceremonial* of 1365 contains minute directions for its conduct[2]. On December 17 the *sclafardi et clericuli* chose an *abbas stultus* to be responsible, as at Auxerre, for the decorum of the choir throughout the year. He was shouldered and borne to a place of honour at a drinking-bout. Here even the bishop, if present, must do him honour. After the drinking, the company divided into two parts, one composed of inferior clergy, the other of dignitaries, and sang a doggerel song, each endeavouring to sing its rival down. They shouted, hissed, howled, cackled, jeered and gesticulated; and the victors mocked and flouted the vanquished. Then the door-keeper made a proclamation on behalf of the 'abbot,' calling on all to follow him, on pain of having their breeches slit, and the whole crew rushed violently out of the church. A progress through the town followed, which was repeated daily until Christmas eve[3]. On the three post-Nativity feasts,

---

[1] Pilot de Thorey, i. 178 (*Statuta*, c. 40) 'Item statuimus et ordinamus, quod ex nunc cessent abusus qui fieri consueverunt per abbatem vulgariter vocatum stultorum seu sociorum . . . Item statuimus et ordinamus, cum in ecclesia Dei non deceat fieri ludibria vel inhonesta committi, quod, in festis Sanctorum Stephani, Iohannis evangelistae, Innocentium et Epiphaniae, domino de cetero officiatur et desserviatur in divinis, prout in aliis diebus infra fieri statuetur, et quod nullus, de cetero, ut quandoque factum fuisse audivimus, portetur in Rost, et quod, de nulla persona ecclesiastica vel seculari cuiuscumque status existat, inhonesti vel diffamatorii rithmi recitentur, et quod nullus pignoret aut aliena rapiat quovisimodo.' A Vienne writer, in Leber, ix. 259, adds that the performance of the office on the three post-Nativity feasts by deacons,

priests, and choir in the high stalls was continued by these Statutes, but suppressed about 1670.

[2] Lancelot, in *Hist. de l'Académie des Inscriptions* (ed. 4to), vii. 255, (ed. 12mo), iv. 397; Ducange, s. v. *Kalendae*; Du Tilliot, 46.

[3] '. . . *Te Deum*, et tunc per consocios subtollitur, et elevatur, ac super humeros ad domum, ubi caeteri pro potu sunt congregati, laetanter deportatur, atque in loco ad hoc specialiter ornato et praeparato ponitur, statuitur et collocatur. Ad eius introitum omnes debent assurgere, etiam dominus Episcopus, si fuerit praesens, ac impensa reverentia consueta per consodales et consocios electo, fructus species et vinum cum credentia ei dentur, &c. Sumpto autem potu idem Abbas vel maior succentor ex eius officio absente Abbate incipit cantando ea quae secuntur; ab ista enim parte sclafardi, clericuli ceterique de

a distinct *dominus festi*, the *episcopus stultus*, apparently elected the previous year, took the place of the *abbas*. On each of these days he presided at Matins, Mass, and Vespers, sat in full pontificals on the bishop's throne, attended by his 'chaplain,' and gave the Benedictions. Both on St. Stephen's and St. John's days these were followed by the recitation of a burlesque formula of indulgence [1]. The whole festivity seems to have concluded on Innocents' day with the election of a new *episcopus*, who, after the shouldering and the drinking-bout, took his stand at a window of the great hall of the bishop's palace, and blessed the people of the city [2]. The *episcopus* was bound to give a supper to his fellows. In 1406 one William Raynoard attempted to evade this obligation. An action was brought against him in the court of the bishop's official, by the then *abbas* and his predecessor.

suptus chorum debent esse simulque canere, ceteri vero desuper chorum ab alia parte simul debent respondere . . . Sed dum eorum cantus saepius et frequentius per partes continuando cantatu tanto amplius ascendendo elevatur in tantum quod una pars cantando, clamando, *è fort cridar*, vincit aliam. Tunc enim inter se ad invicem clamando, sibilando, ululando, cachinnando, deridendo ac cum manibus demonstrando, pars victrix quantum potest partem adversam deridere conatur ac superare, iocosasque trufas sine taedio breviter inferre.

A parte Abbatis. *Heros.*
Alter chorus. *Et nolic. nolierno.*
A parte Abbatis. *Ad fons sancti bacon.*
Alii. *Kyrie Eleison.*
Quo finito illico gachia ex eius officio facit praeconizationem sic dicendo: *De par Mossenhor Labat è sos Cosselliers vos fam assaber que tot homs lo sequa, lay on voura anar, ea quo sus la pena de talhar lo braye.* Tunc Abbas aliique domum exeunt impetum facientes. Iuniores canonici chorarii scutiferique domini Episcopi et canonicorum Abbatem comitantur per urbem, cui transeunti salutem omnes im-

pertiunt. In istis vero visitationibus (quae usque ad vigiliam Natalis Domini quotidie vespere fiunt) Abbas debet semper deportare habitum, sive fuerit manta, sive tabardum, sive cappa una cum capputio de variis folrato.' It is curious how the characteristic meridional love of sheer noise and of gesture comes out.

[1] *De indulgentiis dandis :*
[St. Stephen's Day]
De par Mossenhor l'Evesque,
Que Dieus vos donne gran mal al bescle,
Avec una plena balasta de pardos
E dos das de raycha de sot lo mento.
[St. John's Day]
Mossenhor ques ayssi presenz
Vos dona xx balastas de mal de dens,
Et à vos autras donas atressi
Dona 1ᵃ coa de rossi.
[2] ' Deinde electus per sclafardos subtollitur et campanilla precedente portatur ad domum episcopalem, ad cuius adventum ianuae domus, absente vel praesente ipso domino Episcopo, debent totaliter aperiri, ac in una de fenestris magni tinelli debet deponi, et stans dat ibi iterum benedictionem versus villam.'

It was referred to the arbitration of three canons, who decided that Raynoard must give the supper on St. Bartholomew's next, August 24, at the accustomed place (a tavern, one fears) in the little village of Gras, near Viviers[1].

Finally, there are examples of the Feast of Fools in Provence. At Arles it was held in the church of St. Trophime, and is said to have been presented, out of its due season, it may be supposed, for the amusement of the Emperor Charles IV at his coronation in 1365, to have scandalized him and so to have met its end[2]. Nevertheless in the fifteenth century an 'archbishop of Innocents,' *alias stultus*, still sang the ' *O* ' on St. Thomas's day, officiated on the days of St. John and the Innocents, and on St. Trophime's day (Dec. 29) paid a visit to the *abadesse fole* of the convent of Saint-Césaire. The real abbess of this convent was bound to provide chicken, bread and wine for his regaling[3]. At Fréjus in 1558 an attempt to put down the feast led to a riot. The bishop, Léon des Ursins, was threatened with murder, and had to hide while his palace was stormed[4]. At Aix the chapter of St. Saviour's chose on St. Thomas's day, an *episcopus fatuus vel Innocentium* from the choir-boys. He officiated on Innocents' day, and boys and canons exchanged stalls. The custom lasted until at least 1585[5]. Antibes, as late as 1645, affords a rare example of the feast held by a religious house. It was on Innocents' day in the church of the Franciscans. The choir and office were left to the lay-brothers, the *quêteurs*, cooks and gardeners. These put on the vestments inside out, held the books upside down, and wore spectacles with rounds of orange peel instead of glasses. They blew the ashes from the censers upon each other's faces and heads, and instead of the proper liturgy chanted confused and inarticulate gibberish. All this is

---

[1] Ducange, s.v. *Kalendae*; Bérenger-Féraud, iv. 14.

[2] Papon, *Hist. de Provence* (1784), iv. 212.

[3] Rigollot, 125.

[4] Bérenger-Féraud, iv. 131, quoting Mireur, *Bull. hist. et philos. du Comité des Travaux hist.* (1885), Nᵒˢ. 3, 4.

[5] Rigollot, 171 ; Fauris de Saint-Vincent, in *Magasin encyclopédique* (1814), i. 24. A chapter inventory mentions a 'mitra episcopi fatuorum.' The *Council of Aix* in 1585 (Labbé, xv. 1146) ordered the suppression of 'ludibria omnia et pueriles ac theatrales lusus' on Innocents' day.

recorded by the contemporary free-thinker Mathurin de Neuré in a letter to his leader and inspirer, Gassendi [1].

It will be noticed that the range of the Feast of Fools in France, so far as I have come across it, seems markedly to exclude the west and south-west of the country. I have not been able to verify an alleged exception at Bordeaux [2]. Possibly there is some ethnographical reason for this. But on the whole, I am inclined to think that it is an accident, and that a more complete investigation would disclose a sufficiency of examples in this area. Outside France, the Feast of Fools is of much less importance. The Spanish disciplinary councils appear to make no specific mention of it, although they know the cognate feast of the Boy Bishop, and more than once prohibit *ludi, choreae*, and so forth, in general terms [3]. In Germany, again, I do not know of a case in which the term 'Fools' is used. But the feast itself occurs sporadically. As early as the twelfth century, Herrad von Landsberg, abbess of Hohenburg, complained that miracle-plays, such as that of the *Magi*, instituted on Epiphany and its octave by the Fathers of the Church, had given place to

---

[1] Thiers, *Traité des Jeux et des Divertissements*, 449; Du Tilliot, 33, 39, quoting [Mathurin de Neuré] *Querela ad Gassendum, de parum Christianis Provincialium suorum ritibus . . . &c.* (1645) 'Choro cedunt omnes Therapeutae Sacerdotes, et ipse Archimandrita; in quorum omnium locos sufficiuntur Coenobii mediastini viles, quorum aliis manticae explendae cura est, aliis culina, aliis hortus colendus: Fratres Laicos vocant, qui tunc occupatis hinc et inde Initiatorum ac Mystarum sedibus, ... Sacerdotalibus nempe induuntur vestibus, sed laceris, si quae suppetant, ac praepostere aptatis, inversisque ; inversos etiam tenent libros in quibus se fingunt legere, appensis ad nasum perspicillis, quibus detractum vitrum, eiusque loco mali aurati putamen insertum ... Thuricremi Sanniones in cuiusque faciem cineres exsufflarunt, et favillas ex acerris, quas per ludibrium temere iactantes, stolidis quandoque capitibus affundunt ; sic autem instructi non hymnos, non Psalmos, non liturgias de more concinunt, sed confusa ac inarticula verba demurmurant, insanasque prorsus vociferationes derudunt.' The same M. de Neuré (whose real name was Laurent Mesme) says more generally that in many towns of the province on Innocents' day, 'Stolidorum se Divorum celebrare festa putant, quibus stolide litandum sit, nec aliis quam stolidis illius diei sacra ceremoniis peragenda.' He quotes (p. 72) from a *Rituale* a direction for the singing of the *Magnificat* to the tune 'Que ne vous requinquezvous, vielle? Que ne vous requinquez-vous donc?'

[2] Bérenger-Féraud, iv. 17.

[3] *C. of Toledo*, Nº. 38, in 1582 (Aguirre, *Coll. Conc. Hisp.* vi. 12) ; *C. of Oriolana*, in 1600 (Aguirre, vi. 452) : cf. pp. 162, 350.

licence, buffoonery and quarrelling. The priests came into the churches dressed as knights, to drink and play in the company of courtesans[1]. A Mosburg *Gradual* of 1360 contains a series of *cantiones* compiled and partly written by the dean John von Perchausen for use when the *scholarium episcopus* was chosen at the Nativity[2]. Some of these, however, are shown by their headings or by internal evidence to belong rather to a New Year's day feast, than to one on Innocents' day[3]. A *festum baculi* is mentioned and an *episcopus* or *praesul* who is chosen and enthroned. One carol has the following refrain[4]:

> 'gaudeamus et psallamus
> novo praesuli
> ad honorem et decorem
> sumpti baculi.'

[1] Pearson, ii. 285 ; C. M. Engelhardt, *H. von Landsberg* (1818), 104; C. Schmidt, *H. von Landsberg*, 40. Herrad was abbess of Hohenburg, near Strasburg, 1167–95. The MS. of her *Hortus Deliciarum* was destroyed at Strasburg in 1870, but Engelhardt, and from him Pearson, translated the bit about the Epiphany feasts : cf. ch. xx.

[2] Dreves, *Anal. Hymn.* xx. 22 (from the Gradual, *Cod. Monacens.* 157, f. 231vo); after quoting a decree against *cantiones* of the *C. of Lyons* in 1274; 'ne igitur propter scholarium episcopum, cum quo in multis ecclesiis a iuniore clero ad specialem laudem et devotionem natalis Domini solet tripudiari, saecularia parliamenta nec non strepitus clamorque et cachitus mundanarum cantionum in nostro choro invalescant ... ego Iohannes, cognomine de Perchausen, Decanus ecclesiae Mosburgensis, antequam in decanum essem assumptus ... infra scriptas cantiones, olim ab antiquis etiam in maioribus ecclesiis cum scholarium episcopo decantatas, paucis modernis, etiam aliquibus propriis, quas olim, cum rector fuissem scholarium, pro laude nativitatis Domini et beatae Virginis composui,

adiunctis, coepi in unum colligere et praesenti libro adnectere pro speciali reverentia infantiae Salvatoris, ut sibi tempore suae nativitatis his cantionibus a novellis clericulis quasi ex ore infantium et lactentium laus et hymnizans devotio postposita vulgarium lascivia possit tam decenter quam reverenter exhiberi.'

[3] The following may all be for Jan. 1, and I do not think that there was a *scholarium episcopus* on any other day at Mosburg : *Gregis pastor Tityrus* (Dreves, *op. cit.* 110), *Ecce novus annus est* (Dreves, 131, headed in MS. 'ad novum annum'), *Nostri festi gaudium* (Dreves, 131, 'in circumcisione Domini'), *Castis psallamus mentibus* (Dreves, 135, 251, 'cum episcopus eligitur'), *Mos florentis venustatis* (Dreves, 135 'dum itur extra ecclesiam ad choream'), *Anni novi novitas* (Dreves, 136 'cum infulatus et vestitus praesul inthronizatur'). Some other New Year *cantiones* found elsewhere by Dreves (pp. 130, 131) have no special reference to the feast.

[4] Dreves, *op. cit.* 136 (beginning *anni novi novitas*), 250, with musical notation.

Another is so interesting, for its classical turn, and for the names which it gives to the 'bishop' and his crew that I quote it in full [1].

1. Gregis pastor Tityrus,
   asinorum dominus,
   noster est episcopus.

R°. eia, eia, eia,
    vocant nos ad gaudia
    Tityri cibaria.

2. ad honorem Tityri,
   festum colant baculi
   satrapae et asini.

R°. eia, eia, eia,
    vocant nos ad gaudia,
    Tityri cibaria.

3. applaudamus Tityro
   cum melodis organo,
   cum chordis et tympano.

4. veneremur Tityrum,
   qui nos propter baculum
   invitat ad epulum.

The reforms of the council of Basle were adopted for Germany by the Emperor Albrecht II in the *Instrumentum Acceptationis* of Mainz in 1439. In 1536 the council of Cologne, quoting the decretal of Innocent III, condemned *theatrales ludi* in churches. A Cologne *Ritual* preserves an account of the sub-deacons' feast upon the octave of Epiphany [2]. The sub-deacons were *hederaceo serto coronati*. Tapers were lit, and a *rex* chosen, who acted as *hebdomarius* from first to second Vespers. Carols were sung, as at Mosburg [3].

John Huss, early in the fifteenth century, describes the Feast of Fools as it existed in far-off Bohemia [4]. The revellers,

---

[1] Dreves, *op. cit.* 110, 254, with notation.

[2] Wetzer und Welte, *Kirchen-lexicon*, s. v. *Epiphany*, quoting Crombach, *Hist. Trium Regum* (1654), 752; Galenius, *de admir. Coloniae* (1645), 661. The date of

the *Ritual* is not given, but the ceremony had disappeared by 1645.

[3] 'Admiscent autem natalitias cantiones, non sine gestientis animi voluptate.'

[4] *Tractatus de precatione Dei,* i. 302 († 1406-15), in F. Palacký,

of whom, to his remorse, Huss had himself been one as a
lad, wore masks. A clerk, grotesquely vested, was dubbed
'bishop,' set on an ass with his face to the tail, and led to
mass in the church. He was regaled on a platter of broth
and a bowl of beer, and Huss recalls the unseemly revel
which took place[1]. Torches were borne instead of candles,
and the clergy turned their garments inside out, and danced.
These *ludi* had been forbidden by one archbishop John of
holy memory.

It would be surprising, in view of the close political and
ecclesiastical relations between mediaeval France and England,
if the Feast of Fools had not found its way across the channel.
It did; but apparently it never became so inveterate as
successfully to resist the disciplinary zeal of reforming bishops,
and the few notices of it are all previous to the end of the
fourteenth century. It seems to have lasted longest at
Lincoln, and at Beverley. Of Lincoln, it will be remembered,
Pierre de Corbeil, the probable compiler of the Sens *Officium*,
was at one time coadjutor bishop. Robert Grosseteste, whose
attack upon the *Inductio Maii* and other village festivals
served as a starting-point for this discussion, was no less
intolerant of the Feast of Fools. In 1236 he forbade it to

*Documenta Mag. Ioannis Hus
vitam illustrantia* (1869), 722:
'Quantam autem quamque mani-
festam licentiam in ecclesia com-
mittant, larvas induentes — sicut
ipse quoque adolescens proh dolor
larva fui—quis Pragae describat?
Namque clericum monstrosis vestibus indutum facientes episcopum,
imponunt asinae, facie ad caudam
conversa, in ecclesiam eum ad missam ducunt, praeferentes lancem
iusculi et cantharum vel amphoram
cerevisiae; atque dum haec prae-
tendunt, ille cibum potionemque in
ecclesia capit. Vidi quoque eum
aras suffientem et pedem sursum
tollentem audivique magna voce
clamantem: bú! Clerici autem
magnas faces cereorum loco ei
praeferebant, singulas aras obeunti
et suffienti. Deinde vidi clericos
cucullos pellicios aversa parte induentes et in ecclesia tripudiantes.

Spectatores autem rident atque haec
omnia religiosa et iusta esse putant;
opinantur enim, hos esse in eorum
rubricis, id est institutis. Prae-
clarum vero institutum: pravitas,
foeditas!—Atque quum tenera aetate
et mente essem, ipse quoque talium
nugarum socius eram; sed ut primum
dei auxilio adiutus sacras literas
intelligere coepi, statim hanc ru-
bricam, id est institutum huius insaniae, ex stultitia mea delevi. Ac
sanctae memoriae dominus Ioannes
archiepiscopus, is quidem excommunicationis poena proposita hanc
licentiam ludosque fieri vetuit, idque
summo iure, &c.'
[1] The quotation given above is
a translation by J. Kvíčala from the
Bohemian of Huss. There seems
to be a confusion between the
'bishop' and his steed. It was
probably the latter who lifted up
his leg and cried *bú*.

be held either in the cathedral or elsewhere in the diocese[1];
and two years later he included the prohibition in his formal
Constitutions[2]. But after another century and a half, when
William Courtney, archbishop of Canterbury, made a visitation
of Lincoln in 1390, he found that the vicars were still in the
habit of disturbing divine service on January 1, in the name
of the feast[3]. Probably his strict mandate put a stop to the
custom[4]. At almost precisely the same date the Feast of
Fools was forbidden by the statutes of Beverley minster,
although the sub-deacons and other inferior clergy were still
to receive a special commons on the day of the Circumcision[5].
Outside Lincoln and Beverley, the feast is only known in
England by the mention of paraphernalia for it in thirteenth-

---

[1] Grosseteste, *Epistolae* (ed.
Luard, R. S.), 118 'vobis mandamus in virtute obedientiae firmiter
iniungentes, quatenus festum stultorum cum sit vanitate plenum et
voluptatibus spurcum, Deo odibile
et daemonibus amabile, ne de caetero in ecclesia Lincolniensi die
venerandae circumcisionis Domini
nullatenus permittatis fieri.'

[2] Ibid. *op. cit.* 161 'execra-
bilem etiam consuetudinem, quae
consuevit in quibusdam ecclesiis ob-
servari de faciendo festo stultorum,
speciali authoritate rescripti aposto-
lici penitus inhibemus; ne de domo
orationis fiat domus ludibrii, et acer-
bitas circumcisionis Domini Iesu
Christi iocis et voluptatibus subsan-
netur.' The 'rescript' will be Innocent III's decretal of 1207, just
republished in Gregory IX's *Decretales* of 1234; cf. p. 279.

[3] *Lincoln Statutes*, ii. 247 'quia
in eadem visitacione nostra coram
nobis a nonnullis fide dignis de-
latum extitit quod vicarii et clerici
ipsius ecclesiae in die Circumcisionis Domini induti veste laicali
per eorum strepitus truffas garula-
ciones et ludos, quos festa stultorum
communiter et convenienter appellant, divinum officium multipliciter
et consuete impediunt, tenore pre-
sencium Inhibemus ne ipsi vicarii
qui nunc sunt, vel erunt pro tempore, talibus uti de caetero non

praesumant nec idem vicarii seu
quivis alii ecclesiae ministri publicas potaciones aut insolencias alias
in ecclesia, quae domus oracionis
existit, contra honestatem eiusdem
faciant quouismodo.' Mr. Leach,
in *Furnivall Miscellany*, 222, notes
'a sarcastic vicar has written in
the margin, "Harrow barrow. Here
goes the Feast of Fools (*hic
subducitur festum stultorum*)." '

[4] What was *ly ffolcfeste* of which
Canon John Marchall complained
in Bishop Alnwick's visitation of
1437 that he was called upon to
bear the expense? Cf. *Lincoln
Statutes*, ii. 388 'item dicit quod
subtrahuntur ab ipso expensae per
eum factae pascendo ly ffolcfeste
in ultimo Natali, quod non erat in
propria, nec in cursu, sed tamen
rogatus fecit cum promisso sibi
facto de effusione expensarum et
non est sibi satisfactum.'

[5] *Statutes* of Thos. abp. of York
(1391) in *Monasticon*, vi. 1310 'in
die etiam Circumcisionis Domini
subdiaconis et clericis de secunda
forma de victualibus annis singulis,
secundum morem et consuetudinem
ecclesiae ab antiquo usitatos, debite
ministrabit [praepositus], antiqua
consuetudine immo verius corruptela regis stultorum infra ecclesiam et extra hactenus usitata
sublata penitus et extirpata.'

century inventories of St. Paul's[1], and Salisbury[2], and by a doubtful allusion in a sophisticated version of the St. George play[3].

A brief summary of the data concerning the Feast of Fools presented in this and the preceding chapter is inevitable. It may be combined with some indication of the relation in which the feast stands with regard to the other feasts dealt with in the present volume. If we look back to Belethus in the twelfth century we find him speaking of the Feast of Fools as held on the Circumcision, on Epiphany or on the octave of Epiphany, and as being specifically a feast of sub-deacons. Later records bear out on the whole the first of these statements. As a rule the feast focussed on the Circumcision, although the rejoicings were often prolonged, and the election of the *dominus festi* in some instances gave rise to a minor celebration on an earlier day. Occasionally (Noyon, Laon) the Epiphany, once at least (Cologne) the octave of the Epiphany, takes the place of the Circumcision. But we also find the term Feast of Fools extended to cover one or more of three feasts, distinguished from it by Belethus, which immediately follow Christmas. Sometimes it includes them all three (Besançon, Viviers, Vienne), sometimes the feast of the Innocents alone (Autun, Avallon, Aix, Antibes, Arles), once the feast of St. Stephen (Châlons-sur-Marne)[4]. On the other hand, the definition of the feast as a sub-deacons' feast is not fully applicable to its later developments. Traces of a connexion with the sub-deacons appear more than once (Amiens, Sens, Auxerre, Beverley); but as a rule the feast is held by the inferior clergy known as vicars, chaplains, and choir-clerks, all of whom are grouped at Viviers and Romans under the general term of *esclaffardi*. At Laon a part is taken in it by the *curés* of the various parishes in the city.

---

[1] *Inventory* of St. Paul's (1245) in *Archaeologia*, l. 472, 480 'Baculus stultorum est de ebore et sine cambuca, cum pomello de ebore subtus indentatus ebore et cornu: ... capa et mantella puerorum ad festum Innocentum et Stultorum sunt xxviij debiles et contritae.'

[2] Sarum *Inventory* of 1222 in W. H. R. Jones, *Vetus Registr. Sarisb.* (R. S.), ii. 135 'Item baculi ii ad "Festum Folorum."'

[3] N°. 27 in the list given for ch. x. Father Christmas says 'Here comes in "The Feast of Fools."'

[4] Cf. the further account of these post-Nativity feasts in ch. xv.

The explanation is, I think, fairly obvious. Originally, perhaps, the sub-deacons held the feast, just as the deacons, priests, and boys held theirs in Christmas week. But it had its vogue mainly in the great cathedrals served by secular canons[1], and in these the distinction between the canons in different orders—for a sub-deacon might be a full canon[2]—was of less importance than the difference between the canons as a whole and the minor clergy who made up the rest of the cathedral body, the hired choir-clerks, the vicars choral who, originally at least, supplied the place in the choir of absent canons, and the chaplains who served the chantries or small foundations attached to the cathedral[3]. The status of spiritual dignity gave way to the status of material preferment. And so, as the vicars gradually coalesced into a corporation of their own, the Feast of Fools passed into their hands, and became a celebration of the annual election of the head of their body[4]. The vicars and their associates were probably an ill-educated and an ill-paid class. Certainly they were difficult to discipline[5]; and it is not surprising that their rare holiday, of which the expenses were met partly by the chapter, partly by dues levied upon themselves or upon the bystanders[6], was an occasion for popular rather

---

[1] The *C. of Paris* in 1212 (p. 279) forbids the Feast of Fools in religious houses. But that in the Franciscan convent at Antibes is the only actual instance I have come across.

[2] There were *canonici presbiteri, diaconi, subdiaconi* and even *pueri* at Salisbury (W. H. Frere, *Use of Sarum*, i. 51).

[3] On the nature and growth of vicars choral, cf. Cutts, 341; W. H. Frere, *Use of Sarum*, i. xvii; *Lincoln Statutes*, passim; A. R. Maddison, *Vicars Choral of Lincoln* (1878); H. E. Reynolds, *Wells Cathedral*, xxix, cvii, clxx. Vicars choral make their appearance in the eleventh century as choir substitutes for non-resident canons. At Lincoln they got benefactions from about 1190, and in the thirteenth century formed a regularly organized *communitas*. The *vicarii*

were often at the same time *capellani* or chantry-priests. On chantries see Cutts, 438.

[4] The Lincoln vicars chose two Provosts yearly (Maddison, *op. cit.*); the Wells vicars two Principals (Reynolds, *op. cit.* clxxi).

[5] Reynolds, *op. cit.*, gives numerous and interesting notices of chapter discipline from the Wells *Liber Ruber*.

[6] In Leber, ix. 379, 407, is described a curious way of raising funds for choir suppers, known at Auxerre and in Auvergne, and not quite extinct in the eighteenth century. It has a certain analogy to the *Deposuit*. From Christmas to Epiphany the Psalm *Memento* was sung at Vespers, and the anthem *De fructu ventris* inserted in it. When this began the ruler of the choir advanced and presented a bouquet to some canon or *bourgeois*

than refined merry-making [1]. That it should perpetuate or absorb folk-customs was also, considering the peasant or small *bourgeois* extraction of such men, quite natural.

The simple psychology of the last two sentences really gives the key to the nature of the feast. It was largely an ebullition of the natural lout beneath the cassock. The vicars hooted and sang improper ditties, and played dice upon the altar, in a reaction from the wonted restraints of choir discipline. Familiarity breeds contempt, and it was almost an obvious sport to burlesque the sacred and tedious ceremonies with which they were only too painfully familiar. Indeed, the reverend founders and reformers of the feast had given a lead to this apishness by the introduction of the symbolical transference of the *baculus* at the *Deposuit* in the *Magnificat*. The ruling idea of the feast is the inversion of status, and the performance, inevitably burlesque, by the inferior clergy of functions properly belonging to their betters. The fools jangle the bells (Paris, Amiens, Auxerre), they take the higher stalls (Paris), sing dissonantly (Sens), repeat meaningless words (Châlons, Antibes), say the *messe liesse* (Laon) or the *missa fatuorum* (Autun), preach the *sermones fatui* (Auxerre), cense *praepostere* (St. Omer) with pudding and sausage (Beauvais) or with old shoes (Paris theologians). They have their chapter and their proctors (Auxerre, Dijon). They install their *dominus festi* with a ceremony of *sacre* (Troyes), or shaving (Sens, Dijon). He is vested in full pontificals, goes in procession, as at the *Rabardiaux* of Laon, gives the benedictions, issues indulgences (Viviers), has his seal (Lille), perhaps his right of coining (Laon). Much in

---

as a sign that the choir would sup with him. This was called 'annonce en forme d'antienne,' and the suppers *defructus*. The *C. of Narbonne* (1551), c. 47, forbade 'parochis ... ne ... ad commessationes quas defructus appellant, ullo modo parochianos suos admittant, nec permittant quempiam canere ut dicunt: Memento, Domine, *David sans truffe*, &c. Nec alia huiusmodi ridenda, quae in contemptum divini officii ac in dedecus et probrum totius cleri et fiunt et cantantur.'

[1] When, however, Ducange says that the feast was not called *Subdiaconorum*, because the sub-deacons held it, but rather as being 'ebriorum Clericorum seu Diaconorum: id enim evincit vox *Soudiacres*, id est, ad litteram, *Saturi Diaconi*, quasi *Diacres Saouls*,' we must take it for a 'sole joke of Thucydides.' I believe there is also a joke somewhere in Liddell and Scott.

all these proceedings was doubtless the merest horseplay; such ingenuity and humour as they required may have been provided by the wicked wit of the *goliardi*[1].

Now I would point out that this inversion of status so characteristic of the Feast of Fools is equally characteristic of folk-festivals. What is Dr. Frazer's mock king but one of the meanest of the people chosen out to represent the real king as the priest victim of a divine sacrifice, and surrounded, for the period of the feast, in a naïve attempt to outwit heaven, with all the paraphernalia and luxury of kingship? Precisely such a mock king is the *dominus festi* with whom we have to do. His actual titles, indeed, are generally ecclesiastical. Most often he is a 'bishop,' or 'prelate' (Senlis); in metropolitan churches an 'archbishop,' in churches exempt from other authority than that of the Holy See, a 'pope' (Amiens, Senlis, Chartres). More rarely he is a 'patriarch' (Laon, Avallon), a 'cardinal' (Paris, Besançon), an 'abbot' (Vienne, Viviers, Romans, Auxerre)[2], or is even content with the humbler dignity of 'precentor,' '*bacularius*' or '*bâtonnier*' (Sens, Dijon). At Autun he is, quite exceptionally, 'Herod.' Nevertheless the term 'king' is not unknown. It is found at Noyon, at Vienne, at Besançon, at Beverley, and the council of Basle testifies to its use, as well as that of 'duke.' Nor is it, after all, of much importance what the *dominus festi* is called. The point is that his existence and functions in the ecclesiastical festivals afford precise parallels to his existence and functions in folk-festivals all Europe over.

Besides the 'king' many other features of the folk-festivals may readily be traced at the Feast of Fools. Some here, some there, they jot up in the records. There are dance and *chanson*, *tripudium* and *cantilena* (Noyon, Châlons-sur-

---

[1] Cf. p. 60; Gautier, *Les Tropaires*, i. 186; and *C. of Treves* in 1227 (J. F. Schannat, *Conc. Germ.* iii. 532) 'praecipimus ut omnes Sacerdotes non permittant trutannos et alios vagos scolares aut goliardos cantare versus super *Sanctus* et *Agnus Dei*.'

[2] The 'abbot' appears to have been sometimes charged with choir discipline throughout the year, and at Vienne and Viviers exists side by side with another *dominus festi*. Similarly at St. Omer there was a 'dean' as well as a 'bishop.' The vicars of Lincoln and Wells also chose two officers.

Marne, Paris theologians, council of Basle). There is eating
and drinking, not merely in the refectory, but within or
at the doors of the church itself (Paris theologians, Beauvais, Prague). There is ball-playing (Châlons-sur-Marne).
There is the procession or cavalcade through the streets
(Laon, Châlons-sur-Marne, &c.). There are torches and
lanterns (Sens, Tournai). Men are led *nudi* (Sens); they
are whipped (Tours); they are ceremonially ducked or
roasted (Sens, Tournai, Vienne, *les Gaigizons* at Autun)[1].
A comparison with earlier chapters of the present volume
will establish the significance which these points, taken in
bulk, possess. Equally characteristic of folk-festivals is the
costume considered proper to the feasts. The riotous clergy
wear their vestments inside out (Antibes), or exchange dress
with the laity (Lincoln, Paris theologians). But they also
wear leaves or flowers (Sens, Laon, Cologne) and women's
dress (Paris theologians); and above all they wear hideous
and monstrous masks, *larvae* or *personae* (decretal of 1207,
Paris theologians, council of Basle, Paris, Soissons, Laon,
Lille). These masks, indeed, are perhaps the one feature of
the feast which called down the most unqualified condemnation from the ecclesiastical authorities. We shall not be far
wrong if we assume them to have been beast-masks, and to
have taken the place of the actual skins and heads of sacrificial animals, here, as so often, worn at the feast by the
worshippers.

An attempt has been made to find an oriental origin for
the Feast of Fools[2]. Gibbon relates the insults offered to
the church at Constantinople by the Emperor Michael III,
the 'Drunkard' (842–67)[3]. A noisy crew of courtiers
dressed themselves in the sacred vestments. One Theophilus or Grylus, captain of the guard, a mime and buffoon,
was chosen as a mock 'patriarch.' The rest were his twelve

---

[1] I suppose that 'portetur in
rost' at Vienne means that the
victims were roasted like the fags
in *Tom Brown.*

[2] Ducange, s. v. *Kalendae.*

[3] Gibbon - Bury, v. 201. The
Byzantine authorities are Genesius,
iv. p. 49 B (*Corp. Hist. Byz.* xi. 2. 102);
Paphlagon (Migne, *P. G.* cv. 527);
Theophanes Continuatus, iv. 38
(*Corp. Hist. Byz.* xxii. 200); Symeon
Magister, p. 437 D (*Corp. Hist. Byz.*
xxii. 661), on all of whom see Bury,
App. I to tom. cit.

'metropolitans,' Michael himself being entitled 'metropolitan of Cologne.' The 'divine mysteries' were burlesqued with vinegar and mustard in a golden cup set with gems. Theophilus rode about the streets of the city on a white ass, and when he met the real patriarch Ignatius, exposed him to the mockery of the revellers. After the death of Michael, this profanity was solemnly anathematized by the council of Constantinople held under his successor Basil in 869[1]. Theophilus, though he borrowed the vestments for his mummery, seems to have carried it on in the streets and the palace, not in the church. In the tenth century, however, the patriarch Theophylactus won an unenviable reputation by admitting dances and profane songs into the ecclesiastical festivals[2]; while in the twelfth, the patriarch Balsamon describes his own unavailing struggle against proceedings at Christmas and Candlemas, which come uncommonly near the Feast of Fools. The clergy of St. Sophia's, he says, claim as of ancient custom to wear masks, and to enter the church in the guise of soldiers, or of monks, or of four-footed animals. The superintendents snap their fingers like charioteers, or paint their faces and mimic women. The rustics are moved to laughter by the pouring of wine into pitchers, and are allowed to chant *Kyrie eleison* in ludicrous iteration at every verse[3]. Balsamon, who died in 1193, was almost

---

[1] *C. of Constantinople* (869-70), c. 16 (Mansi, xvi. 169, *ex versione Latina, abest in Graeca*) 'fuisse quosdam laicos, qui secundum diversam imperatoriam dignitatem videbantur capillorum comam circumplexam involvere atque reponere, et gradum quasi sacerdotalem per quaedam inducia et vestimenta sacerdotalia sumere, et, ut putabatur, episcopos constituere, superhumeralibus, id est, palliis, circumamictos, et omnem aliam Pontificalem indutos stolam, qui etiam proprium patriarcham adscribentes eum qui in adinventionibus risum moventibus praelatus et princeps erat, et insultabant et illudebant quibuscue divinis, modo quidem electiones, promotiones et consecrationes, modo autem acute calum-

nias, damnationes et depositiones episcoporum quasi ab invicem et per invicem miserabiliter et praevaricatorie agentes et patientes. Talis autem actio nec apud gentes a saeculo unquam audita est.'

[2] Cedrenus, *Historiarum Compendium*, p. 639 B (ed. Bekker, in *Corp. Hist. Byz.* xxiv. 2. 333), follows verbatim the still unprinted eleventh-century John Scylitzes (Gibbon-Bury, v. 508). Theophylactus was Patriarch from 933 to 956.

[3] Theodorus Balsamon, *In Can. lxii Conc. in Trullo* (*P. G.* cxxxvii. 727) Σημείωσαι τὸν παρόντα κανόνα, καὶ ζήτησον διόρθωσιν ἐπὶ τοῖς γινομένοις παρὰ τῶν κληρικῶν εἰς τὴν ἑορτὴν ἐπὶ τῆς γεννήσεως τοῦ Χριστοῦ, καὶ τὴν ἑορτὴν τῶν Φώτων [Luminarium, Candlemas] ὑπεναντίως τούτῳ·

precisely a contemporary of Belethus, and the earlier Byzantine notices considerably ante-date any records that we
possess of the Feast of Fools in the West. A slight cor-
roboration of this theory of an eastern origin may be derived
from the use of the term ' patriarch ' for the *dominus festi*
at Laon and Avallon. It would, I think, be far-fetched to
find another in the fact that Theophilus, like the western
'bishops' of Fools, rode upon an ass, and that the *Prose de
l'Âne* begins :

> ' Orientis partibus,
> adventavit asinus.'

In any case, the oriental example can hardly be responsible
for more than the admission of the feast within the doors
of the church. One cannot doubt that it was essentially
an adaptation of a folk-custom long perfectly well known
in the West itself. The question of origin had already presented itself to the learned writers of the thirteenth century.
William of Auxerre, by a misunderstanding which I shall
hope to explain, traced the Feast of Fools to the Roman
Parentalia: Durandus, and the Paris theologians after him,
to the January Kalends. Certainly Durandus was right.
The Kalends, unlike the more specifically Italian feasts,
were coextensive with the Roman empire, and were naturally
widespread in Gaul. The date corresponds precisely with that
by far the most common for the Feast of Fools. A singular
history indeed, that of the ecclesiastical celebration of the

καὶ μᾶλλον εἰς τὴν ἁγιωτάτην Μεγάλην
ἐκκλησίαν . . . ἀλλὰ καί τινες κληρικοὶ
κατά τινας ἑορτὰς πρὸς διάφορα μετα-
σχηματίζονται προσωπεῖα. καὶ ποτὲ μὲν
ξιφήρεις ἐν τῷ μεσονάῳ τῆς ἐκκλησίας
μετὰ στρατιωτικῶν ἀμφίων εἰσέρχονται,
ποτὲ δὲ καὶ ὡς μοναχοὶ προοδεύουσιν,
ἢ καὶ ὡς ζῶα τετράποδα. ἐρωτήσας οὖν
ὅπως ταῦτα παρεχωρήθησαν γίνεσθαι,
οὐδέν τε ἕτερον ἤκουσα ἀλλ' ἢ ἐκ
μακρᾶς συνηθείας ταῦτα τελεῖσθαι.
τοιαῦτά εἰσιν, ὡς ἐμοὶ δοκεῖ, καὶ τὰ
παρά τινων δομεστικευόντων ἐν κλήρῳ
γινόμενα, τὸν ἀέρα τοῖς δακτύλοις κατὰ
ἡνιόχους τυπτόντων, καὶ φύκη ταῖς
γνάθοις δῆθεν περιτιθεμένων καὶ ὑπορ-
ρινομένων ἔργα τινὰ γυναικεῖα, καὶ ἕτερα

ἀπρεπῆ, ἵνα πρὸς γέλωτα τοὺς βλέ-
ποντας μετακινήσωσι. τὸ δὲ γελᾶν
τοὺς ἀγρότας ἐγχεομένους τοῦ οἴνου
τοῖς πίθοις, ὡσεί τι παρεπόμενον ἐξ
ἀνάγκης ἐστὶ τοῖς ληνοβατοῖσιν· εἰ
μήτις εἴπῃ τὴν σατανικὴν ταύτην ἐργα-
σίαν καταργεῖσθαι διὰ τοῦ λέγειν τοὺς
ἀγρότας συχνότερον ἐφ' ἑκάστῳ μέτρῳ
σχεδὸν τό, Κύριε ἐλέησον. τὰ μέντοι
ποτὲ γινόμενα ἀπρεπῆ παρὰ τῶν νοταρίων παιδοδιδασκάλων κατὰ τὴν ἑορτὴν
τῶν ἁγίων νοταρίων, μετὰ προσωπείων
σκηνικῶν διερχομένων τὴν ἀγοράν, πρὸ
χρόνων τινῶν κατηργήθησαν, καθ' ὁρι-
σμὸν τοῦ ἁγιωτάτου ἐκείνου πατριάρχου
κυρίου Λουκᾶ.

First of January. Up to the eighth century a fast, with its mass *pro prohibendo ab idolis*, it gradually took on a festal character, and became ultimately the one feast in the year in which paganism made its most startling and persistent recoil upon Christianity. The attacks upon the Kalends in the disciplinary documents form a catena which extends very nearly to the point at which the notices of the Feast of Fools begin. In each alike the masking, in mimicry of beasts and probably of beast-gods or 'demons,' appears to have been a prominent and highly reprobated feature. It is true that we hear nothing of a *dominus festi* at the Kalends ; but much stress must not be laid upon the omission of the disciplinary writers to record any one point in a custom which after all they were not describing as anthropologists, and it would certainly be an exceptional Germano-Keltic folk-feast which had not a *dominus*. As a matter of fact, there is no mention of a *rex* in the accounts of the pre-Christian Kalends in Italy itself. There was a *rex* at the *Saturnalia*, and this, together with an allusion of Belethus in a quite different connexion to the *libertas Decembrica*[1], has led some writers to find in the *Saturnalia*, rather than the Kalends, the origin of the Feast of Fools[2]. This is, I venture to think, wrong. The *Saturnalia* were over well before December 25 : there is no evidence that they had a vogue outside Italy: the Kalends, like the *Saturnalia*, were an occasion at which slaves met their masters upon equal terms, and I believe that the existence of a Kalends *rex*, both in Italy and in Gaul, may be taken for granted.

But the parallel between Kalends and the Feast of Fools cannot be held to be quite perfect, unless we can trace in the latter feast that most characteristic of all Kalends customs, the *Cervulus*. Is it possible that a representative of the *Cervulus* is to be found in the Ass, who, whether introduced from Constantinople or not, gave to the Feast of Fools one of its popular names? The Feast of Asses has been the sport of controversialists who had not, and were at no great pains

---

[1] Belethus, c. 120, compares the ecclesiastical ball-play at Easter to the *libertas Decembrica*. He is not speaking here of the Feast of Fools.

[2] e.g. Du Tilliot, 2.

to have, the full facts before them. I do not propose to
awake once more these ancient angers[1]. The facts themselves are briefly these. The 'Prose of the Ass' was used
at Bourges, at Sens, and at Beauvais. As to the Bourges
feast I have no details. At Sens, the use of the Prose by
Pierre de Corbeil is indeed no proof that he allowed an ass
to appear in the ceremony. But the Prose would not have
much point unless it was at least a survival from a time when
an ass did appear ; the feast was known as the *asinaria festa*;
and even now, three centuries after it was abolished, the Sens
choir-boys still play at being *âne* archbishop on Innocents'
day[2]. At Beauvais the heading *Conductus quando asinus
adducitur* in the thirteenth-century *Officium* seems to show
that there at least the ass appeared, and even entered the
church. The document, also of the thirteenth century, quoted
by the editors of Ducange, certainly brings him, in the
ceremony of January 14, into the church and near the altar.
An imitation of his braying is introduced into the service
itself. At Autun the leading of an ass *ad processionem*, and
the *cantilena super dictum asinum* were suppressed in 1411.
At Châlons-sur-Marne in 1570 an ass bore the 'bishop' to
the theatre at the church door only. At Prague, on the
other hand, towards the end of the fourteenth century, an
ass was led, as at Beauvais, right into the church. These,
with doubtful references to *fêtes des ânes* at St. Quentin about
1081, at Béthune in 1474, and at Laon in 1527, and the
Mosburg description of the 'bishop' as *asinorum dominus*,
are all the cases I have found in which an ass has anything
to do with the feast. But they are enough to prove that an
ass was an early and widespread, though not an invariable
feature. I may quote here a curious survival in a *ronde* from
the west of France, said to have been sung at church doors
on January 1[3]. It is called *La Mort de l'Âne*, and begins :

---

[1] S. R. Maitland, *The Dark Ages*,
141, tilts at the Protestant historian
Robertson's *History of Charles V*,
as do F. Clément, 159, and A. Walter,
Das Eselsfest in *Caecilien-Kalender*
(1885), 75, at Dulaure, *Hist. des
Environs de Paris*, iii. 509, and
other 'Voltairiens.'

[2] Chérest, 81.
[3] J. Bujeaud, *Chants et Chansons
populaires des Provinces de l'Ouest*,
i. 63. The *ronde* is known in Poitou,
Aunis, Angoumois. P. Tarbé, *Ro-
mancero de Champagne* (2ᵉ partie),
257, gives a variant. Bujeaud, i. 61,
gives another *ronde*, the *Testament*

'Quand le bonhomme s'en va,
Quand le bonhomme s'en va,
Trouvit la tête à son âne,
Que le loup mangit au bois.

Parlé. O tête, pauvre tête,
        Tâ qui chantas si bé
        L'Magnificat à Vêpres.

Daux matin à quat' léçons,
La sambredondon, bredondaine,
Daux matin à quat' léçons,
        La sambredondon.'

This, like the Sens choir-boys' custom of calling their 'arch-bishop' *âne*, would seem to suggest that the *dominus festi* was himself the ass, with a mask on; and this may have been sometimes the case. But in most of the mediaeval instances the ass was probably used to ride. At Prague, so far as one can judge from Huss's description, he was a real ass. There is no proof in any of the French examples that he was, or was not, merely a 'hobby-ass.' If he was, he came all the nearer to the *Cervulus*.

It has been pointed out, and will, in the next volume, be pointed out again, that the ecclesiastical authorities attempted to sanctify the spirit of play at the Feast of Fools and similar festivities by diverting the energies of the revellers to *ludi* of the miracle-play order. In such *ludi* they found a place for the ass. He appears for instance as Balaam's ass in the later versions from Laon and Rouen of the *Prophetae*, and at Rouen he gave to the whole of this performance the name of the *festum* or *processio asinorum*[1]. At Hamburg,

de l'Âne, in which the ass has fallen into a ditch, and amongst other legacies leaves his tail to the *curé* for an *aspersoir*. This is known in Poitou, Angoumois, Franche-Comté. He also says that he has heard children of Poitou and Angoumois go through a mock catechism, giving an ecclesiastical significance to each part of the ass. The tail is the *goupillon*, and so forth. Fournier-Verneuil, *Paris, Tableau moral et philosophique* (1826),

522, with the Beauvais *Officium* in his mind, says 'Voulez-vous qu'au lieu de dire, *Ite, missa est*, le prêtre se mette à braire trois fois de toute sa force, et que le peuple réponde en chœur, comme je l'ai vu faire en 1788, dans l'église de Bellaigues, en Périgord?'

[1] Cf. ch. xx. Gasté, 20, considers the Rouen *Festum Asinorum* 'l'origine de toutes les Fêtes de l'Âne qui se célébraient dans d'autres diocèses': but the Rouen MS. in

by a curious combination, he is at once Balaam's ass and the finder of the star in a *ludus Trium Regum*[1]. His use as the mount of the Virgin on January 14 at Beauvais, and on some uncertain day at Sens, seems to suggest another favourite episode in such *ludi*, that of the Flight into Egypt. At Varennes, in Picardy, and at Bayonne, exist carved wooden groups representing this event. That of Varennes is carried in procession; that of Bayonne is the object of pilgrimage on the *fêtes* of the Virgin[2].

Not at the Feast of Fools alone, or at the miracle-plays connected with this feast, did the ass make its appearance in Christian worship. It stood with the ox, on the morning of the Nativity, beside the Christmas crib. On Palm Sunday it again formed part of a procession, in the semblance of the beast on which Christ made his triumphal entry into Jerusalem[3]. A Cambrai *Ordinarium* quoted by Ducange directs that the *asina picta* shall remain behind the altar for four days[4]. Kirchmeyer describes the custom as it

which it occurs is only of the fourteenth century, and the Balaam episode does not occur at all in the more primitive forms of the *Prophetae*, while the Sens Feast of Fools is called the *festa asinaria* in the *Officium* of the early thirteenth century.

[1] Tille, *D. W.* 31. In Madrid an ass was led in procession on Jan. 17, with anthems on the Balaam legend (Clément, 181).

[2] Clément, 182; Didron, *Annales archéologiques*, xv. 384.

[3] Dulaure, *Hist. des Environs de Paris*, iii. 509, quotes a legend to the effect that the very ass ridden by Christ came ultimately to Verona, died there, was buried in a wooden effigy at Sᵗᵃ-Maria in Organo, and honoured by a yearly procession. He guesses at this as the origin of the Beauvais and other *fêtes*. Didron, *Annales arch.* xv. 377, xvi. 33, found that nothing was known of this legend at Verona, though such a statue group as is described above apparently existed in the church named. Dulaure gives as his

authorities F. M. Misson, *Nouveau Voyage d'Italie* (1731), i. 164; *Dict. de l'Italie*, i. 56. Misson's visit to Verona was in 1687, although the passage was not printed in the first edition (1691) of his book. It is in the English translation of 1714 (i. 198). *His* authority was a French merchant (M. Montel) living in Verona, who had often seen the procession. In *Cenni intorno all' origine e descrizione della Festa che annualmente si celebra in Verona l' ultimo Venerdì del Carnovale, comunamente denominata Gnoccolare* (1818), 75, is a mention of the 'asinello del vecchio padre Sileno' which served as a mount for the 'Capo de' Maccheroni.' This is probably Misson's procession, but there is no mention of the legend in any of the eighteenth-century accounts quoted in the pamphlet. Rienzi was likened to an 'Abbate Asinino' (Gibbon, vii. 269).

[4] Ducange, s. v. *Festum Asinorum*; cf. Leber, ix. 270; Molanus, *de Hist. SS. Imaginum et Picturarum* (1594), iv. 18.

existed during the sixteenth century in Germany [1] ; and the stray tourist who drops into the wonderful collection of domestic and ecclesiastical antiquities in the Barfüsserkirche at Basle will find there three specimens of the *Palmesel*, including a thirteenth-century one from Bayern and a seventeenth-century one from Elsass. The third is not labelled with its *provenance*, but it is on wheels and has a hole for the rope by which it was dragged round the church. All three are of painted wood, and upon each is a figure representing Christ [2].

The affiliation of the ecclesiastical New Year revelries to the pagan Kalends does not explain why those who took part in them were called 'Fools.' The obvious thing to say is that they were called 'Fools' because they played the fool ; and indeed their mediaeval critics were not slow to

[1] T. Naogeorgus (Kirchmeyer), *The Popish Kingdom*, iv. 443 (1553, transl. Barnabe Googe, 1570, in New Shakspere Society edition of Stubbes, *Anatomy of Abuses*, i. 332) ; cf. *Beehive of the Roman Church*, 199. The earliest notice is in Gerardus, *Leben St. Ulrichs von Augsburg* (ob. 973), c. 4. E. Bishop, in *Dublin Review*, cxxiii. 405, traces the custom in a Prague fourteenth-century *Missal* and sixteenth-century *Breviary* ; also in the modern Greek Church at Moscow where until recently the Czar held the bridle. But there is no ass, as he says, in the Palm Sunday ceremony described in the *Peregrinatio Silviae* (Duchesne, 486).

[2] A peeress of the realm lately stated that this custom had been introduced in recent years into the Anglican church. Denials were to hand, and an amazing conflict of evidence resulted. Is there any proof that the *Palmesel* was ever an English ceremony at all ? The Hereford riding of 1706 (cf. *Representations*) was not in the church. Brand, i. 73, quotes *A Dialogue : the Pilgremage of Pure Devotyon* (1551 ?), 'Upon Palme Sondaye they play the foles sadely, drawynge after them an Asse in a rope, when

they be not moche distante from the Woden Asse that they drawe.' Clearly this, like Googe's translation of Naogeorgus, is a description of contemporary continental Papistry. W. Fulke, *The Text of the New Testament* (ed. 1633), 76 (*ad Marc.* xi. 8) quotes a note of the Rheims translation to the effect that in memory of the entry into Jerusalem is a procession on Palm Sunday 'with the blessed Sacrament reverently carried as it were Christ upon the Asse,' and comments, 'But it is pretty sport, that you make the Priest that carrieth the idoll, to supply the roome of the Asse on which Christ did ride. . . . Thus you turn the holy mysterie of Christ's riding to Jerusalem to a May - game and Pageant - play.' Fulke, who lived 1538–89, is evidently unaware that there was an ass, as well as the priest, in the procession, from which I infer that the custom was not known in England. Not that this consideration would weigh with the mediaevally-minded curate, who is as a rule only too ready to make up by the ceremonial inaccuracy of his mummeries for the offence which they cause to his congregation.

draw this inference. But it is noteworthy that pagan Rome already had its Feast of Fools, which, indeed, had nothing to do with the Kalends. The *stultorum feriae* on February 17 was the last day on which the *Fornacalia* or ritual sacrifice of the *curiae* was held. Upon it all the *curiae* sacrificed in common, and it therefore afforded an opportunity for any citizen who did not know which his *curia* was to partake in the ceremony[1]. I am not prepared to say that the *stultorum feriae* gave its name to the Feast of Fools; but the identity of the two names certainly seems to explain some of the statements which mediaeval scholars make about that feast. It explains William of Auxerre's derivation of it from the *Parentalia*, for the *stultorum feriae* fell in the midst of the *Parentalia*[2]. And I think it explains the remark of Belethus, and, following him, of Durandus, about the *ordo subdiaconorum* being *incertus*. The sub-deacons were a regular *ordo*, the highest of the *ordines minores* from the third century[3]. But Belethus seems to be struggling with the notion that the sub-deacons' feast, closing the series of post-Nativity feasts held by deacons, priests and choir-boys, was in some way parallel to the *feriae* of the Roman *stulti* who were *incerti* as to their *curia*.

---

[1] Marquardt-Mommsen, vi. 191; Jevons, *Plutarch's Romane Questions*, 134; Fowler, 304, 322; Ovid, *Fasti*, ii. 531 :

'stultaque pars populi, quae sit
    sua curia, nescit ;
sed facit extrema sacra relata
    die.'

[2] Fowler, 306.   [3] Schaff, iii. 131.

CHAPTER XV

THE BOY BISHOP

[*Bibliographical Note.*—Most of the authorities for chh. xiii, xiv, are still available, since many writers have not been careful to distinguish between the various feasts of the Twelve nights. The best modern account of the Boy Bishop is Mr. A. F. Leach's paper on *The Schoolboys' Feast* in *The Fortnightly Review*, N. S. lix (1896), 128. The contributions of F. A. Dürr, *Commentatio Historica de Episcopo Puerorum, vulgo vom Schul-Bischoff* (1755); F. A. Specht, *Geschichte des Unterrichtswesens in Deutschland*, 222 sqq. (1885); A. Gasté, *Les Drames liturgiques de la Cathédrale de Rouen*, 35 sqq. (1893); E. F. Rimbault, *The Festival of the Boy Bishop in England* in *The Camden Miscellany*, vol. vii (Camden Soc. 1875), are also valuable. Dr. Rimbault speaks of 'considerable collections for a history of the festival of the Boy Bishop throughout Europe,' made by Mr. J. G. Nichols, but I do not know where these are to be found. Brand (ed. Ellis), i. 227 sqq., has some miscellaneous data, and a notice interesting by reason of its antiquity is that on the *Episcopus Puerorum, in Die Innocentium*, in the *Posthuma*, 95 sqq., of John Gregory (1649).]

JOANNES BELETHUS, the learned theologian of Paris and Amiens, towards the end of the twelfth century, describes, as well as the Feast of Fools, no less than three other *tripudia* falling in Christmas week[1]. Upon the days of St. Stephen, St. John the Evangelist, and the Holy Innocents, the deacons,

---

[1] Belethus, c. 70 'Debent ergo vesperae Natalis primo integre celebrari, ac postea conveniunt diaconi quasi in tripudio, cantantque *Magnificat* cum antiphona de S. Stephano, sed sacerdos recitat collectam. Nocturnos et universum officium crastinum celebrant diaconi, quod Stephanus fuerit diaconus, et ad lectiones concedunt benedictiones, ita tamen, ut eius diei missam celebret hebdomarius, hoc est ille cuius tum vices fuerint eam exsequi. Sic eodem modo omne officium perficient sacerdotes ipso die B. Ioannis, quod hic sacerdos fuerit, et pueri in ipso festo Innocentium, quia innocentes pro Christo occisi sunt, . . . in festo itaque Innocentium penitus subticentur cantica laetitiae, quoniam ii ad inferos descenderunt.' Cf. also c. 72, quoted on p. 275. Durandus, *Rat. Div. Off.* (1284), vii. 42, *De festis SS. Stephani, Ioannis Evang. et Innocentium*, gives a similar account. At Vespers on Christmas Day, he says, the deacons 'in tripudio convenientes cantant antiphonam de sancto Stephano, et sacerdos collectam. Nocturnos autem et officium in crastinum celebrant et benedictiones super lectiones dant: quod tamen facere non debent.' So too for the priests and boys on the following days.

the priests, the choir-boys, held their respective revels, each body in turn claiming that pre-eminence in the divine services which in the Feast of Fools was assigned to the sub-deacons. The distinction drawn by Belethus is not wholly observed in the ecclesiastical prohibitions either of the thirteenth or of the fifteenth century. In many of these the term 'Feast of Fools' has a wide meaning. The council of Nevers in 1246 includes under it the feasts of the Innocents and the New Year; that of Langres in 1404 the 'festivals of the Nativity'; that of Nantes in 1431 the Nativity itself, St. Stephen's, St. John's, and the Innocents'. For the council of Basle it is apparently synonymous with the 'Feast of Innocents or Boys'; the Paris theologians speak of its rites as practised on St. Stephen's, the Innocents', the Circumcision, and other dates. The same tendency to group all these *tripudia* together recurs in passages in which the 'Feast of Fools' is not in so many words mentioned. The famous decretal of Pope Innocent III is directed against the *ludibria* practised in turns by deacons, priests, and sub-deacons during the feasts immediately following upon Christmas. The *irrisio servitii* inveighed against in the *Rememoratio* of Gerson took place on Innocents' day, on the Circumcision, on the Epiphany, or at Shrovetide.

Local usage, however, only partly bears out this loose language of the prohibitions. At Châlons-sur-Marne, in 1570, the 'bishop' of Fools sported on St. Stephen's day. At Besançon, in 1387, a distinct *dominus festi* was chosen on each of the three days after Christmas, and all alike were called *rois des fous*. At Autun, during the fifteenth century, the *regna* of the 'bishop' and 'dean' of Innocents and of 'Herod' at the New Year were known together as the *festa folorum*. Further south, the identification is perhaps more common. At Avallon, Aix, Antibes, the Feast of Fools was on Innocents' day; at Arles the *episcopus stultorum* officiated both on the Innocents' and on St. John's, at Viviers on all three of the post-Nativity feasts. But these are exceptions, and, at least outside Provence, the rule seems to have been to apply the name of 'Feast of Fools' to the *tripudium*, originally that of the sub-deacons, on New Year's day or the Epiphany, and to distinguish from this, as does Belethus, the *tripudia* of the deacons, priests, and choir-boys in Christmas week.

We may go further and say, without much hesitation, that the three latter feasts are of older ecclesiastical standing than their riotous rival. Belethus is the first writer to mention the Feast of Fools, but he is by no means the first writer to mention the Christmas *tripudia*. They were known to Honorius of Autun[1], early in the twelfth century, and to John of Avranches[2], late in the eleventh. They can be traced at least from the beginning of the tenth, more than two hundred and fifty years before the Feast of Fools is heard of. The earliest notice I have come across is at the monastery of St. Gall, hard by Constance, in 911. In that year King Conrad I was spending Christmas with Bishop Solomon of Constance. He heard so much of the Vespers processions during the *triduum* at St. Gall that he insisted on visiting the monastery, and arrived there in the midst of the revels. It was all very amusing, and especially the procession of children, so grave and sedate that even when Conrad bade his train roll apples along the aisle they did not budge[3]. That the other Vespers processions of the *triduum* were of deacons and priests may be taken for granted. I do not know whether the *triduum* originated at St. Gall, but the famous song-school of that monastery was all-important in

---

[1] Honorius Augustodunensis, *Gemma Animae*, iii. 12 (*P. L.* clxxii. 646).

[2] Ioannes Abrincensis (bishop of Rouen †1070), *de Eccl. Offic.* (*P. L.* cxlvii. 41), with fairly full account of the 'officia.'

[3] Ekkehardus IV, *de Casibus S. Galli*, c. 14 (ed. G. Meyer von Knonau, in *Mittheilungen zur vaterländischen Gesch.* of the Hist. Verein in St. Gallen, N.F., v.; *M. G. H. Scriptores*, ii. 84) 'longum est dicere, quibus iocunditatibus dies exegerit et noctes, maxime in processione infantum ; quibus poma in medio ecclesiae pavimento antesterni iubens, cum nec unum parvissimorum moveri nec ad ea adtendere vidisset, miratus est disciplinam.' Ekkehart was master

of the song-school, and von Knonau mentions some *cantiones* written by him and others for the feast, e. g. one beginning 'Salve lacteolo decoratum sanguine festum.' He has another story (c. 26) of how Solomon who was abbot of the monastery, as well as bishop of Constance, looking into the song-school on the 'dies scolarium,' when the boys had a 'ius . . . ut hospites intrantes capiant, captos, usque dum se redimant, teneant,' was duly made prisoner, and set on the master's seat. 'Si in magistri solio sedeo,' cried the witty bishop, 'iure eius uti habeo. Omnes exuimini.' After his jest, he paid his footing like a man. The 'Schulabt' of St. Gall is said to have survived until the council of Trent.

the movement towards the greater elaboration of church ceremonial, and even more of chant, which marked the tenth century. This gave rise to the tropes, of which much will be said in the next volume; and it is in a tropary, an English tropary from Winchester, dating from before 980, that the feasts of the *triduum* next occur. The ceremonies of those feasts, as described by Belethus, belong mainly to the Office, and the tropes are mainly chanted elaborations of the text of the Mass: but the Winchester tropes for the days of St. Stephen, St. John, and the Holy Innocents clearly imply the respective connexion of the services, to which they belong, with deacons, priests, and choir-boys[1]. Of the sub-deacons, on Circumcision or Epiphany, there is as yet nothing. John of Avranches, Honorius of Autun, and Belethus bridge a gap, and from the thirteenth century the *triduum* is normal in service-books, both continental and English, throughout the Middle Ages[2]. It is provided for in the Nantes *Ordinarium* of 1263[3], in the Amiens *Ordinarium* of 1291[4], and in the Tours *Rituale* of the fourteenth century[5]. It required reforming at Vienne in 1385, but continued to exist there up to 1670[6]. In the last three cases it is clearly marked side by side with, but other than, the Feast of Fools. In Germany, it

---

[1] Frere, *Winch. Troper*, 6, 8, 10. The deacons' sang ' Eia, conlevitae in protomartyris Stephani natalicio ex persona ipsius cum psalmista ouantes concinnamus'; the priests, ' Hodie candidati sacerdotum chori centeni et milleni coniubilent Christo dilectoque suo Iohanni ' ; the boys, ' Psallite nunc Christo pueri, dicente propheta.'

[2] Rock, iii. 2. 214; Clément, 118; Grenier, 353; Martene, iii. 38. These writers add several references for the *triduum* or one or other of its feasts to those here given: e. g. Martene quotes on St. Stephen's feast *Ordinarium of Langres*, 'finitis vesperis fiunt tripudia'; *Ordinarium of Limoges*, 'vadunt omnes ad capitulum, ubi Episcopus, sive praesens, sive absens fuerit, dat eis potum ex tribus vinis '; *Ordinarium of Strasburg* (†1364),

' propinatur in refectorio, sicut in vigilia nativitatis.'

[3] Martene, iii. 38 ' tria festa, quae sequuntur, fiunt cum magna solemnitate et tripudio. Primum faciunt diaconi, secundum presbiteri, tertium pueri.'

[4] Grenier, 353 ' si festa [S. Stephani] fiant, ut consuetum est, a diaconis in cappis sericis . . . fit statio in medio choro, et ab ipsis regitur chorus . . . et fiant festa sicut docent libri '; and so for the two other feasts.

[5] Martene, iii. 38 ' cum in primis vesperis [in festo S. Stephani] ad illum cantici *Magnificat* versiculum *Deposuit potentes* perventum erat, cantor baculum locumque suum diacono, qui pro eo chorum regeret, cedebat'; and so on the other feasts.

[6] Cf. p. 315.

is contemplated in the *Ritual* of Mainz [1]. In England I trace it at Salisbury [2], at York [3], at Lincoln [4], at St. Albans [5]. These instances could doubtless be multiplied, although there were certainly places where the special devotion of the three feasts to the three bodies dropped out at an early date. The Rheims *Ordinarium* of the fourteenth century, for instance, knows nothing of it [6]. The extent of the ceremonies, again, would naturally be subject to local variation. The germ of them lay in the procession at first Vespers described by Ekkehard at St. Gall. But they often grew to a good deal more than this. The deacons, priests, or choir-boys, as the case might be, took the higher stalls, and the whole conduct of the services; the *Deposuit* was sung; *epistolae farcitae* were read [7]; there was a *dominus festi*.

The main outlines of the feasts of the *triduum* are thus almost exactly parallel, so far as the divine *servitium* is concerned, to those of the Feast of Fools, for which indeed they probably served as a model. And like the Feast of Fools, they had their secular side, which often became riotousness. Occasionally they were absorbed in, or overshadowed by, the more popular and wilder merry-making of the inferior clergy.

---

[1] Durr, 77. Here the sub-deacons shared in the deacons' feast.

[2] The *Consuetudinarium* of †1210 (Frere, *Use of Sarum*, i. 124, 223) mentions the procession of deacons after Vespers on Christmas day, but says nothing of the share of the priests and boys in those of the following days. The *Sarum Breviary* gives all three (Fasc. i. cols. cxcv, ccxiii, ccxxix), and has a note (col. clxxvi) 'nunquam enim dicitur Prosa ad Matutinas per totum annum, sed ad Vesperas, et ad Processionem, excepto die sancti Stephani, cuius servitium committitur voluntati Diaconorum; et excepto die sancti Iohannis, cuius servitium committitur voluntati Sacerdotum; et excepto die sanctorum Innocentium, cuius servitium committitur voluntati Puerorum.'

[3] *York Missal*, i. 20, 22, 23 (from fifteenth-century MS. *D* used in

the Minster) '*In die S. Steph.* . . . finita processione, si Dominica fuerit, ut in Processionali continetur, Diaconis et Subdiaconis in choro ordinatim astantibus, unus Diaconus, cui Praecentor imposuerit, incipiat Officium. . . . *In die S. Ioann.* . . . omnibus Personis et Presbyteris civitatis ex antiqua consuetudine ad Ecclesiam Cathedralem convenientibus, et omnibus ordinate ex utraque parte Chori in Capis sericis astantibus, Praecentor incipiat Officium. . . . *In die SS. Innoc.* . . . omnibus pueris in Capis, Praecentor illorum incipiat.' There are responds for the 'turba diaconorum,' 'presbyterorum' or 'puerorum.'

[4] *Lincoln Statutes*, i. 290; ii. ccxxx, 552.

[5] Gasquet, *Old English Bible*, 250.

[6] Martene, iii. 40.

[7] Ibid. iii. 39.

But elsewhere they have their own history of reformations or suppression, or are grouped with the Feast of Fools, as by the decretal of Innocent III, in a common condemnation. The diversity of local practice is well illustrated by the records of such acts of discipline. Sometimes, as at Paris[1], or Soissons[2], it is the deacons' feast alone that has become an abuse ; sometimes, as at Worms, that of the priests'[3] ; sometimes two of them[4], sometimes all three[5], require correction.

[1] In his second decree of 1199 as to the feast of the Circumcision at Paris (cf. p. 276), Bishop Eudes de Sully says (*P. L.* ccxii. 73) ' quoniam festivitas beati protomartyris Stephani eiusdem fere subiacebat dissolutionis et temeritatis incommodo, nec ita solemniter, sicut decebat et martyris merita requirebant, in Ecclesia Parisiensi consueverat celebrari, nos, qui eidem martyri sumus specialiter debitores, quoniam in Ecclesia Bituricensi patronum habuerimus, in cuius gremio ab ineunte aetate fuimus nutriti ; de voluntate et assensu dilectorum nostrorum Hugonis decani et capituli Parisiensis, festivitatem ipsam ad statum reducere regularem, eumque magnis Ecclesiae solemnitatibus adnumerare decrevimus ; statuentes ut in ipso festo tantum celebritatis agatur, quantum in ceteris festis annualibus fieri consuevit.' Eudes de Sully made a donative to the canons and clerks present at Matins on the feast, which his successor Petrus de Nemore confirmed in 1208 (*P. L.* ccxii. 91). Dean Hugo Clemens instigated a similar reform of St. John's day (see p. 276).

[2] Martene, iii. 40 ; Grenier, 353, 412. The *Ritual* of Bishop Nivelon, at the end of the twelfth century, orders St. Stephen's to be kept as a triple feast, ' exclusa antiqua consuetudine diaconorum et ludorum.'

[3] Schannat, iv. 258 (1316) 'illud, quod . . . causa devotionis ordinatum fuerat ... ut Sacerdotes singulis annis in festivitate Beati Iohannis Evangelistae unum ex se eligant,

qui more episcopi illa die Missam gloriose celebret et festive, nunc in ludibrium vertitur, et in ecclesia ludi fiunt theatrales, et non solum in ecclesia introducuntur monstra larvarum, verum etiam Presbyteri, Diaconi et Subdiaconi insaniae suae ludibria exercere praesumunt, facientes prandia sumptuosa, et cum tympanis et cymbalis ducentes choreas per domos et plateas civitatis.'

[4] At Rouen in 1445 the feast of St. John, held by the *capellani*, was alone in question. The chapter ordered (Gasté, 46) ' ut faciant die festi sancti euangelistae Iohannis servicium divinum bene et honeste, sine derisionibus et fatuitatibus ; et inhibitum fuit eisdem ne habeant vestes difformes, insuper quod fiat mensa et ponantur boni cantores, qui bene sciant cantare, omnibus derisionibus cessantibus.' But in 1446 the feast of St. Stephen needed reforming, as well as that of St. John (A. Chéruel, *Hist. de Rouen sous la Domination anglaise*, 206) ; and in 1451 all three (Gasté, 47) ' praefati Domini capitulantes ordinaverunt quod in festis solemnitatis Nativitatis Domini nostri Ihesu Christi proxime futuris, omnes indecencie et inhonestates consuete fieri in dedecus ecclesie, tam per presbyteros dyaconos quam pueros chori et basse forme, cessent omnino, nec sit aliquis puer in habitu episcopi, sed fiat servicium devote et honorifice prout in aliis festis similis gradus.'

[5] *C. of Toledo* (1473), c. 19 (Labbé, xiii. 1460) ' Quia vero quaedam tam in Metropolitanis quam in

I need only refer more particularly to two interesting English examples. One is at Wells, where a chapter statute of about 1331 condemns the tumult and *ludibrium* with which divine service was celebrated from the Nativity to the octave of the Innocents, and in particular the *ludi theatrales* and *monstra larvarum* introduced into the cathedral by the deacons, priests, sub-deacons, and even vicars during this period [1]. Nor was the abuse easy to check, for about 1338 a second statute was required to reinforce and strengthen the prohibition [2]. So, too, in the neighbouring diocese of Exeter. The register of Bishop Grandisson records the mandates against *ludi inhonesti* addressed by him in 1360 to the chapters of Exeter cathedral, and of the collegiate churches of Ottery,

Cathedralibus et aliis Ecclesiis nostrae próvinciae consuetudo inolevit ut videlicet in festis Nativitatis Domini nostri Iesu Christi et sanctorum Stephani, Ioannis et Innocentium aliisque certis diebus festivis, etiam in solemnitatibus Missarum novarum dum divina aguntur, ludi theatrales, larvae, monstra, spectacula, necnon quamplurima inhonesta et diversa figmenta in Ecclesiis introducuntur . . . huiusmodi larvas, ludos, monstra, spectacula, figmenta et tumultuationes fieri . . . prohibemus . . . Per hoc tam honestas repraesentationes et devotas, quae populum ad devotionem movent, tam in praefatis diebus quam in aliis non intendimus prohibere'; *C. of Lyons* (1566 and 1577), c. 15 (Du Tilliot, 63) 'Es jours de Fête des Innocens et autres, l'on ne doit souffrir ès Églises jouer jeux, tragédies, farces, &c.'; cf. the Cologne statutes (1662) quoted on p. 352.

[1] H.E. Reynolds, *Wells Cathedral*, 75 '*Quod non sint ludi contra honestatem Ecclesiae Wellensis*. Item a festo Nativitatis Domini usque ad octavas Innocentium quod Clerici Subdiaconi Diaconi Presbiteri etiam huius ecclesiae vicarii ludos faciant theatrales in ecclesia Wellensi et monstra larvarum introducentes, in ea insaniae suae ludibria exercere praesumunt contra honestatem clericalem et sacrorum prohibitionem canonum divinum officium multipliciter impediendo; quod de cetero in ecclesia Wellensi et sub pena canonica fieri prohibentes volumus quod divinum officium in festo dictorum sanctorum Innocentium sicuti in festis sanctorum consimilibus quiete ac pacifice absque quocunque tumultu et ludibrio cum devotione debita celebretur.'

[2] Reynolds, *op. cit.* 87 '*Prohibitio ludorum theatralium et spectaculorum et ostentationum larvarum in Ecclesia*. Item, cum infra septimanam Pentecostes et etiam in aliis festivitatibus fiant a laicis ludi theatrales in ecclesia praedicta et non solum ad ludibriorum spectacula introducantur in ea monstra larvarum, verum etiam in sanctorum Innocentium et aliorum sanctorum festivitatibus quae Natale Christi secuntur, Presbyteri Diaconi et Subdiaconi dictae Wellensis ecclesiae vicissim insaniae suae ludibria exercentes per gesticulationem debacchationes obscenas divinum officium impediant in conspectu populi, decus faciant clericale vilescere quem potius illo tempore deberent praedicatione mulcere....' The statute goes on to threaten offenders with excommunication.

Crediton, and Glasney. These *ludi* were performed by men and boys at Vespers, Matins, and Mass on Christmas and the three following days. They amounted to a mockery of the divine worship, did much damage to the church vestments and ornaments, and brought the clergy into disrepute[1]. These southern prohibitions are shortly before the final suppression of the Feast of Fools in the north at Beverley and Lincoln. The Wells customs, indeed, probably included a regular Feast of Fools, for the part taken by the sub-deacons and vicars is specifically mentioned, and the proceedings lasted over the New Year. But it is clear that even where the term 'Feast of Fools' is not known to have been in use, the temper of that revel found a ready vent in other of the winter rejoicings. Nor was it the *triduum* alone which afforded its opportunities. More rarely the performances of the *Pastores* on Christmas day itself[2], or the suppers given by the great officers of cathedrals and monasteries, when they

---

[1] F. C. Hingeston Randolph, *Bishop Grandison's Register*, Part iii, p. 1213; *Inhibicio Episcopi de ludis inhonestis.* The bishop writes to all four bodies in identical terms. He wishes them 'Salutem, et morum clericalium honestatem,' and adds 'Ad nostram, non sine gravi cordis displicencia et stupore, pervenit noticiam quod, annis praeteritis et quibusdam praecedentibus, in Sanctissimis Dominice Nativitatis, ac Sanctorum Stephani, Iohannis, Apostoli et Evangelistae, ac Innocencium Solempniis, quando omnes Christi Fideles Divinis laudibus et Officiis Ecclesiasticis devocius ac quiescius insistere tenentur, aliqui praedicte Ecclesie nostre Ministri, cum pueris, nedum Matutinis et Vesperis ac Horis aliis, set, quod magis detestandum est, inter Missarum Sollempnia, ludos ineptos et noxios, honestatique clericali indecentes, quia verius Cultus Divini ludibria detestanda, infra Ecclesiam ipsam, inmiscendo committere, Divino timore postposito, pernicioso quarundam Ecclesiarum exemplo, temere praesumpserunt; Vestimenta et alia Ornamenta

Ecclesie, in non modicum eiusdem Ecclesie nostre et nostrum dampnum et dedecus, vilium scilicet scenulentorumque (*or* scev.) sparsione multipliciter deturpando. Ex quorum gestis, seu risibus et cachinnis derisoriis, nedum populus, more Catholico illis potissime temporibus ad Ecclesiam conveniens, a debita devocione abstrahitur, set et in risum incompositum ac oblectamenta illicita dissolvitur; Cultusque Divinus irridetur et Officium perperam impeditur. . . .'

[2] On the *Pastores* cf. ch. xix. Gasté, 33, gives several Rouen chapter acts from 1449 to 1457 requiring them to officiate 'cessantibus stultitiis et insolenciis.' These orders and those quoted on p. 341 above were prompted by the *Letter* of the Paris theologians against the Feast of Fools and similar revels. In 1445 (or 1449) a committee was chosen 'ad videndum et visitandum ordinationem ecclesiae pro festis Nativitatis Domini et deliberationes Facultatis Theologiae super hoc habitas et quod tollantur derisiones in ipsis fieri solitas.'

sang their '*Oes*,' on the nights between December 16 and Christmas[1], were the occasions for excesses which called for reprehension.

Already, when Conrad visited St. Gall in 911, the third feast of the *triduum* was the most interesting. In after years this reached an importance denied to the other two. The Vespers procession was the germ of an annual rejoicing, secular as well as ritual, which became for the *pueri* attached as choir-boys and servers to the cathedrals and great churches very much what the Feast of Fools became for the adult inferior clergy of the same bodies. Where the two feasts were not merged in one, this distinction of *personnel* was retained. A good example is afforded by Sens. Here, from the middle of the fourteenth century, the chapter accounts show an *archiepiscopus puerorum* side by side with the *dominus* of the Feast of Fools. Each feast got its own grant of wine from the chapter, and had its own prebend in the chapter woods. In the fifteenth century the two fell and rose together. In the sixteenth, the Feast of Boys was the more flourishing, and claimed certain dues from a market in Sens, which were commuted for a small money payment by the chapter. Finally, both feasts are suppressed together in 1547[2]. It is to be observed that the original celebration of the Holy Innocents' day in the western Church was not of an unmixed festal character. It commemorated a martyrdom which typified and might actually have been that of Christ himself, and it was therefore held *cum tristitia*. As in Lent or on Good Friday itself, the 'joyful chants,' such as the *Te Deum* or the *Alleluia*, were silenced. This characteristic

---

[1] At Sarum a *Constitutio* of Roger de Mortival in 1324 (Dayman and Jones, *Sarum Statutes*, 52) forbade drinking when the antiphon 'O Sapientia' was sung after Compline on Dec. 16. John of Avranches (†1070) allowed for the feast of his 'O' at Rouen 'unum galonem vini de cellario archiepiscopi,' and the 'vin de l'O' was still given in 1377 (Gasté, 47). On these 'Oes,' sung by the great functionaries of cathedrals and monasteries, see E.

Green, *On the words 'O Sapientia' in the Kalendar* (*Archaeologia*, xlix. 219); Cynewulf, *Christ* (ed. A. S. Cook), xxxv. Payments 'cantoribus ad ludum suum' or 'ad' or 'ante natale' appear in Durham accounts; cf. *Finchale Priory* ccccxxviii (Surtees Soc.,) and *Durham Accounts, passim* (Surtees Soc.). I do not feel sure what feast is here referred to.

[2] Chérest, 49 sqq.

of the day was known to Belethus, but even before his time it had begun to give way to the festal tendencies. Local practice differed widely, as the notices collected by Martene show, but even when John of Avranches wrote, at the end of the eleventh century, the 'modern' custom was to sing the chants[1].

Many interesting details of the Feast of Boys, as it was celebrated in France, are contained in various ceremonial books. The *Officium Infantum* of Rouen may be taken as typical[2]. After second Vespers on St. John's day the boys marched out of the vestry, two by two, with their 'bishop,' singing *Centum quadraginta*. There was a procession to the altar of the Holy Innocents, and *Hi empti sunt* was sung[3]. Then the 'bishop' gave the Benediction. The feast of the following day was 'double,' but the boys might make it 'triple,' if they would. There was a procession, with the *Centum quadraginta*, at Matins. At Mass, the boys led the choir. At Vespers the *baculus* was handed over, while the *Deposuit potentes* was being sung[4]. At Bayeux the feast followed the same general lines, but the procession at first Vespers was to the altar, not of the Holy Innocents, but of St. Nicholas[5]. Precise directions are given as to the functions of the 'bishop.' He is to wear a silk tunic and cope, and to have a mitre and pastoral staff, but not a ring. The boys are to do him the same reverence that is done to the real

---

[1] Ioannes Abrincensis, *de Eccl. Offic.* (*P. L.* cxlvii. 42) 'Licet, ut in morte Domini, *Te Deum* et *Gloria in excelsis* et *Alleluia* in aliquot ecclesiis, ex more antiquo, omittantur; quia ut Christus occideretur tot parvuli occidi iubentur; et illis occisis fit mors Christi secundum aestimationem Herodis; tamen quia placuit modernis, placet et nobis ut cantentur'; cf. the passage from Belethus quoted on p. 336; also Honorius Augustodunensis, *Gemma Animae*, iii.14 (*P. L.* clxxii.646), and Martene, iii. 40.

[2] *Ordinarium* of Rouen (fourteenth century) in Ducange, s. v. *Kalendae*; *P. L.* cxlvii. 155; Gasté, 35. On the Rouen feast cf. also Gasté, 48.

[3] These chants are taken from *Revelation*, xiv. 3 'nemo poterat dicere canticum, nisi illa centum quadraginta quatuor millia, qui empti sunt de terra. Hi sunt, qui cum mulieribus non sunt coinquinati, virgines enim sunt. Hi sequuntur Agnum quocumque ierit.' This passage is still read in the 'Epistle' at Mass on Holy Innocents' day. Cf. the use of the same chants at Salisbury (Appendix M).

[4] 'Et tamdiu cantetur *Deposuit potentes* quod baculus accipiatur ab eo qui accipere voluerit.'

[5] *Ordinarium* of Bayeux (undated) in Gasté, 37. On the Bayeux feast and its *parvus episcopus* or *petit évêque* cf. F. Pluquet, *Essai sur Bayeux*, 274.

bishop. There are also to be a boy *cantor* and a boy 'chaplain.'
The 'bishop' is to perform the duties of a priest, so long
as the feast lasts, except in the Mass. He is to give the
benediction after *Benedicamus* at first Vespers. Then the
boys are to take the higher stalls, and to keep them
throughout the following day, the 'bishop' sitting in the
dean's chair. The boys are to say Compline as they will.
The 'bishop' is to be solemnly conducted home with the
prose *Sedentem*, and on the following day he is to be
similarly conducted both to and from service. At Mass
he is to cense and be censed like the 'great bishop' on
solemn occasions. He is also to give the benediction at
Mass. There is a minute description of the ceremony of
Deposuit, from which it is clear that, at Bayeux at least, the
handing over of the *baculus* was from an incoming to an
outgoing 'bishop,' to whom the former was in turn to act
as 'chaplain [1].' The rubrics of the Coutances feast are even
more minute [2]. The proceedings began after Matins on
St. John's day, when the boys drew up a *tabula* appointing
their superiors to the minor offices of the coming feast. This,
however, they were to do without impertinence [3]. The
vesting of the 'bishop' and the Vespers procession are
exactly described. As at Bayeux the boys take the high
stalls for Compline. The canon who holds a particular

---

[1] 'Dum perventum fuerit ad illum : *Deposuit potentes*, vadunt omnes ad medium ecclesiae et ibi qui in processione stant ordinate eumdem versum, episcopo inchoante, plures replicantes. Qui dum sic cantatur, offert ipse episcopus sociis suis de choro baculum pastoralem. Post multas itaque resumptiones dicti versus, revertuntur in chorum, *Te Deum laudamus*, si habent novum episcopum, decantantes, et ita canendo deducunt eum ad altare, et mitra sibi imposita et baculo cum capa serica, revertuntur in chorum, illo qui fuerat episcopus explente officium capellani, creato nihilominus novo cantore. Tunc chorus, si non fuerit ibi novus episcopus, vel novus episcopus qui baculum duxerit capiendum, cum suis sociis resumit a capite psalmum *Magnificat*, et sic cantant vesperas usque ad finem.'

[2] *Novus Ordinarius* of Coutances (undated) in Gasté, 39.

[3] 'Post Matutinas conveniant omnes pueri ad suam tabulam faciendam, quibus licitum est maiores personas Ecclesiae minoribus officiis deputare. Diaconis et subdiaconis ordinatis, thuribula imponantur et candelabra maiora videlicet et minora. Episcopo vero, cantori et aliis canonicis aquam, manutergium, missale, ignem et campanam possunt imponere pro suae libito voluntatis. Nihil tamen inhonestum aut impertinens apponatur; antiquiores primi ponantur in tabula et ultimi iuniores.'

prebend is bound to carry the candle and the *collectarium*
for the 'bishop.' After Compline the 'bishop' is led home
with *Laetabundus,* but not in pontificals. Throughout the
services of the following day the 'bishop' plays his part,
and when Vespers comes gives way to a 'bishop'-elect at the
Deposuit[1]. The 'bishop' of St. Martin of Tours was installed in the neighbouring convent of Beaumont, whither all
the *clericuli* rode for the purpose after Prime on St. John's
day. He was vested in the church there, blessed the nuns,
then returned to Tours, was installed in his own cathedral,
and blessed the populace[2]. The secular side of the feast
comes out in the Toul *Statutes* of 1497[3]. Here it may be
said to have absorbed in its turn the Feast of Fools, for the
'bishop' was a choir-boy chosen by the choir-boys themselves
and also by the sub-deacons, who shared with them the name
of *Innocentes*[4]. The election took place after Compline on
the first Sunday in Advent, and the 'bishop' was enthroned
with a *Te Deum.* He officiated in the usual way throughout
the Innocents' day services. In the morning he rode at the
head of a *cortège* to the monasteries of St. Mansuetus and
St. Aper, sang an anthem and said a prayer at the door
of each church, and claimed a customary fee[5]. After Vespers
he again rode in state with mimes and trumpeters through
the city[6]. On the following day, all the 'Innocents' went

[1] 'Quo facto dicat [Episcopus]
Deposuit. Statimque electus Episcopus, tradito sibi baculo pastorali
a pueris ad altare praesentetur, et
osculato altari in domum suam a
dictis pueris deferatur. Et interim,
finito tumultu, eat processio ad
altare S. Thomae martyris.'

[2] *Rituale* (fourteenth century) of
Tours in Martene, iii. 39. There
was a *cantor puerorum* as well as
the *episcopus.* At second Vespers
'quando *Magnificat* canitur, veniunt
clericuli in choro cum episcopo
habentes candelas accensas de proprio et quando *Deposuit* canitur,
accipit cantor puerorum baculum,
et tunc in stallo ascendunt pueri, et
alii descendunt.'

[3] Ducange, s. v. *Kalendae.*

[4] 'Omnes pueri et subdiaconi

feriati, qui in numero dictorum
Innocentium computantur.'

[5] 'Ipsa autem die de mane equi-
tare habet idem episcopus Innocentium ad monasteria SS.
Mansueti et Apri per civitatem
transeundo in comitiva suorum
aequalium, quibus etiam maiores
et digniores personae dignitatum
comitantur per se vel suos servi-
tores et equos, et descendentes
ad fores ecclesiarum praedictarum
intonat unam antiphonam et dicit
episcopus orationem, sibique de-
bentur a quolibet monasteriorum
eorundem xviij den. Tulienses, qui
si illico non solvantur, possunt accipere libros vel vadia.'

[6] 'Cantatis eiusdem diei vesperis,
episcopus ipse cum mimis et tubis
procedit per civitatem cum sua

masked into the city, where, if it was fine enough, farces and
apparently also moralities and miracles were played [1]. On
the octave the 'bishop' and his *cortège* went to the church
of St. Geneviève. After an anthem and collect they adjourned
to the 'church-house,' where they were entertained by the
hospital at a dessert of cake, apples and nuts, during which
they chose disciplinary officers for the coming year [2]. The
expenses of the feast, with the exception of the dinner on the
day after Innocents' day which came out of the disciplinary
fines, are assigned by the statutes to the canons in the order
of their appointment. The responsible canon must give a
supper on Innocents' day, and a dessert out of what is over
on the following day. He must also provide the 'bishop'
with a horse, gloves, and a *biretta* when he rides abroad.
At the supper a curious ceremony took place. The canon
returned thanks to the 'bishop,' apologized for any short-
comings in the preparations, and finally handed the 'bishop'
a cap of rosemary or other flowers, which was then conferred
upon the canon to whose lot it would fall to provide the feast
for the next anniversary [3]. Should the canon disregard his
duties the boys and sub-deacons were entitled to hang up
a black cope on a candlestick in the middle of the choir
in illius vituperium for as long as they might choose [4].

comitiva, via qua fiunt generales
processiones.'

[1] 'In crastino Innocentium, quo
omnes vadunt per civitatem post
prandium, faciebus opertis, in diversis habitibus, et si quae farsae
practicari valeant, tempore tamen
sicco, fiunt in aliquibus locis civitatis, omnia cum honestate.'
Another passage, referring more
generally to the feast, has 'Fiunt
ibi moralitates vel simulacra mi-
raculorum cum farsis et similibus
ioculis, semper tamen honestis.'

[2] 'In octavis Innocentium rursus
vadit episcopus cum omni comitiva
sua in habitibus suis ad ecclesiam
B. Genovefae, ubi cantata antiphona de ipsa virgine cum collecta,
itur ad domum parochialem eius
ecclesiae vel alibi, ubi magister et
fratres domus Dei, quibus ipsa

ecclesia est unita, paraverint foca-
pam unam, poma, nuces, &c. ad
merendam oportuna; et ibi insti-
tuuntur officiarii ad marencias super
defectibus aut excessibus in officio
divino per totum annum com-
missis.'

[3] 'Fit... assignatio post coenam
diei Innocentium; ita quod is qui
illa die festum peregit, gratias refert
episcopo et toti comitivae, ac ex-
cusari petit, si in aliquo defecit; et
finaliter pileum romarini vel alterius
confectionis floreum exhibet ipsi
episcopo, ut tradat canonico in re-
ceptione sequenti constituto ad
futurum annum ipsum festum agen-
dum.' Cf. the bouquets at the
'defructus' (p. 324).

[4] 'Si autem facere contemneret
adveniente festo, suspenderetur
cappa nigra in raustro medio chori,

I cannot pretend to give a complete account of all the French examples of the Boy Bishop with which I have met, and it is the less necessary, as the feast seems to have been far more popular and enduring in England than the Feast of Fools. I content myself with giving references for its history at Amiens[1], St. Quentin[2], Senlis[3], Soissons[4], Roye[5], Peronne[6], Rheims[7], Brussels[8], Lille[9], Liège[10], Laon[11], Troyes[12], Mans[13], Bourges[14], Châlons-sur-Saône[15], Grenoble[16]. Not unnaturally it proved less of a scandal to ecclesiastical reformers than the Feast of Fools; for the choir-boys must have been more amenable to discipline, even in moments of festivity, than the adult clerks. But it shared in the general condemnation of all such customs, and was specifically arraigned by more than one council, rather perhaps for puerility than for

---

et tamdiu ibi maneret in illius. vituperium, quamdiu placeret subdiaconis feriatis et pueris chori; et in ea re non tenerentur nobis capitulo obedire.'
[1] Amiens : Rigollot, 13 and passim ; cf. p. 339.
[2] St. Quentin : Rigollot, 32 ; Grenier, 360.
[3] Senlis : Rigollot, 26 ; Grenier, 360.
[4] Soissons : Matton, *Archives de Soissons*, 75.
[5] Roye : Rigollot, 33 ; Grenier, 359.
[6] Peronne : Rigollot, 34 ; Grenier, 359, 413.
[7] Rheims : Rigollot, 50 ; Petit de Julleville, *Rép. Com.* 348 ; Marlot, *Hist. de Rheims*, ii. 266. In 1479 the chapter undertook the expense, ' modo fiat sine larvis et strepitu tubicinis, ac sine equitatione per villam.' Martene, iii. 40, says that there is no trace of any of the *triduum* ceremonies in the early thirteenth-century Rheims *Ordinarium.*
[8] Brussels : Laborde, *Ducs de Bourgogne*, ii. 2. 286 ' [1378] Item xxi decembris episcopo scholarium sanctae Gudilae profecto Sancti Nycolay quod scholares annuatim faciunt 1½ mut[ones].'
[9] Lille : E. Hautcœur, *Hist. de*

Saint-Pierre de Lille, ii. 217, 223. On June 29, 1501, Guillemot de Lespine 'trépassa évêque des Innocens.' His epitaph is in the cloister gallery (Hautcœur, *Doc. liturg. de S. P. de Lille*, 342).
[10] Liège : Rigollot, 42 ; Dürr, 82. A statute of 1330 laid the expense on the last admitted canon ' nisi canonicus scholaris sub virga existens ipsum exemerit.'
[11] Laon : Rigollot, 21 ; Grenier, 356, 413 ; C. Hidé, *Bull. de la Soc. acad. de Laon*, xiii. 122 ; E. Fleury, *Cinquante Ans de Laon*, 52. A chapter act of 1546 states that the custom of playing a comedy at the election of the Boy Bishop on St. Eloi's day (Dec. 1) has ceased. The Mass is not to be disturbed, but ' si les escoliers veulent faire un petit discours, il seroit entendu avec plaisir.'
[12] Troyes : T. Boutiot, *Hist. de Troyes*, iii. 20.
[13] Mans : Gasté, 43 ; Julleville, *Les Com.* 38.
[14] Bourges : Martene, iii. 40.
[15] Châlons-sur-Saône : Du Tilliot, 20 ; C. Perry, *Hist. de Châlons* (1659), 435.
[16] Grenoble : Pilot de Thorey, *Usages, Fêtes et Coutumes en Dauphiné*, i. 181.

any graver offence [1]. Gradually therefore, it vanished, leaving only a few survivals to recent centuries [2]. As was the case with the Feast of Fools, the question of its suppression sometimes set a chapter by the ears. Notably was this so at Noyon, where the act of his reforming colleagues in 1622 was highly disapproved of by the dean, Jacques Le Vasseur. In a letter written on the occasion he declares that the Boy Bishop had flourished in Noyon cathedral for four hundred years, and brands the reformers as brute beasts masquerading in the robes and beards of philosophy [3].

I have no special records of the Boy Bishop in Spain except the council decrees already quoted. In Germany he appears to have been more widely popular than his rival of Fools. My first notice, however, is two centuries after the visit of Conrad to the *triduum* at St. Gall. The chronicle of the monastery of St. Petersburg, hard by Halle, mentions an accident *in ludo qui vocatur puerorum*, by which a lad was trodden to death. This was in 1137 [4]. The thirteenth and fourteenth centuries yield

---

[1] *C. of Cognac* (1260), c. 2 (Mansi, xxiii. 1033) 'cum in balleatione quae in festo SS. Innocentium in quibusdam Ecclesiis fieri inolevit, multae rixae, contentiones et turbationes, tam in divinis officiis quam aliis consueverint provenire, praedictas balleationes ulterius sub intimatione anathematis fieri prohibemus; nec non et Episcopos in praedicto festo creari; cum hoc in ecclesia Dei ridiculum existat, et hoc dignitatis episcopalis ludibrio fiat.' *C. of Salzburg* (1274), c. 17 (Labbé, xi. 1004) 'ludi noxii quos vulgaris elocutio Eptus puor. appellat'; CC. *of Chartres* (1526 and 1575; Bochellus, *Decr. Eccl. Gall.* iv. 7. 46; Du Tilliot, 66) 'stultum aut ridiculum in ecclesia' on days of SS. Nicholas and Catharine, and the Innocents; *C. of Toledo* (1565), ii. 21 (Labbé, xv. 764) 'ficta illa et puerilis episcopatus electio'; *C. of Rouen* (1581; Hardouin, *Concilia,* x. 1217) 'in festivitate SS. Innocentium theatralia.'

[2] There are traces of it in the eighteenth century at Lyons (Martene, iii. 40) and Rheims (Barthélemy, v. 334); at Sens, in the nineteenth, the choir-boys still play at being bishops on Innocents' day, and name the 'archbishop' *âne* (Chérest, 81).

[3] Grenier, 358, quoting Le Vasseur, *Epistolae,* Cent. ii. Epist. 68; cf. on the Noyon feast, Leach, 135; Du Tilliot, 17; Rigollot, 27; L. Mazière, *Noyon religieux,* in *Comptes-Rendus et Mémoires,* xi. 91, of *The Comité arch. et hist. de Noyon.* Le Vasseur, an ex-Rector of the University of Paris, writes to François Geuffrin 'ecce ludunt etiam ante ipsas aras; internecionem detestamur, execramur carnificem. Ludunt et placet iste ludus ecclesiae. . . . Tam grandis est natu ritus iste, quem viguisse deprehendo iam ante quadringentos annos in hac aede, magno totius orbis ordinum et aetatum plausu fructuque . . . O miserum saeculum! . . . solo gestu externoque habitu spectabiles, sola barba et pallio philosophi, caetera pecudes!'

[4] *Chronicon Montis Sereni* in Pertz, *Scriptores,* xxiii. 144.

more examples. In 1249 Pope Innocent IV complained to the bishop of Ratisbon that the clerks and scholars of that cathedral, when choosing their anniversary 'bishop,' did violence to the abbey of Pruviningen[1]. In 1357 the Ratisbon feast was stained with homicide, and was consequently suppressed[2]. In 1282 the feast was forbidden at Eichstädt[3]. In 1304 it led to a dispute between the municipality and the chapter of Hamburg, which ended in a promise by the *scholares* to refrain from defamatory songs either in Latin or German[4]. Similarly at Worms in 1307 the *pueri* were forbidden to sing in the streets after Compline, as had been the custom on the feasts of St. Nicholas and St. Lucy, on Christmas and the three following days, and on the octave of the Holy Innocents'[5]. At Lubeck the feast was abolished in 1336[6]. I have already quoted the long reference to the *scholarium episcopus* in the Mosburg Gradual of 1360[7]. He may be traced also at Regensburg[8] and at Prague[9]. But the fullest account of him is from Mainz[10]. Here he was called the *Schul-Bischoff*, and in derision *Apffeln-Bischoff*. He was chosen before St. Nicholas' day by the *ludi magister* of the *schola trivialis*. He had his *equites*, his *capellani*, and his *pedelli*. On St. Nicholas' day, and on that of the Holy Innocents', he had a seat near the high altar, and took part in the first and second Vespers. In the interval he paid a visit with his company to the palace of the elector, sang a hymn[11], and claimed a banquet or a donation. The custom

---

[1] *Monum. Boic.* xiii. 214, quoted by Specht, 228 ' in festo nativitatis Dominicae annuatim sibi ludendo constituentes episcopum.'

[2] Vitus Arnpekius, *Chron. Baioariorum*, v. 53, cited by Martene, iii. 40.

[3] Specht, 228.

[4] Ibid. 225 ; Creizenach, i. 391 ; both quoting E. Meyer, *Gesch. des hamburgischen Schul- und Unterrichtswesens im Mittelalter*, 197 ' praeterea scholares nunquam, sive in electione sive extra, aliquos rhythmos faciant, tam in latino, quam in teutonico, qui famam alicuius valeant maculare.' In the

thirteenth century a child-abbot was chosen in Hamburg on St. Andrew's day (Nov. 30). On St. Nicholas' day (Dec. 6) he gave way to a child-bishop, who remained in office until Dec. 28 (Tille, *D. W.* 31, citing Beneke, *Hamburgische Geschichte und Sagen*, 90).

[5] Specht, 229.

[6] Ibid. 228.

[7] Cf. p. 319.

[8] Tille, *D. W.* 31.

[9] Ibid. 299.

[10] Dürr, 67, quoting a *Ritual* of the cathedral (' tempore Alberti ').

[11] It began :
' Iam tuum festum Nicolae dives

was not altogether extinct in Mainz by 1779[1]. In other German towns, also, it well out-lived the Middle Ages. At Cologne, for instance, it was only suppressed by the statutes of Bishop Max Heinrich in 1662[2].

In England, the Boy Bishop weathered the storms of discipline which swept away the Feast of Fools in the thirteenth and fourteenth centuries. He was widely popular in the later Middle Ages, and finally fell before an austerity of the Reformation. The prerogative instance of the custom is in the church of Salisbury. Here the existence of the Boy Bishop is already implied by the notice of a ring for use at the 'Feast of Boys' in an inventory of 1222[3]. A century later, the statutes of Roger de Mortival in 1319 include elaborate regulations for the ceremony. The 'bishop' may perform the *officium* as is the use, but he must hold no banquet, and no visitation either within or without the cathedral. He may be invited to the table of a canon, but otherwise he must remain in the common house, and must return to his duties in church and school immediately after the feast of Innocents. The statute also regulates the behaviour of the crowds which were wont to press upon and impede the boys in their annual procession to the altar of the Holy Trinity, and the rest of their ministry[4]. Two of the

more solemni recolit iuventus,
nec tibi dignus, sacerdotum
    Caesar,
    promere laudes.'
[1] Tille, *D. W.* 31, citing Nork, *Festkalender*, 783. Dürr's tract was published at Mainz in 1755.
[2] Wetzer und Welte, s. v. *Feste* 'consuetudo seu potius detestabilis corruptela, qua pueri a die S. Nicolai usque ad festum SS. Innocentium personatum Episcopum colunt . . . ea puerilibus levitatibus et ineptiis plena coeperit esse multumque gravitatis et decoris divinis detrahat officiis . . . ne clerus se pueris die SS. Inn. submittat ac eorum locum occupet, aut illis functiones aliquas in divinis officiis permittat, neque praesentes aliquis Episcopus benedictiones faciat, aliique pueri in cantandis horariis precibus lectioni-

bus et collectis Sacerdotum, Diaconorum aut Subdiaconorum officia quaedam usurpent ; multo minus convenit ut Canonici aut Vicarii ex collegarum suorum numero aliquem designent Episcopum qui reliquos omnes magnis impendiis liberali convivio excipiat.'
[3] W. H. R. Jones, *Vetus Registr. Sarisb.* (R. S.), ii. 128 ; Wordsworth, *Proc.* 170 'Item, annulus unus aureus ad Festum Puerorum.'
[4] *Constitutiones*, § 45 (Jones and Dayman, *Sarum Statutes*, 75 ; cf. Jones, *Fasti*, 295) 'Electus puer chorista in episcopum modo solito puerili officium in ecclesia, prout fieri consuevit, licenter exequatur, convivium aliquod de caetero, vel visitationem exterius seu interius nullatenus faciendo, sed in domo

great service-books of the Sarum use, the Breviary and the Processional, give ample details as to the 'ministry' of the Boy Bishop and his fellows. The office, as preserved in these, will be found in an appendix[1]. The proceedings differ in some respects from the continental models already described. There is no mention of the *Deposuit*; and the central rite is still the great procession between Vespers and Compline on the eve of the Holy Innocents. This procession went from the choir either to the altar of the Holy Innocents or to that of the Holy Trinity and All Saints in the Lady chapel, and at its return the boys took the higher stalls and kept them until the second Vespers of the feast. For this procession the boys were entitled to assign the functions of carrying the book, the censer, the candles, and so forth to the canons. Some miscellaneous notices of the Salisbury feast are contained in the chapter register between 1387 and 1473. From 1387 the oblations on the feast appear to have been given to the 'bishop.' In 1413 he was allowed a banquet. In 1448 the precentor, Nicholas Upton, proposed that the boys, instead of freely electing a 'bishop,' should be confined to a choice amongst three candidates named by the chapter. But this innovation was successfully resisted[2]. Cathedral documents also give the names of twenty-one boys who held the office[3]. There is in Salisbury cathedral a dwarf effigy of a bishop, dating from the latter part of the thirteenth century. Local

communi cùm sociis conversetur, nisi cum ut choristam ad domum canonici causa solatii ad mensam contigerit evocari, ecclesiam et scholas cum caeteris choristis statim post festum Innocentium frequentando. Et quia in processione quam ad altare Sanctae Trinitatis faciunt annuatim pueri supradicti per concurrentium pressuras et alias dissolutiones multiplices nonnulla damna personis et ecclesiae gravia intelleximus priscis temporibus pervenisse, ex parte Dei omnipotentis et sub poena maioris excommunicationis, quam contravenientes utpote libertates dictae ecclesiae nostrae infringentes et illius pacem et quietem temerarie perturbantes declara-

mus incurrere ipso facto, inhibemus ne quis pueros illos in praefata processione vel alias in suo ministerio premat vel impediat quoquomodo, quominus pacifice valeant facere et exequi quod illis imminet faciendum; sed qui eidem processioni devotionis causa voluerint interesse, ita modo maturo se habeant et honeste sicut et in aliis processionibus dictae ecclesiae se habent qui ad honorem Dei frequentant quando que ecclesiam supradictam.'

[1] Appendix M.
[2] Jones, *Fasti*, 299.
[3] Wordsworth, *Proc.* 259. The *oblationes* vary from lvi*s*. viii*d*. in 1448 to as much as lxxxix*s*. xi*d*. in 1456.

tradition, from at least the beginning of the seventeenth
century, has regarded this as the monument of a Boy Bishop
who died during his term of office. But modern archaeologists
repudiate the theory. Such miniature effigies are not uncommon, and possibly indicate that the heart alone of the
person commemorated is buried in the spot which they mark[1].

The gradual adoption of the use of Sarum by other dioceses
would naturally tend to carry with it that of the Boy Bishop.
But he is to be found at Exeter and at St. Paul's before
the change of use, as well as at Lincoln and York which
retained their own uses up to the Reformation. At Exeter
Bishop Grandisson's *Ordinale* of 1337 provides an *Officium
puerorum* for the eve and day of the Innocents which,
with different detail, is on the same general lines as that of
Salisbury[2]. At St. Paul's there was a Boy Bishop about
1225, when a gift was made to him of a mitre by John de
Belemains, prebendary of Chiswick. This appears, with other
vestments for the feast, in an inventory drawn up some twenty
years later[3]. By 1263 abuses had grown up, and the chapter
passed a statute to reform them[4]. They required the election
of the *praesul* and his chapter and the drawing up of the
tabula to take place in the chapter-house instead of in the
cathedral, on account of the irreverence of the crowds pressing
to see. The great dignitaries must not be put down on the
tabula for the servers' functions, but only the clergy of the
second or third ' form.' The procession and all the proceedings
in the cathedral must be orderly and creditable to the boys[5].

[1] Jones, *Fasti*, 300 ; Rimbault, xxviii; Planché, in *Journal of Brit. Archaeol. Assoc.* xv. 123. Gregory, 93, gives a cut of the statue.
[2] *Ordinale secundum Usum Exon.* (ed. H. E. Reynolds), f. 30.
[3] *Archaeologia*, l. 446, 472 sqq. (*Invent.* of 1245) 'mitra alia alba addubbata aurifrigio, plana est ; quam dedit J. Belemains episcopo innocentum . . . Mitra episcopi innocentum, nullius precii . . . Capa et mantella puerorum ad festum Innocentum et Stultorum [cf. p. 323] sunt xxviij debiles et contritae.' In 1402 there were two little staves

for the Boy Bishop (Simpson, *St. Paul's Cathedral and Old City Life*, 40).
[4] *Statutes*, bk. i, pars vi. c. 9, *De officio puerorum in festo Sanctorum Innocencium* (W. S. Simpson, *Registrum Statutorum et Consuetudinum Ecclesiae Cathedralis Sancti Pauli Londinensis*, 91).
[5] 'Memorandum, quod Anno Domini Millesimo cc lxiij. tempore G. de fferring, Decani, ordinatum fuit de officio Puerorum die Sanctorum Innocencium, prout sequitur. Provida fuit ab antiquis patribus predecessoribus nostris delibera-

Minute directions follow as to the right of the 'bishop' to claim a supper on the eve from one of the canons, and as to the train he may take with him, as well as for the dinner and supper of the feast-day itself. After dinner a cavalcade is to start from the cathedral for the blessing of the people. The dean must find a horse for the 'bishop,' and each canon residentiary one for the lad who personates him [1]. Other statutes of earlier date make it incumbent on a new residentiary to entertain his own boy-representative *cum daunsa et chorea et torchiis* on Innocents' day, and to sit up at night for the 'bishop' and all his *cortège* on the octave. If he is kept up very late, he may 'cut' Matins next morning [2]. The Boy Bishop of St. Paul's was accustomed to preach a sermon which, not unnaturally, he did not write himself. William de Tolleshunte, almoner of St. Paul's in 1329, bequeathed to the almonry copies of all the sermons preached by the Boy

cione statutum, ut in sollennitate Sanctorum Innocencium, qui pro Innocente Christo sanguinem suum fuderunt, innocens puer Presulatus officio fungeretur, ut sic puer pueris preesset, et innocens innocentibus imperaret, illius tipum tenens in Ecclesia, quem sequuntur iuvenes, quocumque ierit. Cum igitur quod ad laudem lactencium fuit adinventum, conversum sit in dedecus, et in derisum decoris Domus Dei, propter insolenciam effrenatae multitudinis subsequentis eundem, et affluentis improborum turbae pacem Praesulis exturbantis, statuendum duximus ut praedicti pueri, tam in eligendo suo Pontifice et personis dignitatum Decani, Archidiaconorum, et aliorum, necnon et Stacionariorum, antiquum suum ritum observent, tabulam suam faciant, et legant in Capitulo. Hoc tamen adhibito moderamine, ut nullum decetero de Canonicis Maioribus vel Minoribus ad candelabra, vel turribulum, vel ad aliqua obsequia eiusdem Ecclesiae, vel ipsius Pontificis deputent in futurum, set suos eligant ministeriales de illis qui sunt in secunda forma vel in tercia. Processionem suam habeant honestam, tam in incessu, quam habitu et

cantu, competenti; ita vero se gerant in omnibus in Ecclesia, quod clerus et populus illos habeant recommendatos.'

[1] 'Die vero solemnitatis post prandium ad mandatum personae Decani convenient omnes in atrio Ecclesiae, ibidem equos ascendant ituri ad populum benedicendum. Tenetur autem Decanus Presuli presentare equum, et quilibet Stacionarius sua personae in equo providere.'

[2] *Statutes*, bk. i, pars vii. c. 6 (Simpson, *op. cit.* 129), a statute made in the time of Dean Ralph de Diceto (1181–†1204) 'Debet eciam novus Residenciarius post cenam die Sanctorum Innocencium ducere puerum suum cum daunsa et chorea et torchiis ad Elemosinariam, et ibi cum torticiis potum et species singulis ministrare, et liberatam vini cervisiae et specierum et candellarum facere, et ibidem ministri sui expectare, quousque alius puer Canonici senioris veniat. Et secundam cenam in octavis Innocencium tenebit, Episcopum cum pueris et eorum comitiva pascendo, et in recessu dona dando, et, si diu expectat adventum illorum nocte illa, ad matutinos non teneatur venire.'

Bishops in his time. Probably he was himself responsible for them[1]. One such sermon was printed by Wynkyn de Worde before 1500[2]. Another was written by Erasmus, and exists both in Latin and English[3]. When Dean Colet drew up the statutes of St. Paul's School in 1512 he was careful to enact that the scholars should attend the cathedral on Childermass day, hear the sermon, and mass, and give a penny to the 'bishop[4].'

The earliest notice of the Boy Bishop at York, or for the matter of that, in England, is in a statute (before 1221), which lays on him the duty of finding rushes for the Nativity and Epiphany feasts[5]. After this, there is nothing further until the second half of the fourteenth century, when some interesting documents become available. The chapter register for 1367 requires that in future the 'bishop' shall be the boy who has served longest and proved most useful in the cathedral. A saving clause is added: *dum tamen competenter sit corpore formosus*[6]. This shows a sense of humour in the chapter, for at York, as at Salisbury, *Corpore enim formosus es, O fili* was a respond for the day. In 1390, was added a further qualification that the ' bishop ' must be a lad in good voice[7]. Doubtless the office was much coveted, for it was a very remunerative one. The visitation forbidden at

---

[1] Rimbault, xxxii.

[2] Printed in Rimbault, 1. Duff, *Handlists*, ii. 5, notes also a *Sermo pro episcopo puerorum* by J. Alcock, printed in the fifteenth century by R. Pynson.

[3] *Concio de puero Iesu pronunciata a puero in nova schola Iohannis Coleti per eum instituta Londini in qua praesidet imago Pueri Iesu docentis specie* (Erasmi *Opera* (1704), v. 599). The English version was printed by W. Redman (Lupton, *Life of Colet*, 176). It is not clear that this *Concio* was preached by a boy bishop, for Colet's school (cf. next note) attended the 'bishop' of St. Paul's song-school.

[4] Lupton, *op. cit.* 175 'Alle these Chyldren shall every Chyldremasse day come to paulis Church and here the Chylde Bisshoppis sermon, and after be at the hye masse, and eche of them offre a 1ᵈ. to the Childe Bisshopp; and with theme the Maisters and surveyours of the scole.'

[5] *Lincoln Statutes*, ii. 98 'Inveniet [thesaurarius] stellas cum omnibus ad illas pertinentibus, preter cirpos, quos inveniet Episcopus Puerorum futurorum [?fatuorum], vnam in nocte Natalis Domini pro pastoribus et ·ijᵃˢ in nocte Epiphanie, si debeat fieri presentacio ·iijᵘᵐ regum.'

[6] Warton, iv. 224 'Ioannes de Quixly confirmatur Episcopus Puerorum, et Capitulum ordinavit, quod electio Episcopi Puerorum in ecclesia Eboracensi de cetero fieret de eo, qui diutius et magis in dicta ecclesia laboraverit, et magis idoneus repertus fuerit, dum tamen competenter sit corpore formosus, et quod aliter facta electio non valebit.'

[7] Warton, iv. 237 'nisi habuerit claram vocem puerilem.'

Salisbury by Roger de Mortival was permitted at York, and
the profits were considerable. Robert de Holme, who was
'bishop' in 1369, received from the choirmaster, John Gisson,
who acted as his treasurer, no less a sum than £3 15s. 1½d.[1]
In 1396 the amount was only £2 0s. 6½d. But this was only
a small portion of the total receipts. The complete *Computus*
for this year happens to be preserved, and shows that the Boy
Bishop made a *quête* at intervals during the weeks between
Christmas and Candlemas, travelling with a 'seneschal,' four
singers and a servant to such distant places as Bridlington,
Leeds, Beverley, Fountains abbey and Allerton. Their
principal journey lasted a fortnight. The oblations on Christmas and Innocents' days and the collection from the dignitaries
in the cloister realized £2 15s. 5d. In the city they got 10s.
and abroad £5 10s. Out of this there were heavy expenses.
The supper given by the 'bishop' cost 15s. 6½d. Purchased
meals had to supplement hospitality at home and abroad.
Horse hire and stable expenses had to be met. There were
the 'bishop's' outfit, candles to be borne in procession, fees to
the minor cathedral officials, gloves for presents to the vicars
and schoolmasters. There was the 'bishop's' own company to
be rewarded for its services. The £2 0s. 6½d. represents the
balance available for his private use[2]. The most generous
contributor to the *quête* was the countess of Northumberland,
who gave 20s. and a gold ring. This is precisely the amount
of the reward prescribed about 1522 for the 'barne bishop' of
York, as well as for his brother of Beverley in the *Household
Book* of the fifth earl of Northumberland[3].

The printed service-books of the use of York do not
deal as fully with the Feast of Boys as do those of Sarum;
but a manuscript missal of the fifteenth century used in the
cathedral itself contains some additional rubrics with regard
to the functions of the 'bishop' and his 'precentor' at
Mass[4]. The names of some of the York 'bishops' are

[1] Warton, iv. 224.
[2] Appendix M. Cf. Rimbault, xi, for further elucidations of the *Computus*.
[3] Percy, *North. H. B.* 340.
[4] *York Missal,* i. 23. The rubric at the beginning of Mass is 'Omni-

bus pueris in Capis, Praecentor illorum incipiat.' There are some responds for the 'Praecentor' and the 'turba puerorum.' After the Kyrie, 'omnibus pueris in medio Chori stantibus et ibi omnia cantantibus, Episcopo eorum interim

preserved, and show that the ceremony prevailed up to the Reformation [1]. And this is confirmed by a list of ornaments for the 'bishop' in a sixteenth-century inventory [2].

I am unable to give such full data for Lincoln as for the cathedrals already named ; but regulations of 1300 and 1527 provide for the supply of candles to the 'bishop' and the rest of the choir at Vespers on the eve and matins on the day of the Innocents [3], and an inventory of 1536 mentions a cope for the 'barne busshop' with a moral 'scriptur' embroidered on it [4]. Nor can I hope to supply any exhaustive list of localities where the Boy Bishop flourished. These include minor cathedrals such as Hereford [5], Lichfield [6], Gloucester [7], and Norwich [8], great collegiate churches such as Beverley minster [9], St. Peter's, Canterbury [10], and Ottery

---

in cathedra sedente; et si Dominica fuerit, dicitur ab Episcopo stante in cathedra *Gloria in excelsis Deo*: aliter non.' · The *Sequentia* for the day is
'Celsa pueri concrepent melodia, eia, Innocentum colentes tripudia, &c.'

[1] Rimbault, xvi. The dates are between 1416 and 1537.

[2] Raine, *Fabric Rolls of York Minster* (Surtees Soc.), 213 sqq. (†1500, the additions in brackets being †1510) 'una mitra parva cum petris pro episcopo puerorum ... [unus annulus pro episcopo puerorum et duo owchys, unus in medio ad modum crucis cum lapidibus in circumferenciis cum alio parvo cum uno lapide in medio vocato turchas] ... Capae Rubiae ... Una capa de tyssue pro Episcopo puerili . . . [duae capae veteres olim pro Episcopo puerorum].' Leach, 132, says 'At York, in 1321, the Master of the Works gave "a gold ring with a great stone for the Bishop of the Innocents." In 1491 the Boy Bishop's pontifical was mended with silver-gilt.'

[3] *Lincoln Statutes*, i. 290 (*Black Book*, †1300) ; ii. ccxxxi.

[4] *Archaeologia*, liii. 25, 50 ; *Monasticon*, viii. 1282 'Item, a coope of Rede velvett wᵗ Rolles & clowdes ordenyd for the barne busshop wᵗ

this scriptur "the hye wey ys best".' The entry is repeated in a later inventory of 1548.

[5] Hereford, *Consuetudines* of thirteenth century (*Lincoln Statutes*, ii. 67) 'Thesaurarius debet invenire . . . in festo Innocencium pueris candelas et ·ijᵒˢ cereos coram parvo Episcopo.'

[6] Lichfield—J. C. Cox, *Sports in Churches*, in W. Andrews, *Curious Church Customs*, 3, quoting inventories of 1345 and of the fifteenth century. The latter uses the term 'Nicholas Bishop.'

[7] Gloucester—Rimbault,14,prints from *Cotton MSS. Vesp.* A. xxv, f. 173, a *Sermon of the Child Bishop, Pronownysed by John Stubs, Querester, on Childermas Day, at Glocester*, 1558.

[8] Norwich—a fourteenth-century antiphonal of Sarum Use, probably of Norwich *provenance* (*Lansd. MS.* 463, f. 16ᵛ), provides for the giving of the *baculus* to the *Episcopus Puerorum* at Vespers on St. John's Day.

[9] Beverley—the fifth earl of Northumberland about 1522 gave xxs. at Christmas to the 'Barne Bishop' of Beverley, as well as to him of York (Percy, *North. H. B.* 340) ; cf. p. 357.

[10] Wordsworth, *Proc.* 52; cf. Appendix M (1).

St. Mary's[1], college chapels such as Magdalen[2] and All Souls[3], at Oxford, the private chapels of the king[4] and the earl of Northumberland[5], and many parish churches both in London[6], and throughout the length and breadth of England[7] and Scotland[8].

Nor is this all. Unlike the Feast of Fools, the Feast of Boys enjoyed a considerable vogue in religious houses. When

[1] Ottery—*Statutes* of Bishop Grandisson (1337), quoted by Warton, ii. 229 'Item statuimus, quod nullus canonicus, vicarius, vel secundarius, pueros choristas in festo sanctorum Innocentium extra parochiam de Otery trahant, aut eis licentiam vagandi concedant.'

[2] Magdalen—see Appendix E.

[3] All Souls—An inventory has 'j chem. j cap et mitra pro Episcopo Nicholao' (Rock, lii. 2. 217).

[4] In 1299 Edward I heard vespers said 'de Sancto Nicholao ... in Capella sua apud Heton iuxta Novum Castrum super Tynam' (*Wardrobe Account*, ed. Soc. of Antiq., 25). In 1306 a Boy Bishop officiated before Edward II on St. Nicholas' Day in the king's chapel at Scroby (*Wardrobe Account* in *Archaeologia*, xxvi. 342). In 1339 Edward III gave a gift 'Episcopo puerorum ecclesiae de Andeworp cantanti coram domino rege in camera sua in festo sanctorum Innocentium' (Warton, ii. 229). There was a yearly payment of £1 to the Boy Bishop at St. Stephen's, Westminster, in 1382 (Devon, *Issues of Exchequer*, 222), and about 1528-32 (Brewer, iv. 1939).

[5] The fifth earl of Northumberland (†1512) was wont to 'gyfe yerly upon Saynt Nicolas-Even if he kepe Chapell for Saynt Nicolas to the Master of his Childeren of his Chapell for one of the Childeren of his Chapell yerely vj⁸. viij^d. And if Saynt Nicolas com owt of the Towne wher my Lord lyeth and my Lord kepe no Chapell than to have yerely iij⁸. iiij^d.' (Percy, *North. H. B.* 343). An elaborate *Contenta de Ornamentis Ep., puer.*, of uncertain *provenance*, is printed by Percy, *op. cit.* 439.

[6] St. Mary at Hill (Brand, i. 233); St. Mary de Prees (*Monasticon*, iii. 360); St. Peter Cheap (*Journal of Brit. Arch. Ass.* xxiv. 156); Hospital of St. Katharine by the Tower (*Reliquary*, iv. 153); Lambeth (Lysons, *Environs of London*, i. 310); cf. p. 367.

[7] Louth (E. Hewlett, *Boy Bishops*, in W. Andrews, *Curious Church Gleanings*, 241)—the payments for the Chyld Bishop include some for 'making his See' (*sedes*); Nottingham (*Archaeologia*, xxvi. 342); Sandwich (Boys, *Hist. of S.* 376); New Romney(*Hist. MSS.* v. 517-28), Yorkshire, Derbyshire, Somersetshire (J. C. Cox, *Sports in Churches*, in W. Andrews, *Curious Church Customs*); Bristol—L. T. Smith, *Ricart's Kalendar*, 80 (1479-1506, Camden Soc.). On Nov. 24, the Mayor, Sheriff, and 'worshipfull men' are to 'receyue at theire dores Seynt Kateryn's pleyers, making them to drynk at their dores and rewardyng theym for theire playes.' On Dec. 5 they are 'to walke to Seynt Nicholas churche, there to hire theire even-song: and on the morowe to hire theire masse, and offre, and hire the bishop's sermon, and have his blissyng.' After dinner they are to play dice at the mayor's counter, 'and when the Bishope is come thedir, his chapell there to synge, and the bishope to geve them his blissyng, and then he and all his chapell to be serued there with brede and wyne.' And so to even-song in St. Nicholas' church.

[8] *L. T. Accounts*, i. ccxlvi record annual payments by James IV (†1473-98) to Boy Bishops from Holyrood Abbey and St. Giles's, Edinburgh.

John Peckham, archbishop of Canterbury, was drawing up his constitutions for such communities in 1279, he found it necessary to limit the duration of this feast to the eve and day of the Holy Innocents[1]. Traces of the Boy Bishop are to be found in the archives of more than one great monastery. A Westminster inventory of 1388 gives minute descriptions of vestments and ornaments for his use, many of which appear to have been quite recently provided by the 'westerer' or *vestiarius*, Richard Tonworthe[2]. There was a mitre with silvered and gilt plates and gems, and the inscription *Sancte Nicholae ora pro nobis* set in pearls. There was a *baculus* with images of St. Peter and St. Edward the Confessor upon thrones. There were two pair of cheveril gloves, to match the mitre. There were an amice, a rochet and a surplice. There were two albs and a cope of blood colour worked with gryphons and other beasts and cisterns spouting water. There was another 'principal' cope of ruby and blood-coloured velvet embroidered in gold, and with the 'new arms of England' woven into it. An older mitre and pair of gloves and a ring had been laid aside as old-fashioned or worn out. Evidently the feast was celebrated with some splendour. Several of the vestments are again inventoried in 1540[3]. A payment for the feast is recorded in a *Computus* of 1413–14[4]. The accounts of the obedientiaries of Durham priory show from 1369 onwards many payments by nearly all these officers to a Boy Bishop of the almonry. He also received a gift up to 1528 from the dependent house or 'cell' of Finchale priory. This payment was made at the office of the *feretrarius* or keeper of Saint Cuthbert's shrine. The 'bishop' is called *episcopus puerilis, episcopus eleemosynariae*, or the like. In 1405 he was not elected, *propter guerras eo tempore*. In 1423 and 1434 there was also an *episcopus de Elvett* or Elvetham,

---

[1] Wilkins, ii. 38 'Puerilia autem solemnia, quae in festo solent fieri Innocentum post vesperas S. Iohannis, tantum inchoari permittimus, et in crastino in ipsa die Innocentum totaliter terminentur.'

[2] *Archaeologia*, lii. 221 sqq.

[3] *Transactions* of *London and Middlesex Arch. Soc.* vols. iv, v.

[4] *Athenæum* (1900), ii. 655, 692 'data Pueris de Elemosinaria ludentibus coram Domino apud Westmonasterium, iijs. iiijd.' Dr. E. J. L. Scott and Dr. Rutherford found in this entry a proof of the existence of the Westminster Latin play at 'a period anterior to the foundation of Eton'!

a manor of the priory[1]. The abbey of Bury St. Edmunds had its *episcopus sancti Nicolai* in 1418 and for at least a century longer[2]. At Winchester each of the great monasteries held a Feast of Boys; the abbey of Hyde on St. Nicholas' day[3]; the priory of St. Swithin's on that of the Holy Innocents. Here, too, the accounts of the obedientiaries contain evidence of the feast in payments between 1312 and 1536 for beer or wine sent to the *episcopus iuvenum*. Nearly all the officers whose rolls are preserved, the chamberlain, the curtarian, the cellarian, the almoner, the sacristan, the *custos operum*, the hordarian, seem to have contributed[4]. A *Computus* of 1441 contains a payment to the *pueri eleemosynariae* who, with the *pueri* of St. Elizabeth's chapel, visited St. Mary's convent, dressed as girls, and danced, sang and sported before the abbess and the nuns[5]. We have had some French instances in which the Boy Bishop visited a neighbouring convent. But the nuns were not always dependent on outside visitors for their revel. In some places they held their own feast, with an 'abbess' instead of a 'bishop.' Archbishop John Peckham, in addition to his general constitution already quoted, issued a special mandate to Godstow nunnery, forbidding the office and prayers to be said *per parvulas* on Innocents' day[6]. Three centuries later, in 1526, a visitation of Carrow nunnery by Richard Nicke, bishop of Norwich, disclosed a custom of electing a Christmas 'abbess' there, which the bishop condemned[7]. Continental parallels to these

[1] Rimbault, xviii; *Finchale Priory* (Surtees Soc.), ccccxxviii; *Durham Accounts* (Surtees Soc.), iii. xliii, and passim.

[2] *Hist. MSS.* xiv. 8. 124, 157.

[3] *Computi* of Cellarer (Warton, ii. 232, iii. 300) '1397, pro epulis Pueri celebrantis in festo S. Nicholai ... 1490, in larvis et aliis indumentis Puerorum visentium Dominum apud Wulsey, et Constabularium Castri Winton, in apparatu suo, necnon subintrantium omnia monasteria civitatis Winton, in festo sancti Nicholai.'

[4] G. W. Kitchin, *Computus Rolls of St. Swithin's* (*Hampshire Rec. Soc.*), passim; G. W. Kitchin and F. T. Madge, *Winchester Chapter Documents* (*H. R. Soc.*), 24.

[5] Warton, ii. 231 '1441, pro pueris Eleemosynariae una cum pueris Capellae sanctae Elizabethae, ornatis more puellarum, et saltantibus, cantantibus, et ludentibus, coram domina Abbatissa et monialibus Abbathiae beatae Mariae virginis, in aula ibidem in die sanctorum Innocentium.'

[6] Harpsfield, *Hist. Eccl. Angl.* (1622), 441, citing Peckham's *Register.* He says the mandate was in French.

[7] *Visitations of Diocese of Norwich* (Camden Soc.), 209 'Domina Iohanna Botulphe dicit ... quod ... habent in festo Natalis Domini

examples are available. An eighth-century case, indeed, which is quoted by some writers, has probably been the subject of a misinterpretation [1]. But the visitation-books of Odo Rigaud, archbishop of Rouen (1248–69) record that he forbade the *ludibria* of the younger nuns at the Christmas feasts and the feast of St. Mary Magdalen in more than one convent of his diocese. One of these was the convent of the Holy Trinity at Caen, in which an 'abbess' was still chosen by the novices in 1423 [2]. All the monastic examples here quoted come from houses of the older foundations. The *Statutes*, however, of the Observant Franciscans made at Barcelona in 1401, expressly forbid the use of secular garments or the loan of habits of the order for *ludi* on St. Nicholas' or Innocents' days [3]; whence it may be inferred that the irregularities provided against were not unknown.

Mediaeval education began with the song-school : and

iuniorem monialem in abbatissam assumptam, vocandi [? iocandi] gratia ; cuius occasione ipsa consumere et dissipare cogitur quae vel elemosina vel aliorum amicorum largitione acquisierit . . . Iniunctum est . . . quod de cetero non observetur assumptio abbatissae vocandi causa.'

[1] Gregory of Tours, x. 16 (*M. G. H. Script. Rerum Meroving.* i. 427), mentions among the complaints laid before the visitors of the convent of St. Radegund in Poitou, that the abbess 'vittam de auro exornatam idem neptae suae superflue fecerit, barbaturias intus eo quod celebraverit.' Ducange, s. v. *Barbatoriae*, finds here a reference to some kind of masquing, and Peter of Blois, *Epist.* 14, certainly uses *barbatores* as a synonym for *mimi*. The *M. G. H.* editors of Gregory, however, explain '*barbatoria*' as '*primam barbam ponere*,' the sense borne by the term in Petronius, *Sat.* lxxiii. 6. The abbess's niece had probably no beard, but may not the reference be to the cutting of the hair of a novice when she takes the vows ?

[2] Ducange, s. v. *Kalendae* ('de monialibus Villae-Arcelli '), ' Item inhibemus ne de caetero in festis Innocentum et B. M. Magdalenae

ludibria exerceatis consueta, induendo vos scilicet vestibus saecularium aut inter vos seu cum secularibus choreas ducendo '; and again ' in festo S. Iohannis et Innocentium mimia iocositate et scurrilibus cantibus utebantur, ut pote farsis, conductis, motulis ; praecepimus quod honestius et cum maiori devotione alias se haberent ' ; Gasté, 36 (on Caen) 'iuniores in festo Innocentium cantant lectiones suas cum farsis. Hoc inhibuimus.' In 1423, the real abbess gave place to the little abbess at the *Deposuit*. Gasté, 44, describes a survival of the election of an ' abbess ' from amongst the *pensionnaires* on the days of St. Catherine and the Innocents in the Abbaye aux Bois, Faubourg St. Germain, from the *Mémoires* of Hélène Massalska. This was about 1773.

[3] Howlett, *Monumenta Franciscana* (R. S.), ii. 93 ' Caveant fratres in festo Sancti Nicolai seu Innocentium, vel quibuscunque aliis festis vestes extraneas religiosas seu seculares aut clericales vel muliebres sub specie devotionis induere ; nec habitus fratrum secularibus pro ludis faciendis accommodentur sub poena amotionis confusibilis de conventu.'

although the universities and other great seats of learning came to be much more than glorified choirs, they still retained certain traces of their humble origin. Amongst these was the Boy Bishop. The students of Paris regularly chose their Boy Bishops on St. Nicholas' day. In 1275, indeed, the Faculty of Arts forbade the torchlight processions which took place on that day and on St. Catherine's, the two great common holidays of the clerks [1]. But in 1367 such processions were held as of ancient custom, and it would appear that every little group of students gathered together under the protection and in the house of a master of arts considered itself entitled to choose a 'bishop,' and to lead him in a rout through the streets. In that year the custom led to a tragic brawl which came under the cognizance of the *Parlement* of Paris [2]. The scholars of one Peter de Zippa, dwelling *in vico Bucherie ultra Parvum Pontem*, had chosen as 'bishop' Bartholomew Divitis of Ypres. On St. Nicholas' eve, they were promenading, with a torch but unarmed, to the houses of the rector of the Faculty and others *causa solacii et iocosa*, when they met with the watch. Peter de Zippa was with them, and the watch had a grudge against Peter. On the previous St. Catherine's day they had arrested him, but he had been released by the *préfet*. They now attacked the procession with drawn swords, and wounded Jacobus de Buissono in the leg. As the scholars were remonstrating, up came Philippus de Villaribus, *miles gueti*, and Bernardus Blondelli, his deputy, and cried '*Ad mortem.*' The scholars fled home, but the watch made an attack on the house. Peter de Zippa attempted to appease them from a window, and was wounded four fingers from a mortal spot. As the watch were on the point of breaking in, the scholars surrendered. The house was looted, and

---

[1] Denifle, i. 532. It was forbidden 'in eisdem festis vel aliis paramenta nec coreas duci in vico de die nec de nocte cum torticiis vel sine.' But it was on Innocents' Day that the *béjaunes* or 'freshmen' of the Sorbonne were subjected to rites bearing a close analogy to the feast of fools ; cf. Rigollot, 172 ' 1476 . . . condemnatus fuit in crastino Innocentium capellanus abbas beiannorum ad octo solidos parisienses, eo quod non explevisset officium suum die Innocentium post prandium, in mundationem beiannorum per aspersionem aquae ut moris est, quanquam solemniter incoepisset exercere suum officium ante prandium inducendo beiannos per vicum super asinum.'

[2] Denifle, iii. 166.

the inmates beaten. One lad was pitched out on his head and driven into the Seine, out of which he was helped by a woman. Peter de Zippa and twenty-four others were rolled in the mud and then carried off to the *Châtelet*, where they were shut up in a dark and malodorous cell. Worst of all, the 'bishop' had disappeared altogether. It was believed that the watch had slain him, and flung the body into the Seine. A complaint was brought before the *Parlement*, and a commission of inquiry appointed. The watch declared that Peter de Zippa was insubordinate to authority and, although warned, as a foreigner, both in French and Latin[1], that they were the king's men, persisted in hurling logs and stones out of his window, with the result of knocking four teeth out of Peter Patou's mouth, and wounding the horse of Philip de Villaribus. This defence was apparently thought unsatisfactory, and a further inquiry was held, with the aid of torture. Finally the court condemned the offending watch to terms of imprisonment and the payment of damages. They had also to offer a humble apology, with bare head and bent knee, to the bishop of Paris, the rector of the Faculty, Peter de Zippa, and the injured scholars, in the cloister or the chapter-house of St. Mathurin's. The case of the alleged murder of the 'bishop,' Bartholomew Divitis, was not to be prejudiced by this judgement, and Peter de Zippa was warned to be more submissive to authority in future. The whole episode is an interesting parallel to the famous 'town and gown' at Oxford on St. Scholastica's day, 1353[2].

Provision is made for a Boy Bishop in the statutes of more than one great English educational foundation. William of Wykeham ordained in 1400 that one should be chosen at Winchester College, and at New College, Oxford, and should recite the office at the Feast of the Innocents[3]. Some notices

---

[1] 'Verbis nedum gallicis sed eciam latinis, ut ipsi qui de partibus alienis oriundi linguam gallicam nequaquam intelligebant plenarie.'

[2] S. F. Hulton, *Rixae Oxonienses*, 68. There had been many earlier brawls.

[3] *Statute* xxix (T. F. Kirby, *Annals of Winchester College*, 503) 'Permittimus tamen quod in festo Innocencium pueri vesperas matutinas et alia divina officia legenda et cantanda dicere et exsequi valeant secundum usum et consuetudinem ecclesiae Sarum.' The same formula is used in *New College Statute* xlii (*Statutes of the Colleges of Oxford*, vol. i).

in the Winchester College accounts during the fifteenth century show that he also presided at secular revels. In 1462 he is called *Episcopus Nicholatensis*, and on St. Nicholas' day he paid a visit of ceremony to the warden, who presented him, out of the college funds, with fourpence[1]. The example of William of Wykeham was followed, forty years later, in the statutes of the royal foundations of Eton College and King's College, Cambridge. But there was one modification. These colleges were dedicated to the Virgin and to St. Nicholas, and it was carefully laid down that the performance of the *officium* by the 'bishop' was to be on St. Nicholas' day, 'and by no means on that of the Innocents[2].' The Eton 'bishop' is said by the Elizabethan schoolmaster Malim, who wrote a *Consuetudinarium* of the college in 1561, to have been called *episcopus Nihilensis*, and to have been chosen on St. Hugh's day (November 17). Probably *Nihilensis* is a scribal mistake for *Nicholatensis*[3]. The custom had been abolished before Malim wrote, but was extant in 1507, for in that year the ' bishop's ' rochet was mended[4]. Some Eton historians have thought that the Boy Bishop ceremony was the origin of the famous

[1] Cf. Appendix E. Kirby, *op. cit.* 90, quotes an inventory of 1406 ' Baculus pastoralis de cupro deaurato pro Epõ puerorum in die Innocencium . . . Mitra de panno aureo ex dono Dñi. Fundatoris hernesiat (mounted) cum argento deaurato ex dono unius socii coll. [Robert Heete] pro Epõ puerorum.'

[2] *The Charter of King's College* (1443), c. 42 (*Documents relating to the Univ. of Camb.* ii. 569; Heywood and Wright, *Ancient Laws of the Fifteenth Century for King's Coll. Camb. and Eton Coll.* 112), closely follows Wykeham's formula: ' excepto festo Sᵗⁱ Nicholai praedicto, in quo festo et nullatenus in festo Innocentium, permittimus quod pueri . . . secundum usum in dicto Regali Collegio hactenus usitatum.' The Eton formula (c. 31) in 1444 is slightly different (Heywood and Wright (*op. cit.* 560) ' excepto in festo Sancti Nicholai, in quo, et nullatenus in festo Sanctorum Innocentium, divina officia praeter missae

secreta exequi et dici permittimus per episcopum puerorum scholarium, ad hoc de eisdem annis singulis eligendum.'

[3] Warton, ii. 228; Leach, 133. The passage from the *Consuetudinarium* is given from *Harl. MS.* 7044 f. 167 (apparently a transcript from a *C. C. C. C. MS.*) by Heywood and Wright, *op. cit.* 632; E. S. Creasy, *Eminent Etonians*, 91 ' in die Sᵗⁱ Hugonis pontificis solebat Aetonae fieri electio Episcopi Nihilensis, sed consuetudo obsolevit. Olim episcopus ille puerorum habebatur nobilis, in cuius electione et literata et laudatissima exercitatio, ad ingeniorum vires et motus excitandos, Aetonae celebris erat.'

[4] *Eton Audit Book*, 1507-8, quoted by H. C. Maxwell-Lyte, *Hist. of Eton* (ed. 1899), 149 ' Pro reparatione rochet pro episcopo puerorum, xjᵈ.' An inventory of Henry VIII's reign says that this rochet was given by James Denton (K. S. 1486) for use at St. Nicholas' time.

'Montem'; but as the 'Montem' was held on the feast of the Conversion of St. Paul (January 25), and as Malim mentions both customs independently, this is improbable[1].

Smaller schools than Winchester or Eton had none the less their Boy Bishops. Archbishop Rotherham, who founded in 1481 a college at his native place of Rotherham in Yorkshire, left by will in 1500 a mitre for the 'barnebishop[2].' The grammar school at Canterbury had, or should have had, its Boy Bishop in 1464[3]. Aberdeen was a city of which St. Nicholas was the patron, and at Aberdeen the master of the grammar school was paid by a collection taken when he went the rounds with the 'bishop' on St. Nicholas' day[4]. Dean Colet, on the other hand, when founding St. Paul's school did not provide for a 'bishop' in the school itself, but, as we have seen, directed the scholars to attend the mass and sermon of the 'bishop' in the cathedral.

Naturally the Reformation made war on the Boy Bishop. A royal proclamation of July 22, 1541, forbade the 'gatherings' by children 'decked and apparalid to counterfaite priestes, bysshopps, and women' on 'sainte Nicolas, sainte Catheryne, sainte Clement, the holye Innocentes, and such like,' and also the singing of mass and preaching by boys on these days[5]. Naturally also, during the Marian reaction the Boy

---

[1] Maxwell-Lyte, *op. cit.* 450.

[2] Hearne, *Liber Niger Scaccarii*, 674 'Item, unam Mitram de Cloth of goold habentem 2 knoppes arg. enameld, dat. ad occupand. per Barnebishop.'

[3] John Stone, a monk of Canterbury, records in his *De Obitibus et aliis Memorabilibus sui Coenobii* (*MS. C. C. C. C.*, Q. 8, quoted Warton, ii. 230) 'Hoc anno, 1464, in festo Sancti Nicolai non erat episcopus puerorum in schola grammatica in civitate Cantuariae ex defectu Magistrorum, viz. I. Sidney et T. Hikson.'

[4] J. Stuart, *Extracts from Council Registers of Aberdeen* (Spalding Club), i. 186. The council ordered on Nov. 27, 1542, 'that the maister of thair grammar scuyll sell haf iiij^s Scottis, of the sobirest persoun that

resauis him and the bischop at Sanct Nicolace day.' This is to be held a legal fee, 'he hes na uder fee to leif on.'

[5] Wilkins, *Concilia*, iii. 860 'And whereas heretofore dyverse and many superstitious and childysshe observations have been usid, and yet to this day are observed and kept in many and sondry parties of this realm, as upon sainte Nicolas, sainte Catheryne, sainte Clement, the holye Innocentes, and such like; children be strangelye decked and apparelid to counterfaite priestes, bysshopps, and women ; and so ledde with songes and daunces from house to house, bleasing the people, and gatherynge of monye; and boyes doo singe masse, and preache in the pulpitt, with suche other unfittinge and inconvenyent usages, rather to

Bishop reappeared. On November 13, 1554, Bishop Bonner issued an order permitting all clerks in the diocese of London to have St. Nicholas and to go abroad ; and although this order was annulled on the very eve of the festival, apparently because Cardinal Pole had appointed St. Nicholas' day for a great ceremony of reconciliation at Lambeth, yet the custom was actually revived in several London parishes, including St. Andrew's, Holborn, and St. Nicholas Olave, Bread Street [1]. In 1556 it was still more widely observed [2].

the derision than to any true glory of God, or honour of his saints ; the kyng's majestie therefore mynding nothing so moche, as to avaunce the true glorye of God without vayne superstition, willith and commaundeth, that from henceforth all suche superstitions be loste and clyerlye extinguisshed throughowte all this his realmes and dominions, forasmoche as the same doo resemble rather the unlawfull superstition of gentilitie, than the pure and sincere religion of Christe.' Brand, i. 236, suggests that there was an earlier proclamation of July 22, 1540, to the same effect. Johan Bale in his *Yet a Course at the Romyshe Foxe* (1542), says that if Bonner's censure of those who lay aside certain 'auncyent rytes' is justified, 'then ought my Lorde also to suffer the same selfe ponnyshment, for not goynge abought with Saynt Nycolas clarkes.' Thomas Becon, *Catechism*, 320 (ed. Parker Soc.), compares a bishop who does not preach, a 'dumb dog,' to a 'Nicholas bishop.' The *Articles* put to bishop Gardiner in 1550 required him to declare 'that the counterfeiting St. Nicholas, St. Clement, St. Catherine and St. Edmund, by children, heretofore brought into the church, was a mockery and foolishness' (Froude, iv. 550).

[1] *Machyn's Diary*, 75 'The xij day of November [1554] was commondyd by the bysshope of London to all clarkes in the dyoses of London for to have Sant Necolas and to go a-brod, as mony as wold have ytt ... [the v day of December, the which was Saint Nicholas' eve, at evensong time, came a commandment that St. Nicholas should not go abroad, nor about. But, notwithstanding, there went about these Saint Nicholases in divers parishes, as St. Andrew's, Holborn, and St.] Nicolas Olyffe in Bredstret.' Warton, iv. 237, says that during Mary's reign Hugh Rhodes, a gentleman or musician of the Chapel royal, printed in black letter quarto a poem of thirty-six octave stanzas, entitled *The Song of the Chyld-byfshop, as it was songe before the queenes maiestie in her privie chamber at her manour of saynt James in the Feeldes on Saynt Nicholas day and Innocents day this yeare nowe present, by the chylde bysshope of Poules churche with his company.* Warton apparently saw the poem, for he describes it as 'a fulsome panegyric on the queen's devotion, in which she is compared to Judith, Esther, the Queen of Sheba, and the Virgin Mary,' but no copy of it is now known ; cf. F. J. Furnivall, *The Babees Book* (E. E. T. S.), lxxxv.

[2] *Machyn's Diary*, 121 'The v day of Desember [1556] was Sant Necolas evyn, and Sant Necolas whentt a-brod in most partt in London syngyng after the old fassyon, and was reseyvyd with mony good pepulle in-to ther howses, and had myche good chere as ever they had, in mony plasses.' Foxe, *Acts and Monuments*, viii. 726, celebrates the wit of a 'godly matron,' Mrs. Gertrude Crockhay, who shut 'the foolish popish Saint Nicholas' out of her house in this year, and

But upon the accession of Elizabeth it naturally fell again into disuse, and it has left few, if any, traces in modern folk-custom [1].

I need not, after the last two chapters, attempt an elaborate analysis of the customs connected with the Boy Bishop. In the main they are parallel to those of the Feast of Fools. They include the burlesque of divine service, the *quête*, the banquet, the *dominus festi*. Like the Feast of Fools, they probably contain a folk as well as an ecclesiastical element. But the former is chastened and subdued, the strength of ecclesiastical discipline having proved sufficient, in the case of the boys, to bar for the most part such excesses as the adult clerks inherited from the pagan Kalends. . On one point, however, a little more must be said. The *dominus festi*, who at the Feast of Fools bears various names, is almost invariably at the Feast of Boys a ' bishop [2].' This term must have been

told her brother-in-law, Dr Mallet, when he remonstrated, that she had heard of men robbed by ' Saint Nicholas's clerks.' This was a slang term for thieves, of whom, as of children, St. Nicholas was the patron ; for the reason of which cf. *Golden Legend*, ii. 119. Another procession forbidden by the proclamation of 1541 was also revived in 1556 ; cf. *Machyn's Diary*, 119 ' [The xxiv day of November, being the eve of Saint Katharine, at six of the clock at night] sant Katheryn('s) lyght [went about the battlements of Saint Paul's with singing,] and Sant Katheryn gohying a prossessyon.'

[1] At Exton in Rutlandshire, children were allowed at the beginning of the nineteenth century to play in the church on Innocents' Day (*Leicester and Rutland Folk-Lore*, 96). Probably a few other examples could be collected.

[2] At Mainz, not only the *pueri*, but also the *diaconi* and the *sacerdotes*, had their *episcopus* (Dürr, 71). On the other hand at Vienne the term used at all the feasts, of the *triduum* and on January 1 and 6, was *rex* (Pilot de Thorey, *Usages*,

Fêtes et Coutumes en Dauphiné, i. 179). The Boy Bishops received, for their brief day, all the external marks of honour paid to real bishops. They are alleged to have occasionally enjoyed more solid privileges. Louvet (*Hist. et Ant. de Beauvais*, cited Rigollot, 142), says that at Beauvais the right of presentation to chapter benefices falling vacant on Innocents' Day fell to the *pueri*. Jean Van der Muelen or Molanus (*De Canonicis* (1587), ii. 43) makes a similar statement as to Cambrai: ' Immo personatus hic episcopus in quibusdam locis reditus, census et capones, annue percipit : alibi mitram habet, multis episcoporum mitris sumptuosiorem. In Cameracensi ecclesia visus est vacantem, in mense episcopi, praebendam, quasi iure ad se devoluto, conferre ; quam collationem beneficii vere magnifici, reverendissimus praesul, cum puer grato animo, magistrum suum, bene de ecclesia meritum, nominasset, gratam et raram habuit.' At Mainz lost tradition had it that if an Elector died during the tenure of office by a Boy Bishop, the revenues *sede vacante* would fall to him. Unfortunately

familiar by the end of the eleventh century for it lends a point of sarcasm to the protest made by Yves, bishop of Chartres, in a letter to Pope Urban II against the disgraceful nomination by Philip I of France of a wanton lad to be bishop of Orleans in 1099 [1]. In later documents it appears in various forms, *episcopus puerorum*, *episcopellus* [2], *episcopus puerilis* or *parvulus*, 'boy bishop,' 'child bishop,' 'barne bishop.' In some English monasteries it is *episcopus eleemosynariae* ('of the almonry'); in Germany, *Schul-Bischof*, or, derisively, *Apfeln-Bischof*. More significant than any of these is the common variant *episcopus Nicholatensis*, 'Nicholas bishop.' For St. Nicholas' day (December 6) was hardly less important in the career of the Boy Bishop than that of the Holy Innocents itself. At this feast he was generally chosen and began his *quête* through the streets. In more than one locality, Mainz for instance in Germany, Eton in England, it was on this day as well as, or in substitution for, that of the Innocents that he made his appearance in divine service [3]. St. Nicholas was, of course, the patron saint

---

the chapter and verse of history disprove this (Dürr, 67, 79). On the other hand it is certain that the Boy Bishops assumed the episcopal privilege of coinage. Rigollot, 52 sqq., describes and figures a long series of fifteenth- and sixteenth-century coins, or medals mostly struck by 'bishops' of the various churches and monastic houses of Amiens. They are the more interesting, because some of them bear 'fools' as devices, and thus afford another proof of the relations between the feasts of Boys and Fools. Lille *monetae* of the sixteenth century are figured by Vanhende, *Numismatique Lilloise*, 256, and others from Laon by C. Hidé, in *Bull. de la Soc. acad. de Laon*, xiii. 126. Some of Rigollot's specimens seem to have belonged, not to Boy Bishops, but to *confréries*, who struck them as 'jetons de présence' (Chartier, *L'ancien Chapitre de N.-D. de Paris*, 178); and probably this is also the origin of the pieces found at Bury St. Edmunds, which have nothing in their devices to

connect them with a Boy Bishop (Rimbault, xxvi).

[1] Ivo Carnotensis, *Epist.* 67, *ad papam Urbanum* (*P. L.* clxii. 87)
'eligimus puerum, puerorum festa colentes,
non nostrum morem, sed regis iussa sequentes.'
Cf. Rigollot, 143.

[2] Lucas Cusentinus (†1203-24) *Ordinarium* (Martene, iii. 39): ' Puero episcopello pontificalia conceduntur insignia, et ipse dicit orationes.'

[3] The *Ritual* (†1264) of St. Omer (*Mém. de la Soc. des Antiq. de la Morinie*, xx. 186) has the following rubric for St. Nicholas' Day 'in se cundis vesperis . . . a choristis incipitur prosa *Sospitati dedit egros*, in qua altercando cantatur iste versus *Ergo laudes* novies tantum, ne immoderatum tedium generet vel derisum.' The same rubric recurs on St. Catherine's Day. At St. Omer, as at Paris (cf. p. 363), these were the two winter holidays for scholars. Cf. also p. 289, and A. Legrand, *Réjouissances des écoliers*

of schoolboys and of children generally [1]. His prominence in the winter processions of Germany and the presents which in modern folk-belief he brings to children have been touched upon in an earlier chapter. It now appears that originally he took rather than gave presents, and that where he appeared in person he was represented by the Boy Bishop. And this suggests the possibility that it was this connexion with St. Nicholas, and not the profane mummings of Michael the Drunkard at Constantinople, which led to the use of the term 'bishop' for the *dominus festi*, first at the Feast of Boys, and ultimately at the other Christmas feasts as well. For St. Nicholas was not only the boys' saint *par excellence*; he was also, owing to the legend of his divinely ordered consecration when only a layman as bishop of Myra, the bishop saint *par excellence* [2]. However this may be, I think it is a fair guess that St. Nicholas' day was an older date for a Feast of Boys than that of the Holy Innocents, and that the double date records an instance of the process, generally imperfect, by which, under Roman and Christian influence, the beginning of

---

de N.-D. de St. Omer, le jour de St.-Nicholas, leur glorieux patron (*Mémoires, ut cit.* vii. 160). The St. Omer *Episcopus puerorum* also officiated on Innocents' Eve and the octave. Dreves, *Anal. Hymn.* xxi. 82, gives various *cantiones* for St. Nicholas' Day; e.g.

　　'Nicolai praesulis
　　Festum celebremus,

　　　　.　　.　　.　　.

　　In tanto natalitio
　　Patrum docet traditio
　　Ut consonet in gaudio
　　Fidelium devotio,
　　Est ergo superstitio
　　Vacare a tripudio.'

In England it is probable that the Beverley Boy Bishop also officiated on St. Nicholas' Day. A chapter order of Jan. 7, 1313, directs the transfer of the 'servitium sancti Nicholai in festo eiusdem per Magistrum Scholarum Beverlacensium celebrandum' to the altar of St. Blaize during the building of a new nave (A. F. Leach, *Memorials of Beverley Minster*, Surtees Soc. i. 307).

[1] Tille, *D. W.* 32; Leach, 130. The connexion of St. Nicholas with children may be explained by, if it did not rather give rise to, either the legend of his early piety, ' The first day that he was washed and bained, he addressed him right up in the bason, and he wold not take the breast nor the pap but once on the Wednesday and once on the Friday, and in his young age he eschewed the plays and japes of other young children' (*Golden Legend*, ii. 110); or the various other legends which represent him as bringing children out of peril. Cf. *Golden Legend*, ii. 119 sqq., and especially the history of the resurrection of three boys from a pickle-tub narrated by Mr. Leach from Wace. A. Maury, *Croyances et Légendes du Moyen Âge* (ed. 1896), 149) tries to find the origin of this in misunderstood iconographic representations of the missionary saint at the baptismal font.

[2] Leach, 130; *Golden Legend*, ii. 111.

winter customs of the Germano-Keltic peoples were gradually transformed into mid-winter customs [1]. The beginning of winter feast was largely a domestic feast, and the children probably had a special part in it. It is possible also to trace a survival of the corresponding beginning of summer feast in the day of St. Gregory on March 12, which was also sometimes marked by the election of a *Schul-Bischof* [2].

[1] Cf. ch. xi. The position of St. Nicholas' Day in the ceremonies discussed in this chapter is sometimes shared by other feasts of the winter cycle: St. Edmund's (Nov. 20), St. Clement's (Nov. 23), St. Catherine's (Nov. 25), St. Andrew's (Nov. 30), St. Eloi's (Dec. 1), St. Lucy's (Dec. 13). Cf. pp. 349-51, 359, 366-8. The feast of St. Mary Magdalen, kept in a Norman convent (p. 362), was, however, in the summer (July 22).

[2] Specht, 229; Tille, *D. W.* 300; Wetze and Welte, iv. 1411. Roman schoolmasters expected a present at the *Minervalia* (March 18-23); cf. the passage from Tertullian in Appendix N (1).

CHAPTER XVI

GUILD FOOLS AND COURT FOOLS

[*Bibliographical Note.*—The best account of the *Sociétés joyeuses* is that of L. Petit de Julleville, *Les Comédiens en France au Moyen Âge* (1889). Much material is collected in the same writer's *Répertoire du Théâtre comique en France au Moyen Âge* (1886), and in several of the books given as authorities on the Feast of Fools (ch. xiii), especially those of Du Tilliot, Rigollot, Leber, and Grenier. Mme. Clément (née Hémery), *Histoire des Fêtes civiles et religieuses du Département du Nord* (1832), may also be consulted. M. Petit de Julleville's account of the *Sottie* is supplemented by E. Picot, *La Sottie en France*, in *Romania*, vol. vii, and there is a good study of the fool-literature of the Renascence in C. H. Herford, *Literary Relations between England and Germany in the Sixteenth Century* (1886). Amongst writers on the court fool are J. F. Dreux du Radier, *Histoire des Fous en Titre d'Office*, in *Récréations historiques* (1768); C. F. Flögel, *Geschichte der Hofnarren* (1789); F. Douce, *Clowns and Fools of Shakespeare* in *Variorum Shakespeare* (1821), xxi. 420, and *Illustrations of Shakespeare* (1839); C. Leber in Rigollot, xl; J. Doran, *History of Court Fools* (1858); A. F. Nick, *Hof- und Volksnarren* (1861); P. Lacroix (le bibliophile Jacob); *Dissertation sur les Fous des Rois de France*; A. Canel, *Recherches historiques sur les Fous des Rois de France* (1873); A. Gazeau, *Les Bouffons* (1882); P. Moreau, *Fous et Bouffons* (1885). Much of this literature fails to distinguish between the *stultus* and the *ioculator regis* (ch. iii). There is an admirable essay by L. Johnson on *The Fools of Shakespeare* in *Noctes Shakesperianae* (1887).]

THE conclusion of this volume must call attention to certain traces left by the ecclesiastical *ludi* of the New Year, themselves extinct, upon festival custom, and, through this, upon dramatic tradition. The Feast of Fools did not altogether vanish with its suppression in the cathedrals. It had had its origin in the popular celebration of the Kalends. Throughout it did not altogether lack a popular element. The *bourgeois* crowded into the cathedral to see and share in the revel. The Fool Bishop in his turn left the precincts and made his progress through the city streets, while his satellites played their pranks abroad for the entertainment of the mob. The feast was a dash of colour in the civic as well as the ecclesiastical year. The Tournai riots of 1499 show that the *jeunesse* of that city had come to look upon it as a *spectacle* which they were entitled to claim from the cathedral. What happened in Tournai doubtless happened elsewhere. And the upshot of it was that when in chapter after chapter the reforming party got the upper hand and the official celebration was dropped, the city and its *jeunesse* themselves stepped into the breach and took measures to perpetuate the threatened delightful dynasty. It was an easy way to avert the loss of a holiday. And so we find a second tradition of Feasts of Fools, in which the *fous* are no longer vicars but *bourgeois*, and the *dominus festi* is a popular 'king' or 'prince' rather than a clerical 'bishop.' A mid-fifteenth-century writer, Martin Franc, attests the vogue of the *prince des folz* in the towns of northern France:

> 'Va t'en aux festes à Tournay,
> A celles d'Arras et de Lille,
> D'Amiens, de Douay, de Cambray,
> De Valenciennes, d'Abbeville.
> Là verras tu des gens dix mille,
> Plus qu'en la forest de Torfolz,
> Qui servent par sales, par viles,
> A ton dieu, le prince des folz[1].'

The term *Roi* or *Prince des Sots* is perhaps the most common one for the new *dominus festi*, and, like *sots* or *folz* themselves, is generic. But there are many local variants, as the *Prévôt des Étourdis* at Bouchain[2], the *Roi des Braies* at Laon, the *Roi de l'Epinette* at Lille, and the *Prince de la Jeunesse* at St. Quentin[3]. The *dominus festi* was as a rule chosen by one or more local guilds or *confréries* into which the *jeunesse* were organized for the purpose of maintaining the feast. The fifteenth century was an age of guilds in every department of social life, and the *compagnies des fous* or *sociétés joyeuses* are but the frivolous counterparts of religious *confréries* or literary *puys*. The most famous of all such *sociétés*, that of *l'Infanterie Dijonnaise* at Dijon, seems directly trace-

---

[1] Martin Franc, *Champion des dames* (*Bibl. de l'École des Chartes*, v. 58).

[2] Du Tilliot, 87.
[3] Julleville, *Les Com.* 241.

able to the fall of an ecclesiastical Feast of Fools. Such a feast was held, as we have seen, in the ducal, afterwards royal, chapel, and was abolished by the *Parlement* of Dijon in 1552. Before this date nothing is heard of *l'Infanterie*. A quarter of a century later it is in full swing, and the character of its dignitaries and its badges point clearly to a derivation from the chapel feast [1]. The Dijon example is but a late one of a development which had long taken place in many parts of northern France and Flanders. It would be difficult to assert that a *société joyeuse* never made its appearance in any town before the ecclesiastical Feast of Fools had died out therein. Occasionally the two institutions overlap [2]. But, roughly speaking, the one is the inheritor of the other; '*La confrérie des sots, c'est la Fête des Fous sécularisée* [3].' Amongst the chief of these *sociétés* are the *Enfants-sans-Souci* of Paris, the *Cornards* or *Connards* of Rouen and Evreux [4], the *Suppôts du Seigneur de la Coquille*

---

[1] Julleville, *Les Com.* 193, 256 ; Du Tilliot, 97. The chief officers of the chapel *fous* were the 'bâtonnier' and the 'protonotaire et procureur des fous.' In the *Infanterie* these are replaced by the emblematical *Mère Folle* and the 'Procureur fiscal' known as 'Fiscal vert' or 'Griffon vert.' Du Tilliot and others have collected a number of documents concerning the *Infanterie*, together with representations of seals, badges, &c., used by them. These may be compared in Du Tilliot with the *bâton* belonging to the Chapel period (1482), which he also gives. The motto of the *Infanterie* is worth noticing. It was *Numerus stultorum infinitus est*, and was taken from *Ecclesiastes*, i. 15. It was used also at Amiens (Julleville, *Les Com.* 234).

[2] At Amiens the 'feste du Prince des Sots' existed in 1450 (Julleville, *Les Com.* 233), but the 'Pope of Fools' was not finally suppressed in the cathedral for another century. But at Amiens there was an immense multiplication of 'fool'-organizations. Each church and

convent had its 'episcopus puerorum,' and several of these show *fous* on their coins. Rigollot, 77, 105, figures a coin with *fous*, which he assigns to a *confrérie* in the parish of St. Remigius ; also a coin, dated 1543, of an 'Evesque des Griffons.'

[3] Julleville, *Les Com.* 144.

[4] The term *cornard* seems to be derived from the 'cornes' of the traditional fool headdress. Leber, ix. 353, reprints from the *Mercure de France* for April, 1725, an account of a procession made by the *abbas cornardorum* at Evreux mounted upon an ass, which directly recalls the Feast of Fools. A macaronic *chanson* used on the occasion of one of these processions is preserved :
'*De asino bono nostro,*
Meliori et optimo,
Debemus faire fête.
En revenant de Gravignariâ,
Un gros chardon *reperit in viâ* ;
Il lui coupa la tête.
Vir monachus, in mense Iulio,
Egressus est e monasterio,
C'est dom de la Bucaille.

of Lyons [1]. The history of these has been written excellently well by M. Petit de Julleville, and I do not propose to repeat it. A few general points, however, deserve attention. The ecclesiastical Feast of Fools flourished rather in cathedrals than in monasteries. The *sociétés* however, like some more serious *confréries* [2], seem to have preferred a conventual to a capitular model for their organization [3]. The *Cornards*, both at Rouen and Evreux, were under an *Abbé*. Cambrai had its *Abbaye joyeuse de Lescache-Profit*, Chalonssur-Saône its *Abbé de la Grande Abbaye*, Arras its *Abbé de Liesse*, Poitiers its *Abbé de Mau Gouverne* [4]. The literary adaptation of this idea by Rabelais in the *Abbaye de Thélème* is familiar. This term *abbaye* is common to the *sociétés*, with some at least of the *Basoches* or associations of law-clerks to the *Parlements* of Paris and the greater provincial towns. The *Basoches* existed for mutual protection, but for mutual amusement also, and on one side at least of their activity they were much of the nature of *sociétés joyeuses* [5]. At Rheims in 1490 a *Basoche* entered into rivalry of dramatic invective with the celebrants of the ecclesiastical Feast of Fools [6]. The *Basoche* of Paris was in the closest relations to, if not actually identical with, the *société* of the *Enfants-sans-Souci* [7]. Just as

Egressus est sine licentiâ,
Pour aller voir donna Venissia,
Et faire la ripaille.'
Research has identified Dom de la Bucaille and Donna Venissia as respectively a prior of St. Taurin, and a prioress of St. Saviour's, in Evreux.

[1] A *coquille* is a misprint, and this *société* was composed of the printers of Lyon.

[2] *Conc. of Avignon* (1326), c. 37, *de societatibus colligationibus et coniurationibus quas confratrias appellant radicitus extirpandis* (Labbé, xi. 1738), forbids both clerks and laymen 'ne se confratres priores abbatas praedictae societatis appellent.' The charges brought against the *confréries* are of perverting justice, not of wanton revelry, and therefore it is probably not 'sociétés joyeuses' that are in question ; cf. Ducange, s. v. *Abbas*

Confratriae, quoting a Paris example. Grenier, 362, however, mentions a 'confrérie' in the Hôpital de Rue at Amiens (†1210) which was under an 'évêque' ; cf. the following note.

[3] I find an 'évesque des folz' at Béthune, a 'M. le Cardinal' as head of the 'Joyeux' at Rheims (Julleville, *Les Com.* 242; *Rép. Com.* 340), and an 'évesque des Griffons' at Amiens (Rigollot, 105). Exceptional is, I believe, the *Société des Foux* founded on the lines of a chivalric order by Adolphe, Comte de Clèves, in 1380 (Du Tilliot, 84).

[4] Julleville, 236 ; Guy, 471.

[5] Julleville, 88, 136. The Paris *Basoche* was a 'royaume'; those of Chambéry and Geneva were 'abbayes.'

[6] Cf. p. 304.

[7] Julleville, *Les Com.* 152.

the law-clerks of Paris were banded together in their *Basoche*, so were the students of Paris in their 'university,' 'faculties,' 'nations,' and other groups ; and in 1470, long after the regular Feast of Fools had disappeared from the city, the students were still wont to put on the fool habit and elect their *rex fatuorum* on Twelfth night[1]. Yet other guilds of a more serious character, generally speaking, than the *sociétés joyeuses*, none the less occasionally gave themselves over to *joyeuseté*. The *Deposuit* brought rebuke upon religious *confréries* up to a quite late date[2] ; and traces of the *fous* are to be found amongst the recreations of no less a body than the famous and highly literary *puy* of Arras. The *sociétés joyeuses*, like the *puys*, were primarily associations of amateur, rather than professional merry-makers, a fact which distinguishes them from the corporations of minstrels described in a previous chapter[3]. But minstrels and *trouvères* were by no means excluded. The poet Gringoire was *Mère-Sotte* of the Paris *Enfants-sans-Souci*. Clément Marot was a member of the same body. In the *puy* of Arras the minstrels traditionally held an important place ; and as the literary and dramatic side of the *sociétés* grew, it is evident that the men who were

---

[1] Bulaeus, *Hist. Univ. Paris*, v. 690 ; Julleville, *Les Com.* 297 ; Rashdall, *Universities of Europe*, ii. 611. It was probably to this student custom that the Tournai rioters of 1499 appealed (cf. p. 301). In 1470 the Faculty of Arts ordered the suppression of it. Cf. C. Jourdain, *Index Chartarum Paris.* 294 (No. 1369). On Jan. 5 they met 'ad providendum remedium de electione regis fatuorum,' and decreed 'quod nullus scolaris assumeret habitum fatui pro illo anno, nec in collegio, nec extra collegium, nisi forsan duntaxat ludendo farsam vel moralitatem.' Several scholars 'portantes arma et assumentes habitus fatuorum' were corrected on Jan. 24, and it was laid down that 'reges vero fatuorum priventur penitus a gradu quocumque.'

[2] Grenier, 365 ; Ducange, s. v. *Deposuit*, quoting *Stat. Hosp. S.*

Iacobi Paris. (sixteenth century), 'après le diner, on porte le baton au cueur, et là est le trésorier, qui chante et fait le *Deposuit*.' *Stat. Syn. Petri de Broc. episc. Autiss.* (1642) 'pendant que les bâtons de confrérie seront exposez, pour être enchéris, l'on ne chantera *Magnificat*, et n'appliquera-t-on point ces versets *Deposuit* et *Suscepit* à la délivrance d'iceux ; ains on chantera quelque antienne et répons avec l'oraison propre en l'honneur du Saint, duquel on célèbre la feste.'

[3] Cf. ch. iii and Appendix F ; and on the general character of the *puys*, Julleville, *Les Com.* 42 ; Guy, xxxiv ; Paris, 185. Some documents with regard to a fourteenth-century *puy* in London are in Riley, *Liber Custumarum*, xlviii. 216, 479 (*Munim. Gildh. Lond.* in R. S.) ; *Memorials of London*, 42.

professionally ready with their pens must everywhere have been in demand.

The primary function of the *sociétés joyeuses* and their congeners was the celebration of the traditional Feast of Fools at or about the New Year. In Paris, Twelfth night was a day of festival for the *Basoche* as well as for the minor association of exchequer clerks known as the *Empire de Galilée*. In mid-January came the *fête des Braies* at Laon, and the *fête* of the *Abbaye de Lescache-Profit* at Cambrai. That of the *Prince des Sots* at Amiens was on the first of January itself[1]. On the same day three *sociétés joyeuses* united in a *fête de l'âne* at Douai[2]. But January was no clement month for the elaborated revels of increasingly luxurious burghers; and it is not surprising to find that many of the *sociétés* transferred their attention to other popular feasts which happened to fall at more genial seasons of the year. To the celebration of these, the spring feast of the carnival or Shrovetide, the summer feasts of May-day or Midsummer, they brought all the wantonness of the Feast of Fools. The *Infanterie Dijonnaise*, the *Cornards* of Rouen and Evreux, the third Parisian law association, that of the *Châtelet*, especially cultivated the carnival. The three obligatory feasts of the *Basoche* included, besides that of Twelfth night, one on May-day and one at the beginning of July[3]. On May-day, too, a guild in the parish of St. Germain at Amiens held its *fête des fous*[4]. It may be noted that

---

[1] Julleville, *Les Com.* 92, 233, 236, 241.

[2] Clément-Hémery, *Fêtes du Dép. du Nord*, 184, states on the authority of a MS. without title or signature that this *fête* originated in a prose with a bray in it, sung by the canons of St. Peter's. The lay form of the feast can be traced from †1476 to 1668. Leber, x. 135, puts the (clerical) origin before 1282.

[3] Julleville, *Les Com.* 92, 204, 247.

[4] F. Guérard, *Les Fous de Saint-Germain*, in *Mélanges d'Hist. et d'Arch.* (Amiens, 1861), 17. On the Saturday before the first Sunday in May children in the rue St. Germain carry boughs, singing

'Saint Germain, coucou,
Ch'est l'fette d'chés fous, &c.'

In the church they used to place a bottle crowned with yellow primroses, called 'coucous.' The dwellers in the parish are locally known as 'fous,' and an historical myth is told to account for this. Probably May-day has here merged with St. Germain's Day (May 2) in a 'fête des fous.' Payments for decking the church appear in old accounts.

these summer extensions of the reign of folly are not without
parallels of a strictly ecclesiastical type. At Châlons-sur-
Marne, as late as 1648, a chapter procession went to the
woods on St. John's eve to cut boughs for the decking of
the church [1]. At Evreux a similar custom grew into a very
famous revel [2]. This was the *procession noire*, otherwise
known as the *cérémonie de la Saint-Vital*, because the proceedings began on the day of St. Vitalis (April 28) and lasted
to the second Vespers on May 1. Originally the canons,
afterwards the choir-clerks, chaplains, and vicars, went at daybreak on May morning to gather branches in the bishop's
woods. Their return was the signal for riotous proceedings.
The bells were violently rung. Masks were worn. Bran was
thrown in the eyes of passers-by, and they were made to leap
over broomsticks. The choir-clerks took the high stalls, and
the choir-boys recited the office. In the intervals the canons
played at skittles over the vaults; there were dancing and
singing and the rest, 'as at the time of the Nativity [3].' The
abuses of this festival must have begun at an early date, for
two canons of the cathedral, one of whom died in 1206, are
recorded to have been hung out of the belfry windows in
a vain attempt to stop the bell-ringing. Its extension to
St. Vitalis' day is ascribed to another canon, singularly named
Bouteille, who is said to have founded about 1270 a very odd
obit. He desired that a pall should lie on the pavement of
the choir, and that on each corner and in the middle of this
should stand a bottle of wine, to be drunk by the singing-men.
The canon Bouteille may be legendary, but the wine-bottle
figured largely in the festival ceremonies. While the branches
were distributed in the bishop's wood, which came to be
known as the *bois de la Bouteille*, the company drank and
ate cakes. Two bottle-shaped holes were dug in the earth
and filled with sand. On the day of the *obit* an enormous
leather bottle, painted with marmosets, serpents, and other
grotesques, was placed in the choir. These rites were still

---

[1] Guérard, *op. cit.* 46.
[2] Leber, x. 125, from *Mercure de France* for April, 1726; Gasté, 46.
[3] 'ludunt ad quillas super voltas ecclesiae ... faciunt podia, choreas et choros ... et reliqua sicut in natalibus.'

extant at Evreux in 1462, when a fresh attempt to suppress the bell-jangling led to a fresh riot. No explanation is given of the term *procession noire* as used at Evreux, but a Vienne parallel suggests that, as in some other seasonal festivals, those who took part in the procession had their faces blacked. At Vienne, early on May 1, four men, naked and black, started from the archbishop's palace and paraded the city. They were chosen respectively by the archbishop, the cathedral chapter, and the abbots of St. Peter's and St. John's. Subsequently they formed a *cortège* for a *rex*, also chosen by the archbishop, and a *regina* from the convent of St. Andrew's. A St. Paul, from the hospital dedicated to that saint, also joined in the procession, and carried a cup of ashes which he sprinkled in the faces of those he met. This custom lasted to the seventeenth century [1].

But the seasonal feasts did not exhaust the activities of the *sociétés*. Occasional events, a national triumph, a royal entry, not to speak of local *faits divers*, found them ready with appropriate celebrations [2]. The *Infanterie Dijonnaise* made a solemn function of the admission of new members [3]. And more than one *société* picked up from folk-custom the tradition of the *charivari*, constituting itself thus the somewhat arbitrary guardian of burgess morality [4]. M. Petit de Julleville analyses a curious *jeu* filled with chaff against an unfortunate M. Du Tillet who underwent the penalty at Dijon in 1579 for the crime of beating his wife in the month of May [5]. At Lyon, too, *chevauchées* of a similar type seem to have been much in vogue [6].

In the fifteenth and sixteenth centuries the entertainment of the *sociétés joyeuses* was largely dramatic. We find them,

[1] Leber, ix. 261.

[2] Julleville, *Les Com.* 233, quotes a decree of the municipality of Amiens in 1450, ' Il a esté dit et declairié qu'il semble que ce sera tres grande recreacion, considéré les bonnes nouvelles que de jour en jour en disoit du Roy nostre sire, et que le ducée de Normendie est du tout reunye en sa main, de fere la feste du Prince des Sots.'

[3] Ibid. 214.

[4] Cf. ch. vii.

[5] Julleville, *Les Com.* 209.

[6] Leber, ix. 150, reprints the *Recueil de la Chevauchée faicte en la Ville de Lyon le dix septiesme de novembre*, 1578. Another Lyon *Recueil* dates from 1566. Cf. Julleville, *Les Com.* 234 (Amiens), 243 (Lyon), 248 (Rouen).

as indeed we find the participants in the strictly clerical feasts of Fools[1] and of Boys[2], during the same period, occupied with the performance both of miracles and of the various forms of contemporary comedy known as farces, moralities, *sotties* and *sermons joyeux*[3]. Of their share in the miracles the next volume may speak[4] : their relations to the development of comedy require a word or two here. That normal fifteenth-century comedy, that of the farce and the morality, in any way had its origin in the Feast of Fools, whether clerical or lay, can hardly be admitted. It almost certainly arose out of the minstrel tradition, and when already a full-blown art was adapted by the *fous*, as by other groups of amateur performers, from minstrelsy. With the special forms of the *sottie* and the *sermon joyeux* it is otherwise. These may reasonably be regarded as the definite contribution of

[1] Cf. chs. xiii, xiv. The *theatrales ludi* of Pope Innocent III's decree in 1207 probably refers only to the burlesque 'offices' of the feasts condemned ; and even the terms used by the Theological Faculty in 1445—*spectacula, ludi theatrales, personagiorum ludi*—might mean no more, for at Troyes in the previous year the '*jeu du sacre de leur arcevesque*' was called a 'jeu de personnages,' and this might have been a mere burlesque consecration. However, 'jeu de personnages' generally implies something distinctly dramatic (cf. ch. xxiv). It recurs in the Sens order of 1511. The Beauvais *Daniel* was possibly played at a Feast of Fools: at Tours a *Prophetae* and a *miraculum* appear under similar conditions; at Autun a *Herod* gave a name to the *dominus festi*. At Laon there were 'mysteries' in 1464 and 1465; by 1531 these had given way to 'comedies.' Farces were played at Tournai in 1498 and comedies at Lille in 1526.

[2] Cf. ch. xv. The Toul *Statutes* of 1497 mention the playing of miracles, morals, and farces. At Laon the playing of a comedy had been dropped before 1546.

[3] Julleville, *Rép. Com.* 321 (*Cata-*

logue des représentations), and elsewhere, gives many examples. The following decree (†1327) of Dominique Grima, bishop of Pamiers, is quoted by L. Delisle, in *Romania*, xxii. 274 : 'Dampnamus autem et anathematizamus ludum cenicum vocatum *Centum Drudorum*, vulgariter *Cent Drutz*, actenus observatum in nostra dyocesi, et specialiter in nostra civitate Appamiensi et villa de Fuxo, per clericos et laycos interdum magni status ; in quo ludo effigiabantur prelati et religiosi graduum et ordinum diversorum, facientes processionem cum candelis de cepo, et vexilis in quibus depicta erant membra pudibunda hominis et mulieris. Induebant etiam confratres illius ludi masculos iuvenes habitu muliebri et deducebant eos processionaliter ad quendam quem vocabant priorem dicti ludi, cum carminibus inhonestissima verba continentes . . .' The *confrates* and the *prior* here look like a *société joyeuse*, but the 'ludus cenicus' was probably less a regular play than a dramatized bit of folk-ritual, like the Troyes *Sacre de l'arcevesque* and the *Charivaris*. The change of sex-costume is to be noted.

[4] Cf. ch. xx.

the Feast of Fools to the types of comedy. The very name of the *sermon joyeux*, indeed, sufficiently declares its derivation. It is parody of a class, the humour of which would particularly appeal to revelling clerks: it finds its place in the general burlesque of divine worship, which is the special note of the feast [1]. The character of the *sotties*, again, does not leave their origin doubtful ; they are, on the face of them, farces in which the actors are *sots* or *fous*. Historically, we know that some at least of the extant *sotties* were played by *sociétés joyeuses* at Paris, Geneva and elsewhere ; and the analysis of their contents lays bare the ruling idea as precisely that expressed in the motto of the *Infanterie Dijonnaise*— ' *Stultorum numerus est infinitus.*' It is their humour and their mode of satire to represent the whole world, from king to clown, as wearing the cap and bells, and obeying the lordship of folly. French writers have aptly compared them to the modern dramatic type known as the *revue* [2]. The germ of the *sottie* is to be found as early as the thirteenth century in the work of that Adan de la Hale, whose anticipation of at least one other form of fifteenth-century drama has called for comment [3]. Adan's *Jeu de la Feuillée* seems to have been played before the *puy* of Arras, perhaps, as the name suggests, in the *tonnelle* of a garden, on the eve of the first of May, 1262. It is composed of various elements: the later scenes are a *féerie* in which the author draws upon Hellequin and his *mesnie* and the three *fées*, Morgue, Maglore and Arsile, of peasant tradition. But there is an episode which is sheer *sottie*. The relics of St. Acaire, warranted to cure folly, are

[1] Julleville, *Les Com.* 33; *La Com.* 73 'Le premier qui s'avisa, pendant l'ivresse bruyante de la fête, de monter dans la chaire chrétienne et d'y parodier le prédicateur dans une improvisation burlesque, débita le premier sermon joyeux. C'est à l'origine, comme nous avons dit, "une indécente plaisanterie de sacristain en goguette."' A list of extant *sermons joyeux* is given by Julleville, *Rép. Com.* 259.

[2] Julleville, *Les Com.* 32, 145;

La Com. 68 ; E. Picot, *La Sottie en France* (*Romania*, vii. 236). Jean Bouchet, *Épîtres morales et familières du Traverseur* (1545), i. 32, thus defines the *Sottie* :
'En France elle a de *sotie* le nom,
Parce que sotz des gens de grand renom
Et des petits jouent les grands follies
Sur eschaffaux en parolles polies.'
[3] Cf. ch. viii.

tried upon the good burgesses of Arras one by one; and there
is a genuine fool or *dervés*, who, like his lineal descendant
Touchstone, 'uses his folly as a stalking-horse to shoot his
wit' in showers of arrowy satire upon mankind[1]. Of the
later and regular *sotties*, the most famous are those written
by Pierre Gringoire for the *Enfants-sans-Souci* of Paris. In
these, notably the *Jeu du Prince des Sotz*, and in others by less
famous writers, the conception of the all-embracing reign of
folly finds constant and various expression[2]. Outside France
some reflection of the *sottie* is to be found in the *Fastnachtspiele* or Shrovetide plays of Nuremberg and other German
towns. These were performed mainly, but not invariably, at
Shrovetide, by students or artisans, not necessarily organized
into regular guilds. They are dramatically of the crudest,
being little more than processions of figures, each of whom in
turn sings his couplets. But in several examples these figures
are a string of *Narren*, and the matter of the verses is in the
satirical vein of the *sotties*[3]. The *Fastnachtspiele* are probably
to be traced, not so much to the Feast of Fools proper, as to
the spring sword-dances in which, as we have seen, a *Narr* or
'fool' is *de rigueur*. They share, however, with the *sotties*
their fundamental idea of the universal domination of folly.

The extension of this idea may indeed be traced somewhat
widely in the satirical and didactic literature of the later
Middle Ages and the Renascence. I cannot go at length into
this question here, but must content myself with referring to
Professor Herford's valuable account of the cycle, which
includes the *Speculum Stultorum* of Wireker, Lydgate's *Order*

---

[1] Creizenach, i. 395; Julleville,
Les Com. 46; *La Com.* 19; *Rép.
Com.* 20; E. Langlois, *Robin et
Marion*, 13; Guy, 337; M. Sepet,
Le Jeu de la Feuillée, in *Études
romaines dédiées à G. Paris*, 69.
The play is sometimes called *Le
Jeu d'Adam.* The text is printed in
Monmerque et Michel, *Théâtre
français au Moyen Âge*, 55, and
E. de Coussemaker, *Œuvres de
Adam de la Halle*, 297.

[2] The extant *sotties* are catalogued by Julleville, *Rép. Com.* 104,

and E. Picot, in *Romania*, vii.
249.

[3] Creizenach, i. 406; G. Gregory
Smith, *Transition Period*, 317;
Goedeke, *Deutsche Dichtung*, i. 325;
V. Michels, *Studien über die ältes-
ten deutschen Fastnachtspiele*, 101.
The latter writer inclines to con-
sider the *Narr* of these plays as
substituted by fifteenth century for
a more primitive *Teufel*. The plays
themselves are collected by A. von
Keller, *Fastnachtspiele aus dem* 15.
Jahrhundert (1853-8).

of Fools, Sebastian Brandt's *Narrenschiff* and its innumerable imitations, the *Encomium Moriae* of Erasmus, and Robert Armin the player's *Nest of Ninnies* [1].

Wireker was an Englishman, and the 'Order' founded in the *Speculum* by Brunellus, the Ass, was clearly suggested by the *sociétés joyeuses*. Traces of such *sociétés* in England are, however, rare. Some of the titles of local lords of misrule, such as the Abbot of Marrall at Shrewsbury or the Abbot of Bon-Accord at Aberdeen, so closely resemble the French nomenclature as to suggest their existence ; but the only certain example I have come across is in a very curious record from Exeter. The register of Bishop Grandisson contains under the date July 11, 1348, a mandate to the archdeacon and dean of Exeter and the rector of St. Paul's, requiring them to prohibit the proceedings of a certain 'sect of malign men' who call themselves the 'Order of Brothelyngham.' These men, says the bishop, wear a monkish habit, choose a lunatic fellow as abbot, set him up in the theatre, blow horns, and for day after day beset in a great company the streets and places of the city, capturing laity and clergy, and exacting ransom from them 'in lieu of a sacrifice.' This they call a *ludus*, but it is sheer rapine [2]. Grandisson's learned editor

---

[1] C. H. Herford, *Literary Relations of England and Germany*, 323 sqq. ; cf. G. Gregory Smith, *op. cit.* 176. On an actual pseudo-chivalric Order of Fools cf. p. 375.

[2] F. C. Hingeston - Randolph, *Register of Bishop Grandisson*, ii. 1055, *Litera pro iniqua fraternitate de Brothelyngham*. 'Ad nostrum, siquidem, non sine inquietudine gravi, pervenit auditum, quod in Civitate nostra Exonie secta quedam abhominabilis quorundam hominum malignorum, sub nomine Ordinis, quin pocius erroris, de Brothelyngham, procurante satore malorum operum, noviter insurrexit; qui, non Conventum sed conventiculam facientes evidenter illicitam et suspectam, quemdam lunaticum et delirum, ipsorum utique operibus aptissime congruentem, sibi, sub Abbatis nomine, prefecerunt, ipsumque Monachali habitu induentes ac in Theatro constitutum velut ipsorum idolum adorantes, ad flatum cornu, quod sibi statuerunt pro campana, per Civitatis eiusdem vicos et plateas, aliquibus iam elapsis diebus, cum maxima equitum et peditum multitudine commitarunt [sic]; clericos eciam laicos ceperunt eis obviam tunc prestantes, ac aliquos de ipsorum domibus extraxerunt, et invitos tam diu ausu temerario et interdum sacrilego tenuerunt, donec certas pecuniarum summas loco sacrificii, quin verius sacrilegii, extorserunt ab eisdem. Et quamvis hec videantur sub colore et velamine ludi, immo ludibrii, attemptari, furtum est, tamen, proculdubio, in eo quod ab invitis capitur et rapina.' There is no such place as Brothelyngham, but 'brethelyng' 'brethel,' 'brothel,' mean 'good-for-nothing' (*N. E. D.*, s.vv.).

thinks that this *secta* was a sect of mediaeval dissenters, but the description clearly points to a *société joyeuse*. And the recognition of the *droits* exacted as being *loco sacrificii* is to a folk-lorist most interesting.

More than one of the records which I have had occasion to quote make mention of an *habit des fous* as of a recognized and familiar type of dress. These records are not of the earliest. The celebrants of the ecclesiastical Feast of Fools wore *larvae* or masks. Laity and clergy exchanged costumes: and the wearing of women's garments by men probably represents one of the most primitive elements in the custom. But there can be little doubt as to the nature of the traditional 'habit des fous' from the fourteenth century onwards. Its most characteristic feature was that hood garnished with ears, the distribution of which to persons of importance gave such offence at Tournai in 1499. A similar hood, fitting closely over the head and cut in scollops upon the shoulders, re-appears in the *bâton*, dated 1482, of the fools in the ducal chapel of Dijon. Besides two large asses' ears, it also bears a central peak or crest [1]. The eared hood became the regular badge of the *sociétés joyeuses*. It is found on most of the seals and other devices of the *Infanterie Dijonnaise*, variously modified, and often with bells hung upon the ears and the points of the scollops [2]. It was used at Amiens [3], and at Rouen and Evreux probably gave a name to the *Cornards* [4]. Marot describes it as appropriate to a *sot de la Basoche* at Paris [5]. It belongs also to the *Narren* of Nuremberg [6], and is to be seen in innumerable figured representations of fools in miniatures, woodcuts, carvings, the Amiens *monetae*, and so forth, during the later Middle Ages and the Renascence [7].

---

[1] Du Tilliot, pl. 4.
[2] Ibid. pll. 1-12 passim.
[3] Julleville, *Les Com.* 234.
[4] Ibid. 246 ; Rigollot, lxxxiv.
[5] Marot, *Epistre du Coq en l'Asne* (ed. Jannet, i. 224 ; ed. Guiffrey, iii. 352) :

'Attachez moy une sonnette
Sur le front d'un moyne crotté,
Une aureille à chaque costé
Du capuchon de sa caboche ;
Voyla un sot de la Basoche,

Aussi bien painct qu'il est possible.'

For other Paris evidence cf. Julleville, *Les Com.* 144, 147 ; E. Picot, in *Romania*, vii. 242.

[6] Picot, in *Romania*, vii. 245 ; Keller, *Fastnachtspiele*, 258.

[7] Rigollot, 73, 166, and passim ; Strutt, 222 ; Douce, 516 ; Julleville, *Les Com.* 147. There are many examples in the literature referred to on p. 382.

Such a close-fitting hood was of course common wear in the
fourteenth century. It is said to be of Gaulish origin, and
to be retained in the religious cowl. The *differentiae* of the
hood of a 'fool' from another must be sought in the grotesque
appendages of ears, crest and bells [1]. Already an eared hood,
exactly like that of the 'fools,' distinguishes a mask, perhaps
Gaulish, of the Roman period [2]. It may therefore have been
adopted in the *Kalendae* at an early date. But it is not,
I think, unfair to assume that it was originally a sophistication
of a more primitive headdress, namely the actual head of
a sacrificial animal worn by the worshipper at the New Year
festival. That the ears are asses' ears explains itself in view
of the prominence of that animal at the Feast of Fools. It
must be added that the central crest is developed in some
of the examples figured by Douce into the head and neck,
in others into the comb only, of a cock [3]. With the hood, in
most of the examples quoted above, goes the *marotte*. This
is a kind of doll carried by the 'fool,' and presents a replica of
his own head and shoulders with their hood upon the end
of a short staff. In some of Douce's figures the *marotte* is
replaced or supplemented by some other form of bauble, such
as a bladder on a stick, stuffed into various shapes, or hollow
and containing peas [4]. Naturally the colours of the 'fools' were
gay and strikingly contrasted. Those of the Paris *Enfants-
sans-Souci* were yellow and green [5]. But it may be doubted
whether these colours were invariable, or whether there is
much in the symbolical significance attributed to them by

---

[1] Rigollot, lxxix.

[2] F. de Ficoroni, *Le Maschere
sceniche e le Figure comiche d'
antichi Romani*, 186, pl. 72.

[3] Dieterich, 237, traces the coxcomb to Italian comedy of the Atellane type; cf. ch. xxiii, on ' Punch.'

[4] Douce, pl. 3 ; cf. Leber, in
Rigollot, lxi. 164, quoting the pro-
verb 'pisa in utre perstrepentia'
and a statement of Savaron, *Traité
contre les Masques* (1611), that at
Clermont in Auvergne men disguised
' en Fols' ran through the streets at
Christmas 'tenant des masses à la
main, farcies de paille ou de bourre,

en forme de braiette, frappant
hommes et femmes.' I suppose the
bauble, like the hood, was originally
part of the sacrificial *exuviae* and
the *marotte* a sophistication of it.

[5] Julleville, *Les Com.* 147, quoting
*Réponse d'Angoulevent à l'archi-
poète des pois pillez* (1603):

' Qu'après, dedans le char de la
    troupe idiotte
Ayant pour sceptre en main une
    peinte marotte,
Tu sois parmi Paris pourmené
    doucement,
Vestu de jaune et vert en ton
    accoustrement.'

certain writers[1]. The *Infanterie Dijonnaise* in fact added red to their yellow and green[2]. The colours of the Cléves Order of Fools were red and yellow[3].

It will not have escaped notice that the costume just described, the parti-coloured garments, the hood with its ears, bells and coxcomb, and the *marotte*, is precisely that assigned by the custom of the stage to the fools who appear as *dramatis personae* in several of Shakespeare's plays[4]. Yet these fools have nothing to do with *sociétés joyeuses* or the Feast of Fools ; they represent the ' set,' ' allowed,' or ' all-licensed ' fool[5], the domestic jester of royal courts and noble houses. The great have always found pleasure in that near neighbourhood of folly which meaner men vainly attempt to shun. Rome shared the *stultus* with her eastern subjects and her barbarian invaders alike; and the 'natural,' genuine or assumed, was, like his fellow the dwarf, an institution in every mediaeval and Renascence palace[6]. The question arises how far the *habit* of the *sociétés joyeuses* was also that of the domestic fool. In France there is some evidence that from the end of the fourteenth century it was occasionally at least taken as such. The tomb in Saint Maurice's at Senlis of Thévenin de St. Leger, fool to Charles V, who died in 1374, represents him in a crested hood with a *marotte*[7]. Rabelais describes the fool

[1] Leber, in Rigollot, lxviii.
[2] Julleville, *Les Com.* 195, 203.
[3] Du Tilliot, 84.
[4] See e. g. the plate (p. 9) and description (p. xii) of Touchstone in Miss E. Fogerty's ' costume edition' of *As You Like It*.
[5] *Twelfth Night*, i. 5. 95, 101 ; *Lear*, i. 4. 220.
[6] To the English data given by the historians of court fools may be added *Wardrobe Account* 28 *Edw. I*, 1299-1300 (Soc. Antiq.), 166 ' Martinetto de Vasconia fatuo ludenti coram dicto domino Edwardo,' and *Lib. de Comp. Garderobae*, temp. Edw. II (*MS. Cotton, Nero*, C. viii. ff. 83, 85), quoted by Strutt, 194 'twenty shillings paid to Robert le Foll to buy a *boclarium ad ludendum* before the king.' Robert le Foll had also a *garcio*.

For fools at the Scottish court of James IV cf. *L. H. T.* i. cxcix, &c.; iii. xcii, &c. ; and on Thomas, the fool of Durham Priory in the fourteenth century, Appendix E (1).

[7] Rigollot, 74 ; Moreau, 180, quoting a (clearly misdated) letter of Charles V to the municipality of Troyes, which requires the provision of a new ' fol de cour ' by that city as a royal *droit*. The king's eulogy of his fool is rather touching : 'savoir faisons à leurs dessus dictes seigneuries que Thévenin nostre fol de cour vient de trespasser de celluy monde dedans l'aultre. Le Seigneur Dieu veuille avoir en gré l'âme de luy qui oncques ne faillit en sa charge et fonction emprès nostre royale Seigneurie et mesmement ne voult si trespasser sans faire quel-

Seigni Joan, apparently intended for a court fool, as having a *marotte* and ears to his hood. On the other hand, he makes Panurge present Triboulet, the fool of Louis XII, with a sword of gilt wood and a bladder [1]. A little later Jean Passerat speaks of the hood, green and yellow, with bells, of another royal fool [2]. In the seventeenth century the green and yellow and an eared hood formed part of the fool's dress which the duke of Nevers imposed upon a peccant treasurer [3]. But in France the influence of the *sociétés joyeuses* was directly present. I do not find that the data quoted by Douce quite bear out his transference of the regular French *habit de fou* to England. Hoods were certainly required as part of the costume for 'fools,' 'disards,' or 'vices' in the court revels of 1551–2, together with 'longe' coats of various gay colours [4]; but these were for masks, and on ordinary occasions the fools of the king and the nobles seem to have worn the usual dress of a courtier or servant [5]. Like Triboulet, they often bore, as part of this, a gilded wooden sword [6]. A coxcomb, however, seems to have been a recognized fool ensign [7], and once, in a tale, the complete *habit* is described [8]. Other fool costumes include a long petticoat [9], the more primitive calf-skin [10],

que joyeuseté et gentille farce de son métier.'
[1] Moreau, 177, 197.
[2] Quoted by Julleville, *Les Com.* 148 :
'L'un [le poète] a la teste verte ; et l'autre va couvert
D'un joli chapperon, fait de jaune et de vert ;
L'un s'amuse aux grelots, et l'autre à des sornettes.'
[3] *Requestes présentées au Roy . . . par le S. de Vertau* (1605), quoted by Leber, in Rigollot, lxvi ; Julleville, *Les Com.* 147 'un habit . . . qui estoit faict par bandes de serge, moitié de couleur verte et l'autre de jaune ; et là où il y avoit des bandes jaunes, il y avoit des passemens verts, et sur les vertes des passemens jaunes . . . et un bonnet aussi moitié de jaune et vert, avec des oreilles, &c.'
[4] Kempe, *Loseley MSS*, 35, 47, 85.
[5] Douce, 512 ; Doran, 293.

Lodge, *Wits Miserie* (1599), describes a fool as 'in person comely, in apparell courtly.' The Durham accounts (Appendix E (1)) contain several entries of cloth and shoes purchased for the fool Thomas, but there is no mention of a hood.
[6] Douce, 510.
[7] Ibid. 510, 511. Hence the common derived sense of 'coxcomb' for a foolish, vain fellow.
[8] Douce, 509, quoting 'the second tale of the priests of Peblis,' which, for all I know, may be a translation, 'a man who counterfeits a fool is described "with club and bel and partie cote with eiris"; but it afterwards appears that he had both a club and a bauble.'
[9] Douce, 510.
[10] Douce, 512, quoting *Gesta Grayorum*, 'the scribe claims the manor of Noverinte, by providing sheepskins and calves-skins to wrappe his highness wards and idiotts in';

and a fox-tail hanging from the back[1]. The two latter seem
to bring us back to the sacrificial *exuviae*, and form a link
between the court fool and the grotesque ' fool,' or ' Captain
Cauf Tail' of the morris dances and other village revels.
Whatever may have been the case with the domestic
fool of history, it is not improbable that the tradition of the
stage rightly interprets the intention of Shakespeare. The
actual texts are not very decisive. The point that is most
clear is that the fool wears a ' motley' or ' patched ' coat[2].
The fool in *Lear* has a ' coxcomb[3]'; Monsieur Lavache in
All's Well a ' bauble,' not of course necessarily a *marotte*[4];
Touchstone, in *As You Like It*, is a courtier and has a sword[5].
The sword may perhaps be inherited from the 'vice' of the
later moralities[6]; and, in other respects, it is possible that
Shakespeare took his conception of the fool less from contemporary custom, for indeed we hear of no fool at Elizabeth's
court, than from the abundant fool-literature, continental and
English, above described. The earliest of his fools, Feste in
Twelfth Night, quotes Rabelais, in whose work, as we have
just seen, the fool Triboulet figures[7]. It is noticeable that
the appearance of fools as important *dramatis personae* in the
plays apparently coincides with the substitution for William
Kempe as ' comic lead ' in the Lord Chamberlain's company
of Robert Armin[8], whose own *Nest of Ninnies* abounds in
reminiscences of the fool-literature[9]. But whatever outward

cf. *King John*, iii. 1. 129 'And
hang a calf's-skin on those recreant
limbs.'
[1] Douce, 511.
[2] *Twelfth Night*, i. 5. 63 ; *As
You Like It*, ii. 7. 13, 43 ; *King
Lear*, i. 4. 160; *Midsummer Night's
Dream*, iv. 1. 215. But the 'long
motley coat guarded with yellow'
of *Hen. VIII*, prol. 16, does not
quite correspond to anything in the
' habit de fou.'
[3] *King Lear*, i. 4. 106. Cf.
Taming of the Shrew, ii. 1. 226
' What is your crest? a coxcomb ? '
[4] *All's Well that Ends Well*, iv.
5. 32. There are *double entendre's*
here and in the allusion to the
' bauble' of a ' natural' in *Romeo*

and Juliet, ii. 4. 97, which suggest
less a ' marotte ' than a bauble of
the bladder type ; cf. p. 197.
[5] *As You Like It*, ii. 4. 47.
[6] Cf. ch. xxv.
[7] *Twelfth Night*, ii. 3. 22.
[8] Fools appear in *As You Like
It* (†1599), *All's Well that Ends
Well* (†1601), *Twelfth Night*
(†1601), *King Lear* (†1605) ; cf.
the allusion to Yorick, the king's
jester in *Hamlet*, v. 1. 198 (†1603).
Kempe seems to have left the Shake-
spearian company in 1598 or 1599.
[9] According to Fleay, *Biog.
Chron.* i. 25, Armin's *Nest of Ninnies*, of 1608 (ed. Shakes. Soc.), is
a revision of his *Fool upon Fool* of
1605.

appearance Shakespeare intended his fools to bear, there can be no doubt that in their dramatic use as vehicles of general social satire they very closely recall the manner of the *sotties*. Touchstone is the type : ' He uses his folly like a stalking-horse, and under the presentation of that he shoots his wit [1].'

[1] *As You Like It*, v. 4. III. Cf. Lionel Johnson, *The Fools of Shakespeare*, in *Noctes Shakespearianae* (Winchester Sh. Soc.) ; J. Thümmel, *Ueber Sh.'s Narren* (*Sh.-Jahrbuch*, ix. 87).

CHAPTER XVII

MASKS AND MISRULE

[*Bibliographical Note.*—On the history of the English Masque A. Soergel, *Die englischen Maskenspiele* (1882); H. A. Evans, *English Masques* (1897); J. A. Symonds, *Shakespeare's Predecessors*, ch. ix; A. W. Ward, *English Dramatic Literature*, passim; W. W. Greg, *A List of Masques, Pageants, &c.* (1902), may be consulted. Much of the material used by these writers is in Collier, *H. E. D. P.* vol. i, and P. Cunningham, *Extracts from the Accounts of the Revels at Court* (Shakespeare Soc. 1842). For the early Tudor period E. Hall's *History of the Union of Lancaster and York* (1548) and the Revels Accounts in J. S. Brewer and J. Gairdner, *Letters and Papers of the Reign of Henry VIII*, vols. ii, iii, are detailed and valuable. R. Brotanek's very full *Die englischen Maskenspiele* (1902) only reached me when this chapter was in type.]

ALREADY in Saxon England Christmas was becoming a season of secular merry-making as well as of religious devotion[1]. Under the post-Conquest kings this tendency was stimulated by the fixed habit of the court. William the Bastard, like Charlemagne before him, chose the solemn day for his coronation; and from his reign Christmas takes rank, with Easter, Whitsuntide, and, at a much later date, St. George's day, as one of the great courtly festivals of the year. The *Anglo-Saxon Chronicle* is at the pains to record the place of its celebration, twelvemonth after twelvemonth[2]. Among the many forgotten Christmassings of mediaeval kings, history lays a finger on a few of special note: that at which Richard II, with characteristic extravagance and the consumption of '200 tunns of wine and 2,000 oxen with their appurtenances,' entertained the papal legate in 1398; and that, more truly royal, at which Henry V, besieging Rouen in 1418,

---

[1] Tille, *Y. and C.* 162; Sandys, 20. At Christmas, 1065, Edward the Confessor 'curiam tenuit' at London, and dedicated Westminster Abbey on Innocents' day (Florence of Worcester, *Chronicle*, ed. Thorpe, i. 224).

[2] Tille, *Y. and C.* 160; Ramsay, *F. of E.* ii. 43.

'refreshed all the poore people with vittels to their great comfort and his high praise [1].' The Tudors were not behindhand with any opportunity for pageantry and display, nor does the vogue of Christmas throughout the length and breadth of ' merrie England' need demonstration [2]. The Puritans girded at it, as they did at May games, and the rest of the delightful circumstance of life, until in 1644 an ordinance of the Long Parliament required the festival to give place to a monthly fast with the day fixed for which it happened to coincide [3].

The entertainment of a mediaeval Christmas was diverse. There was the banquet. The Boy Bishop came to court. Carols were sung. New Year gifts were exchanged. *Hastiludia*—jousts or tournaments—were popular and splendid. Minstrels and jugglers made music and mirth. A succession of gaieties filled the Twelve nights from the Nativity to the Epiphany, or even the wider space from St. Thomas's day to Candlemas. It is, however, in the custom of masquing that I find the most direct legacy to Christmas of the Kalends celebrations in their *bourgeois* forms. *Larvae* or masks are prominent in the records and prohibitions of the Feast of Fools from the decretal of Innocent III in 1207 to the letter of the Paris theologians in 1445 [4]. I take them as being, like the characteristic hood of the ' fool,' sophistications of the *capita pecudum*, the sacrificial *exuviae* worn by the rout of worshippers at the *Kalendae*. Precisely such *larvae*, under another name, confront us in the detailed records of two fourteenth-century Christmasses. Amongst the documents of the Royal Wardrobe for the reign of Edward III are lists of stuffs issued for

[1] Sandys, 23; Ashton, 9.
[2] Sandys, 53; Ashton, 14; Drake, 94.
[3] Ashton, 26; Stubbes, i. 173. Cf. Vaughan's *Poems* (*Muses Library*, i. 107):
' Alas, my God! Thy birth now here
Must not be number'd in the year.'
[4] Cf. ch. xiii. There is much learning on the use of masks in seasonal festivals in C. Noirot, *Traité de l'origine des masques* (1609, reprinted in Leber, ix. 5);

Savaron, *Traité contre les masques* (1611); J. G. Drechssler, *de larvis natalitiis* (1683); C. H. de Berger, *Commentatio de personis vulgo larvis seu mascheratis* (1723); Pfannenschmidt, 617; Fr. Back, *de Graecorum caeremoniis in quibus homines deorum vice fungebantur* (1883); W. H. Dall, *On masks, labrets and certain aboriginal customs* (*Third Annual Report of American Bureau of Ethnology*, 1884, p. 73); Frazer, *Pausanias*, iv. 239.

the *ludi domini regis* in 1347-8 and 1348-9 [1]. For the Christmas of 1347, held at Guildford, were required a number of 'viseres' in the likeness of men, women, and angels, curiously designed 'crestes,' and other costumes representing dragons, peacocks, and swans [2]. The Christmas of 1348 held at Ottford and the following Epiphany at Merton yield similar entries [3]. What were these 'viseres' used for? The term *ludi* must not be pressed. It appears to be distinct from *hastiludia*, which comes frequently in the same documents, although in the *hastiludia* also 'viseres' were used [4]. But it

---

[1] *Archaeologia*, xxxi, 37, 43, 44, 120, 122.

[2] 'Et ad faciendum ludos domini Regis ad festum Natalis domini celebratum apud Guldefordum anno Regis xxj°, in quo expendebantur iiij. iiij. tunicae de bokeram diversorum colorum, xlij viseres diversorum similitudinum (*specified as* xiiij similitudines facierum mulierum, xiiij similitudines facierum hominum cum barbis, xiiij similitudines capitum angelorum de argento) xxviij crestes (*specified as* xiiij crestes cum tibiis reversatis et calciatis, xiiij crestes cum montibus et cuniculis), xiiij clocae depictae, xiiij capita draconum, xiiij tunicae albae, xiiij capita pavonum cum alis, xiiij tunicae depictae cum oculis pavonum, xiiij capita cygnorum cum suis alis, xiiij tunicae de tela linea depictae, xiiij tunicae depictae cum stellis de auro et argento vapulatis.' The performers seem to have made six groups of fourteen each, representing respectively men, women, angels, dragons, peacocks, and swans. A notion of their appearance is given by the cuts from miniatures († 1343) in Strutt, 160.

[3] 'Et ad faciendum ludos Regis ad festum Natalis domini anno Regis xxij^do celebratum apud Ottefordum ubi expendebantur viseres videlicet xij capita hominum et desuper tot capita leonum, xij capita hominum et tot capita elephantum, xij capita hominum cum alis vespertilionum, xij capita de wodewose

[cf. p. 185], xvij capita virginum, xiiij supertunicae de worsted rubro guttatae cum auro et lineatae et reversatae et totidem tunicae de worsted viridi . . . Et ad faciendum ludos Regis in festo Epiphaniae domini celebrato apud Mertonum ubi expendebantur xiij visers cum capitibus draconum et xiij visers cum capitibus hominum habentibus diademata, x c^r tepies de bokeram nigro et tela linea Anglica.'

[4] *Archaeologia*, xxxi. 29, 30, 118. The element of semi-dramatic *spectacle* was already getting into the fourteenth-century tournament. In 1331 Edward III and his court rode to the lists in Cheap, 'omnes splendido apparatu vestiti et ad similitudinem Tartarorum larvati' (*Annales Paulini* in *Chron. Edw. I and II*, R. S. i. 354). In 1375 'rood dame Alice Perrers, as lady of the sune, fro the tour of London thorugh Chepe; and alwey a lady ledynge a lordys brydell. And thanne begun the grete justes in Smythefeld' (*London Chronicle*, 70). These ridings closely resemble the 'mummings' proper. But they were a prelude to *hastiludia*, which from the fourteenth to the sixteenth century constantly grew less actual and more mimetic. In 1343 'fuerunt pulchra hastiludia in Smethfield, ubi papa et duodecim cardinales per tres dies contra quoscumque tirocinium habuerunt' (Murimuth, *Continuatio Chronicarum*, R. S. 146). And so on, through the jousts of Pallas and Diana at the coronation of Henry VIII (Hall, 511)

does not necessarily imply anything dramatic, and the analogies suggest that it is a wide generic term, roughly equivalent to 'disports,' or to the 'revels' of the Tudor vocabulary[1]. It recurs in 1388 when the Wardrobe provided linen coifs for twenty-one counterfeit men of the law in the *ludus regis*[2]. The sets of costumes supplied for all these *ludi* would most naturally be used by groups of performers in something of the nature of a dance; and they point to some primitive form of masque, such as Froissart describes in contemporary France[3], the precursor of the long line of development which, traceable from the end of the following century, culminates in the glories of Ben Jonson. The vernacular name for such a *ludus* in the fourteenth century was 'mumming' or 'disguising[4].' Orders of the city of London in 1334, 1393, and 1405 forbid a practice of going about the streets at Christmas *ove visere ne faux visage*, and entering the houses of citizens to play at dice

to the regular Elizabethan 'Barriers,' such as the siege of the 'Fortress of Perfect Beauty' by the 'Four Foster Children of Desire,' in which Sidney took part in 1581.

[1] This seems to be clearly the sense of the *ludi Domini Prioris* in the accounts of Durham Priory (cf. Appendix E). The Scottish Exchequer Rolls between 1446 and 1478 contain such entries as 'iocis et ludis,' 'ludis et interludiis,' 'ioculancium et ludencium,' 'ludos et disportus suos,' where all the terms used, except 'interludiis' (cf.ch.xxiv), appear to be more or less equivalent (*Accounts of the Treasurer of Scotland*, i. ccxxxix). The *Liber Niger* of Edward IV declares that in the *Domus* of Henry I were allowed 'ludi honesti,' such as military sports 'cum ceterorum iocorum diversitate' (*Household Ordinances*, 18). 'Ioca' is here exactly the French 'jeux.' Polydore Vergil, *Hist. Anglica* (ed. Thysius), 772, says of the weddings of the children of Henry VII 'utriusque puellae nuptiae omnium generum ludis factae.' For 'disports' cf. Hall, 774, 'enterludes... maskes and disportes,' and *Paston Letters*, iii. 314, where Lady Morley is said to have ordered in 1476 that on account

of her husband's death there should be at Christmas 'non dysgysyngs, ner harpyng, ner lutyng, ner syngyn, ner non lowde dysports, but pleyng at the tabyllys, and schesse, and cards. Sweche dysports sche gave her folkys leve to play, and non odyr.' I find the first use of 'revels' in the Household Books of Henry VII for 1493 (Collier, i. 50). In 1496 the same source gives the Latin 'revelliones' (Collier, i. 46). Sir Thomas Cawarden (1545) was patented 'magister iocorum, revellorum et mascorum' (Rymer, xv. 62). Another synonym is 'triumph,' used in 1511 (Arnold, *Chronicle*, xlv). The latter means properly a royal entry or reception; cf. ch. xxiii.

[2] Warton, ii. 220, from *Compotus Magn. Garderobae*, 14 Ric. II, f. 198[b] 'pro xxi coifs de tela linea pro hominibus de lege contrafactis pro ludo regis tempore natalis domini anno xii.'

[3] Froissart (ed. Buchon, iii. 176), Bk. iv, ch. 32, describes the dance of 1393, in which Charles VI dressed in flax as a wild man was nearly burnt to death.

[4] The English *William of Palerne*, 1620 (†1350, ed. Skeat, E. E. T. S.), has 'daunces disgisi.'

therein [1]. In 1417 'mummyng' is specifically included in a similar prohibition [2]; and in a proclamation of the following year, 'mommyng' is classed with 'playes' and 'enterludes' as a variety of 'disgisyng [3].' But the disport which they denied to less dignified folk the rulers of the city retained for themselves as the traditional way of paying a visit of compliment to a great personage. A fragmentary chronicle amongst Stowe's manuscripts describes such a visit paid to Richard II at the Candlemas preceding his accession in 1377. The 'mummers' were disguised with 'vizards' to represent an emperor and a pope with their *cortèges*. They rode to Kennington, entered the hall on foot, invited the prince and the lords to dice and discreetly lost, drank and danced with the company, and so departed [4]. This is the first of several

[1] H. T. Riley, *Liber Albus* (R. S. xii), i. 644, 645, 647, 673, 676; *Memorials of London*, 193, 534, 561. For similar orders elsewhere cf. L. T. Smith, *Ricart's Calendar*, 85 (Bristol), and *Harl. MS.* 2015, f. 64 (Chester).

[2] Riley, *Memorials*, 658.

[3] Ibid. 669. It was proclaimed 'that no manere persone, of what astate, degre, or condicioun that euere he be, duryng this holy tyme of Cristemes be so hardy in eny wyse to walk by nyght in any manere mommyng, pleyes, enterludes, or eny other disgisynges with eny feynyd berdis, peyntid visers,diffourmyd or colourid visages in eny wyse ... outake that hit be leful to eche persone for to be honestly mery as he can, with in his owne hous dwellyng.'

[4] Stowe, *Survey* (ed. Thoms), 37, from a fragment of an English chronicle, in a sixteenth-century hand, in *Harl. MS.* 247, f. 172ᵛ (cf. *Archaeologia*, xxii. 208). I print the original text, which Stowe paraphrases, introducing, e.g., the term 'maskers': 'At yᵉ same tyme yᵉ Comons of London made great sporte and solemnity to yᵉ yong prince: for upon yᵉ monday next before yᵉ purification of our lady at night and in yᵉ night were 130 men disguizedly aparailed and well mounted on horsebacke to goe on mumming to yᵉ said prince, riding from Newgate through Cheape whear many people saw them with great noyse of minstralsye,trumpets, cornets and shawmes and great plenty of waxe torches lighted and in the beginning they rid 48 after yᵉ maner of esquiers two and two together clothed in cotes and clokes of red say or sendall and their faces covered with vizards well and handsomely made: after these esquiers came 48 like knightes well arayed after yᵉ same maner: after yᵉ knightes came one excellent arrayed and well mounted as he had bene an emperor: after him some 100 yards came one nobly arayed as a pope and after him came 24 arayed like cardinals and after yᵉ cardinals came 8 or 10 arayed and with black vizardes like deuils appearing nothing amiable seeming like legates, riding through London and ouer London bridge towards Kenyton wher yᵉ yong prince made his aboad with his mother and the D. of Lancaster and yᵉ Earles of Cambridge, Hertford Warrick and Suffolk and many other lordes which were with him to hould the solemnity, and when they were come before yᵉ mansion they alighted on foot and

such mummings upon record. Some chroniclers relate that it was at a mumming that the partisans of Richard II attempted to seize Henry IV on Twelfth night in 1400 [1]. In the following year, when the Emperor Manuel of Constantinople spent Christmas with Henry at Eltham, the ' men of London maden a gret mommyng to hym of xij aldermen and there sons, for whiche they hadde gret thanke [2].' In 1414 Sir John Oldcastle and his Lollards were in their turn accused of using a mumming as a cloak of sedition [3]. Thus the London distrust of false

entered into ye haule and sone after ye prince and his mother and ye other lordes came out of ye chamber into ye haule, and ye said mummers saluted them, shewing a pair of dice upon a table to play with ye prince, which dice were subtilly made that when ye prince shold cast he shold winne and ye said players and mummers set before ye prince three jewels each after other : and first a balle of gould, then a cupp of gould, then a gould ring, ye which ye said prince wonne at thre castes as before it was appointed, and after that they set before the prince's mother, the D. of Lancaster, and ye other earles euery one a gould ringe and ye mother and ye lordes wonne them. And then ye prince caused to bring ye wyne and they dronk with great joye, commanding ye minstrels to play and ye trompets began to sound and other instruments to pipe &c. And ye prince and ye lordes dansed on ye one syde, and ye mummers on ye other a great while and then they drank and tooke their leaue and so departed toward London.' Collier, i. 26, speaks of earlier mummings recorded by Stowe in 1236 and 1298 ; but Stowe only names ' pageants ' (cf. ch. xxiii). M. Paris, *Chronica Maiora* (R. S. lvii), v. 269, mentions 'vestium transformatarum varietatem ' at the wedding of Alexander III of Scotland and Margaret of England in 1251, but this probably means ' a succession of rapidly changed robes.'

[1] *A Chronicle of London* (†1442,

ed. N. H. Nicolas or E. Tyrrell, 1827), 85 'to have sclayn the kyng ... be a mommynge'; *Incerti Scriptoris Chronicon* (before 1455, ed. J. A. Giles), 7 ' conduxerunt lusores Londoniam, ad inducendum regi praetextum gaudii et laetitiae iuxta temporis dispositionem, ludum nuncupatum Anglice Mummynge'; Capgrave, *Chronicle of England* (†1464, R. S.), 275 'undir the coloure of mummeris in Cristmasse tyme ' ; *An English Chronicle* (†1461-71, C. S.), 20 ' to make a mommyng to the king ... and in that mommyng they purposid to sle him' ; Fabian, *Chronicle*, 567 ' a dysguysynge or a mummynge.' But other chroniclers say that the outbreak was to be at a tournament, e. g. *Continuatio Eulogii* (R. S. ix), iii. 385 ; *Annales Henrici* (R. S. xxviii), 323 ' Sub simulatione natalitiorum vel hastiludiorum.' I suppose ' natalitia ' is 'Christmas games' and might cover a mumming. Hall, *Chronicle* (ed. 1809), 16, makes it 'justes.' So does Holinshed (ed. 1586), iii. 514, 516, but he knew both versions ; ' them that write how the king should have beene made awaie at a justs ; and other that testifie, how it should have been at a maske or mummerie ' ; cf. Wylie, *Henry the Fourth*, i. 93 ; Ramsay, *L. and Y.* i. 20.

[2] Stowe, *Survey* (ed. Thoms), 37, doubtless from *A Chronicle of London* (†1442, *ut supra*), 87. I do not find the mumming named in other accounts of the visit.

[3] *Gregory's Chronicle* (before

visages had its justification, and it is noteworthy that so late as 1511 an Act of Parliament forbade the visits of mummers disguised with visors to great houses on account of the disorders so caused. Even the sale of visors was made illegal[1].

So far there is nothing to point to the use of any dialogue or speeches at mummings. The only detailed account is that of 1377, and the passage which describes how the mummers 'saluted' the lords, 'shewing a pair of dice upon a table to play with the prince,' reads rather as if the whole performance were in dumb show. This is confirmed by the explanation of the term 'mummynge' given in a contemporary glossary[2]. The development of the mumming in a literary direction may very likely have been due to the multifarious activity of John Lydgate. Amongst his miscellaneous poems are preserved several which are stated by their collector Shirley to have been written for mummings or disguisings either before the king or before the lord mayor of London[3]. They all seem to belong to the reign of Henry VI and probably to the years

---

1467, in *Hist. Collections of a Citizen of London*, C. S.), 108 'the whyche Lollers hadde caste to have made a mommynge at Eltham, and undyr coloure of the mommynge to have destryte the Kynge and Hooly Chyrche.'

[1] *Acte against disguysed persons and Wearing of Visours* (3 Hen. VIII, c. 9). The preamble states that 'lately wythin this realme dyvers persons have disgysed and appareld theym, and covert theyr fayces with Vysours and other thynge in such manner that they sholde nott be knowen and divers of theym in a Companye togeder namyng them selfe Mummers have commyn to the dwellyng place of divers men of honor and other substanciall persones; and so departed unknowen.' Offenders are to be treated as 'Suspectes or Vacabundes.'

[2] The *Promptorium Parvulorum* (†1440 C. S.), ii. 348, translates 'Mummynge' by 'mussacio vel mussatus' ('murmuring' or 'keeping silence,' conn. *mutus*), and gives

a cognate word 'Mummӯn, as they that noȝt speke *Mutio*.' This is of course the ordinary sense of *mum*. But Skeat (*Etym. Dict.* s.v.) derives 'mummer' from the Dutch through Old French, and explains it by the Low German *Mumme*, a 'mask.' He adds 'The word is imitative, from the sound *mum* or *mom*, used by nurses to frighten or amuse children, at the same time pretending to cover their faces.' Whether the fourteenth-century mumming was silent or not, there is no reason to suppose that the primitive folk-procession out of which it arose was unaccompanied by dance and song; and silence is rarely, if ever (cf. p. 211) *de rigueur* in modern 'guisings.'

[3] They are in *Trin. Coll. Camb. MS.* R. iii. 20 (Shirley's; cf. E. P. Hammond, *Lydgate's Mumming at Hertford* in *Anglia*, xxii. 364), and copied by or for Stowe 'out of þe boke of John Sherley' in *B. M. Add. MS.* 29729, f. 132 (cf. E. Sieper, *Lydgate's Reson and Sensuallyte*, E. E. T. S. i. xvi).

1427-30. And they show pretty clearly the way in which verses got into the disguisings. Two of them are 'lettres' introducing mummings presented by the guilds of the mercers and the goldsmiths to lord mayor Eastfield [1]. They were doubtless read aloud in the hall. A *balade* sent to Henry and the queen mother at Eltham is of the same type [2]. Two 'devyses' for mummings at London and Windsor were probably recited by a 'presenter.' The Windsor one is of the nature of a prologue, describing a 'myracle' which the king is 'to see [3].' The London one was meant to accompany the course of the performance, and describes the various personages as they enter [4]. Still more elaborate is a set of verses used at

The Hertford verses have been printed by Miss Hammond (*loc. cit.*) and the others by Brotanek, 306. I do not find any notice of disguisings when Henry VI spent the Christmas of 1433 at Lydgate's own monastery of Bury St. Edmunds (F. A. Gasquet, *A Royal Christmas* in *The Old English Bible*, 226). Devon, *Issues of the Exchequer*, 473, notes a payment for the king's 'plays and recreations' at Christmas, 1449.

[1] 'A lettre made in wyse of balade by daun Johan, brought by a poursuyant in wyse of Mommers desguysed to fore þe Mayre of London, Eestfeld, vpon þe twelffeþe night of Cristmasse, ordeyned Ryallych by þe worthy Merciers, Citeseyns of london' and 'A lettre made in wyse of balade by ledegate daun Johan, of a mommynge, whiche þe Goldesmythes of þe Cite of London mommed in Right fresshe and costele welych desguysing to þeyre Mayre Eestfeld, vpon Candelmasse day at nyght, affter souper; brought and presented vn to þe Mayre by an heraude, cleped ffortune.' The Mercer's pursuivant is sent from Jupiter; the Goldsmiths' mummers are David and the twelve tribes. The Levites were to sing. William Eastfield was mayor 1429-30 and 1437-8. Brotanek, 306, argues that, as a second term is not alluded to, this was probably the first. Fairholt, *Lord Mayors'*

Pageants, ii. 240, prints a similar letter of Lydgate's sent to the Sheriffs at a May-day dinner.

[2] 'A balade made by daun John Lidegate at Eltham in Cristmasse for a momyng tofore þe kyng and þe Qwene.' Bacchus, Juno and Ceres send gifts 'by marchandes þat here be.' The same collections contain a balade, 'gyven vnto þᵉ Kyng Henry and to his moder the quene Kateryne sittyng at þe mete vpon the yeares day in the castell of Hertford.' Some historical allusions make 1427 a likely date (Brotanek, 305).

[3] 'Þe devyse of a momyng to fore þe kyng henry þe sixte, beinge in his Castell of wyndesore, þe fest of his crystmasse holdyng þer, made by lidegate daun John, þe munk of Bury, howe þampull and þe floure delys came first to þe Kynges of ffraunce by myrakle at Reynes.' An allusion to Henry's coming coronation in Paris fixes the date to 1429-30.

[4] 'Þe deuyse of a desguysing to fore þe gret estates of. þis lande, þane being at London, made by Lidegate daun Johan, þe Munk of Bury, of dame fortune, dame prudence, dame Rightwysnesse and dame ffortitudo. beholdeþe, for it is moral, plesaunt and notable.' A fifth dame is 'Attemperaunce.' The time is 'Cristmasse.' An elaborate pageant in which Fortune dwelt is described. A song is directed at the close. Henry V is spoken of as dead.

Hertford. The first part of these is certainly spoken by a presenter who points out the 'vpplandishe' complainants to whom he refers. But the reply is in the first person, and apparently put in the mouths of the 'wyues' themselves, while the conclusion is a judgement delivered, again probably by the presenter, in the name of the king[1].

Whether Lydgate was the author of an innovation or not, the introduction of speeches, songs, and dialogues was common enough in the fully-developed mummings. For these we must look to the sumptuous courts of the early Tudors. Lydgate died about 1451, and the Wars of the Roses did not encourage revelry. The *Paston Letters* tell how the Lady Morley forbade 'dysguysyngs' in her house at Christmas after her husband's death in 1476[2]. There were *ludi* in Scotland under James III[3]. But those of his successor, James IV, although numerous and varied[4], probably paled before the elaborate 'plays' and 'disguisings' which the contemporary account-books of Henry VII reveal[5]. Of only one 'disguising,' however, of this period is a full account preserved. It took place in Westminster Hall after the wedding of Prince Arthur with Katharine of Spain on November 18, 1501, and was 'convayed and showed in pageants proper and subtile.' There was a castle, bearing singing children and eight disguised ladies, amongst whom was one 'apparelled like unto the Princesse of Spaine,' a Ship in which came Hope and Desire as

---

[1] 'Nowe foloweth here the maner of a bille by weye of supplycation put to the kynge holdinge his noble fest of crystmasse in the castell of hartford as in dysguysinge of þe rude vpplandishe people complayninge on their wyues with the boystrus answere of ther wyues deuysed by lidgate at þe requeste of the countrowlore Brys slain at louiers.' Louviers was taken by the French in 1430 and besieged next year (Brotanek, 306). The text has marginal notes, 'demonstrando vj rusticos,'&c.

[2] Cf. p. 393. There is a disguising of 1483 in the Howard Accounts (Appendix E, vii).

[3] *L.H.T.Accounts*, i. ccxl 'Iohanni Rate, pictori, pro le mumre regis' (1465-6); ad le mumre grath' (1466-7).

[4] Ibid. i. lxxix, cxliv, ccxxxix; ii. lxxi, cx; iii. xlvi, lv, and passim, have many payments for dances at court, of which some were morris dances, with 'leg-harnis,' and also to 'madinnis,' 'gysaris,' or 'dansaris' who 'dansit' or 'playit' to the king in various parts of the country.

[5] Campbell, *Materials for a Hist. of Henry VII* (R.S.), *passim*; Collier, i. 38-64; Bentley, *Excerpta Historica*, 85-133; Leland, *Collectanea*, iii. 256.

Ambassadors, and a Mount of Love, from which issued eight
knights, and assaulted the castle. This allegorical compliment, which was set forth by 'countenance, speeches, and
demeanor,' ended, the knights and ladies danced together and
presently 'avoided.' Thereupon the royal party themselves
fell to dancing[1]. 'Pageants' are mentioned in connexion
with other disguisings of the reign, and on one occasion the
disguising was 'for a moryce[2].' Further light is thrown upon
the nature of a disguising by the regulations contained in
a contemporary book of 'Orders concerning an Earl's House.'
A disguising is to be introduced by torch-bearers and accompanied by minstrels. If there are women disguised, they are
to dance first, and then the men. Then is to come the
morris, 'if any be ordeynid.' Finally men and women are to
dance together and depart in the 'towre, or thing devised for
theim.' The whole performance is to be under the control of
a 'maister of the disguisinges' or 'revills[3].'

It is possible to distinguish a simpler and a more elaborate
type of masked entertainment, side by side, throughout the
splendid festivities of the court of Henry VIII. For the
more or less impromptu 'mumming,' the light-hearted and
riotous king had a great liking. In the first year of his reign
we find him invading the queen's chamber at Westminster 'for
a gladness to the queen's grace' in the guise of Robin Hood,
with his men 'in green coats and hose of Kentish Kendal'
and a Maid Marian[4]. The queen subsequently got left out,
but there were many similar disports throughout the reign.
One of these, in which the king and a party disguised as
shepherds broke in upon a banquet of Wolsey's, has been
immortalized by Shakespeare[5]. Such mummings were com-

---

[1] Collier, i. 58, from *Harl. MS.*
69. A word which Collier prints
'Maskers' is clearly a misprint for
'Masters,' and misleading.

[2] Ibid. i. 53. The 'morris'
provided a grotesque element,
analogous to the 'antimasque' of
Jonson's day.

[3] Ibid. i. 24, from *Fairfax MSS.*
Of this *Booke of all manner of
Orders concerning an Earle's house*

'some part is dated 16 Henry VII,
although the handwriting appears
to be that of the latter end of the
reign of Henry VIII.'

[4] Hall, 513; Brewer, ii. 1490.

[5] *Hen. VIII*, i. 4; Hall, 719;
Stowe, *Chronicle*, 845; Cavendish,
Life of Wolsey, 112; Boswell-Stone,
Shakespeare's Holinshed, 441;
R. Brown, *Venetian Papers*, iv.
3, 4.

paratively simple, and the Wardrobe was as a rule only called
upon to provide costumes and masks, although on one occasion
a lady in a 'tryke' or 'spell' wagon was drawn in [1]. But the
more formal 'disguisings' of the previous reign were also
continued and set forth with great splendour. In 1527 a
'House of Revel' called the 'Long House' was built for their
performance and decorated by Holbein [2], and there was
constant expenditure on the provision of pageants. 'The
Golldyn Arber in the Arche-yerd of Plesyer,' 'the Dangerus
Fortrees,' 'the Ryche Mount,' the Pavyllon un the Plas
Parlos,' 'the Gardyn de Esperans,' 'the Schatew Vert' [3] are
some of the names given to them, and these well suggest the
kind of allegorical spectacular entertainment, diversified with
dance and song, which the chroniclers describe.

The 'mumming' or 'disguising,' then, as it took shape at
the beginning of the sixteenth century, was a form of court
revel, in which, behind the accretions of literature and pageantry,
can be clearly discerned a nucleus of folk-custom in the entry
of the band of worshippers, with their sacrificial *exuviae*, to
bring the house good luck. The mummers are masked and
disguised folk who come into the hall uninvited and call upon
the company gathered there to dice and dance. It is not
necessary to lay stress upon the distinction between the two
terms, which are used with some indifference. When they
first make their appearance together in the London proclamation of 1418 the masked visit is a 'mumming,' and is included
with the 'enterlude' under the generic term of 'disguising.'
In the Henry VII documents 'mumming' does not occur,
and in those of Henry VIII 'mumming' and 'disguising' are
practically identical, 'disguising,' if anything, being used of
the more elaborate shows, while both are properly distinct
from 'interlude.' But I do not think that 'disguising' ever
quite lost its earlier and widest sense [4]. It must now be added

[1] Brewer, iii. 1552.
[2] Ibid. iv. 1390–3 ; Hall, 722.
[3] Ibid. ii. 1495, 1497, 1499, 1501,
1509; iii. 1558.
[4] Hall, 597, speaks of a disguising
in 1519, which apparently included
'a goodly commedy of Plautus' and

a mask. Away from court in 1543
four players were committed to the
Counter for 'unlawful disguising'
(*P. C. Acts*, i. 109, 110, 122). They
surely played interludes. It may
be further noted (i) the elaborate
disguisings of Henry VII and

that early in Henry VIII's reign a new term was introduced which ultimately supplanted both the others. The chronicler Hall relates how in 1513 'On the daie of the Epiphanie at night, the kyng with a xi other were disguised, after the maner of Italie, called a maske, a thyng not seen afore in Englande, thei were appareled in garmentes long and brode, wrought all with gold, with visers and cappes of gold & after the banket doen, these Maskers came in, with sixe gentlemen disguised in silke bearyng staffe torches, and desired the ladies to daunce, some were content, and some that knewe the fashion of it refused, because it was not a thyng commonly seen. And after thei daunced and commoned together, as the fashion of the Maske is, thei tooke their leaue and departed, and so did the Quene, and all the ladies[1].'

The good Hall is not particularly lucid in his descriptions, and historians of the mask have doubted what, beyond the name, was the exact modification introduced 'after the maner of Italie' in 1512. A recent writer on the subject, Dr. H. A. Evans, thinks that it lay in the fact that the maskers danced with the spectators, as well as amongst themselves[2]. But the mummers of 1377 already did this, although of course the custom may have grown obsolete before 1513. I am rather inclined to regard it as a matter of costume. The original Revels Account for this year—and Hall's reports of court revels are so full that he must surely have had access to some such source— mentions provision for ' 12 nobyll personages, inparylled with

---

Henry VIII, with much action and speechifying besides the dancing, are difficult to distinguish when merely described from interludes. What Hall, 518, calls in 1511 an interlude, seems from the Revels Accounts (Brewer, ii. 1495) to have been really a disguising. Hall, 641, speaks of a 'disguisyng or play' in 1522, and Cavendish, *Life of Wolsey*, i. 136, of a 'disguising or interlude' in 1527; (ii) a disguising or dance might be introduced, as *entr'acte* or otherwise, into an interlude. In 1514 an interlude 'conteyned a moresk of vj persons and ij ladys' (Collier, i. 68). In 1526

a moral play was 'set forth with straunge deuises of Maskes and Morrishes' (Hall, 719). The interlude of *The Nature of the Four Elements* (early Hen. VIII) has after the *dramatis personae* the direction, 'Also yf ye lyst ye may brynge in a dysgysynge'; cf. Soergel, 21.

[1] Hall, 526.

[2] Evans, xxi. Other not very plausible suggestions are made by Ward, i. 150; Soergel, 13. There is a good account of the Italian *mascherata* from about 1474 in Symonds, *Shakespeare's Predecessors*, 321.

blew damaske and yelow damaske long gowns and hoods with hats after the maner of maskelyng in Etaly [1].' Does not this description suggest that the 'thing not sene afore in England' was of the nature of a domino? In any case from 1513 onwards 'masks,' 'maskelers' or 'maskelings' recur frequently in the notices of the revels [2]. The early masks resembled the simpler type of 'mumming' rather than the more elaborate and spectacular 'disguising,' but by the end of the reign both of the older terms had become obsolete, and all Elizabethan court performances in which the visor and the dance played the leading parts were indifferently known as masks [3]. Outside the court, indeed, the nomenclature was more conservative, and to this day the village performers who claim the right to enter your house at Christmas call themselves 'mummers,' 'guisers' or 'geese-dancers.' Sometimes they merely dance, sing and feast with you, but in most places, as

---

[1] Brewer, ii. 1497. There is a further entry in an account of 1519 (Brewer, iii. 35) of a revel, called a 'masklyne,' after the manner of Italy.

[2] 'Maske' first appears in 1514 (Collier, i. 79 'iocorum larvatorum, vocat. Maskes, Revelles, and Disguysings'); 'masque' is not English until the seventeenth century (Evans, xiii). Skeat derives through the French masque, masquer, masquerer, and the Spanish mascara, mascarada (Ital. mascherata) from the Arabic maskharat, a buffoon or droll (root sakhira, 'he ridiculed'). The original sense would thus be 'entertainment' and that of 'face-mask' (larva, 'vizard,' 'viser') only derivative. But late Latin has already masca, talamasca in this sense; e.g. Burchardus of Worms, Coll. Decretorum (before 1024), bk. ii. c. 161 'nec larvas daemonum quas vulgo Talamascas dicunt, ibi ante se ferri consentiat'; cf. Ducange, s.v. Talamasca; Pfannenschmidt, 617, with some incorrect etymology. And the French masque is always the face-mask and never the performance; while se masquier, masquillier,

maschurer, are twelfth- to thirteenth-century words for ' blacken,' ' dirty.' I therefore prefer the derivation of Brotanek, 120, from a Germanic root represented by the M.E. maskel, 'stain'; and this has the further advantage of explaining 'maskeler,' 'maskeling,' which appear, variously spelt, in documents of †1519-26. Both terms signify the performance, and 'maskeler' the performer also (Brotanek, 122). Face-masks were de rigueur in the Mask to a late date. In 1618 John Chamberlain writes ' the gentlemen of Gray's Inn came to court with their show, for I cannot call it a masque, seeing they were not disguised, nor had vizards' (Nichols, James I, iii. 468).

[3] Ben Jonson, iii. 162, Masque of Augurs (1623) ' Disguise was the old English word for a masque, sir, before you were an implement belonging to the Revels'; ii. 476, A Tale of a Tub (1634), v. 2:
' Pan. A masque! what's that?
    Scriben. A mumming or a shew,
With vizards and fine clothes.
    Clench. A disguise, neighbour,
Is the true word.'

a former chapter has shown, they have adopted from another season of the year its characteristic rite, which in course of time has grown from folk-dance into folk-drama [1].

I now pass from the mask to another point of contact between the Feast of Fools and the Tudor revels. This was the *dominus festi*. A special officer, told off to superintend the revels, pastimes and disports of the Christmas season, is found both in the English and the Scottish court at the end of the fifteenth century. In Scotland he bore the title of Abbot of Unreason [2]; in England he was occasionally the Abbot, but more usually the Lord of Misrule. Away from court, other local designations present themselves: but Lord of Misrule or Christmas Lord are the generic titles known to contemporary literature [3]. The household accounts of Henry VII make mention of a Lord or Abbot of Misrule for nearly every Christmas in the reign [4]. Under Henry VIII a Lord was annually appointed, with one exception, until

---

[1] Cf. ch. x. Less dramatic performances are described for the 'guizards' of the Scottish Lowlands by R. Chambers, *Popular Rhymes of Scotland*, 169, for the 'mummers' of Ireland in *N. and Q.* 3rd series, viii. 495, for the 'mummers' of Yorkshire in *F. L.* iv. 162. The latter sweep the hearth, humming 'mumm-m-m.'

[2] *L. H. T. Accounts*, i. ccxl, 270, 327; ii. cx, 111, 320, 374, 430, 431; iii. 127. In 1504 is a payment 'to the barbour helit Paules hed quhen he wes hurt with the Abbot of Unresoun.' Besides the court Abbot, there was an 'Abbot of Unresone of Linlithgow' in 1501, who 'dansit to the king,' and an 'Abbot of Unresoun of the pynouris of Leith' in 1504. Such entries cease after the Scottish Act of Parliament of 1555 (cf. p. 181).

[3] Stowe, *Survey*, 37 'There was in the feast of Christmas in the King's house, wheresoever he was lodged, a Lord of Misrule or Master of Merry Disports; and the like had ye in the house of every nobleman of honour or good worship, were he

spiritual or temporal. Among the which, the Mayor of London and either of the Sheriffs had their several Lords of Misrule, ever contending, without quarrel or offence, who should make the rarest pastimes to delight the beholders. These Lords beginning their rule on Allhollons eve, continued the same til the morrow after the feast of the Purification, commonly called Candlemas-day. In all which space there were fine and subtle disguisings, masks and mummeries'; Holinshed (ed. 1587), iii. 1067 'What time [at Christmas], of old ordinarie course, there is alwaies one appointed to make sport in the court, called commonlie lord of misrule: whose office is not unknowne to such as haue beene brought up in noble mens houses, & among great house keepers which use liberall feasting in that season.' The sense of 'misrule' in this phrase is 'disorder'; cf. the 'uncivil rule' of *Twelfth Night*, ii. 3. 132.

[4] Collier, i. 48–55; Bentley, *Excerpt. Historica*, 90, 92; Leland,

1520[1]. From that date, the records are not available, but an isolated notice in 1534 gives proof of the continuance of the custom[2]. In 1521 a Lord of Misrule held sway in the separate household of the Princess Mary[3], and there is extant a letter from the Princess's council to Wolsey asking whether it were the royal pleasure that a similar appointment should be made in 1525[4]. Little information can be gleaned as to the functions of the Lord of Misrule during the first two Tudor reigns. It is clear that he was quite distinct from the officer known as the 'Master of the Revels,' in whose hands lay the preparation and oversight of disguisings or masks and similar entertainments. The Master of the Revels also makes his first appearance under Henry VII. Originally he seems to have been appointed only *pro hac vice*, from among the officials, such as the comptroller of the household, already in attendance at court[5]. This practice lasted well into the reign of Henry VIII, who was served in this capacity by such distinguished courtiers, amongst others, as Sir Henry Guildford and Sir Anthony Browne[6]. Under them the preparation of the revels and the custody of the properties were in the hands

---

Collectanea (ed. Hearne), iv. 255. The 'Lords' named are one Ringley in 1491, 1492, and 1495, and William Wynnesbury in 1508. In this year the terms 'Lordship' and 'Abbot' are both used. The 'Lord' got a fee each year of £6 13s. 4d. Also the queen (1503) gave him £1.

[1] Collier, i. 74, 76; Brewer, i. cxi. Wynnesbury was Lord in 1509, 1511 to 1515, and 1519, Richard Pole in 1516, Edmund Trevor in 1518, William Tolly in 1520. The fees gradually rise to £13 6s. 8d. and a 'rewarde' of £2. Madden, *Expenses of Princess Mary*, xxvi, enters a gift in 1520 'domino mali gubernatoris [? gubernationis] hospicii domini Regis.'

[2] Brewer, vii. 589.

[3] Madden, *op. cit.* xxviii. He was John Thurgood.

[4] Ellis, *Original Letters* (1st series), i. 270.

[5] Campbell, *Materials for Hist. of Hen. VII* (R. S.), i. 337; ii. 60,

83; Collier, i. 50; Yorke, *Hardwicke Papers*, 19. Payments are made for 'revels' or 'disguisings' to Richard Pudsey 'serjeant of the cellar,' Walter Alwyn, Peche, Jaques Haulte, 'my Lord Suff, my Lord Essex, my Lord Willm, and other,' John Atkinson, Lewes Adam, 'master Wentworth.' In 1501 Jaques Hault and William Pawne are appointed to devise disguisings and morisques for a wedding. The term 'Master of the Revels' is in none of these cases used. But in an 'Order for sitting in the King's great Chamber,' dated Dec. 31, 1494 (*Ordinances and Regulations*, Soc. Antiq. 113), it is laid down that 'if the master of revells be there, he may sit with the chaplains or with the squires or gentlemen ushers.'

[6] *Revels Accounts* (Brewer, ii. 1490; iii. 1548), s. ann. 1510, 1511, 1512, 1513, 1515, 1517, 1522; Brewer, i. 718; ii. 1441; xiv. 2. 284; Kempe, 69; Collier, i. 68.

of a permanent minor official. At first such work was done in the royal Wardrobe, but under Henry VIII it fell to a distinct 'serjeant' who was sometimes, but not always, also ' serjeant ' to the king's tents. In 1545, however, a permanent Master of the Revels was appointed in the person of Sir Thomas Cawarden, one of the gentlemen of the privy chamber [1]. Cawarden formed the Revels into a regular office with a clerk comptroller, yeoman, and clerk, and a head quarters, at first in Warwick Inn, and afterwards in the precinct of the dissolved Blackfriars, of which he obtained a grant from the king. This organization of the Revels endured in substance until after the Restoration [2]. Not unnaturally there were some jealousies and conflicts of authority between the permanent Master of the Revels and the annual Lord of Misrule, and this comes out amusingly enough from some of Cawarden's correspondence for 1551–3, preserved in the muniment room at Loseley. For the two Christmases during this period the Lordship of Misrule was held by George Ferrers, one of the authors of the *Mirrour for Magistrates* [3] ; and Cawarden seems to have put every possible difficulty in the way of the discharge of his duties. Ferrers appealed to the lords of the council, and it took half a dozen official letters, signed by the great master of the household, Mr. Secretary Cecil, and a number of other dignitaries, to induce the Master of the Revels to provide the hobby horses and fool's coat and what not, that were required [4]. Incidentally this correspondence and the account books kept

---

Guildford is several times called 'master of the revels'; so is Harry Wentworth in 1510. In 1522 Guildford is 'the hy kountrolleler.' It was the 'countrowlore' at whose request Lydgate prepared one of his disguisings (p. 398).

[1] Rymer, xv. 62 'dedimus et concessimus eidem Thomae officium Magistri Iocorum Revelorum & Mascorum omnium & singularium nostrorum vulgariter nuncupatorum Revells & Masks.' The tenure of office was to date from March 16, 1544, and the annual fee was £10.

[2] Collier, i. 79, 131, 139, 153;

Kempe, 69, 73, 93, 101 ; *Molyneux Papers* (Hist. MS. Comm., seventh Rep.), 603, 614 ; Brewer, ii. 2. 1517; xiii. 2. 100 ; xiv. 2. 159, 284 ; xvi. 603 ; Halliwell, *A Collection of Ancient Documents respecting the Office of Master of the Revels* (1870); P. Cunningham, *Extracts from the Accounts of Revels at Court* (Sh. Soc. 1842).

[3] Kempe, 19; Collier, i. 147 ; Holinshed (*ut cit. supra*, p. 403) ; W. F. Trench, *A Mirror for Magistrates, its Origin and Influence*, 66, 76.

[4] Kempe, 23. One of Ferrers' letters to Cawarden is endorsed

by Cawarden give some notion of the sort of amusement which the Lord of Misrule was expected to organize. In 1551 he made his entry into court 'out of the mone.' He had his fool ' John Smith ' in a ' vice's coote ' and a ' dissard's hoode,' a part apparently played by the famous court fool, Will Somers. He had a 'brigandyne'; he had his 'holds, prisons, and places of execuc'on, his cannypie, throne, seate, pillory, gibbet, hedding block, stocks, little ease, and other necessary incydents to his person'; he had his ' armury' and his stables with ' 13 hobby horses, whereof one with 3 heads for his person, bought of the carver for his justs and challenge at Greenwich.' The masks this year were of apes and bagpipes, of cats, of Greek worthies, and of 'medyoxes' ('double visaged, th' one syde lyke a man, th' other lyke death ')[1]. The chief difficulty with Cawarden arose out of a visit to be paid by the Lord to London on January 4. The apparel provided for his ' viij counsellors' on that occasion was so 'insufficient' that he returned it, and told Cawarden that he had ' mistaken y° persons that sholde weere them, as Sr Robt Stafford and Thom^s Wyndesor, w^h other gentlemen that stande also upon their reputacõn, and wold not be seen in London, so torche-berer lyke disgysed, for as moche as they are worthe or hope to be worthe[2].' After all it took a letter from the council to get the fresh apparel ready in time. It was ready, for Machyn's *Diary* records the advent of the Lord and his 'consell' to Tower Wharf, with a 'mores danse,' and the 'proclamasyon' made of him at the Cross in Cheap, and his visit to the mayor and the lord treasurer, 'and so to Bysshopgate, and so to Towre warff, and toke barge to Grenwyche[3].' Before the following Christmas of 1552 Ferrers was careful to send note of his schemes to Cawarden in good time[4]. This year he would come in in 'blewe' out of ' *vastum vacuum*, the great waste.' The 'serpente with sevin

---

' Ferryrs, the Lorde Myserable, by the Cunsell's aucketorryte.' Ferrers solemnly heads his communications ' Qui est et fuit,' and alludes to the king as ' our Founder.'

[1] Kempe, 85.
[2] Ibid. 28.
[3] Machyn, 13.
[4] Kempe, 32; Collier, i. 148;

W. F. Trench, *op. cit.* 21; D. N. B. s. v. *William Baldwin*; G[ulielmus] B[aldwin] *Beware the Cat* (1570, reprinted by Halliwell, 1864). In this pamphlet Baldwin tells a story heard by him at court 'the last Christmas,' where he was with ' Maister Ferrers, then maister of the King's Majesties pastimes.' The

heddes called hidra' was to be his arms, his crest a 'wholme bush' and his 'worde' *semper ferians*. Mr. Windham was to be his admiral, Sir George Howard his master of the horse, and he required six councillors, 'a divine, a philosopher, an astronomer, a poet, a phisician, a potecarie, a m^r of requests, a sivilian, a disard, John Smyth, two gentleman ushers, besides jugglers, tomblers, fooles, friers, and suche other.' Again there was a challenge with hobby horses, and again the Lord of Misrule visited London on January 6, and was met by Sergeant Vauce, Lord of Misrule to 'master Maynard the Shreyff' whom he knighted. He then proceeded to dinner with the Lord Mayor[1]. As he rode his cofferer cast gold and silver abroad, and Cawarden's accounts show that 'coynes' were made for him by a 'wyer-drawer,' after the familiar fashion of the Boy Bishops in France[2]. These accounts also give elaborate details of his dress and that of his retinue, and of a 'Triumph of Venus and Mars[3]. In the following year Edward was dead, and neither Mary nor Elizabeth seems to have revived the appointment of a Lord of Misrule at court[4].

But the reign of the Lord of Misrule extended far beyond the verge of the royal palace. He was especially in vogue at those homes of learning, the Universities and the Inns of Court, where Christmas, though a season of feasting and *ludi*, had not yet become an occasion for general 'going down.' Anthony à Wood records him in several Oxford colleges, especially in Merton and St. John's, and ascribes his downfall, justly, no doubt, in part, to the Puritans[5]. At Merton he

---

date seems fixed to 1552 by a mention of 'Maister Willott and Maister Stremer, the one his [Ferrers'] Astronomer, the other his Divine' (cf. Kempe, 34). The pamphlet was probably printed in 1553 and suppressed.

[1] Machyn, 28; Stowe, *Annals*, 608. Abraham Fleming in Holinshed (ed. 1587), copying Stowe, transfers the events of this Christmas by mistake to 1551-2.

[2] Kempe, 53; cf. p. 369.

[3] Ibid. 47.

[4] The letter from Ferrers dated in

Kempe, 37 'Saynt John's Daye, ano 1553,' clearly belongs to the Christmas of 1552. The additional garments asked for therein are in the accounts for that year (Kempe, 52).

[5] A. Wood, *Athenae Oxonienses* (ed. Bliss), iii. 480 'The custom was not only observed in that [St. John's] college, but in several other houses, particularly in Merton College, where, from the first foundation, the fellows annually elected, about St. Edmund's day, in November, a Christmas lord, or lord of misrule, styled in their registers *Rex*

bore the title of *Rex fabarum* or *Rex regni fabarum* [1]. He
was a fellow of the college, was elected on November 19, and
held office until Candlemas, when the winter festivities closed
with the *Ignis Regentium* in the hall. The names of various
Reges fabarum between 1487 and 1557 are preserved in the
college registers, and the last holder of the office elected in
the latter year was Joseph Heywood, the uncle of John Donne,
in his day a famous recusant [2]. At St. John's College
a ' Christmas Lord, or Prince of the Revells,' was chosen up
to 1577. Thirty years later, in 1607, the practice was for one
year revived, and a detailed account of this experiment was
committed to manuscript by one Griffin Higgs [3]. The Prince,
who was chosen on All Saints' day, was Thomas Tucker. He

Fabarum and *Rex Regni Fabarum*;
which custom continued until the
reformation of religion, and then,
that producing puritanism, and
puritanism presbytery, the profession of it looked upon such laudable
and ingenious customs as popish,
diabolical and antichristian'; *Hist.
and Antiq. of the Univ. of Oxford*,
ii. 136, 's. a. 1557' mentions an ora-
tion ' de ligno et foeno' made by
David de la Hyde, in praise of
' Mr. Jasper Heywood, about this
time King, or Christmas Lord, of
the said Coll. [Merton] being it
seems the last that bore that com-
mendable office. That custom hath
been as ancient for ought that I
know as the College itself, and the
election of them after this manner.
On the 19th of November, being the
vigil of S. Edmund, king and martyr, letters under seal were pre-
tended to have been brought from
some place beyond sea, for the
election of a king of Christmas, or
Misrule, sometimes called with us
of the aforesaid college, Rex Fabarum. The said letters being put
into the hands of the Bachelaur
Fellows, they brought them into the
Hall that night, and standing,
sometimes walking, round the fire,
there reading the contents of them,
would choose the senior Fellow that
had not yet borne that office,
whether he was a Doctor of Divin-

ity, Law, or Physic, and being so
elected, had power put into his
hands of punishing all misdemean-
ours done in the time of Christmas,
either by imposing exercises on the
juniors, or putting into the stocks
at the end of the Hall any of the
servants, with other punishments
that were sometimes very ridiculous.
He had always a chair provided for
him, and would sit in great state
when any speeches were spoken, or
justice to be executed, and so this
his authority would continue till
Candlemas, or much about the time
that the Ignis Regentium was celebrated in that college'; *Life and
Times* (O. H. S.), i. 423 'Fresh
nights, carolling in public halls,
Christmas sports, vanished, 1661.'
   [1] The title is borrowed from the
Twelfth - Night King; cf. p. 260.
Perhaps ' Rex de Faba ' was an
early name for the Lord of Misrule
at the English court. In 1334
Edward III made a gift to the
minstrels ' in nomine Regis Fabae'
(Strutt, 344).
   [2] G. C. Brodrick, *Memorials of
Merton College*, 46 and *passim*;
B. W. Henderson, *Merton College*,
267.
   [3] *The Christmas Prince* in 1607,
printed in *Miscellanea Antiqua
Anglicana* (1816); M. L. Lee,
*Narcissus: A Twelfth Night Merri-
ment*, xvii.

was installed on November 5, and immediately made a levy
upon past and present members of the college to meet the
necessary expenses. Amongst the subscribers was 'Mr. Laude.'
On St. Andrew's day, the Prince was publicly installed with
a dramatic 'deuise' or 'showe' called *Ara Fortunae*. The hall
was a great deal too full, a canopy fell down, and the 'fool'
broke his staff. On St. Thomas's day, proclamation was made of
the style and title of the Prince and of the officers who formed
his household[1]. He also ratified the 'Decrees and Statutes'
promulgated in 1577 by his predecessor and added some
rather pretty satire on the behaviour of spectators at college
and other revels. On Christmas day the Prince was attended
to prayers, and took the vice-president's chair in hall, where
a boar's head was brought in, and a carol sung. After supper
was an interlude, called *Saturnalia*. On St. John's day 'some
of the Prince's honest neighbours of St. Giles's presented him
with a maske or morris'; and the 'twelve daies' were brought
in with appropriate speeches. On December 29 was a Latin
tragedy of *Philomela*, and the Prince, who played Tereus,
accidentally fell. On New Year's day were the Prince's
triumphs, introduced by a 'shew' called *Time's Complaint*; and
the honest chronicler records that this performance 'in the
sight of the whole University' was 'a messe of absurdityes,'
and that 'two or three cold plaudites' much discouraged the
revellers. However, they went on with their undertaking.
On January 10 were two shews, one called *Somnium Fundatoris*, and the other *The Seven Days of the Weeke*. The
dearth in the city caused by a six weeks' frost made the President inclined to stop the revels, as in a time of 'generall wo
and calamity'; but happily a thaw came, and on January 15
the college retrieved its reputation by a most successful public

[1] The Prince's designation was
'The most magnificent and re-
nowned THOMAS by the fauour of
Fortune, Prince of Alba Fortunata,
Lord St. Iohn's, high Regent of
ye Hall, Duke of St. Giles, Mar-
quesse of Magdalens, Landgraue
of ye Groue, County Palatine of
ye Cloisters, Cheife Bailiffe of ye
Beaumonts, high Ruler of Rome,
Maister of the Mañor of Waltham,
Gouernour of Gloster-greene, Sole
Coṁaunder of all Titles, Turnea-
ments and Triumphes, Super-
intendent in all Solemnities what-
soeuer.' His seal, a crowned and
spotted dog, with the motto *Pro
aris et focis*, bears the date 1469.
Amongst his officers was a 'Mr
of ye Reuells.' His Cofferer was
Christopher Wren.

performance of a comedy *Philomathes*. *The Seven Days of the Weeke*, too, though acted in private, had been so good that the vice-chancellor was invited to see a repetition of it, and thus Sunday, January 17, was 'spent in great mirth.' On the Thursday following there was a little *contretemps*. The canons of Christ Church invited the Prince to a comedy called *Yuletide*, and in this 'many things were either ill ment by them, or ill taken by vs.' The play in fact was full of satire of 'Christmas Lords;' and it is not surprising that an apology from the dean, who was vice-chancellor that year, was required to soothe the Prince's offended feelings. Term had now begun, but the revels were renewed about Candlemas. On that day was a *Vigilate* or all-night sitting, with cards, dice, dancing, and a mask. At supper a quarrel arose. A man stabbed his fellow, and the Prince's stocks were requisitioned in deadly earnest. After supper the Prince was entertained in the president's lodging with 'a wassall called the five bells of Magdalen church.' On February 6, 'beeing egge Satterday,' some gentlemen scholars of the town brought a mask of *Penelope's Wooers* to the Prince, which, however, fell through ; and finally, on Shrove Tuesday, after a shew called *Ira seu Tumulus Fortunae*, the Prince was conducted to his private chamber in a mourning procession, and his reign ended. Even yet the store of entertainment provided was not exhausted. On the following Saturday, though it was Lent, an English tragedy of *Periander* was given, the press of spectators being so great that '4 or 500' who could not get in caused a tumult. And still there remained 'many other thinges entended,' but unperformed. There was the mask of *Penelope's Wooers*, with the *State of Telemachus* and a *Controversy of Irus and his Ragged Company*. There were an *Embassage from Lubberland*, a *Creation of White Knights of the Order of Aristotle's Well*, a *Triumph of all the Founders of Colleges in Oxford*, not to speak of a lottery 'for matters of mirth and witt' and a court leet and baron to be held by the Prince. So much energy and invention in one small college is astonishing, and it was hard that Mr. Griffin Higgs should have to complain of the treatment meted out to its entertainers by the University at large. 'Wee found ourselves,' he says, '(wee will say justly) taxed for any the least errour (though ingenious spirits would have pardoned many things, where all things were entended for their owne pleasure) but most vnjustly censured, and envied for that which was done (wee daresay) indifferently well.'

Amongst other colleges in which the Lord of Misrule was regularly or occasionally chosen, Anthony à Wood names, with somewhat vague references, New College and Magdalen[1]. To these may certainly be added Trinity, where the *Princeps Natalicius* is mentioned in an audit-book of 1559[2]. But the most singular of all the Oxford documents bearing on the subject cannot be identified with any particular college. It consists of a series of three Latin letters[3]. The first is addressed by *Gloria in excelsis* to all mortals *sub Natalicia ditione degentibus*. They are bidden keep peace during the festal season and wished pleasant headaches in the mornings. The vicegerent of *Gloria in excelsis* upon earth is an annually constituted *praelatia*, that so a longer term of office may not beget tyranny. The letter goes on to confirm the election to the kingly dignity of Robertus Grosteste[4], and enjoins obedience to him *secundum Natalicias leges*. It is *datum in aere luminoso supra Bethlemeticam regionem ubi nostra magnificentia fuit pastoribus promulgata*. The second letter is addressed to *R[obert] Regi Natalicio* and his *proceres* by *Discretio virtutum omnium parens pariter ac regina*. It is a long discourse on the value of moderation, and concludes with a declaration that a moderate *laetitia* shall rule until Candlemas, and then give way to a moderate *clerimonia*. The third is more topical and less didactic in its tone. It parodies a papal letter to a royal

---

[1] Wood, *Hist. of Oxford* (*ut supra*, p. 408), ii. 136, has the following note ' New Coll. in Cat. MSS., p. 371 ... Magd. Coll. v. Heylin's Diary, an. 1617, 1619 et 1620.'

[2] Warton, iii. 304 'pro prandio Principis Natalicii eodem tempore xiii[s]. ix[d].'

[3] H. H. Henson, *Letters relating to Oxford in the fourteenth century* in the Oxford Hist. Soc.'s *Collectanea*, i. 39. The learned editor does not give the MS. from which

he takes the letters, but the rest of his collection is from the fourteenth-century *Brit. Mus. Royal MS.* 12 D, xi.

[4] ' Quocirca festi praesentis imminenti vigilia, vos ut accepimus in loco potatorio, hora extraordinaria prout moris est, unanimiter congregati, dominum Robertum Grosteste militem in armis scolasticis scitis [Ed. satis] providum et expertum, electione concordi sustulistis ad apicem regiae dignitatis.'

sovereign. *Transaetherius, pater patrum ac totius ecclesiasticae monarchiae pontifex et minister* complains, *R. Regi Natalicio,* of certain abuses of his rule. His *stolidus senescallus, madidus marescallus* and *parliamenti grandiloquus sed nugatorius prolocutor* have *ut plura possent inferre stipendia* assaulted and imprisoned on the very night of the Nativity, *Iohannem Curtibiensem episcopum.* In defence of these proceedings the Rex has pleaded *quasdam antiquas regni tui, non dico consuetudines, sed potius corruptelas.* Transaetherius gives the peccant officials three hours in which to make submission. If they fail, they shall be excommunicated, and Iohannes de Norwico, the warden of Jericho, will have orders to debar them from that place and confine them to their rooms. The letter is *datum in vertice Montis Cancari, pontificatus nostri anni non fluxibili sed aeterno.* I think it is clear that these letters are not a mere political skit, but refer to some actual Christmas revels. The waylaying of *Iohannes Curtibiensis episcopus* to make him 'pay his footing' is exactly the sort of thing that happened at the Feast of Fools, and the *non consuetudines, sed potius corruptelas* is the very language of the decretal of 1207 [1]. But surely they are not twelfth- or early thirteenth-century revels, as they must be if 'Robertus Grosteste' is taken literally as the famous bishop of Lincoln [2]. There was no *parliamenti prolocutor,* for instance, in his day. They are fourteenth-, fifth-teenth-, or even sixteenth-century fooling, in connexion with some *Rex Natalicius* who adopted, to season his jest, the name of the great mediaeval legislator against all such *ludi.*

At Cambridge an order of the Visitors of Edward VI in 1549 forbade the appointment of a *dominus ludorum* in any college [3]. But the prohibition did not endure, and more than one unsuccessful Puritan endeavour to put down Lords of Misrule is recorded by Fuller [4]. Little, however, is known of

---

[1] Cf. p. 279.

[2] Grosseteste probably became a student at Oxford before 1196. About 1214 he became Chancellor, and it seems hardly likely, as Mr. Stevenson thinks, that he would have been *rex natalicius* as late as †1233 (F. S. Stevenson, *Robert Grosseteste,* 8, 25, 110). There

were of course no colleges †1200; if *rex,* he was *rex* at a hall. But 1200 is an early date even in the history of the Feast of Fools.

[3] Cooper, *Annals of Cambridge,* ii. 32; *Stat. Acad. Cantab.* 161.

[4] Fuller, *Good Thoughts in Worse Times* (1646), 193 'Some sixty years since, in the University of Cam-

the Cambridge Lords ; their bare existence at St. John's[1] and Christ's Colleges[2] ; and at Trinity the fact that they were called *imperatores*, a name on the invention of which one of the original fellows of the college, the astronomer John Dee, plumes himself[3]. At schools such as Winchester and Eton, the functions of Lord of Misrule were naturally supplied by the Boy Bishop. At Westminster there was a *paedonomus*, and Bryan Duppa held the office early in the seventeenth century[4].

The revels of the Inns of Court come into notice in 1422, when the *Black Book* of Lincoln's Inn opens with the announcement *Ceux sont les nouns de ceux qe fuerunt assignes de con-*

---

bridge it was solemnly debated betwixt the Heads to debarre young schollers of that liberty allowed them in Christmas, as inconsistent with the Discipline of Students. But some grave Governors mentioned the good use thereof, because thereby, in twelve days, they more discover the dispositions of Scholars than in twelve moneths before'; *Hist. of Cambridge* (ed. M. Prickett and J. Wright), 301 (s. a. 1610–11), describing a University Sermon by Wm. Ames, Fellow of Christ's, who 'had (to use his own expression) the place of a watchman for an hour in the tower of the University; and took occasion to inveigh against the liberty taken at that time, especially in such colleges who had lords of misrule, a pagan relic which (he said) as Polidore Vergil showeth, remaineth only in England.' W. Ames had, in consequence, to 'forsake his college.' Polydore Vergil, *de Inventoribus Rerum*, v. 2 (transl. Langley, f. 102ᵛ), speaks of ' the Christemass Lordes' of England.

[1] Cooper, *op. cit.* ii. 112 ; Baker, *St. John's*, ii. 573. Lords in 1545 and 1556.

[2] Ibid. ii. 111. A lord in 1566. Peile, *Christ's College*, 54, quotes payments of the time of Edward VI 'for sedge when the Christenmasse lords came at Candlemas to the Colledge with shewes'; ' for the lordes of S. Andrewes and

his company resorting to the Colledge.' These were perhaps from the city ; cf. p. 419.

[3] Dee, *Compendious Rehearsal* (*Chronicle of John of Glastonbury*, ed. T. Hearne, 502), ' in that College also (by my advice and by my endeavors, divers ways used with all the other colleges) was their Christmas Magistrate first named and confirmed an Emperor. The first was one Mr. Thomas Dun, a very goodly man of person, stature and complexion, and well learned also.' Warton, iii. 302, describes a draught of the college statutes in *Rawl. MS.* 233, in which cap. xxiv is headed ' de Praefecto Ludorum qui Imperator dicitur,' and provides for the superintendence by the Imperator of the *Spectacula* at Christmas and Candlemas. But the references to the Imperator have been struck out with a pen, and the title altered to ' de Comoediis Ludisque in natali Christi exhibendis.' This is the title of cap. xxiv as actually issued in 1560 (Mullinger, *University of Cambridge*, 579). The earlier statutes of 1552 have no such chapter.

[4] H. King, *Funeral Sermon of Bishop Duppa* (1662), 34 ' Here he had the greatest dignity which the School could afford put upon him, to be the Paedonomus at Christmas, Lord of his fellow scholars : which title was a pledge and presage that, from a Lord in jeast, he

tinuer yci le nowel [1]. They are mentioned in the *Paston Letters* in 1451 [2], and in Sir Fortescue's *De laudibus Legum Angliae* about 1463 [3]. Space compels me to be very brief in summarizing the further records for each Inn.

Lincoln's Inn had in 1430 its four revels on All Hallows' day, St. Erkenwold's (April 30), Candlemas and Midsummer day, under a ' Master of the Revels.' In 1455 appears a ' marshal,' who was a Bencher charged to keep order and prevent waste from the last week of Michaelmas to the first of Hilary term. Under him were the Master of the Revels, a butler and steward for Christmas, a constable-marshal, server, and cupbearer. In the sixteenth century the ' grand Christmassings ' were additional to the four revels, and those of Candlemas were called the ' post revels.' Christmas had its ' king.' In 1519 it was ordered that the ' king ' should sit on Christmas day, that on Innocents' day the ' King of Cokneys ' [4] should ' sytt and haue due seruice,' and that the marshal should himself sit as king on New Year's day. In 1517 some doors had been broken by reason of ' Jake Stray,' apparently a popular anti-king or pretender, and the order concludes, ' Item, that Jack Strawe and all his adherentes be from hensforth uttrely banyshed and no more to be used in Lincolles Inne.' In 1520 the Bench determine ' that the order of Christmas shall be broken up'; and from that date a ' solemn Christmas ' was only occasionally kept, by agreement with the Temples. Both Lincoln's Inn and the Middle Temple had a ' Prince,' for instance, in 1599. In 1616 the choice of a ' Lieutenant ' at Christmas was forbidden by the Bench as ' not according to the auncyant Orders and usages of the House.' In 1624 the Christmas vacation ceased to be kept. There were still ' revels ' under ' Masters of the Revels ' in Michaelmas and Hilary terms, and there are notices of disorder at Christmas in 1660 and 1662. But the last ' Prince '

should, in his riper age, become one in earnest' ; cf. J. Sargeaunt, *Annals of Westminster School*, 64.

[1] *Records of Lincoln's Inn : Black Books*, i. 1.

[2] *Paston Letters*, i. 186. The names of two gentlemen chosen stewards this year at the Middle and Inner Temples are mentioned.

[3] Fortescue, *de Laudibus*, cap. xlix.

[4] *N. E. D.* s. v. *Cockney*, supposes the word to be here used in the sense of ' cockered child,' ' mother's darling.'

of Lincoln's Inn, was probably the Prince de la Grange of 1661, who had the honour of entertaining Charles II[1].

The Inner Temple held 'grand Christmasses' as well as 'revels' on All Saints', Candlemas, and Ascension days. The details of the Christmas ceremonies have been put together from old account books by Dugdale. They began on St. Thomas's day and ended on Twelfth night. On Christmas day came in the boar's head. On St. Stephen's day a cat and a fox were hunted with nine or ten couple of hounds round the hall[2]. In the first few days of January a banquet with a play and mask was given to the other Inns of Court and Chancery. The Christmas officers included a steward, marshal, butler, constable-marshal, master of the game, lieutenant of the tower, and one or more masters of the revels. The constable-marshal was the Lord of Misrule. He held a fantastic court on St. Stephen's day[3], and came into hall 'on his mule' to devise sport on the banquetting night. In 1523 the Bench agreed not to keep Christmas, but to allow minstrels to those who chose to stay. Soon after 1554 the Masters of Revels cease to be elected[4]. Nevertheless there was a notable revel

[1] *Records of Lincoln's Inn : Black Books*, i. xxx, 181, 190 ; ii. xxvii, 191 ; iii. xxxii, 440; W. Dugdale, 246; W. Herbert, 314; J. A. Manning, *Memoirs of Rudyerd*, 16 ; J. Evelyn, *Diary* (s. ann. 1661-2). As an appendix to vol. iii of the Black Book is reprinted 'Εγκυκλο-χορεία, or *Universal Motion*, Being part of that Magnificent Entertainment by the noble Prince de la Grange, Lord Lieutenant of Lincoln's Inn. Presented to the High and Mighty Charles II' (1662). Evelyn mentions the ' solemne foolerie' of the Prince de la Grange.

[2] Cf. p. 257.

[3] 'Supper ended, the Constable-Marshall presenteth himself with Drums afore him, mounted upon a Scaffold, born by four men ; and goeth three times round about the Harthe, crying out aloud "A Lorde, a Lorde, &c."—Then he descendeth and goeth to dance, &c., & after he calleth his Court, every one by name, in this manner : " Sir Francis Flatterer, of Fowleshurst, in the county of Buckingham. Sir Randle Rackabite, of Rascall Hall, in the County of Rakehell. Sir Morgan Mumchance, of Much Monkery, in the County of Mad Mopery. Sir Bartholmew Baldbreech, of Buttocke-bury, in the County of Brekeneck ". . . . About Seaven of the Clocke in the Morning the Lord of Misrule is abroad, and if he lack any Officer or attendant, he repaireth to their Chambers, and compelleth them to attend in person upon him after Service in the Church, to breakfast, with Brawn, Mustard, and Malmsey. After Breakfast ended, his Lordship's power is in suspence, until his personal presence at night ; and then his power is most potent.'

[4] W. Dugdale, 153 ; Herbert, 205, 254 ; F. A. Inderwick, *Calendar of the I. T. Records*, i. xxxiv, 3, 75, 171, 183.

in 1561 at which Lord Robert Dudley, afterwards earl of Leicester, was constable-marshal. He took the title of 'Pala-philos, prince of Sophie,' and instituted an order of knights of Pegasus in the name of his mistress Pallas [1]. In 1594 the Inner Temple had an emperor, who sent an ambassador to the revels of Gray's Inn [2]. In 1627 the appointment of a Lord of Mis-rule led to a disturbance between the 'Temple Sparks' and the city authorities. The 'lieutenant' claimed to levy a 'droit' upon dwellers in Ram Alley and Fleet Street. The lord mayor inter-vened, an action which led to blows and the committal of the lieutenant to the counter, whence he escaped only by obtain-ing the mediation of the attorney-general, and making sub-mission [3]. A set of orders for Christmas issued by the Bench in 1632 forbade 'any going abroad out of the Circuit of this House, or without any of the Gates, by any Lord or other Gentleman, to break open any House, or Chamber; or to take anything in the name of Rent, or a distress [4].'

The Middle Temple held its 'solemn revels' and 'post revels' on All Saints and Candlemas days, and on the Saturdays between these dates; likewise its 'solemn Christ-masses [5].' An account of the Christmas of 1599 was written by Sir Benjamin Rudyerd under the title of *Noctes Templariae: or, A Briefe Chronicle of the Dark Reigne of the Bright Prince of Burning Love*. 'Sur Martino' was the Prince, and one 'Milorsius Stradilax' served as butt and buffoon to the company. A masque and barriers at court, other masques and comedies, a progress, a mock trial, a 'Sacrifice of Love,' visits to the Lord Mayor and to and from Lincoln's Inn, made up the entertainment [6]. In 1631 orders for Christmas

---

[1] G. Legh, *Accedens of Armory* (1562), describes the proceedings; cf. Dugdale, 151; Herbert, 248; Inderwick, *op. cit.* lxiv, 219. Machyn, 273, mentions the riding through London of this 'lord of mysrull' on Dec. 27.

[2] Cf. references for *Gesta Grayo-rum* in p. 417.

[3] Ashton, 155, quoting *The Reign of King Charles* (1655) 'A Lieu-tenant, which we country folk call a Lord of Misrule.' In the sixteenth

century the lieutenant was only an officer of the constable-marshal.

[4] Dugdale, 149; Herbert, 201.

[5] Dugdale, 202, 205; Herbert, 215, 231, 235.

[6] J. A. Manning, *Memoirs of Rudyerd*, 9. Carleton wrote to Chamberlain on Dec. 29, 1601, that 'Mrs. Nevill, who played her prizes, and bore the belle away in the Prince of Amour's revels, is sworn maid of honour' (*Cal. S. P. Dom. Eliz.* 1601-3, 136).

government were made by the Bench [1]. In 1635 a Cornish
gentleman, Francis Vivian, sat as Prince d'Amour. It cost
him £2,000, but after his deposition he was knighted at
Whitehall. His great day was February 24, when he entertained the Princes Palatine, Charles, and Rupert, with
Davenant's masque of the *Triumphs of the Prince d'Amour* [2].

There is no very early mention of revels at Gray's Inn, but
they were held on Saturdays between All Saints and Candlemas
about 1529, and by 1550 the solemn observation of Christmas
was occasionally used. In 1585 the Bench forbade that any
one should 'in time of Christmas, or any other time, take
upon him, or use the name, place, or commandment of *Lord*,
or any such other like [3].' Nevertheless in 1594 one of the
most famous of all the legal 'solemn Christmasses' was held
at this Inn. Mr. Henry Helmes, of Norfolk, was 'Prince of
Purpoole [4],' and he had the honour of presenting a mask
before Elizabeth. This was written by Francis Davison, and
Francis Bacon also contributed to the speeches at the revels.
But the great glory of this Christmas came to it by accident.
On Innocents' day there had been much confusion, and the
invited Templarians had retired in dudgeon. To retrieve the
evening 'a company of base and common fellows' was brought
in and performed 'a Comedy of Errors, like to Plautus his
Menaechmus [5].' In 1617 there was again a Prince of Purpoole,
on this occasion for the entertainment of Bacon himself as
Lord Chancellor [6]. Orders of 1609 and 1628 mention re-

[1] Dugdale, 191.
[2] G. Garrard to Strafford (*Strafford Letters*, i. 507); Warton, iii. 321; Ward, iii. 173.
[3] Dugdale, 285; Herbert, 333; R. J. Fletcher, *Pension Book of Gray's Inn* (1901), xxviii, xxxix, xlix, 68 and passim.
[4] His full title was 'The High and Mighty Prince Henry, Prince of Purpoole, Arch-duke of Stapulia and Bernardia, Duke of High and Nether Holborn, Marquis of St. Giles and Tottenham, Count Palatine of Bloomsbury and Clerkenwell, Great Lord of the Cantons of Islington, Kentish Town, Paddington and

Knightsbridge, Knight of the most heroical Order of the Helmet, and Sovereign of the same.'
[5] Halliwell-Phillipps, i. 122; Ward, ii. 27, 628; Sandys, 93; Spedding, *Works of Bacon*, viii. 235; S. Lee, *Life of Shakespeare*, 70; W. R. Douthwaite, *Gray's Inn*, 227; Fletcher, 107. A full description of the proceedings is in the *Gesta Grayorum* (1688), reprinted in Nichols, *Progresses of Elizabeth*, iii. 262.
[6] Douthwaite, *op. cit.* 234; Fletcher, 72, 299; Nichols, *Progresses of James I*, iii. 466. To this year belong the proceedings of 'Henry

spectively the 'twelve' and the 'twenty' days of Christmas as days of license, when caps may be doffed and cards or dice played in the hall [1]: and the duration of the Gray's Inn revels is marked by notices of Masters of the Revels as late as 1682 and even 1734 [2].

Nobles and even private gentlemen would set up a Lord of Misrule in their houses. The household regulations of the fifth earl of Northumberland include in a list of rewards usually paid about 1522, one of twenty shillings if he had an 'Abbot of Miserewll' at Christmas, and this officer, like his fellow at court, was distinct from the 'Master of the Revells' for whom provision is also made [3]. In 1556 the marquis of Winchester, then lord treasurer, had a 'lord of mysrulle' in London, who came to bid my lord mayor to dinner with 'a grett mene of musysyonars and dyssegyssyd' amongst whom 'a dullvyll shuting of fyre' and one 'lyke Deth with a dart in hand [4].' In 1634 Richard Evelyn of Wotton, high sheriff of Surrey and Sussex, issued 'Articles' appointing Owen Flood his trumpeter 'Lord of Misrule of all good Orders during the twelve dayes [5].' The custom was imitated by more than one municipal ape of gentility. The lord mayor and sheriffs of London had their Lords of Misrule until the court of common council put down the expense in 1554 [6]. Henry Rogers, mayor of Coventry, in 1517, and Richard Dutton, mayor of Chester, in 1567, entertained similar officers [7].

I have regarded the Lord of Misrule, amongst the courtly and wealthy classes of English society, as a direct offshoot from the vanished Feast of Fools. The ecclesiastical suggestion in the alternative title, more than once found, of 'Abbot

the Second,' Prince of Purpoole, printed by Nichols, *Eliz.* iii. 320, as the 'Second Part' of the *Gesta Grayorum* ; cf. Hazlitt, *Manual*, 95, 161. 'Henry the Second, Prince of Graya and Purpulia,' was a subscriber to Minsheu's *Dictionary* (1617). An earlier Prince of Purpoole is recorded in 1587 (Fletcher, 78).

[1] Dugdale, 281, 286 ; Herbert, 334, 336.

[2] Douthwaite, *op. cit.* 243, 245.
[3] Percy, *N. H. B.* 344, 346.
[4] Machyn, 125.
[5] *Archaeologia,* xviii. 333 ; Ashton, 144. Other passages showing that lords of misrule were appointed in private houses are given by Hazlitt-Brand, i. 272.
[6] Ashton, 144 ; cf. p. 407.
[7] *Hist. of Cov.* in Fordun, *Scoti-chronicon*, ed. Hearne, v. 1450 ; Morris, 353.

of Misrule,' seems to justify this way of looking at the matter. But I do not wish to press it too closely. For after all the Lord of Misrule, like the Bishop of Fools himself, is only a variant of the winter 'king' known to the folk. In some instances it is difficult to say whether it is the folk custom or the courtly custom with which you have to do. Such is the ' kyng of Crestemesse' of Norwich in 1443 [1]. Such are the Lords of Misrule whom Machyn records as riding to the city from Westminster in 1557 and Whitechapel in 1561 [2]. And there is evidence that the term was freely extended to folk 'kings' set up, not at Christmas only, but at other times in the year [3]. It was a folk and a Christmas Lord whose attempted suppression by Sir Thomas Corthrop, the reforming curate of Harwich, got him into trouble with the government of Henry VIII in 1535 [4]. And it was folk rather than courtly Lords which, when the reformers got their own way, were hardest hit by the inhibitions contained in the visitation articles of archbishop Grindal and others [5]. So this discussion, *per ambages atque aequora vectus*, comes round to the point at which it began. It is a far cry from Tertullian to Bishop Grosseteste and a far cry from Bishop Grosseteste to Archbishop Grindal, but each alike voices for his own day the relentless hostility of the austerer clergy during all ages to the ineradicable *ludi* of the pagan inheritance.

---

[1] Cf. p. 261.

[2] Machyn, 162, 274. The Westminster lord seems to have been treated with scant courtesy, for ' he was browth in-to the contur in the Pultre; and dyver of ys men lay all nyght ther.'

[3] Cf. p. 173.

[4] Brewer, ix. 364. The lord of misrule was chosen in the church ' to solace the parish' at Christmas.

[5] Cf. p. 181.

END OF VOL. I